TIME AND PLACE
IN NEW ORLEANS

The Crescent City in the middle of the twentieth century. *The Historic New Orleans Collection, accession no. 1979.89.7289*

TIME AND PLACE IN NEW ORLEANS

PAST GEOGRAPHIES IN THE PRESENT DAY

Richard Campanella

PELICAN PUBLISHING COMPANY

Gretna 2002

The word "Pelican" and the depiction of a pelican are trademarks
of Pelican Publishing Company, Inc., and are registered
in the U.S. Patent and Trademark Office.

Library of Congress Cataloging-in-Publication Data

Campanella, Richard.
    Time and place in New Orleans : past geographies in the present day / Richard Campanella.
        p. cm.
    Includes bibliographical reference and index.
    ISBN 1-56554-991-0 (alk. paper)
    1. New Orleans (La.)—History. 2. New Orleans (La.)—Geography. 3. Human
geography—Louisiana—New Orleans. 4. Historic sites—Louisiana—New Orleans. 5.
Historic districts—Louisiana—New Orleans. I. Title.

F379.N557 C24 2002
979.3'35—dc21

                                                                                2001052041

Printed in Korea

Published by Pelican Publishing Company, Inc.
1000 Burmaster Street, Gretna, Louisiana 70053

To my parents,
Mr. and Mrs. Mario and Rose Campanella
Brooklyn, New York

and

To Marina's parents,
Sr. and Sra. Ernesto López and Porfiria Morán de López
San Juan Trujano, Oaxaca, Mexico

"By its commanding position in this vast country, New Orleans will assemble in its port a huge amount of commodities from the Torrid Zone for exportation along with products from the Temperate Zone. It will offer the most advantageous assortments of goods from European and West Indian cargoes. It can, in fact, expect to become one of the richest markets in the New World."

—James Pitot, 1802

Above New Orleans in 1972 (top left), 1983 (top right), 1986 (bottom left), and 1987. *U.S. Army Corps of Engineers—New Orleans District*

Contents

Roofscapes of the Vieux Carré, 2000. *Photographs by author*

Preface

Lofting through the Southern twilight on a connector flight from Dallas, I take note of passengers' reactions to the enigmatic deltaic geography below as we approach for landing in New Orleans. Many are business travelers anticipating tomorrow's convention; others are reading, asleep, or terminally oblivious. But an interested few gaze motionlessly out their scratched little windows on the world, peering through the subtropical haze into one of the most dynamic, precarious, and storied places on Earth. Ten thousand feet beneath us lies the watery lithosphere and earthy hydrosphere formed by a great river flailing methodically at its terminus, spilling sediments gathered from the western slopes of the Appalachians to the eastern ramparts of the Rockies into a gulf of a sea of a great ocean. It is a fantastic show, startlingly distinct from the familiar patchwork quilt of woods and fields characterizing most of our journey over the region. The rectilinear landscape of township-and-range America has disappeared; man has arranged things differently in this exceptional terrain. We are now south of the South.

To the west, what first appeared to be a stolid forest is suddenly intersected with orange rays of the setting sun, producing a blinding glint in the form of an enormous spoked wheel. It is the remnant cypress swamp of the Manchac wilderness; loggers a century ago extracted trees along canals radiating from a hub, creating the bizarre pattern. Through this swamp two centuries prior passed French explorers seeking a strategic toehold at the clutch of what would become the richest valley on Earth.

Directly below us is a large body of gray water that confuses some passengers. A bay? Gulf of Mexico? Hurriedly unfurled maps reveal it to be Lake Pontchartrain, a lesson to newcomers who knew since grade school that New Orleans was "on the Mississippi" but until now were unaware of this enormous and well-proportioned lake. Now we swing about and gain views of the swamps to the west, which bear a disconcerting resemblance to the northern *taiga* landscape for their cypress trees killed by salinity and bleached gray by the sun. A passenger on one side of the plane points out a flock of white egrets gliding in formation over the wild-looking terrain, a common scene in televised nature shows but incomparably beautiful from this perspective. By this time, the setting sun casts a golden glow from behind us, making the vegetation more verdant, the swamp water blacker, and every tree and stump salient. A futuristic superhighway, raised on pilings and penetrating the environs like twin laser beams, jars the prehistoric sense of the scene; the visitors will soon get firsthand knowledge of this highway as Interstate 10. An occasional camp deep in the swamps is the object of someone's marvel; *imagine* living out there. . . .

Suddenly, across the cabin, someone exclaims, *"There's the Mississippi!"* Heads bob up and turn toward windows; a murmur arises. Satisfied smiles cross once-perplexed faces. This they've been anticipating: the mighty Mississippi . . . steamboats heading for New Orleans . . . Dixieland. . . . A lifetime's worth of clichés and images registers. Even the preoccupied conventioneer peers out the window to see the great river. And great it is, absolutely unmistakable, meandering in magnificently yawning bends and clung to tenaciously by what appears to be all the human existence in the area. Roads, properties, industry, and agriculture all address the river in the way that ribs adhere to a snake's vertebrae. The passengers are witnessing settlement patterns first surveyed by French colonial engineers over a quarter-millennium ago. Now we start to follow the river, and a sense of confident satisfaction registers with our engaged passengers, some of whom turn about occasionally in the hope of sharing their discoveries with their apathetic seatmates. They have gained an initial geographical comprehension of life in this deltaic landscape: most human existence here clings to the Mississippi River. We have locked on to the homestretch of that river, wending toward the sea on a slurry plain of sediment and water. Inevitably there will be a great city near the mouth of this river, and in a matter of moments we will find that city, sprawled out in splendid isolation amid an inhospitable and ephemeral geography.

All eyes remain on the river. Smokestacks and grain towers shadow serene fields and densely canopied forests; linear communities of chimneyed shacks intersperse with the occasional columned mansion; vessels of various size and purpose engage at this fleeting moment in their ancient endeavor. A glance toward the southern horizon, through air pregnant with humidity, reveals an intricate labyrinth of marsh, water, and forest fraying out into a black infinity that says, *we are nearing the edge of the continent*. Finally, the aircraft swings into orientation with the runway, giving one side of the plane a concatenated vista down three or four meanders of the Mississippi, those in the foreground shrouded in dusk but a particularly spectacular crescent in the distance glittering in a million lights. *"There it is,"* someone says resolutely. *"There's New Orleans."* Vivacious and sparking in its solitude, cast upon a watery surface such that it looks as though it's floating, this place cannot be mistaken for Dallas or Atlanta or anywhere else.

Truth be told, it usually ends there. Most flights plunge into the suburbs of Kenner, where the mystical twilight milieu abruptly submits to strip malls with Winn-Dixies and Burlington Coat Factories. But every so often, circumstances require an aerial revolution around the metropolis, giving lucky passengers a grand tour of this destination of which they have heard so much all their lives. Leafy suburbs of ubiquitous ranch houses and commercial arteries of fast-food restaurants (disappointing those passengers who subconsciously expected narrow streets and iron-lace balconies to characterize the entire metropolitan area) give way to a busier cityscape, where some houses are grander and others more tightly clustered, where the trees are more exuberant and sprawling, and where the streets radiate outward toward the Mississippi. Almost everyone with a window seat is now rapt with attention.

The scene intensifies as we continue downriver. Foliage diminishes to reveal a nineteenth-century streetscape of multifaceted silver-gray slate rooftops and countless chimneys, which just as quickly disappears for wharves, industrial facilities, and superhighways. Then a surprisingly lofty skyscraper district delivers yet another surprise to the observers, whose eyes take in the modern city but fix on the hypnotic mathematics of the Superdome. The syllables of its name float around the cabin, mixed with snippets of *"there it is," "Jackson Square," "see the cathedral?" "that's the French Quarter."* A hush falls over the observers: even first-time visitors get a sense that the symmetrical grid-pattern urban village now below us is the heart of it all, the original city, New Orleans at its most historical and classical, perched so dramatically at a cusp of the Mississippi. The panoply of steep rooftops, courtyard gardens, and narrow streets alive with pedestrians spans an area larger in size and more uninterrupted in its distribution than some had expected. Further banking reinforces recently learned lessons in the local geography, as views of other intriguing neighborhoods, canals, bridges, wharves, and parks are gained. As the aircraft returns to the lake, passengers indulge in one last panoramic vista of the city, looking directly into the Mid-City crux from which streets radiate out to the arcuate river. A final approving whisper of *"Crescent City"* is heard. The anticlimactic ritual of landing and deplaning allows those attentive passengers to absorb their new spatial understanding of New Orleans and its region, spicing their desire to finally know this city on their all-too-brief visit.

Time and Place in New Orleans explores the influence of this exceptional landscape on the Crescent City, and the geographical patterns humans have formed while making history in this exceptional place. It examines the history behind the geography, and the geography behind the history, of the first and last great city on the Father of Waters of the North American continent. But on a more fundamental level, this book addresses the wonder and curiosity evoked by this splendid, tragic, festive, and distinguished American city, in those fortunate enough to live within its limits and in those who only get to view it from a connector flight from Dallas.

> "I never could find out exactly where New Orleans is. I have looked for it on the map without much enlightenment. It is dropped down there somewhere in the marshes of the Mississippi and the bayous and lakes. It is below the one and tangled up among the others, or it might some day float out to the Gulf and disappear. How the Mississippi gets out I never could discover. When it first comes in sight of the town it is running east; at Carrollton it abruptly turns its rapid, broad, yellow flood and runs south, turns presently eastward, circles a great portion of the city, then makes a bold push for the north in order to avoid Algiers and reach the foot of Canal Street, and encountering then the heart of the town, it sheers off again along the old French quarter and Jackson Square due east, and goes no one knows where."
>
> —Charles Dudley Warner, 1887 (308)

A Note on Terminology

Local lexicon reflects New Orleans' geographical and cultural peculiarities and, like the city, evolves over time. The following notes clarify usage of certain terms throughout the book.

French Quarter: "French Quarter," "the Quarter," *Vieux Carré* (Old Square), *Vieux Carré de la Ville* (Old Square of the City), "old city," and "original city" all refer to those blocks bounded by present-day Iberville Street, North Rampart Street, Esplanade Avenue, and the Mississippi River. In certain contexts, it also includes the blocks between Iberville and Canal, though this strip of land is historically and technically not in the French Quarter. The blocks between Barracks Street and Esplanade Avenue were also not in the original plat but are now officially part of the French Quarter, and are considered so here. In discussions focusing on the late eighteenth and early nineteenth centuries, the present-day French Quarter is also referred to as "the city," since all other areas were either rural or only recently subdivided.

Faubourg: *Faubourg* or *fauxbourg* ("false town") is French for suburb, namely inner suburb. It described the subdivisions of old plantations beyond the limits of the original city starting in 1788 and was commonly used into the early 1900s. Its use diminished for many decades but was revived in the 1970s by the historic-preservation movement and neighborhood organizations (not to mention real-estate agents), starting with the Faubourg Marigny. The term is now commonly used as a synonym for "historic neighborhood" in New Orleans, but excluding (by definition) the Vieux Carré.

Central Business District: *Faubourg Ste. Marie*, "Faubourg St. Mary," "St. Mary," "American Sector," "Central Business District," and "CBD" all generally refer to the area loosely bordered by present-day Iberville Street, Loyola Avenue, Howard Avenue, and the Mississippi River, although in certain discussions, the "Canal Street corridor" (between Iberville and Common) may be considered separate, since this remained a commons for twenty years after the 1788 subdivision of *Faubourg Ste. Marie*. This latter term is generally used for discussions recounting the late 1700s and early 1800s, while Faubourg St. Mary, St. Mary, and the American Sector are utilized in antebellum and postbellum contexts, and Central Business District and CBD refer to the area in the twentieth and twenty-first centuries.

Directions: The cardinal directions only serve to confuse in crescent-shaped New Orleans. Instead, *lakeside, riverside, upriver* (or *uptown*), and *downriver* (or *downtown*) are used as surrogates for northward, southward, westward, and eastward—despite the compass's needle.[1] I prefer *upriver/downriver* to *uptown/downtown*, because references to the flow direction of the river remain true no matter where you are in the metropolitan area. Confusing at first, the system works well (except perhaps in the Mid-City/Bayou St. John area) and makes more sense locally than allusions to distant poles and stars.

Downtown/Uptown: Everyone has their own feel of where *downtown* becomes *uptown* in New Orleans (and, relatedly, whether the words should be capitalized as distinct places or lower-cased as general areas). This is the way it should be. Most people today would divide the two places-of-mind somewhere near Howard Avenue and Lee Circle, perhaps along the Pontchartrain Expressway, which roughly separates the harder, congested streets of the commercial sector from the softer, leafier environs of the residential section. Others refer exclusively to the Garden District or the University area as uptown and the French Quarter and Central Business District as downtown. Years ago, Canal Street would have been seen as the demarcation. Understanding the two distinctive yet nebulous areas is enabled more through the rich variety of people's adamantly defended definitions of them than in a dogmatic attempt to formalize them.

Neighborhoods: Neighborhoods are delineated and named historically, colloquially, officially by the city, and by local and federal agencies for historic-preservation purposes. Rarely do all boundaries and names concur. Neighborhoods are referenced all five ways in this volume, but primarily by the official city designations. See pages 82-83 for official names (city designations, National Register Historic Districts, and local Historic District Landmarks Commission districts) and pages 89, 93, and 95 for historic names.

Historical Eras: The French colonial era refers to the years from 1682 to 1762 in regional contexts and 1718 to 1762 for New Orleans discussions. The Spanish colonial era of New Orleans started secretly in 1762, publicly in 1764, politically in 1766, and militarily in 1769; it concluded secretly in 1800 and officially in November 1803. The second French colonial era started secretly in 1800 and formally in November 1803, and ended with the Louisiana Purchase in December 1803, when the colonial era drew to a close and the American era commenced. The American territorial era lasted until 1812, when Louisiana became a state. The antebellum era generally refers to the years after the Battle of New Orleans (1815) to the outset of the Civil War, with

the latter decades of this time span often described as the Golden Age. The city's internal subdivision into three semiautonomous units (1836-52) is sometimes referred to as the "municipality era." The Confederate era commenced with secession in 1861 and lasted until New Orleans' surrender in 1862 (though some close this era with the end of the Civil War), after which the era of occupation and Reconstruction lasted until 1877.

Geography: *Geography* is defined and discussed in the introduction, but this opportunity is taken to emphasize that geography not only considers the physical lay and shape of the land but also the distributions and patterns of phenomena, including human activity, upon it.

Sea Level: Topographic elevation being so minute (yet so historically significant) in this region, the methods of measuring the varying level of the sea as a standard of comparison are relevant. Most elevations cited in this volume are in reference to the National Geodetic Vertical Datum of 1929 (NGVD 1929, formerly called the Sea Level Datum of 1929), which is a mean-sea-level estimate fixed among twenty-six measurements at coastal sites throughout the United States and Canada taken over a number of years starting in 1929. Thus, "three feet below sea level" means three feet below the sea's average level as measured by this vertical datum, which is close to, but not the same as, the level of the Gulf of Mexico where the Mississippi discharges. NGVD 1929 was superceded by the North American Vertical Datum of 1988 but is still commonly used. Recent studies by researchers at Louisiana State University revealed that, because of subsidence on the existing set of benchmarks, true elevations in southern Louisiana are possibly up to four feet lower than previously thought. The establishment of a new set of high-accuracy benchmarks will provide updated elevations for Louisiana as well as up-to-the-minute measurements of subsidence.

Maps in This Volume

Maps in this volume were made by the author using geographic information systems (GIS), computer cartography, remote sensing, and image-processing technology. Information depicted in the maps (topography, historical aerial photographs, neighborhoods, etc.) was processed, interpreted, and mapped from raw data derived from a wide range of sources listed in the acknowledgments and references.

Acknowledgments

I gratefully acknowledge and thank the following institutions and people for access to the research materials cited in this volume, and for information on specific topics.

Louisiana Collection and Special Collections, Earl K. Long Library, University of New Orleans; New Orleans City Planning Commission; Special Collections, Howard-Tilton Library, Tulane University; U.S. Army Corps of Engineers—New Orleans District Aerial Photo Archive and Library; Center for Bioenvironmental Research at Tulane and Xavier Universities; The Historic New Orleans Collection—Williams Research Center (especially curator Sally Stassi); City of New Orleans; Monroe Library, Loyola University; U.S. Geological Survey; U.S. Department of Agriculture; Preservation Resource Center of New Orleans; Historic District Landmarks Commission; Library of Congress American Memory Database; New Orleans Public Library; Port of New Orleans; the *New Orleans Times-Picayune*; Sewerage and Water Board of New Orleans; Mr. Herman S. Kohlmeyer, Jr.; Mr. Carl McArn Corbin; Mr. and Mrs. Harold and Doris Ann Gorman; Dr. Peirce Lewis; Tulane University School of Architecture; Louisiana State University Department of Geography and Anthropology; Louisiana State University Computer-Aided Design and Geographic Information Systems (CADGIS) Lab; University of Southeastern Louisiana; University of Southern Mississippi; Vieux Carré Commission; National Aeronautics and Space Administration; Louisiana Department of Environmental Quality; New Orleans Notarial Archives; Louisiana State Museum; and the people of New Orleans.

I would also like to thank Dr. Milburn Calhoun and the Calhoun family, owners of Pelican Publishing Company, for their support of my work and for their immense contributions to the body of literature on New Orleans and Louisiana; editor in chief Nina Kooij, for her careful and insightful review of my manuscript; and Tracey Clements and the Pelican staff, for the design layout of this book.

1. Before the turn-of-the-century drainage project opened up the Lakefront and made Lake Pontchartrain more relevant to the local citizenry, people referred to the *woods side* versus *riverside* for north and south.

Introduction

The Geographical Perspective

Many people perceive geography as a variation of geology or a collection of Earth facts, an antiquated discipline with little to offer in the modern world. This is unfortunate, because geography provides a perspective—a spatial perspective—fundamentally relevant to a wide range of interests, from the physical to the cultural. Geography is a broadly defined discipline that identifies, analyzes, and interprets the spatial distributions of phenomena as they occur on the surface of the Earth.[2] It addresses the questions of "where" and "why there,"[3] complementing the historian's questions of "when," "who," and "what impact," or the physical scientist's questions of "how" and "why." This, of course, is oversimplification: there are branches within geography that ask all these questions and other disciplines that would be remiss in neglecting geographical dimensions. Nevertheless, the revelation and explanation of spatial relationships are fundamental to geography. "The geographic method is concerned with examining the localization on the Earth of any phenomena," said Carl O. Sauer, a preeminent figure in cultural geography. "The Germans have called this the *Standortsproblem*—the problem of terrestrial position—and it represents the most general and most abstract expression of [the task of the geographer]."[4]

The academic discipline of geography is divided into the physical and human realms. Physical geography investigates the biosphere, lithosphere, hydrosphere, and atmosphere through specialties such as biogeography, geomorphology, oceanography, and climatology. Human geographers specialize in urban studies, economics, culture, history, and other areas, seeking to understand "the areal differentiation of human activities."[5] Geographers of any stripe may investigate at the regional level, in which numerous questions about one particular place are considered, or at the topical level, in which one particular question is studied across various places. Because the concept of spatial distribution is fundamental to all geographical research, the metrics and tools of the discipline, such as cartography, geographic information systems (GIS), remote sensing, geodesy, and spatial statistics, are considered specialties in and of themselves. Geography in general is interdisciplinary and synthesizing, and may be employed qualitatively or quantitatively. Broadness is its strength.

Time and Place in New Orleans is a historical geography—a history of past geographies—of New Orleans and its environs. Parts of it, namely the discussion of the siting of the city in chapter 1, may also be described as geographical history, in that "its aim is the better and truer explanation of historical events by reference to those facts of Geography which have influenced them."[6] Geography investigates both physical and human phenomena, hence this book is as interested in natural levees, battures, and subsidence as it is in Creole residential patterns, the rise and fall of the Cotton District, and why Audubon Park is shaped like a wedge. While traditional histories of New Orleans may identify the colonial era, Louisiana Purchase, and Civil War as major milestones, this historical geography views the subdivision of rural plantations, construction of the drainage system, and excavation of the Industrial Canal as watershed events (sometimes literally) in the city's past. As the St. Louis Cathedral, jazz, Mardi Gras, and Creole cuisine figure prominently in other books about New Orleans, less-famous but equally important features such as the Esplanade Ridge, the St. Mary Batture, the Rigolets, and the New Basin Canal play starring roles here.

Historical geography emerged as a subfield within geography over the past two centuries and has proven both fascinating and enigmatic. The term has variously referred to the history of geography as a discipline; of exploration, discovery, and mapping; and of changing political boundaries. By the 1900s, as geographical thought grew more sophisticated, historical geography came to its current meaning, which is, in more or less words, the reconstruction of past geographies of a place.[7] Represented graphically, historical geography's realm of interest occupies the three-dimensional matrix formed by time (history) on one axis, location (geography) on another, and phenomena of interest on the third axis.[8] In a more utilitarian explanation, imagine a series of thirty maps depicting an important theme of a city, with each map showing the theme's geographical imprint in 10-year increments

spanning the city's 300-year history. This theme may be industry locations, distribution of ethnic groups, transportation networks, topography, locations of churches, green space, government land, or countless other phenomena. Now imagine cycling through each theme's series of maps through time and visualizing the dynamic expansion, contraction, dispersion, erosion, aggradation, shift, or disappearance of those themes over the years. Finally, consider comparing the dynamic cycling of one theme to those of related themes, or to those of other cities or in other eras, or to other data in the historical record. The effort to reconstruct, measure, map, explain, and ultimately understand the spatial patterns of the past, up to the present day, is one way to conceive of historical geography. The subtitle of this book, *Past Geographies in the Present Day*, derives from this concept.

The contributions of historical geography to the understanding of such topics as the origins of agriculture, the evolution of land-division systems, the development of Latin America, and sundry other topics are significant and unique. But some scholars view the term as a redundancy—"*all* geography is historical geography"—while others see it as paradoxical, arguing that history narrates variation through time and geography describes variation through space, two distinct axes, one linear and the other multidimensional.[9] (See the appendix for more reflections on historical geography.) Scholars routinely squabble about the nature and role of their respective fields, but the yearning to formalize a definition for this somewhat nuanced concept obfuscates the indisputable fact that a cognizance of the lay of the land and patterns of human activity adds greatly to the understanding of historical events, *and vice versa*, leading ultimately to a richer appreciation of the present state and appearance of a place. This is the stance assumed in this book, however it may be categorized.

The goal of *Time and Place in New Orleans* is to explore and track myriad geographical circumstances that humans have exploited, enjoyed, tolerated, battled, and created throughout the tumultuous three-century history of this city of great and renowned character. It pursues this goal by examining three premier circumstances influencing the city we know today: situation, topography, and culture. In "Situation," we discuss the most fundamental geographical circumstance of New Orleans and any city, its physical location, from its geological origins, to its discovery by Europeans, to the conceptualization of New Orleans, to the controversy of its siting and foundation. A comparative analysis is presented of the sites in the running to be the capital of French Louisiana ca. 1720: the present-day French Quarter site, Bayou Manchac, Natchez, English Turn, Lake Pontchartrain, and sites along the Gulf Coast. The chapter concludes with a speculative discussion of what New Orleans might have been like had it been sited elsewhere.

In "Topography," we examine the remarkable influence that a few dozen inches of elevation have on a city built upon a deltaic plane straddling the level of the sea. "Major" topographic features—some barely above the swamp, but the less there is, the more it's worth—and the revealing cityscape built upon them are discussed and mapped in detail. Then we look at episodes of topographic change in the city, executed to keep water out (the river levees, the Lakefront, and the hurricane-protection levees), to remove water (the drainage system), to create new land (the St. Mary and French Quarter batture), and to improve navigation (Carondelet Canal, New Basin Canal, Industrial Canal, and Mississippi River-Gulf Outlet Canal). The positive and negative impacts of these engineering projects are discussed.

In "Culture," a dauntingly vast and interwoven influence, we focus the discussion on five elements of a city identified by Dr. Kevin Lynch in his 1960 book, *The Image of the City*: paths, edges, districts, nodes, and landmarks. For paths, we explain the ancient origins of New Orleans' distinctive radiating street pattern in the crescent of the Mississippi, and how each path through uptown New Orleans from Mid-City to the river fell into place from plantation days to the present sans the guidance of central planning authority. For edges, we discuss and debate the oft-heard legend that Canal Street formed a cultural barrier between the city's Creole and American populations. For districts, we review the "where" and "why" behind New Orleans' industry clusters, focusing on the Cotton District, the Sugar District, and Newspaper Row. For nodes, we set forth criteria for identifying "geographical nodes" in the city—specific points that serve as metaphors for New Orleans' historical mission as a nexus between the exterior world beyond the Gulf of Mexico and the interior world accessed by the Mississippi River. Six sites are presented as qualifiers for this title. Finally, for landmarks, we present a photographic collection of those quirky and majestic elements of the New Orleans cityscape that send clues of geographical identity to observers traversing its storied streets and distinctive neighborhoods. A graphical thread throughout this historical geography is a series of maps, satellite and aerial images, historical and modern photos, bird's-eye perspectives, graphs, and charts presented to emphasize and quantify the relevance of the spatial dimension. One of the thrills enjoyed by those who appreciate the geographical perspective is the sense of discovery that arises from a careful analysis of a simple street pattern or feature in an aerial photo that turns out to be a direct descendent of a centuries-year-old influence.

---

2. Haring, Lounsbury, and Frazier, 5.
3. East, 4.
4. Sauer, "Foreword to Historical Geography," 6.
5. Ibid., 7.
6. Fawcett, 7.
7. Smith, 84-85, 91-95.
8. Cant, 134-37.

9. Guelke, 3, 6, 7, citing the interpretations of Immanuel Kant, Richard Hartshorne, and others.

That said, *Time and Place in New Orleans* is decidedly focused in its breadth. It is not by any means intended to be a comprehensive history *or* geography of New Orleans. It does not cover every square mile of Orleans Parish proportionally throughout all its history. Rather, it concentrates on selected aspects of the city's physical and human geography and examines their characteristics, influences, and transformations over time, with an emphasis on the older (pre-twentieth-century) part of the city. The book makes no pretenses of being a scholarly work, because it is based largely on secondary sources of data. Rather, it is a synthesis of secondary and primary historical data (in a ratio of roughly three to one) infused with descriptive and quantified geographical information and interpretations. The liberal use of footnotes is designed to direct the reader to additional sources of information.

City (topic of research)	Number of Geography Ph.D.s	Rank
Los Angeles	59	1
Chicago	48	2
New York City	36	3
Columbus	25	4
San Francisco	24	5
Detroit	22	6
Phoenix	18	7
Boston	17	8
Denver	17	8
Baltimore	16	10
Milwaukee	16	10
Wash., D.C.	16	10
Houston	15	13
San Diego	14	14
Portland	14	14
Austin	11	16
Dallas	9	17
Seattle	9	17
New Orleans	9	17
Oklahoma City	9	17
Memphis	8	21
Philadelphia	7	22
Cleveland	7	22
Nashville	7	22
San Antonio	5	25
Jacksonville	5	25
El Paso	5	25
Indianapolis	4	28
San Jose	3	29
Fort Worth	3	29

City (topic of research)	Geography Ph.D.s per 100,000 Population	Rank
Columbus	4.0	1
Denver	3.6	2
San Francisco	3.3	3
Portland	3.2	4
Boston	3.0	5
Washington, D.C.	2.6	6
Milwaukee	2.5	7
Austin	2.4	8
Baltimore	2.2	9
Detroit	2.1	10
Oklahoma City	2.0	11
Phoenix	1.8	12
New Orleans	1.8	12
Los Angeles	1.7	14
Chicago	1.7	14
Seattle	1.7	14
Cleveland	1.4	17
Nashville	1.4	17
San Diego	1.3	19
Memphis	1.3	19
El Paso	1.0	21
Houston	0.9	22
Dallas	0.9	22
Jacksonville	0.8	24
Fort Worth	0.7	25
New York City	0.5	26
San Antonio	0.5	26
Indianapolis	0.5	26
Philadelphia	0.4	29
San Jose	0.4	29

A Measure of Geographical Research on New Orleans
Number of Ph.D. dissertations with keyword "geography," for the 30 largest U.S. cities (left), and same data normalized for every 100,000 population (right, 1990 population data). These data were derived from keyword searches of the city, state, and "geography" in the Bell & Howard dissertation database. The data show that, although New Orleans is widely recognized as a culturally unique city in a geographically exceptional area, it has not enjoyed a corresponding amount of attention from geographers. (Note: Both city and state were used along with "geography" as keywords, to minimize the number of false positives that would result from city names such as Phoenix or San Jose. To hold all data to the same standard, city and state were used consistently, even though this strategy undercounted some cities. This explains why New Orleans is listed with nine Ph.D.s in this table but fifteen in the text.) *Source: Bell & Howard Information and Learning. Dissertation Abstracts Online/OCLC FirstSearch (2000), Ann Arbor, Michigan*

Despite the plethora of historical and cultural literature on New Orleans, there seems to be a paucity of geographical analyses of the city—a paradox because the Crescent City, down to its very sobriquet, exudes geography, from its exceptional deltaic landscape to its strategic situation on the river to its diverse population and port economy. It is the flattest, lowest, and geologically youngest major American city, populated by arguably America's oldest multicultural society, occupied by a phenomenally large inventory of historical structures laid out in a fascinating urban design, credited with deeply influential cultural and economic contributions to the nation. It is the gatekeeper of one of the world's great rivers, master of a major river and sea port, and an urban enclave in *the* most dynamic ecological region in the nation. For well over a century, it was the unquestioned powerhouse of the South and among the nation's top cities; today, it is a major node in the world shipping system, regional home to 1.34 million people, and a travel destination of over 10 million visitors annually. One would think that New Orleans would thence attract keen attention from geographers of all specializations. This does not seem to be the case.

An unscientific survey of scholarly geographies about American cities gives this author the distinct impression that New Orleans gets short-changed in such analyses, sometimes not even earning a listing in the index. Case in point: the 596-page *Historical Geography of the United States* treats New Orleans *and* Louisiana in all of five brief paragraphs, in the context of a discussion on sugar cultivation. They are barely mentioned in the chapter on the South.[10]

The best geographical profile of the city is Dr. Peirce F. Lewis's 1976 *New Orleans: The Making of an Urban Landscape*, a 115-page monograph that imparts more true understanding of the Crescent City than any other study its size. Dr. Lewis noted the general "scarcity of serious scholarly work" on New Orleans, especially "comprehensive studies of the contemporary city," geographical or otherwise.[11] The works of Dr. Robert A. Sauder and others at the University of New Orleans' Department of Geography, as well as those of researchers at the College of Urban and Regional Planning, are also excellent sources of geographical analyses on the New Orleans area.

Author, Year	Dissertation Title	University
Murphy, Linda K., 1999	The Shifting Economic Relationships of the Cotton South: A Study of the Financial Relationships of the South During Its Industrial Development, 1864-1913	Texas A&M University
Owens, Jeffrey A., 1999	Holding Back the Waters: Land Development and the Origins of Levees of the Mississippi, 1720-1845	Louisiana State University
Hogue, James K., 1998	Bayonet Rule: Five Street Battles in New Orleans and the Rise and Fall of Radical Reconstruction	Princeton University
Komins, Benton J., 1998	A Reading of Cultural Diversity: The Island of New Orleans	Harvard University
Kelman, Ari, 1998	A River and Its City: Critical Episodes in the Environmental History of New Orleans	Brown University
Choi, Youngeun, 1998	Urban Effects on Precipitation in the Southern United States of America	Louisiana State University
Bixel, Patricia B., 1997	Working the Waterfront on Film: Commercial Photography and Community Studies	Rice University
Cheek, Ronald G., 1996	The Development of a Methodology to Visualize the Cancer Risk Potential from Industrial Releases of Air Carcinogens	University of New Orleans
Rohli, Robert V., 1995	The Association between Anticyclonic Weather Changes over the Central Gulf Coast and Large-Scale Circulation Changes	Louisiana State University
Knopp, Lawrence M., 1989	Gentrification and Gay Community Development in a New Orleans Neighborhood	The University of Iowa
Kim, Soon Tae, 1980	A Quantitative Evaluation of Landsat for Monitoring Suspended Sediments in a Fluvial Channel	Louisiana State University
Francis, Barbara M., 1975	Journey-to-Work Patterns: Their Spatial Dimensions in Selected Inner City Areas of New Orleans	University of Cincinnati
Sauder, Robert A., 1973	Geographic Change on the Downtown Waterfronts of Boston, New Orleans, and San Francisco	University of Oregon
Johnson, Eric S., 1968	The Latin American Foreland of the Port of New Orleans	University of Kansas
Campbell, Edna F., 1931	The Port of New Orleans	Clark University

Ph.D. dissertations with keywords "New Orleans" and "geography" listed in the Bell & Howard database. While the degrees conferred were not necessarily in geography, the titles reflect the diversity of topics unified by the discipline. Only one degree was granted by a local university, with four others from LSU in Baton Rouge. *Source: Bell & Howard Information and Learning. Dissertation Abstracts Online/OCLC FirstSearch (2000), Ann Arbor, Michigan*

10. Ralph H. Brown, 40-41, 130-50.
11. Lewis, 3. See also xiii.

Other geographical treatises on the city are hard to find: a query of the Bell & Howard dissertation database, which covers 1,560,000 studies written from 1861 to the present, yielded only fifteen Ph.D. dissertations with keywords "New Orleans" and "geography," listed in the accompanying chart. ("New Orleans" and "history" produced 239 hits.) This is as much a statement on the paucity of New Orleans geographical research as it is on the lack of geographical research in general.

Perhaps this open niche is beginning to be discovered: from 1931 to 1980, an average of one dissertation on New Orleans geography per decade was written; from 1995 to 1999, the pace increased to almost two per year. Other sources of information on New Orleans' spatial dimension are occasional articles in professional journals such as the *Louisiana Historical Quarterly*, *The Geographical Review*, and *The Journal of Southern History*, vignettes such as Tulane University School of Architecture's *The New Orleans Guide* (1984), and government documents for civil engineering and urban planning projects that often do commendable research in historical geography without employing that term. Perhaps the reason for the lack of research on New Orleans geography is that there is only one academic geography department in the city, at the University of New Orleans, and, though an excellent department, it does not currently confer Ph.D.s in the field. (Louisiana State University's geography program in Baton Rouge is nationally known but, until recently, has specialized in rural and folk geography rather than urban topics.) Geographers, plying a discipline predicated on location, tend to focus on their own stomping grounds, thus places with few geographers tend to get few geographies. There may also be the factor of exceptionalism: New Orleans is often viewed as an exception to the national norm, and thus may be eschewed by scholars intent on proposing unifying theories. Similarly, some researchers may assume that New Orleans is more anomalous from other American cities than it actually is, and thus may shy away from analyzing it through methods developed elsewhere.

Countering this scarcity of geographic work is the recognition by other students of the city, particularly in architecture and history, of the relevance of geographical factors and patterns in their areas of interest. The outstanding Friends of the Cabildo *New Orleans Architecture* series, started in 1971 with the landmark *Lower Garden District* and now eight volumes strong, is especially cognizant in this regard. Dr. Joseph Tregle's research on Creoles and Americans in nineteenth-century New Orleans revealed residential patterns of these ethnic groups that countered conventional thinking. John Churchill Chase's classic *Frenchmen, Desire, Good Children . . . and Other Streets of New Orleans!* (1949, now in its third edition) adeptly tells the history behind the city's peculiar street names with equal doses of humor and keen geographical observation. James S. Janssen's *Building New Orleans: The Engineer's Role* (1984) is one of the few books to focus on this fundamentally important but underappreciated aspect of local history.

In the area of literary fiction, one must recognize the role of novelists and playwrights in instilling a sense of place in the mystique of New Orleans. Recall Tennessee Williams' clever and poignant metaphor in his greatest play, in which a puzzled Blanche DuBois, upon arriving at her sister's house from the L & N train station, recounts that "they told me to take a street-car named Desire, and then transfer to one called Cemeteries and ride six blocks and get off at—Elysian Fields!"[12] *A Streetcar Named Desire* (1947) "returned New Orleans to a preeminent place on the literary map of America,"[13] and may have also placed a map of New Orleans, (artistic license and all) in the mind of literary America, casting its streets and neighborhoods in an aura of mystery and poignancy. Other works do fine jobs of capturing sundry elements of New Orleans such as its Carnival traditions, music, food, politics, and society. It is hoped that *Time and Place in New Orleans* will add a tiny bit of the neglected geographical perspective to the wealth of literature on this city.

Analyzing the history of a place through the contours of its geography provides intriguing insights and hypotheses but sometimes leads to overstatement of the role of geography in history. Approached rationally, a geographical understanding imparts a spatial perspective in deciphering the history of a city or any human endeavor. How can one interpret New York City history without understanding its harbor? Or Dutch history without considering the country's low seaside elevation? Or Jewish history without understanding the distribution of Jews throughout the world? Or the Appalachian region without its rugged terrain? To illustrate further, imagine a hypothetical city portrayed as simply a dot on a blank piece of paper. If viewers of this primitive map were asked to speculate on the history of that city, they would be guessing about everything except its existence. If lines indicating rivers and streams were added to the map, viewers may make slightly more informed speculations as to the city's history: perhaps it was founded at the confluence of two rivers, where accessibility would make it an optimal trade center, or perhaps it used the river for irrigation. If topography were added to the map, the viewers may gain a better understanding of the "where" and "why" of the city, and

if soil types, transportation corridors, demographic distributions, street networks, political boundaries, climatic trends, and other "overlays" were added to the map, the viewers may pose initial hypotheses about the history of the city. This illustrates the power of geography as well as its shortfalls in historical analysis: geography provides a fundamental, macroscopic setting and circumstance affecting and reflecting the human events that play out upon them, but many profoundly important historical events would be beyond the reach or explanation of geography. The presence of rich alluvial soils or well-drained uplands may geographically explain the siting and development of a community—major components of its history—but it may not explain a local economic crash that impoverished its people or a historic event that characterized the place for decades. The geographical perspective is valuable—indeed, critical—when synthesized with a parallel historical perspective but misleading when overstated as the "master key to history."[14]

Another fallacy in geography is the overindulgence in deterministic explanations, e.g., "above-ground cemeteries are an adaptation to New Orleans' high water table," or "New Orleans' crescent-shaped street network was designed to conform to the sinuous Mississippi." The high water table was only partially the motivation to bury above ground; cultural factors weighed more heavily. Likewise, the city's streets were not designed to conform to the river any more than Denver's were laid out to match the mountains or San Francisco's to the bay. In fact, the radiating pattern formed gradually as wedge-shaped long-lot plantations were subdivided independently by their owners, passing on the geography of the rural *arpent* land-division system to urban subdivisions. The role of the river is indirect. There are some cases in which geography truly does play a deterministic, causal role in history—natural disasters come to mind—but most situations are more complex and multifaceted, and one should be wary of easy explanations.

A constant theme throughout the discipline of geography is the interrelationship and intertwining of phenomena, akin to ecology in the natural world. For example, it is difficult to describe the impact of the Mississippi River on New Orleans without mentioning the natural levees created by the river (thus providing dry ground for the city) that were subdivided into long-lot plantations (thus providing the basis for modern New Orleans' fan-shaped street network). A single geographic feature may have myriad repercussions, which are rarely related in a linear, univariate, and deterministic manner but rather in complex, multivariate relationships, indirectly affecting any number of consequences. Yet when we examine New Orleans' geographical circumstances here, we itemize each one—situation, topography, culture—like an ingredient in a recipe. Is this an ideal way to analyze the historical geography of a place? In short, no. The itemized, thematic approach runs contrary to the contention of interrelation. Nevertheless, any complex topic can and must be broken down into manageable subtopics to achieve understanding, otherwise we would be stalled at the surficial level, fumbling with semantics as we try to detail the effect of every ripple upon every other ripple when a thousand figurative pebbles are tossed into a pond.[15] The notion of the itemized geographical circumstance, as useful and as flawed as it may be, is illustrated by the concept of the "data layer." A state road map, for example, may contain a half-dozen or so data layers—roads, towns, state and county boundaries, rivers and streams, place names, and recreational areas—which are overlaid at a constant scale and depicted in various symbols to form a map. This is the task of the cartographer. Taking these spatial data layers to another level—explaining their provenances, characteristics, effects, evolutions, and interrelationships—is the task of the geographer.

And that is the goal of this book: to identify and explain, through words and images, the web of geographical circumstances and patterns that humans have exploited, enjoyed, tolerated, battled, and created over a span of three centuries, thus producing this city of great and renowned character, New Orleans.

---

14. East, 2.

15. "If we imagine a series of air photos taken of a single area . . . and viewed as a motion picture film by geographers and historians, the historians would quite possibly consider it a historical picture, but certainly geographers would call it geographic." To analyze these complex data through both time and space dimensions, "the ambitious student must seek ways of reducing some of the difficulties to the minimum . . . by selecting a relatively small region of restricted variation in area and affected by a limited number of factors producing historical change" (Hartshorne, 49).

---

12. Williams, 15. In the 1951 movie, the character speaks these words in a memorable sequence filmed on location at the foot of Canal Street.
13. W. Kenneth Holditch, "South Towards Freedom: Tennessee Williams," in Kennedy, 62.

1 Situation

An aerial perspective serves as a reminder of the intimate relationship between the Mississippi River and the greater New Orleans metropolitan area, viewed here in 1966 from a point above English Turn looking upriver. The river created New Orleans' terrain, sculpted its topography, deposited its rich soils, attracted natives and settlers to its banks, gave access to the interior and the rest of the world, provided water for both residents and industries, and has served as the foundation for its economy and the taproot of its unique culture. *Photograph by Sam R. Sutton, The Historic New Orleans Collection, accession no. 1984.166.2.889*

Casual and veteran observers of New Orleans may cite the Mississippi River as the premier geographical circumstance defining the Crescent City. They are correct. But Baton Rouge and Memphis are also on the river and, though interesting and historical in their own regard, lack the cultural singularity of New Orleans. The premier geographical circumstance that has earned New Orleans its various reputations, forming and affecting it in ways physical, economic, and cultural, is its situation on the Mississippi *nearest the river's mouth,* closest to the Gulf of Mexico and the greater water bodies that communicate with the rest of the world. It is one of those cities that must exist, an inevitable[1] metropolis that guards the gate between the richest valley on Earth and the worldwide demand for its resources, between millions of people in the American heartland and the global market that both supplies their economic demands and consumes the fruits of their productivity. New Orleans' situation makes it both a riverport and a seaport, inwardly impressionable via the river and the vast hinterland it drains and outwardly influenced via the sea and the scores of nations it touches. In this regard, New Orleans' geographical situation differs from most other American ports, which generally serve either a river or an ocean/gulf/sea/lake, but not both on large and roughly equal scales.[2]

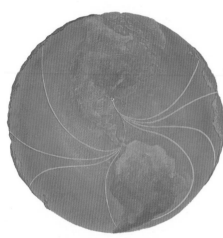

New Orleans' strategic geographical situation—near the mouth of a great river, draining a vast and fertile basin, and convenient to navigation from the rest of the world—underlies much of the city's history and character. *The International Relations Committee of International House, "New Orleans, World Trade Center" (ca. 1965)*

It also differs in the magnitude of its river—the 2,340-mile-long Mississippi drains 600,000 cubic feet of water per second from a 1,125,910-square-mile watershed interspersed with 14,500 miles of navigable waterways—and in the isolation of its perch, where for over a century it had little of the trade competition that characterized Eastern Seaboard ports. "All ports, of course, enjoy a certain worldly quality that comes from the constant mingling of products and people from far-off places," wrote Peirce Lewis in 1976, but "New Orleans is not even ordinary as a port. . . . The port of New Orleans is big—ranking second only to New York in volume and value of cargo handled—[but unlike New York], which does a good many things besides handling cargo, New Orleans embraces marine commerce with the same single-minded enthusiasm as Detroit makes automobiles . . . thoroughly relishing her bigamous marriage to the river and the ocean."[3] New Orleans' keystone geographical situation between the North American interior and the southern seas affected it in a manner so fundamental that many of the city's defining traits stem from it in some manner or another. To characterize the role of geography in the development of New Orleans, we begin by investigating the geological origins of this geographical situation, the historical events that led to the siting of New Orleans *in* this situation, and the myriad consequences *of* this situation.

"By repeated admeasurement upon the best constructed maps, the Mississippi river and its tributary streams drain more than 1,400,000 square miles. If this expanse was peopled [by] about 60 persons to each square mile, the aggregate would be 84,000,000. . . . At a period not more than two centuries distant, more than 100,000,000 of human beings will send the surplus fruits of their labour to New-Orleans."

—William Darby (as quoted by Paxton, 1822, 32)

1. I use "inevitable" with caution. As we shall see, a number of other sites could have hosted New Orleans; moreover, the concept of inevitability in this context gives perhaps too much credit to geography and too little to man in the siting of a city. Nevertheless, the junction of a great river with the sea provides a strong incentive for the founding of an important settlement in the general vicinity. For further thoughts on this subject, see Kidder, 9-21.

2. On a continental scale, Montreal and Québec probably come closest to sharing New Orleans' river/sea juxtaposition; not coincidentally, the three cities share a common cultural heritage. One writer, Oliver Evans, observed that New Orleans resembled a cross between Québec and Havana. For a substantial comparative review, see Hero.

3. Lewis, 7. Since Dr. Lewis penned these words, petroleum and tourism rose to greater importance in the local economy, but not yet to the

Geological Origins of New Orleans' Precarious Perch

New Orleans was established during 1717-22 but was first conceptualized about two decades earlier, giving the city a current life span of roughly 300 years. Going back in time 240,000 times New Orleans' life span—72 million years ago—the city's now-strategic location at 30° north latitude 90° west longitude was an indistinct watery spot far off the coast of what would later become the southeastern United States. The coast in the Cretaceous Period traced a line 200-300 miles inland from its present location (excluding Florida), punctuated by a series of folds in the Earth's crust that allowed gulf waters to penetrate inland an additional few hundred miles.[4] The largest of these synclines was a sagging trough intruding 500 miles up what is now the Mississippi Valley to Cairo, Illinois, a formation known as the Mississippi Embayment.[5] This subsiding indentation drained sediment-laden waters shed by adjacent terrain and deposited the sediments at a pace faster than its natural subsidence. Gradually, the salty gulf waters flooding the Mississippi Embayment receded and were replaced by the sediments that would later form the Mississippi Valley. Sand, silt, and clay were also deposited along the margins of the shrinking Gulf of Mexico such that, during the Miocene Epoch—about 18 million years ago, or 60,000 times the life span of New Orleans—the once-indented coastline of the future southeastern United States formed a smooth curve from present-day Texas, around Georgia, and up to New York.[6] At this point, however, New Orleans' future location was still a geographically undistinguished component of the hydrosphere, a hundred miles offshore.

Around 6,000 New Orleans life spans ago (the Pleistocene Epoch, 1.5 to 2 million years ago), the Louisiana coastline traversed the "Florida parishes" above modern Lake Pontchartrain, about forty miles north of New Orleans' location. This coastal region comprised tilted layers of sedimentary rock—compacted clays, silts, sands, and gravel—gradually leaning into the sea. But continental-scale processes at the opposite end of the Mississippi Embayment (fully sedimented at this point in time) would transform this relatively stable portion

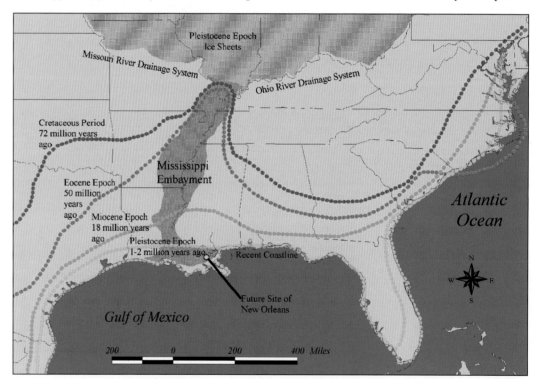

Historic coastlines of the present-day southeastern United States and development of the Mississippi River Valley since the Cretaceous Period, 72 million years ago. *Map by author.*

level of the port. The petroleum sector has since diminished by more than half since the early 1980s, while tourism and the convention trade have steadily and significantly increased. New Orleans remains a port city.

4. Hunt, 209-19.

5. Sibley, 20.

6. Hunt, 218, and Lower Mississippi Region Comprehensive Study Coordinating Committee, 118-22.

of the Gulf Coast into a profoundly dynamic geological region, one that man would exploit as a strategic location for a city and struggle to maintain against the forces of nature. The agent of transformation was the vast ice sheet advancing, melting, depositing, and gouging the upper half of the North American continent. Glaciation reached as far south as present-day Cairo, Illinois, not coincidentally the northern tip of the Mississippi Embayment and later the lower Mississippi Valley. The ice sheet blocked old drainage basins and forced its melting water to seek new paths to the sea; what is now the Missouri River provided one such path, the Ohio River another. These two rivers conflowed near Cairo to form the rapidly developing and suddenly enlarged Mississippi River system. Waters of the Mississippi, laden with sediment once embedded in the glaciers, followed the gradient towards the Gulf of Mexico, where the load would be deposited to form the precarious deltaic plain that would eventually host New Orleans. Steamy, silty New Orleans, hundreds of miles from glaciated terrain and devoid of a single pebble, is an offspring of the Ice Age.

The ice sheets impacted the Gulf Coast not only by creating the Mississippi River and loading it with sediments, but also by fluctuating the level of the sea nine times throughout the Pleistocene Epoch, from 2 million years ago to the end of the Ice Age, 10,000 years ago. When the ice melted, sea level rose; when global temperatures chilled and the glaciers advanced, sea level dropped. During times of glacial augmentation, gulf waters dropped as low as 450 feet below present levels. It was during these times that New Orleans' future site at 30° north 90° west emerged from the hydrosphere (a few hundred feet above sea level) and joined the lithosphere—temporarily. But its location would have been of little geographical value to man: the river and gulf waters, two key reasons for the siting of the city, converged far south of this site, near the Continental Shelf.

Ten thousand years ago—less than thirty-five New Orleans life spans—marked the end of the Ice Age, the beginning of the Recent Epoch in geological time, and the commencement of hyperactive geomorphological processes in what is now southeastern Louisiana.[7] The melting of the ice sheets on a massive scale put three major processes in overdrive: increased flow in the Mississippi River, increased sediment load in the flow, and a rising sea level. The rising sea level would push the coastline inland, the increased sediment load in the river would form more deltaic lands faster near the mouth the river, and the increased flow in the river would deliver more load from the interior to the coast.

By 5,000 years ago, New Orleans' site was once again flooded by rising gulf waters, forming a coastline along the southern shore of not-yet-formed Lake Pontchartrain.[8] At this time the local land-building agent, the Mississippi River, emptied its muddy waters a hundred miles to the west, in the Salé-Cypremort Delta southeast of Lafayette, Louisiana.[9] A thousand years later, gulf water levels rose an additional forty feet to their present level, forming a bay (Pontchartrain Embayment) that would eventually become Lake Pontchartrain.

Cupping the southeastern quadrant of this bay was a sandbar, formed and nudged along by longshore currents, that currently underlies the Interstate 10 corridor from Hancock County in Mississippi to City Park in New Orleans. This barrier spit (Pine Island Trend)[10] was soon smothered by Midwestern topsoil, the first such land-building in this area during the Recent Epoch, as the Mississippi changed courses and formed the Cocodrie Delta directly upon New Orleans' future site. For a millennium (4,500 to 3,500 years ago), this delta established the nexus between the Mississippi River and the Gulf of Mexico, the fundamental premise for the future city of New Orleans.

But the lower Mississippi River is a tumultuous, roiling current flowing upon a broad, flat, malleable basin (meander belt), indicating that channel changes are an inevitable part of the river's dynamics. Around 1500 B.C., the Mississippi jumped channels toward the west and emptied into the gulf near present-day Houma (Teche Delta) for the next 700-1,000 years. Then it acquired its current channel and formed the St. Bernard Delta for the next millennium (roughly 2,600-1,500 years ago), building upon lands created during the days of the Cocodrie Delta in Orleans and neighboring parishes while creating the remote marshlands of eastern St. Bernard Parish.

About A.D. 500, three New Orleans life spans ago, the river diverted near Donaldsonville to form the twin lobes of the Lafourche Delta; a few centuries later, a second delta developed below New Orleans' future site, near Pointe a la Hache (Plaquemines Delta). For about 400 years, almost up to historical times, the lower Mississippi diverted in these two directions. The diversion near Donaldsonville was still prominent enough in 1699 for Pierre Le Moyne, sieur d'Iberville to name the distributary *Lafourche,* "the fork,"[11] a name that remains today. But by this time, in fact at the time of Columbus's discovery of the New World, the main flow

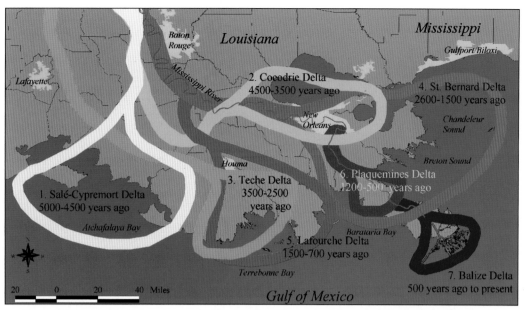

Deltas of the Mississippi River over the past 5,000 years overlaid on present-day coastline, parish/county boundaries, and major cities. Darker shades of red indicate chronology. Note that the terminus of the Mississippi River channel occurred at the future New Orleans site (St. Bernard Delta) around the time of Christ. *Map by author based on U.S. Army Corps of Engineers data in Kniffen and Hilliard, 54, and other sources.*

of the Mississippi returned to its primary and current channel, plowing into the warm gulf waters at the modern Balize Delta, 100 miles southeast of the city that was about to be established.

In the centuries since, the distributary that is now the Atchafalaya River presented an increasingly attractive alternative channel (that is, a steeper gradient to the sea) for the Mississippi, by means of nature and the inadvertent hand of man. That alternate channel nearly seized the Father of Waters in the last century of the second millennium, but a technologically advanced society had since assembled along its banks and would not allow the deprivation of its most important resource. In the late 1950s, the Army Corps of Engineers constructed the Old River Control Structure, an immense engineering project that stopped geological time by maintaining the Mississippi River in its present channel while feeding the Atchafalaya River a government-approved rate of flow.[12] With this project (plus centuries of levee construction and damming of distributaries), the river's meandering ways ended for the foreseeable future—but, of course, not forever. The result of the Mississippi's rambles and deposits during the Recent Epoch was the 13,000-square-mile deltaic plain[13] that is southeastern Louisiana, characterized by natural-levee uplands no more than a few feet in elevation paralleling the river and its distributaries, built up by sediment deposited during seasonal floods. Among and between these natural levees—the only well-drained features in the deltaic plain—lay a complex network of forested wetlands (swamps), open wetlands, marshes of varying amounts of salinity, mudflats, sandbars, brackish-water bays, and waterways.

Hence through this geological and climatic tumult, by means of the alluvium carried by this methodically flailing river, was formed the geographical situation that New Orleans was founded to exploit. Europeans recognized the criticality of this situation, as a way to access the promise of the North America interior from the Gulf Coast and Caribbean, as early as 1678 and certainly following the La Salle expedition of 1682.[14] But identifying a key geographical situation is a broader "phase-one" consideration in the positioning of a city, whereas site selection is a more involved and careful "phase-two" decision. *Situation* connotes the

7. In *Roadside Geology of Louisiana* (49), Darwin Spearing describes southeastern Louisiana as "one of the most dynamic landscapes in the world," accentuating "human interaction with the forces of nature as perhaps no other place can, not even California with its earthquakes." The region's relentless geological forces "create a drama on a scale unmatched in virtually any other natural environment."

8. Snowden, Ward, and Studlick, 5-7.

9. Kolb and Van Lopik, 120, as quoted and interpreted by Snowden, Ward, and Studlick and Kniffen and Hilliard.

10. Spearing, 59-61.

11. Newton, 44-47.

12. See John McPhee's classic essay, "Atchafalaya," in *The Control of Nature.*

13. See Newton, 44-45, for a discussion on the various definitions of *delta* and *deltaic plain* as applied to Louisiana. The figure of 13,000 square miles measures the general area traversed by the seven deltas of the Mississippi over the past 5,000 years.

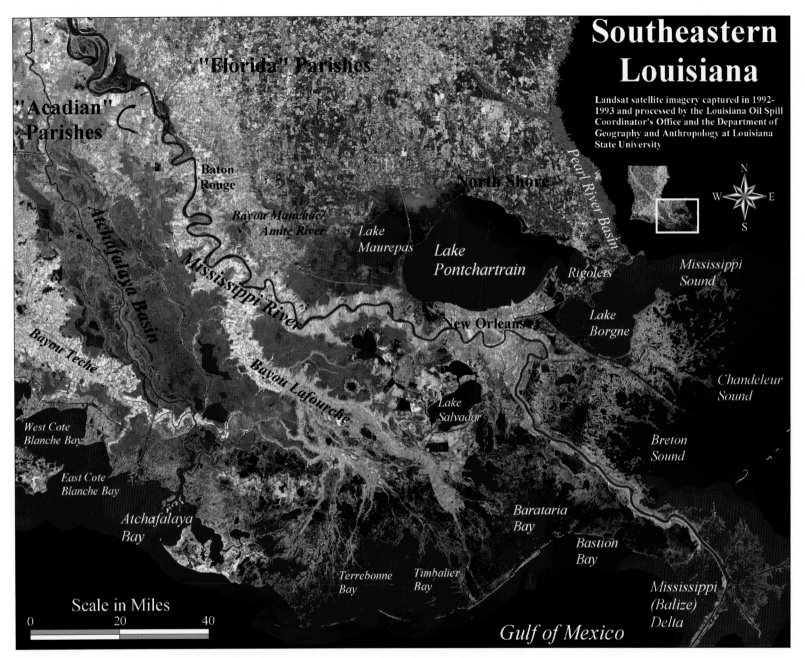

Southeastern Louisiana

Landsat satellite imagery captured in 1992-1993 and processed by the Louisiana Oil Spill Coordinator's Office and the Department of Geography and Anthropology at Louisiana State University

"Florida" Parishes

"Acadian" Parishes

Baton Rouge

Bayou Munchac/ Amite River

Atchafalaya Basin

Mississippi River

Lake Maurepas

Lake Pontchartrain

North Shore

Pearl River Basin

Rigolets

Mississippi Sound

N W E S

Bayou Teche

Bayou Lafourche

New Orleans

Lake Borgne

Lake Salvador

Chandeleur Sound

West Cote Blanche Bay

Breton Sound

East Cote Blanche Bay

Atchafalaya Bay

Barataria Bay

Bastion Bay

Terrebonne Bay

Timbalier Bay

Mississippi (Balize) Delta

Scale in Miles

0   20   40

Gulf of Mexico

Mississippi approaches the Gulf of Mexico proved to be a complex and controversial question.

Early European Cognizance of the New Orleans Region

European cognizance (or conjecture) of the Mississippi River possibly commenced as early as 1502, when an Italian diplomatic agent in Lisbon by the name of Alberto Cantino secretly obtained a Portuguese planispheric map that depicted a *Rio de las Palmas* flowing into what appeared to be a very sketchy Gulf of Mexico. This cartographic squiggle probably represents a river westward toward Mexico, but if it were meant to mark the Mississippi, the source of this information is unknown. Some accounts record that Americus Vespucius sailed the Caribbean and Gulf of Mexico in 1497-98, possibly finding the mouth of the Mississippi, but documentation is lacking.[16] More likely, Western knowledge of the great river resulted from Spanish explorer Alonso Álvarez de Pineda's expedition along the Gulf Coast in 1519, in search of a western passage. Reports by the patron of the expedition, Francisco de Garay, tell of a "very large and very deep"[17] river, named *Río del Espíritu Santo,* that Pineda ascended for six leagues. For centuries Pineda was credited by many for discovering the Mississippi, until research indicated that the river in question may have been the Mobile. Nevertheless, Pineda's expedition made the important contribution of revealing a great river in the region and the general geography of the Gulf Coast, as well as the nonexistence of a western passage.[18]

Nine years later, an ill-planned imperialistic expedition led by Pánfilo de Narváez, a rival of Hernán Cortés, struggled by sea and land from Cuba to Florida (April 1528) and westward towards the mouth of the Mississippi, where the famished soldiers imbibed the river's fresh water as they maneuvered around the geologically nascent bird-foot delta (October-November 1528). Upon entering a strong current west of the delta, two boats drifted away and were never recovered, then Narváez's boat was lost off the southwestern coast of Louisiana. The two surviving vessels drifted westward and landed in the vicinity of present-day Galveston, Texas.

The disastrous expedition was then redeemed in the eyes of history when the remnants of the crew, led by Álvar Núñez Cabéza de Vaca, reorganized and com-

---

surrounding region and adjacent features of a place, observed at a distance and considered in geographical context; *site* is the actual terrain chosen for development, the specific location of the city proper.[15] The distinction is one of scale: situation is to site what neighborhood is to house or what climate is to weather. Selecting a site for the city that would be named *La Nouvelle Orléans* within the outstanding geographical situation where the

menced an epic 2,000-mile odyssey across the wilderness of present-day Texas, possibly New Mexico and Arizona, and northern Mexico, arriving in the Pacific coastal settlement of Culiacán, Mexico in 1536.[19] Cabéza de Vaca's great contribution was his account of the journey, published in 1542, which provided splendid detail

---

14. "Memoir of M. Cavelier de La Salle" (ca. 1684) and "Memoir of the Sieur de La Salle Reporting to Monseigneur de Seignelay" (ca. 1684), as reproduced in Falconer, 3 and 21 of appendix. These memoirs recount Colbert's call for a French port in the Gulf of Mexico, to which La Salle responded with the recommendation of a settlement on the lower Mississippi—among the first official recognitions of the strategic geography of this region and the importance of a colony to control it.

15. Jordan and Rowntree, 366, and Lewis, 17.
16. Ogg, 9-10; Rivera Novo and Martín-Merás, 73; and Sauer, *Sixteenth Century North America*, 25.
17. Ogg, 16.
18. Ibid., 13-21.
19. Sauer, *Sixteenth Century North America*, 36-46. See also map of various hypothesized routes in Hallenbeck.

of the geography of sixteenth-century North America as well as the first descriptions of the Mississippi River delta and adjacent formations. Cabéza de Vaca's reports refueled Spanish interest in the exploration of the North American interior and motivated Hernando de Soto, a former comrade of Peruvian *conquistador* Francisco Pizarro, to launch a gold- and empire-seeking expedition to the region.

De Soto and his 600 soldiers landed near present-day Tampa, Florida in May 1539 and proceeded to explore a circuitous 4,000-mile route through the coastal plain, piedmont, and Appalachian region of the future American South. The expedition came upon the Mississippi River near modern-day Memphis in May 1541, making them the first Europeans to sight and explore the inland channel of the river and first to recognize its "magnitude and importance."[20] The arduous journey cost the expedition over 40 percent of its men, including the De Soto, who died probably near present-day Vidalia, Louisiana and was interred in the Mississippi. The remnants of the expedition, under the rule of Luis de Moscoso, headed overland toward Texas then returned to the Mississippi, floating down the river in July 1543 and possibly passing the future site of New Orleans during the second week of that month. (A 1544 map resulting from the expedition depicts a *Río del Espíritu Santo* that resembles the Mississippi in size and importance but not in shape and form, leading some to believe that the expedition took the Atchafalaya River or other fork to the gulf.[21] If this is true, then no Spaniard nor any other European left documented evidence of sighting the future New Orleans region in the sixteenth century or earlier.)

The wild ride of the 322 survivors of the De Soto expedition in seven rough-hewn vessels, at times under severe Indian attack as they sailed down the untamed Mississippi and escaped, ragged and starved, to Tampico, Mexico,[22] marked the ignominious departure of the Spanish from the Mississippi Valley for centuries to come. They sought not settlement and colonization but power and riches; finding none, they left no permanent mark. How different the region's history would be if the Spanish came with different motives. Pineda, Narváez, Cabéza de Vaca, De Soto, and their men did, however, reveal the region's geography to the Western world, and while these revelations languished on maps and documents for decades, the future New Orleans region and the lower Mississippi Valley persisted and evolved for the final century and a half of its primeval state.

The Arrival of the French

The French in seventeenth-century North America also sought riches, but, invested as they were in the colonies of New France, pursued a means—trade routes and empire—towards that end, not the end alone. Throughout the middle years of the 1600s, rumors circulated among the French in Canada of a "great water" to the west, an equivalent to the St. Lawrence River that would give them claim to distant lands and trade access possibly to the Orient. Explorations of the Great Lakes region in the mid-seventeenth century and the discovery of the upper Mississippi by Jacques Marquette and Louis Joliet (1673) helped demystify the western frontier and put to rest the notion of a nearby Pacific Ocean, but no French explorer had yet confirmed the connection between the upper Mississippi and the Gulf of Mexico and the implications of such a nexus.

René-Robert Cavelier, sieur de La Salle, an ambitious young Norman who migrated to New France in 1666, recognized the likelihood and importance of this connection and set out in 1682 to explore the full length of the River Colbert (Mississippi) and expand the French empire. His name for the river honors Jean Baptiste Colbert, a financial minister for Louis XIV who in 1678 foresaw the importance "for the glory and service of the King to discover a port for his vessels in the Gulf of Mexico,"[23] one of the first documented visions of the city that would become New Orleans. La Salle, his chief lieutenant Henri de Tonti (Henry de Tonty), and their crew sailed down the Mississippi and past New Orleans' future site[24] in the winter and early spring of 1682;

upon reaching the delta on April 9, La Salle claimed the vast drainage basin for his country and named it for his king, Louis XIV. After over 160 years of speculation, the existence and significance of the Mississippi River was finally fully proven, and thus began the French presence in Louisiana and the seed for the eventual city of New Orleans.

Upon returning to France, La Salle recommended to the king the establishment of a fortification sixty leagues[25] above the mouth of the Mississippi in the Gulf of Mexico, for its "excellent position," "favourable disposition of the savages," fertile land, mild climate, advantages of military offense and defense, and opportunity to "harass the Spaniards in those regions from whence they derive all their wealth"[26]—a reminder that France's exertions in this region in these early days were largely driven by competition with the Spanish.[27] The fortification would also serve as a base for preaching the Gospel, conquering the silver-rich provinces of Mexico, storing supplies, harboring and building ships, and exploiting the vast resources of newly claimed Louisiana.[28] In selling the colonization of the lower Mississippi to his king, La Salle boldly declared that "a port or two [here] would make us masters of the whole of this continent."[29] He explained the linchpin position of a settlement on the lower Mississippi in no uncertain—and fairly accurate—terms: while other colonies are vulnerable to attack from "as many points as their coasts are washed by the sea," in this region, "one single post, established towards the lower part of the river, will be sufficient to protect a territory extending more than 800 leagues from north to south, and still farther from east to west, because its banks are only accessible from the sea through the mouth of the river, the remainder of the coast being impenetrable inland for more than 20 leagues."[30] La Salle's conceptualization of this settlement may have foreseen the riverbanks below Baton Rouge, perhaps at the Bayougoula Indian camp near Bayou Manchac, as its location.

La Salle returned to France in late 1683 and, motivated by national strategic and economic factors, confidently set out in 1684 with greenhorn settlers as well as experienced crew to found this envisioned city near the mouth of the great river. What happened over the next three years is the subject of a controversy among some historians, though La Salle's tragic fate is not. The conventional hypothesis holds that the marshy labyrinth of the delta region obscured the Mississippi River channel, setting La Salle on an increasingly desperate search for the river that landed him hundreds of miles to the west, at present-day Matagorda Bay in Texas. Indeed, in the lower Mississippi Valley and deltaic plain, a swollen river, a series of mud lumps,[31] or a foggy day can spell the difference between the successful establishment of a colony and the inability to find North America's greatest river.

The alternate hypothesis casts La Salle in a more sinister role, in which he knowingly reported and mapped the mouth of the Mississippi well west of its actual position to accommodate his true plan: conquest of the Spanish in Mexico. La Salle's mismeasurement of the length and direction of the river and cartographic mislocation of its lower channel and mouth may raise questions of a deception designed to sway financial backers.[32] In any case, the expedition degenerated at Matagorda Bay; La Salle was murdered in March 1687 by mutinous crew members, and most survivors died of disease or were massacred by Indians in January 1688 at

20. Ogg, 27-28, 44.
21. Kniffen and Hilliard, 116.
22. Hudson, 387-97. Ogg put the number of the surviving crew at 372.
23. "Memoir of the Sieur de La Salle," as reproduced in Falconer, 21 of appendix.
24. According to historian Villiers du Terrage (161), La Salle may have first beheld the future site of New Orleans around March 31-April 2, 1682, when his men came upon a recently destroyed Tangibaho (sic) village in Quinipissas territory, situated upon a portage that was probably associated with Bayou St. John.

25. A league at that time measured between 2.4 and 3.0 miles.
26. "Memoir of M. Cavelier de La Salle," as reproduced in Falconer, 3 of appendix.
27. The original communication from King Louis XIV in 1678 granting permission to La Salle to discover the western part of New France stated that "there is nothing we have more at heart than the discovery of this country, *through which it is probable a road may be found to penetrate to Mexico*" (emphasis added). "Letter Patent Granted by the King of France to the Sieur de La Salle, on the 12th of May, 1678," as reproduced in Falconer, 18 of appendix.
28. "Memoir of the Sieur de La Salle," as reproduced in Falconer, 24-27 of appendix.
29. Ibid., "Memoir of M. Cavelier de La Salle," 4 of appendix.
30. Ibid., "Memoir of the Sieur de La Salle," 27-28 of appendix.
31. McWilliams, "Iberville," 127-40. This contains an interesting discussion on the historical impact of mud lumps in the Mississippi delta. These features are extrusions of mud pushed to the surface through fissures in the sea floor by pressure created by compacting sediments.
32. De Vorsey, 5-23.

the Fort St. Luis they had founded about a hundred miles southwest of present-day Houston. (Incredibly, La Salle's ship, the *Belle,* was discovered in Matagorda Bay in 1995; a year later, the Fort St. Luis site was finally found at a ranch near Victoria, Texas, about fifteen miles from the shipwreck.)

We can only hypothesize about La Salle's motives and speculate on the city he might have founded on the Mississippi. But his legacy was significant:[33] first to explore the entire Mississippi River, claimer of its vast basin for France, and first true believer in the criticality of controlling the North American hinterland through a settlement near the mouth of the river.[34] In effect, La Salle executed the phase-one consideration in the positioning of the city that would be New Orleans: identification of a key geographical situation.

La Salle's vision might have died had it not been for his colleagues and competitors, who kept the issue of Mississippi River/Gulf of Mexico exploration in front of the French government. Chief among them was La Salle's friend and lieutenant, Henri de Tonti, the Italian nobleman in service of France who accompanied him on the 1682 expedition and searched for him in 1686. During this fruitless search, Tonti formed important alliances with the natives along the Mississippi, established a post upriver, and left a letter for La Salle with the Bayougoulas (Quinipissas) in the hope that it would someday find him. Tonti later advocated to the French court "the completion of the discovery of the late M. de La Salle,"[35] recognizing, like La Salle, the importance of a settlement on the lower Mississippi for ship building and harboring, communication with the Gulf of Mexico, conquest of Mexican silver mines, agriculture, and fur trading—a business of personal interest to Tonti. Throughout the 1690s, Tonti and other prominent Frenchmen warned their government about the English threat to the Mississippi River from the gulf, the Spanish threat from Texas and Florida,[36] and other perils and lost opportunities in delaying the French settlement of Louisiana.

It was not until 1697 that the French government came around and began to actively pursue the exploration and colonization of Louisiana. In that year, Tonti's memoirs were published, representing "the immediate expression of the growing interest which the occupation of Louisiana aroused."[37] Gabriel Argoud, a Paris lawyer in the employ of the Court, authored an influential plan to colonize Louisiana, alluding to the English threats of invasion from the south and colonial settlement from the north. The plan included commercial aspects offered by Antoine Alexandre de Rémonville, ship owner and former explorer of the upper Mississippi, who foresaw the commercial viability of a Louisiana enterprise and participated in the effort to convince the government to colonize. Scientific, patriotic, and religious elements in French society also began to direct their attention to Louisiana.[38]

France's worries of foreign intervention were further exacerbated that same year by the publication in Utrecht of Father Louis Hennepin's *A New Discovery of a Vast Country in America,* a voyage narrative of the upper Mississippi first published under the title *Description of Louisiana* in France in 1683, which urged William of Orange to take possession of Louisiana.[39] A cessation of hostilities between England and France (King William's War) in 1697 and the growing rivalry of the old foes in the New World returned the French government's attention to colonial matters. With an heirless Carlos II near death in Spain, Louis XIV envisioned a potential reshuffling of the colonial landscape and sought to position France strategically, between the English on the Atlantic seaboard and the Spanish in Mexico.[40] That strategic position was at the mouth of the Mississippi, and the message was increasingly clear: *seize it or lose it.* Minister of Marine (Navy) Louis

Phélypeaux, Count de Pontchartrain finally resolved to settle Louisiana, and in late 1697 charged Pierre Le Moyne, sieur d'Iberville, a thirty-six-year-old mariner and warrior who gained fame in Canada for his exploits against the English in the recently ended war, to seek "the mouth [of the Mississippi River,] . . . select a good site that can be defended with a few men, and block entry to the river by other nations."[41] Thus commenced the phase-two consideration in the positioning of the city that New Orleans would come to be: selection of an actual site within the key geographical situation that La Salle identified almost sixteen years earlier.

Enter the Le Moyne Brothers

Iberville, his teenaged brother, Jean Baptiste Le Moyne, sieur de Bienville, and their crew landed on a barrier island (now Ship Island) off the present-day Mississippi Gulf Coast in February 1699 and proceeded to search for the elusive mouth of the Mississippi. On March 2-3, they entered a swift current of fresh water[42] and eventually the main channel of the Mississippi, naming a point along the banks "Mardi Gras" for the pre-Lenten feast they observed that day. But proof that this channel was indeed La Salle's river eluded Iberville until his crew discovered among the Mougoulachas—who along with the Bayougoulas were referred to as the Quinipissas by Henri de Tonti—the letter Tonti left during his futile search for La Salle in 1686.

While seeking this important piece of evidence during the month of March 1699, Iberville and Bienville gained crucial knowledge (courtesy of their Indian guides) of the geography of the lower Mississippi and deltaic plain, naming features along the way. This information included the existence of shortcut portages[43] to the Gulf Coast via the present-day Bayou Manchac-Amite River-Lake Maurepas-Pass Manchac-Lake Pontchartrain-Rigolets-Lake Borgne route and via Bayou St. John between the Mississippi River and Lake Pontchartrain, marking the future site of New Orleans. It was on March 9, 1699, that Iberville offhandedly described this humble portage that would become the geographical link between the European colonial powers and the North American interior, unwittingly alluding to the area's value as a commercial port:

> The Indian who accompanied me revealed a terminus of the portage from the southern shore of the bay, where the Indian boats land in order to descend to this river. They drag their canoes along a fine path, where we found the baggage of people who are either leaving or returning by way of this portage. This Indian, our guide, took a parcel there. He remarked that the distance between one end of the trail and the other is indeed inconsiderable.[44]

(This "fine path" followed a slight ridge through the swamps that would later become Bayou Road, the oldest road in New Orleans and the prehistoric connection between Bayou St. John and thence Lake Pontchartrain and the Gulf of Mexico at the northern end and the Mississippi River at the southern end.) These navigable shortcuts would allow explorers to bypass the treacherous Mississippi bird-foot delta and access the river from the Gulf Coast in less time, shorter distance, and less risk; credit for their discovery belongs largely, if not entirely, to the indigenous peoples who shared this critical information with the French.

After the explorations, Iberville's expedition then returned to Ship Island and, after a brief site-selection survey, established in early April 1699 Fort Maurepas (Biloxi) in present-day Ocean Springs, Mississippi, the first tangible French effort to develop La Salle's claim from seventeen years earlier.[45] Iberville's selection of

33. Giraud, vol. 1, 3-4. Giraud states that "the expeditions of La Salle, preceding as they did the decisive intervention of France in the Mississippi Basin by only ten years, were the determining factor in establishing a firm foothold there."

34. Edwin Adams Davis (29-30) offers an alternate interpretation: "La Salle deserves a place with the great French colonial explorers . . . but for his expedition to the mouth of the Mississippi he should be placed as just another explorer along with his Spanish predecessors." He cites a Spanish diplomat who in 1818 complained to the French government that "La Salle did nothing more than traverse . . . through territories which, although included in the dominions of the Crown of Spain, were still desert, and without forts or garrisons to check the incursions of that French adventurer; and that nothing resulted from them."

35. Letter of Henri de Tonti, as quoted by Dufour, *Ten Flags in the Wind*, 29, and Giraud, vol. 1, 10.

36. The Spanish were greatly alarmed by La Salle's claims and sent a number of expeditions from 1686 to 1693 to gain back the Mississippi Valley advantage. Two of these expeditions—one by Juan Jordán de Reina and another by Carlos de Sigüenza y Góngora—left documentary evidence of a "palisade" that kept them from entering the *Rio de la Palizada* (Mississippi River). According to one researcher, this barrier comprised not a jam of trees and logs but a series of "mud lumps," extrusions of mud pushed to the surface by the pressure of compacting sediments, a geomorphological peculiarity of the delta region. Once again, the restless geography of the lower Mississippi changed the course of history: had the Spanish found their way around this obstacle, "they might have held not only the lower valley but much of the southern area of North America east of the river for the next seventy years or even longer" (McWilliams, "Iberville," 127-32).

37. Giraud, vol. 1, 19-20.

38. Ibid., 15-20.

39. Brasseaux, "The Image of Louisiana," 153-54; Giraud, vol. 1, 15; and Cross, v-xv.

40. Jerah Johnson, 28-29.

41. Tennant S. McWilliams, as quoted in Richebourg Gaillard McWilliams, *Iberville's Gulf Journals*, 4. The Historic New Orleans Collection recently acquired a hitherto-unknown manuscript that appears to reflect Iberville's thinking around this time—early 1698—after he learned of his appointment to Louisiana but had yet to depart. Iberville proposed the establishment of a colony on the Mississippi for, among other reasons, a strategic military advantage in the event of war with Mexico. The seven-page prospectus may be the earliest documented proposal of Iberville to occupy Louisiana (Arnold, 2-3).

42. McWilliams, "Iberville," 138. Iberville "became aware of a river" while being chased ashore by foul weather and approaching nightfall, a lucky break that evaded his predecessors in their searches for the mouth of the Mississippi. In reaching the fresh water, he encountered countless "rocks" (probably a combination of mud lumps and mud-encrusted logs), the same features that kept Spanish explorers out of the Mississippi a few years earlier. Iberville correctly presumed that these features led the Spanish to name the river *Rio de la Palizada* (Palisade River) and was thus convinced that he had found La Salle's river.

43. "In Louisiana, the dominant usage of the term *'portage'* signified a land route between navigable waterways [as well as] 'small intervening waterways along a route that provided relief in that they served the same function as a land portage'" (Detro, 255). Throughout this book, we will use the term *portage* to reflect both meanings, land and water route.

44. Brasseaux, *A Comparative View of French Louisiana,* 44.

45. Wilson, "Colonial Fortifications," 381-83.

This photograph shows the vicinity of the Indians' landing site on Bayou St. John, near present-day Bell Street. "The bay" that Iberville mentioned would be called Lake Pontchartrain, "this river" was the Mississippi, the "fine path" would become Bayou Road, and the "other" end of the trail would become the original city of New Orleans, now the French Quarter. *Photograph by author, 2000*

First capital of French Louisiana, Fort Maurepas was founded by Iberville in 1699 on the eastern shore of Biloxi Bay. This historical marker and replica fort in Ocean Springs, Mississippi (left) commemorate a site south of the Highway 90 bridge as the location of this first settlement, but it is more likely that Fort Maurepas was located north of the present-day bridge, somewhere along this coast (right). *Photographs by author, 1999*

At this bend in the Mississippi River, somewhere in these woods near Phoenix, lies the site of Fort de Mississippi (Fort de la Boulaye), founded by the young Bienville in 1700. The fort, first European settlement within the current state of Louisiana, reflected French recognition of the importance of a presence on the lower Mississippi River, a role that New Orleans would play decades later. *Photographs by author, 1999*

this site was one of last resort; it had an adequate channel and provided some protection from storms but lacked a great river, good soils, and even drinking water. It would suffice for now. The fort built, Iberville set sail for France in early May to report to his superiors, leaving Bienville chief lieutenant of the nascent colony.

During the next year, with Iberville in France for some months and the colony under development, Bienville and his men made continued use of the Bayou St. John portage for sojourns between the Gulf Coast and the Mississippi River. The lordly youth was apparently impressed with the strategic and convenient situation of this area, for he would later found a city here and govern it for many years. But immediate threats loomed. On September 15, 1699 (August 3, according to Tonti), while sailing the lower river, Bienville encountered a shocking sight: an English frigate, the *Carolina Galley,* heading straight into French Louisiana on a mission of colonization. Bienville famously bluffed the English captain, Louis Bond, into believing that the French would forcibly expel them from the region; the departure of the vessel gave English Turn, the last great meander of the Mississippi, its name.

The incident convinced Iberville,[46] who returned in January 1700, that while coastal Fort Maurepas had its advantages, it neither guarded nor exploited the true geographical prize of the region—the Mississippi River— from English invasion and other considerations. He sent his brother to select a site for a riverside fort, which Bienville located on the east bank about fifty miles above the delta, where the Rivière aux Chênes neared the Mississippi, probably between the present-day towns of Burbridge and Phoenix.[47] Bienville probably selected this site because the Rivière aux Chênes provided a backdoor shortcut to the gulf and because the slight natural-levee crest was said by an Indian to be safe from flooding.

Fort de Mississippi (later named Fort de la Boulaye, or Boulaix), really a crude blockhouse erected in matter of days in February 1700, was the first European establishment within the current boundaries of Louisiana. It marked the French realization of the need of a garrison *on* the Mississippi, and provided the young Bienville with his first experience in site selection in the challenging conditions of the lower Mississippi. (The site proved problematic, prone to floods and lacking in pure fresh water because of tidal influences.) For the next few months, before again returning to France in late May 1700, Iberville resumed exploration of the Mississippi, reaching the Natchez region and its tangential Red River into Spanish territory, then returning to the Gulf Coast and heading to Mobile Bay, all the while making and renewing contact with various Indian tribes.

The dawn of the eighteenth century was characterized by instability and indecisiveness regarding the future of Louisiana. The king and others in France stalled at the idea of increasing investment in the area, expressing disappointment at the progress and promise of the colony to date. Then the ascension of a grandson of Louis XIV to the Spanish throne (Philip V) allied France and Spain under Bourbon rule against England and its allies, eventually triggering the War of the Spanish Succession (Queen Anne's War) and renewing French interest in securing the Gulf Coast against the English.

Iberville sought to collaborate with the Spanish to reinforce Pensacola against this threat; Spain's rejection of the idea led Iberville to propose a new post on nearby Mobile Bay, which, together with a fort on the Mississippi and the alliance of Indian tribes, would form a broad bulwark against the English. In 1702 he and his brother established Fort Louis de Louisiana (Fort Louis de la Mobile), to which the seat of colonial government was transferred from Fort Maurepas at the Bay of Biloxi, which was never intended to be a permanent colony, and laid out a street network adjacent to the fortification. This settlement was located about fifteen miles up the Mobile River from present-day Mobile on a site called Twenty-Seven-Mile Bluff, near the tiny present-day town Axis, Alabama. French investment in the colony concentrated on this establishment over the next few years, creating an impressive settlement with a solid fort, nearly one hundred structures, and eighty-one resident families.[48] One might have predicted at that time that this Mobile would emerge as the principal city of French Louisiana.

Meanwhile, Fort de Mississippi languished in inundated isolation, so poorly sited that Iberville suggested to Bienville, whom he designated commandant of the Louisiana territory, that he relocate it closer to Lake

46. Sauvole, commandant of the Post of Biloxi in Iberville's absence, recorded in his journal (1699-1701), "The meeting of the English frigate in the Mississippy has made [Iberville] decide to keep all peoples from the river, so that no one could take it by force. . . . He instructed me to go find a proper place to change the colony and to put it half way up to the portage which is twenty-two leagues lower than the Bayogoulas [sic], in a river of calm water that I found to have enough current." According to Jay Higginbotham, translator and editor of the journal, Sauvole is refering to the future New Orleans area as the optimal location for Iberville's new river fort. Although this is not entirely clear in the journal, the river fort (Fort de Mississippi) was eventually located downriver, near Phoenix. Sauvole later makes a clearer reference to the future New Orleans area: "We have discovered a land which is not inundated. It is about ten leagues above [Fort de Mississippi]. There are seven to eight cabins of savages at the present time. One can communicate there by the great lake; but it is not well to locate men there, because of its small extent; it is a quarter of a league from the Miciscipi." Sauvole is not describing the future site of the French Quarter but the area where Bayou St. John meets the uplands of the Metairie/Gentilly distributary, which is indeed "small" in extent. Higginbotham, *The Journal of Sauvole*, 38, 54.

47. Artifacts possibly from the old fort (actually a two-story blockhouse with outlying structures) were found in the 1930s after the Gravolet Canal was excavated, but research in the 1980s suggested that this may not have been the exact site. U.S. Army Corps of Engineers, *Final Report of Cultural Resource Investigations*, C-1-4.

48. Descendents of these families formed the Founders of Old Mobile Society in 1999 (http://Foundersofoldmobile.com) (Veach).

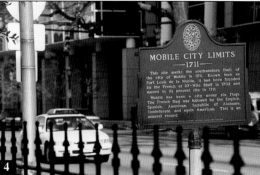

1. Behind this aptly named Le Moyne Water System tower is Twenty-Seven-Mile Bluff, site of Fort Louis de la Mobile (1702), located about fifteen miles up the Mobile River from present-day Mobile near the tiny community of Axis, Alabama. It was to this riverside site—described as the "Jamestown" of French Louisiana—that Iberville moved the colonial capital from Fort Maurepas (present-day Ocean Springs, Mississippi) in 1702. The actual site was discovered in 1989 and has since been under archeological excavation by the University of South Alabama.

2-3. Sentinel of Mobile Bay, Dauphin Island played a key role as port and gateway to the Louisiana colony during the early French years and served as headquarters for its governor in the 1710s, before New Orleans was cleared out of the forest. Its historical criticality is reflected in the Civil War-era Fort Gaines. Today, the island attracts sportsmen, tourists, and retirees.

In 1711, Bienville relocated Fort Louis de la Mobile to a more commanding and strategic position on Mobile Bay, site of present-day Mobile. It was a good move: Mobile has prospered by the bay for nearly three centuries, despite numerous changes of government during the first half of its history. Mobilians cringe when they hear their city described as "a small version of New Orleans," but the two cities exhibit undeniable parallels in their history, geography, culture, and built environments, with most differences related to the disparate sizes of their hinterlands.

4. Southwestern city-limit marker on Government Street in downtown Mobile.

5-6. Historic houses in downtown Mobile with Mobile Bay in the background.

7. Barton Academy, designed by James Gallier, Sr., in a style very similar to his famous St. Charles Hotel (1837-51) on St. Charles Avenue in New Orleans.

8. Antebellum townhouse like hundreds in New Orleans.

9. Port facilities on Mobile Bay seen from the convention center.

10. Montage of historic and modern buildings, of renovation and ruin, all common sights in both Mobile and New Orleans.

11. Three centuries of Mobile architecture. *Photographs by author, 1999*

Pontchartrain.[49] The advice came from Rémonville, the Illinois-country explorer whose knowledge of the coastal region predated the Le Moyne brothers' initial visit. Rémonville wrote on August 6, 1702:

> The fort which was in [sic] the Mississippi River . . . should be transferred eleven leagues higher, to the eastward, in a space of land twelve leagues long and two leagues wide (at barely a quarter of a league from the Mississippi, which is very fine) beyond the insulting reach of floods and near a small river [Bayou St. John]. The latter flows into Lake Pontchartrain and, by means of the canal [probably the Rigolets or Chef Menteur Pass,] . . . joins the sea about a dozen leagues from Mobile. This will make communications much shorter and easier than by sea.[50]

Rémonville is of course describing the New Orleans area and its strategic attributes. Over the next two decades, he would champion the exploitation of the Bayou St. John portage as a site for a settlement. One might ask why did Iberville not relocate the main colony from Biloxi directly to this attractive site on the Mississippi, rather than to Mobile. The answer probably lay in Iberville's concerns regarding the spread of the English along the Atlantic Coast and into the interior and Gulf Coast. Iberville's plan "called for the French to evolve a strong position on the Mississippi, remove themselves from the unimportant position of Biloxi Bay to the far more strategic Mobile Bay-Mobile River area, and, at the same time, urge his government to persuade the Spaniards to cede Pensacola to France," according to historian Glenn R. Conrad. "[Thus] three major Gulf portals to the interior of the present United States would be securely sealed to English supplies and communications."[51] With Fort de Mississippi providing as least *some* presence on the Mississippi, Iberville's immediate concern was to secure the valuable and vulnerable Mobile Bay, hence the Biloxi colony was moved there. Iberville probably passed his vision of a Mississippi stronghold on to his brother Bienville, who would act on it with resolution in later years.

Outposts in the Wilderness

At this time (ca. 1702) there were about 140 subjects of the French crown—mostly Canadians, many sailors, soldiers, craftsmen, and freebooters from the mother country and Saint-Domingue and some *coureurs de bois* from the upper Mississippi—strewn out between the forts on Mobile Bay and the Mississippi River. Iberville lamented the lack of colonizers, especially families that would settle down and cultivate the land, and complained that the French lacked the "colonizing spirit" that he witnessed in the English.[52] Despite the importation of marriageable French women to Mobile in 1704, the population hardly grew over the next four years, due in large part to the debilitating effects of the War of the Spanish Succession on France and the inherent risks to life in a subtropical wilderness.

Among the casualties were Henri de Tonti, who died of yellow fever in Mobile in 1704, and Iberville, who succumbed to the same disease while on war-related duties in Havana two years later. "Louisiana thus lost its principal guiding force" and suffered in isolation for the next few years, having been visited by a mere three supply ships from 1706 to 1711.[53] During these difficult times Bienville was forced to abandon Fort de Mississippi (1707) and relocate Mobile to its present-day location (1711), because of limited resources and poor site selection.

An effort to encourage agricultural production led to the granting of land concessions at Bayou St. John[54] to some Mobile colonists in 1708, the first development by Europeans in the future New Orleans area. These early long-lot plantations, which would come to dominate the Louisiana landscape for centuries, fronted the bayou by 2.5 to 4 arpents and extended back by 36 to 40 arpents along the natural levees of the now-extinct bayous of Metairie and Gentilly (Sauvage).[55] (A linear arpent measures about 192 English feet. See page 85 for a detailed discussion of the unit *arpent.*) The pioneers' wheat crop at Bayou St. John proved to be yet another disappointment, but the venture helped put the site "on the map," literally and figuratively, throughout the 1710s.

Despite these failures, Jérôme Phélypeaux de Maurepas, Count de Pontchartrain[56] maintained a keen interest in Louisiana during this period and began to cast his eyes toward the private sector to enable further development. The decision was finally made by King Louis XIV in 1712 to cede a commercial monopoly of Louisiana to a prominent financier and colonial investor named Antoine Crozat. Promised ownership of all land developments and no taxation on exports, Crozat accepted the fifteen-year charter on September 14, 1712, and formed the Company of Louisiana with two associates. Louisiana was now a private enterprise, with only a few obligations to the government: Crozat would have to import ten colonists and twenty-five tons of goods on each of two ships per year, and the king would provide a governor to represent the crown.[57]

The concession was a logical move, akin to the numerous modern-day efforts to privatize inefficient government endeavors, in that it removed the onus of development from the government's coffers yet allowed the country to reap benefits if the venture proved successful. But Crozat's venture was largely speculative, and failure was probably inevitable. "Bad country, bad people" is how Gov. Antoine de La Mothe Cadillac described his Louisiana colony in 1713.[58] The lack of mineral riches and scarcity of settlers for agriculture, coupled with mismanagement, feuding among the governors, and increased tensions with the Indians, forced Crozat out of business in five years. "My three principal projects: discovery of mines of gold and silver, the establishment and maintenance of workers for plantations of tobacco, [and] commerce with Spain were dissipated,"[59] wrote Crozat to the Ministry of Marine in 1717, upon retroceding his Louisiana monopoly to the crown.

Despite the commercial failure, a number of important events occurred in the region during the Crozat years. First, in 1714, Louis Juchereau de Saint-Denis (former commandant of Fort de Mississippi and one of the recipients of the 1708 Bayou St. John concessions) founded Natchitoches on high ground along the Red River, "to assert the French claim to lower Louisiana and to develop trade with the Spaniards in Texas and to the south."[60] Second, at about the same time, La Mothe Cadillac established Fort Toulouse and Fort Tombecbe on key rivers in Alabama, to guard against English incursions from the north and east. Third, in 1716, Bienville founded a garrison—Fort Rosalie, now Natchez—at the bluffs along the Mississippi above the Red River confluence, providing the French with a commanding presence on the river with fine soils nearby and an opportunity to keep

Four years before Bienville founded New Orleans and hundreds of miles inland from the site he selected, Louis Juchereau de Saint-Denis established Natchitoches on an upland along a branch of the Red River. The settlement was mentioned as a possible capital of French Louisiana. Natchitoches today is beautifully preserved, full of historic homes within its limits and others along the nearby Cane River. *Photograph by author, 1999*

49. Giraud, vol. 1, 38-47.
50. M. de Rémonville's *Historical Letter Concerning the Mississippi*, as quoted by Villiers du Terrage, 166.
51. Conrad, 27.
52. Giraud, vol. 1, 91-97.
53. Ibid., 109-10.
54. This settlement is sometimes (confusingly) referred to as Bilochy, or Biloxi, for the Indian tribe that lived there since 1700. The historic effort in 1708 to settle Bayou St. John was preceded eight years earlier by very meager attempts by Iberville and one Father du Ru to clear land and farm in this same area; both failed to get off the ground and made no lasting impact (Giraud, vol. 1, 190, 99, and Freiberg, 33).
55. Ekberg, *French Roots in the Illinois Country*, 22, and Freiberg, 29-30.

56. Jérôme Phélypeaux de Maurepas, Count de Pontchartrain served as an important advisor to his father, Louis Phélypeaux, Count de Pontchartrain, since 1693 (when the son was the Marquis de Phélypeaux) and formally assumed the post of Minister of Marine from him in 1699. Confusingly, both men are often referred to as "Pontchartrain." Father and son are commemorated today by the lakes Pontchartrain and Maurepas. Rule, 179.
57. Giraud, vol. 1, 249-50.
58. Lemann, 360.
59. As quoted by Dufour, *Ten Flags in the Wind*, 75.
60. Kniffen and Hilliard, 120. The Spanish countered by founding a post at Los Adaïs, twelve miles west of Natchitoches, making this obscure strip of land in modern-day north-central Louisiana an interface between the French and Spanish colonial empires.

an eye on the potentially hostile Natchez Indians. Together with Mobile, Biloxi, and a smattering of outposts on the upper Mississippi, these new French bases formed clutches in the effort to control the unwieldy and problematic Louisiana claim. Fourth, while Crozat's monopoly starved the colony of both competing commercial investment and government financing, it kept Louisiana in the private sector—a status that would soon be exploited and that would eventually lead to the founding of New Orleans. Finally, it was during the Crozat years that Louis XIV died (1715) and left the throne to his five-year-old great-grandson, Louis XV, for whom Philippe, duc d'Orléans would act as Regent of France. During his company's five-year life, Crozat kept alive the idea of a garrison "at the point where [Bayou St. John] runs from the Mississippi River into Lake Pontchartrain,"[61] but it would be up to the next regime of Louisiana mavericks to finally seize the site.

Founding of New Orleans, Phase I: 1717-18

Those mavericks were the Scottish rogue businessman John Law and his French royal patron Philippe, duc d'Orléans. John Law was a flamboyant character of almost cinematic proportions, "handsome and personable, a mathematical wizard, a gambler in the grand manner," and "a fantastic promoter and speculator" skilled in banking and finance.[62] Born in Edinburgh in 1671, Law roved the great cities of Europe and hobnobbed with their aristocracy while dueling, gambling, wheeling and dealing along the way.

Settling with his millions in Paris in the early 1710s, he allied himself with a kindred spirit, Philippe, duc d'Orléans, and received his authorization to establish the *Banque Generale* in 1716. The bank prospered just as Crozat surrendered his Louisiana monopoly, providing an opportunity that the gambler Law seized by proposing to the duc d'Orléans a land-development scheme for the Mississippi Valley that would enrich all investors and the country. On August 13, 1717, Crozat formally relinquished Louisiana; on September 6, John Law, head of the new Company of the West, received a twenty-five-year monopoly charter for the land that he promised to populate with 6,000 settlers and 3,000 slaves during the next ten years.

The Company then launched a marketing campaign of historic dimensions across France and the continent to drum up investment in Louisiana stock and land, and to entice the lower classes to emigrate to the riches of the New World. Speculation in the grossly exaggerated claims of Louisiana's mineral wealth and commercial potential eventually inflated the "Mississippi Bubble" to the bursting point, rendering early Louisiana one of history's great real-estate hoaxes and John Law a fraud for the ages. These judgments aside, Law and his Company of the West, unlike the ambivalent dabblers of previous years, thrust Louisiana into the forefront of European attention and, more importantly and more permanently, decided resolutely to found a city to be called *La Nouvelle Orléans*. The resolution appeared in the Company's register with a probable date of September 9, 1717[63]—only three days into its charter—and read, "Resolved to establish, thirty leagues up the river, a burg which should be called New Orleans, where landing would be possible from either the river or Lake Pontchartrain."[64] The name *Nouvelle Orléans* probably came from a May 1717 report by Bienville and Jean Michelle Seigneur de L'Epinet, which suggested founding a new post and naming it after Philippe, duc d'Orléans;[65] the specified situation between the river and the lake presumably came from Bienville's recommendations and knowledge of the area. (It should be noted that this instruction could imply numerous locations between the river and lake, not necessarily the site eventually chosen.)

Working with information-age speed, the Company declared Bienville "Commander General of the Louisiana Company" and appointed, on October 1, a man named Bonnaud as a cashier "at the counter [office] which is to be established at New Orleans, on the St. Louis [Mississippi] River."[66] Sometime during the next six months—the historical record is scant here—Bienville drew upon his twenty years' experience and his employer's instructions to decide and act upon the siting of New Orleans at its present-day location. Perhaps

he was carrying on the vision of his deceased elder brother, Iberville, who, in the days before private-sector management of Louisiana, always recognized the importance of a key river position as a bulwark against English advancement in the Mississippi Valley.

"I myself went to the spot, to choose the best site," recalled Bienville on June 10, 1718, as his forty men cleared the area. Jean-Baptiste Bénard de La Harpe recorded:

> In the month of March, 1718, the New Orleans establishment was begun. It is situated at 29°50', in flat and swampy ground. . . . The Company's project was, it seems, to build the town between the Mississippi and the St. John river [Bayou St. John] which empties into Lake Pontchartrain; the ground there is higher than on the banks of the Mississippi. This river is at a distance of a league from Bayou St. John, and the latter brook is a league and half from the Lake. A canal joining the Mississippi with the Lake has been planned which would be very useful even though this place served only as warehouse and the principal establishment were made at Natchez. The advantage of this port is that ships of [left blank] tons can easily reach it.[67]

La Harpe's passage recognizes this site's key position between the lake and the river to the point of mentioning a canal proposed to connect the two.[68] It also reveals that the founding of New Orleans did not necessarily imply that this new settlement would be *the* main French city in the Louisiana territory.

Historian Marc de Villiers du Terrage surmised that work commenced on New Orleans sometime between mid-March and mid-April 1718,[69] and the popular consensus seems to be that the initial clearing of forest implies "founding"[70] and therefore New Orleans was founded in 1718 by Jean Baptiste Le Moyne, sieur de Bienville. However, Villiers du Terrage opined that "the date for the foundation of New Orleans may be fixed at pleasure anywhere between the spring of 1717 and the month of June, 1722, when Le Blond de La Tour [ratified the city plan] drawn up a year before by Adrien de Pauger."[71] During those five years—starting with Bienville's report and the Company's resolution and ending with the surveying of the French Quarter—a geographical debate ensued as to which locale should indeed emerge as *the* French city in the effort to develop the wilderness of Louisiana. At stake, of course, was the nature, design, role, and character of the future city of New Orleans.

Where to Site the Principal City?

Controversy surrounded the siting of New Orleans for two reasons: geography and partisanship. The lower Mississippi Valley and coastal region provided numerous potential sites, each with its advantages and disadvantages, but no clearly superior sites,[72] as Havana offered to Cuba or Charleston the Carolina coast. Hence, worthwhile debate emerged purely on geographical grounds. Some candidate sites were under development for

---

61. Crozat, as quoted by Giraud, vol. 2, 42.
62. Dufour, *Ten Flags in the Wind*, 76-77.
63. Villiers du Terrage, 174. The register lists the resolution to establish New Orleans next to an incomplete date ("9th"). It is probable that the date was September 9, 1717, since the company received its charter on September 6 and made a clear reference to the proposed city on October 1, 1717. The register also called for a port at Ship Island, a town at Natchez, and forts in Illinois and Natchitoches country.
64. As quoted by Villiers du Terrage, 174.
65. Villiers du Terrage, 173, 175, and Freiberg, 36.
66. As quoted by Villiers du Terrage, 173-74. After nearly two decades of vacillation in both the government and private sectors, why did the final decision to found New Orleans come about so rapidly, within a single month? Perhaps because the Company, like any enterprise gathering venture capital, strove to impress potential investors with a flurry of tangible activity—essentially the establishment of offices and the hiring of staff.
67. As quoted by Villiers du Terrage, 179.
68. This vision would finally come to fruition 200 years later in the form of the Inner Harbor Navigational Canal (Industrial Canal).
69. Villiers du Terrage, 180. André Pénicaut, carpenter and chronicler of the early years of French Louisiana, describes initial settlement at New Orleans occurring in the latter half of 1717, rather than the spring of 1718: "M. de Bienville had told M. de l'Épinet that on his last trip down from the Natchez he had noticed a place quite suitable for the site of a settlement on the bank of the Missicipy [*sic*] thirty leagues above the embouchure of the river, on the right side going upstream. . . . M. de l'Épinet sent . . . eighty salt smugglers . . . and a great many carpenters with M. de Bienville to show them the place he had chosen on the bank of the Missicipy for this new post. . . . Some living quarters were built and two large warehouses" (Pénicaut, 208-9). This account was later picked up by Father Charlevoix in his history of the area. However, Villiers du Terrage describes Pénicaut's information as "very unreliable . . . filled with errors so gross that they would be incomprehensible, if they were not evidently deliberate" (177). Indeed, Pénicaut seems to paint an overly optimistic picture of New Orleans and Louisiana, citing numerous new land claims and developments but little of the accompanying challenges and controversies.
70. This seems to be the local consensus, although the Bienville statue at the fork of Decatur Street and North Peters, the city's foremost tribute to its founder, identifies 1717 as the founding year. Also, in Paris, the 200th anniversary of the founding of New Orleans was celebrated in 1917, a recognition of the Company's decision to found the city as the city's beginning. Davis, 56-57.
71. Villiers du Terrage, 158.
72. Perhaps this is too kind. "Almost uniformly obnoxious" and "slightly more repulsive as one moved downstream" is how geographer Peirce F. Lewis characterized the suitability of the banks of the lower Mississippi for a city, in his classic *New Orleans: The Making of an Urban Landscape*, 30.

Ascending the Mississippi River from its mouth was slow, difficult, and dangerous. Instead, early settlers gained access to the river from the gulf by penetrating mazes of bays, bayous, and marshes (almost all generously revealed to them by the Indians) to reach high ground leading to the Mississippi. The major route that accomplished this goal led directly to the founding of New Orleans at its present-day site and cannot by overemphasized in its importance to the city's history. It is generally known as the Bayou St. John portage or the Bayou Road portage, but those names reflect sections of a larger route. The route began when sailors exited the salty waters of Lake Borgne at the edge of the Gulf of Mexico, entered the Rigolets (1) or Chef Menteur Pass (2) into Lake Pontchartrain, and followed the south shore of the lake (3) to the mouth of Bayou St. John, seen here at the Spanish Fort ruins (4). "If there is one element of geographic knowledge that makes [New Orleans] inevitable, it is this sluggish bayou," wrote Tulane anthropologist T. R. Kidder. The voyagers would then ascend narrow, log-strewn Bayou St. John to the general vicinity of Moss Street (5a) from about Grand Route St. John (5b-c) to Bell Street (5d), then disembark and walk down this slightly elevated ridge. Continuing down *Le Chemin au Bayou St. Jean* ridge toward the river, they would pass through the present-day Esplanade Ridge neighborhood (6-7), the streets of Faubourg Tremé (8), North Rampart Street at the edge of the original city (9), what is now the French Quarter's Governor Nicholls Street (10-11), and finally to the vicinity of the present-day French Market fruit, vegetable, and flea market (12-13) on the banks of the Mississippi. *Photographs by author, 1999-2000. Paths taken from the bayou to the riverbank during the early years may have varied within one to two blocks of the route described here.*

Bienville strongly advocated this site—at the cusp of a sharp bend of the Mississippi on the relatively high ground of the river's natural levees—to host the city to be called *La Nouvelle Orléans*, which the Company of the West first proposed to create in September 1717. Bienville founded his settlement in the spring of the following year, at the point near the center of the left photo, and started clearing the forest around present-day Decatur Street just upriver from Jackson Square (middle photo) in March-April 1718, but it was not until December 1721 that the site was selected as the capital of the Louisiana colony and its future was somewhat more assured. Viewed from a skyscraper on Canal Street (right), Bienville's settlement in the wilderness, now the world-famous French Quarter, lies perched on the Father of Waters. *Photographs by author, 1996-2000*

a number of years by 1718 and therefore had advocates with something to lose by the rise of a new and inevitably competing city.[73] Hence, timeless hometown partisanship accounted for some of the opposition to New Orleans as well. An analysis of each site that vied to be the premier city in French Louisiana (that is, its principal port or its capital or both), and its advantages and disadvantages as recognized at the time, provides insight into the historical development of the region and the emergence of the city of New Orleans:

1. French Quarter Site Previous discussion described Bienville's personal knowledge of the Bayou St. John portage and his eventual selection of a riverside site to exploit that connection. Bienville was *the* iron-willed advocate of that locale—the French Quarter site[74]—as the home for New Orleans, at times against strong opposition from partisans on the coast and Company directors in France.[75]

Advantages of the French Quarter Site

- **Shortcut Route**   The premier advantage to the French Quarter site was its location on a least-cost/minimum-distance route between the Gulf of Mexico and the Mississippi River. Instead of taking the long and perilous route from the mouth of the river, mariners could slip through the protected waters of the Mississippi Sound and Lake Borgne, and traverse the Rigolets land bridge via the Rigolets or Chef Menteur Pass, to gain access to Lake Pontchartrain and eventually the placid waters of Bayou St. John. Three miles up this bayou lay a slight upland (Bayou Road/Esplanade Ridge) that rose above the swamps and led to the natural levee of the Mississippi River, where Bienville selected his site. In grandiose terms, this site represented the optimal connection between the Old World, where schemed the Company of the West and its investors and government, and the New World, where lay the unknown riches of the Louisiana territory. In plainer words, the French Quarter site was simply on the quickest and safest route to get from point A to point B.
- **Topography**   Sediments deposited by periodic floods over the centuries formed natural levees paralleling the river and bayous throughout the deltaic plain. These uplands provided the French Quarter site with just enough relief—perhaps five to seven feet above average river stage and ten to fourteen feet above sea level at the time—to host a settlement. The French Quarter site being at a cutbank portion of a

river meander, the natural levee here tended to be broader than in other areas. Slight uplands along the Bayou Road/Esplanade Ridge (the back slope of the broad natural levee) and the extinct distributaries of Bayou Metairie and Gentilly formed other transportation advantages. Although Bienville was mistaken in believing this land to be safe from high water, tidal waves (storm surges), and hurricanes,[76] he was right in that the gradual relief of the natural levees and the distance from the coast provided *some* protection from all three threats.

- **Riverside Guard**   A presence on the Mississippi River guarded the artery against foreign—namely English—penetration of Louisiana. Iberville was motivated by this concern in the early years of French Louisiana and probably instilled it in his younger brother, Bienville. Father Charlevoix, writing in 1722, cited New Orleans' location above *le Détour aux Anglois* (English Turn Bend) as an important reason for the city's location, since this great bend in the river "may cause a retardment" in the approach of foreign vessels, which city founders judged "very advantageous to prevent a surprise."[77] Adrien de Pauger made the same observation in 1724. The sweeping crescent of the Mississippi at this site also provided ample opportunities for river access and port activity.
- **Relative Location**   The French Quarter site was roughly halfway between two of the most important assets in French Louisiana, Mobile and Natchez, and thus fit in well with overall development plans.
- **Soils**   Proponents of French Quarter site pointed to the area's rich alluvial soils for agricultural production.

Le Page du Pratz, eyewitness to the early years of French Louisiana, described the attributes of the future French Quarter site in *The History of Louisiana:* "As the principal settlement was then at Mobile, it was proper to have the capital fixed at a place from which there could be an easy communication with this post: and thus a better choice could not have been made, as the town being on the banks of the Missisip, vessels, tho' of a thousand ton, may lay their sides close to the shore even at low water. . . . This town is only a league from St. John's creek [Bayou St. John], where passengers take water for Mobile, in going to which they pass Lake St. Louis [Pontchartrain], and from thence all along the coast."[78]

73. Villiers du Terrage, 172, 186-87.
74. In this particular discussion, we will refer to the final site selected for New Orleans as the *French Quarter site*, rather than as *New Orleans*, to distinguish the site from the "theoretical" New Orleans—the envisioned principal city and capital of Louisiana—that could have been sited in a number of locations. *French Quarter site* implies the riverside location selected by Bienville in 1718 that is known today as the French Quarter, or Vieux Carré.
75. It is probably safe to assume that Bienville, like his adversaries in the competing settlements, was motivated by both a sense of professional responsibility and personal gain. After all, Bienville owned two vast concessions near the French Quarter site (see pages 86-88) and would benefit personally from the relocation of the capital to that area. Then again, he had selected the French Quarter site prior to the acquisition of these concessions. Charles T. Soniat, 9, and Freiberg, 39, 52-53.

76. Davis, 55.
77. Charlevoix, 178. In this particular journal entry, Father Charlevoix listed the Bayou St. John portage and the adjacency to English Turn as the two main reasons for New Orleans' siting. He was, however, duly unimpressed with both.
78. Pratz, 53.

Disadvantages of the French Quarter Site

- **Topography**   The natural levees provided protection from flood only when compared to other areas along the river that had even less elevation. Relative to the bluffs of Natchez and Natchitoches, the French Quarter site was most certainly threatened by rising river waters and in fact suffered from them in 1719.
- **General Environs**   While all prospective sites for New Orleans suffered from heat, humidity, and fetid summertime conditions, the French Quarter site was disadvantaged in that it was almost surrounded by mosquito-infested swamplands, deprived of both the breezes of the coast and the cooler temperatures of the inland.
- **Distance from Coast**   While guarding the river, the French Quarter site neglected the coast by a distance of at least fifty miles and added travel time for ships arriving from the Gulf Coast, the Caribbean, and France. Alternately, distance from the sea may be viewed as a protective measure for a port against enemy raids and a buffer against frontal assaults by hurricanes in the Gulf of Mexico.
- **Sandbars at the Delta**   All Mississippi River sites suffered from constraints on accessibility rendered by the periodic silting of the mouth of the Mississippi. Some observers considered this problem to be insurmountable, reason to exclude the possibility of a river capital.

2. Bayou Manchac Site   A strong and reasonable contender to host New Orleans was the area where Bayou Manchac flowed off from the Mississippi, between Lake Maurepas and the river, southeast of present-day Baton Rouge and northwest of Gonzales.[79] Valued for its position on the busiest route[80] between the gulf and the river, Bayou Manchac's champions included the Company of the West, Bénard de La Harpe, Drouot de Valdeterre, and others, though some of these supporters were more interested in denouncing the French Quarter site than backing Bayou Manchac. Apparently unaware of Bienville's work already under way at the French Quarter site, the Company itself instructed Chief Engineer Perrier on April 14, 1718, "to find the most convenient place for trading with Mobile, whether by sea or by Lake Pontchartrain, . . . in the least danger from inundation when floods occur, and as near as possible to the best agricultural lands. These various considerations convince us, as far as we can judge, that the most convenient site is on the Manchac brook; the town limits should stretch from the river-banks to the edge of the brook."[81] Perrier died en route to Louisiana (in Havana), allowing Bienville to continue his progress at the French Quarter site. But in late 1720 New Orleans was very nearly relocated to the Bayou Manchac site.

Advantages of the Bayou Manchac Site

- **Shortcut Route**   Like the Bayou St. John portage, Bayou Manchac ("Manchac" has been translated as "rear entrance")[82] provided a fairly direct east-west shortcut from the coast to the river. Mariners could enter Lake Pontchartrain as they would traveling to the French Quarter site, but instead of hugging the southern shore of the lake, a westward route was followed through Pass Manchac and across Lake Maurepas to reach the Amite River and finally Bayou Manchac,[83] bringing sailors to within a few miles of the Mississippi, depending on river conditions. By one later estimate, traveling the Manchac route to

this site from the gulf was about six times faster than sailing up the Mississippi.[84] "If [this site] is suitable," continued the Company's directions to Perrier, "then New Orleans will be better there than elsewhere, because of the convenience for communications with Mobile by the brook."[85]

- **Topography**   The natural levee at the head of Bayou Manchac, about three times higher than the French Quarter site relative to sea level but still only a few feet above normal river level, might have provided some flood protection, but the presence of the low spot on the natural levee presumably nullified this advantage.[86] Bluffs at Baton Rouge, ten miles to the northwest, afforded better protection as well as a commanding perch on the river.
- **Other Attributes**   The Company recognized the Bayou Manchac site's proximity to the Red River and the Yazoo region (a potential wheat-growing area) as advantages, as well as its inland position, hunting, and "healthiness of the air."[87] As with the French Quarter site, good soils abounded nearby, and the surrounding marshes provided some protection from hurricanes.

Disadvantages of the Bayou Manchac Site

- **Distance from the Coast**   "The sole difficulty remaining before New Orleans can be built on the Manchac brook, is its distance from the sea, sixty-five leagues."[88]
- **Neglect of the Lower River**   A city at the Bayou Manchac site would expose about two hundred miles of riverbanks below it to foreign ships and footholds. The Company suggested a fort at English Turn Bend to guard against this threat[89]—but might this proposed fort evolve into a settlement in its own right, thus competing with Bayou Manchac?
- **Navigability**   The Company thought Bayou Manchac to be "navigable at all times and at slight expense,"[90] but this was usually not the case. Iberville noted that the bayou was but six feet wide when he encountered it in 1699; Bienville's subsequent exploration determined the waterway to be nearly clogged with debris and difficult to navigate.[91] In the early developmental years of the French Quarter site, the Bayou Manchac/Amite River system (known as the Iberville River at the time) was "practically dry for half the year, [such] that all boats passed through Bayou St. John."[92] Only when the river was high did water flow from the Mississippi through Bayou Manchac's channel; under normal circumstances, a terrestrial portage of about five to ten miles was required between the river and the bayou.[93]
- **Port Limitations**   The Bayou Manchac site lacked the sweeping crescent that characterized the French Quarter site; riverbank access for port activity was relatively limited.
- **Distributary**   The Bayou Manchac site was essentially a crevasse—a low point in the natural levee through which high waters would spill and distribute via the bayou, posing a threat to a settlement. This crevasse could have been (and eventually was) sealed off, but such a project might have represented a major undertaking for a nascent city in the wilderness.

3. Natchez   The rugged loess bluffs overlooking the Mississippi about thirty miles above the Red River confluence, where in 1716 Bienville founded Fort Rosalie, formed a third contender to host New Orleans. Natchez's tenacious promoter was Marc Antoine Hubert, commissary general of Louisiana from 1716 to 1720 and director general of the New Orleans Counter in 1718, a counterpart to Bienville. Hubert acquired land near Bayou St. John and once promoted that area to host New Orleans, but switched his allegiance to Natchez when he received a grant at St. Catherine's Creek and moved there in 1720, quickly establishing an impressive plantation.[94]

79. Bayou Manchac was a distributary of the Mississippi, formed by a low point along the natural levee through which water passed during times of flooding. The waterway, never easily navigable in its upper reaches, was dammed by Andrew Jackson's men in 1814 and permanently closed off from the river in 1824-28, severing the only major eastward distributary of the lower Mississippi. Dalrymple, 12, and Kniffen, "Bayou Manchac," 462. See also Chambers, 107.
80. *The Louisiana Historical Quarterly*, 372.
81. As quoted by Villiers du Terrage, 184.
82. Bragg, 213, and Detro, 193.
83. Iberville christened the Bayou Manchac/Amite River system the "Iberville River" in 1699, a name that was used until the nineteenth century. Bayou Manchac now refers to the distributary that joins the Amite River (a system that drains the hills of southern Mississippi and the Florida parishes) near Port Vincent. Brasseaux, *A Comparative View of French Louisiana*, 65.

84. "The voyage from Pensacola to the Manchac settlement was accomplished in about eight to ten days, as opposed to the seven or eight weeks usually required to go by the Mississippi River" (summarized from a ca.-1779 source by Dalrymple, 7).
85. As quoted by Villiers du Terrage, 184.
86. Kniffen, "Bayou Manchac," 463-64.
87. As quoted by Villiers du Terrage, 184.
88. Ibid.
89. Ibid.
90. Ibid.
91. Brasseaux, *A Comparative View of French Louisiana*, 52, 63.
92. Villiers du Terrage, 193.
93. Kniffen, "Bayou Manchac," 462-66.
94. Villiers du Terrage, 186; Pénicaut, 237-39; and Freiberg, 39.

Looking south toward the Highway 51/I-55 bridges over Pass Manchac (left) and east from the Highway 51 bridge into Pass Manchac and the Manchac Swamp. Pass Manchac (an Indian word loosely translated as "rear entrance"), connecting Lake Pontchartrain and Lake Maurepas, allowed explorers from the Gulf of Mexico to sail across these lakes and reach the Mississippi by means of Bayou Manchac. That site was eyed as a potential location for New Orleans. Years later, Pass Manchac was a segment of a series of international colonial-era borders; it is now a parish line. *Photographs by author, 2001*

There were times in 1718-20 when New Orleans was almost relocated to the point where Bayou Manchac flowed off from the Mississippi, a few miles south of present-day Baton Rouge. The original riverside site has been swept away by the river, but had that decision been executed, these cornfields along Highway 327 at the East Baton Rouge/Iberville Parish line (above) might have hosted part of the initial grid of streets. Instead, New Orleans flourished at Bienville's site far downriver, today's French Quarter. The British realized the commercial potential of the Bayou Manchac site, as a portage from the Mississippi to Lakes Maurepas and Pontchartrain and thence to the gulf, and established the community of Manchac and Fort Bute here in the 1760s (to the left of the forested area in the above photograph, marking the channel of Bayou Manchac). To the right of the forest in the above photograph was Spanish territory, guarded by Fort San Gabriel de Manchack. The British village of Manchac (not to be confused with the modern community of Manchac south of Ponchatoula) was rocked by the Revolutionary War and disappeared by the end of the century, leaving us to speculate what might have become of these cornfields. The photograph below shows the Mississippi at the Manchac Bend; somewhere in the river lies the spot that could have hosted New Orleans. *Photographs by author, 1999-2000*

Headwaters of Bayou Manchac today (left). Bayou Manchac was formed by a crevasse in the natural levee that allowed high river water to spill over and flow toward Lake Maurepas and eventually the gulf. The barely navigable channel was widened by the British in 1764, dammed from the Mississippi by Andrew Jackson in an effort against the British fifty years later, then permanently sealed off from the Mississippi in 1824-28. Upper Bayou Manchac is now a placid stream in a narrow channel shaded by dense vegetation. An international boundary between Spanish and French colonial territories until 1763, British West Florida and Spanish Louisiana from 1763 to 1783, and Spanish West Florida and American Louisiana from 1803-10, Bayou Manchac as shown in the photographs at left now forms the East Baton Rouge/Iberville Parish line. Its present-day circumstance belies its importance in colonial history. *Photographs by author, 1999*

Advantages of Natchez
- **Topography**   At over 200 feet above sea level and 175 feet above the river, Natchez is high enough to view the horizon westward over the Mississippi Valley, completely protected from river floods and well suited for guarding the river.
- **Other Attributes**   Proximity to the Red River confluence, rich agricultural soils (though not as vast and accessible as areas on the lower river), and slightly less hot and muggy conditions than the low country made Natchez an attractive site. Le Page du Pratz, overseer of Company plantations, friend of Hubert, and a Natchez plantation owner, quoted Father Charlevoix's defense of the place in Pratz's *History of Louisiana:*

> Fort Rosalie, in the country of the Natchez, was at first pitched upon for the metropolis of this colony. But though it be necessary to begin by a settlement near the sea . . . it appears to me, that the capital . . . cannot be better situated than in this place. It is not subject to inundations of the river; the air is pure; the country very extensive; the land fit for every thing, and well watered; it is not at too great a distance from the sea, and nothing hinders vessels to go up to it. . . . It is within reach of every place intended to be settled.[95]

Mississippi historian J. F. H. Claiborne also extolled the attributes of Natchez in his 1880 account of the debate, describing the area (perhaps with a bit of home-state bias) as "elevated, healthy, picturesque, contiguous to the alluvions on the west of the river [and] the highlands beyond, sufficiently removed from the sea to be inaccessible to an invader [yet] near enough for all commercial purposes, and three hundred miles nearer the posts of the Illinois! These were the recommendations that presented themselves to [Hubert's] practical and comprehensive mind, and it is a great misfortune that they did not prevail. The proudest city of the new world would now have stood on the ancient village of the Natchez."[96]

Disadvantages of Natchez
- **Distance from the Coast and Neglect of the Lower River**   Like the Bayou Manchac site, only more so, Natchez was simply too removed from the coast to serve as the gatekeeper and port that the envisioned city of New Orleans needed to be. Its perch on the inland hills of present-day Mississippi would have left hundreds of miles of banks along the lower river open to either competition or invasion. In brief, Natchez's *site* was attractive, but its *situation* did not fulfill the requirements—despite the advocacy of Hubert and others.

4. English Turn   English Turn, the first hairpin meander of the Mississippi for travelers heading up from the delta, earned its name from Bienville's 1699 encounter with the *Carolina Galley*. The ten-mile-long 200° swerve (English Turn Bend)[97] around the narrow point bar made it a navigational challenge and a potential strategic opportunity for the French—if not for a capital then at least for a garrison or a counter.

Advantages of English Turn
- **Riverside Guard**   A stronghold at English Turn would achieve excellent military control of the lower river, close enough to the delta to preclude the establishment of a substantial settlement lower down the river. The French eventually would build two forts here, one on each side of the river.

- **Other Attributes**   The slowing of river traffic might have made English Turn a logical harbor or depot. A naval officer recognized this potential in 1717, describing the meander as "a cove where an excellent port could be made."[98] Three years later, another naval officer proposed English Turn as the site for the capital, citing the straightness of the river up to this point (implying, incidentally, an approach from the delta—the slow and often arduous route from the coast) and depth of the river at the turn.[99] Even Adrien de Pauger, engineer of the street network at the French Quarter site, pondered whether the navigational difficulty of English Turn would eventually lead "to the necessity for building stores below the bend, and perhaps even for transporting thither the principal seat of the Colony."[100] (Father Charlevoix identified the aspect of slowing ship movement at English Turn Bend as one of the reasons for the selection of the French Quarter site, since it was located *above* the bend and allowed time to prepare against surprise attacks; Pauger concurred with this view in 1724.)[101] The area was also surrounded by fine agricultural land.

Disadvantages of English Turn
- **Lack of Coastal Access**   Had an adequate waterway connected Lake Borgne with English Turn Bend[102] in the same manner that Bayou Manchac, Pass Manchac, and Bayou St. John linked Lakes Maurepas and Pontchartrain with the Mississippi, English Turn may have been a serious contender to host New Orleans. But compared with these other shortcuts, the trip from the coast to English Turn would have been serpentine and difficult through the shallow bayous of the Lake Borgne marshes or slow and dangerous through the mouth of the Mississippi. It may have required using the Bayou St. John portage—lending more credence to a city at that location.

This point at the sharp eastward bend of English Turn was suggested as a site for a settlement and even a capital. Despite its prominent location from the perspective of river traffic, no substantial city ever developed along English Turn, due in part to the lack of adequate shortcuts to the Gulf of Mexico. Nevertheless, it remained an important military fortification into the early 1800s. *Photograph by author, 1999*

---

95. Pratz, 26.

96. Claiborne, 37.

97. Colonial manuscripts refer to this area as *Détour à l'Anglois, Détour aux Anglois, Détour de l'Anglois,* and *Détour des Anglois,* translated variously as English Turn, English Reach, and English Bend. "English Turn" as used here refers to the east-bank point bar known as Shingle Point, while "English Turn Bend" implies the ten-mile-long river meander shared by the parishes of Orleans, St. Bernard, and Plaquemines. Many people refer to this entire region simply as English Turn. Ekberg, "The English Bend," 212-13.

98. As quoted from *Le Nouveau Mercure* by Villiers du Terrage, 171.

99. As quoted from *Relation de la Louisiane ou Mississipy* by Villiers du Terrage, 198.

100. As quoted by Villiers du Terrage, 223-24.

101. Father Charlevoix nevertheless disputed this alleged advantage to the French Quarter site: "In whatever place the city is situated, must not the mouth of the river be defended by good batteries . . . ?" (178-79). See also Ekberg, "The English Bend," 215.

102. In fact there was a waterway between English Turn Bend and Lake Borgne—Bayou Dupre—but at the time it was a mere inlet through the swamp, small and difficult to navigate, adjoining the shallow backwaters of Lake Borgne. The waterway was enough of a "back door" into the interior to warrant the construction of a fort—Tower Dupre, which still stands—in the 1800s. Bayou Dupre was enlarged in 1886 and 1900 (Lake Borgne Canal) in pursuit of the same goal from two centuries prior—to connect the river and the lake—but was superceded by New Orleans' successful effort to do the same thing at the Inner Harbor Navigational Canal (1923). Since 1947 the Lake Borgne Canal (also called the Violet Canal) has been used mostly by commercial fishermen. U.S. Army Corps of Engineers, *Research Design for the Violet Site Alternative,* 55.

- **Topography**   The natural levee is fairly narrow on both banks along English Turn Bend, measuring only about a mile wide and less than five feet high. The natural levee of the crescent near the French Quarter site is more than twice as broad in some places and a few feet higher.

Bayou Dupre transected the marshes between English Turn and Lake Borgne and thus provided a gulf/river shortcut, a key factor in siting settlements in the Louisiana wilderness of the early 1700s. But the waterway was narrow, shallow, and difficult to navigate; for this and other reasons, no major settlement developed on English Turn. Bayou Dupre was enlarged and opened in 1890 as the Lake Borgne Canal, and since 1947, the waterway (also called the Violet Canal) has been used mostly by commercial fishermen. This photograph shows the lock of the Violet Canal seen from the St. Bernard Parish community of Violet, looking toward Bayou Dupre and Lake Borgne. *Photograph by author, 1999*

5. Lake Pontchartrain Shore   Historian Marc de Villiers du Terrage recounts the obstinacy of François Le Maire, a "geographer-missionary" who stalled in his recognition of the site selected for New Orleans apparently because he hoped "that New Orleans may be created on Lake Pontchartrain, so that its counter may be tributary to Biloxi." Perhaps this site would have been located at the mouth of Bayou St. John (present-day Spanish Fort), as erroneously indicated by a 1721 map of the area stored at the Archives Hydrographiques.[103]

This is the point at which Bayou St. John flowed into Lake Pontchartrain, once suggested as a site for New Orleans. It would have been a terrible choice: too low in elevation, too far from the river, and poor for agriculture. Nevertheless, its strategic location warranted the erection of a series of bastions during the colonial era and early American years, including Fort St. John (Spanish Fort), which survives in ruins. The construction of the lakefront in the 1920s and 1930s moved the bayou's mouth into the lake by a half-mile. New Orleanians know this general area as Spanish Fort. *Photographs by author, 1999*

Advantages of Lake Pontchartrain Shore
- **Shortcut Route**   Like the French Quarter site, a settlement on the shore of Lake Pontchartrain would have exploited the Bayou St. John portage between the lake and the river.

Disadvantages of Lake Pontchartrain Shore
- **Topography**   Neither Bayou St. John nor Lake Pontchartrain were rimmed by natural levees, hence this site—a backswamp partially below sea level—would have been highly susceptible to flooding.

---
103. Villiers du Terrage, 180-81.

- **Lack of Coastal or Riverside Guard**   This position would have guarded neither the river (five miles away) nor the coast (fifty miles away).
- **Soils**   While good soils lay a few miles away, the swamplands by the lake were unsuitable for agriculture.

6. Other Sites   For a while after the 1719 flood of the French Quarter site and the French seizure of Pensacola, some Company directors (now Company of the Indies) cast their eyes upon Pensacola as the main port of Louisiana. Biloxi partisans supported the Pensacola idea as well as their own site's candidacy because it bolstered the role of the coast at the expense of the river and kept their settlement "in the loop." One prominent Biloxi advocate was Chief Engineer Le Blond de La Tour,[104] who designed a series of plans for the site in 1721. (In fact Biloxi became the capital in 1719-22 but failed to attain commercial importance.) Mobile and nearby Dauphin Island, capitals of French Louisiana throughout the 1710s, and Natchitoches, founded inland on the Red River in 1714 by Saint-Denis, were also mentioned as potential headquarters.

Advantages of These Sites
- **Coastal Guard**   Locating New Orleans at a coastal site would have maintained a guard against English and Spanish expansion in the area. But since the Company was more interested in economic development than military defense, this attribute is not weighty. Alternately, a principal city on the sea would have made it vulnerable to enemy attack, thus making a coastal position a potential disadvantage.
- **Establishment**   In all four cases, the settlements were already established in sound geographical sites and with rudiment societies in place. All four cities thrive today.
- **Avoidance of the Mississippi Delta**   Silting of the mouth of the Mississippi impeded access to river sites during certain seasons. A coastal site would circumvent this obstacle, although most existing sites had silting problems of their own.

Sites considered by the Company of the West (later Company of the Indies) and its various stakeholders for the capital and principal city of the Louisiana territory had their share of advantages, disadvantages, proponents and critics.
1a. The "French Quarter site" (it was called *La Nouvelle Orléans* starting in 1718 but had no assurance that it would keep that name and ascend in its status) was the point at which the Rigolets-Lake Pontchartrain-Bayou St. John-Bayou Road shortcut route intersected with the Mississippi River, providing relatively well drained terrain and a strategic position on the river.
1b. The site eventually succeeded in gaining the status of capital in late 1721-early 1722 and was promptly laid out with a grid-pattern street network that is now the French Quarter.
2a. A strong contender to become *La Nouvelle Orléans* was the point at which the Rigolets-Lake Pontchartrain-Bayou Manchac shortcut intersected with the Mississippi, south of present-day Baton Rouge.
2b. In 1720, officials proposed to relocate *La Nouvelle Orléans* to the area outlined here, where Bayou Manchac once flowed off from the Mississippi.
3a. Natchez (Fort Rosalie) in present-day Mississippi was favored by Marc Antoine Hubert, commissary general of Louisiana and a major landowner in the area.
3b. Natchez's main advantage was its lofty bluffs, composed of fine silt called loess. This is not an image but a digital elevation model of the Natchez region (brighter areas representing higher elevations), depicting a range from twenty-five feet above mean sea level at the river to over two hundred feet in downtown Natchez and higher to the east. These elevations are over ten times the range found at the other sites.
4a. Some suggested English Turn as a fine site for a capital and principal port. It had some shortcut access to the Gulf of Mexico via a labyrinth of bayous in the marshes.
4b. Most attractive about English Turn was its commanding position on a hairpin turn of the Mississippi, where incoming ships slowed.
5. One commentator suggested relocating *La Nouvelle Orléans* from its nascent riverside site to the Lake Pontchartrain shore, where Bayou St. John flowed into the lake. It would have been a disaster.
6.-10. Others advocated concentrating resources and power in the older coastal sites of Biloxi, Mobile and Dauphin Island (a), and Pensacola (b). The inland settlement of Natchitoches was also mentioned. At stake for these men were the lives and livelihoods they had built up at their respective locations. At stake for France was the control it would exert over its vast North American claim. At stake for the region was the course it would take through history. *Map by author*

---
104. Chambers, 107.

Sites Competing To Be the Premier City/Capital of French Colonial Louisiana, circa 1720

1. French Quarter Site

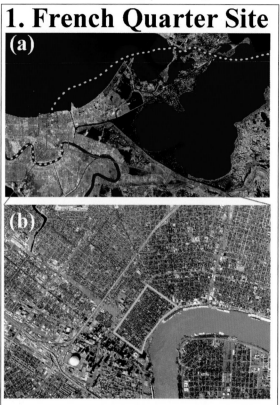
(a)
(b)

Satellite images courtesy Louisiana State University Department of Geography and Anthropology, Landsat, National Air and Space Museum, and Arizona State University Department of Geological Sciences

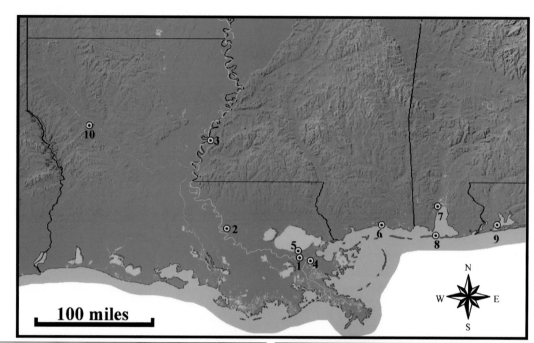
100 miles

5. Lake Pontchartrain

6. Biloxi

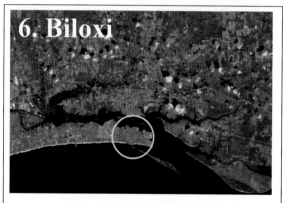

2. Bayou Manchac Site

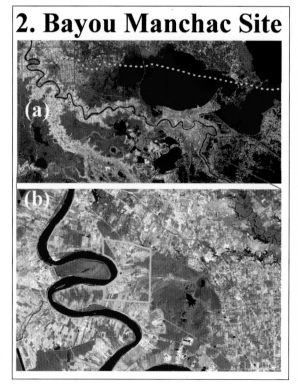
(a)
(b)

3. Natchez

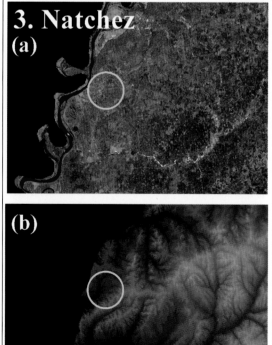
(a)
(b)

4. English Turn Site

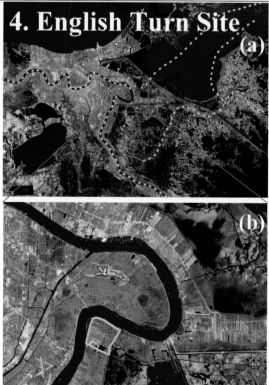
(a)
(b)

7-9. Mobile, Dauphin Island, Pensacola

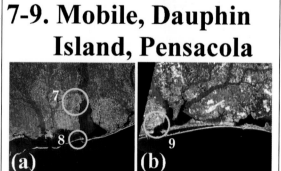
(a)
(b)

10. Natchitoches

Disadvantages of These Sites

- **Neglect of the River** Any coastal site and Natchitoches would have sacrificed the strategic value of the Mississippi River and complicated the flow of goods, probably only delaying, not eliminating, the eventual emergence of a major river port. Had Pensacola been selected, "merchandise from Illinois would have had not one single transshipment at New Orleans, but four: at Pensacola, at Biloxi, at Bayou St. John or Manchac, and finally on the banks of the Mississippi."[105]

- **Distance from French Louisiana** Pensacola's location beyond the far eastern edge of French Louisiana made it politically and militarily vulnerable. Originally a Spanish settlement created in response to La Salle's exploration of the Mississippi Valley for France, Pensacola was seized by the French, regained by the Spanish, recaptured by the French, and returned to the Spanish after the Franco-Spanish War of 1719-22[106]—not a good track record for a principal city. Natchitoches marked the far western edge of southern French Louisiana, near the Spanish Texas frontier, and suffered from the same disadvantage compounded by extreme isolation.

- **Soils** Biloxi and Pensacola lack the rich alluvial soil of the river valley and are better known for their infertile clay earth and spindly pine forests.

- **Other Disadvantages** Biloxi's waters were too shallow for larger vessels to dock or anchor, requiring the use of longboats to ferry seamen from ship to shore.[107] Le Gac also mentions a sort of worm in the waters of Biloxi that apparently damaged ship hulls,[108] and La Harpe claimed that "contrary winds" made Old Biloxy (Ocean Springs) an unfavorable port.[109] But most disadvantageous of all, coastal sites would have been much more prone to hurricane damage than inland sites; in fact, a storm in 1717 damaged the headquarters at Dauphin Island and silted up its harbor, providing Bienville with another reason to cast his eyes toward the French Quarter site.

In sum, Pensacola, Biloxi, Mobile, Natchitoches, and other sites outside the lower Mississippi Valley failed to address the original purpose of occupying Louisiana—"to ensure for France the domination of the Mississippi"[110]—while Natchez and Bayou Manchac may have been too far upriver, and English Turn and Lake Pontchartrain inadequate and inconvenient for other reasons. Although the capital of Louisiana shifted from the Biloxi area (Fort Maurepas, later called Old Biloxy and now Ocean Springs) to two sites near Mobile Bay (Fort Louis, Mobile, and a headquarters and port at Dauphin Island) and back to two sites in the Biloxi area (Old Biloxy and New Biloxy)[111] from 1699 to 1722, it became apparent that the principal economic and political city needed to command a more strategic location.

Competition and Indecision, 1718-21

Hence in the four years following Bienville's selection of the French Quarter site in the spring of 1718, stakeholders in France and throughout Louisiana vied to relocate *La Nouvelle Orléans* to their particular corner of the land. Governor Bienville was practically the sole proponent on the Company board of the French Quarter site.[112] "He pitched upon this spot in preference to many others, more agreeable and commodious," recalled Le Page du Pratz of Bienville's advocacy of the site, concluding thoughtfully, "it is not every man that can see so

Downtown Biloxi in 2000. The first capital of French Louisiana, Fort Maurepas (1699), was located across Biloxi Bay (at a site in the distant upper left) in present-day Ocean Springs. A later capital (1719-22) was located on the peninsula in the foreground, now Biloxi proper. In 1722, the headquarters was relocated to the French Quarter site. *Photograph by author*

far as some others."[113] The other members "were interested in ventures at the old trading posts . . . and they encouraged the coalition of Mobile colonists, of Biloxi tradesmen, and of Lake Pontchartrain boatmen whose business was threatened by rivalry from the Mississippi." The board members "would tolerate no word about New Orleans,"[114] and the "majority of the Superior Council [of the colony] objected to any movement by which the prestige of Biloxi and Mobile might be destroyed."[115]

During those years, progress at the French Quarter site labored under a series of challenges that would put a modern-day chamber of commerce into overtime damage control. Pratz saw only "a palmetto-thatched hut"[116] on the riverside site in January 1719, and three months later Bienville himself reported that "only four houses were under way."[117] Then in the spring of 1719 the waters of the Mississippi rose to levels that even the Indians had not seen before, flooding the muddy outpost and delighting its foes in the competing settlements. The resilient Bienville acknowledged the disaster and suggested building levees and a canal; Hubert, champion of Natchez and enemy of Bienville, seized the moment and transferred company goods to "where the land lies higher and the heat is less severe."[118]

News of the flood and other factors persuaded the Company (called after 1719 the Company of the Indies, after a three-way merger) to suspend work temporarily at New Orleans—that is, the French Quarter site—and cast its eyes toward the excellent harborage at Pensacola, which France had seized, lost, and regained during the Franco-Spanish War of 1719-22. Pensacola was retroceded to the Spanish after the war, rendering moot any talk of making Pensacola the capital of Louisiana, but proponents for a coastal capital had already won out when the Superior Council, opposing both Bienville's New Orleans and Hubert's Natchez, compromised by relocating Company headquarters from the storm-damaged Dauphin Island port near Mobile back to old Fort Maurepas (November 1719) and then across the bay to New Biloxi (January 1720). This decision was something of a blow to Bienville's New Orleans, but at least it drew the capital closer to his site.[119]

105. Villiers du Terrage, 192.
106. Holmes, "Dauphin Island," 103-25.
107. Pénicaut, 208.
108. Villiers du Terrage, 195. Writing almost two centuries later, James S. Zacharie reported that "the waters of the Gulf [near Biloxi] are infested with 'Teredo,' a species of barnacle, which fastens itself to wood under the water and bores into it until it becomes honey-combed." Zacharie, *New Orleans Guide* (1893), 11.
109. La Harpe, 44.
110. Giraud, vol. 2, 137.
111. Higginbotham, *Fort Maurepas*, 69-73.
112. Claiborne, 36-37, and Villiers du Terrage, 196.
113. Pratz, 53.
114. Villiers du Terrage, 186.
115. Chambers, 105.
116. As quoted by Villiers du Terrage, 186.
117. Ibid., 182.
118. Ibid., 190.
119. Howell, 126-27.

Governor Bienville reluctantly obeyed by leaving some of his command to continue working at the French Quarter site and taking the others to build the new fort at the Bay of Biloxi. Chief Engineer Le Blond de La Tour,[120] a pro-Biloxi adversary of Bienville and his French Quarter site, presented plans for New Biloxi in January 1721—a rectangular grid surrounding a *Place d'Armes*—that, ironically, would later evolve into the plat for New Orleans,[121] which survives today at the site La Tour disdained. New Biloxi was established across the bay (present-day Biloxi) from old Fort Maurepas (now Ocean Springs), and with Ship Island as its harbor, this new capital received the first major wave of immigrants to French Louisiana. Thousands of settlers recruited by the Company from Germany, Switzerland, and France arrived through Biloxi from 1719 to 1721, dispersing throughout the territory and increasing its population from mere hundreds to 5,420 whites and 600 blacks[122] (numbers vary in different sources). Many of these immigrants, naturally drawn to the rich agricultural lands of which Biloxi had none, settled in or near New Orleans, which rebounded a year after the 1719 flood with a company store, hospital, houses for the governor and director, over 100 employees, and 250 concession holders ready to take possession of their land.[123]

But adversity countered prosperity in equal or greater doses throughout the venture in these years: thousands died en route or upon arriving to the subtropical frontier; financial return on the Company of the Indies' investment was practically nonexistent; and in 1720, concerned investors began to withdraw their gold and silver deposits, rendering worthless the increasing amount of paper money circulating in France and nearly bankrupting the country in the process. The once-flamboyant tycoon John Law was chased out of Paris, and as the Company struggled to reorganize, settlers in Louisiana grappled with economic and political uncertainty as well as physical hardship. According to historian Edwin Adams Davis, it was the German, Swiss, and other non-French immigrants, who had come not "to make quick riches and return home or because they had been shipped out as criminals or moral lepers," but "to build homes and to make a new life for themselves and their families, [who] probably saved the Louisiana colony."[124] Many Germans settled just upriver and west of New Orleans (*La Côte des Allemands,* or German Coast), bringing industriousness and a sense of stability to the river area at the expense of the coast.

As the "Mississippi Bubble" was bursting in 1720, the struggling Company of the Indies again addressed the issue of where their principal city should be located, deciding on September 15 of that year to build an establishment at the Bayou Manchac site; either it or Bienville's New Orleans would serve as "general warehouse for the interior of the Colony," answering to Biloxi, "the Company's first counter and [its] business-centre."[125] Jean-Baptiste Bénard de La Harpe favored the Bayou Manchac plan—"best place to establish the principal bastion in Louisiana"—and derided the French Quarter site as "flooded, impractical, unhealthy, unfit for the cultivation of rice," fearing that its founders "were not informed of [its] true geographical situation."[126] Le Drouot de Valdeterre echoed these sentiments, endorsing the need for "changing and transporting New Orleans to the Manchac Plain, on the little river between the stream and Lake Maurepas, to establish the principal seat there."[127] "The capital city must be at Manchac, where the high lands begin," wrote one M. de Beauvais in another memoir.[128] But in fact, the Company was mired in indecision regarding this potentially expensive relocation decision, perhaps because it was preoccupied with the larger problems of the faltering business and impending economic chaos in France. So in the time-honored tradition of countless institutions, the Company procrastinated the decision by instructing Chief Engineer Le Blond de La Tour to send his assistant engineer to study the situation some more. This proved to be a turning point for New Orleans.

120. Le Blond de La Tour replaced Perrier as chief engineer of Louisiana. Perrier, who carried with him instructions from the Company to consider the Bayou Manchac area as the site of New Orleans, died in Havana en route to Louisiana in 1718. Wilson, "Colonial Fortifications," 385, and Villiers du Terrage, 184-86.
121. Wilson, "Colonial Fortifications," 385.
122. Claiborne, 38.
123. As quoted from *Etat de la Louisiane* (June 1720) by Villiers du Terrage, 194.
124. Davis, 58.
125. As quoted by Villiers du Terrage, 218.
126. It should be noted that in his report, La Harpe "merged" the sites at Bayou Manchac and Natchez, calling it *Manchae [sic] in Natchez*, either by generalization, mistake, or intention. In any case, he spoke highly of both sites' qualifications for a capital. La Harpe's interesting review of sites appears in a section entitled "Ports and Harbours to be Protected on the Coasts of Louisiana," in which he listed *Pansacolle* (Pensacola), *L'Ille aux Vaisseaux* (Ship Island, near Biloxi), *Biloxy* (Ocean Springs), *New Orleans* (French Quarter site), and *Natchez* (which he fused with the Bayou Manchac site). La Harpe, 43-46.
127. As quoted by Villiers du Terrage, 219.
128. Ibid., 220.

Founding of New Orleans, Phase II: 1721-22

La Tour's assistant, Adrien de Pauger, arrived in New Orleans on March 29, 1721, and resolutely began adapting his superior's rough design for New Biloxi (never executed) to the geography of the French Quarter site. Within a month, Pauger sent his plans for New Orleans to La Tour in Biloxi, who claimed he had in turn sent them on to Paris, but historian Marc de Villiers du Terrage suspects that La Tour, a Biloxi proponent and opponent of New Orleans, shelved them and pursued his own project at Biloxi's nearby port of Ship Island. Yet the plans made it to Paris anyway, perhaps sent by Bienville in collusion with Pauger.

Why the significance of the New Orleans plans arriving in Paris? Villiers du Terrage hypothesized that these plans probably "had weight in the Company's final decision, since the regent [Philippe, duc d'Orléans], godfather to the new capital, was necessarily flattered to see the project put into effect."[129] Indeed, the gridiron street network, with its town square perched high on the riverbank and its fortifications inspired by the influential French military engineer Sebastien Le Pietre de Vauban,[130] must have impressed the Parisians, who for three years had heard little more about New Orleans than its haphazardly arranged palmetto huts and inundated conditions.

Adrien de Pauger also contributed to the credibility of New Orleans as capital through his study of the navigability of the lower Mississippi River by large ships (barred from shallow, narrow Bayou St. John) that until now had been harboring at Dauphin Island and Ship Island.[131] His report emphatically recommended the utilization of the river route and scorned the "stubbornness" and "arrogance" of Company managers who forced "ships from France to be stopped at Biloxi, rather than enter the Mississippi . . . keystone of the country's establishment."[132] Also in 1721, the Council of Regency decided to found a Capuchin convent in New Orleans, and the Company designated New Orleans the first of the nine districts of the Louisiana territory, home to its commandant general.

While some of Pauger's activities in New Orleans in 1721 aroused controversy both locally and in competing posts, the groundswell of opinion among those who mattered finally started to shift toward New Orleans as the capital and principal city of French Louisiana. "The year 1721 had been generally favourable to New Orleans. From a military post, a sales-counter, and a camping-ground for travellers, it had become, in November, a small town, and the number of its irreconcilable enemies began to decrease."[133]

Bienville and his colleagues had created enough of an oasis in the threatening wilderness to surmount that most difficult hurdle in an organization's decision-making process, the phase at which nebulous ideas solidify into definite plans. On December 23, 1721, the Company of the Indies officially transferred the general management of Louisiana from Biloxi to New Orleans. Word of the decision to relocate the capital reached Biloxi on May 26, 1722, and suddenly New Orleans had nothing but friends and allies. Even Biloxi supporter Le Blond de La Tour and Natchez advocate Marc Antoine Hubert imparted kind words about the worthiness of New Orleans and the wisdom of the Company. Starting with an initial *Plan de la Ville de la Nouvelle Orleans* dated April 23, 1722, La Tour and Pauger worked together for the next year in developing the plan for New

At left is one of Le Blond de La Tour's plans for a fort at New Biloxi, drawn in January 1721 but never executed; at right is his (and Adrien de Pauger's) April 1722 design for New Orleans, laid out starting in that year and well preserved (sans the ramparts) today. *Graphic by author based on historic maps*

129. Villiers du Terrage, 222-23.
130. Wilson, "Colonial Fortifications," 378, 386.
131. Chambers, 108.
132. Villiers du Terrage, 223.
133. Ibid., 229.

Orleans that survives today as the French Quarter (*Vieux Carré,* or Old Square), one of the best-preserved colonial city plans in America and a direct link between the modern metropolis and its earliest days in the wilderness.

As if to wipe the slate clean, a hurricane struck the Gulf Coast from Mobile to New Orleans in September 1722, destroying dozens of makeshift structures in New Orleans but allowing Pauger to commence surveying the streets of the newly planned city. By November, "the streets of the old quarter had received the names they still bear."[134] Recalled one observer a few years later, "New-Orleans began to assume the appearance of a city, and to increase in population, . . . in 1722."[135]

More hardship lay ahead: the Company of the Indies lost interest in unproductive Louisiana and finally relinquished it in 1731; a massacre of settlers by Indians at Natchez in 1729 frightened the isolated city; and the everyday struggle of life under subtropical conditions took its toll. In future decades exasperated settlers would occasionally suggest relocating the city and, in time, even its status as capital would move on. But after 1722, New Orleans was firmly established at the site that Bienville first saw nearly a quarter-century earlier, as a youth under the wing of his long-gone brother, Iberville, and at this site New Orleans would grow into Louisiana's premier city and one of the world's great ports. Through the efforts of four principal parties—John Law, who made the business decision to found a city named for the duc d'Orléans thirty leagues up the river; the indigenous peoples of the area, who had discovered the critical portage and passed this knowledge on to the French; Jean Baptiste Le Moyne, sieur de Bienville, who founded the city, defended its attributes, and governed the colony for thirty of the years spanning 1701-43; and Adrien de Pauger, whose engineering turned the sloppy outpost into an organized and serious contender for a capital city[136]—New Orleans was sited on the great crescent near the Bayou St. John portage linking Lake Pontchartrain and the Mississippi River, situated between the Gulf of Mexico and North America's Father of Waters.

Influence of Geographical Situation on the Character of New Orleans

So what of this situation, this site? How has this controversial and geologically precarious perch between two worlds contributed to the formation of New Orleans, this most idiosyncratic and memorable of cities, source of cultural icons and mental images unique in its nation? First it is necessary to identify exactly what makes so many people characterize New Orleans as unique and interesting: those attributes that have physically, economically, and culturally isolated it from the American mainstream for most of its three centuries and even today set it apart from Atlanta and Dallas and Houston and all the rest. Itemizing the character of a city is like measuring the personality of an individual—a difficult and debatable exercise—but certain traits do predominate and those are what we seek to identify here. Many of these traits are now trivialized on postcards and stereotyped in cinema, others are underappreciated, but all are relevant.

> "During most of the nineteenth century, New Orleans remained in counterpoint to the rest of urban America. Newcomers from the South as well as the North recoiled when they encountered the prevailing French language of the city, its dominant Catholicism, its bawdy sensual delights, or its proud free black population—in short, its deeply rooted creole traditions."
>
> —Arnold R. Hirsch and Joseph Logsdon, 1992 (xi)

First, there is the port. The great and ancient effort to route resources between the world within the Mississippi Valley and the world beyond the Gulf of Mexico is the fountainhead of New Orleans as an urban place and as a multicultural society. For almost a century and a half, the port of New Orleans, "Key of the Great Valley,"[137] enjoyed a transportation monopoly in the region, buttressed not only by the criticality of the gulf/river situation but by the isolation from its competitors. Today, the Port of New Orleans handles 88 million tons of freight annually, behind only Houston and New York/New Jersey; when combined with other south

Louisiana ports, it is by far the biggest in the nation, handling 285 million tons—almost 70 and 90 percent more than Houston and New York, respectively.[138] Just as the physical geography of New Orleans is mother to its port, the port is mother to most of the city's unique characteristics, in some derivative or another.

Second, there is the French and Spanish heritage. More so than on any other city in the nation, these two colonial cultures, exceptions to the Anglo-American norm, have left their intertwined imprints on New Orleans and are apparent today in the population's bloodlines, the city's architecture, the state's European-based civil-law legal system, and the society's customs.

Third, there is the African and Caribbean heritage. Through bondage, freedom, immigration from the islands, and emigration from the rural South, these cultures diversified the city with a quality not found in other American ports, making New Orleans an apogee city of the circum-Caribbean cultural region.

Caribbean look and feel: Steep rooftops with chimneys, wooden cottages with shuttered windows, cramped streetscapes, tropical vegetation, and majestic church towers impart a distinctly Caribbean ambience to streets in the old part of town, especially neighborhoods such as Faubourg Marigny, Tremé, Bywater, St. Roch, and the French Quarter. These scenes, unique vistas for an American city, are on Dauphine Street and Chartres Street in the Faubourg Marigny and on St. Claude Avenue in Faubourg Tremé (St. Augustine, bottom right). *Photographs by author, 1999-2000*

Fourth, there is the immigrant heritage. The influx of over a half-million immigrants from Germany, Ireland, and other lands between 1820 and 1860, plus southern and eastern Europeans in later years and Latin Americans and Vietnamese today, makes New Orleans not the most multicultural city in the nation but probably the *oldest historically* multicultural city in the nation. Add to this melting pot the Anglo-American, French, Spanish, African, and Caribbean heritage to produce a truly cosmopolitan society, especially in relation to the interior South. "No city perhaps on the globe, in an equal number of human beings, presents a greater contrast of national manners, language, and complexion, than does New Orleans,"[139] wrote one observer in 1816.

Fifth, there is the religious heritage. New Orleans is one of the most Catholic cities in a Protestant nation, and Catholicism influences the city in manners ranging from the apparent—the Ursuline Nuns, St. Louis Cathedral, the Catholic schools—to the abstract: the Carnival traditions, the votives left for St. Roch, and the pervasive and paradoxical atmosphere of godliness mixed with worldliness, of dogma tempered by tolerance.

---

134. Henry P. Dart, "Allotment of Building Sites," 564-65.
135. Dumont, 41.
136. Said Pauger in 1723, "If I had not taken upon myself all that could be done to overcome ill-will, things would not yet have got beyond the stage of sending ships into the river, and the principal seat would have remained at Biloxi, where the country could not provide sufficient food, as it does here [at New Orleans]." As quoted by Villiers du Terrage, 246. Bienville served as colonial governor of Louisiana during 1701-13, 1716-17, 1718-25, and 1733-43.
137. Ingraham, 96.

138. U.S. Army Corps of Engineers, *Waterborne Commerce of the United States, Part 5,* 5.4.
139. Darby, 186.

New Orleans' prominent Jewish congregation and numerous Protestant faiths further enrich the city's religious dimension.

Sixth, there is the urban layout. La Tour's and Pauger's design for the French Quarter survives today as a reminder of the European instinct for order through engineering in a threatening wilderness; later developments in neighboring *faubourgs* show the influence of classical design, American ideas, the arpent land surveying system, and the hydrologically based geography of the city. "The city of New-Orleans," wrote Joseph Holt Ingraham in 1835, "is planned on a magnificent scale, happily and judiciously combining ornament and convenience. Let the same spirit which foresaw and provided for its present greatness, animate those who will hereafter direct its public improvement, and New-Orleans, in spite of its bug-bear character and its unhealthy location, will eventually be the handsomest, if not the largest city in the United States."[140]

Seventh, there is the architecture. New Orleans' building styles and their glorious adornments are the most ubiquitous and photogenic of its local signatures, the ones most likely to burn themselves into memory and evoke the essence of the city. Architecture is New Orleans' greatest contribution to the national material culture, and it is a truly substantial contribution: tens of thousands of structures, covering about half the developed portion of New Orleans and a quarter of the metropolitan area, may be described as architecturally or historically interesting components of the cityscape. Much, if not most, of this inventory comprises styles and embellishments rarely found beyond the city limits: camelback shotgun houses, Creole townhouses with iron-lace balconies, brick-between-post cottages with center chimneys and double-pitched roofs, double-gallery houses, "jigsaw Victorian" cottages. . . .

Eighth, there is the food. While all places have local specialties, New Orleans is often described as the only city in America with an indigenous cuisine, distinct from its deep-fried neighbors by a rich menu of complex dishes that draws heavily from the heritage of the place and its people. While the prevalence of local dishes has diminished in recent decades, the art and appreciation of New Orleans cooking—"as brilliantly idiosyncratic as it gets"[141]—is still deeply embedded in the city's soul and is one of its two great cultural exports to the nation and the world.

Ninth, there is the music—New Orleans' other great cultural export, probably *the* greatest. Jazz epitomizes the creative and whimsical impulse of New Orleans and is, not coincidentally, often recognized as the only major art form born and developed entirely in America. The magnitude of its influence on American and world culture throughout the course of the twentieth century is only now being fully appreciated. Beyond jazz, New Orleans was famous for its opera in the nineteenth century and was a national hearth for rhythm and blues in the 1950s and early 1960s. Today it is a mecca for funk, blues, brass bands, gospel, Cajun, zydeco, local variations of rock, and both traditional and modern jazz. For a relatively small city, New Orleans' local music scene is disproportionately big and vivacious—practically a sub-economy and a subculture, with its own newspapers, community-supported radio stations, unions, activists, and factions. Broadly possessed musical genius spanning generations within the confines of a single city speaks volumes about the dynamic and creative character of a community.

> "[New Orleans] is destined by its very situation to be the centre of an immense commerce between all nations, and the vast continent bathed by the rivers Misisipi, Misuri, San Francisco, Colorado, etc."
> —Baron de Carondelet, in a 1794 letter recommending fortification of the Spanish colony against the threat of invasion (Turner, 495)

Finally, New Orleans is distinguished from other American cities by sundry traditions and images that have become clichés, mined mercilessly by the tourism industry, but nevertheless play an important role in enriching the overall fabric of the city. Carnival, streetcars on St. Charles, café au lait and beignets, potted ferns spilling from galleries, a jazz funeral—these and other icons impart *character* to *place* in New Orleans, rescuing the city from the modern descent toward placelessness that has homogenized most other American cities.

Behind these distinguishing attributes of New Orleans are geographical influences. The port, of course, is an exploitation of a fundamentally geographical circumstance, and is the taproot of much of the city's history and economics. The port attracted the French and Spanish colonial interests, which in turn brought the African influence and eventually attracted the Caribbean, Anglo-American, and immigrant elements. These groups, at first largely Catholic in religion and Latin by culture, laid out their city with urban-planning methods and architectural styles brought from the mother countries and adapted to local conditions (geographical and otherwise) that gave it an appearance that was both colonial and indigenous.

From this isolated multicultural society, dependent on the constant stream of vessels arriving at all hours from distant lands, emerged local customs—elements of character—ranging from cuisine to music to nightlife to dialect. The birth of jazz in the late nineteenth and early twentieth century derived from traditions that landed in the city due to its nexus position: African and Caribbean rhythms from beyond the Gulf of Mexico, blues melodies from the Mississippi Delta, and ragtime from the Midwestern cities, to which were added local parade tunes and martial music. These elements intermingled in New Orleans—"musical gumbo" is the favored metaphor—and from it emerged a totally new music, one that would change America and influence the world.

Likewise, New Orleans' world-famous Mardi Gras celebration, described by one local historian as "French Catholic by tradition but Yankee Protestant by implementation,"[142] is another example of how the assemblage of cultures (from places as varied as the nations of France and Spain and the American cities of Mobile and Philadelphia) in a single geographical location may produce a distinguishing cultural trait. These sequences of events and factors stem from the port, and the port stems from the physical geography of New Orleans—its situation on the least-cost path between the Gulf of Mexico and the Mississippi Valley and its site on the crescent that facilitates the harboring of ships and the breaking of bulk.

Many large cities share some of these attributes, but few if any exhibit all of them as does New Orleans; perhaps for this reason, visitors often comment that the Crescent City strikes them as a cross between distinct places: Québec and Havana according to one writer; Paterson, New Jersey, and Port-au-Prince, Haiti according to another.[143] Appreciation of the role of geographical situation in the cultural differentiation[144] of New Orleans from other American cities is dramatized by speculating on the possible character of the city had it been located at one of the other proposed sites. Would New Orleans be the peculiar city it came to be had it been located at Bayou Manchac, or Natchez, or Biloxi?

> "There is on the globe one single spot, the possessor of which is our natural and habitual enemy. It is New Orleans, through which the produce of three-eighths of our territory must pass to market, and from its fertility it will ere long yield more than half of our whole produce and contain more than half our inhabitants."
> —Thomas Jefferson, in a letter to American minister in France Robert R. Livingston, April 18, 1802 (As quoted by Farber and Garrett, 159-61. Jefferson, who long recognized the criticality of New Orleans and the Mississippi River for access to the West, was responding to the news that Spain had secretly retroceded Louisiana to France in the Treaty of San Ildefonso [October 1800], replacing a passive, declining colonial power with an aggressive and powerful one in the hands of Napoleon Bonaparte. The alarming situation, which could have led to war between France and the United States for New Orleans, instead led to a diplomatic resolution: the Louisiana Purchase, and the beginning of the Americanization of New Orleans.)

Would New Orleans be *New Orleans* if it were located at the Bayou Manchac site, where Bayou Manchac distributed from the Mississippi south of Baton Rouge, as favored by the Company of the West and Company of the Indies in 1718-20? In this exercise of pure speculation, we may assume that an equivalent sequence of events would have occurred—the French would have laid out streets and built structures in their style, attracted immigrants in a similar manner, and eventually produced as unique an enclave as New Orleans is today at Bienville's French Quarter site. But then again, perhaps the formation of a city fully 200 miles up the Mississippi and 80 miles from the coast—much farther than Bienville's site—would have led to the development of smaller cities below the Bayou Manchac site, which would compete with the larger city and, being more convenient to the coast, draw off the port trade and immigration that were so fundamental to New Orleans' history. (Even as the French were first establishing their presence in Louisiana, other nations probed the lower Mississippi for settlement opportunities: witness the incident at English Turn.) Perhaps these competing cities on the lower river[145]

---

140. Ingraham, 147.
141. Hahn.
142. Errol Laborde, 47.
143. The references are to Oliver Evans and A. J. Liebling.

144. Again, a word of caution is in order regarding "deterministic" explanations: It should be clearly understood that people, not place, created New Orleans. Every one of the ten attributes previously discussed is the product of humans; the geography of New Orleans did not "determine" that a port should arise or that jazz would emerge. But geography presents a set of circumstances that humans exploit, enjoy, adapt to, suffer, or change, and thus *contributes* to the formation of a city's character.
145. The urge to build a port closest to the river's mouth persists today. In 1999-2001, Louisiana officials debated the merits of constructing a "Millennium Port" at any one of ten locations between English Turn Bend and the delta, far below New Orleans, to exploit deep-sea shipping lanes. By June 2000, the Millennium Port Authority had narrowed the selection down to five potential sites for the containerized cargo terminal: Myrtle Grove, Woodland, Magnolia, and Head of Passes, all along the lower river in Plaquemines Parish, and Port Fourchon, at the Bayou Lafourche delta. Later that year, the Army Corps suggested building an island in Barataria Bay to host the port, an amazing example of man's drive to improve a bad geographical site to exploit a fantastic geographical situation, which is essentially the story of New Orleans. Whatever the final choice, port activity will not soon depart New Orleans: earlier plans suggested the expansion of the Napoleon Avenue Wharf and the France Road Container Terminal, both within city limits, and in June 2000, the Dock Board decided to expand and consolidate three river terminals to create a "mega-wharf" in uptown New Orleans, which may eventually supercede the Millennium Port concept. All proposals aim at competing with rival ports at Gulfport, Mobile, Miami, Houston, and beyond. In some regards the great debate on the siting of New Orleans in the early 1700s continues into the twenty-first century. Darcé, "N.O. Port Plans Huge Uptown Expansion," "Prompt Steps Urged," "Officials Take to Air," and "Dock Board Chooses Design"; and the Associated Press.

would have diminished the effect of isolation from which New Orleans benefited, and would have dispersed the cultural traits that were concentrated in New Orleans and consequently became enduring icons. Additionally, perhaps the Bayou Manchac site would have lacked adequate riverside harboring opportunities,[146] and the navigability of the bayou itself might have proven limiting.

A similar case may be made for Natchez, advocated by Hubert and lauded as a superb site for a major city but not necessarily offering an optimal situation. If New Orleans were located at the Natchez site, hundreds of miles of the lower Mississippi (prime plantation country) would have been left open for the development of smaller cities, which might have siphoned off resources and population from the city at Natchez. The bluffs at Natchez do not provide for major port facilities, and the later preeminence of the Spanish and English in this region (if this would have come to pass under these speculative circumstances) may have erased the imprint of the French and made the hypothetical city less distinctive in America today.

Coastal sites at Biloxi, Mobile, or Pensacola probably would have only delayed, not replaced, the establishment of a city on the Mississippi; most major rivers have important cities near their mouths. But had New Orleans been sited on the coast, as a seaport and not a riverport, it would have been deprived of most Mississippi Valley influences. The "Kaintock" flatboatsmen of the early 1800s would not have arrived, the cotton factors and sugar and rice traders of the antebellum years might have settled elsewhere, and the fruits of the plantation economy would not have enriched a coastal city to the degree that they sustained the river city.

> "New Orleans will be forever, as it is now, the mighty mart of the merchandise brought from more than a thousand rivers, unless prevented by some accident in human affairs. This rapidly increasing city will, in no distant time, leave the emporia of the Eastern World far behind. With Boston, Baltimore, New York, and Philadelphia on the left; Mexico on the right; Havana in front, and the immense valley of the Mississippi in the rear, no such position for the accumulation and perpetuity of wealth and power ever existed."
> —Thomas Jefferson, 1887 (As quoted in House Executive Documents, 185. While New Orleans' national influence waned with the diminished criticality of Mississippi River shipping, the cultural fruits reaped during its early-nineteenth-century heyday remain in the city's modern-day character.)

A city at Natchitoches would have been too distant from both the coast and the Mississippi to have fostered the development of a major port that was so rudimentary to New Orleans' history. If New Orleans were sited on the shore of Lake Pontchartrain, it probably would have migrated over to the higher banks of the Mississippi and developed in manner equivalent to what eventually came to pass. Likewise, if New Orleans were sited at English Turn, it too might have migrated or spread upriver to the more convenient portage and broader natural levees of the French Quarter site, and developed accordingly.

In short, had New Orleans been sited too far upriver, competing cities might have usurped its seaport advantage; had it been sited on the coast or in the interior, it might have been supplanted by some other city that seized the riverport advantage; and had it been sited too far downriver, it would have been constricted by a limiting topography and accessibility.

Although this exercise is based entirely on speculation (and the dubious assumption that history would have progressed generally within the channel that it eventually took), a case may be made that New Orleans' geographical situation and site comprised critical ingredients in the formation of the city that we cherish today as a unique component of the world's built environment. "The lower [Mississippi] valley contains the one truly cosmopolitan city, New Orleans, itself in turn a product of its geographical position," wrote the distinguished cultural geographer Dr. Fred B. Kniffen.[147] That geographical position may have imparted to New Orleans just

the right mix of (1) coastal accessibility, (2) river accessibility, (3) portage between the lake and river, (4) proximity to the mouth of the river, (5) port and harbor opportunities, (6) partial protection from flood and hurricane, (7) rich agricultural soils; and (8) geographical isolation to offer an opportunity that humans would make into a distinctive and great city. This is not to say that New Orleans' site is a particularly good one—its shortcomings have challenged engineers and frightened citizens for centuries, and even today the threats of soil subsidence, swarming Formosan termites, coastal erosion, and a Category-5 hurricane over Lake Pontchartrain shroud the otherwise festive city in a surreal sense of foreboding.[148] But New Orleans' *situation* is outstanding, and regardless of the merits of its situation and site, both these variables unquestionably have weighted heavily in the historical development of the Crescent City. *New Orleans* as the distinct cultural and historical phenomenon we recognize today probably could not have happened just anywhere; it might have only happened upon a swath of riverside land somewhere along the lower Mississippi and maybe only at the great crescent selected by Bienville in the early eighteenth century. To those who say, "This is no place for a major city; New Orleans should have been sited elsewhere," one may respond, "But then it wouldn't have become *New Orleans*." Perhaps it is this notion that inspires many observers to evoke the enigmatic phrase "a sense of place" in trying to articulate exactly what makes this city so extraordinary, and what gives even the most oblivious newcomer a tingle and a

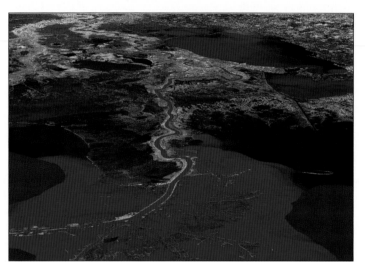

thrill upon beholding the spectacular breadth of Canal Street, or sighting the spires and cupolas above Jackson Square, or seeing the great freighters navigate the meanders of the Mississippi, bound for the sea.

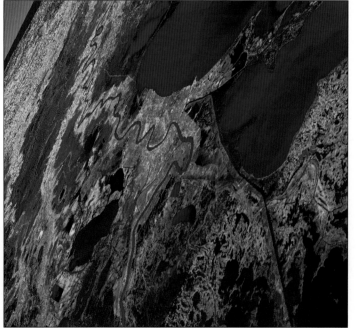

Amid this tangle of lithosphere and hydrosphere was situated New Orleans; upon this unique geographical circumstance, viewed here from space, it earned the enviable reputation of being one of the most fascinating cities in the world. *Oblique perspectives by author based on satellite imagery from Louisiana State University*

146. Although Baton Rouge was founded nearby, no major city ever developed at the Bayou Manchac site. However, in the 1760s and 1770s, the British, realizing the potential of this area, formed a small community called Manchac (Point Iberville) and proceeded to excavate the clogged bayou to establish a permanent connection with the Mississippi. British governor Johnstone declared in 1764, "There is no place of so much Consequence, to this Province, as that Settlement now [that] the Iberville [River] is open'd, & which will command the whole Trade of the Mississippi." British plans in ensuing years foresaw Manchac growing to compete with New Orleans for Mississippi River trade. Their Fort Bute and the Spaniards' Fort San Gabriel de Manchack, on the other side of the bayou, attested to the perceived value of this place. But the American Revolution intervened, and tiny Manchac became embroiled in the conflict, even in the actual fighting, "the only land clash between British and American forces to take place in Louisiana." This site that might have become the premier city in the region—French, English, or Spanish—instead dwindled by the close of the century and was eventually swept away by the Mississippi River. Dalrymple, 11-33; quotes from 12, 26.
147. Kniffen, "The Lower Mississippi Valley," 3.

148. See Lewis, 27, for a "Catalogue of Difficulties" of New Orleans' site.

2 Topography

Algiers and Gretna (lower left) in the 1950s, before the construction of the Mississippi River bridge. While elevational range is imperceptibly slight in the deltaic environment of southeastern Louisiana, topography has had a major influence on the historical development of the region. Elevations of the area shown here range from ten feet above sea level along the river (with the exception of the manmade levees, which now rise to almost twenty-five feet) to sea level at lower right. *U.S. Army Corps of Engineers—New Orleans District*

Picture an enormous three-dimensional graph placed upon greater New Orleans, with the x-axis running west to east, the y-axis running south to north, and the z-axis running upward from the ground toward the sky. In chapter 1, we investigated how and why New Orleans was sited upon the x-y plane of this cubic volume—the surface of the Earth—and the consequences of that geographical decision. Now we consider the z-dimension—elevation, or more accurately, topography[1]—and its influence upon the development of New Orleans, as well as the city's impact upon its topography, for in New Orleans, more so than in any other city in the nation, man and nature have played roughly equal roles in sculpting the local terrain. While greater New Orleans sprawls out grandly and conspicuously in the x- and y-directions, spread-eagled nearly twenty miles across and ten miles wide, its expanse into the z-direction is almost imperceptible, from about 10 feet below mean sea level to a mere 20 feet above it[2] (with the highest lands—the artificial levees and battures—built up by the hand of man, and the tallest buildings 165 feet higher than the highest natural point—Driskill Mountain, 535 feet—in the entire *state*). But those few feet of elevation played a major role in the city's history, as a natural constraint to urban development, as an all-too-breachable barrier against rising river water or surging lake water, and as a saucerlike basin from which trapped rainwater had to be extracted. Paradoxically, the city that both newcomers and old-timers declare to be utterly and incurably *flat* has, in fact, a history of urban development that is closely associated with topographic elevation. An inch of terrain in a riverside city that straddles the level of the sea is substantially more important than a dozen feet of terrain in a high, hilly city in the interior. New Orleans is *not* flat.

Original Topographic Circumstance of the New Orleans Region

"As the traveler proceeds down the Mississippi river from its source to its mouth," said Martin Behrman, mayor of New Orleans, "a unique phenomenon attracts his attention. The river seems to grow higher as he descends."[3] The phenomenon that Mayor Behrman observed in 1914 often startles newcomers to the Mississippi deltaic plain, who are usually more familiar with the excavating power of moving water than with its depositional capacity.

Indeed, the Mississippi River does grow higher (relative to surrounding terrain, not the sea) as one descends south of Baton Rouge toward the mouth, where the banks of the river, stretching back a mile or so, form the highest lands around. To understand this phenomenon, imagine tossing a bucket of muddy water into a backyard gully. The water erodes some soil and makes the gully slightly smoother and deeper. Repeated a million times, the gully will deepen into a ravine. But now imagine tossing the same muddy water onto a flat surface. The water will spill in a certain pattern, lose energy, puddle, and eventually evaporate, leaving behind a thin layer of sediment. Repeated constantly, a channel will emerge through which most of the water flows, while surplus ("flood") water will disperse and leave behind more and more layers of sediment. Eventually a fairly significant deposit of soil will rise above our flat surface, not exactly mountainous but nevertheless the highest terrain around. After a while, enough sediment will accumulate in the bed such that the flow will spill over the thin layer of sediment and run off in a new direction.

This simplification illustrates the fundamental force underlying New Orleans' topographical circumstance: when sediment-laden water flows down a weak slope, its kinetic energy decreases and is overtaken by the gravitational pull upon the waterborne sediments, causing the particles to settle. In times of flood, fast-moving river water stirs up bottom sediments, then spills over the banks and floods the adjacent countryside, suddenly losing velocity and depositing the coarsest particles (sand) first, the finer particles (silt) farther on, and the finest particles (clay and smaller) last and farthest. With repeated floods every few years for millennia, the lands paralleling the river rise to form natural levees, which are higher in elevation, coarser in soil texture, higher in fertility, and better-drained during rainstorms. Meandering portions of the river, such as the New Orleans crescent, tend to produce wider natural levees, while straight sections of the river (such as the area downriver from English Turn) create relatively narrow ones. Cutbank portions of meanders, those convex sections where the flow of the river bears into the bank before wending around the next meander, generally create the broadest natural

levees. (The French Quarter site is at the crest of a cutbank natural levee.) Natural levees slope downward like a ramp as one moves away from the river toward the backswamp, where fewer and thinner layers of fine-grain soils accumulate during floods and where rainwater puddles to form a marshy environment.[4] In southeastern Louisiana, the entire elevational range between the natural levees and the backswamps of the Mississippi is about ten to twenty feet, spanning a width of about 1 to 2 miles on each side of the river, and it is along this geographical vertebra and others following smaller bayous that most human settlement exists,[5] even today. Because heavier particles generally settle early on, southeastern Louisiana's soils contain little sand and no rocks whatsoever; soils in New Orleans proper range from silty loams along the higher natural levees to clays and mucks in the lower backswamps (now drained).[6]

In sum, the 13,000-square-mile Mississippi deltaic plain is a landscape formed by soils eroded from the 1,125,910-square-mile North American interior, then transported and deposited by the Mississippi. The river, flailing like a deranged serpent and depositing, silting up, jumping channels, and depositing again from Terrebonne to St. Bernard Parish over the past 5,000 years, *created* southeastern Louisiana and is a profoundly fundamental component of the region's geography. Just as a drop of rainwater that fell in South Dakota may flow past Decatur Street, soil particles that once clung to the ramparts of the Rockies may now underlie Rampart and Dumaine streets—all courtesy the Mississippi River.

> "The upper surface [of the soil on which New Orleans stands] is a marsh mud, extremely slippery as soon as wet, with a small mixture of sand, & below this surface are decayed vegetables, water at 3 feet, & as I am told by others, abounding in large logs, or in large vacancies, apparently occupied formerly by logs which have rotted. Such a soil [is] the result of the gradual accumulation of the deposition of the river, & of the logs & trees which in astonishing quantities & of immense size are constantly descending the stream at every fresh."
>
> —Benjamin Latrobe, 1819 (68)

The natural levees of the Mississippi are the most prominent natural topographic features in New Orleans, but not the only ones. These riverside uplands sometimes contained saddles or crevasses that remained dry under normal conditions but allowed a plume of river water to shoot over the bank in times of high water. The resulting distributaries[7] flowed down the back slope in a generally shallow and dispersed manner but formed well-defined bayous upon reaching the backswamp. One such distributary, born through a crevasse in the natural levee near present-day Kenner, wended eastward across what is now the entire metropolitan area during prehistoric times. Like the river from which it came, this distributary—known as Bayou Metairie in its western portion, Bayou Gentilly in the middle, and Bayou Sauvage toward the east—deposited sediments and formed natural levees of its own. (The three bayous, all really branches of a single dendritic drainage pattern that flowed out of Bayou St. John, were adjoined by a small rivulet called Bayou Fanchon, also called Bayou Clark, which created the slight upland beneath Grand Route St. John, Desoto Street, and Bell Street.) The upland was, logically, not nearly as high and wide as the Mississippi River's natural levees, but it rose far enough above the swamps to serve as an east-west transportation route from prehistoric times to the present. Although the Mississippi abandoned this distributary before historic times, its channel still carried water into the nineteenth century and remnant portions of its waters still exist today in the lagoons of lower City Park. The distributary's natural levee, known as Metairie Ridge to the west and Gentilly Ridge (or Terrace) to the east, was utilized as a foot trail since prehistoric times and, into the early twentieth century, served as the *de*

---

1. *Elevation* is simply the vertical distance above a datum plane, such as the spheroid (sea level) or the ellipsoid (a mathematical construct defining the shape of the Earth). *Topography* is a broader term that considers the shape and form of the land, measured by elevation, slope, aspect, curvature, drainage, and other parameters.

2. This is the general elevational range within Orleans Parish. There are certain places where canal beds and underpasses dip as low as 18 feet below sea level, and where levees and landscaping features rise as high as 41 feet above sea level. All topographic measurements in this analysis are derived from 1-foot elevation contours compiled in 1994 using Global Positioning Systems technology based on second-order, class-1 survey standards using the North American Datum of 1983-86 and the National Geodetic Vertical Datum of 1929. These contours are maintained and distributed as .DXF files by the New Orleans City Planning Commission through its New Orleans Geographic Information System (NOGIS). The author compiled the contours from 231 separate files and developed a surface from the isolines using the Triangulated Irregular Network (TIN) program in ERSI ARC/INFO software. This TIN was then rasterized into a digital elevation model with an x-y resolution of 2 feet and a z-resolution of 1 foot. The NOGIS at the City Planning Commission is partially funded by a federal grant through NOAA.

3. Behrman, "New Orleans . . . Utilities."

4. Under natural conditions, these areas are usually forested wetlands, which is the definition of a swamp. The term *back*swamp reflects early New Orleanians' perspective that all life in this threatening wilderness fronted the river, where high, arable, and accessible land lay; the swamps, on the other hand, were useless, dangerous, and remote and were described only in relation to the good land. *Backswamp* is not often heard today in common speech, because modernization has shifted our mental map of where this feature may lie, and environmental awareness has changed our view of these areas as wastelands.

5. The recent suburban development in the backswamps around New Orleans comprises the only major exception, and only since the 1920s, after the construction of the drainage system.

6. U.S. Department of Agriculture Soil Conservation Service, 11-24 and maps. Sand particles are by definition far coarser and heavier than silt or clay. Most sand that reaches the delta region settles either in the river (sandbars), on the sides of the river (battures), or on the crests of natural levees. The Louisiana and Mississippi Gulf Coast has few natural sandy beaches.

7. The Mississippi River collects runoff throughout its vast drainage basin via *tributaries* that flow into the main channel. But below the Old River region, between Natchez and Baton Rouge, the topography changes from that of a valley to that of a deltaic plain, where the river flows through the highest land in the area and therefore sheds local rainfall and its own floodwaters, forming *distributaries*.

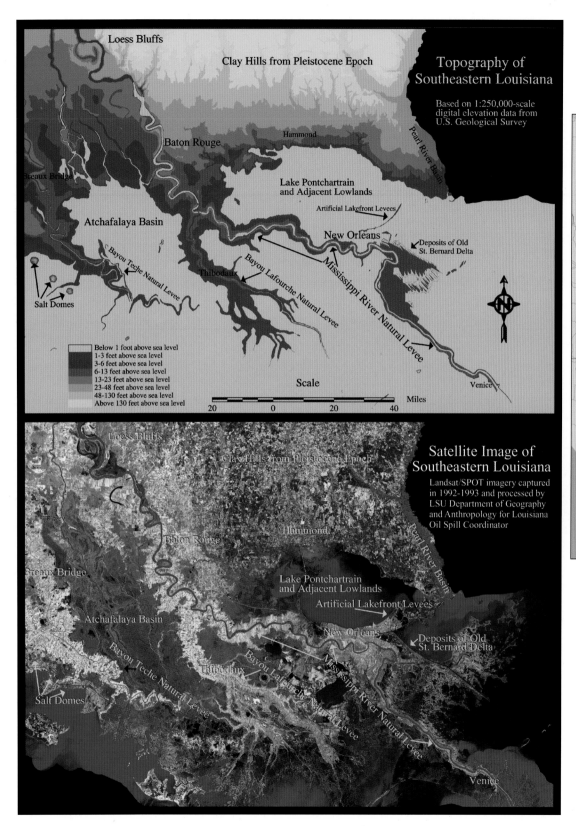

Topography of Southeastern Louisiana

Based on 1:250,000-scale digital elevation data from U.S. Geological Survey

Loess Bluffs

Clay Hills from Pleistocene Epoch

Baton Rouge

Hammond

Breaux Bridge

Lake Pontchartrain and Adjacent Lowlands

Pearl River Basin

Atchafalaya Basin

Artificial Lakefront Levees

New Orleans

Deposits of Old St. Bernard Delta

Bayou Teche Natural Levee

Thibodaux

Bayou Lafourche Natural Levee

Mississippi River Natural Levee

Salt Domes

Below 1 foot above sea level
1-3 feet above sea level
3-6 feet above sea level
6-13 feet above sea level
13-23 feet above sea level
23-48 feet above sea level
48-130 feet above sea level
Above 130 feet above sea level

Venice

N

Scale

20   0   20   40   Miles

Satellite Image of Southeastern Louisiana

Landsat/SPOT imagery captured in 1992-1993 and processed by LSU Department of Geography and Anthropology for Louisiana Oil Spill Coordinator

Loess Bluffs

Clay Hills from Pleistocene Epoch

Baton Rouge

Hammond

Breaux Bridge

Lake Pontchartrain and Adjacent Lowlands

Pearl River Basin

Atchafalaya Basin

Artificial Lakefront Levees

New Orleans

Deposits of Old St. Bernard Delta

Bayou Teche Natural Levee

Thibodaux

Bayou Lafourche Natural Levee

Mississippi River Natural Levee

Salt Domes

Venice

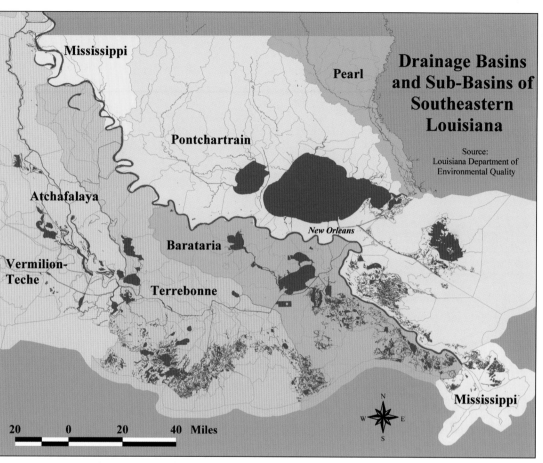

Drainage Basins and Sub-Basins of Southeastern Louisiana

Source: Louisiana Department of Environmental Quality

Mississippi

Pearl

Pontchartrain

Atchafalaya

Barataria

New Orleans

Vermilion-Teche

Terrebonne

Mississippi

N   W   E   S

20   0   20   40   Miles

(Left) Comparison of southeastern Louisiana's topography with its surface features, as seen from space. (Above) Drainage basins of southeastern Louisiana. Note that, despite the domination of the Mississippi River in the region's life, only two small basins actually contribute their runoff to the river. New Orleans is in the Lake Pontchartrain Basin; raindrops falling on the ramparts of the Rockies are more likely to flow past the French Quarter than those falling on the Quarter's own streets and rooftops. *Maps by author based on data from U.S. Geological Survey, Louisiana State University, and Louisiana Department of Environmental Quality*

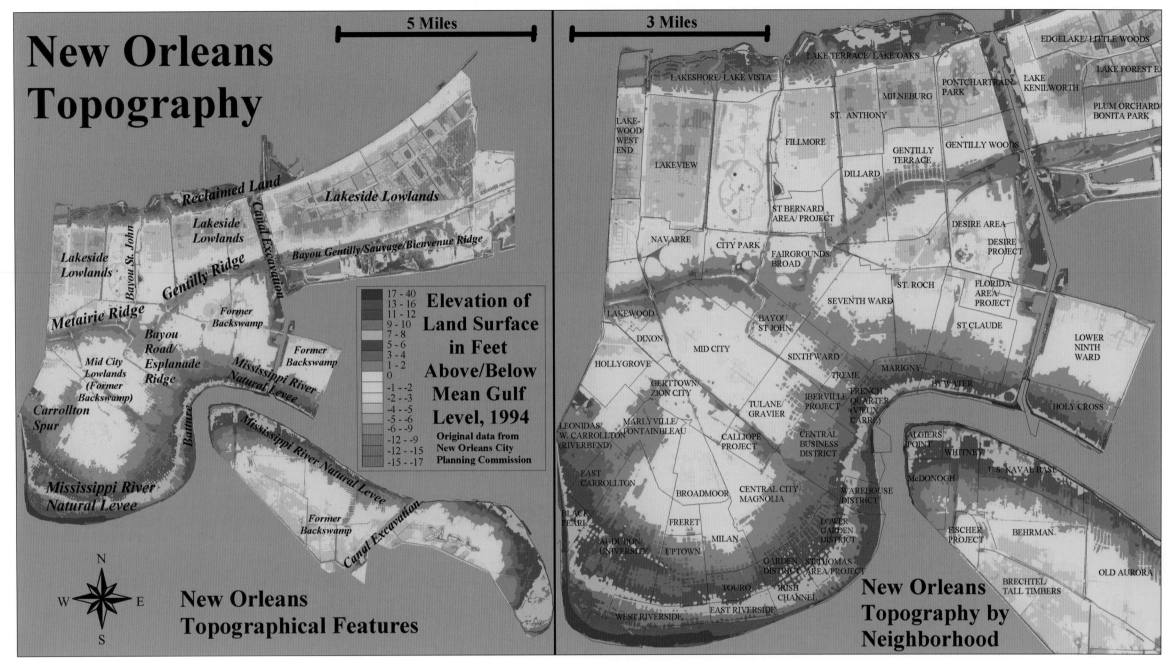

New Orleans Topography

5 Miles

3 Miles

New Orleans Topographical Features

Reclaimed Land

Lakeside Lowlands

Lakeside Lowlands

Canal Excavation

Bayou Gentilly/Sauvage/Bienvenue Ridge

Bayou St. John

Gentilly Ridge

Lakeside Lowlands

Metairie Ridge

Former Backswamp

Mid City Lowlands (Former Backswamp)

Bayou Road/Esplanade Ridge

Former Backswamp

Mississippi River Natural Levee

Carrollton Spur

Batture

Mississippi River Natural Levee

Mississippi River Natural Levee

Former Backswamp

Canal Excavation

N W E S

Elevation of Land Surface in Feet Above/Below Mean Gulf Level, 1994

Original data from New Orleans City Planning Commission

17 - 40
13 - 16
11 - 12
9 - 10
7 - 8
5 - 6
3 - 4
1 - 2
0
-1 - -2
-2 - -3
-4 - -5
-5 - -6
-6 - -9
-12 - -9
-12 - -15
-15 - -17

New Orleans Topography by Neighborhood

EDGELAKE/ LITTLE WOODS
LAKE TERRACE/ LAKE OAKS
LAKESHORE/ LAKE VISTA
LAKE FOREST E.
PONTCHARTRAIN PARK
LAKE KENILWORTH
MILNEBURG
PLUM ORCHARD BONITA PARK
ST. ANTHONY
LAKE-WOOD WEST END
FILLMORE
GENTILLY TERRACE
GENTILLY WOODS
LAKEVIEW
DILLARD
ST BERNARD AREA/ PROJECT
DESIRE AREA
NAVARRE
CITY PARK
FAIRGROUNDS/ BROAD
DESIRE PROJECT
ST. ROCH
FLORIDA AREA/ PROJECT
SEVENTH WARD
LAKEWOOD
BAYOU ST JOHN
ST CLAUDE
DIXON
MID CITY
SIXTH WARD
LOWER NINTH WARD
HOLLYGROVE
TREME
MARIGNY
GERTTOWN ZION CITY
BYWATER
IBERVILLE PROJECT
FRENCH QUARTER (VIEUX CARRE)
HOLY CROSS
TULANE GRAVIER
LEONIDAS/ W. CARROLLTON (RIVERBEND)
MARLYVILLE/ FONTAINBLEAU
CALLIOPE PROJECT
CENTRAL BUSINESS DISTRICT
ALGIERS POINT
WHITNEY
EAST CARROLLTON
CENTRAL CITY MAGNOLIA
WAREHOUSE DISTRICT
McDONOGH
U.S. NAVAL BASE
BROADMOOR
BLACK PEARL
FRERET
LOWER GARDEN DISTRICT
FISCHER PROJECT
BEHRMAN
AUDUBON UNIVERSITY
MILAN
GARDEN DISTRICT
ST. THOMAS AREA/PROJECT
UPTOWN
TOURO
IRISH CHANNEL
BRECHTEL/ TALL TIMBERS
OLD AURORA
WEST RIVERSIDE
EAST RIVERSIDE

A game of inches: New Orleans' topographic variation is decidedly minute, but in this deltaic environment, a few inches of elevation can determine whether a certain area was developed in 1800 or 1920. Topographic data in this map and throughout this volume are derived from one-foot elevation contours compiled in 1994 by Vernon F. Meyer for the New Orleans City Planning Commission through Global Positioning Systems technology based on second-order, class-1 survey standards using the North American Datum of 1983-1986 and the National Geodetic Vertical Datum of 1929. *GIS processing and cartography by author. Reproduction prohibited without written consent of the Executive Director, the New Orleans City Planning Commission. The New Orleans Geographic Information System at the New Orleans City Planning Commission is partially funded by a federal grant through NOAA*

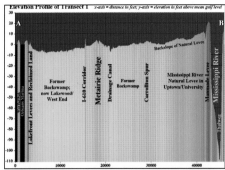
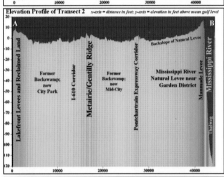
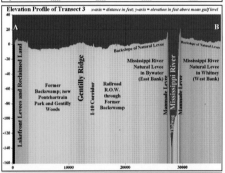
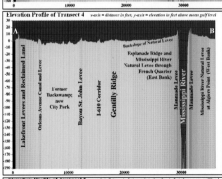
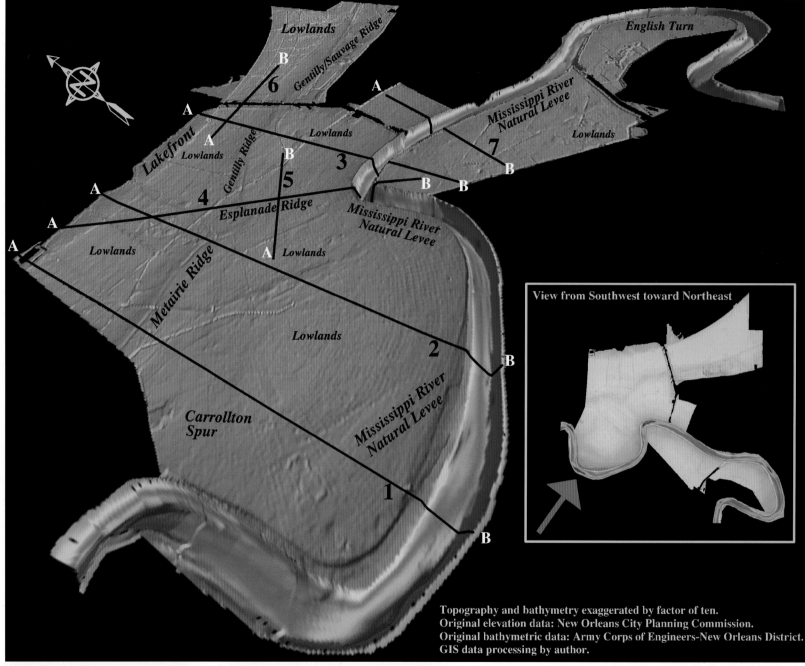
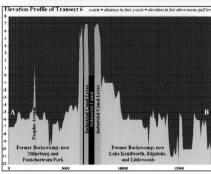
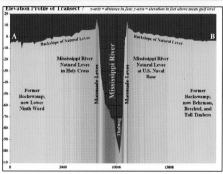
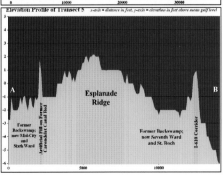

Topography and bathymetry exaggerated by factor of ten.
Original elevation data: New Orleans City Planning Commission.
Original bathymetric data: Army Corps of Engineers-New Orleans District.
GIS data processing by author.

Profiles of New Orleans topography and Mississippi River bathymetry (depth), derived from New Orleans City Planning Commission elevation data and Army Corps of Engineers bathymetric data. *GIS processing and cartography by author. Reproduction prohibited without written consent of the Executive Director, the New Orleans City Planning Commission. The New Orleans Geographic Information System at the New Orleans City Planning Commission is partially funded by a federal grant through NOAA*

Sights along the Metairie and Gentilly (Sauvage) Ridge, an upland formed by sediments deposited by distributaries of the Mississippi and wending west to east through the metropolitan area about four to five feet above mean sea level (seven to ten feet above adjacent lowlands):

1. Note the bend in Metairie Road—a rarity in these twentieth-century Jefferson Parish suburbs—following the curving Metairie Ridge. It is one of the oldest roads in the metropolitan area.

2. City Park Avenue follows the Metairie Ridge past Greenwood Cemetery (left). The plethora of cemeteries along the ridge reflects the fact that, in the late 1800s, this area marked the rural edge of New Orleans and the only well-drained land in the marshes surrounding the city, two driving factors for such land uses.

3.-5. This lagoon in City Park is the last remnant of Bayou Metairie, a prehistoric distributary of the Mississippi that deposited sediments across a curving band through the modern-day metropolitan area. Its channels and branches were gradually filled in and drained off during the nineteenth century, but its natural levee remains, home to the world's largest ancient live oak grove (5) in beautiful City Park.

6. This marker commemorates the historically significant intersection of the Metairie/Gentilly Ridge with Bayou St. John.

7. Gentilly Terrace neighborhood, developed from 1909 to World War II on the once-remote Gentilly Ridge, is known for its Craftsman-style California bungalows, Spanish Revival homes, and English cottages. It was declared a National Historic District in 1999, the first in New Orleans to be entirely a product of the twentieth century.

8. The Fair Grounds (1872), as well as the older portion of City Park and the former Metairie Race Track, all occupy the Metairie/Gentilly Ridge. These establishments needed well-drained land and proximity to urban populations but lacked space in the city; the semirural Metairie/Gentilly Ridge provided the perfect solution.

9. Looking down Franklin Avenue riverside of Gentilly Boulevard. Note the very slight slope into the distance: we are looking down the Gentilly Ridge into the lowlands of the Desire/St. Roch area, a total elevation range of about seven to eight feet spanning two miles. Unnoticeable to a pedestrian or cyclist, these slight topographic differences have had major impacts on the development of New Orleans.

10. Hebrew Rest Cemetery, Elysian Fields Avenue on the Gentilly Ridge, is another example of how this once-distant upland was utilized before residential development. Note the predominance of below-ground graves in this Jewish cemetery: this is *not* due to the fact that this area is historically well drained but rather to the Jewish custom of subterranean burial.

11. This spot by Xavier University on South Carrollton Avenue is a topographic "saddle" between the Metairie Ridge and the "Carrollton Spur." Had this spot been higher in elevation, it would have connected the Bayou St. John area and the Mississippi River near Carrollton with a passable upland (as did the Bayou Road/Esplanade Ridge on the opposite side of the New Orleans crescent). The historical development of New Orleans might have been quite different were it not for this low spot.

12. The Bayou Road/Esplanade Ridge rises about two to three feet above mean sea level and four to five feet above nearby lowlands. In this scene, Bayou Road intersects Esplanade Avenue at Gayarré Place (distant center).

13. The French Quarter is one of the highest, though not *the* highest, neighborhoods in New Orleans, occupying the back slope of the Mississippi River's natural levee starting at about 10 feet above mean sea level along Decatur Street (right) and sloping downward to about 1-2 feet near Rampart Street (left), which was just a few blocks from the backswamp in historic times. Visitors often make the mistaken impression that the French Quarter is below sea level because they are told that New Orleans is below sea level (in fact, 45 percent of urbanized New Orleans is above the level of the sea) and because the Mississippi River occasionally swells above the level of the streets, convincing them that the Quarter must be below sea level. In fact, the Quarter is entirely above sea level but not always or entirely above river level. The river level at the French Quarter ranges from as low as 0.71 to as high as 18.4 feet above the mean gulf level, with a typical springtime river level being about 10 feet above the gulf—about the same as Decatur Street. At these levels, only the manmade levee keeps the river from flooding the streets. *Photographs by author, 1999-2000*

facto upper limit of New Orleans' populated area.[8] The ridge system currently hosts the conspicuously curving Metairie Road, City Park Avenue, and Gentilly Boulevard, with their plethora of nineteenth-century cemeteries and racetracks, built there because it was the nearest rural upland to the urbanized area.[9] Major Amos Stoddard described these backcountry roads in his 1812 book, *Sketches, Historical and Descriptive, of Louisiana:*

> The road leading from the back part of the city [Bayou Road], forks two miles from the Mississippi [near present-day Fair Grounds]. The one on the right runs north east on a tongue of land [Gentilly Ridge], about half a mile in width, generally known by the name of Chantilly, and terminates in the marshes and swamps at the distance of about twenty miles [Bayou Sauvage in the Rigolets]. The one on the left [road following Metairie Ridge] extends about west, crosses St. John's creek over a drawbridge, and intersects the river road about fifteen miles above the city [Kenner, at the site of the original crevasse].[10]

Metairie and Gentilly Ridge, about four to five feet above mean sea level (m.s.l.) and seven to ten feet above the adjacent below-sea-level former backswamps, form the second component of New Orleans' original topography.

(Note: Unless otherwise stated, elevations cited in this discussion reflect modern measurements. Because New Orleans has been subsiding at greater-than-natural rates ever since the construction of the levees and the drainage system—it currently sinks at a pace of about seven millimeters per year,[11] faster now than historically—we may estimate that the ca.-1700 topographic surface was about two to four feet higher than it is now. Lower areas probably have fallen at greater rates than higher areas. However, layers of artificial fill and pavement throughout the city have cancelled out some of the losses to subsidence, thus making the current land surface perhaps one to three feet lower than the prehistoric era.)

That the third element in the local z-dimension was actually an offspring of the first two—the natural levees of the Mississippi River and of Bayous Metairie/Gentilly—does not diminish its importance in local history, for the location of New Orleans is largely derived from it. Since the original city occupied a cutbank portion of a Mississippi River meander, its natural levee was especially broad—broad enough to extend into the backswamp and "fuse" with the back slope of the much-smaller Bayous Metairie/Gentilly natural levee, in the vicinity of the present-day Fair Grounds Race Track, to form a faint rise linking the two uplands. This third topographic feature was the "fine path" that Iberville described on March 9, 1699 (see page 20), part of the portage between the lake and the river that the Indians had used for ages. The ancient portage evolved into Bayou Road in the early colonial years and is now generally known as the Esplanade Ridge,[12] about two to three feet above m.s.l. and four to five feet above nearby lowlands, connecting Bayou St. John with the French Quarter. Like Metairie Road and Gentilly Boulevard, Bayou Road curves gently through the orthogonal street patterns of later urban developments, its path determined not by man's sense of order but by his need for dry ground to walk from point A to point B. Had the Bayou Road/Esplanade Ridge not existed, the river would have been divorced from the convenience of Bayou St. John by nearly impenetrable cypress swamps, and New Orleans probably would have been sited elsewhere.

The Bayou Road/Esplanade Ridge topographic feature, jutting as it does from the French Quarter bend of the Mississippi northwest to the crux of the crescent, is mirrored by a similar feature on the flip side of the crescent. Call it the "Carrollton Spur," a two-mile intrusion of silt and clay stretching from the Carrollton bend of the Mississippi northeastward toward the middle of town, probably formed by a crevasse in the natural levee of the present-day Riverbend neighborhood that allowed a plume of sediment-laden water to enter the crescent

8. A 1917 population map shows a very low population density north of the Metairie/Gentilly Ridge, compared to its city side. Allison; see "Map of New Orleans Showing Street Car Lines and Density of Population."

9. Gentilly Boulevard, which splits into Chef Menteur Highway (Highway 90) and Old Gentilly Road as it runs eastward, was *the* gateway in and out of New Orleans from all points eastward on the Gulf Coast until just a few decades ago, when Interstate 10 was completed. The old ridge is still the principal eastern corridor for railroads.

10. Stoddard, 162.

11. Ramsey and Moslow, 1673. The figure of seven millimeters per year is an average of the authors' observations that "subsidence has been greatest on the western deltaic plain (0.36 cm/yr) and along the coast (1.03 cm/yr)."

12. I refer to this feature as the "Bayou Road/Esplanade Ridge," rather than just the "Esplanade Ridge," because Bayou Road is far older and more historically significant than Esplanade Avenue, despite the fact that the former is now a quiet back street and the latter a grand avenue.

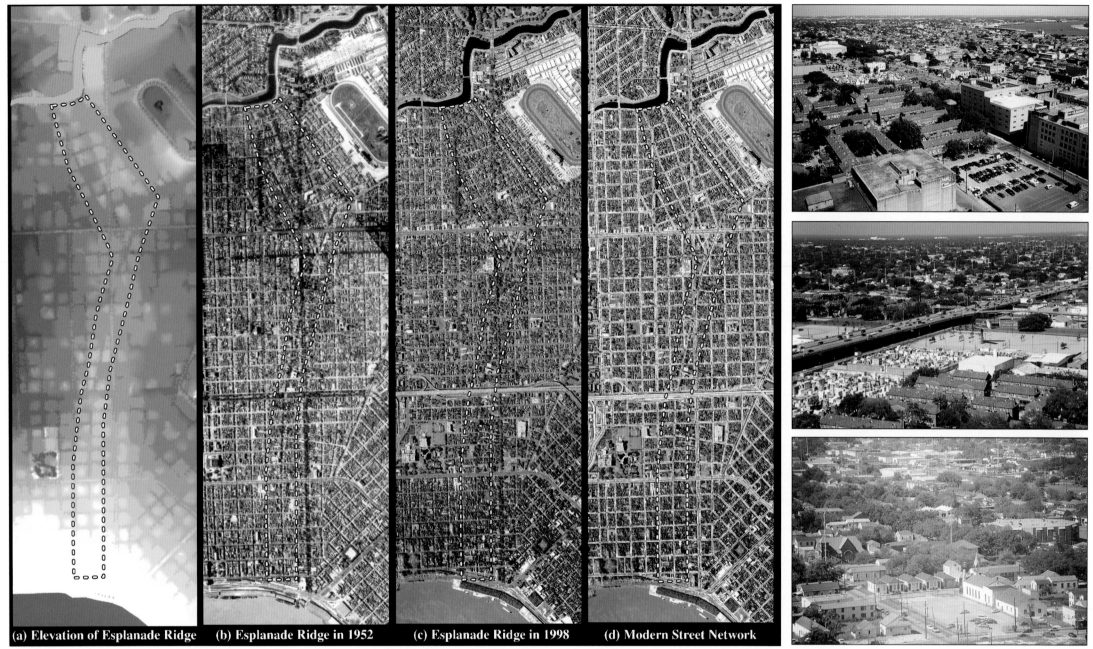

(a) Elevation of Esplanade Ridge (b) Esplanade Ridge in 1952 (c) Esplanade Ridge in 1998 (d) Modern Street Network

These aerial perspectives show the relationship between elevation and development on the historic Bayou Road/Esplanade Ridge. The first scene is not an image but a digital elevation model in which brighter colors represent higher areas. Note the faint ridge connecting the French Quarter (bottom) and Bayou St. John (top). The remaining scenes are aerial photographs showing the curving pattern of ancient Bayou Road through otherwise orthogonal street networks laid out throughout the nineteenth century.

Processing and cartography by author; data from New Orleans City Planning Commission, U.S. Department of Agriculture, and U.S. Geological Survey

Above sea level: Back slope of the Mississippi River natural levee, looking from the Iberville Housing Development (slightly above sea level) to the riverfront, about ten feet above sea level plus another ten to fifteen feet of manmade levees in certain areas. The housing project occupies the site of the famous red-light district Storyville (1897-1917), one of the last surviving structures of which is visible at center, among trees.

Sea level: The I-10/Claiborne Avenue corridor through Faubourg Tremé and the Sixth Ward intersects the area where, in historic times, the well-drained back slope of the natural levee descended into inundated swamp or marsh, known then as the "back-of-town." In the distance, far too subtle to see, lies the slightly elevated Esplanade Ridge. The swath of concrete passing perpendicularly beneath Interstate 10 is the former bed of Carondelet Canal, first dug in 1794; note also St. Louis Cemetery No. 2. In 2001, the New Orleans Saints proposed this area—specifically the Iberville Housing Development—as possible site for a new retractable-roof football stadium.

Below sea level: These Tulane/Gravier/Sixth Ward neighborhoods are slightly below sea level, though not nearly as low as some lakeside areas. The installation of the drainage system around 1900 allowed for the development of these low-lying areas. *Photographs by author, 2000*

periodically and deposit a few inches of earth.[13] About as high as the Bayou Road/Esplanade Ridge (two to four feet above m.s.l.), the Carrollton Spur differs in one fundamental way from its cross-town counterpart: it falls short by about one mile of joining the Metairie Ridge/Gentilly Ridge. Thus what could have been another portage from Bayou St. John to the river instead petered out into the swamp at about the point where Xavier University is located today. Had the Carrollton Spur fused with the Metairie/Gentilly Ridge, as does the Bayou Road/Esplanade Ridge, Bienville would have had two paths between the lake and the river—shaped like a wishbone, with Bayou St. John as the trunk—and perhaps would have founded New Orleans (or an ancillary depot or fort) at the future Carrollton area. Instead, the Carrollton area remained an isolated agricultural tract until the 1830s, when a community developed and prospered as a separate city, finally merging with New Orleans in 1874. The Carrollton Spur did enable the early development of Carrollton Avenue (with a railway and canal) into the middle of the crescent over half a century before other uptown avenues expanded into that area.

These four formations produced the original topographical circumstance of New Orleans. Engineer and writer James S. Janssen observed that although the city's topography is often compared to a saucer, a better analogy might be to those "Blue Plate Special" platters[14] found in mom-and-pop diners, the ones with the sectioning ridges that keep the peas from socializing with the fried okra. This analogy works even better today, when the entire city is ringed by a high rim (like the plate) of artificial levees along the river, lake, and marshes, for flood and hurricane protection. In its primeval state, however, Lake Pontchartrain had no natural levee, since it did not deposit sediment.

Two other topographic elements warrant mention, not for their physical prominence as much as for the access they provided southward and northward of the city, perpendicular to the riverside uplands. To the south of the eventual site of New Orleans, the slight upland paralleling the west-bank distributaries of Bayou des Familles and Bayou Barataria extended narrow fingers of dry land into the marshy wilderness. To the north, no natural levee protruded from the Metairie/Gentilly Ridge to touch the shore of Lake Pontchartrain, but a saddle or fault in said ridge allowed impounded water in the lowlands of present-day Mid-City (cradled by the Mississippi natural levee, Esplanade Ridge, and Metairie Ridge) to spill northward toward the lake in the form of three-mile-long Bayou St. John. The impounded water flowed into the bayou and thence into the lake via a dendritic stream network—*trib*utaries in this case—that drained the back slopes of the crescent (present-day Mid-City with branches reaching as far as Carrollton and Lee Circle) as well as areas to the east (New Marigny/St. Roch). Too meager to have developed its own natural levees, Bayou St. John nevertheless played a crucial role in the founding of New Orleans.

Repercussions of Topography on the Development of New Orleans

Geographers are leery of ascribing the causes of human endeavors solely to physical geography—the overly simplistic notion of environmental determinism has already been discussed—but in the case of topography in New Orleans, an undeniable cause-and-effect relationship exists between the lay of the land and the development of the city. For nearly two centuries, from the earliest European settlements at Bayou St. John in 1708 to the electrified metropolis of the early 1900s, New Orleans clung to the natural-levee uplands of the Mississippi River and its distributaries at the exclusion of the "back-of-town" lowlands, the lake shore, and surrounding marshes. The shape of this built environment—not just the bend in the river—earned New Orleans its enchanting old nickname, Crescent City.[15] Natural levees were the only regularly dry swaths rising above the wetlands, and until the appropriate technology emerged for draining the swamps, the city was naturally constricted to their limits. *Within* this constriction, development was guided by myriad factors, including politics, economics, culture, transportation, and geographic distance, but for almost two hundred years, topography formed the first-tier rule guiding where New Orleanians built New Orleans.

---

13. This is the Macarty Crevasse, which last broke in 1832, just before the Macarty plantation was subdivided as Carrollton. The 150-foot crevasse occurred near present-day Leonidas Street and deposited sediment in the vicinity of Carrollton Avenue. William H. Williams (189) seems to imply that all of the extra sedimentary deposit in this area stems from the 1832 crevasse, but it seems more likely that what we are calling the "Carrollton Spur" was in fact decades, if not centuries, in the making. There had been a prior crevasse here area just a few years earlier, in 1816, which presumably contributed its share of sediments to the Carrollton area. See also Swanson, 91, and Ledet, 227-28.
14. Janssen, 21.
15. "I have termed New-Orleans the crescent city . . . from its being built around the segment of a circle formed by a graceful curve of the river at this place" (Ingraham, 91).

A Trip across the Backswamp, 1854
Toward the end of his tour of the seaboard slave states in 1853-54, a disoriented Frederick Law Olmsted arrived from Mobile via Lake Pontchartrain to the "backdoor" of New Orleans, near the present-day main campus of the University of New Orleans. He described his train trip to the city proper from Milneburg, the resort community located where the Pontchartrain Railroad, following present-day Elysian Fields Avenue, reached the lake, at the present-day intersection of Leon C. Simon.

"There were many small buildings near the jetty, erected on piles over the water—bathing-houses, bowling-alleys, and billiard-rooms, with other indications of a place of holiday resort—and, on reaching the shore, I found a slumbering village [Milneburg]. [Then] a locomotive [Smokey Mary, the famed engine of the Pontchartrain Railroad] backed, screaming hoarsely, down the jetty; and I returned to get my seat.

"Off we puffed, past the restaurant . . . through the little village of white houses . . . and away into a dense, gray cypress forest. For three or four rods [about 60 feet], each side of the track, the trees had all been felled and removed, leaving a dreary strip of swamp, covered with stumps. This was bounded and intersected by broad ditches, or narrow and shallow canals, with a great number of very small punts in them—which, I suppose, are used for shrimp catching [crawfish? crabs?]. So it continued, for two or three miles; then the ground became dryer [Gentilly Ridge], there was an abrupt termination of the gray wood. The fog was lifting and drifting off . . . and liberty of the eye was given over a flat country, skirted still, and finally bounded, in the background, with the swamp-forest [lowlands in present-day Seventh Ward and St. Roch]. There were scattered, irregularly over it, a few low houses, one story high, all having verandahs before them.

"At length, a broad road struck in by the side of the track; the houses became frequent; soon it was a village street [rear edge of natural levee, around the Claiborne Avenue intersection with Elysian Fields], with smoke ascending from breakfast fires; windows and doors opening, girls sweeping steps, bakers' wagons passing, and broad streets, little built upon, breaking off at right angles. . . . I asked the name of the village [Faubourg Marigny], for my geography was at fault. I had expected to be landed at New Orleans by the boat, and had not been informed of the railroad arrangement, and had no idea in what part of Louisiana we might be. . . .

"There was a sign, '*Café du Faubourg,*' and, putting my head out of the window, I saw that we were thundering into New Orleans. . . . We rattled through narrow, dirty streets, among grimy old stuccoed walls; high, arched windows and doors, balconies and entresols, and French noises and French smells [and] French signs, ten to one of English."
                                    —Frederick Law Olmsted, 1856 (225-27. Olmsted would go on to national fame as a landscape architect; his firm, Olmsted and Brothers, landscaped Audubon Park in the early 1900s.)

It was at the upland junction of Bayou St. John and the Metairie/Gentilly waterway-and-ridge system that Europeans first settled in the future New Orleans area, guided there by the Indians who had used the spot since time immemorial for camps and portage. Six land concessions, granted by the government in Mobile to eight colonists on October 28, 1708, were surveyed to exploit the topographic and transportation advantage offered by these features for wheat cultivation. The narrow plots (2.5 to 4 arpents wide and 36 to 40 arpents deep) followed the Metairie/Gentilly Ridge in an east-west direction and intersected Bayou St. John perpendicularly, just as thousands of future long-lot plantations would be oriented to exploit the Mississippi and its uplands. Although the wheat crop at these first concessions did not prosper, the venture brought attention to this backdoor route to the Mississippi, for usage of the Bayou St. John/Bayou Road portage increased in the 1710s[16] and eventually led to the founding of New Orleans later in the decade. The site of the 1708 concessions today spans the beautiful Faubourg St. John neighborhood from lower City Park eastward to the Fair Grounds Race Track, an area that does not even break the five-foot contour above the sea but might approach the ten-foot contour if local lowlands are considered the datum plane. Within this swath, lagoons near City Park Avenue and the nearby kink in Bayou St. John mark the vestiges of Bayou Metairie and Bayou Gentilly, agents of land building and history making in this important district.

---

16. Freiberg, 28-33.

These photographs provide an idea of what Mid-City and lakeside New Orleans looked like throughout the nineteenth century. Swamp—that is, forested wetlands—covered the area in its wilderness state, but a century of timber-felling rendered New Orleans' "back-of-town" an open wetland covered with thick scrub vegetation, occasional stumps, remnant cypress stands, and networks of rivulets. These photographs were taken near the Turtle Cove area in the Manchac Swamp, west of Lake Pontchartrain, which was deforested for housing construction in New Orleans around 1900. Lumber from Manchac's trees now support countless turn-of-the-century shotgun houses and cottages throughout the city. *Photographs by author, 2001*

Perpendicular to a bend in the upper reaches of Bayou St. John was a slight natural levee built up by now-extinct Bayou Gentilly. The upland extended far enough to fuse with the rear edge of the natural levee of the Mississippi River, forming the Bayou Road portage and playing a decisive role in the siting of New Orleans, as previously discussed. The portage did not just follow a topographical feature, it *was* a topographical feature, nary one to two feet above m.s.l. and three to four feet above adjacent swamps but enough to allow for the passage of pedestrian traffic. If one views New Orleans as the historic link between the outside world and the North American interior, and as a cog among extraordinarily diverse cultural regions, then two-mile-long Bayou Road—*Le Chemin au Bayou St. Jean* to the French, *El Camino al Gran Bayou llamado San Juan* to the Spanish—is raised to a lofty symbolic level. See page 160 for more details on the disembarkation point between the bayou and the road.

Bayou Road's shoulders, like the natural levees of waterways in the region, were subdivided into long, narrow *habitations* (plantations)—with backswamps at both ends and the upland in the middle—and conceded to various citizens throughout the French and Spanish colonial years. Though they originally spanned about forty arpents, from present-day Tulane Avenue to St. Bernard Avenue (edges of neighboring plantations that radiated from the bend of the Mississippi and thus intersected the Bayou Road properties perpendicularly), only about three arpents on each side of the road were regularly dry and cultivable, owing to the slender width of the Esplanade Ridge. Houses lining the road, crops growing behind the houses, and dark cypress swamps extending both directions into the horizon: this was the eighteenth-century landscape one encountered when traveling the road from Bayou St. John to the city.

That city—*La Nouvelle Orléans,* announced by the Company of the West in 1717, sited by Bienville in 1718, and surveyed after it became capital of Louisiana in 1722—occupied the intersection of the two-foot-high Bayou Road/Esplanade Ridge corridor with the approximately ten-foot-high natural levee of the Mississippi. The earliest clearing and construction occurred in the vicinity of Conti and Decatur Street (which at the time lay near the riverbank at the crest of the natural levee) and proceeded in a somewhat haphazard fashion until the nascent city, vying for the status of capital, was surveyed by Adrien de Pauger (1721-22) from plans originally developed by his superior, Chief Engineer Le Blond de La Tour. Contrary to New Orleans' *laissez faire* reputation, this first built environment—now the French Quarter, or Vieux Carré—"is actually military in the insistence of its right angles, like the gridded camps Roman soldiers laid out at the wild edges of their empire. . . . The French Quarter looks like what it is—the elaboration of a colonial outpost designed by military engineers."[17] Historically, the French Quarter is the oldest neighborhood in New Orleans and the site of numerous events of national significance; architecturally, the 72-block district is an outdoor museum of

about 1,800 structures[18] ranging stylistically from French Creole to Spanish Colonial to Greek Revival to Art Deco; culturally, it is the hearth of New Orleans, a lively neighborhood and engine behind the tourist industry.[19] The diversity of the half-square-mile cityscape contrasts with the subtlety of its topography.

Historic Roads Following Topographic Ridges in New Orleans		
Modern and Historic Names	**Associated Streets**	**Underlying Topographic Feature**
Bayou Road *Le Chemin au Bayou St. Jean,* *El Camino al Gran Bayou* *llamado San Juan*	Governor Nicholls Street, Esplanade Avenue, Grand Route St. John, Bell Street, Desoto Street, part of Gentilly Boulevard	Two-foot-high ridge connecting natural levee of Metairie/Gentilly Bayou with natural levee of the Mississippi
Metairie Road	City Park Avenue	Natural levee of now-extinct Bayou Metairie, winding through Jefferson Parish and western Orleans Parish, three to four feet high
Gentilly Boulevard *Chantilly, Gentilly Road*	Chef Menteur Highway, Highway 90	Natural levee of now-extinct Bayou Gentilly (Sauvage), winding through eastern New Orleans at three to four feet high and terminating at Chef Menteur Pass
South Carrollton Avenue *Canal Avenue*		Two-foot-high "spur" that is really an extended back slope of the natural levee created by a historic crevasse in the Riverbend neighborhood
Tchoupitoulas Street *Chemin Real, Camino Real,* *Rue de la Levée, Rue de la* *Vieille Levée, Rue des* *Tchoucpicloneas, Levee Street,* *Old Levee Street, Choupitoulas* *Street, Tchapitoulas Street*	North Peters Street, Decatur Street, Chartres Street, Leake Avenue, River Road	Crest of the natural levee of the Mississippi River, ten to twelve feet above m.s.l.

The riverside edge of the French Quarter overlays the crest of the natural levee that is currently about ten feet above m.s.l. (excluding the manmade levee). Toward the lake, the silty-loamy terrain slopes downward at a rate of about one foot per block—a negligible 1 percent slope but enough to shed water backward—so that the five-foot-contour level straggles between Dumaine and Burgundy in the downriver end of the Quarter and Royal and Bourbon in the upriver end.[20] (An extra foot of elevation in the downriver end of the Quarter reflects the emergence of the Bayou Road/Esplanade Ridge.) In adapting Le Blond de La Tour's city plan for Biloxi to the geography of New Orleans, Adrien de Pauger relocated the town square (*Place d'Armes*) from the center of the grid to this higher edge, explaining to his boss "the changes I have been obliged to make because of the situation of the terrain. As it is higher on the bank of the river, I have brought the town square and the sites marked for the houses of the principal inhabitants closer to it, so as to profit not only from the proximity of the landing place, but also from the air of the breezes that come from it."[21] (Were it not for Pauger's topographic observation, today's Jackson Square might be located near the Bourbon/Orleans intersection.) Higher lands

17. Heard, 1.

18. An exact count of the blocks in the French Quarter varies from a historic minimum of 66 to a modern maximum of 108 (as enumerated by the *Vieux Carré Survey*), depending on what one considers to be a block. There are about 1,800 curbside structures in the French Quarter, but this number grows to almost 3,000 if dependencies and outbuildings are included. About 57 percent of the Vieux Carré's buildings pre-date the Civil War, and 78 percent were constructed before 1900.
19. Being the engine behind tourism conflicts with the French Quarter's neighborhood aspects. From 1940 to 1990, the Quarter's full-time residential population declined from 11,053 to 3,991, as the noise and banality of tourism drove locals away, gentrification inflated the rents, and out-of-towners scooped up the scores of condominiums carved out of old mansions and cottages. The decline stabilized in the 1990s: the 2000 census counted 4,176 residents in the Quarter (of whom 92 percent, incidentally, were white), a 5 percent increase. Efforts to strike a balance between this important industry and the authenticity of the feature upon which it is based have been a constant and controversial theme in local politics since the 1960s, and will only intensify in the future.
20. The exact location of a particular contour varies with the scale, accuracy, and precision of the map. These figures are derived from one-foot contour data provided by the New Orleans City Planning Commission Geographic Information Systems, mapped in 1994 using Global Positioning Systems technology. Soil information is based on U.S. Department of Agriculture Soil Conservation Service.
21. Wilson, "Colonial Fortifications," 386.

along the river and near the *Place d'Armes* were developed first, due primarily to convenience but also to elevation, while lower lands near present-day Rampart remained vacant for a number of years and hosted such land uses as an early below-ground cemetery and, later, a palisade and moat. Structures of church and state were erected high on the natural levee by the river, creating "a profound sense of the union between the river and the city . . . the sacralization of the Mississippi."[22] The riverside upland became the most valuable land in town, offering two critical ingredients for local prosperity—transportation accessibility and good drainage—and providing

> the point of ingress and egress for travelers, traders, and residents of New Orleans. The high ground along the waterfront served as the city's front door; it was the first site greeting people as they arrived in New Orleans, and the last site they saw when they left. For social reasons, too, New Orleanians valued their waterfront. Elevated above the city physically, the riverfront provided a breezy waterside promenade, where people [enjoyed] cooling breezes wafting off the Mississippi.[23]

Today, the ten-foot contour runs in front of Jackson Square and is spatially correlated with the majority of "bustle" in the French Quarter—the traffic on Decatur Street, the countless pedestrians strolling by St. Louis Cathedral, the freight trains rumbling past crowded French Market stalls—whereas the lower-elevation Dumaine-Burgundy-Rampart area is decidedly more placid and residential. Artificial fill, pavement, and sidewalks obscure the original topographic circumstance of the French Quarter today, but the general back-sloping trend remains as an underlying factor in the urban geography of this centuries-old world-famous neighborhood.

The Good Friday Fire of 1788 and demand for land prompted the Gravier family, owners of the former Jesuit plantation that originally belonged to Bienville, to subdivide their plantation for the upriver expansion of New Orleans. Faubourg Ste. Marie (St. Mary), the city's first suburb and the only major subdivision during the colonial era, was laid out in the spring of 1788 by Spanish surveyor general Don Carlos Laveau Trudeau and developed slowly at first but then more aggressively in early American years. Like the original city across the commons, Faubourg Ste. Marie exploited the natural levee, hugging the 10-foot-high crest along the riverfront and extending six blocks inland to within sight of the lowland cypress swamps. Nearly every outpost of the Spanish colonial empire had a *Camino Real* (Royal Highway), and in Faubourg Ste. Marie the *Camino Real* naturally ran along the riverside uplands, being dry, elevated, communally held, and accessible via watercraft. This road was an extension of Levee Street (now North Peters and Decatur) on the old side of town, and is now Tchoupitoulas Street, the great arcuate corridor that straddles the 10-foot contour as it encircles the entire crescent of the modern-day city (see page 99). Today, the former *Camino Real* runs fully 1,500 feet inland from the river it used to follow, due to the fortuitous development of a batture—deposition of sediment along the levee/river interface—that occurred around the time of subdivision and altered the geography and topography of this district to the present day. (The St. Mary batture, which also affected the French Quarter, is discussed in more detail on page 62.) Faubourg Ste. Marie developed in the early nineteenth century as the hub of the Anglo-American element that migrated to the city after the Louisiana Purchase, and was at times home to an even larger foreign-born population (mostly Irish and German), comprising fully 51

22. Kelman, 22.
23. Ibid., 21.

(a) French Quarter Streets and Elevation

(b) French Quarter in 1922

(c) French Quarter in 1940

(d) French Quarter in 1952

(e) French Quarter in 1964

(f) French Quarter in 1989

(a) Digital elevation model of the French Quarter shows the relatively higher areas by the river (about ten feet above sea level plus the manmade levee) and the back slope toward Rampart Street (one to two feet high). The aerial photographs (b-f) reveal the subtle increments of change that have transpired within the confines of New Orleans' oldest neighborhood over the twentieth century. *Processing and cartography by author; data from New Orleans City Planning Commission, U.S. Department of Agriculture, and U.S. Geological Survey. Note: The diagonal line across the 1922 photograph is a crease in the original print.*

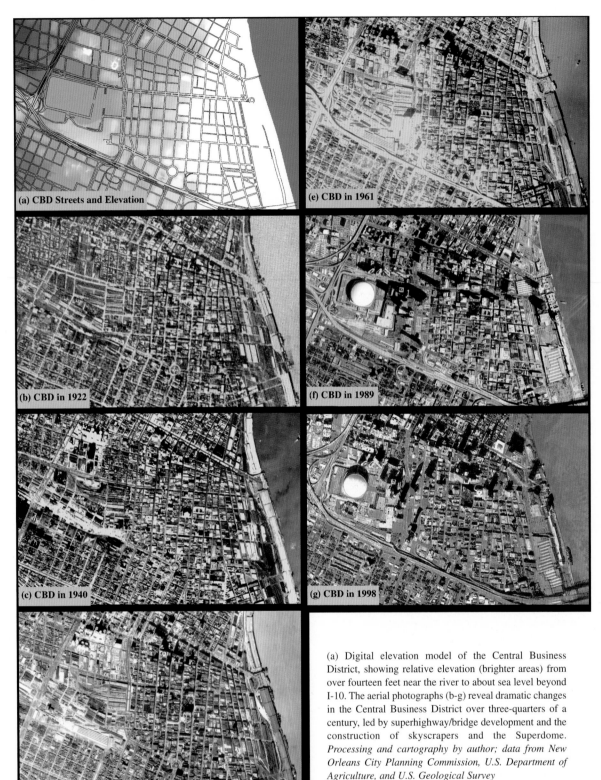

(a) CBD Streets and Elevation

(e) CBD in 1961

(b) CBD in 1922

(f) CBD in 1989

(c) CBD in 1940

(g) CBD in 1998

(d) CBD in 1952

(a) Digital elevation model of the Central Business District, showing relative elevation (brighter areas) from over fourteen feet near the river to about sea level beyond I-10. The aerial photographs (b-g) reveal dramatic changes in the Central Business District over three-quarters of a century, led by superhighway/bridge development and the construction of skyscrapers and the Superdome. *Processing and cartography by author; data from New Orleans City Planning Commission, U.S. Department of Agriculture, and U.S. Geological Survey*

percent of the white population of this faubourg in 1850.[24] With English as its language, business as it dedication, and Northeastern architectural styles as its signature, the district became known as Faubourg St. Mary, the American Sector, and finally, today, as the Central Business District. Now, skyscrapers dominate the old plantation, with rooftops reaching almost 700 feet above ground level and pilings tapping into the firm point-bar sands or hard Pleistocene clays 100 feet below Trudeau's streets. Topographically, the CBD occupies the same 3-to-10-foot-high "ramp" that underlies the French Quarter (except that the CBD extends farther and higher into the river, and farther inland toward that great manmade watershed, the Louisiana Superdome and its surrounding infrastructure); it differs from the French Quarter in that its back slope is somewhat more gradual, its batture is longer and wider, and its street network retains some of the topology of the old plantations from which it was subdivided. These two districts, separated by a barren triangular commons[25] and connected to the outside world by their perch on the Mississippi and by their access to Bayou St. John, formed the remote and isolated city of New Orleans at the close of its colonial era.

Three years after the Louisiana Purchase made New Orleans an American city, two new urban developments were subdivided from adjacent plantations, one upriver from Faubourg Ste. Marie, forming the "Upper Banlieue," and one downriver from the city, toward what would be the "Lower Banlieue."[26] The upriver area was surveyed in 1806-10 out of the late-eighteenth-century long-lot plantations of Delord-Sarpy (later sold to Duplantier), Saulet (Solet), the recently created Robin property, and Livaudais, by surveyor Barthélémy Lafon, and developed into the Faubourg Duplantier, Faubourg Solet, Faubourg de La Course, and Faubourg de L'Annunciation. Together, these four faubourgs (referred to in various ways during the 1800s) became the attractive residential neighborhoods of Coliseum Square and Annunciation Square.[27] Today the general area is known as the Lower Garden District, extending into adjacent neighborhoods and anchored by Lee Circle, a signature component (*Place du Tivoli*) of Lafon's classical city planning and one of the higher spots in the area (15 feet above m.s.l.), albeit landscaped. The plantations subdivided by Lafon and annexed to Faubourg Ste. Marie are topographically significant in that they occupy one of the broadest natural levees within the crescent, with the 5-foot contour about 4,000 feet from the river and the sea-level contour another 4,000 feet away. Contrast this with the French Quarter and downriver communities, where these two isolines are only half as far from the Mississippi, due in large part to the dynamics of the bending river.

Also at this time, the first faubourg downriver from the French Quarter was planned by Nicolas de Finiels and surveyed by Lafon (starting 1805) for, and upon the former plantation of, the famous Creole aristocrat Bernard Xavier Philippe de Marigny de Mandeville. The Faubourg Marigny, the quintessential New Orleans Creole faubourg, is perched slightly beyond a cutbank section of the Mississippi, where the current removes rather than deposits sediment (as in the St. Mary batture), and occupies a fairly narrow natural levee. The land beneath the odd-shaped blocks of this historic community, which conflate the grid of the old city to the new grid below Elysian Fields Avenue (the "Marigny Triangle" and the "Marigny Rectangle"), slopes from ten feet down to five feet above m.s.l. in a span of only three blocks. In upriver neighborhoods, this same elevation range traverses an area up to ten blocks wide.

With faubourgs expanding New Orleans laterally along the natural levee, an opportunity arose to exploit the limited acreage *behind* the French Quarter, at the trunk of the Bayou Road/Esplanade Ridge. In 1810-12, the ten-arpent plantation of Claude Tremé was purchased by the city and surveyed by Jacques Tanesse, creating the community of Faubourg Tremé between present-day St. Bernard Avenue and Carondelet Canal, an important feature excavated in 1794 and discussed on page 66. Faubourg Tremé is one to four feet above m.s.l. and, though suffering from social ills and physical decay, is still fairly intact in terms of its historical architecture,[28] and rejuvenating more and more every day. An adjacent community on the other side of Carondelet Canal was developed at about the same time as Faubourg Tremé (and is often considered a section of the same community), built not upon an upland but on the swampy lowlands (zero to two feet) that were designated as the City Commons in the eighteenth century and used for "public grazing and as a source of free firewood and fill during the dry season."[29] The topographic disadvantage of the City Commons area was mitigated by the drainage provided by the canal, allowing for housing development in the early 1800s, but the area has always been a place apart in New Orleans. In the early years, its backswamp status made it home to things that citizens did not want in their backyards: cemeteries, hospitals, forts, military installations, and the like. In later years, low rents attracted indigents and eventually prostitutes to parts of this so-called "over the basin"[30] area,

24. Tregle, "Creoles and Americans," 164.

25. This commons is now the series of blocks wedged between Iberville and Common Street.

26. "The Upper Banlieue embrac[es] the suburbs of Duplantier, Soulet, La Course, Annunciation, and Religieuses. . . . The Lower Banlieue embrac[es] the suburbs of Daunois and Clouet" (Paxton, 1822, 9). *Banlieue* means a suburb, or in this context, suburban development.

27. Wilson, "Early History of the Lower Garden District," 7-12.

28. A major exception is Armstrong Park, an urban-renewal-era intrusion (demolition 1956-73, park opened 1980) that replaced ten blocks of historic Tremé with bridged lagoons and ersatz topographic relief.

29. Friends of the Cabildo, vol. 6, 56.

30. Claiborne Avenue Design Team, 28.

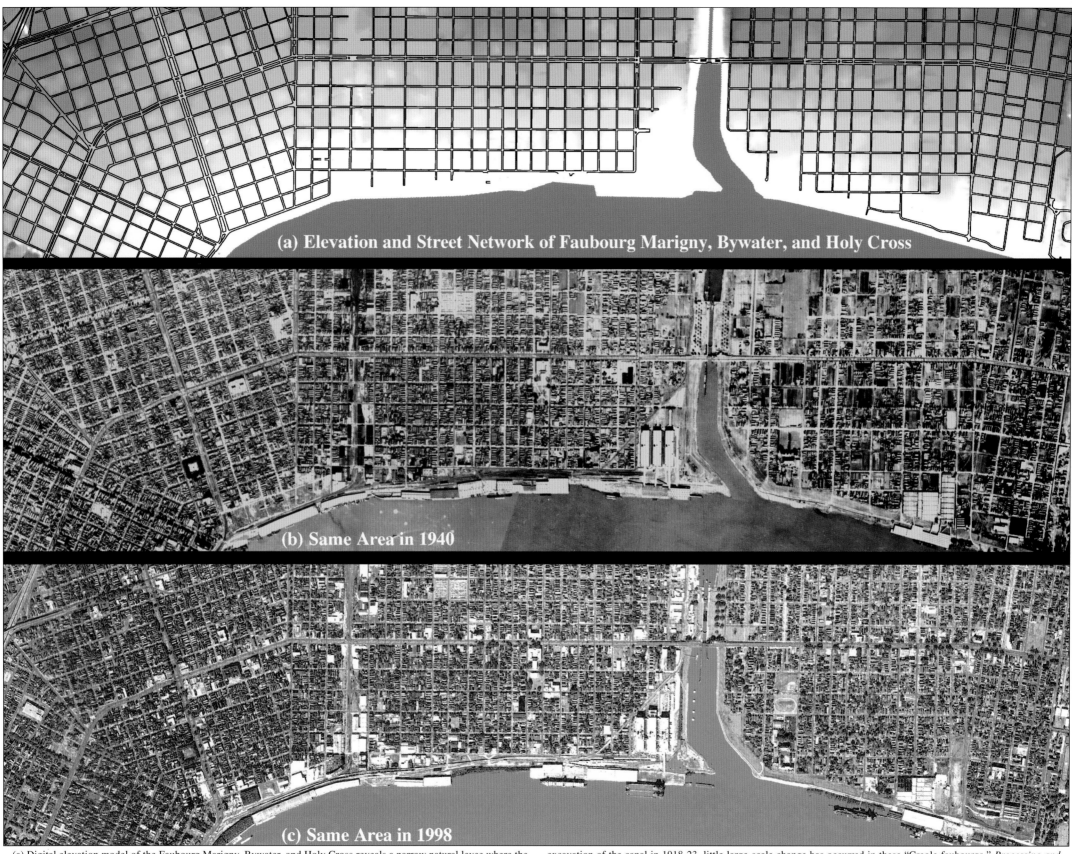

(a) Elevation and Street Network of Faubourg Marigny, Bywater, and Holy Cross

(b) Same Area in 1940

(c) Same Area in 1998

(a) Digital elevation model of the Faubourg Marigny, Bywater, and Holy Cross reveals a narrow natural levee where the river straightens out and has excavated the bank over the centuries, in contrast to the deposition that occurred upriver in the Central Business District. Note the artificially shored up area at the mouth of the Industrial Canal. Since the excavation of the canal in 1918-23, little large-scale change has occurred in these "Creole faubourgs." *Processing and cartography by author; data from New Orleans City Planning Commission, U.S. Department of Agriculture, and U.S. Geological Survey*

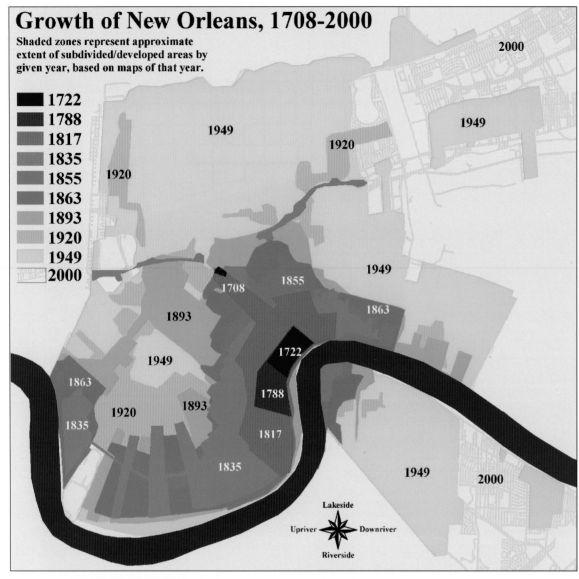

Growth of New Orleans, 1708-2000

Shaded zones represent approximate
extent of subdivided/developed areas by
given year, based on maps of that year.

■ 1722
■ 1788
■ 1817
■ 1835
■ 1855
■ 1863
■ 1893
■ 1920
■ 1949
☐ 2000

Physical growth of New Orleans was driven by economic, cultural, and geographical factors. Starting with the original city in the early eighteenth century, the general trend was to spread mostly upriver along the natural levee (and to a lesser degree downriver) during the course of the nineteenth century, across the river in the late 1800s, and then toward the lake after the installation of the drainage system around 1900. With some exceptions (such as Gentilly), most above-sea-level areas in New Orleans were developed in the nineteenth century or earlier, while most below-sea-level areas urbanized in the twentieth century. This growth map was made by digitally coregistering historical maps and aerial photographs, interpreting them for developed versus undeveloped areas, and overlaying the results. The process is more difficult than it sounds, because surveyors and cartographers through the years employed different standards of what constituted "development," often drawing their lines in contradictory patterns. What one cartographer indicated as rural may have been depicted as developed by another mapmaker years earlier. Some historical maps, usually made for real-estate purposes, show entire neighborhoods, complete with street names and parks, in areas that were not actually developed until generations afterward. Additionally, geometric distortion makes coregistration of the old maps difficult. The patterns shown here are approximate. *Map and analysis by author*

specifically to the blocks that became Storyville, the infamous legalized red-light district (1897-1917) that ensured New Orleans' worldwide reputation for debauchery. Former Storyville was cleared away in 1940 and replaced by what is now the Iberville Housing Development (1941); a few decades later Interstate 10 and its ramps encircled the area, replacing the beautifully foliated neutral ground of Claiborne Avenue. In keeping with its propensity for radical change, the former City Commons area (bordered by Claiborne, Canal, Rampart, and Lafitte) today boasts hardly any intact historic blocks (except for the St. Louis cemeteries), quite unlike the other end of Tremé on the Bayou Road/Esplanade Ridge. Even greater radical change was proposed in the spring and summer of 2001, when the New Orleans Saints, unhappy with the aging Superdome, eyed this area as a potential site for a state-of-the-art football stadium. The retractable-roof arena would sit smack on the old Storyville site, requiring the demolition of the Iberville Housing Development and a number of structures on Canal Street while literally shadowing the two historic St. Louis cemeteries.[31] The identification of the former City Commons for such a colossal project reflects the continued tendency to do things to this area that would not be considered in neighboring areas. The differing histories and modern-day cityscapes of these adjacent neighborhoods, Tremé and the former Commons, correlate to their differing historical topography.

Hence in the late colonial era and the early American years (1788 to 1812), the original city of New Orleans expanded into four new communities: the faubourgs of Ste. Marie, Delord/Duplantier, Marigny, and Tremé. The first three suburbs occupied the natural levee of the Mississippi, while Tremé utilized the trunk of the Bayou Road/Esplanade Ridge at one end and the drained City Commons at the other end; the first two expanded the city in an upriver direction, while Marigny augmented the city downriver and Tremé did so lakeside. "New-Orleans is daily extended by the erection of buildings in the two extremities, and between the city and the Bayou St. John," reported John Adems Paxton in 1822.[32] But the pace was not equal in all directions: New Orleans would grow most strongly in the upriver direction along the broad natural levee of the Mississippi River, with relatively less growth occurring along the constricted uplands below and lakeside of the French Quarter, for the entire nineteenth century. A major reason for this trend was topographic—there was simply more well-drained acreage upriver than downriver or lakeside—and once these new communities grew, a critical mass developed on economic or cultural grounds and thus attracted more development to these areas. Many newcomers to these new upriver communities were English-speaking Americans arriving after the Louisiana Purchase. Their presence attracted their ambitious brethren from the North to join them in this economically booming area—who among them would live among the Creoles, the foreign French, and the immigrants in the crowded old city?—and inject more money and development to the upriver frontier. A table on page 182 of the appendix summarizes the subdivision of new communities in New Orleans with respect to their topographic characteristics, in generalized chronological order.

Topographic Observations

The following observations further characterize the relationships between topography and urban development in New Orleans.

- The trend of New Orleans spreading upon the broader natural levees of uptown had the unintended but nevertheless important effect of "reserving" lower areas for twentieth-century *industrial* development,[33] as well as for modern residential subdivision in eastern New Orleans. This partly explains the survival of expansive historic neighborhoods in the city.

- New communities in the early 1800s generally were subdivided within the borders of former long-lot plantations, which had been delineated and conceded during French colonial times in accordance with the *arpent* system. This land-surveying system allocated two scarce resources—well-drained, fertile soils and river access—in a maximum-benefit manner, such that a large number of plantations would enjoy reasonable quantities of both resources. In a riverine landscape, this is done by dividing the land into narrow lots perpendicular to the river. Where the river meanders, lots diverge on the convex side of the bend and converge on the concave side, like wedges in a pie. The Crescent City occupies the concave side of a meander and thus its original long-lot plantations converged in the former backswamp of Mid-City. That these patterns are readily apparent in the modern street network of New Orleans testifies to the fact that New Orleans grew in a sectionalized manner sans a central planning authority, with new subdivisions simply conforming to "the antecedent cadaster."[34] (*Within* each section, however, the subdivision of lots was

31. Greg Thomas, "Favored Stadium Site Off-Limits, Morial Says," and Duncan.
32. Paxton, 10.
33. Chase, 136.
34. Newton, 211.

planned, producing roughly orthogonal blocks.) No matter—the resulting arpent-system-based pattern of the streets of New Orleans has produced a unique and beautiful pattern that reflects both the history and topography of the city and is easy and interesting to navigate (with the possible exception of Mid-City, where all the river-perpendicular streets converge). Today, motorists commuting upriver and downriver along arteries such as Claiborne Avenue, St. Charles Avenue, and Tchoupitoulas Street follow constant elevation contours (roughly zero feet, four feet, and twelve feet above m.s.l., respectively) as they cruise around the crescent, across numerous former long-lot plantations from the eighteenth and nineteenth centuries. See pages 86-99 for a detailed discussion of the impact of the arpent system on New Orleans' street network.

- As the highest portions of the natural levee were fully exploited, development would creep closer and closer down into the backswamp, and finally into and across it, once the appropriate technology evolved to drain these areas. The movement toward the backswamps often followed newly established transportation corridors, such as the Pontchartrain Railroad on Elysian Fields, which enabled the development of Faubourg New Marigny.

- Development would also reach toward the minor outlying uplands of the Metairie/Gentilly Ridge, the shoulders of the Esplanade Ridge, the spur of relief between Carrollton and Bayou St. John, the narrow natural levees below the city, and across the river on the west bank. Some of these rural outskirts were used for establishments that served the city's population but were too big to be located there, such as the Fair Grounds Race Course, Louisiana Jockey Club, Oak Land Riding Park (now the New Orleans Country Club), the former racetrack that is now Metairie Cemetery, and numerous adjacent burial grounds (collectively identified as the "Ridge Cemeteries" in an 1878 drainage map).[35] These facilities exploited the well-drained Metairie/Gentilly Ridge, to the envy of modern-day residents in the lowlands surrounding the ridge. Developers today prize open spaces close to the urban market for these types of space-consuming projects, but no longer have well-drained areas among their options. The only remaining undeveloped areas in Orleans Parish are low-lying acreages in the east, where large-scale recreational facilities, dependent on both market proximity and ample, cheap real estate, are proposed regularly. The New Orleans Business & Industrial District—that mostly forested industrial park with the unfortunate acronym of NOBID, sandwiched between Chef Menteur Highway and the MR-GO/Intracoastal Waterway—has recently been eyed as a site for a New Orleans International Speedway and a stadium for a United Soccer Leagues franchise. Whatever comes to fruition for this site will have to deal with its topographic conditions. Farther out, the Jazzland amusement park (2000) solved the drainage problem by creating its own topography: the entire complex rests on a raised wooden platform.

- The neighborhood of Gentilly Terrace was platted in 1909 and developed over the next thirty years to exploit what its developers extolled (inaccurately) as "the most elevated residential section in the City of New Orleans." The ridge, which is perceptibly uplifted relative to its surrounding terrain but hardly hilly, "was caused by the overflows, year after year, of Bayou Sauvage, until perhaps sixty years ago [around 1850] when it was dammed, drained, and filled." Laid out to emulate the "beautiful residential districts . . . which have proven so successful in Los Angeles,"[36] Gentilly Terrace was high enough to enable construction fifteen to sixty inches above the street grade and to allow for a local version of a basement—or a least a flight of stairs to reach the main floor. Gentilly today reflects the aim of its creators: the Craftsman-style California bungalows, Spanish Revival homes, and English cottages are highly reminiscent of the Golden State between the wars, and some of their lawns are steep enough to roll a tractor. Long ignored by architectural historians and stigmatized as the quintessential suburb—Walker Percy set *The Moviegoer* here to symbolize Binx Bolling's sense of anonymity[37]—Gentilly finally gained some respect when, in the last days of the 1900s, it became New Orleans' first completely twentieth-century National Register Historic District.[38]

- Because pre-twentieth-century New Orleans was confined to the uplands described above, it comes as no surprise that the National Register Historic Districts of the city, some among the largest urban units in the country, are spatially correlated with the original topographic uplands of the city (see map on page 82). Of the seventeen National Register Historic Districts in Orleans Parish, only one, Mid-City, lies below sea level, and barely. Thirteen districts occupy the back slope of the river's natural levees (including the Carrollton Spur), two touch the Metairie/Gentilly Ridge, and one covers the Esplanade Ridge. This will probably change in the next few decades, when low-lying Lakeview's time comes for historical and architectural appreciation.

- John Churchill Chase observed that the narrow natural levee (only 1,600 feet wide at the time) below the city facilitated Andrew Jackson's thorough routing of the British in the Battle of New Orleans, providing the Americans with "a short line of concentrated fire power that ranks among the strongest fortified positions in military annals."[39] The outcome of the battle, or at least its decisiveness, may have been different had it occurred on a broad natural levee.

The Battle of New Orleans (January 8, 1815) transpired on a fairly narrow natural levee, allowing the Americans to concentrate their firepower against regimented British troops and possibly influencing the magnitude of the U.S. victory. Natural levees tend to be narrower where the river runs straight, as it does in Chalmette. The National Park Service maintains the distant treeline in its approximate location at the time of the battle, when it marked the edge of the backswamp. This photograph of the Beauregard Plantation House, built on the battlefield years after the war, was captured from the crest of the manmade levee. *Photograph by author, 2000*

"A succession of swampy woods, which the people of the country call the Cypriera, run parallel with the Misisipi at a distance of three or four hundred fathoms . . . ; whence it results that the enemy can only advance to the attack by the Royal road which follows the bank of the river. . . . The enemy being confined to a very narrow space, a highway as it were, in order to approach the fortifications, it is possible to keep up a superior fire."
—Baron de Carondelet, Spanish governor of Louisiana, in a 1794 letter discussing the military implications of the colony's geography (Turner, 484-85)

- Yellow fever, the arbovirus that periodically terrorized the city with biblical-scale epidemics from 1796 to 1905, spread by means of filthy stagnant water collecting in open cisterns, muddy streets, and topographic features. In a fascinating 1854 report, medical researcher Edward H. Barton plotted mortality rates from 1787 to 1853 against soil-disturbance events ("Canal Carondelet dug," "Trenches dug around the City & Swamp exposed," "Drained the rear of 2nd District," "Immense excavations . . . for foundation of Customhouse," etc.) and revealed certain correlations[40] that would, in time, point to the role of drainage in eradicating the habitat of the yellow fever vector (*Aedes aegypti,* a mosquito introduced from Africa possibly via the slave trade), though at the time the public suspected miasmas from the lowlands to be the cause of the plagues. Similar research in Baltimore noted that yellow fever "was localized in low, wet areas" and "did not occur in high, dry areas."[41] The topographic variable in New Orleans' public-health history demonstrates again that in a city with only a few precious feet of relief above sea level, minute changes in topography can make major differences in livability.

- It is commonly held that New Orleans' "cities of the dead," its above-ground cemeteries, were an adaptation to the boggy, low-lying terrain and high water table. But topography cannot be credited with these fascinating elements of the cityscape; they are far more a product of culture. The earliest cemetery in the city (on the upriver side of St. Peter between Burgundy and Rampart, which, in 1725, was the outskirts

35. Hardee.

36. "Where Homes Are Built On Hills" (brochure, ca. 1910), as quoted by Reiff, 1. The author of the brochure claimed that the average elevation of Gentilly Terrace was 27 feet above the Cairo Datum Line, and took this to mean that it was the highest neighborhood in New Orleans. The Cairo Datum was a standard of that time for elevational measurements, based on a benchmark in Cairo, Illinois that was 20.434 feet above sea level, putting Gentilly at 6.6 feet above sea level by this account. In fact, Gentilly today is about 3-4 feet above sea level by today's standards, lower than most older parts of the city but nevertheless higher than immediately adjacent areas.

37. Lewis Lawson, "Pilgrim in the City: Walker Percy," in Kennedy, 55.

38. Fricker, 7.

39. Chase, 135-36.

40. Barton, chart on 101. According to Christine Moe, this same chart appears in City Council of New Orleans' *Report of the Sanitary Commission of New Orleans on the Epidemic of Yellow Fever of 1853* (1854), 314.

41. Moe, 5.

of town) had below-ground graves. Water was drained from the area simply by digging a trench around it and spreading the excavated soil on top to raise the elevation. The St. Peter Street Cemetery served New Orleans for the entire French colonial era and well into the Spanish years, when, in taking stock of the city after the 1788 fire, city leaders created what is now St. Louis Cemetery No. 1 (1789), again on the edge of town. Spanish tradition in the mother country and throughout its colonies determined that this new cemetery would have above-ground tombs. That the raised vaults negated the soil-moisture problem was an added benefit, but not a causative one. The tradition persisted among a remarkably broad ethnic[42] and socioeconomic range and continues today, a truly distinguishing cultural trait of the local population with a distinctive signature in the built environment. New Orleans shares its cemetery traditions not with the United States but with southern Europe and Latin America, where one regularly finds above-ground tombs in all types of terrain. Topography did influence one aspect of cemeteries in New Orleans: their location. Cemeteries tended to be located on the outskirts of the developed area, which meant at the back-swamp edge in the eighteenth century and the Metairie/Gentilly Ridge in the nineteenth and early twentieth century.

- Geographers have documented significant positive correlations between topographic elevation and economic wealth in selected American cities.[43] In the popular image of cities, the splendid mansion high on a hilltop, or the tony neighborhood overlooking the riverside slum, is standard material. This relationship has been observed in hilly cities such as Lexington, Richmond, Atlanta, Durham, Syracuse,[44] and Vicksburg, and is sometimes associated with environmental-justice issues, in which the poor are more likely to be affected by floods and other natural disasters. "Wealth is going to go up [in elevation] and poverty is going to go down. That's a basic tenet of urban geography," said Jonathan Bascom, of East Carolina University, regarding the impact of Hurricane Floyd's flooding in North Carolina in 1999.[45]

But does the topography/prosperity relationship hold true in deltaic New Orleans? Do wealthier people tend to live in higher areas and poorer people in lower areas in the Crescent City? "In New Orleans, income and elevation can be correlated on a literally sliding scale: the Garden District on the highest level, Stanley Kowalski in the swamp," wrote John McPhee on this question in his 1989 book, *The Control of Nature*. "The Garden District and its environs are locally known as uptown."[46] McPhee's words work well in his excellent chapter on the engineering of the Mississippi, but issue may be taken with this particular claim, as with the implication that "uptown" refers to elevation. When New Orleans was limited to its natural levees (prior to the turn-of-the-century drainage system), wealthier people did tend to live on the higher, better-drained natural levees, while those areas lining the backswamps were more likely to be inhabited by the poor. But plenty of poor people also lived on the high natural levees, in riverside areas such as the original Irish Channel.

New Orleans' topographic peculiarity of riverbanks being the highest lands diluted the correlation, since the high levees were often occupied by warehouse and port facilities and were more likely, then and now, to be neighbored by slums.[47] If any elevation-to-prosperity pattern prevailed in uptown in the 1800s, it was likely a second-order relationship in which poorer people lived at the highest and lowest elevations (higher risk) and wealthier people lived in between (lower risk). Even today, windshield surveys of the housing stock in the "belly" of the crescent reveal that the mid-elevation neighborhoods between Magazine and St. Charles are far more prosperous than the higher areas riverside of Magazine and the lower areas lakeside of St. Charles, particularly in Central City.

After the drainage system was installed around 1900, elevation/prosperity correlations were further weakened, as middle- and upper-class residents built comfortable neighborhoods in former swamplands while the poor moved into the older housing stock in higher areas. (It is interesting to note that New Orleans is economically intermixed in the lateral dimension as well as the vertical dimension: the wealthy and the poor live only a few doors away from each other in some areas, and except for the housing developments, the city has no true ghettoes.) Today, for every upraised wealthy or low-lying poor neighborhood, one can name a low-lying wealthy or upraised poor neighborhood.

Nevertheless, there are certain areas where neighborhoods with higher elevations and higher tax brackets intersect lower areas with lower incomes. A prime example is the increasingly prosperous Esplanade Ridge running through the lower, poorer neighborhoods of Tremé, St. Roch, and Sixth and Seventh wards.[48] Additionally, a glance at a map of median household income from recent census data shows poorer blocks neatly nestled in the lowlands between the natural-levee uplands of the Mississippi River and Metairie/Gentilly Ridge, which are more likely to be wealthier. But the inclination to surmise a correlation diminishes when one takes a closer look and notices the numerous small-scale and large-scale exceptions.

- A glance at recent census data shows that, with the exception of the French Quarter, CBD, Warehouse District, and Lower Coast of Algiers, most higher-elevation areas lost population while most lower-elevation increased in residential population between 1990 and 2000 (see page 185). One factor explaining this trend is black family migration from older (higher) neighborhoods in the inner city to lower eastern and lakeside suburbs. Another factor is gentrification, in which households in architecturally rich older neighborhoods (higher in elevation, being closer to the river) that previously housed families with children and sometimes extended families become single-person or childless-couple dwellings. "Generally, older neighborhoods with a rising percentage of white residents tend to lose residents because the white buyers who take the place of black families have no children or reduce the density of a building by tearing out walls and converting doubles into singles."[49]

- Italian immigrants and their descendents in New Orleans historically have been far more integrated into the residential patterns of native-born whites than in any other major American city. In explaining this phenomenon, researchers Anthony V. Margavio and J. Lambert Molyneaux pointed to not only New Orleans' tolerant atmosphere and Catholic heritage but also to its topography. "The scarcity of residential land limited the segregation of immigrants. . . . Topography tended to disperse the Italian population."[50] This phenomenon of topographic restriction leading to dense settlement patterns and ergo to a higher degree of ethnic and racial inter-association was also observed by Arnold R. Hirsch and Joseph Logsdon in their anthology, *Creole New Orleans: Race and Americanization*.[51] But Earl F. Niehaus, an expert on the Irish in New Orleans, noted an opposite phenomenon: that the deficiency of high ground "was the principal reason for the severity of New Orleans' growing pains [during the municipality era of 1836-52], and also explains the bitter and continuous struggle for residential area between the national groups."[52] Topographical and sociodemographic relationships persist today. Note that the areas to which whites fled during the recent middle-class exodus from New Orleans were, in general, low-lying former backswamps that had been rendered developable by modern drainage equipment.

- Where are the highest and lowest points in New Orleans? Identifying these elevational extremes depends on what one regards as the legitimate topographic surface. Are we considering only the natural surface, minus manmade alterations? Or should artificial levees, dry canal beds, and landscaping also be included? Should the presence of a concrete surface or fill disqualify a feature, in favor of earthen surfaces? Finally, should a feature span a certain minimum size to qualify? (There is something misleading about bestowing the title of "highest point" on a tiny manmade mound or single landscaping feature.) Even after agreeing upon these ground rules, subsidence, erosion, and deposition make the exact measurement of elevation in southeastern Louisiana a shifty business. Lack of historical topographic data that is both accurate and precise makes identification of New Orleans' elevational extremes in the eighteenth and nineteenth centuries difficult to ascertain, but with the advent of reliable surveying tools, photogrammetry, and Global Positioning Systems (GPS), far more exact measurements of the New Orleans z-dimension

42. One exception is among New Orleans' Jewish population, who, for reasons of religious tradition, bury their dead. Some early Protestant communities also opted for interment. This further reflects the cultural, rather than topographical, basis of New Orleans' above-ground cemeteries.

43. Meyer, 505-13.

44. Kellogg, 310-21, and Willie, 7-11.

45. Waggoner.

46. McPhee, 59.

47. "Historically the poorer neighborhoods in uptown New Orleans grew up nearer the river. Progressively more well-to-do sections grew further back, especially on the opposite side of Magazine Street. The proximity of port facilities and industries such as cotton processing steadily overtook any of the more upscale housing near the riverfront" (Magill, 19). The cotton processors are gone, but this pattern generally persists today.

48. A zoning controversy in the late 1990s involving a pharmacy on Esplanade Avenue highlighted the economic, philosophical, and geographical differences between the Esplanade Ridge and its adjacent neighborhoods (Fahrenthold).

49. Coleman Warner, "Neighborhoods Win, Lose in '90s," citing Pat Connor, demographic data analyst at the University of New Orleans.

50. Margavio and Molyneaux, 645.

51. Hirsch and Logsdon, 99.

52. Niehaus, "The New Irish, 1830-1862," 379.

are now available.[53] The elevation data cited below and throughout this volume are based on one-foot digital contours derived from GPS surveys conducted in 1994 and maintained by the New Orleans City Planning Commission.

The putative highest point in New Orleans is the famous Monkey Hill in the Audubon Zoological Gardens, a mound built by the Works Progress Administration in 1933 for the enjoyment of children. The hill measured 27.5 feet above m.s.l., depending on the amount of joyous dirt kicking and grass stomping on the "summit," until it was heavily relandscaped in late 2000 with concrete walkways, statues of a pride of lions, and a rope bridge connecting the top to surrounding sidewalks. Because Monkey Hill is based on the high natural levee, about 11 feet above m.s.l., its local relief is only about 16 feet. Despite its fame, Monkey Hill is not the highest earthen point in New Orleans.

A hill in the Couturie Forest Arboretum in the middle of City Park not only "towers" above Monkey Hill but starts at a far lower base elevation (three feet *below* sea level). This massive landscaping feature, spanning more than two acres and rising over thirty feet above m.s.l (forty-two feet according to a 1982 book on the park and fifty-two feet according to other sources), was built of material excavated for Interstate 610 in the 1960s and 1970s. Hiking trails and a platform were built upon "City Park hill" in 2000-2001.[54]

City Planning Commission data show a number of other points throughout the city that are up to forty feet above m.s.l. These are mostly very small spots atop levees and overpasses. In Jefferson Parish, the manmade berm at Zephyr Field may be among the highest earthen spots in the metropolitan area.

Depending on one's definitions of what constitutes the topographic surface, this hill in the Couturie Forest Arboretum in City Park, built of material excavated for Interstate 610, is the highest point in New Orleans. It starts at three feet below sea level and rises to over thirty feet above the sea. Other sources indicate that it is higher. *Photograph by author, 2000*

Riverview Park, between Audubon Zoo and the Mississippi, is one of the highest areas of substantial size in New Orleans, over twenty feet above m.s.l. The Henry Clay Avenue Wharf appears in the foreground. *Photograph by Donn Young, courtesy the Port of New Orleans*

Considering more expansive surfaces, the highest areas in New Orleans are the riverside lands (1) from St. Louis Street to Canal Street in the French Quarter, (2) from Soniat to Broadway near Audubon Zoo (Riverview Park), and (3) from Perrier to Burdette in Carrollton. These areas, which are all over twenty feet above m.s.l. and all adjacent to the Mississippi, consist of some combination of batture, natural levee, manmade levee, and artificial fill. Some artificial levees in Algiers Point and other areas also break the twenty-foot level. All points in the city higher than these areas tend to be minor, isolated landscaping or infrastructural features.

- New Orleans' lowest substantial areas (as measured by the City Planning Commission data, which do not cover the parish east of Paris Road) are mostly within the Lakefront East, Lakefront West, and Little Woods neighborhoods bounded by Jourdan, Morrison, Paris, and Dwyer roads. These recently developed lakeside communities are, in some parts, lower than ten feet below m.s.l. There are lower spots in the city, but they tend to be dry canal beds or underpasses.

- Of urbanized New Orleans—that is, Orleans Parish from Paris Road to the Jefferson Parish line, lakefront to the Lower Coast—about 45 percent is above sea level and 55 percent is at or below sea level. These numbers vary if the low-lying, eroding marshes of eastern Orleans Parish are included, but it is clear that the oft-heard claim that "New Orleans is below sea level" is inaccurate by about half. In fact, New Orleans *straddles* the level of the sea, from about ten feet below it to twenty feet above.

- "As the traveler proceeds down the Mississippi," commented Mayor Martin Behrman in 1914, "the river seems to grow higher as he descends."[55] Exactly how much higher above the land depends on the season: recent measurements recorded river heights as low as 0.71 above sea level on February 11, 1977, to 18.4 feet on April 7, 1973, during the second greatest flood of the century, and to 19.98 feet at the Carrollton gauge on February 10, 1950. A typical springtime river level is 10 feet above the sea.[56] Considering the additional elevation of the ship, one can easily gain the impression of looking down upon the city while sailing down the river. It is no optical illusion.

53. Subsidence has lowered many geodetic benchmarks in southern Louisiana, making almost all current elevational measurements, including those cited here, possibly up to four feet higher than their actual positions. Most of this deviation occurs in low-lying areas, not the higher natural levees upon which pre-1900 New Orleans is built. Researchers at Louisiana State University are currently installing a network of high-accuracy stations throughout the state to track subsidence every thirty seconds. When this system is operational, we will have a new understanding of just how far above or below sea level we are in southern Louisiana. The news will probably not be good. Schleifstein, "Lower Ground."

54. Jensen; Hardy; and Reeves et al., 186. The thirty-foot figure comes from the 1994 City Planning Commission elevation data, the forty-two-foot measurement is from Reeves et al., and the fifty-two-foot figure comes from sources at City Park. The differences may reflect measurement from sea level versus local terrain, inclusion of the platform, approximations, etc.

55. Behrman, "New Orleans . . . Utilities."

56. According to Army Corps of Engineers river stage data, the highest level of the Mississippi River ever recorded at the Carrollton gauge was 21.27 feet on April 25, 1922, while the lowest was -1.6 feet on December 27, 1872. However, these figures are based on a different vertical datum (possibly local sea level at Biloxi) than the National Geodetic Vertical Datum of 1929, upon which the other measurements were based. Also, measurements prior to 1973 "are not comparable to those since then because of changes in the river." See also John Hall, spokesman for the Army Corps of Engineers, as quoted in a staff-authored article, "Room to Spare," *New Orleans Times-Picayune*, June 1, 2000, and Bell.

• Clues to New Orleans' historical topography may be found in the streets—literally. In the Garden District, deep gutters lined with granite paving blocks parallel certain streets, allowing for water shed by the higher blocks to flow through the ditches and eventually backward toward the lake. Cast-iron bollards still stand at many corners, to keep carriages from dropping into these drains. Evidence of subsidence abounds in the French Quarter, from tilted doorways to submerged vents and buried cornerstones, and throughout the city, in the form of buckling pavement and potholes. *Banquettes* ("little benches," raised wooden sidewalks that allowed pedestrians to avoid the low muddy streets) are long gone, but one occasionally hears "bankits" today as a localism for sidewalks. The best reminder of New Orleans' topography comes during a heavy rain, when the rushing runoff demonstrates that indeed there *is* some elevational variation in this deltaic city.

Topographic Change

In a deltaic landscape, nature can perceptibly alter topography well within the span of a human life, substantially faster than most geological change. In response to these threats (or in exploitation of these opportunities), man has resculpted this terrain with equal doses of zeal, so that, in New Orleans, artificial levees rise twice as high as natural ridges, canals flow far below former bottomlands, and rainwater is pumped uphill from subsea levels into surrounding lakes. While other American cities—New York, Miami, Boston in particular[57]—have greatly altered the shape and form of their terrain, New Orleans stands alone in the magnitude of its anthropogenic topographic change relative to its original elevation range. Man has effectively doubled, and in some places tripled, the prehistoric range of its elevations above and below the level of the sea. Topographic change in New Orleans is a hyperactive phenomenon, one of its distinguishing characteristics among urban places, for it and Amsterdam alone are "the only major cities in the world with a large percentage of the urban area located below sea level."[58] This is one of the site-related costs that accompany the benefits of New Orleans' situation.

Episodes of topographic change, some natural but most anthropogenic, have occurred in New Orleans with the objectives of (1) keeping water out of the city, (2) removing water from within the city, (3) creating new land for the city, and (4) improving navigation to link the city with the outside world.

Topographic Change to Keep Water Out

The Mississippi River Levee System, 1722-Present   The objective to barricade out surrounding water from the sea-level-straddling terrain of New Orleans is as old as Bienville's first clearing of the forest and as current as today's suburban sprawl. The artificial levee,[59] the great linear landmark and frontline between man's will to control his environment and nature's obedience to physical law, is, in New Orleans, "a municipal icon . . . inextricably bound with the safety, growth, and history of the city."[60] Acknowledgment of its presence is one of the ingrained distinctions between residents of southeastern Louisiana and their inland compatriots: the latter group may dismiss the grassy berms as a minor landscape feature or unknowingly climb right over them while touring the French Quarter riverfront, but locals always consciously or subconsciously take note when the levee comes into view—*there's the levee*—and orient themselves with respect to the earthwork, the water body in front, and the street network behind. During times of high water or approaching hurricane, the levees assume a civil-defense role of almost biblical proportions, encircling and protecting the city from outside threat like a wall around an ancient city. Few other American cities claim such a clear interface between the controlled urban environment and the uncontrolled natural world.

Topographically, the artificial levee is to the natural levee what the natural levee is to the rest of the city: a high earthen brim along the waterfront, the edge of the "saucer," a reflection of the Mississippi River's dual personality of provider and threat. Whereas New Orleans' natural levees are ten to fourteen feet above m.s.l at the riverfront and decline imperceptibly toward the lowlands, the modern artificial levees rise about as high above the natural levees as the natural levees rise above sea level (peaking at about twenty-five feet) and form steep thirty-degree slopes on both sides. The artificial levees—those lining the river, the lake, and canals in between—are by far the highest, steepest, and most prominent topographic features in the region. They are also the most fundamental to the survival of the city.

While rudimentary levee construction probably occurred in 1719,[61] the first organized effort to build a levee in New Orleans (and in America) began in 1722-23, coinciding with the time when the outpost was promoted to the status of capital of Louisiana. Engineers Le Blond de La Tour and Adrien de Pauger, responsible for the design and layout of the original city, planned an earthen embankment about twelve feet wide atop the crest of the natural levee; Pauger further advocated reinforcing the dike with a double palisade of timbers. Original plans had to be scaled back because of an insufficient labor force and the death of La Tour in late 1723. By 1724, the first levee measured six feet wide, about three thousand feet long, and probably three feet high, but was readily breached by the high waters of the Mississippi that spring.[62] The reconstruction and reinforcement work that followed was constantly hampered by a meager workforce; nevertheless, by 1727, a solid eighteen-foot-wide and three-foot-high levee (plus a parallel ditch to collect seepage water) lined one mile of the town's riverfront. To solve the manpower problem, the city at first obligated slave owners to assign their bondsmen thirty days' labor on public works, then adopted a tax instead.[63] Ensuing efforts addressed not only the strength of the levee along the waterfront but, more importantly, the need to extend the levee system far upriver and downriver, since an overflow in the wilderness may have consequences similar to a breach right at the *Place d'Armes*.

As early as 1724, the French held riverfront landowners responsible for the maintenance of levees bordering their properties.[64] Over the next decade, levees arose along both sides of the river thirty miles above and twelve miles below New Orleans, only to be destroyed by the severe 1735 floods and rebuilt. For the rest of the colonial years and well into the American era, "extension of the levee line (from the city) was almost entirely the work of private land developers supervised at the local level, first by commandants, then by parish and county governments."[65]

During the Spanish administrative years, the construction of levees and associated drainage ditches and roads were the responsibility of each concession recipient[66]—and these were numerous, since the Spanish continued the French tradition of delineating long, narrow lots perpendicular to the levee (see page 98). Problems were such that Spanish governor Carondelet, the great public-works administrator, issued a levee ordinance in 1792 that required syndicated residents to raise levees to the recent high-water mark of the river, while reinforcing their sides by filling in ditches and planting grass to conserve the soil. Livestock grazing was strictly forbidden, and in the most vulnerable places, "the owner will have to have at all times a deposit of pickets, planks, Spanish moss and other articles necessary to stop the crevasses under penalty of a fine of one hundred piastres."[67]

Local responsibility of levee construction and maintenance generally continued after the Louisiana Purchase, when Louisiana became an American territory. An unwise policy, given that the nature of levees demands consistently thorough engineering and construction, the tradition of localism was perhaps to be expected in the isolated lower Mississippi region during this era of weak federal control in the fledgling United States. In New Orleans, the City Council gradually gained control over the waterfront and set standards (1810) for the construction of levees—at least three feet above the river, one foot above the high-water line, and five to six feet wide at the base for each foot in height.

Levee construction at this time was under the direction of City Engineer Jacques Tanesee, who designed revetments that, unlike today's trapezoidal berms, faced the river with a wall of wooden piles reinforced by an earthen back slope that served as a wharf.[68] But levees in nearby communities or in rural areas along the River Road might or might not have conformed to the standards held for levees in New Orleans, thereby reducing the effectiveness of the best levees to those of the worst. Levees of varying quality standards expanded upstream at a rapid pace: pre-1735 levees paralleled the river from English Turn up to present-day Reserve; by 1812 they extended up to Old River; and by 1844 the dikes reached beyond Greenville, Mississippi.[69] Joseph Holt Ingraham described New Orleans' levees in his 1835 travelogue, *The South-West by a Yankee:*

57. This is well documented in Whitehill and Kennedy, first published in 1959.

58. Louisiana Statewide Flood Control Program's Project Evaluation Committee, 107. Approximately 55 percent of New Orleans' eighty-four square miles of urbanized area—excluding the eastern marshes—is at or below sea level. According to the U.S. Geological Survey, Long Beach, California is the only other large American city that dips considerably below sea level, to -7 feet.

59. "The word *levee* is the French word for raised or elevated, while *dike*, which means the same thing, is from an Anglo-Saxon word, *dic*. The words are interchangeable although we tend to think of a levee as paralleling a river or inland lake while dikes are found along oceanfronts or seashores as in Holland." Janssen, 30.

60. Kelman, 309.

61. Kniffen, "The Lower Mississippi Valley," 24.

62. Giraud, vol. 5, 207.

63. Kelman, 310, and Giraud, vol. 5, 208.

64. Cowdrey, 1.

65. Owens (quoted from abstract).

66. Burns, 570.

67. Porteous, 513-14.

68. Orleans Levee District, *The Orleans Levee District—A History.*

69. Kniffen, "The Lower Mississippi Valley," maps adapted from Cowdrey on 6-7.

Topographic Change in New Orleans, 1700-2000

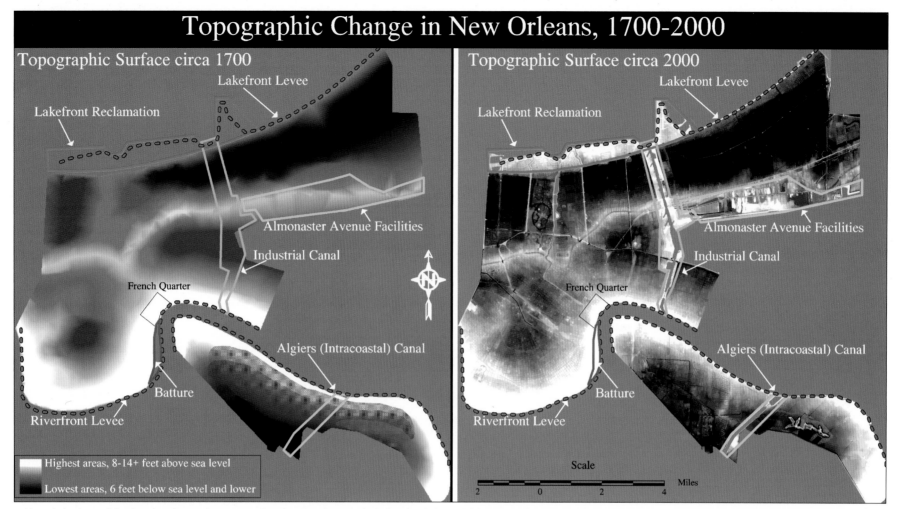

Topographic Surface circa 1700

Lakefront Reclamation

Lakefront Levee

Almonaster Avenue Facilities

Industrial Canal

French Quarter

Algiers (Intracoastal) Canal

Batture

Riverfront Levee

Highest areas, 8-14+ feet above sea level

Lowest areas, 6 feet below sea level and lower

Topographic Surface circa 2000

Lakefront Reclamation

Lakefront Levee

Almonaster Avenue Facilities

Industrial Canal

French Quarter

Algiers (Intracoastal) Canal

Batture

Riverfront Levee

Scale

Miles

2   0   2   4

In a city where topographic variation is as miniscule as its relevance is great, man has played an almost geological-scale role in altering the shape of the land. A number of episodes of topographic alteration stand salient in the history of New Orleans, executed for four reasons: to keep water out (the river levees, the lakefront, and the hurricane-protection levees), to remove water (the drainage system), to create new land (the St. Mary and French Quarter batture), and to improve navigation (Carondelet Canal, New Basin Canal, Industrial Canal, Mississippi River-Gulf Outlet Canal, and Intracoastal Waterway). The scene on the left is an approximated reconstruction of the area's topographic surface before the founding of the city, interpreted by the author from a variety of data. The scene on the right is a digital elevation model of modern New Orleans, with major areas of topographic change identified. *Map and interpretations by author. Reproduction of modern digital elevation model prohibited without written consent of the Executive Director, the New Orleans City Planning Commission. The New Orleans Geographic Information System at the New Orleans City Planning Commission is partially funded by a federal grant through NOAA.*

1-3. Modern-day manmade Mississippi River levee at its place of origin, along the French Quarter riverfront. Note mix of industrial and recreational use. The tourists descending these steps over the levee outside the Riverwalk (3) are probably unaware that they are traversing one of man's most environmentally influential projects in the region, providing protection from floods but starving the land of sediment deposition.
4. Levee in Algiers.
5. Levee above Audubon Park in uptown New Orleans.
6. Lakefront levee. The physical appearance of the manmade levee belies the fact that they require careful engineering and costly construction.
7. Floodgates allowing passage through the levee from West End into the residential neighborhoods of Lakeshore and Lake Vista. *Photographs by author, 2000*

[The levee] extends, on both sides of the river, to more than one hundred and fifty miles above New Orleans. This *levée* is properly a dike, thrown up on the verge of the river, from twenty-five to thirty feet in breadth, and two feet higher than high-water mark; leaving a ditch, or fossé, on the inner side, of equal breadth, from which the earth to form the *levée* is taken. Consequently . . . when the river is full . . . the surface of the river will be *four feet higher* than the surface of the country; the altitude of the inner side of the *levée* being usually six feet above the general surface of the surrounding land.[70]

Impetus for change in flood-control policy materialized after a crevasse in the levee of Pierre Sauvé's plantation (in present-day River Ridge) on May 3, 1849 flooded 220 city blocks in the lower areas of New Orleans between the Metairie/Gentilly Ridge and the natural levee, including portions of the French Quarter. In partial response, legislation in Washington offered federally owned swamplands to states in the Mississippi Valley in exchange for the states' promise to build levees, reclaim the swamps, sell the land, and recoup their investment. The Swamp and Overflow Land Act of 1850 spurred more levee construction in the 1850s but fell far short of expectations. Also at this time, the federal government engaged itself in matters of the navigability and control of the Mississippi with the funding of two landmark (and bitterly competing) surveys—one by Andrew Atkinson Humphreys, which would recommend a levees-only policy to control the Mississippi, and one by Charles Ellet, which suggested a comprehensive approach that included levees but also outlets and reservoirs, mechanisms that accommodate the will of the river. Humphreys' research would lead to increased federal involvement in levee development later in the century (and to great controversy in the wake of the 1927 flood, when the wisdom of Ellet's research proved true).[71] In 1854, the Louisiana state legislature formed four flood districts and a Board of Swamp Land Commissioners that was responsible for levee development; in time, this entity would evolve into the concept of a "levee district," a consortium of governmental bodies that manages levee work and possesses the power to levy taxes.[72] The age of localism was beginning to end. But then war clouds gathered on the horizon and progress in coordinating and standardizing levee construction was derailed for over a decade, while miles of existing levees in Louisiana deteriorated or were damaged or destroyed during the Civil War. In New Orleans, the early surrender (May 1862) to federal troops spared not only its citizens and buildings but also its levees.

"In high-river stage, in the New Orleans region, the water is up to the top of the inclosing levee-rim . . . and as the boat swims along, high on the flood, one looks down upon the houses and into the upper windows. There is nothing but that frail breastwork of earth between the people and destruction."
—Mark Twain, 1883 (265)

Levees, like many other major civil-engineering projects in America, came of age in the final decades of the nineteenth century. Locally, city engineers in New Orleans proposed in 1871 (the year of the Bonnet Carré crevasse flood) an integrated system of protection levees and drainage networks; statewide, in 1886, Louisiana created levee districts to begin coordinating levee management efforts.[73] Nationally, the new era dawned when Congress created the Mississippi River Commission in 1879 and directed the agency to work with the Army Corps of Engineers in controlling the lower Mississippi. During the turn-of-the-century era, with the Mississippi River Commission "offering advice, serving as a clearing house for technical data, and providing two thirds of the funding required for construction, levees in Louisiana reached a new level of sophistication."[74] In 1890, the state created the Orleans Levee District and the Board of Levee Commissioners, charging them with the "construction, repair, control and maintenance of all levees in the District, whether on river, lake, canal or elsewhere."[75]

70. Ingraham, 78-79.
71. Barry, 32-45.
72. Cowdrey, 9.
73. Regional Planning Commission, 6.
74. Kelman, 311.
75. Act 93 of the 1890 General Assembly of the State of Louisiana (July 7, 1890), as quoted by Orleans Levee District, *The Orleans Levee District—A History.*

With the help of the Board of State Engineers and other organizations, the modern Mississippi River levee system on the lower Mississippi and in New Orleans began to take shape. Within two years of the Orleans Levee Board's first meeting in 1890 in the Cotton Exchange Building on Carondelet Street, a half-million cubic yards of New Orleans soil were moved and sculpted to construct five miles of new levees and to strengthen twenty-four miles of existing levees. Over a million more cubic yards were added to the city's levees in 1892-96.

In 1907, earth-moving machines were introduced, reducing construction costs by half while speeding the work and improving the quality of the complex task of levee construction. By the late 1920s, the Orleans Levee Board and its men had moved an additional 15 million cubic yards of soil to the New Orleans riverfront levees, in a careful manner that conformed to the exacting standards of the Mississippi River Commission.[76] The earth moved in this period alone was the equivalent of a blanket of soil more than thirty feet thick over an area the size of the French Quarter, representing a profound change in the topography of the city and ranking as one of the greatest topographic engineering attempts in any American city.

While the massive earthen wall arising around New Orleans gave its citizens a sense of security, the emphasis on levees and levees alone as the defense against floods—the "levees only" policy advocated by Humphreys and others, including the public, since the mid-1800s—backfired famously during the superlative flood of 1927. Levees are critical to the control of a river but, without backup mechanisms, they raise the level and power of the water within the constrained channel and thus worsen both the risk and the consequences of a crevasse. (The dramatic events of the cataclysmic 1927 flood, and their impact on flood-control policy as well as regional and national history, are recounted authoritatively in John M. Barry's 1997 book, *Rising Tide.*)

After the 1927 flood, the Bonnet Carré and Morganza spillways—systems that accommodate the will of the river rather than restrict it—were added to the control policy of the Mississippi. But within New Orleans proper, it is the centuries-old effort to exaggerate the original topographic circumstance by adding artificial levees upon natural levees that keeps Big Muddy from reclaiming the city. Today, the Orleans Levee District controls 28 miles of levees and floodwalls and 73 floodgates just along the Mississippi, plus another 101 miles of levee

Located about twenty terrestrial miles upriver from New Orleans, the Bonnet Carré Spillway was built in response to the misguided over-reliance on levees, made evident by the great Mississippi River Flood of 1927. The spillway comprises a wall of creosote-soaked wooden ties that are extracted individually by a rail-based crane, allowing the muddy, fresh, cold waters of the swollen Mississippi to expel into the clearer, saltier, warmer waters of Lake Pontchartrain and thus relieving pressure on the river levees downstream. The aerial photograph shows the opening of the Bonnet Carré Spillway in 1973; the ground shot shows the opening of March 1997. *Aerial photograph by U.S. Army Corps of Engineers—New Orleans District; ground photograph by author, 1997*

76. Kelman, 311-13.

and 107 floodgates along the lake and canals.[77] The infrastructure is constantly maintained and improved according to the design grades of the U.S. Army Corps of Engineers, whose office commands a symbolically prominent position—one of the highest places in town—upon the levee in Carrollton.

All previous discussion on topographic change to keep water out of New Orleans addressed the artificial levees lining the banks of the Mississippi River, because the river posed the most proximate and dire threat of inundation. When the advanced drainage system came into place in the turn-of-the-century years (see page 59), the city began to grow off the riverside high ground and toward the low ground in the direction of the lake. Now engineers had to consider a second front on which unwanted water could beset the city. In the dynamic 1920s, New Orleans cast its collective eyes toward that "other" waterfront.

The Lakefront, 1926-34-Present The "other" waterfront of historic New Orleans, five miles from the bustling quay of the Mississippi but a world away in every other sense, was the indistinct shore of the semi-brackish inland bay known by the quasi-misnomer of Lake Pontchartrain. Low, marshy, inaccessible, and remote from the principal corridors of ingress and egress that put New Orleans on the map, the lakeshore remained a wilderness in the early decades and a shantytown of fishing camps and jerry-built shacks into the early twentieth century.[78] There were exceptions—the resorts of Milneburg, Spanish Fort, and West End brought economic and cultural life to the shore and served as jumping-off points for towns in the Florida parishes and coastal Mississippi. But even these establishments had to depend on stilts and pilings to rise above the sea-level terrain and tempestuous waters of the lake.

When the turn-of-the-century reclamation of the Mid-City lowlands unleashed the population from the confines of the Mississippi River natural levee toward the lake, the lakeshore took on new significance, and the issue of reinforcing it against potential "storm surges"—the dreaded floods that occur when sustained hurricane-force winds plow high lake or gulf water onto the land—became a pressing one. In the early 1900s, the Orleans Levee Board built a levee about three hundred feet inland from the marshy shore, along portions of present-day Robert E. Lee Boulevard, but the high humus and water content of both the levee and the muck below it resulted in the shrinkage and subsidence of the dike.[79] There had to be a more ambitious solution.

One had been envisioned decades earlier, by city surveyor W. H. Bell, whose *Plan of Property Improvements for the Lake Shore Front of the City of New Orleans* (1873) first broached the idea of combining flood protection with residential and recreational land development for the backwater. Why settle for a flimsy levee when you can build a solid seawall and create high, dry scenic real estate at the same time? The idea lingered among city and state officials until 1921, when changes to the state constitution granted the Orleans Levee Board sweeping powers to reinforce the lakefront. Three years later, chief engineer Col. Marcel Garsaud was commissioned to develop the concept, and within the year he emerged with a plan so ambitious that the Levee Board needed additional constitutional authority to approve and support it.

A curving levee reinforced by a stepped concrete seawall, over five miles long and a half-mile offshore, would be built in the lake; bottom sediments would then be dredged from beyond this barrier and pumped into the bemired enclosure behind it, creating new New Orleans land out of old Lake Pontchartrain water and raising the topography of the lakeshore by over five feet.[80] In effect, the plan represented the exact opposite of the natural land-building process that created the deltaic land of southeastern Louisiana. Whereas under natural conditions, floodwaters would gradually deposit sediments beyond the natural levees of the Mississippi River during a period of hundreds or thousands of years, man along the lakeshore would reach into the bottom of a bay to pump sediments over an artificial levee to create uplands within hundreds or thousands of *days*. Colonel Garsaud's plan also called for the improvement and sale of the reclaimed land to offset the original $27 million project price tag, which the Levee Board was unauthorized to carry out until a 1928 revision to the state constitution, under the title of Lakefront Improvement Project, gave the already powerful organization these additional abilities.[81]

While the actual land-use plan for the proposed lakefront was deliberated, work commenced on the grand civil-engineering project with the construction of the lakeside levee in 1926. This was a temporary wooden

bulkhead constructed 2,500-3,500 feet offshore to an elevation of 2 feet above lake level, designed to confine the fill that would be pumped behind it toward the shore. Partly damaged by storms on the deceptively calm lake, the levee was promptly repaired as sediment from the bottom of the lake was hydraulically pumped behind it until the new land was level with the top of the temporary levee, 2 feet above lake level. Then the bulkhead was strengthened and raised by 4 feet and the filling process was repeated. The entire process took over three years; the result was 2,000 acres of manmade land, 4-6 feet above the level of the lake and the gulf, about 10 feet above adjacent lowlands, higher than the Metairie/Gentilly Ridge, and roughly half as high as the Mississippi River natural levee that for two centuries hosted nearly the entire city of New Orleans. In 1930, the lakeside levee, which now actually formed the shore of the lake, was reinforced by a massive concrete seawall designed after similar structures on the Florida coast. The seawall steps evoke the image of New Orleans as a stage playing to an audience of water; one may step out of the brackish waters of Lake Pontchartrain and up a dozen or so steps to climb about half the entire elevational range of the city.

"It is some measure of the project's scale that a municipal airport was added to the Lakefront scheme almost as an afterthought,"[82] through the efforts of Abe Shushan, the politically connected Levee Board president. Shushan Airport was constructed in 1931-33 within a vertical seawall, unlike the stepped bulkhead around the lakefront, and although it is lower than the lakefront acreage (to 2 feet above the lake), it now extends twice as far into the lake, adding a distinctive peninsula to the physical shape of the city. It was an ideal site for an airport, requiring no real-estate purchase, imposing no interference with existing urban infrastructure, providing obstruction-free approaches and departures for pilots, and allowing for easy and inexpensive expansion farther into the lake.[83] With great Art-Deco styling (unfortunately covered over on the exterior but at its best inside) immortalizing the streamlined 1930s-era image of aviation, Shusan (now Lakefront) Airport was at the time one of the finest airfields in the nation and, along with the Naval Air Station located on the present-day UNO campus, played an important role in training for the air war against Germany and Japan. Today, the 300-acre manmade peninsula jutting into Lake Pontchartrain hosts a 6,879-foot-long airstrip, a busy terminal, and over 200,000 takeoffs and landings a year, mostly by corporate and private aircraft.[84]

With the engineering stage of the lakefront project concluding by 1934, authorities and the public debated what to do with this new land. One plan allocated most of the terrain to recreational parkland use; another proposed the construction of lagoons and canals among parklands and residences. A compromise plan was eventually accepted, enabling the public-access recreational development of lands between Lakeshore Drive and the water, and residential and public-facility development (sans the lagoons) of the remaining acreage.[85] About

Brackish waters of Lake Pontchartrain lapping the stepped lakefront seawall, constructed in 1930. *Photograph by author, 2000*

77. Association of Levee Boards of Louisiana, 44, and Orleans Levee District, *The Orleans Levee District—The Hurricane Levee System.*
78. This precarious lifestyle survives along Hayne Boulevard and the Rigolets in eastern New Orleans, salty and vulnerable communities that recollect the Lake Pontchartrain shore before the reclamation project. Unfortunately, about 100 of the 120 camps along Hayne Boulevard were destroyed by Hurricane Georges in September 1998, effectively ending the history of what might be called New Orleans' most unusual neighborhood.
79. Filipich and Taylor, 12-13.
80. Ibid., 7-11.
81. Association of Levee Boards of Louisiana, 43.

82. Lewis, 65.
83. Orleans Levee Board (unpaginated booklet).
84. Swoboda, "Lakefront Airport," 34-35.
85. Filipich and Taylor, 9-11.

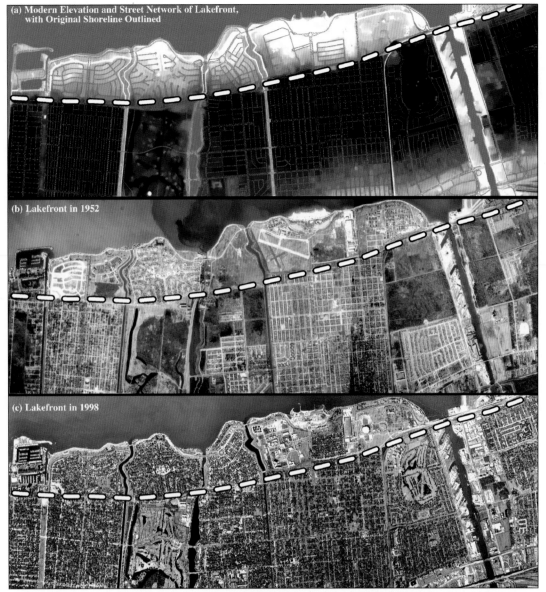

(a) Modern Elevation and Street Network of Lakefront, with Original Shoreline Outlined

(b) Lakefront in 1952

(c) Lakefront in 1998

(a) Digital elevation model of lakefront New Orleans, showing relative elevation (brighter areas) from over seven feet above sea level on the constructed land to under six feet below sea level on the natural terrain. The aerial photographs (b-c) show the steady development of the lakefront from midcentury to the present. *Processing and cartography by author; data from New Orleans City Planning Commission, U.S. Department of Agriculture, and U.S. Geological Survey*

half the new acreage was sold off into the real-estate market to pay off the Levee Board's bonds; new neighborhoods including Lake Vista, Lakeshore, Lake Terrace, and Lake Oaks were planned and constructed between 1939 and 1960 according to mid-twentieth-century urban-planning sensibilities.[86] The lakefront was also home to Pontchartrain Beach, an integral memory of many New Orleanians who grew up in the midcentury decades, plus amusement parks, marinas, and a branch of Louisiana State University that became the University of New Orleans in 1975. "Lakefront was and is an ornament to the city—one of the very few places where twentieth century city planning has truly improved a large area of an American city,"[87] wrote geographer Peirce Lewis in 1976. The reclaimed lakefront currently pads the northern edge of New Orleans from the Jefferson Parish line to the Industrial Canal, with Lakefront Airport extending into the lake on the other side of the canal. While Robert E. Lee Boulevard traces the pre-reclamation lakefront, Lakeshore Drive marks the new extremity. In utter contrast to the historic city along the riverfront, lakefront New Orleans today is spacious, sprawling, suburban, prosperous, and privy to expansive vistas of water and sky, rendering a modern subtropical coastal ambience one might associate with Florida. Its deviation from the New Orleans of cliché and stereotype endears it to locals much more so than to tourists, who hardly ever visit the area. But while its suburban environment creates the greatest impressions, the lakefront's role in protecting the city against the tempestuous waters of Lake Pontchartrain stands as the original purpose of the undertaking;[88] everything else was *lagniappe*. This great episode of topographic change in New Orleans history is better classified as an effort to keep water out of the city than as a scheme to create new land.

The Hurricane-Protection Levees, 1965-Present   With the river levees restraining the Mississippi and the lakefront levees holding back Lake Pontchartrain, New Orleans on the east bank was nevertheless still vulnerable to flooding by outside water on its lateral sides, while the west bank remained relatively unguarded on its southwestern flank. This vulnerability was demonstrated by the 1947 hurricane and more dramatically by Hurricane Betsy in 1965, which passed southwest of the city and pushed gulf waters upon lower-lying neighborhoods, causing extensive destruction. The event accelerated the movement to build hurricane-protection levees around the city, to protect against the surges that accompany storms in the Gulf of Mexico—especially slow-moving and powerful hurricanes juxtaposed such that their counterclockwise rotation pushes the waters of the gulf or nearby lakes directly upon the city. After Betsy, floodwalls were built along the Industrial Canal, followed by an extensive series of levees through the marshes of semiwild but rapidly developing eastern New Orleans. The lakefront levee was raised to twelve feet in 1969, sixteen feet in 1981, and eighteen feet by 1987,[89] reflecting the dire consequences foreseen if a powerful hurricane pushed Lake Pontchartrain upon the city and disabled its drainage system. Additional hurricane-protection levees, floodwalls, and bulkheads were built in surrounding areas in Jefferson Parish and along canals and waterways. Today, New Orleans on the east bank is about 95 percent protected from a Category-3 hurricane, although a worst-case-scenario storm would probably render the hurricane-protection levee system futile.[90] The west bank is much more at risk, even from a minor storm, ranking today as the most densely populated part of the metropolitan area that lacks levee protection from hurricanes. A series of upgrades to this last major gap in the topographic wall around Greater New Orleans is currently under way, prompted by the reminders of Tropical Storm Frances and Hurricane Georges in 1998.[91]

Of the 129 miles of levees under the jurisdiction of the Orleans Levee Board, 101 miles, or 78 percent,[92] guard against the relatively recent priority of hurricane-induced surges from nearby water bodies, while the remainder confronts the centuries-old threat of rising Mississippi River waters. The river levees are generally higher than the hurricane-protection levees, but all levees will probably continue to rise as expectations and safety standards evolve. And for good reason: if New Orleans were ever wiped off the map, as one occasionally suspects it will, the agent of destruction will probably be a direct hit by a slow-moving Category-5 hurricane, one that could rearrange the geography of the deltaic plain and send New Orleans in the direction of

86. Association of Levee Boards of Louisiana, 44.

87. Lewis, 66.

88. Orleans Levee District, *The Orleans Levee District—A History,* and Filipich and Taylor, 5.

89. Orleans Levee District, *The Orleans Levee District—The Hurricane Levee System.*

90. A computer model by Louisiana State University engineering professor Joseph Suhayda predicted "virtual destruction" of the metropolitan area by a hypothetical Category-4 hurricane approaching the city from the southwest at ten miles per hour. Only the high natural levees—the older part of the city—would escape utter inundation, and this is not to mention wind damage. Schleifstein, "Virtual Destruction."

91. Louwagie, and Barbier, "Winds of Change." Hurricane-related articles such as these often appear on June 1 of each year, marking the beginning of hurricane season.

92. Orleans Levee District, *The Orleans Levee District—The Hurricane Levee System.*

New Orleans' aging drainage system bails out the city after every major storm but will prove no match for a direct hit of a major hurricane, whose storm surge is likely to inundate the pumps and their power supplies and raise the lake to a levee above the surrounding floodwaters. This photograph of the Industrial Canal area in the aftermath of Hurricane Betsy in September 1965 gives an idea of the potential havoc. *U.S. Army Corps of Engineers—New Orleans District*

Atlantis.[93] Until then, the topographic change incurred by the construction of the three-front levee system around the problematic old town should provide New Orleans with a fairly secure lease on life.

Topographic Change to Remove Water

The Drainage System, 1893-1915-Present Whereas a historian might point to the Louisiana Purchase or the Civil War as the watershed event in the history of New Orleans, a geographer or urban planner may identify a less-famous but equivalently influential event, at least upon the city's physical growth: the development of the world-class drainage system that removed standing water and rainfall from the backswamps and eventually opened them up for residential development. The reclamation of "back-of-town" not only transformed the central and lakeside portions of the city but also the vast western, eastern, and west bank sections of the metropolitan area—a seven-fold increase in urban acreage—all within the twentieth century. It was New Orleans' answer to the Manifest Destiny ethos that gripped the nation in the previous century. Drainage technologies designed and mastered in New Orleans served as prototypes for other "topographically challenged" cities around the world, a contribution for which New Orleans is rarely credited. That the reclamation concurred with the turn-of-the-century era when modern society emerged—when automobiles, electricity, telephones, radio, new architectural styles, and other technological and societal changes resolutely ended the nineteenth century—helps make this engineering feat an almost literal watershed event in the city's history. While the reclamation was accomplished primarily through infrastructure and not actual alterations of the landform, the "drainage system ecologically had the effect of changing the topography of the city. . . . With drainage, [the land] is perfectly flat and as far as topography is concerned it is all equally desirable for building purposes."[94] *The drainage system neutralized topography as the first-tier rule guiding where New Orleanians would build New Orleans.* Today, the impact has been so great that one may assess the historical-topographical circumstance of a neighborhood simply by glancing at its architecture: stout cottages with dormers and chimneys probably predate the reclamation and are more likely to occupy higher riverside natural levees; spacious ranch houses lining broad suburban avenues probably postdate the reclamation and occupy areas at or below sea level, where cypress swamps lay but a few generations ago. The topographic change that separated old New Orleans from modern New Orleans came to fruition between the years 1893 and 1915 and continues today as what one agency brochure describes, quite accurately, as "the world's toughest drainage problem."[95]

The problem was as simple as its solution was difficult: natural and artificial levees that had the intended effect of keeping river and lake water *out* of the city also had the unintended effect of trapping rainwater *in* the city. New Orleans' levees shed water not into the Mississippi River but backward into the city itself, presenting the curious situation in which raindrops falling in the Wyoming Rockies are more likely to flow past Jackson Square than raindrops falling on Jackson Square. In fact, the lower Mississippi River, from the Red River confluence almost to the bird-foot delta, serves as a ridgeline separating the Pontchartrain Basin on the east bank from the Terrebonne and Barataria basins on the west bank, a function performed by mountain ridges in other environments. "The streets of the city are several feet below the level of the river, and the stranger is at once struck by the novel sight of the surface water running from the river," observed travel writer James S. Zacharie in 1893.[96] The result: muddy streets, stagnant water, horrendously pathological conditions, frequent flooding, and a restriction on the geographical growth of the city. New Orleans suffered these conditions for most of its first two centuries, contributing to the Crescent City's haunting stigma (often suppressed by newspapers of the day)[97] as a "vast necropolis" with among the highest death rates in the nation. Early attempts at drainage included the excavation of ditches around the blocks of the Vieux Carré to feed a makeshift canal network that ushered water away from the city and toward the backswamp; builders accommodated this situation by constructing raised edifices and wooden sidewalks. When the drainage ditches flooded, wooden bridges had to be used just to cross the street.[98] Starting in 1794, Spanish governor Baron de Carondelet had prisoners and slaves excavate a canal for the purposes of drainage and transportation for the city and the area that would later become Faubourg Tremé. Carondelet Canal formed part of the cityscape for 130 years but did little to solve New Orleans' drainage problems. Likewise, the Melpomene Canal and Poydras Canal, dug in the American Sector, and the Marigny Canal, excavated down Elysian Fields Avenue and into Bayou St. John, formed but piecemeal efforts to drain the city and were largely ineffective.[99]

The first serious engineering attempt to drain New Orleans was produced by the New Orleans Drainage Company, granted a twenty-year charter by the city in 1835 to drain a vast area from riverbank to lakeshore. With consultation from state engineer George T. Dunbar, the company proposed a series of underground drainage canals below key downtown streets that would take advantage of the natural levee's back slope and accumulate water back-of-town, where it would flow into the Claiborne Canal and then the Orleans or Girod Canal. Though the ambitious plan was skeptically received by the city and was derailed by the Panic of 1837, the New Orleans Drainage Company did implement a series of ditches in the French Quarter to gather water in the Girod or Orleans Canal, which was then removed into Bayou St. John by a steam-driven pump. The company, and the initiative, died within a few years.

Drainage as a municipal priority arose again in the 1850s in the midst of some of the worst yellow-fever summers in the city's history. By 1859, engineers, guided by a drainage plan envisioned by city surveyor Louis H. Pilié, had built four steam-powered paddlewheels to rush and lift water in a series of brickwork channels throughout the New Orleans, Jefferson City, and Lafayette drainage districts toward the backswamp and Lake Pontchartrain. But this time the Civil War intervened, and the system dilapidated during the chaotic postwar years.

A third attempt at an integrated drainage system was the 1871 effort of the Mississippi and Mexican Gulf Ship Canal Company, which dug thirty-six miles of canals in New Orleans before it too went out of business. Failed experiences with private-sector initiatives landed the formidable task back in municipal hands by the 1880s, at which time the city still depended on inadequate canals and steam wheels that removed water at a rate no faster than that deposited by a foggy drizzle—no more than 1.5 inches of rain per day under optimal circumstances. While lack of an adequate drainage system was everyone's problem, the additional lack of a sewerage system led some private-sector entities, including many prominent downtown buildings and businesses, to install their own underground sewer lines into the Mississippi River.[100]

---

93. The city of Galveston testifies to the history-altering power of Gulf Coast hurricanes: the storm that struck this Texas coastal city on September 8, 1900, killed over five thousand people, the worst natural disaster in U.S. history, and forever robbed it of its position as the most important and affluent city in Texas. Houston ascended in the decades after the catastrophe; Galveston was rebuilt but never fully recovered. A calamitous storm hitting southeastern Louisiana may play out an equivalent scenario on New Orleans and its upriver sister, Baton Rouge.

94. Gilmore, 392.

95. Sewerage and Water Board of New Orleans, *Sewerage and Water Board of New Orleans: Drainage Information.*

96. Zacharie, *New Orleans Guide* (1893), 44.

97. Wrote Benjamin Latrobe in 1819, "I asked one of the editors from what motive this omission [of news of yellow fever deaths] arose; his answer was, that the principal profit of a newspaper arising from advertisements, the merchants, their principal customers, had absolutely forbid the least notice of fever, under a threat that their custom should otherwise be withdrawn" (146). Latrobe himself died of yellow fever in New Orleans the next year.

98. Giraud, vol. 5, 211. These raised wooden sidewalks are the origin of the local term *banquettes* ("little benches") for sidewalks.

99. U.S. Army Corps of Engineers, *National Register Evaluation*, 12. The Marigny Canal extended from the foot of Elysian Fields Avenue toward the lake, elbowing at the intersection of Hope Street and again at St. Bernard Avenue and outflowing into Bayou St. John. The latter stretch of this old drainage canal now hosts a railroad and the part of Interstate 610 just east of City Park.

100. Ibid., 13-19, and Janssen, 23.

Finally, during the progressive years of the 1890s, a public consensus—led by editorialists, activists, and citizen committees—formed in support of a serious drainage effort, shining light on the embarrassing backwardness of this fundamental aspect of city services. The New Orleans City Council responded in February 1893 by directing the new Drainage Advisory Board to gather data and study the situation, funding it with $700,000. No lethargic bureaucratic committee, the Drainage Advisory Board assembled the best and the brightest in the city, "successful engineers, international experts on public health . . . men who believed New Orleans's history of inconclusive skirmishes with its climate, its topography, and the forces of nature could end in a rousing victory for the city."[101] Their findings, presented to the city in January 1895, comprised an assessment of past drainage attempts, the development of a large-scale topographic map, the collection of site-specific meteorological and hydrological data, and finally a proposed solution. Their plan:

- street gutters would collect surface flow and direct it into covered branch drains;
- branch drains would flow into main drains;
- main drains would flow into gravity-fed branch canals;
- branch canals would flow into a central main canal, located at the lowest point in the city to exploit fully the meager natural slope of the city;
- pumping stations would operate along this low central main canal to speed the draw of water into it;
- another set of pumps would raise the water uphill into an outflow canal;
- the outflow canal would empty into a bayou;
- and the bayou would empty into Lake Borgne.[102]

Dr. Ari Kelman made the following observation in his outstanding 1998 dissertation on New Orleans' environmental history:

> In a sense the Drainage Board recommended New Orleans create an artificial river system within the confines of the city: tiny streams (the gutters) led to small tributaries (the branch drains) that linked up with bigger tributaries (the main drains) that eventually coupled with still greater tributaries (the branch canals) of a trunk stream (the main canal) that finally flowed into a major body of water. . . . The key difference, of course, lay in New Orleans's topography. While river systems follow the natural slope of the landscape, the members of the Drainage Commission did not have that luxury for their system. Faced with the city's unique shape, they turned to human innovation— the pumps—to overcome the lay of the land and mimic nature.[103]

With the game plan set, the state legislature organized the Drainage Commission of New Orleans in 1896 to begin work. Despite several legal hurdles, work progressed as work often does when there exists a clear and critical goal: rapidly and efficiently. The effort received an additional mandate when voters (including women, who had the suffrage in this municipal-bond referendum and enthusiastically supported drainage) overwhelmingly approved a property tax of two mills per dollar to fund municipal waterworks, sewerage, and drainage in a special election in June 1899. This led to the creation of the famous Sewerage and Water Board of New Orleans, then and now the organization responsible for these herculean tasks in the subtropical metropolis. With both funding and support on its side, the board and its contractors had by 1905 completed forty miles of canals (mostly lined and covered), many more miles of pipelines and drains, and six operating pumping stations on the east bank, draining a total of 22,000 acres with a maximum capacity of 5,000 cubic feet per second (c.f.s.) and representing about 44 percent of the original proposed plan. Benefits were reaped almost immediately: "Storm water from moderate storms was removed rapidly . . . , mosquitoes decreased noticeably, land within the city limits that had formerly been too wet for building or agricultural use became available for development, and mortality rates for city residents dropped significantly."[104] Wrote George Washington Cable of the emergence of this modern New Orleans:

> There is a salubrity that could not be when the mosquito swarmed everywhere, when the level of supersaturation in the soil was but two and half feet from the surface, where now it is ten feet or more. . . . The curtains of swamp forest are totally gone. Their sites are drained dry and covered with miles of gardened homes.[105]

It became apparent that the drainage system was a victim of its own success, having increased impermeable acreage and thus runoff, so in 1910 the Drainage Advisory Board reconvened to plan improvement and expansion of the fifteen-year-old system.

Among the board employees was a quiet young engineer named Albert Baldwin Wood, a descendent of the prominent Bouligny family and a recent Tulane engineering graduate. He contributed to the drainage system under construction at the time with pump designs and improvements that would increase the capacity of the system. But Wood's greatest contribution came in 1913, when he presented to the board his design for a "screw pump," an enormous impeller that would draw water out of the suction basin and into the discharge basin at phenomenal rates and with mechanical efficiency and simplicity. Eleven were installed by 1915; many are still in use today. The brilliant but modest Wood spent his career devoted to his beloved hometown, continually inventing and improving its drainage system, while his patented Wood screw pumps were utilized in China, Egypt, India, and especially in the Zuyder Zee in Holland. The science and art of draining low-lying cities was born and mastered in New Orleans, and it is fitting that the master of the craft also hailed from the city.

By 1925, the New Orleans drainage system served 30,000 acres with an incredible 560-mile network of canals, drains, and pipes and a total pumping capacity of 13,000 c.f.s. The land rush off the natural levees into the drained backswamp was in full swing: just between 1900 and 1914, assessed property value in the city grew by 80 percent to $250 million, the water table dropped so that cellars and subterranean burials became feasible, new neighborhoods such as Lakeview were platted, and the death rate dropped by 25 percent, and between 1899 and 1925, malaria and typhoid deaths decreased tenfold. The infamous summertime yellow fever epidemics, which plagued the city periodically since colonial times and claimed tens of thousands of lives, last visited New Orleans in 1905. "The lives of thousands of New Orleanians were saved in the first decade of the twentieth century alone by the net effects of drainage, sewerage, and water system modernization."[106]

After two centuries of topographic restriction to the uplands along the Mississippi River, New Orleans engineers had reversed the prehistoric topographic circumstance through canal excavation and mechanized pumping and re-formed both the geography and livability of the city. (The drainage system also increased pollution in nearby lakes, caused subsidence of the once-soaked soils, increased the impermeable acreage, which augmented the amount of runoff, and strained the provision of city services to these new scattered communities.) Today, a century after progressives led the effort to establish a modern drainage system, New Orleans is still a world leader in this department, one of its truly superlative claims to fame. The Sewerage and Water Board today drains over 61,000 acres in Orleans and neighboring Jefferson Parish of their annual average 12.9 billion cubic feet of water, of which "every drop . . . must be pumped and/or lifted from the city's streets and property." Ninety miles of canals (many beneath the grassy "neutral grounds" of broad avenues), eighty-two miles of open canals, twenty east-bank pumping stations, two west-bank stations, and ten underpass pumps combine to siphon rainwater out of the city lowlands, over the levees, and into neighboring water bodies at a rate of 45,000 c.f.s., ten times the 1915 capacity and "enough to fill the Louisiana Superdome in 35 minutes."[107] Runoff from a typical rainstorm departs the city via the Broad-Florida Avenue route to Bayou Bienvenue and finally to Lake Borgne, but severe downpours engage pumps that bail the water through the outflow canals at London Avenue, Orleans Avenue, and Seventeenth Street into Lake Pontchartrain. In eastern New Orleans, rainwater is removed into Lake Pontchartrain or the Mississippi River-Gulf Outlet Canal, while across the river, the Intracoastal Waterway or Bayou Barataria are utilized. Hence the system uses a combination of manmade and natural topographic features to relocate and deposit water (quite polluted) from the streets of basin-shaped New Orleans.

While only the excavation of the canals literally changed the topography of the city, the pumps and the system as a whole had the effect of eliminating topography as a restriction on growth, at just the time when technological change allowed for the rapid development of these newly reclaimed areas. The result was the complete development of the great backswamp between the natural levees of the Mississippi and the artificial lakefront within four decades. The historical-topographic change effected upon New Orleans by its drainage system is easily identified today in a street map—where old New Orleans is parceled into former long-lot plantations radiating from the river and new New Orleans is platted in grid-pattern street networks— and in the street itself, where old New Orleans is characterized by crowded Creole cottages and Greek Revival townhouses while new New Orleans sports sprawling ranch houses and split-level homes with garages. The

101. Kelman, 251-53, 267.
102. *Report on the Drainage of the City of New Orleans by the Advisory Board, Appointed by Ordinance No. 8327, Adopted by the City Council, November 24, 1893,* as summarized by Kelman, 269.
103. Kelman, 269-70.
104. U.S. Army Corps of Engineers, *National Register Evaluation,* 28.
105. Cable, 564, 560, as quoted by Kelman, 281.
106. U.S. Army Corps of Engineers, *National Register Evaluation,* 38.
107. Sewerage and Water Board of New Orleans, *The Sewerage and Water Board of New Orleans: How It Began,* 9-11.

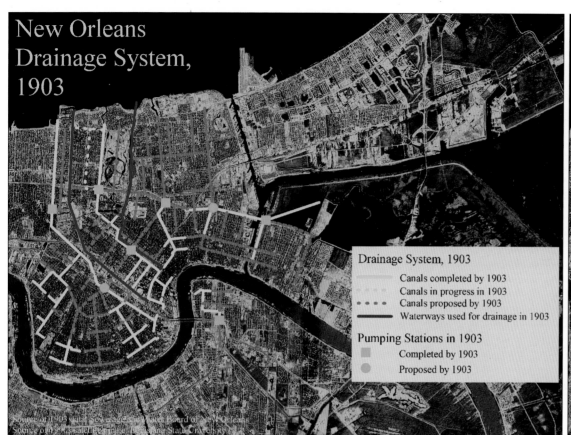

New Orleans Drainage System, 1903

Drainage System, 1903
- Canals completed by 1903
- Canals in progress in 1903
- Canals proposed by 1903
- Waterways used for drainage in 1903

Pumping Stations in 1903
- Completed by 1903
- Proposed by 1903

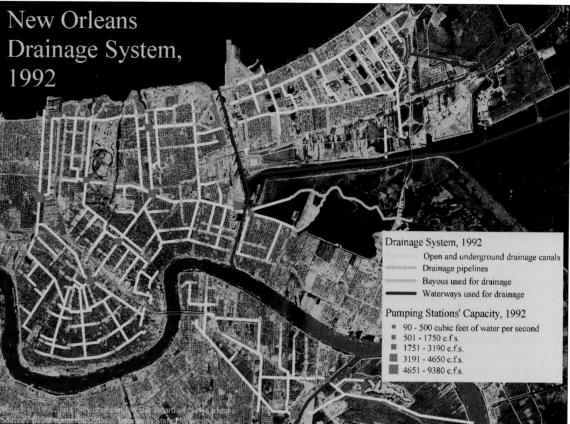

New Orleans Drainage System, 1992

Drainage System, 1992
- Open and underground drainage canals
- Drainage pipelines
- Bayous used for drainage
- Waterways used for drainage

Pumping Stations' Capacity, 1992
- 90 - 500 cubic feet of water per second
- 501 - 1750 c.f.s.
- 1751 - 3190 c.f.s.
- 3191 - 4650 c.f.s.
- 4651 - 9380 c.f.s.

The development of the drainage system in the 1890s and early 1900s allowed the Crescent City to spread beyond its historic confinement to the natural levees and into the backswamp, losing its crescent shape. Today, the New Orleans Sewerage and Water Board operates a vast and complex network of pumps, pipes, and canals (open and underground) to solve "the world's toughest drainage problem." These maps show how the system itself has grown over the years, both causing and responding to increased urban development. *Map by author; satellite image courtesy Louisiana State University. Special thanks to Harold and Doris Ann Gorman for access to source data from the Sewerage and Water Board maps.*

drainage project even affected the local dialect: no longer do locals refer to the *back-of-town* or *the woods side* to mean directions away from the river. "The woods" are gone and "back-of-town" is now *part* of town; now we hear *lakeside* or *on the lake side*.

The task of draining New Orleans has become increasingly challenging with the expansion of urbanized land surfaces, the subsidence of soils, the pollution of nearby lakes, and the inadequacies—despite its success—of the aging drainage system.[108] Many residents would express anything but admiration for the work of the Sewerage and Water Board, amid their legitimate complaints about the common minor flooding that occurs after heavy storms. (One journalist suggested that the Sewerage and Water Board "may be the most vilified public agency in New Orleans," saved only by the intriguingly mystical crescent-and-stars logo on its water meters.[109] The organization may be privatized in the near future.) The riverside of St. Charles Avenue, for example, sometimes accumulates deep puddles because the streetcar tracks embedded in the crested neutral ground trap water that would otherwise flow harmlessly toward the backswamp. For this reason, St. Charles' riverside blocks in the uptown area are in a higher-risk flood-insurance zone than those topographically lower blocks lakeside of the avenue. Even streets following the crest of the natural levee, such as Chartres Street in Bywater and parts of Tchoupitoulas, form deep puddles because the curbs on the lake side of the street trap water like a rice terrace, a miniature version of the city's larger problem of bowl-shaped topography. Residents of New Orleans were reminded of these inadequacies by the deluge of May 8, 1995, which deposited up to eighteen inches of rain in one day (twelve inches in a single hour in some places) and caused $761 million in damage throughout a twelve-parish area. The flood also put the Southeastern Louisiana Urban Flood Control Program (SELA) on the fast track, resulting in over a half-billion dollars of mostly federal funds invested in Orleans, Jefferson, and St. Tammany drainage projects. New Orleans is using the money to increase its

drainage capacity from three inches of rain every five hours to five inches in five hours. At the turn of the twenty-first century, work was under way on new pumps at the Broad Avenue Pump Station and other locations, new canals on Napoleon Avenue, Dwyer Road, and in Hollygrove, box culverts on South Claiborne Avenue, and a backup generator along the Industrial Canal.[110] For as long as New Orleans maintains it tenuous position on the deltaic plain, engineers will battle and resculpt topography to remove water trapped within New Orleans' levees, in what is indeed "the world's toughest drainage problem."

Located in the Mid-City lowlands, the ca.-1900 Melpomene Pumping Station No. 1 (left, South Broad and Martin Luther King Boulevard, formerly Melpomene Avenue), named after local engineering genius Albert Baldwin Wood, pumps runoff out the Washington Avenue Canal and into Lake Pontchartrain in times of heavy rainfall. Enormous intake pipes at another Broad Avenue pump (right) show the magnitude of the draining task. *Photographs by author, 2000*

108. Louisiana Statewide Flood Control Program's Project Evaluation Committee, 107.
109. Grace.
110. Ross.

(Top) Pumps to lift runoff out of a drainage canal, over the lakefront levee, and into Lake Pontchartrain. (Middle) Excavation of underground drainage canal on the neutral ground of South Claiborne Avenue near Napoleon in 2000. (Bottom) Even something as mundane as a water-meter box evokes intrigue in New Orleans. The emblem of the famed New Orleans Sewerage and Water Board, the city agency tasked with one of the world's most difficult urban-drainage projects, has long beguiled visitors and residents with its inexplicably mystical crescent-and-stars design. It has become a signature of New Orleans to observant pedestrians and a favorite design of local artists. *Photographs by author, 2000*

Topographic Change to Create New Land

The Batture, 1790s-1830s   In the early and mid-1700s, the river and its quay paralleled present-day Decatur and North Peters Street (once appropriately called Levee and New Levee Street), flowing much closer to the core blocks of the original city than it does to today's French Quarter. The tremendous Mississippi, lined by a miniscule manmade levee, must have formed an impressive sight virtually across the street from the *Place d'Armes*. Today, the river is more removed from Jackson Square, and from the corner of Iberville and Decatur (which marked the extreme upriver/riverside tick of Pauger's grid), the river is fully 1,600 feet away, four times the distance in 1724.[111] What had happened, during the late colonial and early American years, was the same dynamic sedimentation that had occurred for millennia before the city's founding: slight shifts in the course of the river allowed the roiling current to excavate material from the opposite bank along present-day Gretna and Algiers, deposit it in the zone of weaker flow across the river (Faubourg St. Mary and the upper French Quarter), then cut into the bank again by Esplanade Avenue and the Faubourg Marigny, ricocheting from bank to bank around each meander toward the sea. The result was a sandbar—a batture[112]—a few inches deep and a few hundred feet wide that fortuitously padded the bank during times of low water, from the upper French Quarter to the neighborhood now known as the Lower Garden District (and, to a lesser extent, the underbelly of the crescent toward Audubon Park). This semiland, called the St. Mary batture because it mostly formed in the faubourg of that name (now the Central Business District), was seized and leveed by astute businessmen and became the subject of a nationally famous court case in the early 1800s. "The Batture Case" pitted local public-use traditions of the waterfront against the national sensibility for private ownership and symbolized the larger issues of the roles of the Mississippi River and the recently acquired Louisiana Purchase in the young American nation. Regionally, the controversy would indicate whether European civil law or the American variation of English common law would prevail in this former French

and Spanish colony turned new American territory.[113] And locally, the case would determine land-ownership patterns that would greatly influence the development of downtown New Orleans.

The issue originated when sands started accreting along the bank of the new Faubourg Ste. Marie, which Bertrand Gravier acquired and subdivided in the 1780s and passed on to his brother Jean upon his death in 1797. The accumulation of sand along the banks of the Mississippi was (and is) a common natural phenomenon, and during low-water times when it was exposed, citizens of New Orleans would freely partake of the topographic gift by utilizing its sediments for construction fill, its surface area for storage, and its perch as a promenade.[114] With riverside land a valuable commodity after the American acquisition of the city in late 1803, Jean Gravier saw this *terre d'alluvions* not as a public resource but as a boon to his real-estate holdings. So he seized the developing land by erecting an artificial levee around a portion of it and barring people from utilizing it. This original area is now between St. Joseph and Julia Street, riverside of Tchoupitoulas.

The New Orleans *Conseil de Ville* (City Council) responded in 1804 by declaring the batture public property, in keeping, according to Dr. Ari Kelman's recent analysis of the case, with Louisiana's Spanish- and French-influenced civil law heritage as well as the local customs of the city. It appeared that Jean Gravier had lost his claim to the batture. But that same year arrived to New Orleans a lawyer named Edward Livingston (brother of the famed Robert, who negotiated the Louisiana Purchase and helped develop the steamboat), to escape a bad reputation in New York and to start afresh in what was increasingly viewed as the city of the future. A former mayor of New York City, "Livingston brought with him to New Orleans an American perspective on property rights, a New Yorker's eye for the value of riparian land, a debtor's nose for easy money, and one of the keenest legal minds in the nation."[115] Sensing opportunity, he took the case of Jean Gravier in exchange for a portion of the batture (Julia to Common Street) and, in October 1805, sued to secure his client's right to the controversial mud. The Justices of the Territorial Court ruled in his favor in May 1807, and within days, Livingston planned to shore up the ephemeral topography of his booty by building a levee, a navigation canal, and a structure, thereby turning the semiland into a strategically located private port. But when his laborers arrived to commence work, angry citizens (described as a mob by Livingston) gathered and chased them away. Cognizant of the fact that it was about to lose a valued right, the local community with the support of the city repeatedly confronted Livingston's workers in near riotous situations throughout the summer of 1807, with the nascent batture, scarcely a few inches above river level, at the center of the controversy. Two camps formed, one advocating the public ownership of the batture and generally, but not exclusively, comprising Creoles (that is, New Orleans natives); the other, counting among its ranks many Americans (meaning recent emigrants from the North), supporting obedience to the court's judgment that the batture belonged to Gravier and Livingston.[116]

Both parties appealed to territorial governor William Claiborne for resolution, who, deeply conflicted on the matter,[117] turned to Pres. Thomas Jefferson, warning the chief executive that blood may spill in the new American city if an adequate solution were not found. The issue apparently struck a nerve with Jefferson, for in November 1807 he sided resolutely with the public-use camp, deciding that the batture belonged to the United States. In early 1808, President Jefferson sent the U.S. Marshal to evict Livingston—deemed a squatter, without due process—and seize the batture, making it once again open to the public. Scholars have explained this action as a product of Jefferson's personal disdain for Livingston, his desire to keep the peace in this strategic but exotic city, and his will to maintain a free and open Mississippi River through the lands of the Louisiana Purchase, one of his greatest legacies.[118]

111. "De Pauger's Plan of 1724," as reproduced in Bureau of Government Research, 10, and U.S. Geological Survey New Orleans East Quadrangle.

112. A clear working definition of "batture" was put forth in an 1807 legal document: "Those portions of the bed of the Mississippi, which are entirely covered with water when the River is highest, and are left dry when the waters are low. These Battures, by the accretion of Sand which the Mississippi deposits in its course, often rise to a level with the land, and sometimes are consolidated with it." *Case Submitted to Council, on the City's Claim to the Batture,* as quoted in Padgett, 679.

113. Stewart, 657, and Kelman, 13-15.

114. As controversy over the batture grew, Governor Claiborne tried explaining the local perspective on this geographical phenomenon to his superiors in Washington: The batture case "is indeed a question highly interesting to the inhabitants of this city. From [the batture] has been taken all the earth for constructing the *Levee* that protects New Orleans from the inundations of the river. It has also furnished the earth used in public and private buildings and for improving the streets. In high water the Batture is entirely covered. If reclaimed, it is feared the current of the Mississippi will in some measure change its course, which will not only prove injurious to the navigation, but may occasion depredations on the levees of the city, or those in its vicinity." As quoted by Gayarré, vol. 4, 187.

115. Kelman, 19, 25.

116. The Batture Case is often portrayed as an example of a Creole-versus-American cultural clash, but the details complicate this notion. Gravier, who advocated the presumably American position of privatization of the batture, was a Creole, and his American attorney, Livingston, was in fact an advocate of civil law and later helped form the foundation of Louisiana's French-influenced codified law tradition. A strong advocate of the public's right to the batture, the supposed Creole position, was a prominent American by the name of Pres. Thomas Jefferson. Yiannopoulos, 56.

117. Wrote Claiborne on September 3, 1807, to the secretary of state, "I must confess that I feel much embarrassed what course to pursue. The opposition on the part of the people to a decision of the court is in itself so improper, and furnishes a precedent so dangerous to good order, that it cannot be countenanced. But the opposition on the present occasion is so general, that I feel myself compelled to resort to measures the most conciliatory; as the only means of avoiding still greater tumult, and, perhaps, bloodshed." As quoted by Gayarré, vol. 4, 186.

118. Kelman, 31.

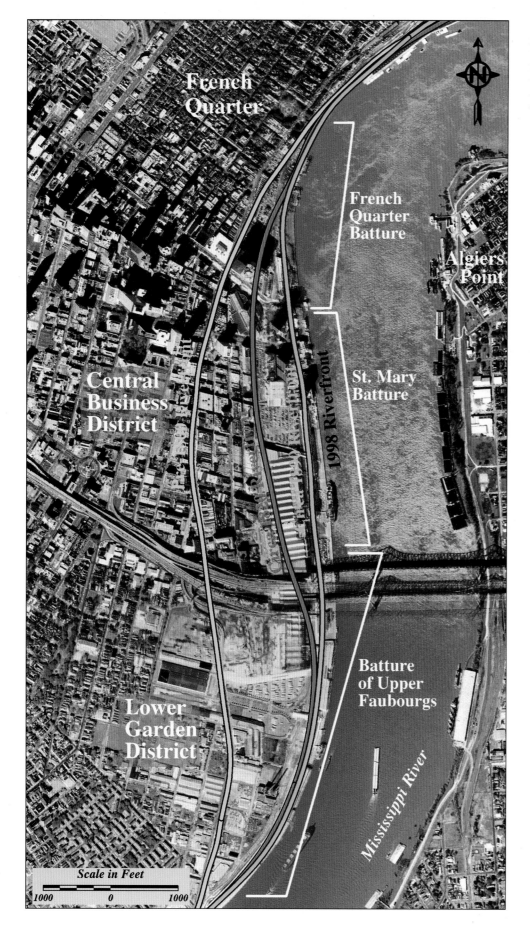

French Quarter

French Quarter Batture

Algiers Point

Central Business District

1998 Riverfront

St. Mary Batture

Lower Garden District

Batture of Upper Faubourgs

Mississippi River

Scale in Feet

1000   0   1000

Natural shifts of the Mississippi River in the late 1700s and early 1800s allowed for sediment deposition along the east bank from the present-day Lower Garden District to the French Quarter. The resulting "batture" (from the French word for "beaten," as in "beaten upon by the river") was the subject of a long series of court battles in the early 1800s, pitting local public-use traditions of the waterfront (associated with the Creole populace) against the American sensibility for private ownership. The court battles continued for decades and ended in a series of compromises. Until a few decades ago, the batture was used mostly for industrial uses, but now hosts a mix of commercial, residential, recreational, and industrial uses, including the fashionable Warehouse District. *Map and analysis by author; aerial image courtesy U.S. Geological Survey*

Detail of bird's-eye perspective of the batture along Faubourg St. Mary and the old city (right) in 1851, from *Bird's Eye View of New-Orleans* (New York: A. Guerber & Co., 1851). *American Memory Panoramic Maps Collection, Library of Congress*

This scene, captioned by the photographer "New Orleans Feb 1890 Steamships New Orleans and other boats at the wharf," shows the riverfront at the northern end of the St. Mary batture looking downriver. *Photographer unknown, New Orleans Views Collection, UNO Special Collections*

"When the cotton press [on Front and Terpsichore] was built in 1832 it stood upon the edge of the Mississippi. It is now distant at least three hundred feet, so rapid is the formation here of the batture. Sixteen years ago, [a gentleman] informed me the site of the press was occupied by the bed of the river whose western bank was then to be found where there are now wide streets and squares covered with buildings. This change is constantly going on. One side of the river is undermined and falls in as the current rushes against it, while the other receives a slow but certain increase from the alluvion which is annually deposited there, so that while the general course of the stream is sensibly changed, the parallelism of its banks remains unaltered. While the batture is forming in the upper faubourg and upper part of the City, the river is working away the bank in the lower part and along the lower faubourg, and it yet remains to be seen what the effect will be upon the port."

—John H. B. Latrobe, 1834 (as quoted by Wilson, *Southern Travels*, 52)

Now the Batture Case was a national issue, with implications reaching as far as public access to the American West. A frustrated Livingston took his case to Washington and then to the American people, with missives detailing the plight of the property owner; Creole lawyers on the opposing side distributed pamphlets describing the civil-law basis for the batture as a public commons. In 1810-13, Livingston again sued to secure his portion of the batture, targeting the former president in a court in Richmond and the marshal who evicted him in 1808 in a court in New Orleans.

Livingston lost the first lawsuit—a case in which an indignant former president Jefferson was deeply involved, having written a scholarly pamphlet on the Batture Case[119]—but won the New Orleans case, in which the court deemed the marshal's actions illegal and Livingston's claim to the batture legitimate. Rather than ending the case, the decision merely gave Livingston new life in firing legal volleys at the city, with the city returning them for the next seven years, during which time Livingston served in the military campaign that culminated in the Battle of New Orleans. Finally, in September 1820, Livingston and the city negotiated a compromise in which Livingston would retain some rights to the batture but the public would maintain the right to cart off landfill sediment, the city would gain a portion of the contested land, and Livingston would be responsible for the construction of a new levee, a market, and a road.[120] Livingston obtained title to portions of the batture in 1823 and was awarded money in 1826, after which he paid off his debts and went on to state and national prominence before his death in 1836. Though litigation would follow for years, "the rights of the city were ultimately upheld, and gradually streets through the batture began to appear on maps."[121] John Adems Paxton provided this status report on the batture in *The New-Orleans Directory and Register* in 1822:

> The Batture was formed by deposits from the river, on which it has a front of about 3400 feet, and an average depth of 470 feet. This piece of property, which has made so great a figure in the history of litigation, is now divided among a great number of proprietors . . . and a liberal arrangement with the corporation of the city has put it in a situation in which it may be improved and made useful to the public, as well as a source of profit to the owners. . . . We understand it is stipulated that all the soil between the present Levée and the river shall in future be held by the city for the purposes of navigation, but that no buildings whatever shall be erected thereon; and the proprietors agree to build none but brick buildings, covered with tile or slate. In consequence of the arrangements, some valuable brick shops and stores have been erected . . . and before the end of this season it is calculated that more than an hundred fine stores will be erected on New Levée. . . . One half of [New Levée Street], next to the city, is exclusively appropriated for steam-boats, of which there are sometimes thirty or forty lying at a time, more than 70 being now employed in bringing down cotton, tobacco, flour, hemp, cordage, beef, pork, corn, lead, peltries, and all the other products which are poured into our harbour from the great rivers which empty into the Mississippi. . . .
>
> All this commerce centres on the Batture, and it would be difficult to select in any city in the world a spot in which more extensive business is done in the same space. The property then must soon become invaluable.[122]

Originally located between the crest of the natural levee (Levee Street, now Tchoupitoulas) and what became New Levee Street (now South Peters), the batture would continue to grow and develop for decades, a product of both physics and the hand of man. With the city-controlled portion of the St. Mary batture used for wharves and dumps[123] and other areas devoted to commercial/residential land use, the city in 1851 decided to relinquish its control of the batture and consequently finalized the subdivision and sale of the lots. By the Civil War era, a layout of long parallelogram-shaped blocks, labeled with rather staid street names (Commerce, South Peters, Fulton, Front, Delta, Water) that suggest the area's functional origins and emergence during the American era, was fully superimposed upon the sandy batture. That these streets were appended to the original street layouts of Faubourg Ste. Marie (1788) and Faubourg Delord (1806) is readily apparent from a glance at a map. It was at this time, just before the Civil War, that the "important transition in this area from a commercial/residential neighborhood to a commercial/industrial district began,"[124] fueled later by the postwar railroad boom. Thus was born the warehouse district, the great industrial zone occupying much of this important area of topographic change in New Orleans. The warehouse district diminished in importance as port activity spread far beyond the downtown riverfront in the twentieth century and the city's economy and demographics shifted; by the 1970s, it was a decaying postindustrial noman's land. Then, in 1984, the former St. Mary batture hosted the Louisiana World Exposition, which—like the 1884 World's Industrial and Cotton Centennial Exposition at present-day Audubon Park—failed financially but succeeded in reviving the zone into the Warehouse District, ground zero for New Orleans' lucrative convention trade and, in the 1990s, the hottest spot in town for the development of condominiums, nightspots, and hotels. Anchored by the vast riverside convention facilities interspersed with upscale condominiums, looming warehouses, acclaimed art studios, clubs, paving-block streets, and trendy hotels that seem to go up almost weekly, the Warehouse District is booming once again. The batture's biggest economic engine today is the Ernest N. Morial Convention Center, originally built as the Great Hall for the 1984 World's Fair, converted to a convention center in 1985, and expanded in 1991 and enormously in 1999, with a fourth ($450 million) phase in the works. This gargantuan facility hosted 111 major conventions and accounted for 886,000 visitors in 1999, close to 10 percent of all city tourism. Jean Gravier's riverside sand flat has come a long way in 200 years.

One can only speculate on how differently downtown New Orleans would have evolved had all those valuable riverside batture lands been in completely private hands, a no-trespassing zone wedged between the business district and the river. Conversely, had the city owned the entire batture and prohibited the subdivision of parcels for sale, downtown would have developed in yet another manner. Legally, the Batture Case, especially the decisions in the early years of the controversy, "played a role in the development of the Louisiana Civil Code of 1808 [and] was the first judicial recognition of what is now the only European-based civil law jurisdiction in the United States,"[125] one of New Orleans' distinguishing cultural characteristics and one that people today may not readily associate with the gloomy warehouses and stark streets riverside of Tchoupitoulas. Today, the batture covers about ninety acres across three historical districts and rises eight to twelve feet above m.s.l., far higher than its original elevation of a few inches above the river. It is a vibrant part of the downtown fabric, yet still a place apart.

Only a small portion of the batture, its northern tip, accumulated on the French Quarter side of Canal Street, bounded today by Canal, North Peters, St. Peter, and the river. Much of this alluvial deposit formed between 1818 and 1835, as indicated by city surveyor Joseph Pilié's maps from that era, and had roughly spanned its modern extent by the 1860s. The batture was wide enough in 1827 to allow for a "New Public Road" to be added, later called New Levee Street and now North Peters.

119. Jefferson wrote and published *The Proceedings of the Government of the United States in Maintaining the Public Right to the Beach of the Mississippi* (1812), described as "a dazzling piece of erudition" by one historian. That Jefferson devoted so much time to the Batture Case demonstrates not only his personal involvement in the suit but the importance he ascribed to New Orleans and to the issues of land ownership in "his" Louisiana. Peterson, 944-46.
120. Kelman, 53, 55.
121. Chase, 194.
122. Paxton, 32-33.
123. According to Hilary S. Irvin (4-5), development of the upriver portion of the batture, in Faubourg Delord, "predates by decades the development of the riverfront of the [Faubourg] St. Mary, the reason being that the City did not possess the use of this batture land."
124. Irvin, "The Site Boundaries," as quoted by Preservation Resource Center.
125. Stewart, 662.

1

5

9

3

8

2

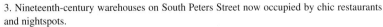

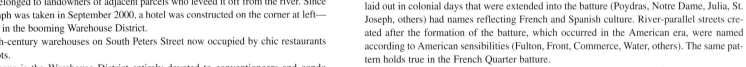

7

4

The St. Mary Batture Today

1. Starting in the late 1700s, the St. Mary batture developed and eventually spanned the area to the left of the stepped-roof hotel (right center). Once leveed off from the river, the batture was gradually enveloped by the urban geography of downtown New Orleans but always remained distinct from it, vis-à-vis street patterns, structures, economic activity, and even street names. No one calls it the St. Mary batture anymore; now it's the Warehouse District, seen here in 1996 when the hotel-construction boom in this former industrial area was just beginning.

2. Intersection of South Peters and St. Joseph. It was in this vicinity that the 1807 showdown transpired between those advocating the traditional public ownership of the batture (generally comprising Creoles) and those supporting the American court decision that the batture belonged to landowners of adjacent parcels who leveed it off from the river. Since this photograph was taken in September 2000, a hotel was constructed on the corner at left—one of many in the booming Warehouse District.

3. Nineteenth-century warehouses on South Peters Street now occupied by chic restaurants and nightspots.

4. By no means is the Warehouse District entirely devoted to conventioneers and condo dwellers: there are still a number of industrial occupants in the old structures, some of which are still warehouses. This particular building on South Peters houses an ironworks, a craft integral to the city's physical heritage.

5. Once at the heart of the batture dispute and later part of a sweaty blue-collar industrial area, this corner in the Warehouse District now serves a more upscale crowd. The change began in 1984, when the area hosted the Louisiana World Exposition, which brought attention, money, and appreciation to this historic industrial area. In the decade and a half that followed, and especially in the booming late 1990s, the Warehouse District became the hottest real-estate market in town, a mecca for condominiums, apartments, topnotch restaurants and art galleries, nightspots, and an amazing array of new hotels.

6. Corner of Notre Dame and Fulton in the old St. Mary batture. River-perpendicular streets laid out in colonial days that were extended into the batture (Poydras, Notre Dame, Julia, St. Joseph, others) had names reflecting French and Spanish culture. River-parallel streets created after the formation of the batture, which occurred in the American era, were named according to American sensibilities (Fulton, Front, Commerce, Water, others). The same pattern holds true in the French Quarter batture.

7. The former St. Mary batture in 2000. Census data shows the Warehouse District (combined with the adjacent CBD) with the fastest-growing residential population of any neighborhood in the city, having increased by 31 percent (to 1,794 people) between 1990 and 2000.

8. Contrasts abound in the Warehouse District: a century-old warehouse cracking with age in front of the Ernest N. Morial Convention Center, one of the largest and best facilities of its type in the nation. The old warehouse was demolished in 2001, while the convention center planned its fourth expansion phase since its construction for the 1984 World's Fair.

9. Despite its trendiness, the Warehouse District still imparts a sense of poignancy and mystery.

Photographs by author, 1996-2000

Portions of this batture were conveyed to the city of New Orleans by the U.S. Supreme Court in 1836, and in the 1860s, Clay and Front streets were added and the resultant blocks were subdivided and sold by the city to the private sector, eventually falling into the hands of the sugar, warehousing, and railroad industry. The Pontchartrain Railroad (later the Louisville & Nashville Railroad) and New Orleans, Mobile, and Texas Railroad laid tracks through the batture in 1867-73 and furthered its industrial development;[126] from this time into the 1930s, New Orleans' "Sugar District" functioned here (see page 133), headquartered at the Louisiana Sugar and Rice Exchange at Bienville and North Front. From a topographic perspective, the French Quarter batture is an undistinguishable plane wedged between the modern manmade levee and the crest of the natural levee (which runs under the Canal Place complex) in the upriver corner of the French Quarter. Had it developed under natural conditions, it would be significantly lower in elevation and sandier in soil texture than adjacent areas, but layers of artificial fill have conflated this area with the surrounding terrain; today the French Quarter batture averages eight to twelve feet above m.s.l., and in parts rises over twenty feet high, making it one of the highest places in town.

That the batture is a relative newcomer to New Orleans geography is dramatically evident today in the land use of this area: never developed in the townhouse-and-storehouse commercial/residential plan that characterized the rest of the Vieux Carré, the batture hosted port-related industrial enterprises in the nineteenth and early twentieth centuries and remained a place apart from the *tout ensemble* of the French Quarter ever since it emerged from the Mississippi River.[127] Thus instead of boasting iron-laces galleries, Creole cottages, and Spanish courtyards, the batture was home to gritty turn-of-the-century warehouses and sugar refineries, far more akin to the Warehouse District than to the Vieux Carré. As in Faubourg St. Mary, even the street names divulge a mundane origin here: compare *Clay, North Front,* and *Wells* in the batture to *Toulouse, Chartres,* and *Ursulines* in the heart of the French Quarter.

The area was initially included in the jurisdiction of the Vieux Carré Commission, charged in 1936 with the protection of the French Quarter's historical architecture and ambience, but was excluded from 1946 to 1964 and subsequently lost many of its old industrial structures, producing today a bleak zone of parking lots, electrical infrastructure, and isolated edifices in the shadow of nearby skyscrapers. Demolitions and a series of blazes in the 1960s and 1970s claimed some of the grander old sugar buildings; today, only the 111 Rue Iberville Building, a row of structures on North Front, the ruins of a Filter House addition, and the heavily remodeled Henry Howard warehouse (now home to theme restaurants and retailers) remain of the batture's lost built environment.[128] Everything else is pavement.

The creation of Woldenberg Park (1989), the Aquarium of the Americas (1990), and other riverside attractions have instilled new life in the batture and reconnected French Quarter visitors with the river. Engineers have even extended the "terrain" into the river via cleverly landscaped docks that were once part of the Bienville Street wharves. Despite its unglamorous heritage, the French Quarter's batture, which added about twenty acres to Bienville's original city and has since been expanded to about thirty-five acres, played an important role in the district's working years and represents a rare opportunity for future development in the Vieux Carré.

Topographic Change to Improve Navigation

The principal motive behind much of New Orleans' manmade topographic change was the (quite accurate) perception of water as a threat. But water, of course, is also the lifeblood of the city; New Orleans would not exist were it not surrounded by convenient and strategic bodies of water. Sited to exploit the connection between the Gulf of Mexico and the Mississippi River, New Orleans has been economically obligated ever since 1718 to streamline this linkage, allowing for the swift passage of vessels and the efficient break of bulk. While many local merchants had for years maintained a reverence for the Mississippi River as *the* transportation link—a complacency, termed "the Mississippi Obsession" by one historian, that led to intense competition from Northern railroads in the late 1800s[129]—others recognized the importance of navigational canals to expedite the flow of goods between the world accessed by the salty waters to the southeast and the very different world served by the muddy fresh waters to the northwest. Historian Gary A. Bolding described this awareness as the

"New Orleans Seaway Movement" in 1969, after the latest component of the movement, the Mississippi River-Gulf Outlet Canal, was completed.[130] The first impulse to join these two worlds surfaced almost concurrently with the founding of the city: the Company of the Indies considered a canal to connect the river and lake even before finally deciding on the New Orleans site, and Bienville himself proposed digging such a canal (for sanitation more so than for transportation) in June 1718. A number of 1720s-era maps of the city depict the canal, complete with locks, in the vicinity of today's Canal Street, and a small defensive moat was actually dug by Pierre Baron around 1730 along a portion of the corridor.[131] The planned navigation canal would have linked Bayou St. John and Lake Pontchartrain, providing a waterborne alternative to the Bayou Road portage for river/lake access. Although proposed a number of times into the mid-1800s, an actual navigation canal was never dug[132] along Canal Street, and no progress on any navigational canals ensued in New Orleans until the late Spanish colonial years, during the administration of Governor Carondelet.

Carondelet (Old Basin) Canal, 1794-1938   Gov. Francisco Luis Hector, Baron de Carondelet, a Belgian in service of Spain, was a skilled and popular administrator credited with bringing various reforms to New Orleans during his tenure of 1792-97. In June 1794, after a series of communications with his superiors in Spain, Carondelet announced the excavation of a canal from the rear of the city to Bayou St. John.[133] Although Carondelet probably had both drainage and navigation in mind when he envisioned the canal,[134] it appears that the canal was initially designed and built primarily for drainage.[135] This would explain its centralized position at the rear of the city. Using the labor of prisoners and about 60 slaves "volunteered" by planters in the region (Spain allowed the project but did not fund it), Governor Carondelet's men had by the end of 1794 excavated a channel three to six feet deep, about six feet wide, and lined with eight-foot embankments from the present-day block of Basin Street between Toulouse and St. Peter straight back 1.6 miles to Bayou St. John. With the canal barely navigable and tangled with roots and cypress stumps, Governor Carondelet called upon the planters again in 1795 to help deepen it; they responded by sending 150 slaves, who widened the channel to fifteen feet with a depth that accommodated small vessels. A third call for help was heeded in November 1795, and by early 1796, the canal was operational and later decreed by the Cabildo to be called *Canal Carondelet.*[136] It was dedicated in August 1796 but fell into disrepair after Carondelet was transferred to Quito a year later, eventually deteriorating into an "unwholesome morass"[137] by the time of the American takeover of the city in late 1803. Despite its condition, Carondelet Canal figured prominently in the many maps made of the city following the Louisiana Purchase.

Its promise was apparent to James Pitot, a Frenchman by birth who migrated to Saint-Domingue (now Haiti), fled to Philadelphia after the 1793 slave insurrection, and finally arrived, like so many other Saint-Domingue refugees, in New Orleans in 1796. He saw in Carondelet Canal and Bayou St. John the promise of trade flowing between the river and the lake, and organized the Orleans Navigation Company in 1805 to exploit the opportunity. (Pitot was also appointed mayor of the city that year, indicative of an era in New Orleans when city business and corporate business were deeply entangled.)

The company cleared out Bayou St. John starting in 1806 and proceeded to widen and deepen Carondelet Canal over the next decade, embroiled in legal battles with the city all during and after the course of the expansion.[138] After over $300,000 in expenditures, the Orleans Navigation Company fully opened the canal for navigation in May 1817, charging $1.25/ton for transporters to avoid the slow, jolting journey on muddy Bayou

126. *Vieux Carré Survey,* Binders for Squares 4-5E and Squares A-3A, and Russell Wright.
127. See time-sequence photographs of the area in Campanella.
128. *Vieux Carré Survey,* Binders for Square 4-5E and Squares A-3A.
129. Clark, "New Orleans and the River," 133-35; Bolding, 51-53; and Mitchell, 944-45.

130. Bolding, 49.
131. Wilson, "Early History of Faubourg St. Mary," 3-6, and Villiers du Terrage, 180.
132. Drainage ditches, though hardly canals, operated on parts of Canal Street periodically in the 1800s. "The 'canal' in Canal Street," wrote Hennick and Charlton (49), "the drainage ditch from North Claiborne to the River, had been filled long before 1866." The name *Canal Street* came from the vision of a navigation canal that never came to be, rather than the drainage canal that once was.
133. Holmes, *A Guide to Spanish Louisiana,* 19-28.
134. The canal would serve "the double purpose of draining the marshes and ponds in [the rear of the city], and establishing a navigable communication with the sea," John Wesley Monette stated in his *History of the Valley of the Mississippi.* "This canal, communicating with the Bayou St. John, would effectually accomplish the latter object, to the great commercial advantages of New Orleans, while it would also remove one great source of annoyance and disease proceeding from the generation of innumerable swarms of mosquitoes and march miasma from the stagnant pools." As quoted by Gayarré, vol. 3, 351-52. See also Burns, 566.
135. Referring to the proposed canal, Carondelet said, "Should this drainage not be executed, it will be necessary to abandon the town in three of four years, for the inundation of the Mississippi or the breaking of any of its levees . . . will cover almost all the streets . . . and thus make the town a sort of sink which will have not outlet for its waters." As quoted by Wood, 37. See also Paxton (1822), 34. Paxton wrote that the canal was dug "for the express purpose of draining the city."
136. Gayarré, vol. 3, 352-53; Friends of the Cabildo, vol. 6, 60; and Janssen, 63-65.
137. As quoted in Clark, *New Orleans, 1718-1812,* 295.
138. Clark, *New Orleans, 1718-1812,* 287-96, and Rowland, 325-26.

Road in favor of a smooth sail on the canal to the rear door of the city. "Where there was formerly a filthy ditch and noisy frog-pond, we find a beautiful canal, with a good road and walks on each side, with gutters to drain off the water, and a large and secure Basin where vessels can lie in perfect safety at all seasons," wrote John Adems Paxton in 1822.[139]

"[Carondelet Canal] facilitates a highly useful communication with Pensacola, Mobile, the lakes, and their settlements. Before it was opened, the ships of that waterway docked about two miles from the city on Bayou St. John, while now they come into a basin at the foot of the fortifications to discharge their goods and load cargoes for the return voyage. If this improvement had been kept up, it would provide great encouragement to the planters of West Florida; but soon through culpable indifference and neglect of maintenance the choked and ruined canal will no longer be navigable."
—James Pitot, 1802 (111-12. Pitot made good on his comments in 1805, when he formed the Orleans Navigation Company.)

The expanded canal was paralleled by towpaths so animals or men could pull vessels through the canal in the event of adverse weather conditions. A drawbridge at Bayou St. John, a lighthouse at the bayou's mouth, and an extrawide timber-reinforced channel at the lakeside port further enabled the promise of commerce, while a surveyor and two inspectors collected revenues for the United States government at the port of delivery. The expansion project was a success: Carondelet Canal developed into a key commercial waterway through which small craft brought in "cotton, tobacco, lumber, wood, lime, brick, tar, pitch, bark, sand, oysters, marketing . . . furs and peltries"[140] and other resources from the communities of Lake Pontchartrain and the gulf, and shipped out sundry merchandise unavailable in the countryside.

Major Amos Stoddard described the recently expanded Carondelet Canal in his 1812 sketch of Louisiana:

This canal rises in a basin directly behind the charity hospital, which is sufficiently capacious to accommodate several small vessels. It extends in a direct line about two miles to St. John's creek [Bayou St. John], and is about twenty feet wide. This is of great advantage to the city, particularly as the products of the lake and back country, such as fish, lime, tar, pitch, and various other articles, find an easy water access to the inhabitants; whereby a difficult and expensive cartage of three miles [along the Bayou Road] from the bridge is avoided.[141]

"We frequently see in the Basin from 70 to 80 sail, of from 550 to 600 barrels, from the West Indies, the northern states, Pensacola, Mobile, Covington and Madisonville," reported Paxton in 1822,[142] providing an idea of the sizable hinterland serviced by this tiny backdoor port. Travelers also used Carondelet Canal to connect with steamers that transported them to Biloxi, Mobile, and beyond.[143] From the 80,000-square-foot turning basin on present-day Basin Street, the total distance to the lake was a little over 5 miles, with 1.6 miles on the manmade rectilinear Carondelet Canal through the swamps west of the Bayou Road/Esplanade Ridge and 3.5 miles on the twisting natural inlet of Bayou St. John. Carondelet Canal became an asset of the Creole community in the heightening competition between the natives and the recently arrived Americans in the former colonial city.

The expansion of Carondelet Canal for navigation not only encouraged the development of the back-of-town area but also initiated the history of New Orleans' greatest thoroughfare, Canal Street. Part of a dusty commons between the old French side of town and the twenty-year-old suburb of Faubourg Ste. Marie, the triangular swath of land was claimed by the city and officially recognized as such by an Act of Congress in 1807, provided that the city "reserve for the purpose, and convey gratuitously for the public benefit . . . as much of the said commons as shall be necessary to continue the canal of Carondelet from the present basin to the Mississippi, and shall not dispose of, for the purpose of building thereon, any lot within sixty feet of the space reserved for building a canal, which shall forever remain open as a public highway." Accordingly, Canal Street was laid out in great width—about 171 feet in most places—to accommodate the right-of-way of the planned Carondelet Canal extension.[144] But disputes between the Orleans Navigation Company and the City Council

139. Paxton, 36.
140. Ibid., 37.
141. Stoddard, 163.
142. Paxton, 37.
143. Friends of the Cabildo, vol. 6, 60-61.
144. "An Act Respecting Claims to Land in the Territories of Orleans and Louisiana" (March 3, 1807), as recorded in *The Debates and Proceedings in the Congress of the United States* (1852), 1283. The planned extension of Carondelet Canal accounts for the great width of Basin Street as well as Canal Street. Burns, 566.

This detail from *Bird's Eye View of New-Orleans* (1851) shows Carondelet (Old Basin) Canal in the distant upper left, connecting the rear of the old city with Bayou St. John and thence to Lake Pontchartrain. *American Memory Panoramic Maps Collection, Library of Congress*

regarding the use of the canal for navigation versus drainage led to the derailment and finally the abandonment of the plans to extend the canal to the river.[145] Were it not for Carondelet Canal, world-famous Canal Street would have been of an entirely different, and probably less spectacular, character. Then again, had the canal actually been expanded down Canal Street, the "Great Wide Way"[146] may have developed into a bleak industrial strip or perhaps a picturesque waterfront thoroughfare.

Carondelet Canal's importance to the city diminished after the 1830s, when the Americans, with Irish-immigrant laborers, completed the rival New Basin Canal. Carondelet Canal became, literally and nominally, the "Old Basin Canal"; its owners since 1805, the Orleans Navigation Company, went bankrupt in 1852, forfeited its charter to extend the waterway down Canal Street, and auctioned off Carondelet Canal. A new company, the New Orleans Canal and Navigation Company, took over the canal that year, followed by the Carondelet Canal and Navigation Company in 1857. The competition between the New Basin and Carondelet canals was reflected in the fact that, although a state act in 1857 allowed the owners of the latter waterway to charge up to $1/ton from the basin to the bayou and another $1/ton from the bayou to the lake, the Carondelet Canal and Navigation Company charged only $0.35/ton for the *entire* trip.[147] Receipts for commerce on the two rival canals in 1865 reveal their commercial relationship:

145. Henry Clement Pitot, *James Pitot (1761-1831): A Documentary Study* (1968), 86-88.
146. This term comes from Peggy Scott Laborde's documentary.
147. H. D. Ogden, 8-10.

1940

1998

Selected Products Arriving during the Year Ending August 31, 1865	Receipts at New Basin Canal	Receipts at Carondelet Canal (Old Basin Canal)	Ratio of receipts between New Basin and Old Basin Canal
Cotton, bales	4,348	767	5.7 to 1
Lumber, feet	6,309,000	965,000	6.5 to 1
Wood, cords	5,894	3,424	1.7 to 1
Bricks	220,000	70,000	3.1 to 1
Sand, bbls.	14,400	3,880	3.7 to 1
Shells, bbls.	10,300	530	19 to 1
Charcoal, bbls.	3,100	27,240	0.1 to 1
Shingles	23*	22,000	.001 to 1*
Staves	24*	28,000	.001 to 1*
Rosin, bbls.	1,814	105	17 to 1
Turpentine, bbls.	76	138	.55 to 1
Tar, bbls.	826	50	17 to 1
Oysters, bbls.	110*	50,200	.002 to 1*

Source: Gardner, 1866, 25. Original data listed a number of livestock products for the New Basin Canal that were not matched for the Old Basin Canal.
*New Basin Canal figures for shingles, staves, and oysters are probably typographical errors, since it seems unlikely that so few of these items arrived in comparison to almost exactly 1,000 times that amount arriving at the Old Basin Canal. Actual figures are probably 23,000; 24,000; and 110,000, respectively, producing more likely ratios of 1:1, .9:1, and 2.2:1.

At the turn of the century, the waterway still served as a local industrial corridor through the fascinating Dickensian cityscape that comprised the Parish Prison, Tremé Market, Storyville, St. Louis Cemeteries, Congo Square, and expansive Creole faubourgs associated with the development of jazz. Sanborn Fire Insurance Maps from the late 1800s and early 1900s record numerous businesses near the turning basin, such as lumberyards and charcoal deposits, that attest to the canal's continuing role as a local port. The right-of-way of the canal was also utilized by the Southern Railroad (whose tracks passed over the western corner of the turning basin, which had been partially filled in around 1900) to transport passengers to the prominent terminal on Basin and Canal that stood from 1908 to 1956.[148] By 1919, the Old Basin Canal (by this time under the control of railroad companies) was doing only about one-third the business of the New Basin Canal, leading only in the lake oyster trade, where it benefited from its proximity to downtown markets.

With its career winding down, New Orleans' first major navigation canal was declared unnavigable in 1927 and was filled in by 1938. The topographic change initiated by slaves and prisoners under Spanish colonial governor Carondelet was reversed 140-odd years later; today, the former bed of Carondelet Canal is now a conspicuously open swath of land through the otherwise densely populated neighborhoods between the French Quarter and Bayou St. John. Traces of its existence may be detected in the modern landscape. a drainage canal still flows beneath parts of its route; city equipment and fenced lots occupy portions of the bed and right-of-way that still belong to the city or railroad; and the grassy corridor still touches the "headwaters" of Bayou St. John exactly where it did in 1796, now at the junction of Lafitte Street with Jefferson Davis Parkway. The former canal bed and adjacent railroad right-of-way, now in the possession of the defunct Alabama Great Southern Railroad, may not remain "perhaps one of largest single chunks of undeveloped land in the heart of the city"[149] for long: in February 2001, plans for a Winn-Dixie Supermarket, sorely needed in this depressed

148. Janssen, 66, and Friends of the Cabildo, vol. 6, 61-66.
149. Greg Thomas, "Grocery Store."

The Old Basin Canal (1794) was filled in during 1927-38, but its mark on the streetscape in 1940 was just as clear as it is today, forming a conspicuously open swath of concrete and grass through otherwise densely populated neighborhoods. The French Quarter appears at the bottom of these aerial photographs; Bayou St. John appears at the top. Notice the alteration of the Faubourg Tremé neighborhood on both sides of the foot of the canal (bottom). The area to the left, formerly Storyville, was demolished soon after the 1940 photograph was taken and replaced with the Iberville Housing Development (1941). The historic neighborhood to the right was razed in the 1960s-70s for the urban renewal project that included Armstrong Park (1980). Note also Interstate 10. *Map by author; aerial images courtesy U.S. Geological Survey*

This photograph, described as "New Orleans Feb 1890 at Spanish Fort," shows the area where Bayou St. John flowed into Lake Pontchartrain, guarded by a fort since colonial times. Water traffic destined for the rear of the old city would pass through this mouth, sail up the bayou, then turn into Carondelet Canal at the present-day intersection of Jefferson Davis Parkway and Lafitte Street, to arrive and deposit at the turning basin on Basin Street. The ruins of a colonial-era fort may be seen here today, though the site is now a half-mile inland. *Photographer unknown, New Orleans Views Collection, UNO Special Collections*

area, were unveiled for the section near Claiborne Avenue, and in June of that year, the general area was envisioned as a possible site for a major new stadium for the New Orleans Saints. But for now, Governor Carondelet's ambitious project is still apparent, even decades after its elimination. Ironically, the filling of the canal made the former channel slightly higher (one to three feet above m.s.l.) than its adjacent neighborhoods, which fall below sea level in some areas. The canal that gave Basin Street and Canal Street their widths, names, and character helped connect New Orleans with the outside world for well over a century, and still forms a remnant imprint upon the geography of the modern city.

The New Basin Canal, 1832-1950   The expanding economy of New Orleans in the early 1830s inspired a rigorous competition among businessmen to find and exploit commercial opportunities in the strategically located port city. This rivalry extended into the ethnic dimension in multicultural New Orleans, where recently arrived Americans in Faubourg St. Mary and upriver neighborhoods competed with the Creoles in the old city and lower faubourgs. Lake and coastal trade became a treasured prize in this rivalry, such that in 1831 the monopoly enjoyed by Carondelet Canal was challenged by the entrepreneurs who built the Pontchartrain Railroad on Elysian Fields Avenue in the Faubourg Marigny. American businessmen in Faubourg St. Mary responded by forming the New Orleans Canal and Banking Company to connect their faubourg with the lake, well on the American side of town. Not to be outdone, investors in the old city organized the Lake Borgne Navigation Company to excavate a canal to that lake, while farther downriver in St. Bernard Parish, another group formed the St. Bernard Railroad Company (1834) to connect their community with Lake Borgne. The Pontchartrain Railroad weighed back in by proposing to extend their line far into the marshes of eastern New Orleans.[150] All these plans save one fell by the wayside, in large part because of the Panic of 1837.

---
150. Reed, 34-38.

1. This space on Basin Street was occupied by Carondelet Canal's turning basin for over 140 years.

2. Next to that site is the former Southern Railway System office, seen here behind a statue of Central American liberator Francisco Morazon. The railway office postdates the canal but exists because of it: railroad tracks utilized the canal's right-of-way through the crowded neighborhoods of the Sixth Ward and Faubourg Tremé; curving near the turning basin, the trains passed by St. Louis Cemetery No. 1 and the rollicking brothels of Storyville and pulled into the beautiful Southern Railway Station at Basin and Canal. It must have been quite a trip. (The wreath at the base of the statue was left by patriotic Hondurans on their Independence Day, September 15. New Orleans is home to one of the largest expatriate Honduran communities.)

3. The swath of concrete from the upper left to the upper center of this photograph marks the foot of Carondelet Canal; its turning basin was located in the area to the upper right of St. Louis Cemetery No. 1. The Iberville Housing Development (foreground), built in 1941, replaced the slums that operated as Storyville from 1897 to 1917. This area was suggested in 2001 as a possible site for a Saints football stadium.

4. Looking down the former bed of Carondelet Canal at the North Broad Avenue intersection, 207 years after the canal's excavation by slaves and prisoners. The rear of the old city is straight ahead; the "headwaters" of Bayou St. John is directly behind. Although the Spanish-colonial-era canal has been gone for decades, its imprint is still evident: city-owned land lies to the left of the fence, where the canal once passed; a part of the adjacent right-of-way at right was owned by a railroad company, which once ran tracks down the convenient corridor into downtown.

5. Lakeside of North Broad, this drainage canal parallels the disappeared navigation canal, recollecting one of the functions of the old waterway. Note the fence at right, marking the former canal bed.

6. This is the "headwaters" of Bayou St. John, located at North Jefferson Davis Parkway and Lafitte Avenue. From this point, Carondelet Canal extended in a straight shot to the rear of the original city. The open spaces along Lafitte Avenue (trees in distant center) mark its corridor. Here, for well over a century, watercraft of all sorts navigated through the marshes on voyages from the backdoor of the Crescent City to points around Lake Pontchartrain, the Gulf Coast, and beyond. *Photographs by author, 1999-2001*

The exception was the New Orleans Canal and Banking Company, which capitalized in 1831 with the substantial sum of $4 million "solely because of the crying demand for an outlet from the flourishing little city to the shores of Lake Pontchartrain."[151] Its charter called for the construction of "a canal from some part of the city or suburbs of New Orleans, above Poydras street to the Lake Pontchartrain," measuring no less than 60 feet wide, accommodating vessels with a six-foot draft, terminating in a basin, and lined with a levee and paved toll road—all within six years.[152] This colossal undertaking would dwarf Carondelet Canal in length, width, and depth and trace a straighter path to the lake, without the twists and turns of Bayou St. John. A six-mile, 300-foot-wide right-of-way was purchased through city land and parts of the Macarty, Redon, and Augusta plantations, to accommodate the new canal. With a turning basin on present-day South Rampart Street about four blocks above Lee Circle, the canal would run, in three segments, across the Mid-City swamps, through the Metairie Ridge, then straight to the lake. Its first mile from the turning basin would follow the boundary between the former Delord-Sarpy/Duplantier plantation and Saulet plantation, preserving this historical border in the landscape,[153] and continue in a straight line to the middle-of-town marshland spot where extant streets were projected to converge, above which it would angle one more time before heading for the lake. The route would give merchants on the American side of town a competitive advantage by allowing them to circumvent the Creoles' downtown facilities in transporting between the city and the lake. Building materials comprised a chief import from the rural communities across the lake, and the rapidly developing American Sector (Faubourg St. Mary) demanded ample supplies of these goods.

But who would dig this tremendous trench through the backcountry? Local labor was sparse and generally uninterested in the dangerous, low-paying work. Enslaved labor was considered too valuable in agriculture to squander on such treacherous toil. So the New Orleans Canal and Banking Company dipped into the labor pool that nineteenth-century corporate American would often rely on: the desperate indigents of Ireland and their brethren already arrived on the shores of the New World. Thousands of sons of Erin were recruited locally, nationally, and internationally, to serve as "ditchers" in New Orleans.[154] The frightful voyage and the back-breaking dollar-a-day work reflected on just how wretched their conditions must have been back home—and this was *before* the Famine. Work commenced in 1832, a year in which nearly one out of every six New Orleanians died of yellow fever and cholera. An even higher death rate would beleaguer the Irishmen during the six-year excavation of the New Orleans Canal.

Digging entirely by hand and wheelbarrow, the Irishmen excavated a series of basins along the route, then connected them by removing the separating walls. The first half, from the turning basin to the Metairie Ridge, was completed in August 1834; a year later, the remaining portion from the ridge to the lake was completed. By 1838, a million dollars had been expended to dig a canal 60 feet wide at water surface, 3.17 miles long, and deep enough for vessels drawing six feet, for which the New Orleans Canal and Banking Company charged $0.375 per ton for passage.[155] At this time, the canal was turned over to the state; the New Orleans Canal and Banking Company eventually separated, becoming Canal Bank (which would operate until 1933). It took an additional decade after 1838 to expand the canal to its full dimensions of 100 feet wide and 12 feet deep, paralleled with a levee, roads, and right-of-way that measured 100 feet on each side. A dramatized description written a century later provides a sense of the miserable conditions suffered during the construction, as well as the dismay still felt by New Orleanians over the magnitude of this tragedy: "The tale survives that, amazing as it sounds, some 20,000 Irishmen died of the cholera that broke out among them, and that some 8000 survived who drove that ditch through the muck amid the dying, and buried the dead in the 'back dumps' by covering them with the wheelbarrow loads of muck they shoved up slanting planks out of the big ditch from which handpumps strove to drain the seeping water so men could work."[156] It is more likely that 6,000-10,000 died during the project, many of whom were interred in

unmarked backswamp graves. Violence arose among the various labor gangs competing for work on other projects in the city.[157] Wretched as they were, the employment opportunities helped establish the Irish community in New Orleans, which from the riverside slums of the Irish Channel slowly but surely began its ascent from the bottom rung of New Orleans society.

The New Orleans Canal, known widely as the New Basin Canal to distinguish it from Carondelet Canal ("Old Basin Canal"), was a success. For decades, the state-run waterway brought to the city a steady stream of goods such as sand, gravel, and shell for fill; lumber, firewood, and charcoal; fruits, vegetables, cotton, and seafood; and myriad other products and merchandise from the Lake Pontchartrain basin and Gulf Coast. At times, "schooners, luggers, barges, and tugs almost filled the canal from bank to bank,"[158] creating an impressive vista across the open marshes as the vessels approached the bustling port city from its rear door. In 1893-94, for example, the canal was visited by 3,367 vessels carrying 14 million feet of logs, almost 7 million bricks, hundreds of thousands of barrels of charcoal, sand, and resin, and 10,000 cords of firewood, to list but some of its receipts.[159] When the great cypress trees of the swamps southwest of Lake Pontchartrain were felled in the late nineteenth century, it was through the New Basin Canal that those logs reached the city. Countless historic houses in New Orleans today contain wood milled at the many lumber-related businesses (twenty-three in 1883) lining the canal from Claiborne to the turning basin. Tolls charged for tonnage as well as for use of the bridges and related facilities kept the operation financially sound. The regional access provided by the New Basin Canal directly aided the growth of Faubourg St. Mary and uptown New Orleans, delivering a severe but not fatal blow to Carondelet Canal and the Pontchartrain Railroad[160] (another product of Irish labor) in the increasingly *passé* Creole part of town.

This photograph, captioned "New Orleans Feb 1890 Road to Lake Pontchartrain On left is jungle and swamp—On right is the canal and then more swamp," shows the Shell Road and the New Basin Canal in what is now probably in the vicinity of the Lakeview neighborhood. *Photographer unknown, New Orleans Views Collection, UNO Special Collections*

151. Canal Bank and Trust Company, 6-7.
152. Thompson, 24-25.
153. City Planning and Zoning Commission, 23.
154. Niehaus, *The Irish in New Orleans,* 44-47. The Irish drawn to New Orleans in the 1830s-40s, in large part to dig the New Basin Canal, greatly influenced the demographics as well as the geography of the city. Their numbers made New Orleans a white-dominant city in the mid-1830s for the first time since its earliest years, a status it would keep until the mid-1970s. Niehaus, "The New Irish," 388.
155. *Gibson's Guide and Directory,* 237-38.
156. Frost.

157. Niehaus, *The Irish in New Orleans,* 46.
158. Frost.
159. Jackson, 154-55.
160. Reed, Merl E., 37, and Janssen, 66.

Left scene: Dashed yellow line traces the path of the New Basin Canal through the gradually developing backswamps of New Orleans in 1908. (Subdivisions depicted in the top half of this map are mostly speculative: these areas were not developed until decades later, and some were never developed, instead becoming City Park.) The 1998 aerial photograph on the right shows the same area today, in which the Pontchartrain Expressway and West End/Pontchartrain Boulevard follow the former canal bed. *Map by author; historical map courtesy Perry-Castañeda Library Map Collection, University of Texas at Austin; aerial image courtesy U.S. Geological Survey*

This 1922 aerial photograph is one of the few nadir (straight-down) views of the New Basin Canal taken before any of it had been filled (outlined in yellow). Note the presence of as-yet undeveloped land in Mid-City. The 1994 view of the same area shows the vast changes in this area, the least of which is the Superdome and interstates. *Map by author; aerial photographs courtesy the Port of New Orleans and U.S. Geological Survey*

More than a waterway, the New Basin Canal was in fact a bimodal transportation corridor through the low-lands to the lake, lined in 1838 with a fine shell road on the upper bank, a towpath on the lower side, and a levee, connecting the turning basin at Mobile Landing on the edge of Faubourg St. Mary with a jetty-protected harbor (complete with hotel) on the shores of Lake Pontchartrain.[161] In later years, railroads also utilized parts of the corridor, and still do. The Shell Road became a popular route for Sunday rides and horseracing (giving rise to the old harness-racing expression, "2:40 on the Shell Road," as in, "He was traveling like . . . "), and the terminus of the corridor at the lake marked the location of the prestigious Southern Yacht Club and West End resort. West End, formerly New Lake End, was built in the 1870s upon an artificial embankment—a forerunner to the lakefront project of 1926—constructed near the mouth of the New Basin Canal, and formed part of the leisure scene of turn-of-the-century New Orleans. Its neighboring lakeside resorts, Spanish Fort and Milneburg, shared a common origin with West End in that all, quite logically, were constructed where a transportation corridor from the city terminated at the lake. West End was served by the New Basin Canal; Spanish Fort was accessed by Bayou St. John and Carondelet Canal; and Milneburg was reached by the Pontchartrain Railroad. For all three transportation corridors, topography had to be altered to penetrate the swamps. For all three lakeside resorts, structures had to be built on embankments or upon stilts and piers to combat the low-lying terrain.[162] The New Basin Canal also affected urban demographic patterns well into the twentieth century: according to a 1917 population map, areas below the canal from its basin to Metairie Ridge (City Park Avenue) were roughly five times more populous than areas on its uptown side.[163]

Like Carondelet Canal, the right-of-way of the New Basin Canal is still richly evident in the streetscape today, hosting the Pontchartrain Expressway from the I-10/610 split to the Superdome. Seen here is the point at which the canal bed crossed the naturally elevated Metairie Ridge (now City Park Avenue; note Metairie Cemetery at upper right). Above is Interstate 10. This area was once a rural outpost; later, it was home to racetracks and cemeteries too large to be located in the city proper. Today, this vicinity comprises the well-kept neighborhoods of Lakewood, Navarre, and Mid-City. *Photograph by author, 1999*

The New Basin Canal, dug by hand in 1832-38 mostly by Irish immigrants, connected Faubourg St. Mary (Central Business District) with the lake for over a century. Its turning basin, filled in 1937, occupied the neutral ground and surrounding asphalt that is now Loyola Avenue between Julia and Howard, near the base of the Plaza Tower, from which this photograph was taken. *Photograph by author, 2000*

(Upper left) The reclamation of the lakefront in 1926-34 extended the canal into the lake; originally, it met the lake at the present-day intersection of West Robert E. Lee and West End Boulevard. The relatively recent extension of the canal through the lakefront is the last surviving portion of the New Basin Canal.
(Right) In its last two decades, the New Basin Canal outflowed into Lake Pontchartrain at this point in West End, marked by the historic New Canal Lighthouse.
(Lower left) Entrance to the former New Basin Canal from Lake Pontchartrain. *Photographs by author, 2000*

161. *Gibson's Guide and Directory,* 237-38.
162. Baughman, 5-11.
163. Allison; see "Map of New Orleans Showing Street Car Lines and Density of Population."

The New Basin Canal served as an important industrial and transportation corridor well into the twentieth century, but competition from the Industrial Canal, roads, and railways eventually devalued its services. Natural resources and building materials from the North Shore were no longer as valuable to the city as they once were. In 1936, the Louisiana legislature passed a constitutional amendment to close the century-old waterway. Filling of its turning basin began in July 1937; by 1938, the portion between Claiborne and South Rampart was covered over. The remaining section functioned until after World War II but was finally filled in by the early 1950s. The topographic alteration that cost thousands of Irishmen their lives, affecting the growth and prosperity of the city in its formative years, was reversed but not erased from the landscape. During the post-World War II years, when the Mississippi River Bridge was in the planning phase, a portion of the canal's former right-of-way was selected as the corridor for the Pontchartrain Expressway, the first major modern superhighway in the city. Coming in from Jefferson Parish, the highway would attain the former canal bed in the vicinity of the Metairie Ridge and follow the path excavated by the Irishmen straight into downtown New Orleans and over the Mississippi River Bridge (1958) to the west bank. The route made sense: the open swath of the old canal bed through crowded neighborhoods allowed planners to minimize demolition and right-of-way acquisition costs for at least a portion of the route, from the modern-day I-10/610 split to the Superdome. Lakeside of the split, the former bed of the New Basin Canal is now the spacious grassy neutral ground between Pontchartrain and West End Boulevard, owned by the Orleans Levee District. Beyond Robert E. Lee Boulevard, in the lakefront area that was constructed in 1926-34, the final stretch of the waterway still exists, now lined with pleasure craft instead of tugs but still neighbored by the 1850s Southern Yacht Club.

Geographical Impact of the New Basin Canal upon Modern New Orleans		
Segment of Canal	Mileage	Current Status
Turning basin to South Claiborne Avenue	0.5 miles	Footprint of the turning basin is now erased from landscape, occupied by asphalt at the convergence of Julia, Loyola, and South Rampart. Parallel to the former canal bed (though not on top of it) run the railroad tracks leading to the train station.
South Claiborne Avenue to present-day Marguerite Road, north of Metairie Cemetery	3.75 miles	Footprint preserved in the landscape as Interstate 10. The southern end of this segment also reiterates the boundary between the former plantations of Delord-Sarpy/Duplantier and Saulet.
Marguerite Road to present-day West Robert E. Lee Boulevard (original lakefront)	2.0 miles	Footprint preserved as open field between Pontchartrain Boulevard and West End Boulevard.
West Robert E. Lee Boulevard to modern lakefront (post-1934)	0.5 miles	Footprint preserved as last remaining channel of New Basin Canal (though not part of original 1830s-era excavation), associated with Orleans Marina, West End Park, and Southern Yacht Club.

In 1990, the Irish Cultural Society of New Orleans dedicated a Celtic cross monument and park at West End Boulevard and Downs Street, to commemorate the terrible suffering of the immigrants who built the canal and to celebrate the contributions of the Irish to New Orleans. "This is the only such monument in New Orleans to the Irish who helped develop this city," read the flier distributed for the ceremony.[164] Perhaps this is true, but then again, the fruit of their labor is still conspicuous in the urban landscape of modern New Orleans, utilized by millions of motorists annually as the Interstate-10/Pontchartrain Expressway corridor and forming a great entranceway into the heart of the city that the Irish helped enrich through the success of their canal and a multitude of other significant contributions.

The Inner Harbor Navigational Canal (Industrial Canal), 1918-23-Present   For 200 years, the desire to connect the Mississippi River with Lake Pontchartrain via a navigable waterway went unfulfilled. The Company of the West instructed Chief Engineer Perrier to build such a canal in 1718; three years later, a river/lake canal was sketched halfway between present-day Iberville and Canal Street in what may be the earliest city plat, *Plan de la Ville de la Nouvelle Orleans projetteé* [sic] *en Mars 1721*.[165] These and subsequent plans, the later Carondelet Canal, Canal Marigny, New Basin Canal, and other efforts, all failed to make the connection primarily for reasons of engineering (a technologically complex lock system would be needed to account for the different water levels of the river and lake) as well as economics and politics. One design, entitled *Map Plan and Profiles annexed to the Report on a Canal Destined to Connect the Mississippi with Lake Pontchartrain* (1827), proposed to extend the Canal Marigny up present-day Elysian Fields Avenue to the lake, but that path was instead utilized by the famous Pontchartrain Railroad from 1831 to 1932.[166] A canal connection of sorts was finally made in 1886-1904, when Bayou Dupre was widened into the Lake Borgne Canal (today's Violet Canal), connecting English Turn Bend with Lake Borgne in St. Bernard Parish. At seven feet deep and sixty feet wide, with a forty-foot-wide-by-twenty-five-foot-high lock, the 6.75-mile-long Lake Borgne Canal (opened 1890) was the closest to date that man had come to connecting river and sea in the region, transporting through its lock vessels bearing lumber, coal, and fish.[167] Limited in space and distant from the city, the canal had little lasting impact on the region and is now used by fishermen. In the latter decades of the 1800s, few major engineering improvements were pursued to make New Orleans more competitive on the national shipping scene, at a time when eastern transportation networks had aggressed substantially into the Mississippi Valley once commercially controlled by New Orleans. "Big British ships, deep water, the Erie Canal, and the five trans-Mississippi Basin railways have established the commercial supremacy of New York," pointed out one canal activist in 1885, "while the want of deep water, big ships, and the improvement of the Mississippi River underlie the decadence of the commercial prosperity of New Orleans."[168] Some of these wants would be alleviated by an ambitious new deepwater canal with wharf space between the river and lake.

City leaders began clamoring for the likes of this envisioned waterway in the 1910s, inspired by the recent opening of the Panama Canal, the war effort, and a canal planned to connect Chicago with the Mississippi. "The Illinois-Lake Michigan Canal and the New Orleans Industrial Canal are complementary links in a new system of waterways connecting the upper Valley through the Mississippi River and New Orleans with the Gulf and the Panama Canal, [giving] the differential to the Valley cities in trade with the markets of the Orient, our own west coast, and South America," declared the *New Orleans Item* in 1916.[169] Advancing the strategic advantage of geographical situation that Bienville recognized two centuries prior, New Orleans received authorization from the state in July 1914 to locate and build a deepwater canal linking the Mississippi River and Lake Pontchartrain, expediting the maritime connection between New Orleans and the world.

> "The immense advantage of New Orleans and one of the real factors to make it a great industrial center, is the nearness of raw products. . . . But these advantages are nearly all as yet potential only. . . . Nature has placed them at the disposal of New Orleans. Will the people of New Orleans depend on nature alone, or will they assist nature's efforts with real scientific planning and development?"
> —James Z. George (*Why New Orleans Needs an Industrial Canal and Terminal*, New Orleans: Tulane University Special Collections, ca. 1915)

The streamlining of shipping routes was by no means the only motivation or goal behind the project. A committee organized in 1918 identified additional benefits that the Industrial Canal would bring to New Orleans: the creation of shipbuilding sites within a protected, fixed-level harbor; the development of new water frontage that could be privately held (river frontage in New Orleans was traditionally held in the public trust); the creation of space for new facilities to handle, store, and transport cargo; and the extension of the Intracoastal Canal.[170] In May 1918, the corridor for the canal was selected—a swath 5.3 miles long and up to 1,600 feet wide (right-of-way width; the canal would be much narrower) located roughly 2 miles downriver

164. Irish Cultural Society of New Orleans.

165. Map reproduced in Wilson, "Early History of Faubourg St. Mary," 4.
166. The construction of this early railroad and its Port Pontchartrain entailed its own amount of topographic alteration and impact on river/lake transportation. The right-of-way of this old line, long removed from the landscape, explains why Elysian Fields Avenue today traces a perfectly straight line from river to lake, the only thoroughfare in New Orleans with that characteristic. Reed, 34-35.
167. Dabney, *One Hundred Great Years*, 290, and U.S. Army Corps of Engineers, *Research Design for the Violet Site Alternative*, 55.
168. Cowdon, 2 (introduction).
169. As quoted by Dabney, *The Industrial Canal and Inner Harbor of New Orleans*, 8-9.
170. Dabney, *The Industrial Canal and Inner Harbor of New Orleans*, 10-12.

and parallel to Elysian Fields Avenue, where a similar canal was foreseen ninety years earlier. The selected corridor boasted definite advantages, being (1) within Orleans Parish limits, (2) across a relatively narrow land strip between river and lake, (3) mostly undeveloped, (4) convenient to existing shipping lanes and port activity, and (5) either city-owned or readily acquirable. Its riverside half followed the tract of land owned by the Ursuline Nuns since 1821 (plus adjacent Convent Street and some nearby blocks), which the nuns, "with exceptional generosity,"[171] donated to the city in 1911 before they moved uptown. The orientation of the nuns' property and the surrounding street network in the Ninth Ward (present-day Bywater and Holy Cross neighborhoods) determined the northeasterly orientation of the lower portion of the Industrial Canal; once the corridor got past the developed area along the natural levee, designers doglegged the path in a northwesterly direction to achieve a shorter route to the lake. Thus physical, historical, economic, and political geography all played roles in siting the Industrial Canal.

> "The 'Industrial Canal' was primarily conceived because it will: (a) shorten the distance from the city to the Gulf of Mexico by means of Lake Pontchartrain, and (b) because it will afford deep-water locations for manufacturing plants, shipbuilding plants, and other similar enterprises.
>
> "[The construction of the Industrial Canal entails] four separate parts: (a) The Lake End, comprising the bridge for the Northeastern Railroad, and the Doullut & Williams shipyard; (b) The Bridge for the Louisville and Nashville Railroad near Gentilly Terrace; (c) Florida Walk, at which point is located the bridge for the Public Belt Railroad and the siphon for the Florida Walk drainage canal, probably the largest siphon in the world; and (d) The River End of the Canal, about 2000 feet from which point the huge lock is constructed, and the St. Claude Bridge for the Louisiana Southern Railroad and the New Orleans electric street railways."
> —Hibernia Bank & Trust Company (*The New Orleans Inner-Harbor Navigation Canal*, New Orleans: Tulane University Special Collections, 1921, 3-4)

With the Dock Board in charge and the renowned George W. Goethals Company as consulting engineers, ground was broken on June 6, 1918. Digging a major canal through a swamp connecting a powerful river and a vast lake presented numerous engineering challenges. For one, levees had to be built along the new excavations. A lock was necessary since the two water bodies maintained different and changing levels; turning basins were also needed to accommodate larger vessels. Dredges had to enter the dig site via the lake and Bayou Bienvenue to excavate the canal because boring in directly from the Mississippi was too risky. Waterlogged soils proved challenging to restrain from sliding back into the excavation, and the occasional ancient cypress log embedded in the muck jammed the suction dredges and slowed progress.[172] The recently installed drainage system at Florida Walk had to be siphoned beneath the canal, and existing railroads had to be rerouted. Then the Dock Board decided to augment the size of the canal between the lock and the lake to a depth of 30 feet, a width at the top of 300 feet, and a bottom width of 150 feet, double the size of the canal originally planned. With labor gangs, mechanized excavators, pile drivers, dredges, dynamite, and other implements, the largest construction project in New Orleans history was rapidly redefining the geography of the Crescent City. The initial channel, from the lock to the lake, was completed in September 1919.[173] Now attention turned to the lock.

The great lock was the centerpiece of the Industrial Canal, located about two thousand feet in from the Mississippi River and restraining its powerful, average-ten-foot-high waters from pouring into the sea-level lake. It symbolized the point at which, like the intersection of Bayou Road and Bayou St. John in the 1700s, the interior river world met the exterior sea world. Here was one of the geographical nodes that epitomized New Orleans' role in the world (see page 167). The lock was also an engineering landmark, one of the largest locks in the nation at the time and built upon soils far less stable than any previous project of this type. Six hundred forty feet long, only seventy-four feet wide, and originally excavated to a depth of fifty feet during

construction, the five-gate motorized lock was designed to withhold the Mississippi's range of river stages, which could span over twenty feet.

New Orleans finally accomplished its dream of connecting lake and river on January 29, 1923, when work on the canal was completed. Eight days later, the fire tug *Samson* carried Gov. John M. Parker and distinguished guests through the lock, opening the canal for navigation.[174] At the May 5, 1923, dedication ceremony of the Industrial Canal, attended by thousands, Governor Parker declared that the waterway would "equip New Orleans to be, in the broadest sense, the gateway of the Mississippi Valley for its interchange of products with the markets of the world."[175]

Soon after the canal's completion, the Dock Board adapted it into an inner harbor, accommodating not just the passage of vessels but their docking and cargo needs. This change reflected the sentiment that the dispersed, end-to-end nature of Mississippi River wharves would someday necessitate the development of compact, economical dock space somewhere other than the river.[176] The six-block-long shedded Galvez Street Wharf was

Lock of the Industrial Canal under construction, June 3, 1920. *The Port of New Orleans*

added in 1924, and the Florida Avenue Wharf was developed in 1942 as New Orleanians worked arduously for the war effort. Part of that effort occurred at the Gentilly Road section of the Industrial Canal, where the legendary eccentric shipbuilder Andrew Jackson Higgins operated a sprawling facility in which LCM tank carriers, FS ships, and PT boats were built for the World War II effort.[177] Another major addition to the canal came with the excavation of the Intracoastal Waterway (1930s) and the Mississippi River-Gulf Outlet (1960s), giving ships direct sea access to the Industrial Canal sans usage of the river or the lake. In recent decades, the immense France Road Container Terminal Berths and other facilities were constructed, furthering the trend of the migration of port activity away from the Mississippi River. Since the 1930s, the Industrial Canal has worn a second hat as a segment of the Intracoastal Waterway, the peri-coastal barge route running from Texas to Florida.

---

171. U.S. Army Corps of Engineers, New Orleans District, *Architectural and Archeological Investigations,* 83. The Ursulines, in New Orleans since 1727, moved their convent from the ca.-1750 building that still stands on Chartres Street to this eighty-acre tract starting in 1824. After the donation, the nuns relocated in 1912 to their new uptown campus at South Claiborne Avenue and State Street, still very much in service. The Ursuline Academy has been in continual operation since 1727, the oldest girls' school in the nation. For an exact description of the site for the Industrial Canal, see Mayoralty of New Orleans, *New Orleans Industrial and Ship Canal.*

172. This problem was resolved by none other than Albert Baldwin Wood, the genius engineer who helped make the New Orleans drainage system the best in the world. Wood adapted his centrifugal pump impeller, which he designed to handle debris within the sewerage system, to the dredges. Dramatic increases in productivity were realized immediately after installation. Dabney, *The Industrial Canal and Inner Harbor of New Orleans,* 28.

173. Ibid., 17-30.

174. "The Marriage of Mississippi and Pontchartrain," *The Literary Digest,* (New Orleans: Science and Invention Section, Tulane University Special Collections, April 14, 1923), and Dabney, *The Industrial Canal and Inner Harbor of New Orleans,* 40-47.

175. As quoted in Bolding, 53-54.

176. Roberts, 324-25.

177. Mullener, "Ramped Up For War."

After envisioning it for over two hundred years, New Orleans finally connected the Mississippi River and Lake Pontchartrain with the construction of the Inner Harbor Navigational Canal, known more commonly as the Industrial Canal, in 1918-23. The motivation for the massive engineering project included the streamlining of shipping routes, the creation of shipbuilding sites within a protected harbor, the development of new water frontage that could be privately held, and the creation of space for new facilities to handle, store, and transport cargo. This photograph from the mid-1920s provides a rather jarring view of the impact of the recently completed canal on the delicate marshes of lakeside New Orleans, largely undeveloped at the time except for Gentilly Ridge (center left). The New Orleans crescent appears at upper right. *U.S. Army Corps of Engineers*

1952 **1998**

The Industrial Canal and the adjoining Intracoastal Waterway/Mississippi River-Gulf Outlet Canal succeeded in creating expansive and modernized dock space but did not fully draw port facilities off the Mississippi River, as envisioned in the 1970s. In the process, it fueled the development of eastern New Orleans. The patterns of urban development seen in the 1952 aerial image are correlated to topography: the older neighborhoods of Bywater and Holy Cross appear on the natural levee near the Mississippi; the swath of development perpendicular to the canal at upper center follows the Gentilly/Sauvage Ridge; and the subdivisions on the lakefront (extreme upper left) were built upon reclaimed upland. By 1998, the entire swath had been developed. Note the turning basin at the junction of the Industrial Canal and Mississippi River-Gulf Outlet Canal. *Map by author; aerial images courtesy U.S. Geological Survey*

Lock of the Industrial Canal at its junction with the Mississippi River, viewed from Algiers looking toward Lake Pontchartrain. The fork of the canal heading toward the right was, at the time of this photograph (1950s), the Intracoastal Waterway; it was later expanded to also become the Mississippi River-Gulf Outlet Canal. Note the extraordinary narrowness of the lock at the mouth of the canal: an engineering marvel for its time, the lock has since become a serious bottleneck for ship traffic and is currently slated for a controversial expansion. The historic neighborhoods of Bywater and Holy Cross border the canal. *U.S. Army Corps of Engineers*

Today, eighty years after the most dramatic alteration of New Orleans topography and geography, the Industrial Canal (or Inner Harbor Navigational Canal, as it is officially known) is—according to port authorities, waterways operators, and the Army Corps of Engineers—a victim of its own success, while watchdog groups and neighborhood associations dismiss it as a functional antique not worth the cost of improving. The canal's landmark lock, still in operation since the 1920s, has formed a bottleneck restricting barge movement through the channel, forcing barges to park and wait up to thirty-six hours along the riverbank while traffic files through the narrow passage. A view of the mechanism from the St. Claude Avenue Bridge reveals its startlingly constricted proportions (seventy-four feet), less than a quarter the width of the main channel.

The Army Corps of Engineers proposes to triple the width of the current bottleneck and relocate the lock to a widened portion of the canal about a half-mile lakeside of its present location, a controversial and disruptive project that could take twice longer than the original project and cost over twenty-five times more,[178] but one deemed critical to keeping the canal and the port up to competitive standards. In defending the expansion, the Corps used 1990 cargo data (23.5 million tons shipped through the lock) and projected a 1.3 percent annual increase, a scenario that would tip a cost-benefit analysis in favor of proceeding with the project. But opponents such as the Holy Cross Neighborhood Association, who dread years of noise and disruption as well as an adverse impact on their historic neighborhood, pointed to actual data from the 1990s revealing a steady 2 percent annual *decrease* in usage, down to 19.4 million tons in 1999. The Corps countered that the steady drop-off reflects barge pilots avoiding the six- to twenty-two-hour wait at the narrow lock by avoiding the Industrial Canal altogether; opponents responded with data showing that some canal usage actually increased during the 1990s.

Infamously narrow lock of the Industrial Canal, a major factor in port-activity trends between the Mississippi River and the canal since the latter's completion in 1923. *Photograph by author, 2001*

In the same manner that the Industrial Canal represents a geographical crux of shipping between the Mississippi Basin and the Gulf of Mexico, the canal represents a flash point for broad shipping trends determined by the counteracting variables of population growth, economic expansion, decentralization of industrial plants, changes in fossil-fuel usage, agricultural and industrial patterns, growth of Latin American exports, and technological development.[179] While various forecasts produce different cost-benefit ratios, most would agree that the bottleneck has been a burden to the canal, and others would add that the canal's overall performance has not met the Dock Board's original expectations. It did not, for example, foster large-scale development of industrial manufacturing facilities, and it did not by any means replace the Mississippi River as the main site of the city's wharves. And, ironically, after 200 years of anticipation, the first canal to connect the river and the lake did not reroute shipping traffic from and to New Orleans via Lake Pontchartrain (or, more significantly, the later Mississippi-River Gulf Outlet Canal) to the Gulf of Mexico to the extent originally predicted. Instead, the Industrial Canal's success came in the form of the development of dockside freight-handling facilities for vessels traveling the Intracoastal Waterway.[180]

The topographic alteration that created the Industrial Canal also introduced a bold new element to modern New Orleans' cityscape, literally cutting Orleans Parish in half. The canal serves as *the* threshold between the nebulous nowhere of eastern New Orleans and the distinctive sense of place of the main part of the city. Its presence impacted the design and configuration of the lakefront project of 1926-34 and the new neighborhoods developed subsequently. The lofty bridges that carry vehicular traffic over the Industrial Canal provide spectacular views of the New Orleans skyline—and infamous slowdowns for rush-hour traffic. Along the canal, the intense concentration of ships, cranes, gantries, and towers creates a complex port vista that recalls, in function if not in form, the bustling scenes along the French Quarter levee in times past. (Many I-10 motorists unfamiliar with the city confuse the busy canal with the Mississippi!) Most significantly, the Industrial Canal is a direct descendent of New Orleans' original purpose—to serve as a nexus between the river and the sea—reminding us that there is an authentic and important city beneath the increasingly thick layer of clichés and myths shrouding New Orleans in the eyes of the world.

The Mississippi River-Gulf Outlet Canal, 1958-68-Present The most recent manifestation of the seaway movement—"the realization of a century-old dream for a shorter and safer water passage from New Orleans to the open sea"[181]—came with the excavation of the Mississippi River-Gulf Outlet Canal in the marshes of eastern New Orleans and St. Bernard Parish. Cleverly abbreviated as "MR-GO," this seventy-five-mile-long[182] waterway connects the Industrial Canal and the Gulf of Mexico with a 500-foot-wide channel excavated through the delicate marshes deposited by the St. Bernard Delta around the time of Christ. The route of the MR-GO vaguely follows the millennia-old former path of the Mississippi as it empties into the sea (actually the Breton Sound, an obscure backwater of the Gulf of Mexico) about halfway between the Mississippi Gulf Coast and the bird-foot delta of the modern Mississippi River. The 15 percent of the MR-GO that is within Orleans Parish actually predates the rest of the waterway, excavated as part of the Gulf Intracoastal Waterway (GIWW) that forms a protected shipping lane along America's "third coast," from Apalachee Bay, Florida, to the Mexican border.[183] The slender channel was greatly enlarged when the MR-GO was developed.

Just as the notion of the Industrial Canal arose with World War I on the horizon, the idea for the MR-GO originated when war clouds gathered again in the early 1940s. Local government authorities and business leaders met with the U.S. Army Corps of Engineers in 1943 and agreed that a tidewater canal would put New Orleans and the Mississippi Valley's vast inland-waterway network back in competition with routes that utilized the Panama Canal for east-west shipping. Participants disagreed, however, on the route of the seaway: some advocated an east-bank path from the Industrial Canal to the Gulf of Mexico; others favored a west-bank route from the Intracoastal Canal to Grand Isle. The war effort put the plan on the backburner until the late 1940s, when local leaders and politicians in Washington endorsed the construction of New Orleans' connection with the sea. Funding was lost, however, when Sen. Russell Long withdrew an amendment that would have authorized $67 million for the project; he sensed that advocates of the competing St. Lawrence Seaway would ruin the effort. Similar legislation met the same fate twice again by 1953. "Apparently, upper Mississippi Valley supporters of the Louisiana seaway were more interested in the St. Lawrence seaway, which New Orleans opposed, and withdrew their votes until the St. Lawrence project passed Congress. After Congressional approval of the St. Lawrence seaway in 1954, opposition to the New Orleans project faded."[184] It is ironic that two seaways at opposite ends of North America, both connecting former French colonial regions with the sea, would compete with each other in the mid-twentieth century—a competition that reiterated the fact that New Orleans' unrivalled mastery of Mississippi Valley trade through reliance on the Mississippi River was long a thing of the past. A bill for New Orleans' seaway finally passed and was signed into law by President Eisenhower on March 29, 1956.

178. The original canal (1918-23) cost $19 million to build; the canal upgrade is estimated at $500-$600 million and could take ten to twelve years. Various proposals to upgrade the old lock have been circulating for at least three decades; the current plan is vigorously opposed by neighborhood associations, environmentalists, and taxpayer groups, some of whom selected the project for their "25 most wasteful projects" list. Coleman Warner, "Residents Fighting Mad"; Alpert; U.S. Army Corps of Engineers, *The Mitigator;* and Huber, *New Orleans,* 349.
179. Coleman Warner, "Bottleneck."
180. U.S. Army Corps of Engineers, New Orleans District, *Architectural and Archeological Investigations,* 83, and Lewis, 71.

181. Bolding, 49.
182. The MR-GO channel is about seventy-five miles long from its turning basin at the Industrial Canal to its mouth at the edge of the Breton Sound, between the Breton Islands and Grand Gosier Island. However, only forty-five miles pass within the shoreline; the lower thirty miles is a channel beneath the waters of the Breton Sound.
183. The stretch of the GIWW that became the MR-GO in eastern Orleans Parish was planned during the early stages of the Industrial Canal in the 1910s. A map enclosed in the pamphlet from the May 5, 1923, dedication ceremony depicted the future waterway plus two lateral canals parallel to present-day Dwyer and Morrison roads. The latter two were never built. *Inner-Harbor Navigation Canal Dedication Pamphlet,* and U.S. Army Corps of Engineers, New Orleans District, *Water Resources Development in Louisiana,* 133.
184. Bolding, 56-57.

The first phase of the project (1958-59) altered 20 million cubic yards of local topography and bathymetry by enlarging the GIWW between the Industrial Canal and Paris Road, now I-510. Phase two (1959-61) involved the dredging of a narrow access channel from the GIWW to the Breton Sound, affecting 27 million cubic yards in St. Bernard Parish. The third and fourth phases (1960-65 and finalized in 1968) enlarged this access channel to its full dimensions, from Paris Road to the -38-foot bathymetric contour in the Gulf of Mexico, an excavation of 225 million cubic yards of dredged material. Spoil was accumulated on a 4,000-foot-wide strip paralleling the lower MR-GO in St. Bernard Parish, while spoil from the excavation of the spacious turning basin in New Orleans (at the point where the Industrial Canal, MR-GO, and GIWW all intersect) was used to shore up the topography in the area now occupied by the Jourdan Road Terminal.[185] Upon completion, the MR-GO channel measured 36 feet deep and 500 feet wide in its inland stretch and slightly larger in its offshore portion. It eliminated thirty-seven miles from the voyage to New Orleans from the open gulf waters and provided ample opportunities for dockside development within the Port of New Orleans. It also destroyed about eight thousand acres of wetlands. "Sailing time, ship turnaround time, navigation hazards, and congestion all tend to be reduced by the [MR-GO]."[186]

Did the MR-GO live up to expectations? The record is decidedly mixed. Annual traffic on the seaway averaged 7,193,000 tons of freight in 1984-93. But tonnage declined steadily in the 1990s, accounting for 11 percent of Port of New Orleans activity in 1990 down to only 5 percent in 1998.[187] (See page 79.)

In a larger picture, the MR-GO failed to draw the wharves and dockside facilities away from the Mississippi to become the CENTROPORT that was envisioned in the 1970s. At that time, observers predicted that the Mississippi would be free of port facilities by 2000.[188] Instead, by 2000, the vision and the trend had decidedly reversed back to the historical circumstance of riverside wharves. Recognizing the difficulty of large container ships in navigating the MR-GO to dock in the Industrial Canal, the Dock Board decided to create a "mega-wharf" by combining and expanding the uptown terminals at Napoleon and Nashville avenues, at the bottom of the Mississippi River crescent. The trend now is to convert these uptown docks to container wharves, a status once monopolized by Industrial Canal facilities but hindered by narrow and shallow waterways. Currently, the Nashville terminal is the only Mississippi River facility in the Port of New Orleans capable of handling containerized cargo, and, unlike the MR-GO and the Industrial Canal, the deep, wide waters of the river present no bottleneck for large oceangoing vessels. A $300 million redevelopment project of the uptown Napoleon Avenue, Milan Street, and Louisiana Avenue wharves to create containerized facilities is currently under way.[189] While the Industrial Canal and MR-GO have made major gains in relocating the fulcrum of port activity eastward and off the river, a large amount of port activity, including container cargo operations, remains on the Mississippi and will expand there in the near future.

The most ominous legacy of the MR-GO was and is its disastrous impact on the delicate and vulnerable marshland environment. The seaway has eroded to a width of 2,000 feet in places,[190] destroying thousands of acres of wetlands in St. Bernard Parish while constantly silting up and requiring more dredging, costing the federal government about $16 million a year to maintain. Storms and even brisk winds push tides up the canal toward low-lying areas in St. Bernard Parish, threatening them with flooding. The MR-GO also permits salt water from the gulf to intrude upon the brackish and freshwater marsh and swamp ecosystems in Chalmette and eastern New Orleans, converting some areas to unsightly half-dead wastelands. This same plume of salt water invades Lake Pontchartrain, occasionally creating an oxygen-poor water layer near the Industrial Canal that kills organisms and disperses fish. In March 1999, only three decades after its completion, when the MR-GO was predicted to transform the Port of New Orleans, the Army Corps of Engineers and the Environmental Protection Agency proposed its partial closure. If this comes to pass, containerized-cargo ships would utilize the present-day Nashville wharf, the "mega-wharf" under construction between the Napoleon and Louisiana Avenue wharves on the Mississippi River, or a proposed Millennium Port that may be located elsewhere. But bulk-cargo ships would have still have to pass through the narrow 1923 lock that bottlenecks the Industrial Canal.[191] The latest chapter of the New Orleans seaway movement, and the history of topographic change to improve navigation in New Orleans, remains to be written.

185. Brent M. Johnson, 8-9.
186. U.S. Army Corps of Engineers, New Orleans District, *Water Resources Development in Louisiana,* 89-90.
187. Ibid., 90, and U.S. Army Corps of Engineers, *Waterborne Commerce of the United States, Part 2,* 165, 170, 207. See also Schleifstein, "MR-GO Closing Plan."
188. Lewis, 67-75, and Huber, *New Orleans,* 352.
189. Darcé, "Board to Launch First Phase," "Dock Board Chooses Design," and "Cargo Ship a Huge Hit."
190. Turni, "Corps Battles Erosion."
191. Schleifstein, "MR-GO Closing Plan"; Gill, "Goodbye"; Darcé, "Prompt Steps Urged"; and Turni, "Task Force Urges Shutdown."

The Mississippi River-Gulf Outlet (MR-GO) Canal was envisioned in the early 1940s as a means to increase the competitiveness of the Port of New Orleans and the Mississippi Valley's vast inland-waterway network by carving a shortcut from the Industrial Canal to the Gulf of Mexico. It was excavated in 1958-68. Today, the MR-GO's economic record is mixed and its environmental impact decidedly negative; it may be gradually closed off in the near future. *Map by author; Landsat/SPOT satellite image courtesy Louisiana State University*

An oceangoing vessel heading up the MR-GO passes Shell Beach in St. Bernard Parish and approaches New Orleans. In 1999, an average of only three deep-draft ships a day plied the manmade seaway. Originally excavated about 500 feet wide, the MR-GO has eroded to a width of 2,000 feet in some areas. *Photograph by author, 2000*

The Mundane and the Catastrophic: Other Topographic Change in New Orleans

These changes to New Orleans' topography—changes to keep water out, to remove water, to create new land, and to improve navigation—are the macroscopic adjustments that humans have imposed upon the young soils of this old city. They are joined by numerous other projects throughout the region that have endeavored to achieve these four goals. Their impact, of course, goes far beyond the mere movement of soil: the construction of levees allowed new communities to expand into the wilderness; the excavation of canals drew industry and commerce into new areas; the drainage of swamplands enabled thousands of residents to pursue suburban lifestyles. Additional *micro*-scale topographic changes cover nearly every urbanized inch, in the form of artificial landfill and landscaping designed to shore up buildings from the moist and flood-prone soils. Sewage-treatment ponds, lagoons, ornamental lakes, and landscaping in parks (like Monkey Hill in the Audubon Zoo, designed to give local children the rare experience of a hill) represent additional adjustments to the deltaic surface. A typical city block is designed to drain water away from the backyards in the middle and toward the four streets surrounding

Freight Traffic on Port of New Orleans Waterways, 1990-1998

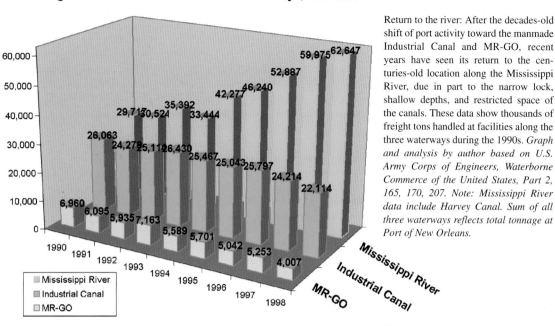

Return to the river: After the decades-old shift of port activity toward the manmade Industrial Canal and MR-GO, recent years have seen its return to the centuries-old location along the Mississippi River, due in part to the narrow lock, shallow depths, and restricted space of the canals. These data show thousands of freight tons handled at facilities along the three waterways during the 1990s. *Graph and analysis by author based on U.S. Army Corps of Engineers, Waterborne Commerce of the United States, Part 2, 165, 170, 207. Note: Mississippi River data include Harvey Canal. Sum of all three waterways reflects total tonnage at Port of New Orleans.*

it, thus making it a square "island" surrounded by street a foot or so lower.[192] Overpasses and underpasses separating roads and railways, constructed in the post-World War II modernization era, provide almost as much topographic relief within a single acre as the entire city boasts in thousands. These are mundane adjustments. At the other end of the spectrum, manmade topographic change in New Orleans and the region has unleashed two forms of natural topographic change—soil subsidence and coastal land loss—that present the potential for catastrophe.

Soil subsidence occurs naturally as wet, loose sediments deposited by periodic floods settle and compact, but the rate of subsidence increases greatly when soils that are normally high in water content are drained of the liquid. Decomposition of organic matter frees up additional space, allowing particles to adjust and settle into the crevices. Like piles of wet towels gradually drained of their moisture, the soil body occupies less and less volume, shrinking and subsiding and lowering anything constructed upon it.[193] At the opposite end of the equation, no new sediments arrive to build up the land because the manmade levees that protect the city from catastrophic floods also deprive it of flood-borne sediment deposition.

Subsidence rates have been measured at about 1.2 millimeters annually in New Orleans over the past 4,400 years, and 10.3 millimeters annually along the Louisiana coast in modern times.[194] Recent research by geodesists at Louisiana State University revealed that benchmarks used in mapping, many of which had not been recalibrated in ten years, have sunk possibly by as much as four feet in southern Louisiana, throwing into question most topographic map data as well as the protection afforded by levees and flood-control projects. The LSU Center for GeoInformatics is currently installing a new network of thirty Continuously Operating Reference Stations to provide precise measurements of subsidence updated every half-minute.

According to the geodesists, some areas in New Orleans are sinking as much as an inch every three years.[195] In a city where a mere two feet of elevation may dictate whether an area was settled in the 1720s or the 1920s, such anthropogenically increased rates represent alarming trends. The rates vary inversely with elevation: high natural levees subside less (because they, being naturally drained, contain less water and organic matter), artificially drained backswamps subside more, and dried peat deposits (which are 95 percent water and organic matter under natural conditions) sink the most. Thus, while old homes in the older natural-levee portion of New Orleans suffer their share of settling, it is the relatively new housing built on concrete slabs in the lakeside lowlands that sustains greater damage. In accordance with a 1987 city requirement, pilings are now used to stabi-

lize slabs under new houses, the same technique that keeps downtown skyscrapers from tumbling.[196] House leveling, or shoring, is big business in New Orleans, and many homeowners are well acquainted with the distressing indications of subsidence: jammed doors, cracks in the brickwork and buckles in the woodwork, floors that send a dropped can of beans rolling crazily across the kitchen. Settling is especially apparent not after heavy rain, when one would think that the soil softens, but during a drought, when the soil dries and compresses. Though subtle, soil subsidence is observable in the cityscape, from the half-sunken vaults in St. Louis No.1 Cemetery to the half-buried wall vents of French Quarter townhouses to the undermined slabs of suburban ranch houses. More often, the effects of subsidence are obscured from view: the cornerstone of the U.S. Custom House, laid amid fanfare in 1849, has sunk thirty inches below Canal Street.

One of subsidence's most odious effects is the buckling and potholing of the city's streets, identified as the worst in the nation in 2000, a situation exacerbated by underfunded and inefficient municipal services (streets in neighboring parishes suffer the same geological processes but are far better maintained than those in Orleans). Subsidence poses a more ominous threat to infrastructure such as gas pipelines, sewer and water lines, bridges and interstates, and industrial facilities. Every now and then, one hears of the bizarre incident of a structure exploding because of a gas line cracked by this geological process. Five houses in Jefferson Parish were destroyed in this manner in 1972-76; all five occupied areas of thick peat and high subsidence.[197] In solving the problem of removing unwanted water from the basin of New Orleans, the city's marvelous drainage system introduced another problem: the removal of *needed* water from the basin of New Orleans. It is safe to say that the subsidence of New Orleans' soils will not be stopped or reversed, only combated by building on pilings or piling on landfill.

Like the levees along the river, the hurricane-protection levees have incurred costs along with their benefits. The ecological health of marshes in eastern New Orleans has suffered since the hurricane-protection levee system was started in the 1960s, closing off natural water flow through the wetlands and making them dependent on rainfall for moisture. In times of drought, the usually verdant waterways of Bayou Sauvage National Wildlife Refuge and other areas are prone to drying up and losing their peat soils to the wind. In the arid summer of 2000, skeletons of fish and dead mussels strewn out over cracked dry-mud river bottoms predominated over 6,000 acres of the refuge, while the 8,000 acres that lay beyond the levees remained well watered. The only realistic mitigation, pumping in Lake Pontchartrain water, is hardly a solution, because lake water is usually too saline for the wetland ecosystem.[198]

Along the fringes of the metropolitan area and all along the Gulf Coast, erosion eats away at the terrestrial realm, a situation so dire that the 2000 Louisiana state highway map had to be revised—not because of a growing road network but because of a shrinking land surface.[199] Louisiana has lost more than 1,500 square miles of marsh since the 1930s and currently loses 25-35 square miles of coastal land per year, for five interrelated reasons. First and foremost, the constraint of the Mississippi and other natural waterways by the construction of levees has starved the marshes of the flood-borne sediments that once replenished them. Second, an extensive network of manmade channels through the marshes (like the MR-GO but also oil- and gas-exploration canals and small trapping canals) has created more land-water interfaces and thus more opportunities for erosion.[200] Third, existing soils that have been drained of their water content are subsiding into the water under their own weight. Fourth, gulf waters are gradually rising. Finally, the dying of coastal saltwater-marsh grasses ("brown marsh"), destroyed by invasive nutria, high salinity levels, or droughts such as those in 2000, renders the dwindling land surface even more vulnerable to erosion.[201]

Like a bank account in which withdrawals exceed deposits, the coastal lands are diminishing at rates that would scare even those ordinarily dubious about incessant environmental foreboding. "How do you describe a disaster on its way to happening?" pondered one observer whose business is threatened by the land loss.[202]

---

192. So topographically distinct are the blocks from the surrounding streets that a high-resolution contour map of New Orleans actually resembles a street map, with many blocks encircled by a number of one-foot contours.

193. Snowden, Ward, and Studlick, 14. Similar problems have been encountered in Venice, Italy and other coastal cities.

194. Ibid. (citing the research of Saucier in 1963), and Ramsey and Moslow, 1673.

195. Schleifstein, "Lower Ground." This article notes that the "one agency that seemed to have accurate records . . . was the New Orleans Sewerage & Water Board, which had done a good job of updating its benchmarks at various pumping stations and other locations in the city."

196. Snowden, Ward, and Studlick, 14-15, and Coleman Warner, "Sinking Homes."

197. Snowden, Ward, and Studlick, 17. The houses were all located within two miles of the Veterans Boulevard/David Drive intersection.

198. Pope.

199. Barbier, "Less Louisiana."

200. Recent research estimated that roughly 10 percent of land loss in southeastern Louisiana may be attributed to canal excavation. The constraint of the Mississippi by levees accounts for the lion's share of land loss; river diversion into the backswamps is the most effective—and costliest—solution. Day et al., 425-38.

201. Marshall.

202. As quoted by Schleifstein, "Wetlands Loss."

Deltaic soils drained of their water content naturally subside, buckling the pavements that overlay them and tilting the buildings constructed upon them. Evidence of soil subsidence in New Orleans abounds, in (1) structural cracks, such as in this building on lower Magazine Street; (2) crooked doorways, such as that of the Boston Club on Canal Street; (3) leaning and listing houses, such as these Mid-City cottages; and, most infamously, the city's streets, regarded as among the worst in the nation. Subsidence is generally more severe in the former backswamps but can be quite bad high on the natural levees, such as here (4) on Chartres Street in Bywater. (This particular moonscape was repaired only after an exasperated resident posted a sign reading S.U.V. TEST AREA—THANKS MORIAL. New Orleanians deal with this axle-cracking, teeth-rattling headache with a sharp eye, a quick swerve, and a sense of humor.) Construction engineers combated the soft soils by inserting cypress or yellow pine pilings into the ground and resting the buildings on them. After 1908, concrete pilings were also used. Near the historic corner of Bourbon and Canal (5), holes are drilled for pilings to underlie a new high-rise hotel, with antebellum French Quarter townhouses on Iberville Street in the background. *Photographs by author, 2000-2001*

engineered to mimic (as best as possible) the natural trait of the river to overflow its banks and inundate the backswamp with sediment-laden fresh water. One project, the Caernarvon Freshwater Diversion Structure in

"New Orleans will, in effect, be a Gulf Coast city, with the Gulf of Mexico just a few miles from the French Quarter," stated a 1999 report by the Coalition to Restore Coastal Louisiana. Coastal erosion also makes the city more vulnerable to storm surges: every 2.7 miles of wetland loss allows an extra foot of sea water to be pushed inland by a hurricane. "The city will lose the wetland buffer that now protects it from many effects of flooding. As a result, severe floods will occur more frequently, and the strain on the area's already overtaxed drainage system will increase."[203] Scenarios like this are predicted to occur within the lifetime of children born today.

That this natural topographic nightmare is largely a result of manmade topographic change imparts a stinging lesson, but not one that points to a ready solution. There's nothing to ban and no one to sue; there's not even a clear target for blame. The main "cause" of the problem, after all, is us, and our not-outlandish desire to live without floods.

A number of small-scale remedial actions have been implemented to slow the loss in certain areas, such as constructing rip-rap barricades to soften wave action or submerging Christmas trees to trap sediment. On a much larger scale, two river-water-diversion projects have been

St. Bernard Parish, has been showing promising results in replenishing the wetlands of the Breton Sound Basin by diverting fresh river water from English Turn Bend into the increasingly brackish-water wetlands. Since its opening in 1991, Caernarvon has succeeded in building 406 acres of marshland, saving existing areas, and pushing the salt water out. Another, the Davis Pond Freshwater Diversion Project, scheduled to open by 2002, will redirect up to 4.8 million gallons of river water per minute from a meander near Luling, upriver from the metropolitan area, through culverts and into waterways leading toward the Barataria Bay region south of New Orleans proper. Costing $106 million and taking four years to complete, Davis Pond has been described as the world's largest coastal restoration project. A third project, still in the planning phase, is the Bonnet Carré Freshwater Diversion Structure, which will parallel the Bonnet Carré Spillway and divert river water into Lake Pontchartrain to reduce marsh loss around the lake and in the western Mississippi Sound.

The Caernarvon, Davis Pond, and Bonnet Carré diversion projects all endeavor to inject fresh water into the delicate wetlands, pushing back the erosive, harmful salt water of the Gulf of Mexico while depositing sediments in the marshes and fertilizing the ecosystems with productivity-enhancing nitrogen. (This excess nitrogen, accumulated from farms, cities, and industries throughout the Mississippi River Basin, helps cause harmful algae blooms—starving salty waters of dissolved oxygen and creating a "dead zone"—in the Gulf of Mexico, so any nitrogen trapped inland has a secondary benefit of being removed from the gulf.) On the negative side, the diversion projects may introduce the problems of Mississippi River water—pollutants, thermal differences, invasive species such as the zebra mussel—into the marshes, while throwing local fishery industries and land activities into a temporary state of volatility. Besides, these costly projects are not really engineered to create new land but rather to save existing land, or at least slow the pace of loss. The land-building potential of three relatively small diversions pales in comparison to the sediments deposited by annual overflows of the entire river. Nevertheless, diverting the river is an important step toward solving this dilemma, and four additional diversion projects are currently in the planning stage.[204] Although none is in New Orleans proper, and their impact will barely affect the marshes of Orleans Parish, all will serve to protect the Crescent City from the terrible fate of isolation on a dwindling deltaic peninsula in the Gulf of Mexico. The *reversal* of topographic change is the next, greatest, costliest, and most critical chapter in the topographic history of New Orleans and the delta region. At stake is the very existence of the place.

The Topographical City

Alluding to the analogy of the bucket of muddy water tossed on a flat surface (page 38), which illustrated how land forms in a deltaic environment, the role of topography in the history of New Orleans may be visualized. In prehistoric times, "buckets" of sediment-laden water intruded in a number of directions (the various historic deltas of the Mississippi) upon southeastern Louisiana, creating high natural levees, backswamps, and a network of distributaries throughout the flat terrain laced with the meandering river. Among these youthful geographical situations was the great crescent that would host New Orleans, sited to exploit a portage to the lake and thence to the sea. A city formed, restricted to the higher lands of the natural levees and dramatically reflecting topography in its shape and growth. The threat of river flooding was fought by the construction of levees atop the natural levees; the opportunity offered by battures was seized and exploited; the threat of storm surges was countered by lakefront reinforcement and the circumscription of the city with hurricane-protection levees. Water trapped within the confines of New Orleans was drained and pumped up and over the basin, allowing the city to grow beyond the natural levees and into the lowlands. Navigation canals were excavated to improve commerce with the world, crisscrossing the city in some areas and penetrating the countryside in others. All the while, residents adjusted their own terrain domains, importing landfill to raise their built environment above their natural environment. As a result, many of New Orleans' topographical problems—the challenges that restrained and threatened the city for centuries and made residents curse Bienville's stubborn attachment to the site—have been conquered. New Orleans today is, for the most part, protected, dry, and reasonably functional if not efficient. But in solving these pressing problems, the topographic adjustments engendered new problems—not sudden, terrifying disasters but gradual and subtle ones that undermine the very soils of the city, gnaw away at its land base, and expose it to the threat of fierce storms. New Orleans may have simply traded today's disaster for tomorrow's. Who wouldn't?

203. Ibid.

204. Swerczek, and U.S. Army Corps of Engineers, New Orleans District, *Freshwater Diversion* informational booklet (2000).

3 Culture

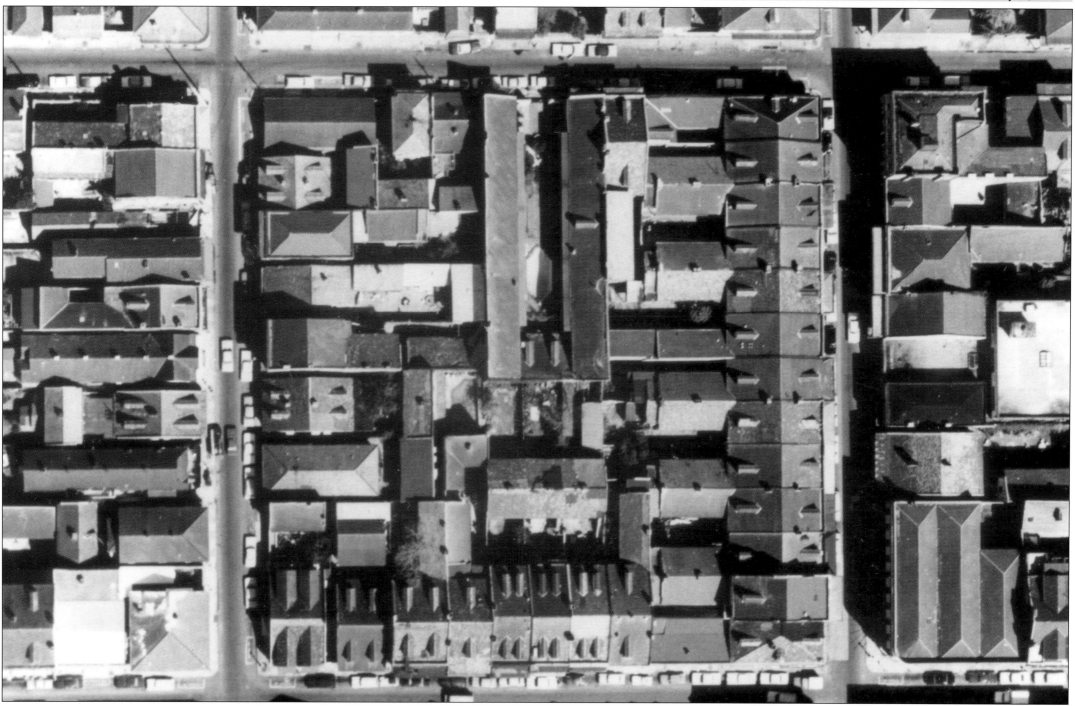

Tout ensemble: 1966 aerial view of the Vieux Carré block bounded by Bourbon (left), Governor Nicholls (top), Royal, and Ursulines. Narrow streets, dense arrangement of structures with no setbacks from the sidewalk, courtyards, servants' quarters, galleries, balconies, and steep hip and gable rooftops peppered with dormers and chimneys make for a fascinating and rare sight in modern America. *Vieux Carre Aerial Survey (1966), Jack Beech of Amman-International, The Historic New Orleans Collection, accession no. 1979.237.6.51*

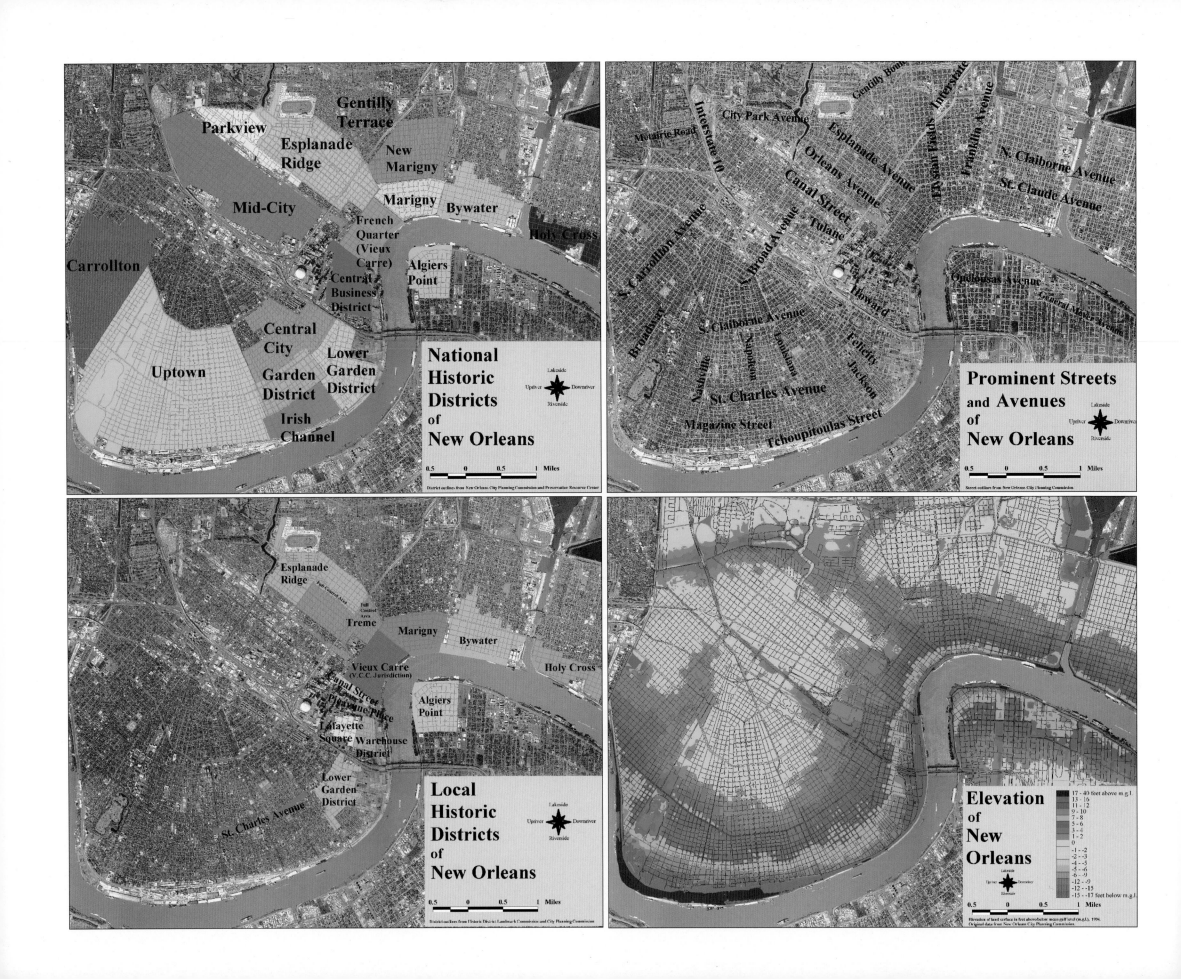

National Historic Districts of New Orleans

Parkview, Gentilly Terrace, Esplanade Ridge, New Marigny, Mid-City, Marigny, Bywater, French Quarter (Vieux Carre), Holy Cross, Carrollton, Central Business District, Algiers Point, Central City, Uptown, Garden District, Lower Garden District, Irish Channel

Lakeside / Upriver / Downriver / Riverside

0.5   0   0.5   1   Miles

District outlines from New Orleans City Planning Commission and Preservation Resource Center

Prominent Streets and Avenues of New Orleans

Gentilly Boulevard, Interstate, City Park Avenue, Metairie Road, Interstate 10, Esplanade Avenue, Orleans Avenue, Franklin Avenue, N. Claiborne Avenue, St. Claude Avenue, Canal Street, Tulane, S. Broad Avenue, Howard, S. Carrollton Avenue, S. Claiborne Avenue, Broadway, Napoleon, Louisiana, Nashville, Felicity, Jackson, General Meyer Avenue, Opelousas Avenue, St. Charles Avenue, Magazine Street, Tchoupitoulas Street

Lakeside / Upriver / Downriver / Riverside

0.5   0   0.5   1   Miles

Street outlines from New Orleans City Planning Commission

Local Historic Districts of New Orleans

Esplanade Ridge, Full Control Area, Treme, Marigny, Bywater, Vieux Carre (V.C.C. Jurisdiction), Canal Street, Picayune Place, Lafayette Square, Warehouse District, Holy Cross, Algiers Point, Lower Garden District, St. Charles Avenue

Lakeside / Upriver / Downriver / Riverside

0.5   0   0.5   1   Miles

District outlines from Historic District Landmark Commission and City Planning Commission

Elevation of New Orleans

17 - 40 feet above m.g.l.
13 - 16
11 - 12
9 - 10
7 - 8
5 - 6
3 - 4
1 - 2
0
-1 - -2
-2 - -4
-4 - -5
-5 - -6
-6 - -9
-9 - -12
-12 - -15
-15 - -17 feet below m.g.l.

Lakeside / Upriver / Downriver / Riverside

0.5   0   0.5   1   Miles

Elevation of land surface is in feet above/below mean gulf level (m.g.l.), 1994.
Original data from New Orleans City Planning Commission.

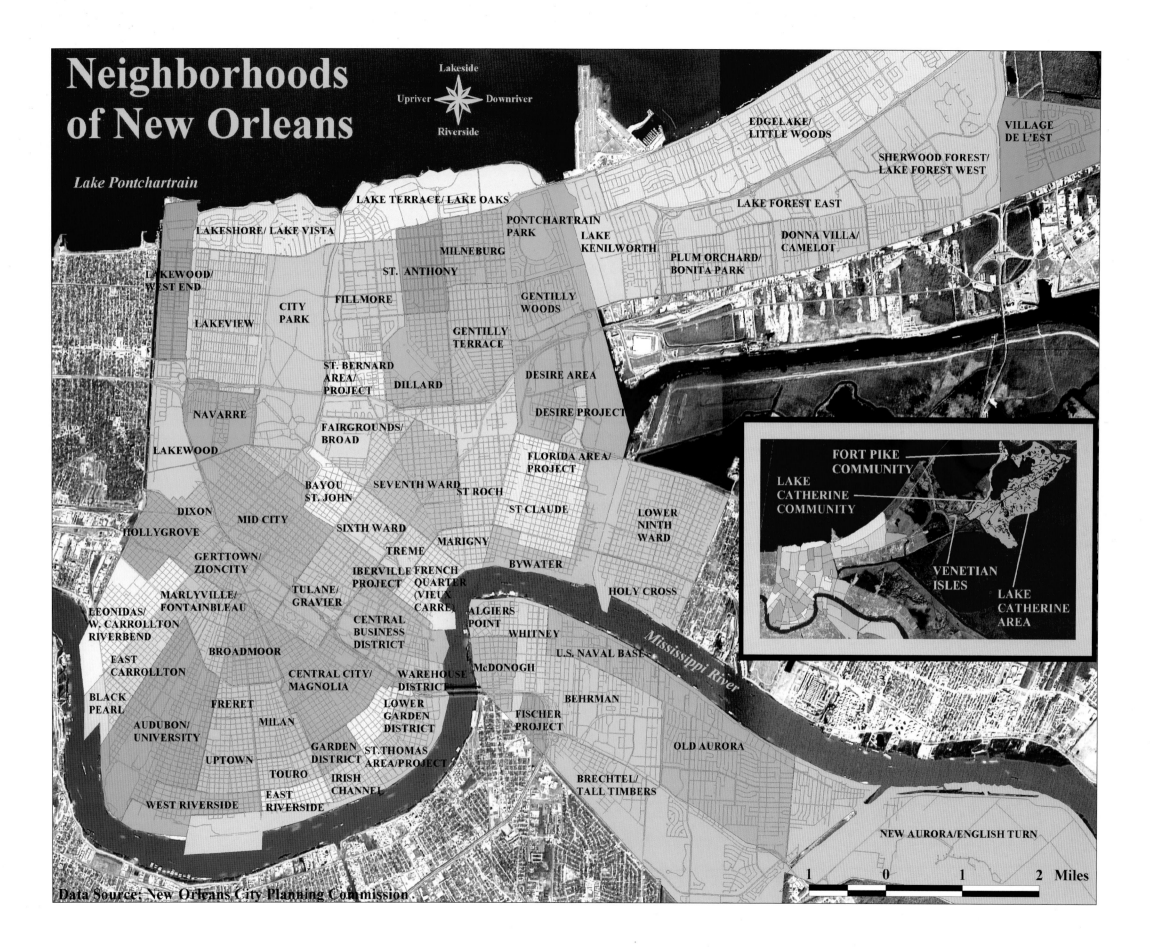

Neighborhoods of New Orleans

Upriver — Lakeside — Downriver — Riverside

Lake Pontchartrain

EDGELAKE/ LITTLE WOODS

VILLAGE DE L'EST

SHERWOOD FOREST/ LAKE FOREST WEST

LAKE TERRACE/ LAKE OAKS

LAKE FOREST EAST

LAKESHORE/ LAKE VISTA

PONTCHARTRAIN PARK

DONNA VILLA/ CAMELOT

MILNEBURG

LAKE KENILWORTH

PLUM ORCHARD/ BONITA PARK

LAKEWOOD/ WEST END

ST. ANTHONY

CITY PARK

FILLMORE

GENTILLY WOODS

LAKEVIEW

GENTILLY TERRACE

NAVARRE

ST. BERNARD AREA/ PROJECT

DILLARD

DESIRE AREA

LAKEWOOD

FAIRGROUNDS/ BROAD

DESIRE PROJECT

FLORIDA AREA/ PROJECT

DIXON

BAYOU ST. JOHN

SEVENTH WARD

ST ROCH

MID CITY

ST CLAUDE

HOLLYGROVE

SIXTH WARD

LOWER NINTH WARD

GERTTOWN/ ZIONCITY

TREME

MARIGNY

MARLYVILLE/ FONTAINBLEAU

TULANE/ GRAVIER

IBERVILLE PROJECT

FRENCH QUARTER (VIEUX CARRE)

BYWATER

LEONIDAS/ W. CARROLLTON RIVERBEND

CENTRAL BUSINESS DISTRICT

ALGIERS POINT

HOLY CROSS

EAST CARROLLTON

BROADMOOR

WHITNEY

U.S. NAVAL BASE

BLACK PEARL

CENTRAL CITY/ MAGNOLIA

WAREHOUSE DISTRICT

McDONOGH

FRERET

LOWER GARDEN DISTRICT

BEHRMAN

AUDUBON/ UNIVERSITY

MILAN

FISCHER PROJECT

OLD AURORA

GARDEN DISTRICT

ST.THOMAS AREA/PROJECT

UPTOWN

TOURO

IRISH CHANNEL

WEST RIVERSIDE

EAST RIVERSIDE

BRECHTEL/ TALL TIMBERS

Mississippi River

NEW AURORA/ENGLISH TURN

FORT PIKE COMMUNITY

LAKE CATHERINE COMMUNITY

VENETIAN ISLES

LAKE CATHERINE AREA

1   0   1   2 Miles

Data Source: New Orleans City Planning Commission.

(Page 82, upper left) New Orleans has some of the largest urban National Register Historic Districts in the nation. Their spatial patterns reflect the topography of the city, because urban development during what we currently consider to be "historic times" occurred on higher ground. In time, this will change, as we come to appreciate the architecture of places such as low-lying Lakeview and other areas. The most recent such district is Gentilly Terrace, declared in November 1999, the first to be entirely a product of the twentieth century. Inclusion in the National Register of Historic Places is largely an honorary designation; other benefits, from the perspective of preservationists, include special consideration of the neighborhood's historical integrity vis-à-vis federally funded projects that occur in or near it, and certain tax credits. The designation does not imply legal protection of historic structures, and is by no means a guarantee against demolition. *Map by author; district boundaries courtesy Preservation Resource Center of New Orleans; aerial image courtesy U.S. Geological Survey*

(Page 82, lower left) Local historic districts have far more "teeth" in protecting architecturally and historically significant structures than do National Register Historic Districts. The French Quarter is the oldest and most protected of these special zones, overseen by the Vieux Carré Commission, a regulatory group constitutionally empowered in 1936 to protect the city's world-famous signature neighborhood. The Irish Channel may be added to the list of local historic districts in the near future. Local historic districts are managed by the Historic District Landmarks Commission, a city agency, with involvement from the City Planning Commission and other groups. Note that the Cotton Garden District and other uptown historic neighborhoods are not among the local historic districts. Despite the high degree of preservationist spirit in these areas, some residents fear restrictions on property rights by such a designation. *Map by author; district boundaries from Historic District Landmarks Commission and digitized by the New Orleans City Planning Commission; aerial image courtesy U.S. Geological Survey*

(Page 82, upper right) New Orleans has perhaps the most intriguing streets of any city in America. Their memorable names, graceful patterns, and fascinating origins and the beauty of the surrounding architecture and foliage give them a mystique that most other cities cannot deliver. *Map by author; aerial image courtesy U.S. Geological Survey*

(Page 82, lower right) This map of the elevation of New Orleans is provided for comparison to the neighborhood and street maps. For more detail on New Orleans topography, see the maps on page 40. *Map by author. Reproduction of modern digital elevation model prohibited without written consent of the Executive Director, the New Orleans City Planning Commission. The New Orleans Geographic Information System at the New Orleans City Planning Commission is partially funded by a federal grant through NOAA.*

(Page 83) Official neighborhoods of New Orleans, according to the city government. These nomenclatures are but one way in which New Orleanians refer to areas in their city; others include traditional or historic names (usually with "soft" geographical boundaries), ward or district numbers, local historic districts as defined by the Historic District Landmarks Commission, or National Register Historic Districts as defined by the Department of the Interior. *Map by author; neighborhood boundaries courtesy New Orleans City Planning Commission*

While situation and topography presented a set of physical circumstances (certainly not the only ones) underlying the development of New Orleans, it was and is, of course, the human element that ultimately exploited these circumstances to form the peculiar metropolis of today. The case was made in chapter 1 that many of New Orleans' distinguishing characteristics—its port, its ethnic and religious heritage, its built environment, its traditions—share a common origin in that they may be traced, directly or indirectly, to the city's riverside situation between the North American interior and the world beyond the Gulf of Mexico. This situation allowed a potpourri of cultures to assemble in a single, remote, and isolated locale and thus gave rise to the myriad melting-pot qualities that the city boasts. In chapter 2, we analyzed the topographical shape of the city and how it affected urban development—and vice versa. Here, we consider selected cultural characteristics of the urban geography of New Orleans. "Cultural" in this context simply implies the human factor: while geographical situation may have allowed for the development of a port, and topographic restriction may have dictated the early growth of the city, cultural factors were responsible for such quintessentially New Orleans attributes as its radiating street network, its splendid architecture, and its neighborhoods and districts.

Depicting the cultural influences upon the built environment of New Orleans is like describing the influences of climate upon a natural ecosystem—the effects are so fundamental, so omnipresent, and so interwoven that a rudimentary framework is needed simply to gain hold of the subject, to focus on a few important features rather than dispersing efforts on many. That framework is provided by the five elements identified by the late Dr. Kevin

Lynch in his influential 1960 book, *The Image of the City,* which define the public image of the physical dimension of a city. Dr. Lynch classified these elements as paths, edges, districts, nodes, and landmarks. We will employ this framework not quite as Lynch originally proposed them—as variables that define a city's image—but rather as a structure to identify important components of New Orleans' geography over the years, and to discuss the cultural influences behind them.

Paths, according to Lynch, are "streets, walkways, transit lines, canals, railroads" and other corridors "along which the observer customarily, occasionally, or potentially moves."[1] We will use the concept of paths to discuss the origins and development of New Orleans' distinctive street network.

Edges are linear features that serve as boundaries of regions, holding together areas with something in common and separating them from differing areas. Edges may be walls, geographical features such as drainage canals or water bodies, or infrastructure like transportation corridors. Canal Street is perhaps New Orleans' most famous "edge," separating the old city from the new city in the early 1800s, the ghetto from the boomtown in the early 1900s, and the world-famous French Quarter from the locally important Central Business District today. We will assess the evidence for the consideration of Canal Street in this role.

Districts are areas that share a "common, identifying character"[2] (and may be separated from adjacent districts by "edges"). We will use the concept to analyze three historical industry districts of times past: the Cotton District, the Sugar District, and Newspaper Row.

Nodes are foci, or nuclei, of activity. They may be parks or squares that epitomize districts, or junctions of paths or edges. We will recast this concept of urban nodes to signify strategic points in the city, rooted in its physical geography, which symbolize the fundamental premise for the existence of New Orleans: the tangency of the exterior world beyond the Gulf of Mexico with the interior world of the Mississippi River and the basin it drains. These "geographical nodes," relevant at different times throughout the 300-year history of the city, include the Rigolets, the Bayou St. John/Bayou Road area, greater Jackson Square, the turning basins of the old navigation canals, the foot of Canal Street, and the lock and turning basin of the Industrial Canal.

Landmarks are "clues of identity"[3] that populate the cityscape and give people a sense of place, direction, and ambience. Like nodes, landmarks are points, but unlike nodes, they are noticed more so than entered, physically prominent more so than functional. Landmarks may include steeples and domes, hilltops and monuments, prominent buildings and nostalgic signs. New Orleans is chock-full of landmarks, ranging from the dignified to the odd to the downright bizarre. Presented in this section is a photographic inventory of landmarks characterizing New Orleans' neighborhoods and regions.

Paths: Origin and Development of New Orleans' Radiating Street Pattern

To the pedestrian, it is hardly noticeable. To the motorist or streetcar rider, it is vaguely apparent—a periodic sway, a gentle but consistent pull on the steering wheel, a perception that two streets that were only a couple of blocks apart in Mid-City span half-a-dozen blocks near the river. To the aviator or map reader, it is striking: the street network of historic New Orleans—that is, the pre-twentieth-century, pre-drainage, pre-automobile city—radiates outward from a nebulous origin in the middle of the crescent toward the river, creating a unique and elegant pattern that evokes the sweeping gesture of opening arms. From Mid-City, a series of corridors (Canal, Tulane, Louisiana, Napoleon, Jefferson, Carrollton, and others) broadcasts outward and terminates perpendicularly to the river, intersecting along the way quiet backstreets and grand avenues such as Claiborne, St. Charles, and Magazine that parallel the river. The radiating streets are deeply ingrained in the way people perceive and experience the city—Lynch's "paths"—providing a sense of magnificence amplified by the accompanying canopies of oak trees and rows of spectacular mansions and picturesque cottages. Observers have compared the pattern to wedges in a pie, spokes in a wheel, blades in a fan, a pinched accordion, a scallop shell, or the skeleton of a sinuous snake. Tour guides often account for the phenomenon as the product of the wending river, explaining with words to the effect that "the streets were surveyed to adapt to the curving Mississippi and thus form a radiating pattern." This explanation ignores cultural influences, implying that surveyors were somehow compelled to conform their street designs to nearby geographical features. (If this were true, then New York City's streets would form a series of concentric ovals within Manhattan Island, and Chicago's streets would curve like the shore of Lake Michigan!) In fact, the origin of New Orleans' radiating street network is

1. Lynch, 47.
2. Ibid.
3. Ibid., 48.

Photograph by Donn Young, courtesy the Port of New Orleans

far more interesting. The pattern is a direct descendent of the *arpent* land-surveying system, a French colonial parceling system derived from centuries-old European methods that, in the New Orleans region, was adopted by the Spanish and American regimes and remains richly evident in the landscape today, one of Louisiana's distinguishing signatures. The arpent system established the method for plantation delineation, and, "in New Orleans, old plantation lines are a determining factor in the arrangement of the street system, [giving] the city a circulation plan that is unique in many respects."[4]

The Arpent System

The antecedent of the arpent system appeared in the lowlands and mountain valleys of north-central Europe, centered around present-day Germany, around the end of the first millennium. (The system may date back as far as Babylonian times.)[5] It spread to present-day Belgium and northern France in later centuries, where the system was called variously *en arête de poisson* (herringbone), *village-route* (street-village), or *hameau-allongé* (string town).[6] Whether this land-division pattern derived from tillage practices or from an organized effort of settlement and tenure, the resultant parcels were consistently shaped as elongated lots, or long lots, defined by various researchers as rectangular land parcels whose depth-to-width ratio is anywhere from 3:1 to 10:1 or more.

It was primarily the French who transferred the concept to the New World, establishing their long lots most prominently between Québec City and Montreal (where they were called *rotures*) but also "everywhere in North America where there was the least bit of French influence, from the St. Lawrence Valley westward to Michilimackinac and to the Detroit region, . . . Green Bay and Prairie du Chien (now in Wisconsin) . . . to the Red River . . . to the Illinois Country (including St. Louis) and to Lower Louisiana,"[7] as well as in the Caribbean island colonies. The logic behind the method is compelling: given (1) a valued resource at one end (usually a waterway or road), (2) unproductive land at the other end (marshes or mountains), and (3) a swath

of well-drained, fertile land in between (natural levees or valley bottoms), then the optimal manner of division is to delineate the fertile land into narrow strips so that a maximum number of farms would enjoy access to at least a small segment of the valued resource.[8] If the lots are too wide, only a few farms would be created. If the lots are demarcated as small squares rather than strips, then numerous lots may be created but many settlers would be deprived of the use of the valued resource, such as the transportation and irrigation benefits of the river. Thus the reasoning behind long-lot division: it is an optimal allocation of two scarce resources, river access and well-drained, fertile land.[9] Longlots are found today throughout southern Louisiana, parts of the central and upper Mississippi Valley, the Great Lakes region, and eastern Canada and in parts of Texas, New Mexico, Brazil, and Argentina.[10] Long lots are also still found in north-central Europe, where, in some areas, the lots project off not a river but a road, and stretch not downward to the swamp but upward to the mountains.

The measurement unit used to delineate long lots throughout French America was the *arpent*, or *arpen*, derived from the Latin *arepennis*, a term used by the Gauls to refer to the Roman areal measurement *semi-jugerum*. By the seventeenth century, the size of an arpent was equal to 10 *perches*, a *perche* measuring anywhere from 18 to 26 French feet (*pied de roi*). In Paris, 18 *pieds* equaled 1 *perche* and 10 *perches* measured 1 *arpent;* therefore an *arpent de Paris* equaled 180 French feet as a lineal measurement and 32,400 square French feet as an areal measurement. The *arpent de Paris* was the unit that the French brought to North America in the division of the landscape. Like most old measurements, the actual size of an arpent in its practical application varied by time, place, administration, and interpretation.[11] Problems arose in Louisiana when American surveyors, unsure of the exact conversion of the French foot to the American foot, determined the length of an arpent by measuring a typical land tract—40 arpents—and deduced that an arpent equaled 191.994 feet. Thus many measurements made in rural areas after the Louisiana Purchase were based on an arpent rounded off to 192 American feet. But in urban areas such as New Orleans, surveyors were more likely to use the more precise measurement of 191' 10" American feet. An arpent is the functional equivalent of the English acre, except that, while an acre measures a superficial area, an arpent measures both lineally and superficially.[12] The U.S. Bureau of Standards characterized the arpent as follows:[13]

Lineal Measure
- 1 French foot = 1.06575 American feet
- 1 American foot = 0.938306 French feet
- 1 arpent = 180 French feet = 191.835 American feet = about 191' 10" American feet

Areal Measure
- 1 square arpent = 0.844827 American acres
- 1 American acre = 1.18367 square arpents
- 1 square arpent = 36,800.667 square American feet

As the long lot spread across France's North American empire, it was almost always measured in arpents but utilized in a variety of ways: in Québec, settlers resided on their lots in the manner of farmsteads; in the Illinois

4. City Planning and Zoning Commission, 22.
5. John Whitling Hall, 25-32, and Knipmeyer, 32-34.
6. Ekberg, *French Roots,* 6.
7. Ibid., 5-6, 9, 12.

8. An added advantage was the fact that an elongated lot minimized the number of times a farmer had to retrack to tend to the next row, thus accommodating the farm implements of the day, especially plows. Cultural geographer Richard C. Harris listed additional benefits to long lots: they offered proximity to neighbors, access to fishing resources, and a diversity of flora and soil types spanning from the waterway to the hinterland, and they were easy to survey. Ibid., 11.
9. Knipmeyer (32) had a somewhat different take on this: "Had those rivers [in southern Louisiana] been without natural levees, and had the land been completely flat but satisfactory for settlement, the land division would undoubtedly have been the same. If rivers had not been available for lines of departure, roads or canals would have served the purpose. The system was not devised to suit the particular topographic conditions even though a system resembling it would probably have been invented if none had existed." For more on the environment-versus-culture debate on Louisiana long lots, see Ekberg, *French Roots,* 24-25.
10. Jordan and Rowntree, 111. Ekberg (*French Roots,* 10-11) also reports linear settlement patterns appearing rather incongruously in Sudbury and Rowley, Massachusetts.
11. Other variations used by the French, Spanish, and others demonstrate the wide range of the arpent's interpreted size: the *arpent d'ordonnance,* the *arpent comun* (sic), and the *arpent belgique* measured 1.26 acres, 1.04 acres, and 4.17 acres, respectively. Holmes, "The Value of the Arpent." 314-20.
12. After the Americanization of Louisiana in the early 1800s, "arpents" and "acres" were sometimes used interchangeably, imparting a new local meaning to "acre" as both a lineal and superficial measure. An ad in an 1832 newspaper (*Louisiana Advertiser*) offered for sale a sugar plantation "measuring about eighty acres front on the Bayou, bounded on the left by the Bayou aux Oies, which line has 40 acres depth; and on the right by [land] which line measures about eighty acres. The whole being about eight hundred acres of land." The seller of the land, incidentally, had an American name: Andrew Hodge, Jr. *Whitney's New-Orleans Directory* (1810-11), a bilingual publication, translated "arpent" as "acre" and—confusingly—described both as being synonymous with "hectare," all with the same measurements. Whitney, 78-79.
13. Henry P. Dart III, 96-97. See also John Whitling Hall, 24, and John E. Walker, "Surveyors and Surveying," in Friends of the Cabildo, vol. 7, 52.

country, a tripartite settlement pattern reminiscent of medieval France recurred, in which a central village was surrounded by commons and long-lot plow lands.[14] This village-commons-plow lands arrangement was not appropriate in Louisiana because of a variety of factors. The initial years of French sovereignty in the lower Mississippi region were characterized by a weak, distant governing authority and a plethora of land, hence only rudimentary attempts were made to standardize and document the distribution of land. Further, the scarcity of settlers, the business goals of the Company of the West, and the type of agriculture supported in this region precluded the adoption of the Illinois model. This era in early Louisiana is described by geographer Milton B. Newton, Jr., as the time in which land apportionment was conducted by *concessions,* large land grants by the Government of Louisiana to important and wealthy people aimed at developing the wilderness and benefiting the nascent colony. Concessions were erratically distributed, inconsistently sized and shaped, and frequently unsurveyed and unsanctioned by a public authority. But concessions did have some key features that connected them with their ancient antecedents: they were oriented perpendicularly to the river, they extended backward toward the *ciprières* (cypress swamps), and they were generally deeper than they were wide.[15]

"By a peculiarity perhaps unique, the highest places in all these lands are the banks of the Mississippi and of the bayous, as well as the shores of the lakes. This high ground provides the only means they have of establishing plantations; and it generally consists of good soil, rarely with too much clay in it, more often loamy with an adequate mixture of sand, varying considerably in depth, and only in certain circumstances connecting with the high ground along another lake or river. Because of this unique situation, concessions of land are granted in arpents measured fronting on the waterways and going back as far as possible to the muddy lands at the rear. . . . To the planter's greatest advantage, arable land fortunately extends quite a distance along both banks of the river to the rear; however, this depth can vary from a fraction of an arpent to thirty ordinarily, rarely as much as sixty, and in unusual cases up to one hundred arpents."

—James Pitot (101-2)

Some land grantees used their expansive concessions not for agriculture but for timber and real-estate sales, "entirely contrary to the establishment of the colony."[16] When King Louis XV (represented by the duc d'Orléans, since the king was but a child) learned of the Government of Louisiana's excessive land concessions and the resulting abuses, he issued the Edict of October 12, 1716, the first law regulating land grants in Louisiana. The edict provided for the return of certain lands to the public domain for distribution to inhabitants "in the proportion of two to four arpents front by forty to sixty in depth."[17] The land-redistribution clause of the Edict of 1716 was only partially enforced, but its stipulation "that the concessions be cultivated in accordance with the same pattern of long, narrow fields that prevailed in the country along the St. Lawrence River [and] Cape Breton Island . . . would henceforth be the rule for all lands in the colony."[18] This represented a drastic cutback from the 50- or 100-arpent frontages of the large-scale concessions. From this early reference, the indefinite concession tradition slowly matured into the well-defined arpent system. The transformation occurred as the strength of the local governmental authority increased, the population grew, and the abundance of virgin land decreased in comparison to the early years. Newton describes the implementation of the arpent system in his *Louisiana: A Geographical Portrait:*

[The arpent system] was implemented under a definite set of rules. The first rule required that, in principle at least, a line be drawn parallel to the low water mark of each navigable stream. This line, placed at a distance of 40 arpents from the stream's edge, served as the "back" line of all grants made on that side of the river. . . . Such a line is still commonly known as the forty-arpent line. . . . Where the stream was fairly straight, the forty-arpent line follows a smooth path, neatly mirroring the shape of the river bank. Where, however, the stream meanders sharply, the forty-arpent line follows a wide arc around the cut bank side, but cuts sharply in to form a point on the point bar side. The tell-tale clue to the presence of the arpent system of land allocation is the forty-arpent line.[19]

With the forty-arpent line tracing a buffer about 7,680 American feet from both sides of the river toward the backswamp, the *arpenteur*[20] demarcated elongated lots for settlers, one by one in successive order, with no gaps or overlaps in between. Settlers were allotted a portion of river frontage, perhaps two to eight *arpents de face* (frontage arpents) and extending back to the forty-arpent line. (On broader natural levees, lots might extend back to an eighty-arpent line.) Where the river meandered, lots diverged on the exterior of the bend and converged on the interior, thus evoking comparisons to a snake skeleton or a pinched accordion—not coincidentally the same similes used to describe New Orleans' modern street pattern. Although the concession of large lots would continue for years, the arpent system[21] began to trace the landscape of the lower Mississippi as early as the 1720s. The nearly one hundred parcels along the Mississippi ten leagues above and below New Orleans, mapped in the remarkably accurate *Carte Particuliere de la Nouvelle Orleans au Mississipy* (ca. 1723), are mostly long and narrow in shape, generally perpendicular to the river, and about forty arpents in depth.[22]

Initial Appearance of the Radiating Pattern

The first application of the long lot in the New Orleans area came with the granting of concessions to a group of Mobile colonists to grow wheat along Bayou St. John in 1708, the first European settlers in the area. These four-by-thirty-six-arpent long lots seemed to carry on the French Canadian cadastral tradition, where properties had roughly 1-to-10 width-to-depth ratios, with which Jean Baptiste Le Moyne, sieur de Bienville had become familiar during his youth in the St. Lawrence Valley.[23] But it was not for another decade that the pattern would be imposed upon the crescent of the Mississippi, initializing the radiating street pattern that we see today.

On March 27, 1719, a year after work commenced on New Orleans, city founder Bienville granted himself (with the concurrence of Hubert, the Ordonnateur of the Colony) the sweep of land in the crescent from about present-day Bienville Street in the upper French Quarter to beyond Carrollton, stretching from the river to the backswamp along present-day Broad Avenue, plus another tract across the river in the present-day Lower Coast neighborhoods of Algiers, Behrman, and Aurora.[24] The vast concession of what was then called the "Chapitoulas Coast"[25] was tentatively approved by Company representatives in Paris in February 1720. The Bienville concession represented the first large-scale land distribution in what would become metropolitan New Orleans, dwarfing tenfold any one of the nearly hundred plantations near New Orleans that appeared in the ca. 1723 map cited above.[26]

Concurrent with the Company's approval of Bienville's grant, however, a royal edict issued in November 1719 forbade colonial governors from owning such plantations, allowing only for vegetable gardens. Bienville complied by subdividing some of his holdings and renting out parcels to various settlers, among them a dozen or so German families displaced by the 1722 hurricane, and Swiss and French-Canadian families. By 1724, a series of parcels was delineated from the limits of the city upriver for about three miles. Bienville's "vegetation garden" occupied the first lot, a 53.5-arpent expanse from about present-day Bienville Street to Felicity Street between Claiborne Avenue and the river, and nine other families settled upriver parcels, measuring from 5 to 18 arpents in frontage, with various depths. "These were the first European inhabitants of what is now uptown New Orleans."[27] In April 1726, Bienville sold his house and 20 arpents of land to the Jesuits.

14. Ekberg, *French Roots,* 54, and "The Illinois Country."
15. Newton, 210-12, and John Whitling Hall, 33.
16. The Edict of October 12, 1716, as translated by Henry P. Dart, "The First Law," 346.
17. Ibid., 347.
18. Giraud, vol. 2, 136. (This quote is by Giraud himself.)
19. Newton, 213. See also Kniffen, "The Lower Mississippi Valley," 15.

20. Literally, one who measures arpents. In modern French, *arpenteur* translates as land surveyor and *arpentage* as land surveying. John E. Walker, "Surveyors and Surveying," in Friends of the Cabildo, vol. 7, 52, and *Webster's New World French Dictionary,* 21, 444.
21. On this term, Ekberg (*French Roots,* 23) makes an important point: "In Louisiana nomenclature the longlot is often called the 'arpent lot' or the 'arpent system,' for the obvious reason that all surveys throughout the colonial period (Spanish as well as French) employed the French arpent as the basic unit of measure. This terminology is rather confusing, however, for although longlots in French North America were almost always surveyed in arpents, not all property surveyed in arpents was laid out in longlots." While we will continue to use the traditional Louisiana terminology here, Ekberg's observation should be kept in mind.
22. It was probably this map that James W. Taylor (277) was referring to when he stated that "a map of unknown authorship of the lower Mississippi drawn in 1723 shows ninety-one landholdings along the banks of the river; of these holdings only eighteen exceed forty arpents in depth, and only four are of a shape other than a long narrow strip, and these four are variations of that type."
23. Ekberg, *French Roots,* 22.
24. Cruzat and Dart, no. 1, 8-17.
25. The term *Chapitoulas Coast* referred to the entire crescent between the original city of New Orleans and the Chapitoulas Indian camp across from Nine Mile Point. *Chapitoulas* became *Tchoupitoulas,* and today Tchoupitoulas Street traverses most of the old Chapitoulas Coast. Meloncy C. Soniat, "The Tchoupitoulas Plantation," 308-10.
26. *Carte Particuliere.*
27. Wilson, "Early History of the Lower Garden District," 3-4, and Briede, 898.

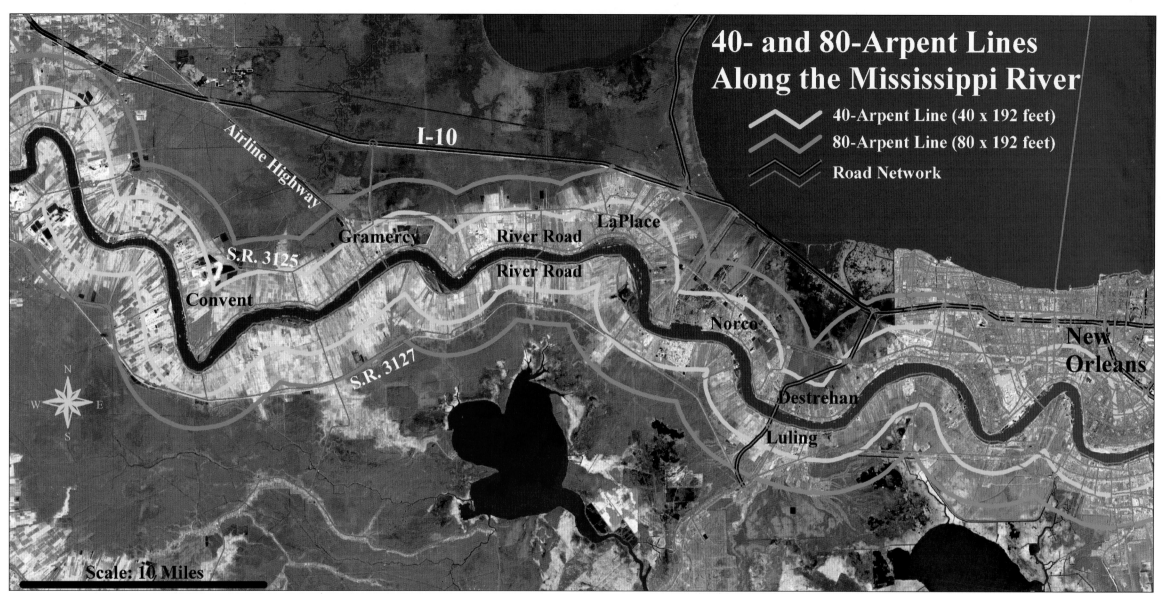

40- and 80-Arpent Lines Along the Mississippi River

40-Arpent Line (40 x 192 feet)
80-Arpent Line (80 x 192 feet)
Road Network

I-10

Airline Highway

Gramercy

River Road

LaPlace

S.R. 3125

River Road

Convent

Norco

New Orleans

S.R. 3127

Destrehan

Luling

N W E S

Scale: 10 Miles

Since French colonial times, plantations along the lower Mississippi were delineated as long, narrow lots perpendicular to the river, such that the two limited resources—rich, well-drained alluvial soils for agriculture and access to the river for transportation—were distributed in a maximum-benefit manner. This surveying method, based on centuries-old European traditions, is called the *arpent* system, named for the unit (equal to just under 192 American feet) used to measure them. Plantations were demarcated from the river to the so-called forty-arpent line—about a mile and half—unless the natural levee was especially wide, in which case the eighty-arpent line was used to mark the edge of the backswamp. The forty- and eighty-arpent lines overlaid on this satellite image show that these historic patterns persist in the Louisiana landscape, influencing the locations of streets, properties, and towns. Note how Interstate 10 and parts of Airline Highway "violate" the pattern because they were built in an era when technology allowed construction in low-lying areas. Greater New Orleans sprawled beyond the natural levee when drainage systems made former swamps available for development. *GIS processing and cartography by author; Landsat/SPOT satellite image courtesy Louisiana State University*

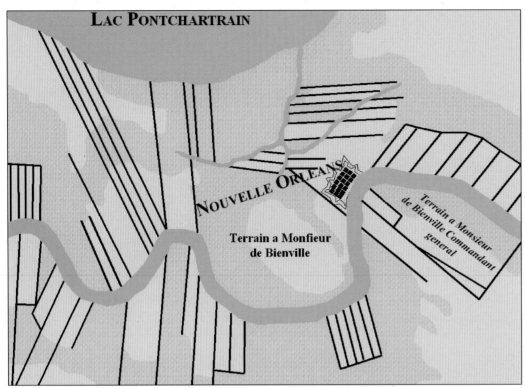

LAC PONTCHARTRAIN

NOUVELLE ORLEANS

Terrain a Monfieur
de Bienville

Terrain a Monfieur
de Bienville Commandant
general

These are among the earliest plantation delineations in the New Orleans region, mapped just after the surveying of the city, ca. 1723. The map shows the relative importance of the Bayou St. John region at the time, having been cultivated since 1708, ten years before the founding of the city. Note the lack of plantations in the future New Orleans crescent, because the entire area, plus land on the opposite bank, was granted to city founder Bienville. *Map by author based on Carte Particuliere*

Despite the rental arrangements, Bienville's massive self-grant was controversial in colonial Louisiana and was soon reconsidered by the Company and the French government.[28] As another milestone in the movement away from large concessions and toward small surveyed long lots, the Council of State (the highest court in France) issued the Edict of August 10, 1728, "Annulling All Concessions from Manchac to the Sea and Providing a Method of Re-establishing Titles Thereto."[29] Its intention was to ensure that grants along the lower Mississippi would be made "in small parcels to ex-soldiers or to settlers under semi-feudal conditions with the object of creating a body of retainers who would be subject to military duty in defense of New Orleans."[30] Bienville, who fell out of favor with his superiors at the Company of the Indies and was recalled to France in 1723-25, had lost his valuable concession because of this edict. He was reinstated as governor for the fourth time in 1733—after the Company of the Indies retroceded Louisiana to the French government (June 1731), ending the private-sector management of the colony—and strove to reinstate ownership over his former grants.[31] He succeeded. A survey in 1737 revealed the status and usage of the various parcels: Bienville was "'Seigneur et proprietaire' (lord and proprietor) and conveyed possession to his tenants at a yearly rental in money, in capons and in free labor."[32] In essence, the parcels surveyed out of Bienville's original vast grant of 1719 and lost in 1728 had operated by 1737 under a feudal system of forced labor as well as payment of rent and produce—a consequence not quite anticipated by the Edict of 1728.

28. Charles T. Soniat, 9.
29. The Edict of August 10, 1728, as reproduced, translated, and interpreted by Cruzat and Dart, no. 2, 166.
30. Cruzat and Dart, no. 2, 162.
31. Cruzat and Dart, no. 3, 364-70.
32. Cruzat and Dart, no. 4, 538-39.

Still, many of the parcels described in these Certificates of Survey or shown on an ancillary map measured "six arpents fronting on the [Mississippi River], by forty in depth," reflecting the growing institutionalization of what we now call the arpent system.[33] A 1737 map of the Bienville's concession shows the east bank (covering present-day uptown) subdivided into twenty-two long lots with frontages averaging 7 arpents wide and 40 to 45 arpents deep; the fourteen long lots on the west bank (from present-day Algiers Point downriver toward English Turn Bend) averaged 9.6 arpents wide and 40 to 60 arpents deep.[34] Settlers with names like *Le Sr. Estienne Langlois, Andre Kerchement,* or simply *Les trois freres Larche* are associated with various parcels within Bienville's subdivided concession. As per the arpent system, this historic map shows those lots delineated within concave bends of the river as converging in the backswamp, while lots delineated along straight stretches of river form elongated rectangles. The 1737 map provides a first glimpse at the antecedent cadastral pattern that eventually evolved into the radiating street pattern of modern New Orleans.

Spokes in the Crescent

The Jesuits increased their holdings from the twenty frontage arpents purchased from Bienville in 1726 to a property measuring thirty-two frontage arpents by fifty arpents in depth by 1743, giving them ownership of the valuable swath from the city to present-day Felicity Street. The fathers developed their land into a fine and prosperous plantation (see page 133), but following the French and Indian War in 1763, the order was exiled from the colony and deprived of all its assets. The former Jesuit plantation was divided into six lots, five of five arpents in width and one of seven arpents, and promptly auctioned off.[35] But unlike Bienville's plantation, which extended into the present-day French Quarter (Bienville Street), the Jesuit plantation at the time of its seizure bordered "the slopes of the fortifications of Fort St. Louis, above the City of New Orleans."[36] Construction of these early fortifications had moved the lower limit of the Jesuit plantation upriver by a few blocks, creating a triangular swath of the land that would remain as a fortified area—cleared of structures so as not to obstruct firing lines—into the early American years.[37] The two parcels of the former Jesuit plantation closest to the fortifications, spanning a total of twelve arpents, served as a sugar plantation in the Spanish colonial years (the first significant sugar venture in the region) and eventually came into the possession of the Gravier family, who decided to subdivide it after the catastrophic fire of 1788. Spanish surveyor general Don Carlos Laveau Trudeau sketched the street network in a plan drafted only ten days after the fire and updated in the weeks following. The Gravier plantation became New Orleans' first suburb, Faubourg Ste. Marie, starting from the *terre commune* (present-day Common Street) and expanding upriver to the limit of the neighboring Delord-Sarpy plantation (parallel to, though not exactly coinciding with, the former Delord Street, now Howard Avenue). The streets of Faubourg Ste. Marie—Gravier, Poydras, Girod, Julia—formed the first "spokes" in the Crescent City's street network, intersecting the first arcs: Magazine, St. Charles, Carondelet, and others (more on the arcs later). Subdivision of Faubourg Ste. Marie also burned the lower line of the old Jesuit plantation and the recent Gravier plantation into the landscape as today's Common Street, and ergo imprinted the triangular fortified zone between Common Street and present-day Iberville Street into New Orleans' urban geography.[38]

Fortifications were rebuilt along the city edge of this triangular area in 1793-94, during the busy administration of Spanish governor Carondelet.[39] But a decade later, after the American takeover of the city, the growth of the community enveloped the deteriorating ramparts, rendering them a worthless obstacle impeding "the communication between the town and the suburb St. Mary," lined with trenches that "were receptacles of stagnant water and of all manner of filth which engender disease."[40] In 1805, the City Council petitioned the federal

33. Copies of Certificates of Survey of the Bienville Land in 1737, as reproduced, translated, and interpreted by Cruzat and Dart, no. 4, 540.
34. From "Map of Bienville's Concessions," reproduced and interpreted by Cruzat and Dart, no. 1, 8-9. Width measurements of the parcels are recorded exactly in the legend of this map; depth measurements were approximated by the author using the scale on the map.
35. The division was mandated on November 24, 1763, and carried out by City Engineer Olivier Duvezin, who ascertained the plantation's measurements as thirty-two acres (arpents) fronting the river by fifty acres in depth. Padgett, 680-81.
36. Charles T. Soniat, 19.
37. This area, between Common Street and the present-day French Quarter, was an open commons at this time, but it was not completely publicly owned. Surveyor Barthélémy Lafon owned a portion of it (for a foundry), between present-day Camp and Carondelet, as did others. On account of the fort, however, owners were restricted in their rights to develop their land. Maduell, 5, and Wilson, "Early History of Faubourg St. Mary," 10.
38. Trudeau, *Plan of the City,* and Wilson, "Early History of Faubourg St. Mary," 6-8.
39. Holmes, *A Guide to Spanish Louisiana,* 22. According to James Pitot (106), these forts were more "intended to serve as a refuge for the friends of the government in case of an insurrection, so dreaded from 1793 to 1796, than to guard against an enemy attempting to capture the city."
40. As quoted in Gayarré, vol. 4, 194.

government to recognize the city's claim to the commons, and by an Act of Congress on March 3, 1807, the claim was accepted, with the stipulation that a sixty-foot right-of-way be established on both sides of a canal that was to be dug to connect Carondelet Canal with the river (see page 67).[41] The canal was never excavated, but its dimensions and name live on in Canal Street, the widest and perhaps most famous "path" leading nowadays from the Metairie Ridge to the Mississippi River and famously separating—to various degrees (see page 110)—the old Creole French Quarter from the new American Sector. New streets and properties were subdivided between Canal and Common in 1810, filling in the gap between the old and new city while reserving the imprint of both the plantations and the fortified zone in the landscape. A glance at a map reveals the twin thoroughfares of Canal Street and Common Street/Tulane Avenue, born as two legs of the same right triangle, as the downriver-most spokes in the Crescent City's radiating street pattern, intersecting with the farthest-upriver spoke (Carrollton Avenue) at points in the crux of the crescent.

S. Frederick Starr described the growth of Faubourg Ste. Marie and its adjacent commons, from Canal to present-day Howard Avenue, as the "first phase of Americanization of New Orleans," occurring after the Louisiana Purchase and lasting until the 1830s.[42] The second phase of Americanization in the Creole City occurred upon the remainder of the former Jesuits holding—the "Upper Banlieue"—which became the Delord-Sarpy/Duplantier plantation (later Faubourg Duplantier), the Solet plantation (Faubourg Solet), the Robin property (Faubourg de La Course), and the Livaudais plantation (Faubourg de L'Annunciation).[43] Surveyor Barthélémy Lafon's classical urban plan for this area, designed in 1806-10 and well preserved in today's Lower Garden District, unified these parcels and obscured the boundaries that separated them—thus these particular plantation lines are among the few in New Orleans *not* transferred to the street network[44]—but the upriver edge of L'Annunciation remains imprinted in the modern cityscape as Felicity Street.

Chemin de la Félicité (Felicity Road) was approximately the upper border of the former Jesuits plantation, and in 1810 it formed an exact boundary between Lafon's previously mentioned subdivisions and his current work in the neighboring Ursuline Nuns' plantation, which was about to become Faubourg des Religieuses. Felicity Street was also a prominent political boundary, forming the upper edge of New Orleans until 1852, and the lower edge of the Jefferson Parish city of Lafayette from 1832 to 1852. Felicity Street is prominent today not from a pedestrian scale but from a cartographic scale, in which one can readily see where the former plantations abutted and exactly how Lafon changed his street designs in the two areas. Nearly every river-parallel street, including St. Charles Avenue, angles when it intersects with Felicity (see page 105). The shape of the former Ursuline Nuns plantation is perfectly preserved today—a long, narrow pie wedge about five arpents (~1,000 feet) wide at the river and 40 arpents (~1.5 miles) in depth—nestled among three streets named for the nuns involved in the sale: Felicity (Félicité), St. Mary (Marie), and St. Andrew (André).[45] Extra room at the river end of the "fan blade" allowed for the inclusion of a short street called Nuns and part of a river-parallel street called Religious, further reminders of the heritage of this area.

Because the Ursulines only had their own property to subdivide, the limits of their plantation[46] became the limits of the faubourg, and the edges of the faubourg became new streets. With the subdivision of Faubourg des Religieuses, a pattern was unintentionally established in the development of uptown New Orleans: the "antecedent cadaster"[47] would generally dictate the geometry of future streets as former plantations were developed for city life. "When cities begin to grow beyond their limits into formerly agricultural areas," observed John Whitling Hall, "the most convenient way to divide the newly acquired land is according to existing cadastral divisions."[48] Because of the division of land into converging or diverging long lots, the resultant street network would radiate accordingly. In this incremental manner, planned at the microlevel but unplanned at the macrolevel, New Orleans' famous and unique street pattern was born.

41. "An Act Respecting Claims to Land in the Territories of Orleans and Louisiana" (March 3, 1807), as recorded in *The Debates and Proceedings in the Congress of the United States* (1852), 1283.

42. Starr, 13-15.

43. Wilson, "Early History of the Lower Garden District," 7-12.

44. One interesting exception is the inland boundary between the former plantations of Delord-Sarpy/Duplantier and Solet, which, about twenty-five years after their subdivision, was reiterated by the New Basin Canal for a distance of about one mile. The canal was filled in by 1950 but its right-of-way was later used for the Pontchartrain Expressway/Interstate 10. Today, motorists on I-10 heading toward the Crescent City Connection parallel this old plantation boundary, and straddle the former canal bed, from about South Rocheblave to South Claiborne Avenue. City Planning and Zoning Commission, 23.

45. Wilson, "Early History of the Lower Garden District," 30-31.

46. According to Briede (907), there is no evidence that the Ursuline Nuns cultivated or even inhabited this property, so perhaps "plantation" is not an accurate term. The Ursulines decided to subdivide their parcel to enhance its sellability, as they needed the money to purchase a property below the city to which they would relocate their downtown convent (the buzz of activity at the Chartres Street convent, which still stands, interfered with the nuns' cloister tradition). That downriver property remained in the Ursulines' hands until 1911, when they donated it to the city; in 1918, it was used for the construction of the Industrial Canal (see page 74). Thus the Ursulines' historic land dealings had significant impacts on modern-day New Orleans geography.

47. Newton, 211.

48. John Whitling Hall, 67-71.

Historic plantation boundaries in the lower portion of the New Orleans crescent and their relationship to the modern city. Green type indicates prominent owners (not necessarily all owners) during plantation days; yellow type indicates the name of the development at the time of its subdivision; blue type shows present-day streets derived from the edges or centers of old plantations. The earliest plantations delineated above the original city (upper right, now the French Quarter) belonged to city founder Jean Baptiste Le Moyne, sieur de Bienville and were partially sold to the Jesuits in 1726; these areas are indicated by the arrows on the right. *Map and analysis by author based on various historical maps and data; aerial image courtesy U.S. Geological Survey. Locations of lateral boundaries of plantations are certain, but rear boundaries (along the backswamp) varied over the years, depending on conditions, and were often not depicted on historical maps.*

This detail of a panoramic photograph of the Central Business District, captured in 1919 from the roof of the Hotel Grunewald (now the Fairmont), shows the triangular shape of the former commons between Iberville Street (extreme left, one block behind Canal Street) and Common Street (right, directly behind the dome of the Church of the Immaculate Conception). The vertex of the triangle is at the Mississippi River (distant center). From 1788 to about 1810, this swath of land was a terre commune between the old city and Faubourg Ste. Marie, occupied only by aging fortifications from the colonial era. *Library of Congress*

Similar perspective today, taken from Tulane University's Tidewater Building. The shape of the old commons is permanently incorporated into the street network of downtown New Orleans. *Photograph by author, 2000*

The Gravier plantation covered the lower three-quarters of the area seen in this photograph. Today, it forms the upper section of the Central Business District, featuring the classic American townhouses called the Thirteen Sisters of Julia Street (center) and the Gothic-style St. Patrick's Cathedral (1840) at right. *Photograph by author, 1996*

The St. Charles Avenue streetcar swivels around the angle of Common Street, once the lower edge of the Jesuits plantation, subsequently the Gravier plantation, and finally Faubourg Ste. Marie (1788). Common Street is also the logical (though not official) terminus of Highway 61, the famous artery following the Mississippi River from Minnesota to a point a few blocks to the right of this photograph. *Photograph by author, 2000*

This area was part of the Delord-Sarpy, later Duplantier, plantation into the early 1800s. When the D-Day Museum was under construction in spring 2000, excavations to plant palm trees on this traffic island near Howard and Camp uncovered these old bricks, possibly belonging to the magnificent Delord-Sarpy mansion that stood on this exact spot from about 1815 to 1957, when it was demolished for an off-ramp for the Mississippi River bridge. Despite its appearance, this Delord-Sarpy mansion actually postdated the subdivision of the area and was thus not a plantation house. An earlier Delord-Sarpy *plantation* house stood much closer to the river (to the right) as did almost all plantation houses in this region. *Photograph by author, 2000*

This area was the lower edge of Faubourg Ste. Marie, subdivided in 1788 out of the Gravier plantation as the first *fauxbourg* ("false town," or suburb) of New Orleans. Between this faubourg and the city (to the right) lay the undeveloped commons. The designs and names of these streets derive from eighteenth-century history: in this perspective, we are looking up *Gravier* Street and *Common* Street. In the 1720s, city founder Bienville had his plantation home roughly at the center of this photograph, corner of Magazine and Common. Harrah's Casino (bottom), seen here under construction, occupies a spot that was in the Mississippi River 200 years ago. *Photograph by author, 1996*

Street angles in New Orleans often originate from old plantation boundaries delineated according to the French *arpent* land-division system. These old agrarian patterns were passed on to the urban environment as the city expanded into the old plantations and were thence passed on to architects and builders, who accommodated their structures to the odd shapes and angles of blocks. Glances up at the modern New Orleans skyline reflect these historical-geographical patterns: the angle between the foreground structures on St. Charles and the Sheraton skyscraper on Canal is formed by Common Street, a former plantation boundary. *Photograph by author, 2000*

The late-eighteenth-century boundary between the Gravier plantation (later Faubourg Ste. Marie) and the Delord (later Duplantier) plantation passed from the lower left corner to the upper center of the area seen in this photograph. Unlike many other old plantation lines in the city, this particular one is not "burned" into the modern street network. But Howard Avenue (which used to be called Delord), the wide street at right, comes close to marking the old boundary. Note Lee Circle at upper right. *Photograph by author, 2000*

Clues to the Plantation Past in New Orleans' Modern Cityscape

Above present-day St. Andrew Street was the Panis plantation, bought by Don Jacinto Panis in 1779, subdivided in 1813 (river end) and 1818 (swamp end), and developed in the following two decades as part of the city of Lafayette. Through the center of this parcel ran a broad thoroughfare named *Cours Panis,* paralleled by two lesser streets probably named after the children of Madame Panis, Philip and Josephine.[49] The broad river end of this wedge-shaped faubourg accommodated the surveying of two additional shorter streets, Soraparu and Adele, which would form part of the original Irish Channel neighborhood in ensuing decades. The remaining unsold portion of the plantation was sold by Madame Panis's daughter, Madame Rousseau, to John

This detail of Currier & Ives' *The City of New Orleans* (1885) depicts the growth (or "sprawl," as we might call it today) of New Orleans into the former plantations of the Mississippi River crescent and, to a lesser extent, backward into the wooded swamplands. Note Lee Circle at right, the New Basin Canal at upper right, the World's Industrial and Cotton Centennial Exposition buildings (present-day Audubon Park) at left, and the train traveling the tracks on Metairie Road (the only upland in that area) at upper left. *American Memory Panoramic Maps Collection, Library of Congress*

Poultney in 1818, who developed it. The former Panis plantation became Faubourg Lafayette in 1824, part of the city of Lafayette in 1832, and finally part of New Orleans in 1852. Today, Philip and Josephine streets mark the outline of the former Panis plantation; Jackson Avenue—formerly *Cours Panis*—still runs through the middle; and Soraparu and Adele still anchor it to the river. Treelined Jackson Avenue was a prestigious address in the nineteenth century and today boasts some of the most splendid mansions in the area. Now the lower limit of the Garden District, it forms an impressive path to the river and a prominent spoke in the radiating street pattern of uptown New Orleans. The river ends of Jackson Avenue and adjacent communities, however, have always been far less prosperous, even poverty stricken, than the interior streets. The historic neighborhoods built upon the river ends of both the Nuns and Panis plantations were viewed as horrific slums about 125 years after their birth and were obliterated for the St. Thomas Housing Development during a series of phases from the 1930s to the 1950s;[50] in 2000, the St. Thomas complex was in turn viewed as a horrific slum and was demolished for a mixed public/private housing experiment.

49. According to Chase (124), Philip Street might have been named for Celeste Philippe Marigny Livaudais, sister of the famed Bernard Marigny and owner of the adjacent Livaudais plantation. In either case, Philip Street marks a former plantation boundary. See Wilson, "Early History of the Lower Garden District," 31-33.
50. Magill, 18-19.

The next blade in the fan of New Orleans' streets started as the expansive Livaudais plantation, a sixteen-arpent-wide lot that, unlike most other plantations within the crescent, formed an elongated shape more rectangular than triangular. It was sold by Celeste Philippe Marigny Livaudais to four businessmen, who had it subdivided in 1832. The rectangular shape of Faubourg Livaudais explains why the streets of the present-day neighborhoods that overlay the old Livaudais plantation—portions of the Garden District, Irish Channel, and Central City, between Philip and Harmony—constitute grid-pattern blocks with few angular intersections or other odd shapes. This serves as a reminder that, while there was no central planning authority overseeing the development of the plantation country into urban units (allowing the old plantation boundaries to become the skeleton of the new street network), there was indeed a planning authority governing the street layout *within* new faubourgs. That authority was usually the surveying engineer tasked with the design of the new subdivision. "The result . . . is a fan that has a checkerboard on each blade of the fan. Thus did the firm hand of the historic cadaster, through the legal reality of the concession, guide the physical formation of Louisiana's greatest city."[51]

Purchased out of the Livaudais plantation was the Delassize property, a small triangular lot measuring three arpents in front and stretching back only about half the distance of the neighboring plantations. Subdivided prior to 1834, the compact wedge-shaped Faubourg Delassize (previously used for a sawmill more so than a plantation) explains the acute angles that Harmony and Pleasant streets make with Eighth, Ninth, and Toledano streets.[52] The shape of this area reflects the fact that when a long-lot plantation was partially sold or divided among heirs for continued non-urban use, the new unit was almost always sliced off perpendicularly to the river, not parallel to it, so as to maintain mutual access to the river. Adjoining the Delassize and Livaudais properties was the Wiltz plantation, a tapered rectangular parcel about 8 arpents wide and extending back, like most plantations in the crescent, to the 40-arpent line near present-day Claiborne Avenue. The downriver portion of the Wiltz plantation, measuring 4 arpents wide at the river and about 4.5 at one point inland, was subdivided surprisingly early in the development of uptown (1807) and called Faubourg Plaisance (or Quartier de Plaisance), later part of Jefferson City (1850) and eventually New Orleans (1870). Through its middle ran *Gran Cours Wiltz,* much as *Cours Panis* (Jackson Avenue) bisected Faubourg Lafayette; today this thoroughfare is Louisiana Avenue, a major path and spoke in the crescent and the dividing line between Central City and Milan, the Garden District and Touro, and the Irish Channel and Riverside. The well-preserved limits of the former Faubourg Plaisance are today's Toledano Street on the downtown side and Delachaise Street on the uptown side.[53] S. Frederick Starr described the peopling of this area, from Felicity to Louisiana Avenue, as the third phase of the Americanization of New Orleans (1820s-50s), after Faubourg Ste. Marie (Phase I, 1800-30s) and Faubourg Delord and its neighbors (Phase II, 1806-40s).[54]

The upriver portion of the Wiltz plantation, shaped like a slightly crooked isosceles triangle, was inherited by Wiltz's son and daughter in 1811 and eventually purchased piecemeal by Philippe Auguste Delachaise in 1820-23. To this 4.3-arpent parcel, Delachaise added the neighboring 2.5-arpent Le Breton plantation in 1831, essentially enlarging the isosceles triangle. After Delachaise's death in 1838, his heirs maintained a plantation (complete with house, gardens, outbuildings, eighty-seven slaves at one point, and a brickworks) until 1855, making the Delachaise plantation the last agricultural operation in the central crescent. When Faubourg Delachaise was subdivided that year and incorporated into Jefferson and later New Orleans, the former plantation's lower and upper limits were already inscribed into the street network (as Delachaise and Amelia streets) on account of the prior development of neighboring faubourgs. The terminus of the former Delachaise plantation, tangential to the 40-arpent line that marked the edge of the backswamp, became the acute-angled intersection of these two streets near present-day Magnolia Street. Even the slight crookedness of the frontage of the old cadaster may be witnessed today, in the incrementally lengthening blocks between Annunciation and Tchoupitoulas as one walks from Amelia to Delachaise. (These riverside blocks, incidentally, mark the site of the brickyard and the long-demolished Delachaise plantation house, located in the vicinity of the Foucher/Annunciation intersection.) Other streets within Faubourg Delachaise commemorated Delachaise

51. Newton, 211. The only major exception to this checkerboard-on-a-fan-blade phenomenon in historic New Orleans is the Lower Garden District, where Barthélémy Lafon designed irregularly shaped parks and circles to complement his interesting arrangement of streets. Lafon's mythological street names also distinguish this neighborhood from adjacent areas.
52. According to Meloncy C. Soniat ("The Faubourgs," 200), the plan by which Faubourg Delassize was subdivided was created in April 1836. However, Zimpel's *Topographical Map of New Orleans and Its Vicinity,* published in 1834, shows Delassize already subdivided.
53. Samuel Wilson, Jr., "Early History," in Friends of the Cabildo, vol. 7, 16-18, and Meloncy C. Soniat, "The Faubourgs," 201-2.
54. Starr, 13-15.

Felicity Street, covered with old granite paving blocks, runs straight as an arrow through some of most imaginative urban designs in America, created by Barthélémy Lafon in 1806-10. Its straightness, which is more striking from a remote or cartographic perspective than from a pedestrian view, reflects its origins as a plantation boundary. Surrounding this part of Felicity Street today is the Lower Garden District, a great historic neighborhood filled with mansions and cottages of remarkable architectural variety, sans the aloof air and astronomical housing prices of the more famous Garden District a few blocks uptown. Note the imprint of streetcar tracks, removed long ago. *Photographs by author, 2000*

The foot of Felicity Street (right) intersects with block-long Nuns Street (left) at Tchoupitoulas Street. Land to the left of Felicity Street comprised the Ursuline Nuns plantation until 1809. This general area is currently a rough industrial district intermixed with impoverished residential areas, but great change looms with the construction of the large Saulet apartment complex between Annunciation and Tchoupitoulas and the demolition of the St. Thomas Housing Development for an innovative mixed private/public residential experiment. In the summer of 2001, Wal-Mart proposed locating a "big box" supercenter in this area, indicative of changing times. *Photograph by author, 2000*

Most bends in present-day St. Charles Avenue correspond to old plantation lines. As old plantation boundaries became river-perpendicular streets and the former croplands were subdivided into grids during the early 1800s, new river-parallel streets tended to "kink" every time they crossed a plantation boundary. One such example is St. Charles Avenue, originally laid out as a railroad route, at the Felicity intersection, seen here. Felicity Street is a vestige from the mid-1700s, when it was the upper line of the Jesuits plantation; later, the street marked the boundary between Barthélémy Lafon's subdivisions (1806) and the Ursuline Nuns plantation. Until the annexation of Lafayette, Felicity Street was the upper limit of New Orleans. Today, most river-parallel streets in the crescent, including St. Charles Avenue, make an approximately ten- to twenty-degree bend when they intersect with Felicity. *Photograph by author, 2000*

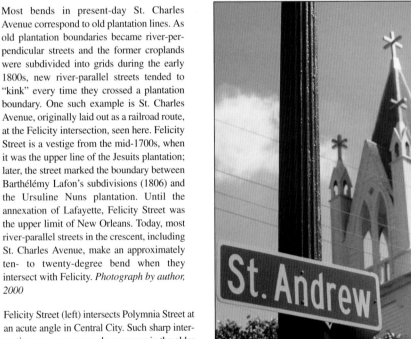

St. Andrew Street was the upper line of the Ursuline Nuns plantation, subdivided in 1809 as Faubourg des Religieuses. The shape of the former plantation is perfectly preserved in the modern street network—a long, narrow pie wedge about five arpents (~1,000 feet) wide at the river and 40 arpents (~1.5 miles) in depth, nestled among three streets named for the nuns involved in the transaction: Felicity (Félicité), St. Mary (Marie), and St. Andrew (André). *Photograph by author, 2000*

Felicity Street (left) intersects Polymnia Street at an acute angle in Central City. Such sharp intersections are a common phenomenon in the older section of New Orleans, as plantations were developed whenever the owner decided to get out of agriculture and however the surveyor decided to subdivide lots and streets. Because of the sectionalized nature of growth in New Orleans and the lack of a centralized planning authority, the shapes of old long-lot plantations were incorporated into the street network and are evident today in the radiating pattern of the New Orleans map. A byproduct of this process was the creation of the occasional acute-angle intersection, occurring when surveyors "squeezed" a grid of streets into a wedge-shaped parcel. They are a signature of New Orleans' unique urban geography. *Photograph by author, 2000*

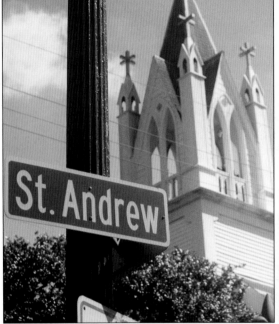

Religious Street gets its name from the property once owned by the Ursuline Nuns on these outskirts of early-nineteenth-century New Orleans, now near the St. Thomas Housing Development and the Lower Garden District. The sisters' parcel was subdivided in 1809 as Faubourg des Religieuses. Only the upper two blocks of this short street were actually within the Ursuline plantation; the rest of it, including this intersection, was subdivided three years earlier as Faubourgs de L'Annunciation and La Course. *Photograph by author, 2000*

Historic plantation boundaries in the middle portion of the New Orleans crescent and their relationship to the modern city. Green type indicates prominent owners (not necessarily all owners) during plantation days; yellow type indicates the name of the development at the time of its subdivision; blue type shows present-day streets derived from the edges or centers of old plantations. *Map and analysis by author based on various historical maps and data; aerial image courtesy U.S. Geological Survey. Locations of lateral boundaries of plantations are certain, but rear boundaries (along the backswamp) varied over the years, depending on conditions, and were often not depicted on historical maps.*

family members, and, like the ghostly geographical imprint of the old plantation, endure today. The last surviving structure of the Delachaise plantation's initial subdivision, an immense ca.-1850s double townhouse at 1722-24 Delachaise Street, was recently restored and now stands like a monarch over the community that has developed on these former sugar fields.[55]

Upriver from the Delachaise property was a 3-arpent remnant of Valentin Robert Avart's original 38-arpent-wide plantation from the early 1800s, owned by Mme. Louis Robert Avart (Claude Augustine Eugénie Delachaise) at the time of its 1849 subdivision as Faubourg St. Joseph. The two-block-wide rectangular plantation is today bounded by General Taylor and Amelia. By 1816, the original Avart tract had been whittled down to 23.5 arpents, forming a symmetrical trapezoid oriented perfectly in the belly of the crescent. In that year, the large estate was acquired by Gen. Wade Hampton, who operated it as "The Cottage" plantation until 1829, when he sold it to Louis Bouligny.[56] Businessmen Laurent Millaudon and Samuel Kohn recognized this area as a valuable real-estate investment, especially in light of the planned New Orleans & Carrollton Rail Road (in which they were also invested), which would bisect the parcel; they purchased a half-interest in it

Detail of bird's-eye perspective of uptown New Orleans, the city of Lafayette, and the backswamp around 1850, from *Bird's Eye View of New-Orleans* (New York: Guerber & Co., 1851). Note the New Basin Canal turning basin at extreme center right, Coliseum Square at bottom center, and Place du Tivoli (later Lee Circle) at lower right. *American Memory Panoramic Maps Collection, Library of Congress*

from Bouligny. In 1834, the substantial lot was subdivided by Pierre-Benjamin Buisson and mapped by Charles F. Zimpel as "L. Millaudon - S. Kohn" for the lower half and "Bouligny" for the upper half. Later, the two sections would be called East and West Bouligny, and together they formed Faubourg Bouligny, heart of Jefferson City and still the core of uptown New Orleans.[57] The Cottage plantation and Faubourg Bouligny, formed and designed with such symmetry, are perfectly preserved today in both shape and balance. Down the middle runs graceful Napoleon Avenue, a major path and spoke in the crescent and similar in origin to Jackson and Louisiana avenues. Crossing Napoleon perpendicularly is magnificent St. Charles Avenue, the premier arc of the crescent and spinal column of the city. Bounding Bouligny upriver and downriver are the former plantation limits of Upperline and its mirror image, General Taylor (formerly Lowerline,[58] because it formed the lower boundary of the Bouligny tract); bordering it on the river and lake sides are Tchoupitoulas and Clara

55. Samuel Wilson, Jr., "Early History," in Friends of the Cabildo, New Orleans Architecture, vol. 7, 18-19, and Donze. See also Zimpel; B. F. Ogden; and W. Walter, *Plan of New Orleans and Environs* (1855), the latter two reproduced in Friends of the Cabildo, vol. 7, 10, 26.
56. Meloncy C. Soniat, "The Faubourgs," 204, and Samuel Wilson, Jr., "Early History," in Friends of the Cabildo, vol. 7, 20.
57. Friends of the Cabildo, vol. 7, 22-23, and the maps of Walter and Zimpel, reproduced on 26, 29.
58. This is not to be confused with the Lowerline Street that still exists in Carrollton, which was the lower line of the Macarty plantation.

Napoleon Avenue is the present-day centerpiece of former Faubourg Bouligny. Like most of the grand river-perpendicular avenues in uptown New Orleans, Napoleon runs down the middle, not the edge, of an old plantation. The edges of former plantations are usually marked by lesser streets today. *Photograph by author, 2000*

The large plantation owned by Valentin Robert Avart and others in the heart of the crescent was subdivided in 1834 as Faubourg Bouligny, with Upperline Street and Lowerline Street forming its edges. Upperline Street (left) survives today, but Lowerline was changed to General Taylor Street a few years later, seen here (right) at the Tchoupitoulas intersection. Some New Orleanians are perplexed why present-day Lowerline Street in Carrollton is "above" Upperline Street in Bouligny. The answer is, of course, that each marked the upper and lower limits of different plantations: the Macarty plantation in the case of Lowerline in Carrollton; the Bouligny plantation in the case of Upperline in Faubourg Bouligny. Note the row of houses a block down General Taylor. These turn-of-the-century cottages were all in ruin until the Preservation Resource Center of New Orleans targeted the entire block for a major renovation effort aimed at rejuvenating the whole neighborhood. The impressive renovations were completed by 2001. *Photographs by author, 2000*

streets, marking the public river road and the edge of the backswamp, respectively. Later development of a batture and wharves allowed for the creation of Leake Avenue riverside of Tchoupitoulas. The Sieurs Laurent Millaudon and Samuel Kohn are commemorated in the cityscape today through the parks of Laurence Square and Samuel Square along Napoleon Avenue at the Magazine and South Saratoga intersections. Other streets in the area denote place names associated with the career of Napoleon Bonaparte. Faubourg Bouligny today embraces the neighborhoods of Milan, Touro, Riverside, Uptown, and Freret, though the name *Bouligny* is also used, as is the designation of Uptown National Register Historic District. In sum, the Bouligny area is a masterpiece example of how the dimensions of a nineteenth-century sugarcane plantation would evolve into a beautiful urban layout and a keystone component of New Orleans' radiating street pattern.

The third part of the original Avart plantation, upriver from Faubourg St. Joseph and Faubourg Bouligny, was an 8.5-arpent parcel known by the name of the original lot from which it was delineated. Like the Delachaise plantation, this Avart plantation was an agricultural enterprise with a house, garden, appendages, and brickworks located near the river. The Avart family had the property subdivided in 1841 as Faubourg Avart, naming the streets after family members. Today, this 8.5-arpent-wide upriver remnant of the original Avart plantation, which once spanned over 20 modern-day blocks in the core of the crescent, survives between Upperline and Valmont Street.[59]

The next segment of the radiating street pattern originated as the Ducros plantation in the late 1700s and later became the property of the Beale family (1818), with a portion sold to Daniel Treadwell Walden in 1831. The ensuing story of the Beale family's financial and legal tumult in their relationship with a maverick interloper named Samuel Ricker, Jr., is expertly told by Sally Kittredge Reeves in her history of the founding families of Jefferson City.[60] The eight-arpent plantation, used for a while as a cattle ranch, was owned by the City Bank of New Orleans and seven other parties at the time of its subdivision as Rickerville in 1849. As the uppermost district of Jefferson City, Rickerville was settled only by a handful of families, mostly working class or poor, by the years following the Civil War, though it would rise in prominence (as the edge of the "Silk-Stocking Ward") in the turn-of-the-century years and remains a well-off neighborhood today. Rickerville today is the fan blade between Valmont and Joseph Street, including Jefferson Avenue (formerly Peters Avenue), another classic treelined path and spoke through uptown New Orleans, running from Mid-City to the Mississippi.

Upriver from Rickerville was the ten-arpent LeBreton plantation that was purchased by Cornelius Hurst, Pierre Joseph Tricou, and Julia Robert Avart in 1832 and divided among the threesome the following year.[61] Hurst acquired Tricou's tract later that year, forming a parcel of just under seven arpents wide (two-thirds the LeBreton parcel), and built a mansion in its lowermost corner.[62] An initial subdivision of the lot was done by 1834—Zimpel's *Topographical Map of New Orleans and Its Vicinity* (1834) shows the Hurst property as the only subdivided lot between Bouligny and Carrollton—but was updated in 1837 by Pierre-Benjamin Buisson to include a wide avenue down the middle of this new suburb of Hurstville. The thoroughfare was designed to host a spur of the New Orleans and Nashville Rail Road that would connect these two cities and increase the value of the new residential real estate. The Panic of 1837 sank the railroad project, but the idea lives on in the name and width of today's Nashville Avenue. The Hurst plantation's lower line is now Joseph Street; its upper line is not a street but a demarcation running between the slightly angled streets of Eleonore and State that is known as the Bloomingdale line (more on this later).

The remaining third of the LeBreton plantation, the three-arpent lot owned by Julia Robert Avart, was sold to John Green in 1834 and subdivided by Pierre-Benjamin Buisson in 1836.[63] Called Bloomingdale, this narrow subdivision had as its axis State Street, another grand spoke in the radiating street pattern. But what is unusual about Bloomingdale is the fact that its boundaries are among the few former plantation or faubourg limits in uptown New Orleans *not* fixed into the modern transportation network as streets. The lower Bloomingdale line, which separated Hurstville from Bloomingdale, now runs midblock between Eleonore and State Street; the upper Bloomingdale line, which separated Bloomingdale from Burtheville, today runs between State and Webster.[64] In other sources, these boundaries are called the line of Hurstville and the line of

Laurence Square on Napoleon Avenue at Magazine commemorates businessman Laurent Millaudon, who played an important role in the development of Faubourg Bouligny and Carrollton. His business partner, Samuel Kohn, is remembered through another neighborhood park, Samuel Square Playground, on Napoleon at South Saratoga. Napoleon Avenue runs through the middle of Faubourg Bouligny and is one of the most splendid pathways through uptown New Orleans. St. Stephen (1868-87), one of the largest churches in the city, is a landmark of the present-day neighborhoods of Touro/ Bouligny. *Photograph by author, 2000*

Jefferson Avenue, seen here near the Magazine intersection, is the main thoroughfare of the 1849 subdivision known as Rickerville, part of Jefferson City until its annexation into New Orleans in 1870. The area was earlier part of plantations belonging to the Ducros and Beale families. As the uppermost district of Jefferson City, Rickerville was mostly settled by working-class and poor families; in later decades, it rose in affluence and remains prosperous today. The former subdivision of Rickerville covers the present-day "fan blade" between Valmont and Joseph Street, with Jefferson Avenue (formerly Peters Avenue) running down the middle. *Photograph by author, 2000*

Napoleon Avenue, shaded with live oaks and lined with beautiful homes, comes alive during Carnival season, when it serves as the assembly point and staging ground for most uptown parades. Bands rehearse, floats are rigged up and organized, tractor engines are started, and the great ritual begins. *Photograph by author, 2001*

59. Friends of the Cabildo, vol. 7, 23-24. According to Meloncy C. Soniat ("The Faubourgs," 204), the original Avart plantation "began at Valmont Street and extended to a line running between Antonine and Foucher streets," which is about 1.5 blocks downriver from Amelia. Three major components of the original 38-arpent Avart plantation—Faubourg St. Joseph (3 arpents), Faubourg Bouligny (23.5 arpents), and Faubourg Avart—(8.5) arpents—account for 35 of the original 38 arpents; the remainder were probably obtained by Le Breton and eventually came into the hands of Delachaise in 1831, becoming part of Faubourg Delachaise.
60. Sally Kittredge Reeves, "The Founding Families and Political Economy, 1850-1870," in Friends of the Cabildo, vol. 7, 41-46.
61. This general area was originally the Jean Etienne Boré plantation, where the granulation of sugar in 1795 led to the birth of the Louisiana sugar industry.
62. The Cornelius Hurst House still exists, one of the few surviving presubdivision mansions of present-day Uptown, but not in its original location: it was dismantled and moved to 3 Garden Lane, near the New Orleans Country Club, in 1922. Wilson, "The Uptown Faubourgs," 15.
63. Friends of the Cabildo, vol. 7, 19.
64. Ibid., xiii.

Burtheville, respectively.[65] But whatever the names, neither line became a modern street, unlike so many other old property boundaries in the crescent. Why? One may hypothesize that, since these properties were united at various times and in various combinations under the ownership of Boré, LeBreton, and others, and since Pierre-Benjamin Buisson had a hand in subdividing at least two lots at roughly the same time (1836-37), there may have been a tendency to design the blocks with less regard toward existing property lines. Indeed, the Zimpel map (1834) shows blocks in the initial Hurst subdivision as being sliced off midblock at the edge of the property—the lower Bloomingdale line—in a manner that suggests an expectation that the layout would proceed upriver in the near future. And it did. Whatever the reason, the narrow Bloomingdale subdivision would develop into an affluent neighborhood and maintain its quirky shape, with slightly up-bent and elongated blocks between Eleonore and Webster Street, to this day. Odd angles and kinks in Laurel Street (for Gilmore Park) and Annunciation Street line up with the otherwise-erased upper and lower Bloomingdale lines, and Alonzo Street actually follows the lower line in its two-block length.

The upper portion of the old Boré sugar plantation was acquired by Dominique François Burthe in 1831 and subdivided in 1854 as an eight-arpent development called Burtheville. (Boré's impressive plantation compound, which originated in 1781 and once served a twenty-one-arpent estate, was located between present-day Annunciation and Constance Street within the sliver of land that later became Burtheville; it was probably here that the first major granulation of sugar occurred in 1795.)[66] The upper Bloomingdale line marked the lower limits of Burthe's plantation, while the Foucher tract (now Audubon Park, bordered by Exposition Boulevard) delineated its upper limit. Like its neighbors, the old Burthe plantation's classic long-lot shape is very well preserved today, extending from the river to the crux of the crescent among Webster, Henry Clay, and Calhoun Street.

The old Foucher tract is the arpent system's most prominent signature in the radiating street pattern of modern New Orleans, not because of the street network it engendered but because its current occupants—park, campuses, and residential parks—distinguish it from the dense urban cityscape that has encroached upon all other long-lot plantations in the crescent. This lot came into the Foucher family during colonial times as a 10.5-arpent lot purchased by Pierre Foucher from Jacques Fontenot (1793) and expanded to 12.5 arpents in 1825. Its location in the upriver "corner" of the crescent afforded it a depth of about 70 arpents from the river to the backswamp, making it one of the larger properties in the area. (Additionally, the riverside end of the Lebreton plantation, a 7-arpent long lot immediately upriver to the original acquisition, was acquired by Foucher in 1800 and sold in 1836, becoming Greenville.)[67]

The main 12.5-arpent tract is today the only former plantation in the crescent that, with some minor exceptions, was never subdivided for residential development. That its shape as a 200-year-old long lot persists today despite the lack of subdivision derives from a series of factors. First, subdivision of the neighboring parcel as Greenville in 1836 established the upper line, bordering this new community and the Foucher tract, into the landscape.[68] Second, the subdivision of Burtheville in 1854 imprinted the lower line, separating the Burthe and Foucher properties. Third, the dismal and later colorful history that would unfold on the Foucher tract would ensure that it remain a place apart in uptown New Orleans.

Louis Frederic Foucher, Pierre's son, struggled in his management of the plantation and eventually departed for France prior to the Civil War, leaving his property in a state of absentee ownership and neglect that would subject it to wartime abuse and real-estate scam. Following the sale of the property by Foucher's widow in 1871, a series of dubious dealings involving Reconstruction-era state legislators and land speculators ended up making the portion of the former Foucher tract riverside of St. Charles Avenue a park for the citizens of New Orleans. Upper City Park, established in 1879, remained a muddy cow pasture lined with old live-oak alleys left over from plantation days, until its watershed moment: its selection as the site for the World's Industrial and Cotton Centennial Exposition of 1884-85.[69] The park's status as the only sufficiently large and accessible open public area made it a natural candidate for such a site.

Though the exposition was a financial failure, it had a profound effect on the growth of uptown New Orleans, spurring the residential development of nearly all surrounding subdivisions and bringing attention and elaborate (though temporary) structures to the Foucher tract itself. "Without the decision to have the exposition in this city, on the old Foucher estate," wrote Hilary Somerville Irvin, "the Olmsted-inspired park, two

65. Meloncy C. Soniat, "The Faubourgs," 206.
66. Ibid., and Wilson, "The Uptown Faubourgs," 25.
67. Friends of the Cabildo, vol. 7, 30-33.
68. This line is now near, but not quite coincident with, today's Walnut Street. The subdivision of Greenville was executed in a manner "so that near the river there is, between Walnut Street and the Greenville-Foucher line, space for about six lots; this is gradually reduced so that at St. Charles there is only a sliver of land." Wilson, "The Uptown Faubourgs," 33.
69. Hilary Somerville Irvin, "Foucher Tract," in Friends of the Cabildo, vol. 8, 39-45.

Historic plantation boundaries in the upper portion of the New Orleans crescent and their relationship to the modern city. Green type indicates prominent owners (not necessarily all owners) during plantation days; yellow type indicates the name of the development at the time of its subdivision; blue type shows present-day streets derived from the edges or centers of old plantations. *Map and analysis by author based on various historical maps and data; aerial image courtesy U.S. Geological Survey. Locations of lateral boundaries of plantations are certain, but rear boundaries (along the backswamp) varied over the years, depending on conditions, and were often not depicted on historical maps.*

Among the few plantation boundaries that were not preserved in the street network were those subdivided as Hurstville, Bloomingdale, and Burtheville in the 1830s. The lower Bloomingdale line, which separated Hurstville from Bloomingdale, now runs midblock between Eleonore and State Street; the upper Bloomingdale line, which separated Bloomingdale from Burtheville, today runs between State and Webster. Although these old delineations do not survive as streets, there are certain clues in the streetscape that apparently line up with the old plantation boundaries and may derive from them in some distant way.

1. This photograph looks up Laurel Street between Eleonore and State. Note the very slight angle in the sidewalk at center right and the offshoot street visible at center left. These two artifacts line up with the lower Bloomingdale line. The park at center is Gilmore Park, which fills in the awkward space.

2. This photograph looks down the short offshoot street that lines up with the old lower Bloomingdale line. The river is about a half-mile straight ahead.

3. Farther up Laurel Street, between State and Webster, we encounter possible vestiges of the upper Bloomingdale line. In the foreground is Gilmore Park; at center, we see again a vague angle in the street plus an offshoot to the left, both of which line up with the upper Bloomingdale line.

4. Looking up the upper Bloomingdale line, toward the lake, from the offshoot street on Laurel, between State and Webster. *Photographs by author, 2000*

Looking downriver from the former Greenville subdivision into the Foucher tract (now Audubon Park and the Zoological Gardens), along what was once the River Road, lined with plantation homes and dependencies. This particular area was first subdivided in 1836 but was not fully populated with homes until the end of the nineteenth century. The Foucher tract was never fully subdivided for residential dwelling. This photograph was taken from the Lambeth House at Broadway and Leake Avenue. *Photograph by author, 2000*

The St. Charles Avenue Streetcar Line, formerly the New Orleans & Carrollton Rail Road (1835), made the distant subdivision of Carrollton (1833) accessible to New Orleanians and thus increased its real-estate value, resulting in its incorporation as a town in 1845. It was a symbiotic relationship: some investors in the railroad were also invested in the subdivision. The oldest continually operating rail system in the world, the streetcar is deeply embedded into the New Orleans ambience, especially in uptown. Here, a 1920s-era Perley Thomas car negotiates the ninety-degree turn from South Carrollton Avenue onto St. Charles Avenue. *Photograph by author, 2000*

The Carrollton Courthouse, now a school, is a vestige of Carrollton's days as a separate city anchoring the opposite end of the crescent from the original city of New Orleans. In 1874, New Orleans annexed Carrollton and completely filled the sweeping crescent formed by the Mississippi. The Carrollton Courthouse is among the oldest structures in the United States currently used as a public grade school. *Photograph by author, 2000*

Looking directly across the crescent from the former subdivision of Greenville toward downtown, viewed from the Lambeth House. Two hundred years ago, this vista would have incorporated a vast expanse of about a dozen long-lot plantations, with a compact city of New Orleans in the distance. A hundred and fifty years ago, about half this expanse would have been developed with new houses and streets. A hundred years ago, most of this area would have been developed. *Photograph by author, 2000*

important universities, and a large church might have been located elsewhere."[70] Add to this list most of the beautiful residential homes built here, and their influential occupants who settled in this area at the turn of the century, bringing a prosperity that the area still exudes today. Upper City Park was renamed Audubon Park in 1886 and finally landscaped by the famed Olmsted and Brothers firm from 1897 until the early 1920s, followed by the creation of Audubon Zoo at the river end of the former tract. Thus, Louis Foucher's neglect of his property in the mid-1800s led to a sequence of events that would freeze this land into the cityscape as a beautiful park within the configuration of an old plantation.

As for a fourth factor for the perseverance of the old property lines, the development spurred by the exposition led to, among other things, the eventual acquisition of the former Foucher tract "on the woods side" (lakeside) of St. Charles Avenue by the Jesuits in 1889 and by the Board of Administrators of Tulane University in 1891. Construction of the twin campuses of Loyola University (starting with Marquette Hall, 1910) and Tulane University (Gibson Hall, 1894), both of which moved from downtown locations, commenced in the 1890s and continues today. The attractive campuses are necessarily compact and elongated, since they are located in the increasingly narrow section of a wedge-shaped parcel surveyed under the arpent system. The most historically interesting architecture and attractive campus ambience of Tulane and Loyola tend to be closest to St. Charles Avenue, becoming progressively more modern and undistinguished as one heads toward the former backswamp near Claiborne Avenue. The campuses fill most but not all of the old tract lakeside of St. Charles; the remainder, upriver and adjacent to Tulane, is occupied by the residential parks of Audubon Place (1894), Audubon Boulevard (1909), and Versailles Boulevard (1925), as well as Newcomb College, which moved to this site from the Garden District in 1918.[71] These affluent residential parks plus a few narrow blocks lakeside of them are the only portions of the old Foucher plantation that were subdivided.

Part of the neighboring Lebreton plantation came into the possession of the Foucher family in 1800 but was sold by his son Louis to James Ogilvie, who in turn partnered with two other men in 1836 to subdivide it as Greenville.[72] This suburb was named for one of the partners, the same John Green behind Bloomingdale, and subdivided by the same surveyor, Pierre-Benjamin Buisson. Buisson laid out square blocks between the lower line of the neighboring Macarty plantation (still called Lowerline Street today) and the Greenville/Foucher property line. As he did in Bloomingdale, Buisson laid out a street along this line in a not-perfectly-coincident manner, such that small sections of river-parallel streets spill over past Walnut Street and now appear to be "in" Audubon Park. Thus the former Greenville/Foucher line counts among those few historic property lines in uptown New Orleans that was not precisely transferred to the street network—but nevertheless very nearly so. Greenville was laid out with Broadway as its primary thoroughfare, now a major spoke in the crescent and "main street" in the local college scene, paralleled by Pine and Chestnut (now called Audubon), and then Walnut on the lower edge. Another oddity about this particular wedge in the crescent is the fact that, in the 1830s, three parties owned roughly equal portions of the long rectangular parcel: the Foucher family owned the riverside end; the Derbigny-Lebreton clan maintained ownership of the middle section from about present-day Freret to about Claiborne Avenue; and Pierre Marly, a free man of color, owned "the woods end" from Claiborne to the crux of the crescent.[73] Faubourg Marly (Marlyville) was subdivided in 1834 and the Derbigny-Lebreton section was subdivided as Friburg in 1837, although these areas were not fully developed until well into the twentieth century. All three developments—Greenville, Friburg, and Marlyville—demarcate the eighteenth-century Lebreton plantation in today's radiating street pattern. One of Greenville's earliest structures, a spacious raised Greek Revival country home built by Christian Roselius in 1839, still stands at 515 Broadway, now one of the oldest structures in the area.

Thus far we have examined the piecemeal embossment of the old arpent land-surveying system into the modern street network of New Orleans, starting with Canal Street and wrapping around the crescent to this last upriver corner of the city, Carrollton. If modern-day Carrollton looks and feels like a city unto itself, with its main-street bustle on South Carrollton Avenue and quaint business district on Oak Street, there are geographical and historical reasons to support the impression. The area was attractive for a number of reasons: it had excellent river access, it occupied a slight ridge extending into backswamp ("Carrollton Spur"; see page 43)

70. Friends of the Cabildo, vol. 8, 43, 47.

71. Ibid., 57-66.

72. Ibid., 31-33.

73. Dorothy G. Schlesinger, "Introduction," xiii, and Robert J. Cangelosi, Jr., "Residential Parks," 90, both in Friends of the Cabildo, vol. 8. See also detail of Zimpel's *Topographical Map*, 12.

Tulane and Loyola universities occupy the rear half of the former Foucher tract, an old plantation and typical French long lot in what is now uptown New Orleans. The campuses, laid out starting in the 1890s, have since crammed into the slender strip of land starting from St. Charles Avenue (foreground, where the oldest buildings are located) and expanding back toward South Claiborne Avenue. Tulane Stadium (1926), home to forty Sugar Bowls and three Super Bowls, practically spills over the confines of the former long-lot plantation into surrounding residential neighborhoods in this 1966 photograph. After its expansion to a seating capacity of 82,000 (three and a half times its original size) in 1947, Tulane Stadium became the largest steel-structured arena in the country. Pressure for space led to the demolition of the landmark in 1979-80. *Photograph by Sam R. Sutton, The Historic New Orleans Collection, accession no. 1984.166.2.624*

that connected it with the New Basin Canal, and most importantly, it was reachable—by design—from downtown via the New Orleans & Carrollton Rail Road. These two key transportation facilities were built in the 1830s and fostered the early growth of Carrollton. In fact, many investors in Carrollton were also investors in the New Orleans & Carrollton Rail Road (see page 93). The community incorporated as a town in 1845 and became the Jefferson Parish seat in 1852 and a city in 1859, complete with its own courthouse, until it was absorbed into New Orleans in 1874. Carrollton was originally the upper flank of Bienville's immense concession from 1719 and later part of the Lebreton family plantation until 1781, when thirty-two arpents—the entire western edge of the crescent—were acquired by Barthelemy Macarty.[74] Owing to both its size and its location on a straight river section between the sharp Greenville Bend and Carrollton Bend of the Mississippi, the Macarty sugar plantation had not the traditional triangular shape of a long lot but rather an irregular parallelogram shape spanning from the river practically to the Metairie Ridge, and from Lowerline Street to Upperline Street (now called Monticello Avenue and coincident with the Orleans/Jefferson Parish line).[75] A consortium of buyers, including the New Orleans Canal and Banking Company (builders of the New Basin Canal), Laurent

74. Accounts vary as to exactly how and when—as early as 1771 to as late as 1795—this plantation passed from the Lebreton family to the Macarty family. See Ledet, 225, and William H. Williams, 187-88.

75. Chase (45, 229) states that the upper limit of Bienville's concession also coincided with Monticello Avenue, although it is unclear whether he meant *exactly* or *approximately*. A 1737 map of Bienville's property shows its upper line intersecting the foot of Monticello Avenue at the river—known as the Chapitoulas area at the time—but not coincident with the modern street. See also Cruzat and Dart, no. 1, 8-9.

Millaudon and Samuel Kohn (who would later invest in the Bouligny area), and John Slidell, purchased the Macarty plantation in 1831 and had it subdivided by the chief engineer of the New Orleans & Carrollton Rail Road, Charles F. Zimpel, in 1833.[76] The main thoroughfare through the subdivision was called Canal Avenue, which exploited the "Carrollton Spur" upland into the crux of the crescent to the New Basin Canal, from which the avenue got its name. It was later changed to South Carrollton Avenue on the riverside of the New Basin Canal (filled in since the early 1950s and now overlaid by Interstate 10) and North Carrollton Avenue on the lake side. Carrollton Avenue is today the uppermost major spoke in the radiating street pattern of New Orleans, forming a perfect *X* with downtown's Canal Street at the bull's eye of the crescent and the heart of the great present-day neighborhood of Mid-City. Together, these two paths anchor the grand diffusion of streets spanning over seven miles (about two hundred linear arpents) of spectacular Mississippi riverfront in a manner so perfect that it is hard to believe there was no urban planner overseeing the 120-odd-year development period[77] in which the wedge-shaped pieces of this puzzle fell into place.

"To a degree probably true of no other American city the history of New Orleans is reflected in its street nomenclature. The haphazard way in which the community expanded has led to an exceedingly complicated street plan. Part of its irregularity arose from conditions imposed upon the builders by the location of the city in a bend of the Mississippi. The original town was laid out with mathematical exactitude. But when it outgrew its swaddling clothes it did not spread beyond the original boundaries regularly into the adjacent country. The people went far afield, built up little isolated groups of homes, with street systems and parks of their own. When the growing metropolis ultimately encircled these villages, the eccentricities of their maps were accepted without correction. The result is seen in a curious, fan-like radiation of streets, crossed in every direction by diagonals. Not merely in the older part of the city, but in the newest quarters, streets merge into one another and squares taper into triangles, in a fashion which is bewildering even to the native."

—John Smith Kendall, 1922 (672)

Endurance of the Arpent-System Pattern

It may seem paradoxical that arbitrary and cryptic cadastral patterns often have a greater and longer-lasting impact on the landscape than massive structures of brick and mortar. But buildings come and go, subject to the elements and the whims of their owners, whereas parcel delineation is inscribed in legal and political realms and rooted in fundamental national philosophies. Even with changes of government—at least nonrevolutionary changes—extant cadastral patterns are often respected and maintained by new administrations, and continue their stamp upon the landscape.

Despite the fact that the Spanish used a wide range of cadastral systems elsewhere in the New World, ranging from circular patterns to square *sitios* to elongated lots based on the unit *vara* (both once found in southwestern Louisiana), they generally continued the French arpent-based system upon taking possession of the Louisiana colony—technically theirs since 1762—in 1769.[78] Spanish governor Don Alexandro O'Reilly decreed in 1770 that land grants would be allocated to qualified parties in lots of "four, six, or eight arpens" (*sic*) in front but "never to exceed eight hundred arpens in superficies"[79] along the banks of the Mississippi, roughly the size of the parcels within the New Orleans crescent. Spanish governor Manuel Luis Gayoso also mandated that land grants must adjoin each other, leaving no gaps in between, for reasons of security, policing, and economic development. This stipulation may have impacted the eventual pattern of parcels delineated within the crescent and hence the eventual street network. The Spanish were also the first to appoint official surveyors throughout Louisiana, bringing precise measurements (at least in frontage; side lines were surveyed less carefully, and rear lines even less so) to properties that were often loosely defined and disputed under the French regime. By the end of the Spanish era, about 3 million arpents, or roughly 10 percent of the land area, were delineated in "Lower Louisiana,"[80] the vast majority along riverine environments, by means of the French arpent system, and measured almost exclusively by the French arpent (de Paris), not Spanish units. This is not to say that the specific regulations of land distribution, stipulating acquisition, disposition, and conditions of ownership,[81] were the same under Spanish rule; rather, it was the geographical patterns of the system (long lots perpendicular to the river) that persisted. The underlying reasons for the prevalence of the French land-division system under the Spanish administration were simply that (1) most of populace remained French in every way[82] and (2) the Spanish presence in Louisiana was generally benign, even lax, and certainly nonrevolutionary, often making it amenable to the inclinations of its new subjects.

Louisiana was secretly retroceded by Spain to France in 1800 and formally transferred to the original mother country on November 30, 1803. Twenty days later, the Louisiana Purchase was made official, finally ending the French presence as well as the European colonial years, and making the vast Louisiana hinterland plus the very foreign New Orleans region American territories. The federal government of the United States promptly sent out its contract surveyors to delineate the unoccupied lands of Louisiana in the standard American rectangular grid pattern.

This sufficed in the piney wild lands that covered most of the territory, but was met with resistance in the riverine agricultural lands of southern Louisiana, which had been settled for decades and were thoroughly French Creole (meaning French in ancestry and native to Louisiana) in culture. "Inhabitants simply refused to buy lands which were so divided," wrote John Whitling Hall in his 1970 dissertation on the subject. "The new patterns were counter to the established culture, disrupting the familiar long settlements with their attached fields running perpendicular to the streams, the main transportation arteries. They complained that much land they might be forced to buy under the American system might well be useless, inundated land."

Aware of the controversy, Secretary of the Treasury Gallatin mandated in 1805 to survey in a manner "having as much front in proportion to their depth as has been usual in Lower Louisiana."[83] One American surveyor even consulted with the former Spanish surveyor general Don Carlos Laveau Trudeau, designer of Faubourg Ste. Marie, to issue a set of rules on long-lot division along meandering waterways. In this manner, the French and later Spanish surveying heritage was passed on to the American regime.

An Act of Congress in 1807 confirmed most titles of settlers from colonial times,[84] and a second Act of Congress in 1811 further formalized the transition of land-division systems, providing that surveyors in the Territory of Orleans "be authorized, in surveying and dividing such of the public lands . . . as are adjacent to any river, lake, creek, bayou, or water course, *to vary the mode heretofore prescribed by law . . . and to lay out* [the tracts] fifty-eight poles in front and four hundred and sixty-five poles in depth, of such shape, and bounded by such lines as the nature of the country will render practicable."[85] This 58-by-465-pole measurement equates to the classic 5-by-40-arpent lots of colonial times.[86] The American variation of the arpent parcels was not quite identical to the French system—sizes and shapes were more regulated; rear lines along the backswamps tended to be more squared off; a variety of units was used—and for this reason Hall proposes the term "American long lot" to describe the new adaptation. In most literature, however, one sees the terms "arpent lots" and "long lots" and their variations used in both historical contexts.

Survival of long-lot division in Louisiana from the French to Spanish to American administrations[87] allowed the cadastral pattern to thrive throughout the former French zone in Louisiana, including the Acadian (Cajun) settlements west of the New Orleans region. One may debate whether the new governments continued the practice because they sought to keep the peace among the contentious Creoles, because they considered it a superior way to divide riverine lands, or simply because it would have been pointless to force a complicated switch to an unwanted system, incurring the wrath of new citizens and logistical problems for new authorities. Whatever the reason, the result is that the long-lot division of the natural levees of the Mississippi, Bayou Lafourche, Bayou Teche, and numerous other waterways is splendidly prominent today, detectable even from

---

76. Meloncy C. Soniat, "The Faubourgs," 208-10, and Guilbeau, 2-3.

77. The period of uptown development started with the subdivision of Faubourg Ste. Marie in 1788 and ended in the early years of the twentieth century, when Audubon Park was landscaped and its neighboring communities were populated with residences.

78. James W. Taylor, 278; John Whitling Hall, 34, 44; and Holmes, "The Value of the Arpent," 317. See also Burns.

79. As quoted in John Whitling Hall, 36-37.

80. This percentage is based on data from Major Amos Stoddard (259), who, writing around 1810-12, probably used "Lower Louisiana" to mean the Louisiana Purchase south of the Arkansas River, east of the Red/Atchafalaya, and west of the Mississippi, plus the New Orleans area, an area of roughly 44,000 square miles. Stoddard's approximation of 3 million delineated arpents presumably means *superficial* arpents, which equals about 4,000 square miles. If these presumptions are correct, then roughly 10 percent of Lower Louisiana was delineated by the end of the colonial era. The figure would be in the 15-20 percent range if a more restrictive definition of "Lower Louisiana" was implied. See also 205-6, where Stoddard defines Upper Louisiana.

81. See Burns.

82. Jerah Johnson, 45. James Pitot (31), writing in 1802, stated that "the population of Louisiana, Spanish by its government, is still generally French in its tastes, customs, habits, religion, and language. Gay, noisy, hospitable, and easy to govern, it would need more education to moderate its passions."

83. As quoted in John Whitling Hall, 56.

84. This was the same Act of Congress that granted New Orleans the commons surrounding the city and stipulated the construction of a canal that, in its absence, eventually became Canal Street. Much of New Orleans' modern urban geography stems from this 1807 legislation. "An Act Respecting Claims to Land in the Territories of Orleans and Louisiana" (March 3, 1807), as recorded in *The Debates and Proceedings in the Congress of the United States* (1852), 1283, section 2. See also Burns, 581.

85. As quoted in John Whitling Hall, 56-57 (emphasis added).

86. A pole, equivalent to a perch and a rod, is 16.5 linear American feet. John Whitling Hall, 209.

87. Again, it should be noted that it was the *geography* of the French and Spanish systems that endured into the American years, not necessarily the rules and regulations of land ownership.

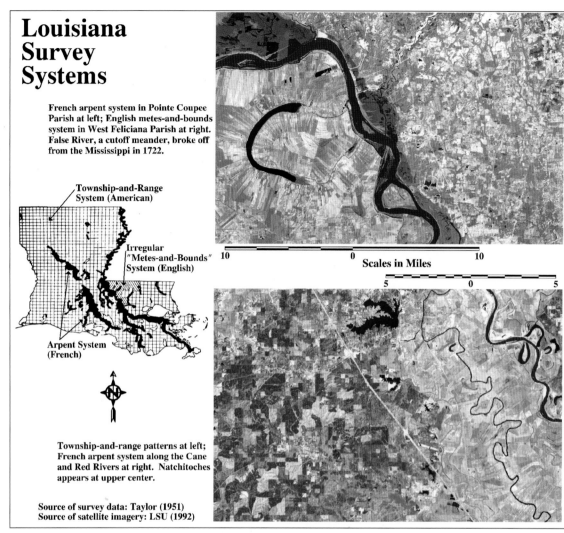

Louisiana Survey Systems

French arpent system in Pointe Coupee Parish at left; English metes-and-bounds system in West Feliciana Parish at right. False River, a cutoff meander, broke off from the Mississippi in 1722.

Township-and-Range System (American)

Irregular "Metes-and-Bounds" System (English)

Arpent System (French)

Township-and-range patterns at left; French arpent system along the Cane and Red Rivers at right. Natchitoches appears at upper center.

Source of survey data: Taylor (1951)
Source of satellite imagery: LSU (1992)

10   0   10
Scales in Miles
5   0   5

Major survey systems of Louisiana and their patterns in the landscape. *Map by author based James W. Taylor; Landsat/SPOT satellite imagery courtesy Louisiana State University*

space-borne imaging satellites, and clearly influential in the layout of hundreds of towns and villages in the deltaic region, including modern subdivisions.[88] It contrasts with the old Spanish *sitios* in pockets of southwestern Louisiana, the English metes-and-bounds surveying system employed in the "Florida parishes" north of Lake Pontchartrain, and the Americans' orderly township-and-range system predominating throughout most of the state. All these surveying systems have influenced the development of road networks and communities throughout the state, but it is in New Orleans' radiating street pattern that the French arpent land-surveying system has left its largest and most magnificent urban imprint. Given this pattern of land-ownership parcels and the absence of a central planning authority, private-sector developers implemented community growth within the crescent by incrementally filling in these parcels, one by one, respecting their irregular outer boundaries because they had to, but designing fairly regular street patterns within the boundaries because they could.

88. John Whitling Hall, 67-68.

Contrast this situation to the one in Manhattan in the early 1800s, when Dewitt Clinton oversaw the imposition of a famously rigid grid upon the countryside in the central and northern parts of the island. In this case, a central authority controlled the development of a rural area adjacent to a growing city and did so regardless of property boundaries, replacing the old systems with an overriding grid. Even in the lakeside half of New Orleans, developed entirely in the twentieth century under the regulatory eye of local agencies, one sees a large-scale orthogonal grid with streets following cardinal directions—just like Manhattan. It is no surprise that this area lies beyond the reach of the natural levee of the Mississippi, north of the point at which the eighteenth-century arpent lots converged in present-day Mid-City.

Arcs in the Crescent

While it is the spokes in the crescent—streets like Felicity, Jackson, Jefferson, and others perpendicular to the river—that reflect the plantation delineations and form the radiating street pattern, it is the transcrescent streets parallel to the river—"arcs"—that serve as the primary transportation routes between downtown and uptown, as well as the paths through which most people experience the image of the city. The principal arcuate paths in the crescent, Tchoupitoulas, St. Charles Avenue, and Claiborne, were designed and surveyed with partial regard to physical and human geography and total regard to expediency. The first arc in the crescent, dating from prehistoric times, logically followed the crest of the natural levee—the highest, driest, and most accessible land around—and served the Chapitoulas Indian camp located across from Nine Mile Point, above present-day Carrollton. Lands downriver from the campsite comprised Bienville's concession, while the site itself was conceded to the Chauvin brothers almost concurrently with Bienville's grant (March 1719). Thus within a year of the founding of New Orleans, new upriver land grants established an initial need among the French for a road along the "Chapitoulas Coast"—the riverbank around the great crescent. The old Indian path grew into the *Chemin de Tchoupitoulas* in the French era, the *Camino Real* in Spanish times, variously *Rue de la Levée, Rue de la Vieille Levée, Rue des Tchoucpicloneas* (sic), *Levee Street, Old Levee Street, Choupitoulas Street,* and *Tchapitoulas Street* throughout the 1800s, and finally *Tchoupitoulas Street* in the late 1800s to today. The various names for this great riverside path all describe what was essentially the first few miles of the River Road, which, then and now, parallels the Mississippi River from New Orleans to Baton Rouge. It was along the course of this road that surveyors traced out the frontage arpents demarcating the many long-lot plantations in the crescent, and it was on this road that inhabitants of those early plantations communicated with New Orleans and each other. One can trace the original crest of the natural levee through downtown New Orleans by following Tchoupitoulas Street: areas riverside of this 5.5-mile corridor comprise natural battures or man-made land added to the riverbanks well after the founding of the city; areas lakeside of the street host the majority of the historic city and slope gently from about ten feet above m.s.l. to below sea level in the middle of the crescent. It is one of the longest streets in the city and certainly the longest, *highest* street in town. If New Orleans' elevation were exaggerated tenfold, the great arc of Tchoupitoulas Street would circumscribe the upper rim of a deep, coliseum-shaped basin.

In the 100-year heyday of the cotton industry, starting in the early 1800s, Tchoupitoulas was increasingly lined with enormous cotton warehouses and presses, specializing in compressing bales, through horse and hydraulic power at first and later steam power, to about half their original size after all transactions and measurements were made on the lint and just before it was shipped out to its buyer. First-generation presses fronted Tchoupitoulas in the vicinity of Poydras around 1806; by 1873, twenty-six cotton presses, "immense brick store-houses," lined Tchoupitoulas from St. Joseph to Louisiana.[89] "Tchoupitoulas street was white with loose cotton that had dropped from bales in transit," recalled one observer in 1885 of the street in earlier decades.[90] So dominant was this industry that another writer (1893) referred to this portion of Tchoupitoulas as the "Cotton Press quarter of the city."[91] With competition from railroads and changes in the cotton industry and marketplace, New Orleans' mastery of the cotton trade would fade by World War II, and Tchoupitoulas's "Cotton Press quarter" would retool for other port-city tasks.

Today, Tchoupitoulas Street defies categorization. In its downtown stretch, it resembles other streets of the Central Business District, lined with nineteenth-century storehouses interspersed with modern structures and parking lots. Through the Warehouse District, century-old industrial buildings share the streetscape with the

89. Paxton (1823), 118, and Arnesen, 39.
90. New Orleans Press, 274.
91. Zacharie, *New Orleans Guide* (1893), 84.

This early aerial photo mosaic of New Orleans (1922), taken only nineteen years after the Wright Brothers commenced the era of aviation, shows some of the very last undeveloped land in the crux of the New Orleans crescent (upper center), now covered by parts of the Broadmoor, Fontainbleau, and Gert Town neighborhoods. Note the rural nature of the west bank, where Algiers and Gretna seemed to be as tiny and isolated as nineteenth-century villages. A sharp eye can find the New Basin Canal, Old Basin Canal, and former Storyville in the upper right center. *Image processing by author; mosaic courtesy the Port of New Orleans*

Comparison of the 1922 mosaic to this 1998 scene brings to light some major elements of macroscopic change: the total development within the New Orleans crescent, accomplished by the 1930s; the suburban development of eastern Jefferson Parish and most areas on the west bank, by the 1970s; the construction of skyscrapers and the Superdome (1975) in downtown New Orleans from the mid-1960s to the mid-1980s; the installation of the expressways and bridges (1958-88); and the development of convention and port facilities along the Mississippi from Canal Street to Audubon Park. *Image processing by author; aerial image U.S. Geological Survey*

Street patterns of New Orleans above (top) and below sea level. The above-sea-level streets are older and tend to form a radiating pattern, with the exception of the artificial lakefront uplands built in the late 1920s. The below-sea-level streets generally postdate the turn-of-the-century drainage system and are more orthogonal in their layout, with the exception of Mid-City streets, which are really extensions of older high-ground streets. *GIS processing and cartography by author based on street and topographic data from New Orleans City Planning Commission*

expansive convention facilities that now envelope the piers of the Crescent City Connection, where a bewildered convention-eer can end up in Algiers if he takes a wrong turn in the snarl of ramps and exits entangling the bridges. Above the bridges, Tchoupitoulas Street serves the modern Port of New Orleans facilities occupying the southern tip of the batture that first formed over two hundred years ago (see page 62). A major change currently in the making in this area is the immense Saulet apartment complex arising on the once-empty lots between Annunciation and Tchoupitoulas just above the expressway; the hundreds of future residents promise to change the barren, post-industrial nature of this area for the better. Near the Felicity Street intersection, Tchoupitoulas finally draws near the river again, a proximity it formerly maintained for its entire length in centuries past. From this point in the Lower Garden District upriver to Audubon Park, the ancient road now serves thoroughly mixed neighborhoods,[92] industrial and commercial in some areas, residential in others, populated with structures that are variously humble, dignified, deteriorated, robust, historic, modern, abandoned, and bustling. Though never visible from the street, the presence of the Mississippi is palpable, with shipping facilities exploiting the great continental drainage a short distance from the levees and floodwalls that fight it, symbolic of the city's dual relationship with the river as friend and foe. There are few graceful live oaks, no clanging streetcars, and but a handful of historical structures, yet traveling on gritty, unromantic Tchoupitoulas Street, one gets the sense that this is among those places that people mean—or should mean—when they speak of the "real" New Orleans. "Real" in the workingman's defini-tion, too: as in the days of the Chapitoulas and the early settlers, Tchoupitoulas Street is still a crucial riverside transportation route today. Recent years have seen the creation of the Tchoupitoulas Trucking Corridor (Clarence Henry Truckway), an unobstructed artery for eighteen-wheelers (hidden from sight behind the flood-wall) designed to minimize truck traffic in residential neighborhoods while streamlining the port and facilitating its shift from rail to road transportation.[93] The high-speed truckway is a functional descendent of the old

92. Master Planning Consortium, Inc., 29-33.
93. Master Planning Consortium, Inc. and Burk-Kleinpeter, Inc.

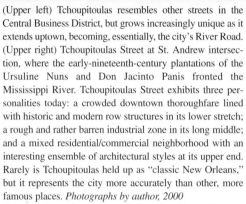

(Upper left) Tchoupitoulas resembles other streets in the Central Business District, but grows increasingly unique as it extends uptown, becoming, essentially, the city's River Road. (Upper right) Tchoupitoulas Street at St. Andrew intersection, where the early-nineteenth-century plantations of the Ursuline Nuns and Don Jacinto Panis fronted the Mississippi River. Tchoupitoulas Street exhibits three personalities today: a crowded downtown thoroughfare lined with historic and modern row structures in its lower stretch; a rough and rather barren industrial zone in its long middle; and a mixed residential/commercial neighborhood with an interesting ensemble of architectural styles at its upper end. Rarely is Tchoupitoulas held up as "classic New Orleans," but it represents the city more accurately than other, more famous places. *Photographs by author, 2000* (Bottom) Latest incarnation of the River Road: Clarence Henry Truckway provides speedy access to wharves lining the Mississippi along Tchoupitoulas Street. *Photograph by Donn Young, courtesy the Port of New Orleans*

River Road and the prehistoric paths that also exploited this convenient riverside high ground. Railroads, the historical nemesis of river transportation, now collaborate with shipping on tracks between Tchoupitoulas and the Mississippi. In a city that still ultimately depends on its keystone geographical situation first appreciated 300 years ago, the importance of this transportation route is no trivial matter. Tchoupitoulas Street, from Canal Street to Audubon Park, has served riverside traffic in New Orleans constantly from prehistoric times to the present, and forms the first great river-parallel arc in the radiating street pattern of New Orleans.

At the opposite end of the natural levee, straddling the sea-level contour clear across Orleans Parish from Jefferson to St. Bernard Parish, runs the southern and northern portions of Claiborne Avenue. Present-day Claiborne Avenue generally marks the rear zones (though not quite the rear edges) of the forty-arpent-deep long-lot plantations that divided up the crescent. Here began the backswamp in prehistoric times up to about the 1880s: riverside of Claiborne, the periodically flooding Mississippi deposited its silt as soon as gravity would allow it, building land up to ten to fifteen feet in elevation, but lakeside of Claiborne, little remained to be deposited, leaving only water and a small amount of fine-grained sediments to accumulate. Timber in this cypress swamp was "mostly felled" by the Civil War[94] and probably much earlier, making the natural levee/backswamp interface somewhat variable according to seasonal weather conditions, standards applied by different surveyors, and the impacts of local canals and drainage ditches. In many cases, rear lines of long-lot plantations were either not surveyed or not depicted accurately in maps, relegating the "back-of-town" to the status of *terra incognita* during the plantation era of present-day uptown.

94. Abbot.

Claiborne Avenue, named for William Charles Cole Claiborne, the only governor of the new American Territory of Orleans (1804-12) and later Louisiana's first state governor (1812-16), is something of a barometer of New Orleans' progress in drainage and uptown growth. It was first surveyed as Claiborne Street within Faubourg Tremé in the late 1820s, and by 1834 it spanned from present-day Tulane Avenue to Bayou Road, really the only portion of its current route that was drained and subdivided at the time. By the early 1850s, with the city expanding in both directions (see page 50), Claiborne extended in two separate portions from present-day Tulane down to St. Bernard and from the New Basin Canal up to Felicity Street. An 1861 city directory described the growing street united as one span from St. Bernard to Felicity; the 1866 edition had it reaching all the way down to Poland Avenue.[95]

By the 1870s, Claiborne expanded uptown to Toledano Street, and later that decade, it extended clear across the crescent to Carrollton, where it was called Tenth Street and later Mobile Street.[96] But, though it appeared in maps conspicuously crossing barren swamplands, Claiborne Street (or Avenue) was really no more than a rural dirt road following a drainage canal, the Claiborne Canal, excavated in the late 1850s as part of the drainage plan of city surveyor Louis H. Pilié (see page 59). The Claiborne Canal drained the rears of the crescent's plantations and faubourgs into the Melpomene Canal by means of the Melpomene Drainage Machine, located at the present-day intersection of Martin Luther King, Jr., and South Claiborne Avenue.[97] The layout of the Claiborne Canal first manifested the segmented shape of future South Claiborne Avenue, and it comes as no surprise that the joints of the segments generally occur when the thoroughfare intersects a former plantation boundary. Angles at modern-day Claiborne's intersections with "Lowerline, Upperline, Delachaise, Felicity, St. Bernard, and Almonaster all indicate ancient property lines."[98] Here, again, we see the indirect repercussions of the arpent system upon the radiating street pattern of New Orleans. The angles are also "echoes" of the bends of St. Charles Avenue (see page 105), laid out in the 1830s about fifteen blocks away.

It was not until the first decade of the twentieth century that Claiborne Avenue assumed its full span and was named South Claiborne above Canal Street and North Claiborne downriver from Canal. In the Sanborn Fire Insurance Maps of 1908-9, the uptown portion of the street appears fully platted but unpaved, dominated by its old drainage canal, and devoid of structures from about Toledano to Lowerline. Even in the early 1920s, that same span was only about 60 percent developed, with the area between Nashville and Upperline on the lakeside of Claiborne completely empty—one of the

last major remnants of the old vacant backswamp. South Claiborne Avenue was finally fully developed for residential and commercial use later in the 1920s through 1940s, a fact richly evident in the architecture and streetscape of this broad transcrescent thoroughfare.

As a path from which New Orleans may be experienced, this great arc of Claiborne Avenue exhibits four principal characters after emerging from the lower Ninth Ward. First there is *old Claiborne,* a narrow, one-way, two-lane artery lined with decaying cottages running from the Industrial Canal to Elysian Fields Avenue and then to St. Anthony Street, where it widens and surrounds the last surviving portion of its famous forested neutral ground. From St. Anthony to the Pontchartrain Expressway is what one might call *lost Claiborne.* Once described as the "Main Street of Black New Orleans," this oldest portion of the street, serving Faubourg Tremé and the Sixth Ward, was dealt what some deemed a crushing blow in 1966-69 when its beautiful oak-alley neutral ground was bulldozed and overlaid with Interstate 10. The street below, shadowy and thunderously noisy, is utterly devastated as a historical streetscape. Yet all is not truly lost: local residents hold weekend markets on the vestiges of their neighborhood's lost neutral-ground park, and on Mardi Gras, the interstate becomes probably the only one in the nation below which revelers enjoy generations-old Shrove Tuesday festivities and traditions. The Orleans Avenue intersection with North Claiborne has been one of the favorite gathering places of the famed Mardi Gras Indians.[99] Reminders of lost Claiborne's days in the sun may be seen in the past splendor of a few surviving nineteenth-century structures, the poignant St. Louis Cemetery No. 2, and what remains of St. Bernard Circle, a downtown rotary balancing out uptown's Lee Circle.

Crossing Canal, North Claiborne becomes South Claiborne, providing access to the city's extensive medical district clustered along the intersecting Tulane Avenue, then ramps over the Pontchartrain Expressway corridor, which interrupts Claiborne Avenue as it did in historical times when it hosted the New Basin Canal. One now lands among the palm trees and subtropical sun of Central City. Call it *gritty Claiborne* here: this rough-edged commercial/residential neighborhood contains a hodgepodge of architectural styles and a mix of locally owned mom-and-pop stores and national chains. Between the busy lanes of traffic is a wide, grassy neutral ground, hilly in some areas despite the fact that the general area is at sea level and Claiborne itself is underlaid by a drainage canal. The view of the Superdome from South Claiborne in Central City is especially spectacular. Gritty Claiborne changes to *tony Claiborne* after the Napoleon Avenue intersection, past Memorial Hospital, where early-twentieth-century residences prevail in a

The three great arcs of the New Orleans crescent. Transecting numerous old plantations from downtown to uptown—Tchoupitoulas Street at the crest of the natural levee, St. Charles Avenue halfway down the back slope, and South Claiborne Avenue near the former backswamp edge—each provides an utterly distinct profile of New Orleans' society and built environment. *Map by author based on street data from New Orleans City Planning Commission; aerial image courtesy U.S. Geological Survey*

95. Gardner, *Gardner's New Orleans Directory for 1861,* 19. See also 1866 edition.

96. This is based on inspection of various maps dated 1815, 1834, ca. 1853, 1863, 1869, 1873, 1880, 1891, 1895, 1896, 1908, and 1909, plus aerial photographs from 1922 and 1940. Many of these maps are stored in the Louisiana Collection at the University of New Orleans Earl K. Long Library.

97. U.S. Army Corps of Engineers, *National Register Evaluation,* 14.

98. Chase, 205.

99. Claiborne Avenue Design Team, 32. This document identified the "Dumaine and Claiborne intersection [as] **the** spot to enjoy the soul and excitement of Black Carnival" prior to the mid-1950s. See also Dericki Johnson, and Elie.

The neutral ground of North Claiborne Avenue from Elysian Fields to Tulane Avenue was once shaded by hundreds of beautiful oak trees, a green oasis in a densely populated neighborhood and an integral memory of those who grew up here. Almost the entire stretch was destroyed starting in 1966, when the elevated Interstate-10 superhighway was built over it (left). Today, the thunderously noisy and dark neutral ground is an urban eyesore but is nevertheless still utilized by residents for markets and social events, especially on Mardi Gras. This stretch (right) of North Claiborne from St. Anthony to Elysian Fields in the Seventh Ward is the last reminder of the long-gone oak alley. *Photographs by author, 2000*

comfortable upper-middle-class neighborhood that includes the Ursulines Nuns' campus (only their third location in the city since arriving in 1727), the rear campus of Tulane University, and the prosperous World War I-era residential parks of Broadmoor, Fontainbleau, University, and others.

Taken in its entirety, Claiborne Avenue is a cross-section of New Orleans beyond the clichés, far from the internationally recognized city symbols of iron-laced French Quarter balconies and pearl-white Garden District mansions. The avenue, being on the interior of the crescent, also provides convenient "backdoor" access to places such as Carrollton, Tulane University, the Central Business District, the Quarter, and the downtown faubourgs, connecting them in a shorter distance and in less traffic than other river-parallel routes. (Traveling around the crescent from Canal Street to South Carrollton Avenue takes 3.73 miles on Claiborne but 5.28 on St. Charles Avenue and 7.40 if Tchoupitoulas Street spanned the entire distance.) In its extraordinary length from St. Bernard to Jefferson Parish, Claiborne Avenue exhibits its own thoroughly local flair and touches at least portions of numerous historic neighborhoods, reflecting the city's geographical history of drainage, growth, and development. Unlike Tchoupitoulas Street, which exploits the natural levee, Claiborne Avenue was a path carved through the swamp, a path dictated in part by drainage needs, cadastral patterns, and existing streets. A very different history lies behind the great arc halfway between Tchoupitoulas and Claiborne, the world-famous path named St. Charles Avenue.

St. Charles Avenue was first etched into New Orleans when Spanish surveyor general Don Carlos Laveau Trudeau designed Faubourg Ste. Marie in 1788. *Calle San Carlos,* named after the patron saint of Trudeau's king, Carlos III, extended from present-day Common to just past Julia Street, unremarkable in every way except that it passed in front of the *plaza* (present-day Lafayette Square) that Trudeau laid out in the center of his subdivision.[100] But it was Barthélémy Lafon's 1806-10 subdivision of the adjacent plantations—Delord-Sarpy/Duplantier, Saulet (Solet), Robin, and Livaudais—that put in place a series of urban designs that established a prominent thoroughfare in a key position, one that would eventually develop into the premier arc around the crescent. He named that thoroughfare *Cours des Nayades* (or *Naiades*)—Walk of the Water Nymphs—and projected it off a circular park (Place du Tivoli) surrounded by a series of semi-ornamental drainage canals following other nearby streets.[101] The position was key because (1) the circular park, now Lee Circle, would allow future traffic to flow relatively smoothly between downtown and uptown and because Nayades was (2) a wide street protruding into the (3) approximate middle of the forty-arpent-deep long-lot plantations that lay upriver from this site.

100. Trudeau, *Plan de la Habitacion.*
101. Wilson, "Early History of the Lower Garden District," 10-11.

Cours des Nayades and its adjacent streets slowly extended uptown over the next twenty-five years as the Ursuline Nuns' property, the Panis plantation, and other parcels were subdivided. Then, on June 2, 1832, an announcement in the *Louisiana Advertiser,* signed by C.F.Z. (Charles F. Zimpel), proposed "a rail road running from Canal street through St. Charles and Nayades street, through suburb Livadais, up to Macarty's Point," for an estimated price tag of under fifty thousand dollars. The route Zimpel had in mind would pass "over a high cleared and almost level road" that was half the distance of a levee route and a third the length of a lakeside route.[102]

A committee formed the next week and put forth in July an initial report describing its intent to build a railroad from Faubourg St. Mary to the Macarty plantation, whose new owners—the New Orleans Canal and Banking Company, Laurent Millaudon, Samuel Kohn, and John Slidell—sought a means of transportation from New Orleans to enhance the economic viability of the isolated community (now Carrollton) they planned to subdivide. The investment strategy was symbiotic: the subdivision would grow in value as the railroad connected new residents with New Orleans, and the railroad would earn revenue as it created new commuters. Some financiers were invested in both projects, and some, like Millaudon and Kohn, were also invested in other uptown plantations (Bouligny) that would stand to benefit from a transcrescent transportation line.[103]

The aptly named New Orleans & Carrollton Rail Road was chartered by the state legislature on February 9, 1833, and two months later, the N.O. & C.R.R.'s chief engineer, Charles F. Zimpel, set out to subdivide the former Macarty plantation into Carrollton. Rather than grant it a private right-of-way, the state legislature decreed that the railroad must share public streets with other travelers,[104] thus ensuring that the route selected for the railroad would eventually become a major street and a major factor in the development of uptown. Working swiftly, the N.O. & C.R.R. obtained on June 1 a 120-foot-wide easement through most plantations above the city, eagerly donated by their owners,[105] who realized the implications of such a transportation line.

A number of factors influenced the selection of the actual route of the New Orleans & Carrollton Rail Road above *Place du Tivoli* (Lee Circle):

1. The first twenty-five or so blocks of the route were already set in place, since *Cours des Nayades* (future St. Charles Avenue) was already formed from *Place du Tivoli* to Faubourg Plaisance by 1833. Zimpel seemed to refer to this when he wrote that "from Tivoli as far as Larisses plantation [the railroad would go] through a street of 127 feet in width, so that not an inch of ground is to be bought."[106]

2. Faubourg Bouligny and Hurstville were also subdivided or slated for subdivision in the early 1830s, indicating (or possibly reflecting) the future route of the railroad through those areas.

3. The company could not route the railroad from *Place du Tivoli* directly across to Carrollton, cutting a minimum distance across the crescent, because such a straight line would have necessitated crossing the backswamp. A lakeside route, potentially connecting the two-year-old Pontchartrain Railroad on Elysian Fields Avenue with the lakefront and thence to the Macarty plantation, was dismissed as far too long.

4. Nor could it route the railroad closer to the river, because this would have created a much longer route and presumably would have interfered with operations at the busy river end of those long-lot plantations still used for agriculture. Zimpel rejected a levee route (following Tchoupitoulas) in his first public announcement of the project: "From Canal street to Macarty's by the Levee road, the distance is about 7½ miles; whereas, by the route I propose, it will only be about 3¾ miles."[107]

5. Thus the optimal route would be halfway between the river and the backswamp, roughly at the twenty-arpent line that crossed each forty-arpent-deep lot. Because the river curved, and because of the convergent nature of the long lots in the crescent, the optimal route would curve as well.

6. Because of the faubourgs already subdivided sporadically throughout the crescent, the railroad would pass within and between each subdivision by means of a straight line. Slight angles would form as the railroad emerged from one subdivision into open land then headed for another, creating a series of slightly angled line segments. These angles influenced the geometry of St. Charles Avenue and were "inherited" by subsequent subdivisions and streets in uptown New Orleans. Almost all are still evident today (see page 105).

102. Zimpel, "RAILROAD." See also Guilbeau, 1-2.
103. Sally Kittredge Reeves, "The Founding Families and Political Economy, 1850-1870," in Friends of the Cabildo, vol. 7, 46.
104. Guilbeau, 4-5.
105. Not all owners were so eager. According to Sally Kittredge Reeves, François-Robert Avart, a Creole country gentleman and owner of the Avart plantation, "felt injured when the New Orleans and Carrollton Rail Road extended its tracks across what was then the rear of his land." A court case ensued. Sally Kittredge Reeves, "The Founding Families and Political Economy, 1850-1870," in Friends of the Cabildo, vol. 7, 34.
106. Zimpel, "RAILROAD" (No. II).
107. Ibid.

This set of circumstances led to the routing of the New Orleans & Carrollton Rail Road along a segmented curve from New Orleans to Carrollton, a route that became at once Nayades Street. The N.O. & C.R.R. constructed the 4.5-mile track beginning in 1834 and officially commenced full scheduled service, for a twenty-five-cent fare, on September 26, 1835.[108] "The route passes through a level and beautiful country," reported *The Bee* after opening day, "very high, dry and arable land; and affording one of the most pleasant drives in the southern states. It passes through the limits of an ancient forest of live oaks; peculiarly interesting as being one of the very few of its kind now remaining in the south."[109] For many, the new railroad provided first glimpses of the plantation country within the crescent as well as forested backswamps behind them.[110] With a single engineering effort, the geography of future St. Charles Avenue was suddenly established, providing "one of the earliest examples of a transportation artery being the determinant of urban growth rather than its servant."[111] Most former plantations along the route were subdivided by 1855 and filled in with residences of the communities of Lafayette, Jefferson, and Carrollton before each was absorbed into New Orleans. Development occurred gradually at first and rapidly after the World's Industrial and Cotton Centennial Exposition took place at present-day Audubon Park in 1884-85, sited there in part because of the access provided by the railroad. The name change of Nayades Street to St. Charles Street (Avenue) first appeared in the City Directory of 1856, but *Nayades* or *Nyades* would appear on maps into the 1870s. In the waning decades of the nineteenth century, St. Charles Avenue began to develop its unmistakably magnificent character as scores of mansions arose, the campuses of Tulane and Loyola were established, graceful live oaks grew, churches were erected, and the streetcar was electrified (1893). "The uniqueness of St. Charles Avenue is brought about by its gradual curvature, which provides a sense of continual anticipation to the traveler," wrote architect Monroe Labouisse, Jr.[112] Underlying that curvature are clues to the historical-geographical significance of this spectacular and quintessential path across the Crescent City: Its location marks the approximate halfway line between the natural levee and the back edge of the arpent lots, its origin and destination (downtown New Orleans and uptown/Carrollton) symbolize the source and destination of urban development in the antebellum "Golden Age," and the slight angles of the avenue's curvature provide insight to the history of subdivision of the old plantations.

Angled Intersections with St. Charles Avenue	Magnitude of Angle[113]	Historical Significance of Intersection (year indicates time of subdivision)
Felicity Street	14 degrees	Boundary between L'Annunciation plantation (1807) and Ursuline Nuns property (1809); once approximate upper edge of Jesuits plantation.
St. Andrew Street	8 degrees	Boundary between Ursuline Nuns property (1809) and Panis plantation (1813).
Philip Street	5 degrees	Boundary between Panis property (1813) and Livaudais plantation (1832).
Pleasant/Toledano Street	10 degrees	Toledano is boundary between Delassize property (ca. 1833) and Wiltz plantation (1807).
Foucher/Amelia/Peniston Street	14 degrees	Amelia is boundary between Delachaise plantation (1855) and Faubourg St. Joseph portion of Avart plantation (1849).
Bordeaux/Upperline/Robert Street	31 degrees	Upperline is boundary between Bouligny plantation (1834) and Faubourg Avart portion of Avart plantation (1841).
Nashville/Eleonore/State Street	10 degrees	"Bloomingdale Line" (between Eleonore and State) separates Hurst plantation (ca. 1833) and the Bloomingdale portion of the Avart plantation (1836).
Lowerline Street	5 degrees	Boundary between Greenville portion of the Foucher plantation (1836) and Macarty plantation (1833).

Note that every bend in St. Charles Avenue above Lee Circle corresponds to a historical plantation boundary. But not every historical plantation boundary corresponds to a bend on St. Charles Avenue; only those plantations that were already subdivided by the time of the engineering-and-construction phase of the N.O. & C.R.R. (1833-35) left their mark on the routing of the railroad and the shape of the avenue.[114] Faubourgs subdivided *after* the railroad abut straight sections of the avenue. In other words, designers of the railroad conformed to the geography of existing subdivisions; after the railroad was built, designers of faubourgs had to conform to the geography of the railroad. In this manner, the N.O. & C.R.R. *created* St. Charles Avenue, serving as the "spine of expansion linking the Uptown faubourgs."[115] Today, the railroad—the St. Charles Avenue Streetcar Line, the oldest continually operating rail line in the world—is just as important to the avenue as it was during their mutual formation.

St. Charles Avenue today forms perhaps the second most recognized symbol of the city of New Orleans (after the iron-lace balconies of the French Quarter), assembling, from Jackson Avenue up to Carrollton, some of the most endearing images of the city: stately mansions, manicured gardens, streetcars, Carnival parades, Audubon Park, the universities, and most of all the poetically beautiful spectacle of graceful live oaks arching over the boulevard. Below Jackson Avenue, the avenue's original residential land use was changed to light-industrial and commercial zoning starting in 1929, allowing retail usage and apartment buildings to dominate the streetscape. Thirty years later, the Pontchartrain Expressway connection to the Mississippi River Bridge further blighted the area and contributed to the residential evacuation of urban neighborhoods in the subsequent decades. Only a handful of historical structures remains on St. Charles between Lee Circle and Jackson Avenue, but the ambience of the great avenue nevertheless prevails. Lower St. Charles through the Central Business District is a fine sampler of what the CBD has to offer: an intriguing mix of the historical and the modern, the opulent and the indigent, the spectacular and the mundane, with magnificent Gallier Hall (City Hall from 1852 to 1957) forming the centerpiece of the streetscape and the center stage of Carnival rituals. Above Jackson Avenue, upper St. Charles Avenue exhibits a *tout ensemble* of history and architecture punctuated by landmarks such as Christ Church Cathedral, Academy of the Sacred Heart, the Brown House, the gates of Audubon Park and Audubon Place, Gibson Hall, and finally the climactic ninety-degree turn onto South Carrollton Avenue. But the overriding memory of the great avenue is one of movement, movement around a gradual curve, movement of streetcars, parades, automobiles, cyclists, joggers, pedestrians, movement up and down the great arc across New Orleans' historically rich and geographically unique radiating street pattern.

New Orleans' Radiating Street Pattern: Some Observations

- New Orleans' street pattern preserves former long-lot plantations in a state fairly close to their original size and shape from centuries past. Long lots in rural areas tend to be far narrower and more numerous now than they were in earlier days, because the Louisiana civil-law tradition of forced heirship—in which land was divided equally among all heirs—had the effect of slicing the narrow lots into increasingly slender strips.[116] This is revealed in aerial photographs of rural long lots along the Mississippi River, Bayou Lafourche, and other waterways, compared to New Orleans' "preserved" parcels. That the parcels within the New Orleans crescent were urbanized before too many generations passed allowed the wider properties to become frozen in time in the modern street network.

- Has the radiating street pattern served well as a system of urban transportation? Writers of a 1927 city street report thought not:

  > Narrow strips running back from the river invite a form of platting that may be entirely opposed to the needs of traffic. The river has ceased to be the objective of travel. The dominant movement today is across the strips or at an angle to them. . . . It is manifest that a broadly conceived plan of streets for the greater New Orleans must ignore, where necessary, the invisible and arbitrary lines marking property ownerships.[117]

108. *The Bee* (September 25 and 28, 1835).

109. *The Bee* (September 28, 1835). See also Guilbeau, 15.

110. The unidentified journalist covering the opening-day trip of the N.O. & C.R.R. reviewed the excursion like a lifelong city dweller on a first trip to the country: "Having partook of the refreshments prepared for about 200 person [in Carrollton], we ascended to the observatory; and were much pleased at the view presented of the Mississippi in its winding course; although we were surprized [*sic*] at the red appearance of the water." He hoped that "next summer the forest of live oaks would be rendered fit for an agreeable ramble for our ladies and their escorts." Such comments serve as anecdotal evidence of the inaccessibility of rural areas above the city prior to the railroad. *The Bee* (September 28, 1835).

111. Monroe Labouisse, Jr., introduction, in Kirk, Smith, and Krentel, xi.

112. Ibid.

113. Angles measured off 1:6000-scale GIS coverages of New Orleans streets from the New Orleans City Planning Commission through its New Orleans Geographic Information System (NOGIS). The author processed these street files and measured the angles using ERSI ARC/INFO software. The NOGIS at the City Planning Commission is partially funded by a federal grant through NOAA.

114. The only exception is the Amelia Street intersection; neither the Delachaise plantation above it nor the Avart plantation below it were subdivided by the time of the railroad, yet there is a fourteen-degree bend in St. Charles here. The reason probably lies in the fact that there were two major extant subdivisions above and below this property line, Livaudais and Bouligny, which already established the path of the railroad and forced the engineers to curve the track at present-day Amelia Street to accommodate both subdivisions.

115. Bernard Lemann, "The Uptown Experience," in Friends of the Cabildo, vol. 7, 3.

116. James W. Taylor, 277-78; John Whitling Hall, 72-74; Newton, 214; and Kniffen and Hilliard, 122.

117. City Planning and Zoning Commission, 22.

St. Charles Avenue:
Scenes along the Transcrescent Arc

1. Grand, foliated St. Charles Avenue, address of mansions and universities, starts as a narrow downtown street in the heart of the Central Business District, designed during the Spanish colonial regime as *Calle San Carlos* in honor of the patron saint of King Carlos III. Today, Rubenstein's, one of the last elegant local stores on Canal, marks St. Charles' riverside corner, while the spectacular Pickwick Club anchors the lakeside corner. *Photograph by author, 1999*

2. Nineteenth-century commercial structures with breathtaking galleries characterize the first block of St. Charles Avenue. Kolb's, the famous German restaurant founded in 1899, closed in 1994, in an era when numerous downtown New Orleans institutions folded. The Pearl, one of those great old-time city diners with carved meat on display in the window, is undergoing extensive renovation in this scene. It reopened in 2001 with a hackneyed retro-modern interior design. The former Kolb's is now slated for renovation into a hotel, joining the modern corner structure, which was hotelized in 2000 (along with many other buildings on St. Charles and adjacent streets). *Photograph by author, 2000*

3. St. Charles takes on a feeling of a special street when it passes Gallier Hall, the former City Hall (1852) and the greatest work of architect James Gallier, Sr. *Photograph by author, 2000*

4. Same spot, viewed from the federal building on South Street. The purple, gold, and green grandstands mean Carnival season in the Crescent City, and it is here on St. Charles Avenue that the mayor toasts Rex on Mardi Gras, culmination of the city's great annual ritual. Lafayette Square appears at lower right. *Photograph by author, 1996*

5. St. Charles Avenue at its character-changing loop around Lee Circle, seen from the base of the Lee Monument looking into the CBD. Below Lee Circle, St. Charles is narrow and urban; above Lee Circle, it widens and becomes progressively more foliated, residential, and prosperous. *Photograph by author, 1995*

6. View up St. Charles Avenue from the Lee Monument, at the point where St. Charles widens and starts to feel like an avenue. The date is June 6, 2000; the occasion is the opening-day parade for the D-Day Museum, an event that brought the world's attention to New Orleans and the aging veterans assembled for the occasion. The military truck at center is carrying veterans of the First Infantry Division past the appreciative crowd. *Photograph by author*

7. Lee Circle, designed by Barthélémy Lafon in 1807 as *Place du Tivoli* and dedicated with the Robert E. Lee Monument in 1884, is seen here from Howard Street (formerly Delord Street) in the early 1900s. General Lee is oriented to address traffic coming up St. Charles Avenue (facing the North, as Southern partisans like to point out). In the background are the Temple Sinai (1872; demolished 1977) and St. John the Baptist, also built in 1872 and still standing at the gateway to Central City. All other structures in this view, save the Lee Monument, are gone. *Frank B. Moore Collection, captioned "145-442 Robert E. Lee Monument," UNO Special Collections*

8. An earlier view (1890) of Lee Circle, from St. Charles Avenue toward downtown, shows the stately homes surrounding the rotary in the late Victorian era. St. Patrick's Church (1840) appears in the distance. The foundations at lower left were laid in 1871 for a Masonic temple that was never built; instead, the prominent St. Charles Avenue site was used for years as a platform for circuses, theaters, amusement rides, and an ornate hall constructed temporarily (1890, soon after this photograph was taken) for the festival of the German-American singing club, *Saengerbund*, used for only four days and demolished by the end of the year. Then, in 1908, the site hosted an appropriately magnificent structure, the domed New Orleans Public Library, which was demolished in 1959 and replaced by the modern K&B Building. *Photographer unknown, captioned "New Orleans Feb. 1890 Lee Circle and Lee Statue," New Orleans Views Collection, UNO Special Collections*

9-10. Somewhere uptown on St. Charles Avenue in Carnival season, 1998. The great avenue provides perhaps the most beautiful stage upon which New Orleans plays out its annual Mardi Gras pageantry. The scenery is spectacular, the crowds are civil, the ambience is joyful, and the parades are up close and accessible. *Photographs by author*

11. Newcomers to New Orleans are struck by the poetic beauty of the live oaks of St. Charles Avenue and other uptown thoroughfares, arching over the street and streetcar tracks like an arboreal cathedral with graceful fingerlike branches touching at the center. The ample foliage allows rays of light to penetrate through the morning mist, creating patterns of mottled sunshine on the ground. Most live oaks along St. Charles are about forty to one hundred years old, and unfortunately many suffer Formosan termite infestations, weakening them structurally and sometimes causing their removal or collapse. *Photograph by author, 2000*

12. The New Orleans & Carrollton Rail Road, proposed in 1832 and started in 1835, followed *Cours des Nayades* (future St. Charles Avenue) for its first twenty-five blocks, up to about present-day Toledano Street. From there to Carrollton, however, the designers of the railroad, in effect, also designed the thoroughfare that would become St. Charles Avenue, routing the tracks in straight segments across the middles of a number of wedge-shaped plantations. The railroad fueled the development of these rural croplands and influenced their urban layouts. Today, the operation, now called the St. Charles Streetcar Line, is the oldest continually running rail system in the world, and a direct link of uptown New Orleans to its origins. It is among the most treasured icons of the city, humming, clanking, and ringing its way through graceful live oak trees and rows of splendid mansions on one of American's great avenues. This is a 1920s-era Perley Thomas car. *Photograph by author, 2000*

Spinal column of New Orleans, leafy St. Charles wends gracefully across the crescent, both a cause and effect of the city's growth from the old city (top) into the former plantations of present-day uptown (bottom). This photograph was taken on Mardi Gras 1967; note the incredible number of truck floats parading on St. Charles Avenue. *Photograph by Sam R. Sutton, The Historic New Orleans Collection, accession no. 1984.166.2.465*

Issue may be taken with the implication that the dominant movement of traffic in the past was down the narrow strips toward the river, and that now (1927), traffic flows "across the strips or at an angle to them." In historic times, traffic was light moving down the strips because few had a reason to commute between the backswamp and the river, save for field hands and hunters; most traffic moved "across the strips," from the city to uptown faubourgs. Additionally, by 1927, new development of lakeside communities increased the flow of traffic "down the strips" between river and lake.

- The same 1927 street report mapped out the numerous dead-ends and jogs (unaligned intersections) throughout New Orleans,[118] brought about by the incremental development of plantations with no overseeing authority. Many such quirky intersections were eliminated in the post-World War II years, but scores remain.

- New Orleans historian John Smith Kendall observed that "the episodic fashion in which the city grew [into neighboring plantations] resulted . . . in the discovery that what was, in fact, a single thoroughfare often had half a dozen names." Many of these confusing names were standardized in a ca.-1860 city ordinance.[119]

- Many river-perpendicular streets iterate property lines, but only a few river-parallel streets do so. Tchoupitoulas, the river road, is the best example; in the rear of the crescent, a good example is that section of South Broad Avenue coinciding with the rear line of those plantations from Livaudais up to Avart. This avenue also traces an edge of the irregular and sprawling Macarty plantation in one of its early permutations (1795).[120] The reason for the lack of streets following rear boundaries of old plantations is simply the nature of the arpent system in this environment, which put such boundaries along the agriculturally useless backswamp, so they were less likely to be surveyed carefully, more likely to be waterlogged or forested, less likely to serve as roads, and much less likely to be developed into faubourgs until twentieth-century drainage technology opened them up for development.

- We have focused attention on the arpent-system-based street network in *uptown* New Orleans, because it was here that the system and physical geography (the crescent) conspired to form the unique radiating pattern. But the system was, of course, employed below the French Quarter as well, in the Faubourg Marigny, St. Roch, Bywater, Holy Cross, across the river in Algiers, and other areas. Here, the river is fairly straight, thus the long lots surveyed normal to the river were not wedge shaped but rectangular, and so no radiating pattern developed. To the extent that the river does bend, we do indeed see some fanning of the modern street network based on old property lines. Franklin/Almonaster Avenue in the Faubourg Marigny and St. Roch is one such example.

- In the Jefferson Parish communities of the west bank, on the opposite side of the Mississippi River from the New Orleans crescent, we see exactly what we would expect: a *diverging* pattern of streets radiating *outward* from the river. Streets in the riverside portions of Metairie, Harahan, Kenner, and other suburbs also reflect the old cadastral pattern: convergence in the concave side of meanders, divergence on the convex side.

- Where were the last large-scale rural long lots within New Orleans (Orleans Parish)? The 1883 Robinson *Atlas* shows the lands paralleling the Bayou Sauvage/Gentilly Road corridor divided into traditional long lots of typical proportions, the only large-scale array of rural lots left in the east bank of Orleans Parish at the time. Almost fifty years later (1931), these same areas were still undeveloped and further divided, through inheritance or sales, into dozens of narrow long lots, fronting the old Gentilly Road and Bayou Sauvage and extending into the swamp by about twenty arpents.[121] These elongated property lines are

118. Ibid., 51.
119. John Smith Kendall, 676.
120. Burns, 568, and City Planning and Zoning Commission, 23.
121. Robinson and Pidgeon, and New Orleans Association of Commerce.

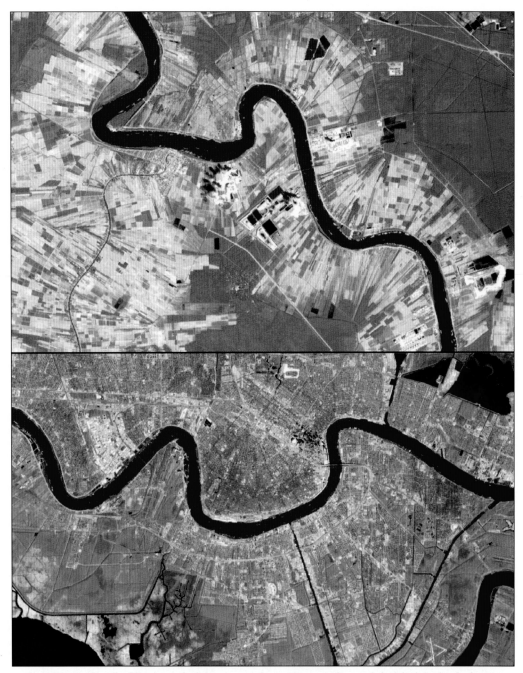

Long lots are often sliced into increasingly narrow parcels over the generations, as heirs inherit land and sales are made. As a result, rural long lots such as those along the Mississippi River and Bayou Lafourche near Donaldsonville (top) tend to be narrower than those embedded into the street system in 1850s New Orleans. *Map by author; Landsat/SPOT satellite imagery courtesy Louisiana State University*

now partially visible in the mid-twentieth-century housing subdivisions that occupy this lower-middle-class area (between Chef Menteur Highway and Interstate 10), one of the last large-scale conversions of long lots to subdivisions in New Orleans proper.

- Is New Orleans' radiating street pattern truly unique in the nation? For its scale and distinctness, the answer is a resounding yes. St. Louis, Missouri comes perhaps the closest in reflecting the pattern, though it is nowhere near New Orleans'. There are, however, some communities in former French Louisiana that have geographically similar circumstances and have passed through equivalent developmental cycles as New Orleans, on a much smaller scale, and also portray radiating patterns in their maps. White Castle, in Iberville Parish, depicts a diverging pattern of streets, while the properties and streets surrounding False River (a broken-off meander of the Mississippi) in Pointe Coupée Parish form distinct diverging and converging patterns. Many other bayou and river communities are spread upon a skeleton of streets derived

(Left) Typical jogged intersection in uptown New Orleans, created when streets surveyed in one former plantation did not line up perfectly with those laid out in the neighboring tract at a different time. Lowerline Street was the lower boundary of the Macarty plantation (foreground, now Carrollton); below it was the Greenville portion of the Foucher plantation (parts of which are now Audubon Park and the campuses of Tulane and Loyola universities). (Right) Typical acute-angle intersection formed when street networks were surveyed within converging long-lot plantations. This particular one comprises Dufossat and Valmont at the Freret Street intersection. Valmont Street was once the upper edge of the Avart plantation, subdivided as Faubourg Avart in 1841. *Photographs by author, 2001*

Franklin Avenue (formerly Almonaster Avenue and originally a plantation line) intersects North Rampart in Faubourg Marigny at an odd angle, another byproduct of New Orleans' growth into the surveying patterns of the arpent system. Many such quirky intersections were "fixed" in the urban-planning era after World War II, but many remain. In some cases, such as this beige cottage behind the public telephone (left), the geography of centuries-old plantation lines are passed on to the houses built upon the lots, and to the parlors and kitchens within. Despite this idiosyncratic network of streets, the older part of the city is fairly easy to navigate. It's not quite as easy where the streets converge, in Mid-City (right). *Photographs by author, 2000*

from arpent-system property lines but form fairly orthogonal street patterns because the corresponding section of waterway is straight.

- Is New Orleans unique in its absorption of old long lots (radiating or not) into new street networks? In fact, this phenomenon is fairly common in cities and towns of former French America. St. Louis incorporates an array of eighteenth- and nineteenth-century "plow-land" long lots into its modern map,[122] as do Winnipeg, Detroit, Green Bay, and other communities in the old French Illinois Country, in Quebec and eastern Canada, and, of course, in Louisiana.

> "Streets and numbers [in New Orleans] are perplexing in the extreme. The plain continuation of many streets have different names, and formerly, before city legislative action, a stranger wound be exceedingly amused to find himself on a strange thoroughfare, though he had never deviated from the one on which he started. Even when the council changed the name of one of these continuations, the old Creoles, their children and children's children, continue to call it by the ancient name. Thus we hear of Greatmen, Love and Bagatelle streets to this day, in face of the fact that the lamp signs for years have been Dauphine, North Rampart and Bourbon. The numbers have always been independent, and have evidently, in some cases, been affixed upon the convictions or fancies of property holders, rather than by the result of surveyors' lines. You may live at 403, and your vis-a-vis will, likely as not, be 320. You may live at 310, and your next door neighbor ten feet away, be 340."
> —*Soards' New Orleans City Directory for 1885* (954. This confusion derived from the sectionalized expansion of the city into former plantations and backswamp. The logical street numbering system we use today was adopted in 1894.)

- Defying traditional senses of direction, the radiating streets of New Orleans impede the use of *south, north, east,* and *west* to indicate bearing. Very few streets in historic (pre-twentieth century) New Orleans follow the cardinal directions of the compass, and if they do, the concurrence lasts but a few blocks. (Elysian Fields is the only true exception.) Instead, locals invoke geographical features to imply direction and location: *riverside, lakeside, downtown* (or *downriver*), and *uptown* (or *upriver*). Thus, the location of the French Quarter batture would be described as the uptown-riverside corner of the Quarter, rather than the southern tip of the Quarter. References to the lake as a direction became more common after the turn-of-the-century drainage project opened up lakeside New Orleans to development; prior to that, New Orleanians used references to the backswamp—*the woods side* or *the back-of-town side*—to mean northward directions toward the lake, while *the riverside* meant south toward the Mississippi. Eradication of the swamps by the early twentieth century made the lake the local bearing for north. Today, this localism is more likely to be heard in the older part of the city, not because it is an old tradition but because those older areas reflect the shape of the Mississippi more so than twentieth-century lakeside neighborhoods, which do follow cardinal directions.[123] Similar wording is used in rural areas in the region: writing in 1970, John Whitling Hall reported that the native population of former French Louisiana often used *la bas* (*la basse,* downstream) and *la haute* (upstream) for direction on one axis, and "front" and "back" for direction on the perpendicular axis.[124] The terminology, one of the distinguishing characteristics of the local lexicon, works well in drawing a mental map of the area and siting places on a locally fitting "coordinate system." It speaks volumes of the subconscious relevance of waterways not only to Louisiana culture but to any selected person on the street, reflected in his common parlance. As the arpent system physically affected New Orleans' street system, it linguistically affected the city's internal compass.

122. Ekberg, *French Roots,* 99.

123. An unscientific survey leads this author to believe that this terminology is also not used much in the Mid-City/Bayou St. John area, presumably because the confusing convergence of streets and the curving Metairie/Gentilly Ridge arteries in this area obscure their spatial relationships with the river and the lake.

124. John Whitling Hall, 71.

Edges: The Porous and Shifting Nature of Canal Street as an Urban Boundary

As a port city with a multicultural populace and a strategic geographical perch, New Orleans is full of "edges"—linear features separating differentiating urban regions. Some edges are physical with ramifications in the social arena, such as the Industrial Canal and its tendency to isolate the impoverished lower Ninth Ward from the rest of the city. Others are physical with ramifications in the economic arena, such as the levee separating city life from port activity. Other edges divide commercial areas from residential areas (the Pontchartrain Expressway between the Central Business District and Central City); prosperous neighborhoods from poor neighborhoods (St. Charles Avenue separating the Garden District from Central City; North Rampart Street between the French Quarter and Faubourg Tremé); and old areas from new areas (riverside and lakeside of the Metairie/Gentilly Ridge).

But perhaps the best-known edge in the Crescent City, one as familiar to lifelong residents as to weekend tourists, is Canal Street, the "Great Wide Way" between the French Quarter and the Central Business District. Its reputation as an edge derives from the general facts that, throughout most of the nineteenth century, (1) Creoles tended to live in downriver neighborhoods, (2) Anglo-Americans gravitated to upriver neighborhoods, (3) the two groups were, for much of the century, in competition and at odds with each other, and (4) Canal Street, at various times and to various degrees, lay between them, in semimythological roles of neutrality and separation. Given that both the Creoles and the Americans were enormously important to the history and development of New Orleans, the alleged role of Canal Street as a cultural edge between them bequeaths the avenue a special significance, but also invites careful consideration and skepticism.

Envisioning New Orleans as a junction of the Old World beyond the Gulf of Mexico and the New World up the Mississippi River, how remarkable it would be if, in Canal Street, those two worlds would indeed form an interface, taut with cultural tension, with Old World Creoles residing below the thoroughfare and ambitious Americans above, as if in allegiance to the water bodies that communicate with their ancestral homes. Such an edge would represent to New Orleans what New Orleans represents to the region: an essential place where one can step from one world to another, traveling far culturally within the confines of a few city blocks. But such geographical symbolism, while cozy and tantalizing, is only as sound as the facts that support it.

The contention—fact? myth? generality?—that Canal Street was a formidable urban edge separating rival Creole and American factions is in fact an involved question that draws into its resolution some of the most fundamental aspects of historic New Orleans. Who was Creole? Who was American? Was there tension, why, how much, and when? Who lived where, and to what degree did they intermingle? What impact did this have on the streetscape? How did these identities and patterns evolve over the decades? And what about Canal Street: was its role one of impervious urban edge—a "demilitarized zone," as the term *neutral ground* implies for its median—or was it a political boundary between districts dominated by one group or the other? Was Canal Street simply a prominent linear geographical feature that more or less correlated with the porous and fuzzy edge between the two groups? Or are we simply mistaken in identifying the 171-foot-wide avenue as the geographical cleavage of New Orleans' famous cultural dichotomy?[125]

Canal Street Corridor before 1810

Canal Street postdates the streets of the French Quarter by almost ninety years and those of the Central Business District (Faubourg Ste. Marie, or St. Mary) by about two decades. During those decades (1788-1807), future Canal Street lay roughly in the middle of a triangular *terre commune* between the old city and the new faubourg. The streets known today as Iberville and Common defined the lower and upper legs of this ten-degree-wide triangle; running jagged between them was the Spanish-colonial-era fortification anchored by Fort San Luis near the river and Fort Burgundy near the back-of-town.

The path through the commons that would become the great Canal Street of the mid-nineteenth century was barely discernible in the landscape at the beginning of that century, marked only by the remains of an old moat, a parallel road built in 1763,[126] and possibly some other indications of a canal that was, at various times, slated to be dug there. After the Louisiana Purchase, Faubourg Ste. Marie grew steadily while the fortification deteriorated in both strength and relevance, pressuring the eventual development of this increasingly attractive

piece of real estate. Determination of its fate would be hurried by a sequence of events involving the Marquis de Lafayette, the French hero of the American Revolution, whom Congress in the early 1800s had decided to reward with a grant of land in gratitude for his service.

The debt-ridden Lafayette, appreciative of the gift and guided by his old friend, Pres. Thomas Jefferson,[127] sought his grant in New Orleans, where the culture was familiar and the land could be developed for quick profit. He appointed Armand Duplantier (Duplantiers), owner of the former Delord-Sarpy plantation and a savvy dealer in the local real-estate market, to act as his agent in the distant city. With most lands adjacent to the city already in private hands, Duplantier filed a warrant for the only other viable option: the former fortifications and commons spanning from present-day Common Street/Tulane Avenue all the way over to Carondelet Canal (minus the city proper) and extending back to the swamp. The most valuable portion was the future Canal Street swath between the city and Faubourg Ste. Marie.

The New Orleans City Council protested forcefully that these commons belonged to the city government, not the federal government,[128] and petitioned Washington in 1805 to recognize the legitimacy of the city's claim. The dispute led to a compromise in the form of the March 3, 1807, Act of Congress, in which the city's claim to the commons and to the 600 yards surrounding the old fortifications was confirmed, though its other land claims had to be relinquished. It was in this milestone legislation that Congress stipulated a right-of-way be reserved for a waterway to connect Carondelet Canal with the river, paralleled by sixty-foot open spaces for a public highway, forming the origins of Canal Street.[129] Denied the choice downtown section, the aging gentleman Lafayette did not pursue the matter, saying graciously, "I do not wish that a single personal advantage prevents my co-citizens at New Orleans from means of realizing humanitarian projects."[130] Lafayette eventually obtained plantation land in the Pointe Coupée region as well as less-than-prime New Orleans property just beyond the 600-yard limit, which, after much changing of hands, eventually was subdivided and sold in 1841 as Faubourg Hagan.[131] "Lafayette was a much better major general than a real estate speculator," concluded John Churchill Chase.[132] Downtown New Orleans and Canal Street would probably look quite different today had the Marquis de Lafayette gained his Revolutionary War booty where Duplantier had originally hoped. Nevertheless, the incident precipitated the 1807 Act of Congress, which pushed the dusty commons into its first urban-development stage.

Canal Street: Three Transitions, 1810-2000

The newly confirmed city property was ingested into New Orleans' urban geography when, in 1810, city surveyor Jacques Tanesse subdivided parts of the former commons, uniting the old and new halves of the city with blocks nestled among Common Street (lower edge of Faubourg Ste. Marie), the new Canal Street, and Customhouse Street (today's Iberville Street; upper edge of the city and today's French Quarter).[133] Properties in what are now known as the "100 blocks" between Canal and Iberville were delineated in a fashion that preserved the old fortification line, traces of which remains today.[134] The stipulation that Carondelet Canal be

---

125. The focus here is on the portion of Canal Street riverside of Claiborne Avenue. Lakeside of Claiborne, an intersection accentuated by the elevated Interstate 10, Canal Street is of an entirely different character.

126. One writer views this 1763 road to be the true origin of Canal Street, claiming the great boulevard as a Spanish contribution to the city. Montero de Pedro, 244-45.

127. President Jefferson had in fact informally offered the governorship of Louisiana to Lafayette in November 1803, just prior to the finalization of the Louisiana Purchase. Lafayette politely did not pursue the offer; instead, William C. C. Claiborne became the first American governor of Louisiana in December 1803. Abbey, 363.

128. The legitimacy of the city's claim to the commons was doubted by Governor Claiborne, Surveyor Barthélémy Lafon, and others. There were, in fact, some private claims to parts of the commons, including one to Lafon, but their rights to develop these parcels were restricted. Ibid., 366; Maduell, 5; and Wilson, "Early History of Faubourg St. Mary," 10.

129. "An Act Respecting Claims to Land in the Territories of Orleans and Louisiana" (March 3, 1807), as recorded in *The Debates and Proceedings in the Congress of the United States* (1852), 1283.

130. Abbey, 366.

131. Faubourg Hagan's boundary lines were "Orleans Street on the north, Common Street on the South; extending between converging lines consisting of Roman and Claiborne on Orleans and Galvez and Robertson on Common." Other maps show the parcel coming to a point at the Claiborne/Bayou Road intersection. President Jefferson was surprisingly involved in the destiny of this parcel, as he was in the Batture Case. Abbey, 373, and Zimpel, *Topographical Map.*

132. Chase, 155.

133. A few years earlier, the present-day streets of Decatur, Chartres, and Royal had been conflated across the commons with Magazine, Camp, and St. Charles, marking the first fusion of the old city's and new city's street network. Wilson, "Early History of Faubourg St. Mary," 11.

134. Large-scale photographs of the 1966 Vieux Carre Aerial Survey, captured by Jack Beech of Amman-International and archived at The Historic New Orleans Collection, reveal five nineteenth- and twentieth-century structures between Decatur and Bourbon whose angled walls line up exactly with the eighteenth-century fortification line. Unfortunately, three of these buildings have since been demolished, their lots subsumed into high-rise hotel lobbies. The clearest vestiges of the old fort line are the rear walls of the parking garage at 720 Iberville (in the building that houses Dickie Brennan's Steakhouse) and the adjacent Acme Oyster House.

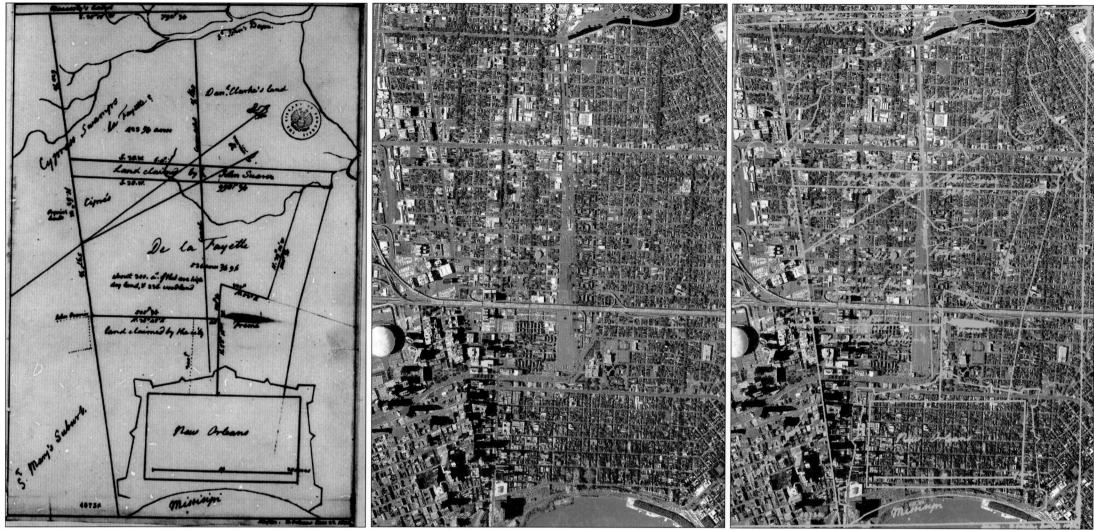

Map at left is a sketch of the Marquis de Lafayette's land holdings in New Orleans, June 23, 1805, in relation to the growing new American city of New Orleans and surrounding areas. Aerial photograph at center covers the same area in 1998. Scene at right depicts the 1805 map superimposed upon the 1998 photograph, revealing relationships between old property lines and modern-day streets. Note the salient corridors of Common Street, Carondelet Canal, and Bayou Road, as well as the natural drainage system that flowed into Bayou St. John. *1805 map courtesy The Thomas Jefferson Papers, Series 1. General Correspondence 1651-1827, and American Memory Panoramic Maps Collection, Library of Congress; 1998 aerial image courtesy U.S. Geological Survey. Image processing and overlaying by author. Note: digital coregistration of the historic map somewhat distorts the original document; it should not be used beyond the context of this graphic. The accuracy of this comparison is roughly within one block of actual locations.*

extended to the Mississippi influenced both the width and path of the street that would host the waterway. Tanesse laid out that street 170 feet six inches[135] wide and routed it parallel to Customhouse (Iberville) Street, a geometry that would, to this day, support popular identification of Canal Street as *the* dividing line between two distinct cultural, historical, and architectural zones. (A case can be made that Common or Iberville also separate those zones, but few would accept these narrow back streets as playing such a lofty role!)

Canal Street's spaciousness and axislike position invited the construction of substantial institutional and residential buildings in its first two decades, marking the first of three transitions the street would make in its history. A custom house (predecessor to the current one) was built near the street's riverside "foot"; churches arose at the intersections with Bourbon and Levee streets; and Charity Hospital was constructed at the Baronne

Street intersection and later enlarged as the Louisiana State House. Elegant residences occupied the blocks among these institutions, with some commercial structures mixed in. The street itself comprised two lanes of traffic separated by a median as wide as both lanes combined and lined with rows of sycamore trees, indicating that plans for the canal had been shelved for the time being.

Canal Street slowly transitioned, for a second time, from a stately street of residences and institutions to a lively commercial "main street" during the 1840s and had fully redefined itself by the boom years of the 1850s, when it replaced Royal and Chartres Street as the primary shopping district in the city.[136] Epitomizing 1850s-era commercial Canal Street was Touro Row, an ensemble of twelve identical four-story Greek Revival commercial units between Royal and Bourbon built for hometown millionaire philanthropist Judah Touro in increments during the decade and distinctive for their spectacular two-story iron-lace gallery, in fashion at the time and almost as much a part of Canal Street as they still are of the French Quarter. Canal Street was renamed Touro Boulevard for its benefactor briefly in the mid-1850s but the name did not stick.

135. This measurement is "from building line to building line, and is divided into two sidewalks 21 feet in width, two roadways 35 feet each in width, and a neutral area 59 feet in width" (Regular Democratic Organization, 29). Such was the case in 1932; some measurements varied over the years. According to one thesis, "Canal Street's right of way for the first four blocks from the river is 190 feet, and from Rampart Street it narrows down to 170 feet which is one foot less than the 171 feet fixed in 1852. This is thought to make Canal Street the widest central city retail street in the United States" (Khorsandi).

136. Some identify the year 1866 as the time by which Canal Street captured the distinction of New Orleans' "grand boulevard" from Chartres Street. The transition was certainly complete by that year. Hennick and Charlton, 49.

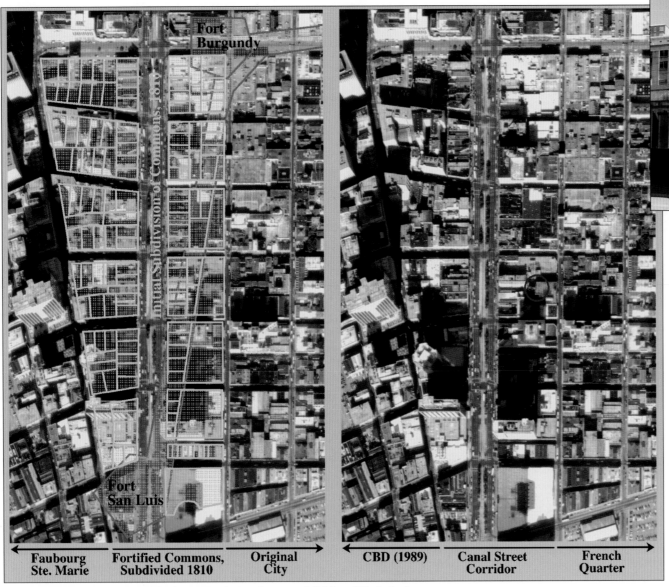

Fort
Burgundy

Initial Subdivision of Commons, 1810

Fort
San Luis

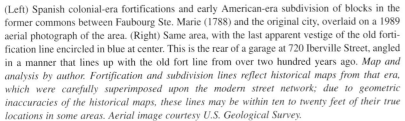

| ← Faubourg Ste. Marie | Fortified Commons, Subdivided 1810 | Original City → | CBD (1989) | Canal Street Corridor | French Quarter |

(Left) Spanish colonial-era fortifications and early American-era subdivision of blocks in the former commons between Faubourg Ste. Marie (1788) and the original city, overlaid on a 1989 aerial photograph of the area. (Right) Same area, with the last apparent vestige of the old fortification line encircled in blue at center. This is the rear of a garage at 720 Iberville Street, angled in a manner that lines up with the old fort line from over two hundred years ago. *Map and analysis by author. Fortification and subdivision lines reflect historical maps from that era, which were carefully superimposed upon the modern street network; due to geometric inaccuracies of the historical maps, these lines may be within ten to twenty feet of their true locations in some areas. Aerial image courtesy U.S. Geological Survey.*

(Aerial scenes) These 1966 aerial photographs of the blocks between Canal (left) and Iberville from Bourbon (top) to Chartres show five structures with angled walls lining up with the eighteenth-century fortification line (arrows) preceding the creation of Canal Street and subdivision of adjacent blocks (1810). The fort line was preserved in the resulting land parcels and passed on to structures constructed many years later. Since 1966, three of these vestiges have been demolished. *Vieux Carre Aerial Survey (1966), Jack Beech of Amman-International, The Historic New Orleans Collection, accession nos. 1979.237.6.41 and 1979.237.6.54*

(Inset) A closer look at the angled walls at 720 Iberville Street (Dickie Brennan's Steakhouse and parking garage) and the Acme Oyster House. Demolition of the former Woolworth's building in 2000 revealed this feature to pedestrians on the first block of Bourbon Street. *Photograph by author, 2000*

Iberville Street, formerly Customhouse, Aduana, and Douane, was the original upriver edge of the city, and remains the upper boundary of the French Quarter, despite the common association of Canal Street with that role. Rear quarters of large structures facing Canal tend to dominate the upriver half of Iberville (left), giving it a warehouse-district feel, but older, more appropriately scaled buildings still predominate on the lower half of the street, thanks to Vieux Carré Commission protection. This is the Bourbon Street intersection, looking toward the lake. *Photograph by author, 2000*

For the century that followed, Canal Street lakeside of approximately the Chartres/Camp intersection would serve as the retail spine of New Orleans,[137] home of its most important department stores and shops, while the blocks riverside of Chartres/Camp hosted warehouses, shipping, and transportation services. Patterns of land use on the avenue were remarkably similar in the years 1887 and 1940,[138] for example, and probably from the 1860s to 1950s as well. The street also assumed a kind of town-square role, as a place where the community assembled in times of both celebration and strife. In happier times, Canal Street hosted the lavish dedication of the Henry Clay statue (1860) and scores of Carnival festivities; in more tragic times, it saw the Battle of Liberty Place (1874) and the assembly of the mob that lynched eleven Sicilians at the Parish Prison (1891). James S. Zacharie's 1885 tour guide of the city not only describes Canal Street as the "main avenue" and "chief promenade" of the city, home to its "principal shops, confectioners, stores, and clubs," but also as the "centre of the city"—specifically at the Clay Statue, where Canal intersects Royal/St. Charles.[139]

The foot of Canal Street, where the Great Wide Way meets the Father of Waters, was a whirlwind of excitement and activity from the late 1800s to the mid-1900s, terminal for railroads, streetcars, ferries, and ships, a real geographical node and jumping-off point for the Crescent City (see page 164). Transportation activity also buzzed a mile inland, where steam locomotives pulled passenger cars along the Old Basin Canal corridor and past the brothels of Storyville to deposit visitors at the Southern Railway Terminal at the Basin Street intersection of Canal Street, two streets originally laid out spaciously to accommodate the planned extension of Carondelet Canal to the river. Designed in the Renaissance Revival style by architect Daniel Burnham, famous for his influential "Great White City" at the 1893 World's Columbian Exposition in Chicago, the Southern Railway Terminal nearly inspired New Orleans to transform Canal Street into a gleaming-white Renaissance Revival thoroughfare.[140] Southern Terminal was opened in 1908 and demolished in 1956; the ca.-1900 L & N Station at the foot of Canal was razed soon after, and the 1920s-era pedestrian viaduct to the ferry was removed in 1965, though the ferry still functions.

During these spans of years, Canal Street was home to a high-end shopping district, anchored by landmark department stores like Maison Blanche, D. H. Holmes, and Godchaux's and populated with locally famous enterprises like Katz and Bestoff, which became the now-sold K&B drugstore chain. The retail offerings of the street attracted a regional and local clientele and had the kind of emporium atmosphere that required dressing up for visits to the better stores. (Most of these stores were racially segregated until the early 1960s, giving rise to an adjacent black retail community on South Rampart above the Common Street intersection. Integration had the ironic effect of depleting this black shopping district of its customers, who headed instead to Canal Street. It was gone by the late 1960s.) While the role of Canal Street as the center of the New Orleanians' world—or at least the white New Orleanians' world—remained fairly constant for a century, its features, of course, changed dynamically: Streetcars arrived at Canal Street in 1861 and were electrified in the 1890s; electric lights illumi-

nated the thoroughfare in the 1880s; telegraph and telephone wires cluttered the airspace since the beginnings of these technologies; distinctive lampposts and terrazzo-style sidewalk paving were installed during the beautification effort of 1929-30; the 1850s-era iron-lace galleries were gradually removed in the 1930s for scrap iron; and many of the ubiquitous three-story row structures from the antebellum era were replaced by taller, more ornate buildings of the early twentieth century.

The third transition of Canal Street began around 1964, the year when most streetcars were removed from the corridor, and is in its latter stages today. The termination of the famous Canal Street streetcar lines—May 31, 1964, a date remembered ruefully by many—symbolized the increasing reliance upon the automobile for transportation and concurred with the beginning of the middle-class flight for suburban communities in neighboring parishes.[141] Automobiles, increasing crime rates, white flight, and competition from suburban malls and office parks starved Canal Street merchants and professionals of their prosperous clients at just the time when tourism to New Orleans, primarily to the French Quarter, increased to over 10 million annually by the late 1990s.

New Orleans held off the demise of its major downtown artery much longer than most other major cities; the street still had a number of major stores and high-end retailers into the 1980s. Then, one by one, Canal Street's old clothing and department stores—Godchaux's, Kreeger's, Gus Mayer, D. H. Holmes, Krauss, Woolworth's, Maison Blanche—closed and were replaced or reoccupied by monuments to the tourist and convention trade. The closings of Canal Street institutions occurred with such steadfast regularity that by 2000, only Rubenstein's and Adler's remained of the elegant local retail community.

Skyscraper hotels arose in the early 1970s, replacing lower Canal's turn-of-the-century port-city motif with a severe and modernistic Times Square look. The most drastic land-use alteration generally occurred in the blocks closest to the river, where uncherished nineteenth-century industrial structures afforded the space, and the nearby French Quarter provided the tourist clientele, for large-scale demolition and construction in the 1960s and 1970s. The 1999 opening of an ostentatious casino on the site of the equally startling (but well-engineered and architecturally more valued) Rivergate Exhibition Hall (1968) further embedded a nonlocal orientation in lower Canal Street. According to urban geographer Anne E. Mosher, the recent changes on Canal Street reflect "the century-long transformation of New Orleans from a postmercantile monocentric to postmodern polycentric city."[142] In other words, Canal Street is no longer the center of the New Orleanians' world.

There is still plenty of bustle on Canal Street, far more than on the main downtown thoroughfares of many other major American cities. A study in the 1980s showed that, between 7:45 and 8:45 A.M., over 1,100 pedestrians traveled the three Canal Street blocks between Royal and Burgundy, while 700-1,100 walked its other blocks between Basin and the river. Another study counted about 80,000 pedestrians on Canal between 10:00 A.M. and 5:00 P.M. in 1987.[143] These figures are probably much higher today. A typical weekday crowd consists of roughly equal portions of office workers on breaks, tourists, and residents of nearby poor neighborhoods (primarily the Iberville Housing Development), who rely on the street for shopping and transportation. On weekends, the crowd is split between mostly poor black residents and middle-class white tourists, to whom the Canal Street retail community responds accordingly.

Canal Street may shift again in the early 2000s, looking this time toward its past: streetcar tracks were reinstalled in 1997 to the great excitement of the city, and plans to convert the upper floors of old commercial structures to condominiums may return a residential element to Canal Street, which may in turn draw nontourist commerce to the thoroughfare. The closing of the nearly century-old department stores of Krauss and Maison Blanche in 1997-98 was a sad loss for the economically depressed section of Canal Street away from the river, but the long-awaited opening of a five-star Ritz-Carlton Hotel in the former Maison Blanche Building may attract quality shops (but not local shoppers) back to this grungy section. In 2000, the Downtown Development District (DDD), the CBD's planning and advocacy agency, proposed a multimillion-dollar beautification program of Canal from the river to Claiborne Avenue, featuring new sidewalks, light fixtures, palm trees, street furniture, and historic markers, though it would take fundamental economic changes to bring back the elegant boulevard that once was.[144] Radical change was proposed in the summer of 2001 by the New Orleans Saints,

137. *White* New Orleans, that is. Most Canal Street stores were segregated into the early 1960s, as was the city in general. Black New Orleanians operated shops for their community along South Rampart Street above Canal. This interesting retail community dissipated after the civil-rights movement opened up Canal Street to all New Orleanians.

138. Mosher, Keim, and Franques, 501, 504.

139. Zacharie, 36.

140. "Architectural Gems of the 20th Century," *New Orleans Times-Picayune,* March 5, 2000.

141. See Hennick and Charlton, 42-44, for an account of the demise of the Canal Street line.

142. Mosher, Keim, and Franques, 515.

143. Olmo, I-10, I-11.

144. Yerton, "Canal's Crown Jewel," and Eggler.

The Canal Street corridor about forty years after its development, when it had seized the status of the city's premier retail thoroughfare from Chartres Street. *Detail of Bird's Eye View of New-Orleans (New York: A. Guerber & Co., 1851), courtesy American Memory Panoramic Maps Collection, Library of Congress*

This detail of Currier & Ives' *The City of New Orleans* (1885) shows the busy Canal Street corridor in the mid-1880s, after the city had emerged from the tumult of the war and Reconstruction. *American Memory Panoramic Maps Collection, Library of Congress*

Looking down Canal Street around 1913, viewed from the Hotel Grunewald toward the river. Note the new Hotel Monteleone in the French Quarter at left center, and the American Sugar Refining Company facilities on the French Quarter batture at upper right. Canal Street at this time was wall-to-wall retailers in these blocks, with professional and specialty service businesses operating on the upper floors and wholesalers in the buildings toward the river. *Detroit Publishing Company, Library of Congress, no. LC D401-15657 LC DLC*

Looking up Canal Street from the Clay Statue at the Royal/St. Charles intersection around 1890, captured by famed Western photographer William Henry Jackson when he was in the employ of the Detroit Publishing Company. The original units of Judah Touro's "Touro Row" appear at right; the Victorian dome of the Mercier Building, home of the first Maison Blanche in 1897, appears in the distant center, and the cupola of Chess, Checkers, and Whist is visible in the distant left. A stroll up Canal Street in the Victorian era must have been a spectacular experience. *Photograph by William Henry Jackson, Detroit Publishing Company, Library of Congress, no. LC-D418-8101 DLC*

Looking up Canal Street around 1910, from the roof of the U.S. Custom House. *Detroit Publishing Company, Library of Congress, no. LC-D4-33060 DLC*

who suggested siting a huge retractable-roof football stadium on the Iberville Housing Development and redeveloping the Canal blocks from Basin to Claiborne as a retail and entertainment center. Such a plan would vastly alter the nature of Canal Street and neighboring Tremé, ameliorating some social problems but extending the ersatz tourist scene in a new direction and further reducing the number of New Orleanians utilizing Canal Street. Despite the "Disneyfication" of the French Quarter that has now encroached on lower Canal Street and that may extend to the Basin-to-Claiborne stretch, hope remains that a local significance will return to the Great Wide Way. The street, after all, is familiar with transition, having evolving from a barren commons to an elegant residential/institutional avenue, then to a bustling and world-famous commercial main street, and now to a mecca of the hospitality industry.

Creoles, Americans, and Canal Street in Nineteenth-Century New Orleans

Who were the Creoles? The answer to this question is one of the most controversial and confusing matters in Louisiana history, one that strikes at the very soul of the place and its people. Into the twenty-first century, spirited discussions on this question occasionally appear in letters to the editor and may be heard in coffee-shop conversations or call-in radio programs.

The meaning of *Creole,* implied or stated, varies on the axes of time and place; ethnicity, race, class, and politics of the speaker; and context in which the word is spoken. In the early nineteenth century, so nuanced was the word that there were slightly different unwritten understandings of the word *creoles* versus *the creoles,* and the more exclusive *ancienne population.*[145] In the late nineteenth and early twentieth centuries, the city's white population of French or Spanish ancestry laid claim to the cherished appellation, adamantly excluding people of color from its definition. In the late twentieth century, *Creole* in New Orleans came to refer to certain segments of the city's African-American population, usually those of mixed ancestry, Catholic faith, Gallic surnames, and deep roots in the city (many of them descendents of the *gens de couleur libres,* free people of color).

For well over a century up to today, the word has been used as both a noun ("the Creoles") and adjective ("Creole cottages," "Creole cooking"), a situation that tends to drive the noun usage astray from earlier meanings. Furthermore, the word has been hijacked, usurped, and misused by people with a heritage to protect, identity to seize, cherished myth to promulgate, or product to sell. To be fair, much of the confusion is understandable—words derive their meaning from usage, and if usage varies, a case may be made that meaning varies.

But such consideration cannot be imposed on past usage. From late colonial times to the post-Civil War era, there was one common denominator in everyday usage of the term "Creole," and that was *native born.*[146] The Creoles—or creoles—were those native to New Orleans, Louisiana, and the Gulf Coast region, meaning those who traced their roots back a few generations to French and Spanish colonial times and who tended to carry on the cultural traits associated with those societies. They were here before the American takeover of the city, before the English-speaking Anglo element emigrated to the region from the North, and before the styles and sensibilities of the American mainstream arrived and took hold.

A Creole, in the usage of the eighteenth and nineteenth centuries, may be white, black, or mixed; he was usually of French or Spanish ancestry, culturally Latin and Catholic, but could also be of German, African, even Anglo or other origin; he may even be Cajun (Acadian)[147]—just so long as he or she was born here, likely descending from stock residing in the region for a generation or more prior to the era of American domination. Some contemporary accounts restrict the term to native whites of French or Spanish ancestry,[148] but many more emphasize that the distinguishing element was nativity, not race, and everyday usage (as recorded in newspapers)

backs up this view. "All who are born here, come under this designation [of Creole], without reference to the birth place of their parents," wrote Benjamin Moore Norman in his 1845 description of New Orleans.[149] Joseph Holt Ingraham, after recounting a crude anecdote in which a Northern uncle understood his nephew's new wife to be mulatto because he described her as a Creole in his letter, reiterated that "'Creole' is simply a synonym for "native." . . . To say 'He is a *Creole* of Louisiana' is to say 'He is a *native* of Louisiana.'"[150] A writer to the Louisiana Courier in 1831 commented that *Creole* is a word by which "we have ever been distinguished from those who have emigrated to the state. . . . [It is also used] to signify such as have been born in the country, whether white, yellow, or black; whether the children of French, Spanish, English, or Dutch, or of any other nation."[151]

Any further identification of the race or ethnicity of a Creole derived from context. For example, antebellum advertisements selling "Fanny, aged 26 years, a creole" and "Mary Ann . . . a creole, aged 7 years, speaks French and English"[152] implied that these Creoles were black, since whites were not enslaved, while an article on Creole voting trends would indicate that these Creoles were white, since blacks could not vote. Nineteenth-century newspapers are loaded with such references, day after day, in classified ads, articles, commentaries, and announcements.

Further clarification may be gained by identifying who would *not* have been considered Creole in the period under discussion. A recent immigrant from Ireland or Germany would not be a Creole (he would be a "foreigner"), although a descendent of the 1720s-era German settlers to *La Côte des Allemands* would be Creole. A French-blooded Saint-Domingue refugee who escaped to New Orleans in the early 1800s would not be Creole, nor would a Paris-born Frenchman residing in the city (both would be "foreign French").[153] The post-Louisiana Purchase Anglo-Saxon American emigrants were absolutely not Creoles, but their Louisiana-born children generally would be. A bondsman of pure African descent enslaved in Louisiana since colonial times would be a Creole, but a mixed-race French-speaking slave from a Caribbean island would not (though a visitor may confuse him with one).

To be sure, many, perhaps most, Creoles in old New Orleans could be described as white people of French and Spanish descent[154] who were Catholic in faith and Latin by culture, but one cannot conclude that these conditions had to be met to be considered Creole in the era under discussion. "In Louisiana, every native, be his parentage what it may, is a Creole. They are convertible terms," explained the author of the 1854 city directory, then adding, "Although the word *Creole* in its usual acceptation means a white person, it applies to all races, as Creole negroes."[155] The key element, in this era, was nativity to the region. Additional understanding may be gained through some analogies put forth in an 1839 note in the *Bee,* a New Orleans newspaper with deep ties to the city's French-speaking community (see page 147): "A Kentuckian is a Creole of Kentucky and a Yankee a Creole of New England . . . and an Irishman of Ireland. . . . A Creole is a native of the state or country where he or she may have been born."[156]

Who were the Americans? Less controversy surrounds this question. The Americans were primarily those new New Orleanians of Anglo-Saxon descent, English speaking, Protestant in faith, citizens of the United States, and resident to their northeastern or upper-South homelands for generations.[157] Significant American penetration into colonial Louisiana began in 1788, when Spain liberalized its immigration policy (part of a halfhearted attempt to augment the population of the colony for defense against potential invaders, including the United States), allowing a handful of Americans to cast their lot with *La Nueva Orleans.*[158]

145. Joseph G. Tregle, Jr., *Louisiana in the Age of Jackson,* 26, and "Creoles and Americans," 140.

146. This definition is based on the careful primary-source research of the renowned historian Joseph G. Tregle, Jr., professor emeritus of history at the University of New Orleans and a leading expert on Louisiana history. Dr. Tregle's work regarding the nature of nineteenth-century Creole society was quite controversial when first published in 1952. Using copious newspaper references, directory listings, and first-person accounts, he deals blow after blow to what turn out to be little more than myths, many of them central to the modern-day perception of historic New Orleans: that the Creoles were necessarily of pure French or Spanish blood; that they were aristocratic, cultured, and pretentious; that they looked down upon the "crass" Americans; that they rejected the Americans from their midst and forced them to live across Canal Street; that Creoles could never also be considered Cajuns (Acadians) or Anglos. Dr. Tregle argues compellingly and with evidence that these images were conjured up in the late nineteenth century by writers and aging Creole partisans intent on establishing a mystique for the remnants of their society, a society smothered over by the greater American culture. "The inevitable pain of final surrender [of the Creoles to American society] . . . found its amelioration in the reassurances of an imagined past," wrote Dr. Tregle in his 1992 article, "Creoles and Americans." A major component of this late-nineteenth-century redefinition involved the adamant exclusion of black blood from the ranks of Creole, and it is of great irony that the understanding of the word "Creole" in the streets of New Orleans today is just about the opposite. See Tregle, "Early New Orleans Society," "On that Word 'Creole' Again," "Creoles and Americans," and *Louisiana in the Age of Jackson.*

147. Tregle, "Early New Orleans Society," 24, and *Louisiana in the Age of Jackson,* 342-43.

148. John H. B. Latrobe, son of the famous architect, upon observing veiled women on a balcony and taking them for quadroons, wrote, "Heavens no, they are creoles—natives, whites—Spanish and French mixed—born in the country—very good society. No indeed they are not quadroons. You must make the distinction." As quoted in Wilson, *Southern Travels,* 43.

149. Norman, 73.

150. Ingraham, footnote on 118-19.

151. *Louisiana Courier,* 28 October 1831, as quoted by Joseph G. Tregle, Jr., "On that Word 'Creole' Again," 194-95.

152. *Louisiana Advertiser,* 20 April 1827, as quoted by Tregle, 197, and flier from New Orleans, May 13, 1835, as reproduced by Walter Johnson, illustration section.

153. Jerah Johnson, 51, and Joseph G. Tregle, Jr., "Early New Orleans Society," 31.

154. Norman, 74.

155. *Cohen's City Directory for 1854,* 34.

156. *New Orleans Bee,* May 19, 1839, as quoted by Joseph G. Tregle, Jr., *Louisiana in the Age of Jackson,* 340. Projected to modern scenarios, the relationship between Creoles and Americans in nineteenth-century Louisiana parallels the association between *Tejanos* and the many transplants currently migrating to the border region in the American Southwest, or between those of the old Spanish bloodline and newly arrived whites in trendy Santa Fe, New Mexico. Equivalent relationships of locals in competition with the newly arrived are found commonly these days: poor residents versus "yuppies" in gentrifying neighborhoods, conservative country people versus urban environmentalists moving to scenic regions, Westerners versus Eastern "dudes" relocating to towns in the Rockies, etc.

157. Both Creoles and Anglo-Americans were citizens of the United States and thus technically "Americans" after the Louisiana Purchase. The Creoles "very properly, and proudly too, assume the national appellation [of American], which we of the English tongue have so haughtily arrogated to ourselves." But the nomenclature of "Creole" as opposed to "American" persisted for years, probably for convenience in speech, but perhaps because the assumption of a radically new national identity is a slow process. Ingraham, 101.

158. Din, 334-47. Spanish colonial administrators in Spain and New Orleans held deeply conflicting views on the encroaching Americans, seeing them variously as potential allies against the English, possible threats to Mexico, able commercial partners, and dangerous inciters of liberation.

American commerce with Spanish New Orleans also increased in this era, from a dozen American flatboats arriving in 1792 to 550 in 1802, guided by 3,200 rough frontier rivermen who circulated and intermingled in this European colonial city of 8,000.[159] Even in that last colonial year, "more than half of the city's mercantile establishments were operated by agents of New York, Philadelphia, and Baltimore merchants."[160]

But the lion's share of serious, long-term-oriented American emigrants to Louisiana arrived after the Louisiana Purchase and before the Civil War, from the Mid-Atlantic states, New England, and the upper South, primarily New York, Pennsylvania, and Virginia.[161] The first wave commenced after Americanization in late 1803 and lasted for about two decades; a second influx occurred in the 1830s up to the economic crash of 1837; and a third wave arrived in the mid-1840s.[162] New York, a kindred city in so many ways, was by far the largest contributor to New Orleans' American population from 1834 to the Civil War,[163] and probably earlier. Later on in the antebellum era, neighboring Southern states also contributed to New Orleans' American transplant population. The 1850 census, the first that recorded place of birth, listed 966 white families with out-of-state American birthplaces living in Orleans Parish, of which 33 percent hailed from New York, 11 percent from Mississippi, 10 percent Alabama, 6 percent Missouri, and the remainder from Ohio, Pennsylvania, Kentucky, Tennessee, Massachusetts, South Carolina, and other states.[164] Another analysis of the 1850 census tabulated 9,461 residents (8.2 percent of the city's total population of 116,000) born in the Northern free states and another 6,616 (5.7 percent) born in the South (excluding Louisiana) and border states.[165] Add to these figures the thousands of children and grandchildren of the early waves of Americans to New Orleans, who had local birthplaces but presumably carried on at least some of the American cultural traits of their elders. "Northerners became leaders in the city's commerce and finance, and by 1851 the New Orleans *Crescent* could report that 'a majority of the business men of this city' were importations from north of Mason and Dixon's line."[166]

Americanization

"Americans are pouring in daily. . . . In a few years therefore, this will be an American town. What is good & bad in the French manners, & opinions must give way, & the American notions of right & wrong, of convenience & inconvenience will take their place. . . . Everything French will in 50 years disappear. Even the miserable patois of the Creoles will be heard only in the cypress swamps."
—Benjamin Latrobe, on New Orleans in 1819 (35)

"To merchants—wants a situation. A young *gentleman* from the north wishes employment in *a respectable mercantile store or counting-room ;* one in the city would be preferred, but would have *no objection to go into the country.* He is a complete and *universal* accountant . . . his principal study for a *number of years,* and practicing it *in the first houses* in New-York and Philadelphia—speaks the French, and understands a little of the *Spanish and Portuguese languages . . .* and is an *excellent* salesman. The most unquestionable references will be given, *as to* character for honesty and sobriety—salary is less an object than a permanent and steady employ."
—advertisement (as quoted by Paxton, 1822, as representative of the enterprising young Yankees arriving to New Orleans at that time, 42-43)

"Much distortion of opinion has existed . . . respecting public morals and manners in New Orleans. Divested of pre-conceived ideas on the subject, an observing man will find little to condemn in New Orleans, more than in other commercial cities ; and will find that noble distinction of all active communities, acuteness of conception, urbanity of manners, and polished exterior. There are few places where human life can be enjoyed with more pleasure, or employed to more pecuniary profit."
—William Darby, 1816 (187)

Like most migrating peoples, the post-Purchase Anglo-Americans (especially the first wave) were self-selected for traits of industriousness and enterprise, arriving "to seek their fortunes in the rich acres of the new territory and in its markets, banks, courts, and thriving trading centers."[167] Prominent men such as Edward Livingston,

John Slidell, Judah Touro, and Samuel Peters all emerged from the first waves of American emigration to New Orleans. The newly acquired city represented a rare opportunity for the ambitious and daring Americans: here was a civilized, century-old society suddenly thrown open for business, and what a business it promised to be! After decades of stifling colonial lethargy and suppressed trade efforts, the gatekeeper city *and* its vast hinterland were now suddenly all in the hands of the American government and available to the American people. Pregnant with economic promise, New Orleans was now in the right place at the right time and in the right hands to exploit its potential. Respected figures routinely predicted that New Orleans would someday be one of the wealthiest and most important cities on earth, "the great emporium of the Western world," "one of the greatest cities the world has ever seen."[168] In droves came Americans to New Orleans and Louisiana.

Creole identity, in the form of an importance attached to being *from here,* did not take shape until these waves of Americans began to arrive after the Louisiana Purchase. Prior changes in government—specifically the Spanish takeover in the 1760s—did not change the essential French nature of the city,[169] and inasmuch as the Spanish and French shared many cultural traits and cohabited in isolation in New Orleans, no great sense of competition nor of native identity prevailed. The American flatboatsmen who arrived from the frontier in 1792-1803 were a gritty and itinerant lot who likewise evoked few feelings of social envy or fear among the natives.

This changed entirely after 1803. For the first time, the natives were threatened by an ambitious people of an alien culture, swarming over their homeland and threatening their hold on institutions of state, business, church, and society. Contrary to popular imagery, the Creoles were hardly the cultured aristocrats who sneered at the uneducated Americans; if anything, the opposite was more likely the case. Native New Orleanians (many of whom descended from settlers of a social status no higher than the working class) lived in a remote outpost of a fading colonial power that held notoriously little value for education, while many post-Purchase Americans buzzed with entrepreneurial spirit and democratic ideals and were often appalled at the ignorance and illiteracy of their new neighbors.[170] Feelings of jealousy, inadequacy, and fear prevailed among the Creoles toward the cocky newcomers. "Fully aware of their deficiencies, the original inhabitants sensed that their most persuasive claim to precedence [over the Americans] lay in the proposition that those born to the region had priority rights within it, a natural endowment flowing from those primal attachments which bind men to the place of their birth,"[171] wrote the eminent historian Dr. Joseph G. Tregle, Jr.

From this growing sense of threat and insecurity arose the Creole identity of native pride, bonding together those who were born in the region against those who recently migrated here. Cognizant that the term *Creole* denoted only nativity to Louisiana and not race nor any sense of exclusivity, a certain class of Creoles called themselves the *ancienne population,* "to designate those white residents whose attachment to Louisiana extended back into colonial times and whose ancestry derived almost certainly from French or Spanish progenitors." But this awkward term was eventually subsumed into the more convenient *Creole.*[172]

Myths aside, the Creoles and the Americans were fundamentally different in culture and outlook—one oriented toward Louisiana and Europe, passive, monarchic, insecure in the company of ambitious outsiders, less educated, and provincial; the other oriented toward the United States and resolutely against Europe, aggressive in business, democratic in government, confident to the point of swaggering, better educated, and worldly. Other groups maneuvered on the ethnic chessboard of New Orleans in this era. There were thousands of enslaved Africans as well as *gens de couleur libres* (free people of color), of whom some were native to Louisiana (Creole) and others to American, Caribbean, or African soil. There were the "foreign French," those recent immigrants from France or Saint-Domingue, many of whom were refugees from revolution and insurrection. And there were numerous German and Irish immigrants, struggling in trades or dangerous manual labor. The 1850 census recorded 925 foreign-born families residing in Orleans Parish, hailing primarily from

159. Whitaker, 150-51.
160. Chenault and Reinders, 232.
161. Joseph G. Tregle, Jr., "Creoles and Americans," 153-54.
162. Chenault and Reinders, 233.
163. Treat, 278-82.
164. Ibid., calculated from data presented on 263-64. Treat notes on 248 that, according to the 1850 census, "[50.5]% of all migrants [to Greater New Orleans] were from foreign countries; 25% from slave states; and 24.5% from free states. In other words, three-quarters of the migrants to New Orleans came from non-slaveholding sources. In the state outside Greater New Orleans only 6.7% came from such sources."
165. Based on James D. B. De Bow's compilations, as quoted by Chenault and Reinders, 233.
166. Chenault and Reinders, 232.
167. Joseph G. Tregle, Jr., *Louisiana in the Age of Jackson,* 26.

168. Paxton (1822), 42, and John McDonogh (1818), as quoted in Clark, "New Orleans and the River," 134.
169. Jerah Johnson, 45, and James Pitot, 31.
170. Joseph G. Tregle, Jr., "Creoles and Americans," 142. The few Americans who arrived to the wharves of New Orleans before the Louisiana Purchase, and the Mississippi "watermen" who frequented the city throughout the early 1800s, were more in line with the stereotype of the crass "Kaintuck," but Dr. Tregle comments that "Louisiana folklore has too greatly stressed this vulgarity and barbarism of the early Americans in Louisiana." The post-Purchase Americans were of an entirely different breed. Tregle, *Louisiana in the Age of Jackson,* 26, and "On that Word 'Creole' Again," 198. See also Norman, 74-75.
171. Joseph G. Tregle, Jr., "Creoles and Americans," 138. Such sentiments may be seen today in bumper stickers proclaiming "CALIFORNIA NATIVE," "WYOMING NATIVE: ENDANGERED SPECIES," and the like, words that speak volumes about perceptions of nativity and its perceived rights and threats.
172. Ibid., 140.

Ireland (41 percent), Germany (23 percent), France (18 percent), Great Britain (9 percent), and other countries.[173] There were also pockets of "Danes, Swedes, . . . Englishmen, Portuguese, Hollanders, Mexicans, . . . and a motley group of Indians"[174] enriching the melting pot of New Orleans. But for the first half of the nineteenth century, the fundamental theme characterizing life in New Orleans was the competition between the Creoles and the Americans, in which each group vied for political, economic, and social supremacy in the community. Most other groups sided with either party of this cultural dichotomy, depending on what was in their best interest.

And down the middle, the legend goes, lay Canal Street. The oft-repeated story goes like this: the proud and aristocratic Creoles lived in the old city and so despised the crass, money-hungry Americans that they forced them to live beyond the city, on the other side of Canal Street, in Faubourg Ste. Marie. Canal Street, it continues, became a veritable cultural barrier between the rival camps in the old and new city. Emphasizing the cultural tension manifested in this urban edge was Canal Street's "neutral ground," a term used to this day for the median of this and other boulevards in the Crescent City. The story is appealing for its neatness and its ability to resolve a number of local clichés into a single anecdote. And it is not without first-person witnesses to its veracity, at least to parts of it. In *Norman's New Orleans and Environs* (1845), Benjamin Moore Norman caricatured the reaction of an old Frenchman, who rarely ventured "three squares beyond [his] favorite cabaret" in the city, upon hearing of the Americans' progress across Canal Street in Faubourg St. Mary: "Ah Monsieur B. dat is too much! You von varry funny fellow—I no believe vat you say—its only von grand—vot you call it—vere de mud, de alligator, and de bull frog live?—von grand—grand—mud swamp, vere you say is von grand city, I no believe it!"[175] The implication that the new American city across Canal Street was *terra incognita* to the French in the old city is clear. But this sense of strict geographical segregation by ethnicity is countered by a passage on the next page (emphasis added): "In taking a lounge through the lower part of the city, the stranger finds a difficulty in believing himself to be in an American city. The older buildings are of ancient and foreign construction, and the manners, customs and languages are various—the population being composed, *in nearly equal portions, of Americans, French, Creoles, and Spaniards,* together with a large portion of Germans, and a good sprinkling from almost every other nation upon the globe."[176]

Other first-person accounts reiterate the case for Canal Street as a hard cultural edge. A. Oakey Hall's *The Manhattaner in New Orleans* (1851) described the crossing of Canal Street as "passing the Rubicon of Creole prejudice, and entering on the American portion of the city."[177] "The lines between the separate sections of colored Society here, are distinctly marked," observed P. B. Randolph, a black community leader from the North

who visited New Orleans during its wartime occupation. "Very few French live above Canal St., very few Americans below it, and save politically, they seldom affiliate."[178] Grace King, the famed "local color" writer, recalled an English visitor to the city in 1839 who said that "below Canal Street everything reminded him of Paris: the lamps hanging from ropes across the streets, the women in gay aprons and caps, the language, the shops . . . the style of living . . . and the amusements, operas, concerts, ballets, balls, and masquerades."[179] Ernst von Hesse-Warteg, the German travel memoirist, gushed on the subject during his 1879-80 visit to the city:

This Mississippi of streets opens onto the Mississippi itself, the street the perfect counterpart to the river. . . . Here the South lies at one end of an international thoroughfare, the tropical West Indies at the other. The contrasts collide in one city, it seems, and in *this* street. Situation, prospect, traffic, the splendor of shops, all of life as lived in a street—in a word, *everything*—says we stand on the boundary between two great but distinct cultures. Anglo-Saxon and Latin meet *here*. Everything says we tread the contiguous edges of geographical zones. Tropical and temperate intersect *here*. . . .[180]

Canal Street divides New Orleans as the Straits of Dover do England from France. Indeed, English culture and French—better called Anglo-Germanic and Latin—could not be more precisely and more surely set at intervals than here, on either side of our broad Canal Street. From the Mississippi inland, everything to the left [of Canal Street] is Anglo-Saxon, and to the right it is Spanish, Italian, and French. . . . West of Canal, then, we hear *street, cents,* and *mister* without exception; east, *rue, centimes,* and *monsieur* also without exception. Ask directions in public and get the answer in English to the left, in French to the right. Each nation dwells as a separate society, isolated from one another, not mingling.[181]

Stated an 1892 photographic book,

Take half a dozen steps either way from Canal street and you are in a town as widely different in race, language, custom and ideas as two races of people living close to each other, and separated only by an imaginary line, can well be. Up town, as the American portion of the city is called, all is bustle and hurry, partaking of the activity of Northern cities. Cross the magic line toward Creole town, and one hears the foreign tongue and sees the signs in French, while groups of men chatter over their cigarettes and gesticulate as only the man can through whose veins Gallic blood flows.[182]

The message was passed on to visitors in an 1893 travel guide to the city and to the next generation in a 1919 schoolbook published by the Orleans Parish School Board:

The two most distinct classes are the Creoles and Americans, the former living mostly below Canal street, and the latter above. Canal street seems to be the dividing line and there are many Creoles who have never crossed that line. The change from the American portion to that of the Creole is very sudden, and in penetrating into the quarter below Canal street, the stranger goes, as it were, into another city. The signs are in French, and the names of the streets also, while French is heard on all sides.[183]

When Louisiana passed under the American flag, the Americans built up a quarter for themselves above the Terre Commune. This Terre Commune is now Canal Street and thus marks the division between the old city and the new, and between the Creoles and the Americans. Below Canal Street is the French or Creole quarter and above Canal Street the American district; the line is not as strictly drawn now as in former times.[184]

173. Treat, calculated from data presented on 263-64.
174. *The Western Gazette, or Emigrant's Directory* (1817), as quoted by Dufour, "The People of New Orleans," 37.
175. Norman, 68.
176. Ibid., 69-70. It appears that Norman may have borrowed these thoughts, and much of the exact phrasing, from *Gibson's Guide,* 285-86, though possibly he authored both passages.
177. Hall, 145.

178. As quoted in Logsdon and Bell, 239-40.
179. King, 272-73.
180. Trautmann, 156.
181. Ibid., 162-63.
182. From introduction written by Carl E. Groenevelt in *New Orleans Illustrated in Photo Etching* (1892).
183. Zacharie, *New Orleans Guide* (1893), 45-46.
184. Orleans Parish School Board, 130.

No one would deny the general veracity of these observations. Residential society in areas below Canal Street was indeed more culturally French than areas above Canal Street, where American culture predominated. But some skepticism is in order regarding the implication that Canal Street was a hard, impenetrable cultural barrier separating Creole and American completely and consistently throughout the nineteenth century. This notion of a stark cultural dividing line carries connotations of exclusivity and segregation (on the part of both Creoles and Americans), which begs for hard evidence before such a fascinating and revealing phenomenon is presumed to be true. A careful investigation of the names and addresses listed in the *Whitney's New-Orleans Directory* for 1811[185] reveals patterns that contradict the conventional wisdom of the Canal Street corridor as such. (Granted, Canal Street barely existed in this year, but the corridor and its two abutting neighborhoods were in place and developing.) This directory, reflecting data captured in 1810, lists heads of households and businesses by their addresses in the few neighborhoods that existed at the time—the city (total free and slave population: 12,225), Faubourg Ste. Marie (2,788), Faubourg Marigny (2,229), Bayou St. John and Gentilly Road (1,615), Faubourg de La Course, and outlying areas in the parish (whose total population was 24,552).[186]

I have categorized every entry in the fifty-five pages into (1) Gallic-, Hispanic-, or otherwise Latin-sounding names versus (2) Anglo-, Germanic-, or Celtic-sounding names, in a dubious (though best available) effort to identify Creoles and Americans.[187] Each entry was further classified according to the household's location, either below or above Canal Street.[188] The very few names that were illegible, indeterminable as to ancestry, or otherwise uncategorizable were excluded, as were residents of Bayou St. John and Gentilly, since these areas are beyond the scope of the Canal Street-focused research question. The results:

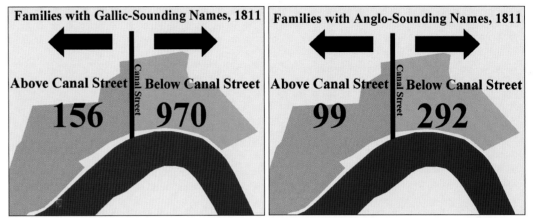

It is an undeniable fact that, for most of the nineteenth century, Creoles generally lived below Canal Street, in the old city and the lower faubourgs, while Americans tended to settle and work above Canal Street, in Faubourg St. Mary and the upper communities. But was Canal Street a hard cultural division separating the two cultures, a "neutral ground" between rival factions, as it is often remembered today? It appears not: an analysis of Gallic-sounding versus Anglo-sounding surnames and their residences in the 1811 city directory, and other directories from later in the antebellum era, reveals that there were plenty of families of either culture on both sides of Canal Street. This method is highly imprecise—for example, it is impossible to distinguish between Creoles and "foreign French" among Gallic-sounding names, and equally difficult to discern American names from Anglicized or immigrant names among Anglo-sounding names. Nevertheless, it appears that the two cultures were a bit more integrated than is usually thought, and that the Canal Street corridor was not quite the cultural Rubicon it is often portrayed as in history books. *Map and analysis of 1811 data by author. See text for details on methodology.*

Categorization of Entries in *Whitney's New-Orleans Directory* for 1811 by Ethnicity and Location						
Category	Number	Percent of Total	Percent among Gallics	Percent among Anglos	Percent below Canal	Percent above Canal
Families with **Gallic**-sounding names living **below Canal Street**	970	64	86	—	77	—
Families with **Gallic**-sounding names living **above Canal Street**	156	10	14	—	—	61
Families with **Anglo**-sounding names living **below Canal Street**	292	19	—	75	23	—
Families with **Anglo**-sounding names living **above Canal Street**	99	7	—	25	—	39

Below Canal Street denotes mostly the city and Faubourg Marigny; *above Canal Street* means mostly Faubourg Ste. Marie and de La Course (present-day CBD and parts of the Lower Garden District).

Although one hesitates to refer to all Gallic-sounding names as "Creole" or to all Anglo-sounding names as "American," it appears that, in 1810-11, there was no stark segregation of these two general cultures on the two sides of Canal Street. As one might expect, 86 percent of the Gallic-named heads of household lived below Canal, in the old city and Marigny, but fully 75 percent of Anglo-named households also lived below Canal Street. In

this year, only one of four Anglo entries lived according to the conventional story—that is, above Canal Street—and roughly the same percentage (23 percent) of the citizens in the supposedly exclusive French-Creole area below Canal Street were in fact Americans. Even more interesting is the number of Gallic-named entries residing above Canal Street, accounting for 61 percent of all those residing in these new suburbs, again in contradiction of the old story. Despite its flaws, this quantification provides some evidence that the Canal Street corridor was not an impermeable cultural edge in 1810—a time at which one might think that post-Purchase American emigrants were the targets of the maximum amount of local disdain, if the old legend bears any truth.

Dr. Tregle, who employed a similar methodology, concluded that French-sounding names clearly outnumbered American-sounding names in Faubourg St. Mary and all other sections of the city in 1810 and 1820. It was not until the 1830 census that American names outnumbered French names in this faubourg, though the French still comprised a full 35 percent of this neighborhood total. Additional investigation into the censuses of 1840, 1850, and 1860 support the contention that significant numbers of Americans indeed lived below Canal Street, in the French Quarter, contrary to legend. Even in 1850, at the height of the antebellum era, less than one in three whites in Faubourg St. Mary were American born, while 19 percent were born in Louisiana. The remaining 51 percent in this so-called American Sector were foreign born.[189]

Victor Hugo Treat's carefully documented 1967 dissertation, *Migration into Louisiana 1834-1880,* records fully 247 white families with out-of-state or foreign birthplaces—by definition non-Creole—living in the supposedly Creole-exclusive French Quarter in 1850. Of these families, 43 percent were American (a third from New York) and 57 percent were foreigners (almost half foreign French). It is interesting to note that 120 of these non-Creole families lived in the twelve blocks of Ward 2, between St. Louis and St. Peter Street, which incorporated such Creole cultural landmarks as the St. Louis Hotel and City Exchange.[190]

The evidence is abundant that American emigrants were *not* excluded from the old city below Canal Street by law, society, lifestyle, nor the availability of living space. Rather, Americans located in the "three- or four-block

185. Whitney, 3-55.
186. Ibid., appendix.
187. This method of determining ethnicity and nativity by surname is flawed for a number of reasons. Many people Gallicized their Anglo, German, or Irish names; others Anglicized their French or Spanish names. Also, members of the foreign French community, through this method, would appear to be Creoles (they were not), and recent German and Irish immigrants would be counted as Americans (they were not). Still other names are simply difficult to categorize. Nevertheless, no better method exists, at least not for this era, since place of birth was not recorded until the census of 1850. See Joseph G. Tregle, Jr., "Creoles and Americans," 154.
188. My original plan was to map out the addresses of each entry at the block level, to discern residential patterns at a finer detail than simply downtown/uptown. But because no comprehensive, reliable house-number maps exist for the city (especially the faubourgs) in this era, the plan had to be abandoned. The early numbering system was quite erratic and confusing: in 1835, for example, the block of Exchange Place between Conti and St. Louis numbered 19 to 37 on the lake side heading downriver, but reversed direction on the river side, going from 38 to 56. By 1876, this particular street was renumbered 111-148; finally, in 1894, the present-day system was adopted, and this became the 400 block of Exchange. *Vieux Carré Survey,* Binder for Squares 29-30.

189. Joseph G. Tregle, Jr., "Creoles and Americans," 154-57, 164.
190. Treat, calculated from data presented on 261-62. Wards 1, 2, 3, and 4 of the First Municipality comprise the modern-day Vieux Carré, according to *Norman's Plan of New Orleans & Environs* (1849), with municipality and ward boundaries as shown in Hirsch and Logsdon, 94-95.

area of the present Vieux Carré just below Canal Street, establishing a dominant presence there which would persist certainly down to the Civil War. Only when that section had become heavily populated did later American arrivals gravitate primarily to [Faubourg St. Mary]."[191] In the area stretching from St. Louis Street (or alternately Conti or Toulouse but certainly not Canal) to the streets of Faubourg St. Mary, the Americans dominated in their presence and in their commercial activity. "Here one found the banks, insurance companies, exchanges, specialty retail stores, commodity brokers, wholesale warehouses, factors . . . American bookshops, jewelry stores, and dry good emporiums."[192] Chartres Street was an especially busy strip of Northern-style retail, described by Joseph Holt Ingraham in 1835 as "the 'Broadway' of New-Orleans"—the exact same metaphor, incidentally, that German travel writer Ernst von Hesse-Wartegg would employ to describe Canal Street forty-five years later.[193] Ingraham's richly detailed travelogue of New Orleans and other Southern cities, *The South-West by a Yankee*, provides this revealing passage concerning the Americanized nature of the present-day upper French Quarter: "After passing Rue Toulouse, the streets began to assume a new character; the buildings were loftier and more modern—the signs over the doors bore English names, and the characteristic arrangements of a northern dry goods store were perceived. . . . We had now attained the upper part of Chartres-street, which is occupied almost exclusively by retail and wholesale dry goods dealers, jewellers, booksellers, &c., from the northern states, and I could almost realize that I was taking an evening promenade in Cornhill, so great was the resemblance."[194]

Upon reaching Canal Street, Ingraham lauded the treelined avenue for its breadth and beauty but made no mention of any sort of stark change of cultural character on the other side of the street. He then proceeded down Canal to Levée Street (now Decatur) and reentered the city, walking downriver. Again: "The stores on our left were all open, and nearly every one of them, for the first two squares, was . . . kept by Americans; that is to say, Anglo Americans as distinguished from the Louisiana French." It was not until he approached the market, about five blocks down, that "French stores began to predominate, till one could readily imagine himself, aided by the sound of the French language, French faces and French goods on all sides, to be traversing a street in Havre or Marseilles."

The extant architecture of the upper city, as alluded to by Ingraham, generally bears out its historic American influence. Here, three- and four-story Greek Revival storehouses line the streets much more so than Creole or colonial styles; were it not for the narrowness of the streets, many blocks in the upper French Quarter, then as now, would resemble certain parts of the Central Business District more so than the classic streetscapes of the lower Quarter.[195] Even that quintessential Creole, Bernard Marigny, identified St. Louis Street as the dividing line between upper and lower New Orleans in 1822, complaining that the Americans were entrenched in their section above St. Louis at the expense of the Creoles living downriver from that street.[196] Henry C. Castellanos, the astute observer of nineteenth-century life in New Orleans, concurred in 1895: "Canal street was not by any means, as some people suppose, the dividing line of the contending factions, inasmuch as many of the most enterprising American merchants and business men of the period . . . had their principal establishments in the French quarter."[197] Newspaper offices of the day also offer clues to the cultural porousness of Canal Street. The famous *L'Abeille de la Nouvelle Orléans (New Orleans Bee)*, a fixture of French culture located on Chartres Street, published in French *and* English, while a newspaper by the name of *Semi-Weekly Creole* was published not below Canal Street but at 94 Camp Street, well into Faubourg St. Mary.[198] Concluded Dr. Tregle, "The old notion of Canal Street as a real if unofficial dividing line separating highly exclusive ethnic populations contains more fancy than fact."[199] "Canal Street never really divided the populations at all, the American presence always remaining dominant in the upper reaches of the City [present-day French Quarter]."[200]

191. Joseph G. Tregle, Jr., "Creoles and Americans," 154.
192. Tregle, page 155.
193. Ingraham, 88, and Trautmann, 156. Ingraham also compared Canal to Manhattan's Broadway (100) but in reference to size, not function or character. He estimated Canal to be wider by half.
194. Ingraham, 93-94.
195. Campanella, 44-51.
196. Joseph G. Tregle, Jr., "Creoles and Americans," 155.
197. Castellanos, 253.
198. *Cohen's City Directory for 1854*, 296.
199. Joseph G. Tregle, Jr., "Creoles and Americans," 154.
200. Joseph G. Tregle, Jr., *Louisiana in the Age of Jackson*, 15.

Origins of the Premise

How, then, did the premise of Canal Street as a cultural Rubicon of nineteenth-century New Orleans come to be so broadly accepted? The concept stems, in large part, from the climactic repercussion of the Creole/American conflict: the 1836 subdivision of New Orleans into three semiautonomous municipalities. In the years leading up to this partition, French-speaking New Orleans—that is, the uncomfortable but useful alliance of the Creoles and the foreign French—boasted a numerical superiority over the Anglo-Americans, rendering the latter group, which dominated in commerce, subject to the political whim of the former. Allegations of financial mismanagement and incompetence flew in one direction; sentiments of jealousy and fear flew back. With the Americans harboring disdain toward the Creoles and suspicion toward the foreigners, with mutual feelings in return, "profound ethnic strife wracked New Orleans for decades, by the mid-1820s coming perilously close to armed violence."[201] The Americans resolved to fix the matter by essentially divorcing their neighborhood from the city. In 1836, after years of effort, they finally won legislative consent to divide New Orleans into three semiautonomous municipalities. A single mayor and constabulary would preside, but most other city functions would fall upon the councils of each municipality. "Each of the three municipalities, two downtown dominated by French-creoles and one uptown controlled by Anglo-Americans, had its own council to draft ordinances and its own municipal court system to enforce the often disparate regulations. Each conducted official business in its own language, and each tried to perpetuate its culture and language through its own public school system."[202] But where to draw the municipal boundaries? Americans generally lived upriver from about St. Louis Street (which also happened to be the line between the First and Second wards); Creoles intermixed throughout the city but prevailed as the clear majority in the lower neighborhoods. Perhaps St. Louis Street would have made an ideal municipal boundary. But it was not selected. Why? Dr. Tregle explained it in this manner: "It proved impossible . . . to overcome the emotional resistance to any plan that would wrench the First Ward from its historic place within the original city, no matter that ethnic identification and economic characteristics tied it more closely to the Faubourg St. Mary than to the lower quarter." Thus the compromise dividing line between the First Municipality (the City) and the Second (St. Mary) was fixed at Canal Street, with Esplanade Avenue serving as the upper boundary of the Third, roughly Faubourg Marigny."[203]

According to some accounts, St. Louis Street, not Canal Street, divided American-dominated areas (to the left) from Creole-dominated neighborhoods, though neither side completely excluded either group. The Royal Orleans Hotel (1960, large building on right) occupies the site of the famous St. Louis Hotel and City Exchange, a landmark of the Creole business community in the antebellum age. *Photograph by author, 2000*

201. Joseph G. Tregle, Jr., "Creoles and Americans," 153.
202. Hirsch and Logsdon, 93.
203. Joseph G. Tregle, Jr., "Creoles and Americans," 156.

So, in 1836, Canal Street became the dividing line between the Creole-dominated First Municipality and the American-dominated Second Municipality, even though Canal Street was clearly not the dividing line of the Creole and American populations. A casual glance at the surnames of the aldermen (they were called councilmen in the Second Municipality) in 1838 provides some clues to both the ethnic domination *and* diversity of each municipality's political arena. Acknowledging the problems of interpreting ethnicity by surname, the general pattern appears to be a Gallic political dominance with a significant Anglo minority in the First Municipality, a clear but not unanimous Anglo prevalence in the Second, and a Gallic/immigrant political preponderance in the Third:

Surnames of Aldermen/Councilmen of the Three Municipalities in 1838			
Ward	**First Municipality** (between Canal and Esplanade)	**Second Municipality** (above Canal)	**Third Municipality** (below Esplanade)
First	Armitage Faures Luzenberg Duplessis Crossman Duplessis Picton	Caldwell Gloyd Meux Nixon	Preux Montamat
Second	Guillot Wiltz Lesseps Lanaux Colson	Peters Yorke Lockett	Marigny Rigaud
Third	Cruzat Lefebvre Vignié Lambert Prados Guesnard	Sewell Whitney Hall	Kilshaw Giquel
Fourth	Correjolles Marsoudet Preval	—	Cucullu
Fifth	Roy Lanaux Colson	—	—
Source: *Gibson's Guide*, 301-4.			

To the extent that the legend of Canal Street as a cultural edge grew out of this political geography, it is fair to acknowledge some truth to the legend, since, for sixteen years, Canal Street would indeed form a hard edge between political units dominated by rival factions. *Neutral ground,* a term originally used to describe many political boundaries in New Orleans, was logically used to describe this new boundary, but came to take on connotations of a "demilitarized zone" between sparring Creoles and Americans. The term survives today to mean street medians throughout the city, which seems to buttress the case that the term was used widely, not just on Canal Street. The 1836 partition also probably explains some of the first-person testimony to the Canal Street legend (often written, incidentally, by visitors to the city who probably knew about as much of New Orleans' inner machinations as present-day tourists do). In any case, the 1836 municipality division had the effect of assuaging ethnic tensions, though it proved impractical and was eventually abandoned in 1852[204]— but only when the Americans were confident that their new alliances with Irish and German immigrants would assure American political dominance in a newly reunited city. In retrospect, the municipal subdivision proved

to be a defeat for the Creoles; never again would they hold sway over the American community or the city in general. Their relative numbers decreased, the binding sense of native identity diminished, their neighborhoods deteriorated, and the use of their language began to abate, though it would be heard in the streets into the early 1900s and among a dwindling number of old-timers into the mid-twentieth century.[205] The old native bloodlines would gradually blend into the American population. Creole cultural decline, coupled with dramatically increased racial tension after the Civil War, led certain writers and commentators in the 1870s and 1880s to recast the Creole and his role in the history of New Orleans into a romanticized, mythological one, in which Creoles were identified as necessarily of white French or Spanish extraction and supposedly known for their aristocratic and gallant ways. The Creole myth was born, and part of that myth was the obligatory mention of Canal Street as the city wall beyond which the aloof Creoles exiled the barbaric Americans. The truth is, as usual, more complicated and less romantic.

A second reason behind the legend of Canal Street as an impermeable cultural edge may stem from the turn-of-the-century era, when conceptions of old Creole society transformed from fact to romanticized fancy and the label of "American" became an antiquated and irrelevant one. In this era, the French Quarter was a decaying slum inhabited by immigrants, many from Sicily and most poor, and stood in sharp contrast to the electrified shopping district of Canal Street and the bustle of commerce in the Central Business District. Below Canal Street, the streetscape resembled a crumbling, ancient Mediterranean village, with foreign tongues and with clotheslines strung from balconies. Above Canal Street existed a modern and thoroughly American business district, characterized by steel-frame high-rises exhibiting nonnative architectural styles and catering to commerce impacting far beyond the limits of the city. The difference was so dramatic that contemporary observers (namely visitors with pen and paper in hand) probably could not help but cast Canal Street in the role of cleavage between old and new, Latin and Anglo, tropical and temperate[206]—and perhaps projected this sentiment on what they considered to be a related dichotomy: *Creole* and *American.* If so, it would not be the first or last time that modern conceptions of Creole and American society would be imposed on the past.

A third explanation for the Canal Street legend comes from the concept of scale. Every historical and geographical discussion assumes a certain level of detail, as a map employs a particular scale, and researchers are generally held to levels of precision that match the accuracy of that scale. (Precision and accuracy are not synonymous.) Few would expect a 1:2,000,000-scale map of Louisiana to even show Canal Street—far too much detail for this representative fraction—and likewise few synoptical histories of New Orleans have the space and inclination to depict the nuanced nature of Canal Street in the ethnic geography of the city. Mapped at 1:250,000 scale, Canal Street would indeed divide a cartographic representation of sections of historic Creole and American domination. But at the much more detailed scale of 1:24,000, the ethnic divide would be off Canal Street by about four blocks and form a porous zone, not a solid line. Though a legitimate explanation for imprecision, many myths are born in this fashion.

The sense of the Canal Street chasm between the new-world Central Business District and the old-world French Quarter remains today, reinforcing the image of the thoroughfare as an urban edge and tempting people to impose that sense on the past. As one crosses the eight lanes of treacherous car, bus, and streetcar traffic on Canal Street in the twenty-first century, that impression of temporal and cultural passage endures, and has no equal in the crossing of, say, Poydras Street, or Loyola Avenue, or St. Charles Avenue, or even Esplanade Avenue, which echoes Canal in its historical geography. Skyscrapers, cell phones, and business characterize one side of Canal—the functionally named *CBD*; iron-lace balconies, whiffs of fine cuisine, and escapism distinguish the other—the euphonically named *Vieux Carré.* (That there are also iron-lace balconies and great restaurants in the CBD, and offices and cell phones in the French Quarter, again reminds us of the gulf between impression and reality and the dangers of overgeneralization.) Canal Street itself is ragged today, shadowed by its glory years but still spectacular and relevant, despite the disfiguration of its famous riverside terminus and other urban-planning assaults.[207] Perhaps that glory will come riding in on a rail: in the last month

204. One contemporary take on the reunification reads, "Within the last year, 1852, New-Orleans has changed her form of municipal government, and organized herself into one community under one administration, a measure which is already telling upon her prosperity. She is greatly modifying her laws obnoxious to capital and progress." De Bow's Review, 559.

205. The steady decline of Creole culture in New Orleans in the nineteenth century may be tracked to some degree by the language choice of local newspapers: French predominated in city periodicals from the 1790s to the 1820s, when New Orleans was still a Creole city; from then to the Civil War, it shared a roughly equal number of speakers and readers with English, and most papers were bilingual. After the conflict, when New Orleans was nearly fully Americanized, Creole French declined in relative and absolute numbers over the next half-century. The last derivative of a French newspaper in New Orleans, L'Abeille, folded in 1923. Creole French is all but extinct in New Orleans today, although Cajun French is still often heard in the Acadian parishes of south-central Louisiana. Marino, 313, 320, and John S. Kendall, 364-65.
206. See Ernst von Hesse-Wartegg's description on page 117.
207. New Orleans Magazine's "1999 Reader's Choice: Best and Worst of New Orleans" selected Canal as its "Worst Street," commenting that "Fewer T-shirt shops and athletic-shoe stores, a bit more quality and this street isn't far from its past glory."

The Clay Statue on Canal Street at the Royal Street intersection, described in an 1885 guidebook as the "centre of [the] city." The tower straddling Canal Street guided wires and held high-powered lights over the thoroughfare. This photograph is captioned "New Orleans Feb 1890 Looking down Canal Street." *Photographer unknown, New Orleans Views Collection, UNO Special Collections*

Lower Canal Street viewed from the World Trade Center in 1996. The triangular wedge of land spanning from narrow Common Street (left) to the right edge of this photograph was an undeveloped commons until an Act of Congress in 1807 created Canal Street. The *terre commune* was subdivided in 1810, filling in the gap between the Faubourg Ste. Marie (1788) and the old city, platted in 1722. *Photograph by author*

These blocks of lower Canal host the urban elements that have characterized the "Great Wide Way" for over a century and half. Once a residential boulevard, Canal Street shifted to retail commerce in the 1840s and developed wall-to-wall multistory shops and stores over the decades that followed, many of which still stand structurally. Larger department stores such as Maison Blanche (left) arose in the early 1900s, while streetcars traveled the expansive neutral ground. Starting in the 1960s, the high-end retail sector began to depart Canal Street, while high-rise hotels arose at the river end, addressing the increasing tourist trade. After three decades of decline, Canal Street is partially returning to its glory days, with new streetcar tracks installed in 1997, continued restoration of old buildings, and improvement of its sidewalks and features. But the days of Canal Street as *the* local retail mecca are over; most shops today cater to tourists and lower-income residents. *Photograph by author, 2000*

(Left) Canal Street viewed from the Tremé Street intersection, looking toward the river. The 171-foot-width of Canal Street was designed to accommodate a 50-foot-wide navigation canal down the middle, with 60 feet of undeveloped space paralleling the waterway on each side. The canal, which would have extended Carondelet Canal down Basin Street and onto Canal at the intersection visible at lower center, would have cast a far different history for downtown New Orleans. But it was never built.

(Right) Canal Street viewed from the Tremé Street intersection, looking toward the lake. Few streets change atmosphere like Canal Street at the Claiborne Avenue/Interstate-10 intersection (upper center). Riverside of this intersection, Canal Street is world famous, commercial, urban, bustling, and both gritty and sophisticated. Lakeside, Canal Street is mixed residential and commercial, foliated, suburban in its look and feel, and decidedly local in its population. *Photographs by author, 2000*

of the 1900s, the first new Canal Street streetcar lines returned to a short section of the Great Wide Way, to be expanded up to City Park Avenue in the near future. With its sweeping history from a dusty commons to an elegant residential avenue, from a political boundary between rival municipalities to a bustling shopping district, from a corridor of great row architecture to a raffish Main Street of past splendor, Canal Street will continue to transition but will always remain an integral part of downtown New Orleans—myths and all.

Districts: Sense of Purpose, Sense of Place

Firms often locate adjacent to their competitors to tap the infrastructure, geographical feature, labor pool, services, data, markets, and clients upon which all in the industry depend. Known as *agglomeration* to geographers, the tendency of like industries to cluster is driven by perceived mutual benefit of some or all involved, or a parasitic benefit of one upon another. Agglomeration creates districts, known more broadly as functional areas,[208] and includes such notable modern entities as New York's Financial District, Garment District, Fashion District, and Diamond District. Some districts' prominence makes them metaphors for their industry, as Madison Avenue, Broadway, and Wall Street represent advertising, theater, and finance. Most other districts are of local importance and occur in pedestrian-scale neighborhoods (especially retail and services enterprises), because potential customers prefer to survey as many offerings as possible in a minimum of time and hassle. Walkable cities like Manhattan are loaded with districts; automobile suburbs surrounding most major cities have few. Like a legend to a map, industry districts reveal much about a city, its relationship with the hinterland or service area, and its role in the nation and the world. Districts also reflect historical eras and their economies and policies; they tend to be transient, but when they disperse, they often leave behind place names, palimpsests in the built environment, and a certain ambience in a particular street corner or block that are legible to observers today. That people find exciting the notion of a concentration of enterprises, completely absorbed in their dedication, is evidenced by the liberal use of the term *district* by sundry chambers of commerce and promotional boards, which declare "Entertainment Districts" and "Arts Districts" and "Antiques Districts" in the hope of attracting a critical mass of the appropriate enterprise.[209] Most older districts, however, formed under their own power, and in doing so instilled a palpable sense of purpose and place in their home cities. Such was the case in New Orleans.

208. Hartshorn, 317-19. Functional areas include industrial districts as well as other clusters of a particular land use, such as public housing, academia, hospitals, and "skid rows."

209. One local example is Fat City, Metairie's effort to form an entertainment district for the suburbanites in answer to downtown's Bourbon Street. Located among the five streets west of the Lakeside Shopping Center between Veterans Memorial Boulevard and West Esplanade Avenue in Jefferson Parish, Fat City was the place to be in the 1970s but petered out in the 1980s and 1990s. Many bars and restaurants from the 1970s have since been refurbished as professional offices and retailers—the opposite trend than prevails in downtown New Orleans.

These three row structures are the best-preserved units of the 1850s-era Touro Row, a magnificent ensemble of twelve Greek Revival commercial buildings on Canal between Bourbon and Royal united by a spectacular two-story iron-lace gallery. Touro Row, a project of one of New Orleans' greatest citizens, Judah Touro, symbolized Canal Street in its antebellum glory years. This is the Royal Street end of former Touro Row. *Photograph by author, 1995*

The Bourbon Street end of Touro Row was altered a number of times, by demolition, fire, and reconstruction, starting in the 1880s. Here, the 1960s-era Woolworth's, which closed like numerous other Canal Street department stores, is being demolished for the construction of a major new hotel. Transition from locally oriented businesses to tourist-oriented enterprises is the trend on Canal Street and throughout downtown New Orleans. *Photograph by author, 2000*

Canal Street Scenes, 1995-2000. *Photographs by author*

1-2. Retail shops on Canal Street at the Dauphine and University Place intersections.

3. Once-prominent Royal/St. Charles intersection of Canal Street, where the Clay Statue once stood. Two years after this photograph was taken, streetcar tracks were reinstalled.

4. One of the most beautiful architectural rows on Canal Street, between St. Charles and Carondelet.

5. Ultimate symbol of New Orleans' mid-nineteenth-century prosperity, the U.S. Custom House (1848-81) processed receipts of cotton, sugar, and myriad other products flowing through the port. One of the largest federal projects of its day, it still represents a major federal presence in New Orleans today, maintaining a sense of importance and relevance in lower Canal Street.

6. This battered building at 1411 Canal Street symbolizes the transitions of lower Canal Street over the past century and a half. It was designed in 1858 as an opulent Italianate townhouse for Col. S. N. Moody, indicative of the era when this part of Canal was a prosperous residential boulevard. Moody owned a well-known men's furnishing store in the Granite Building on the corner of Canal and Royal, symbolic of the time when that part of Canal was the premier retail district in the city (a reputation once held by Chartres Street in the French Quarter). Lower Canal Street's residential element departed long ago, and its fame as the city's high-end retail district petered out gradually starting in the 1960s. Today, only the ornate lintels, adrift on an ugly bare wall, recall the lost splendor of the Moody residence and its surrounding Canal Street neighborhood. As part of the New Orleans Saints' 2001 suggestion to build a new football stadium on the site of the nearby Iberville Housing Development, this building would be demolished for a block-long entertainment strip.

Canal Street starts exuberantly at the river and ends quietly at these cemeteries. Between the two termini lies a literal and figurative cross section of New Orleans. *Photograph by author, 2000*

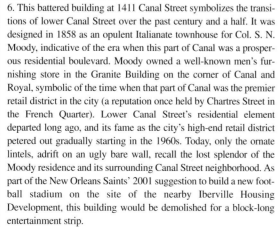

"Concerns Akin Assemble Together": Districts in Historic New Orleans

Industry districts that flourished during the busy antebellum era in New Orleans often traced their origins to the early American years. One example was the "banking district" that formed around the intersection of Royal and Conti streets, comprising the Louisiana Bank (chartered 1804), Planter's Bank (1811), Louisiana State Bank (1818), Bank of Louisiana (1824), and others, most of which, remarkably, structurally still stand.[210] Chartres Street drew early publishers as well as professional offices and retailers in this era, and Gravier Street tended to attract cotton men. But the city was probably too small at this time to see any substantial business agglomeration.

That changed by the end of the antebellum era. The *Picayune* in 1859 noted some industry concentrations and in doing so depicted the street economy of New Orleans at that time: "Carondelet Street was devoted entirely to cotton and shipping; Canal was nearly taken up with the dry goods trade; Chartres was expected to retain the variety trade; St. Charles, with its various places of amusement, could retain only certain classes of offices, besides coffee saloons and cigar stores; Magazine had a near monopoly on the wholesale boot and shoe and a goodly part of the wholesale dry goods trade; from Tchoupitoulas to the levee, Canal to Lafayette, Western produce reigned; Poydras claimed as a specialty bagging and rope."[211] An eventful half-century later, a vignette entitled "Approximate Centers of Districts" on a 1904 streetcar map[212] provided a glimpse of New Orleans' local and regional economy in the midst of the flourishing commercial era between Reconstruction and the Great Depression:

PRINCIPAL SHOPPING DISTRICT. Canal Street, at Bourbon and Dauphine Streets.
GENERAL OFFICE DISTRICT. Carondelet and Common Streets.
SHIPPING DISTRICT. Canal Street, at Canal Street Ferry Landing.
WHOLESALE COTTON DISTRICT. Carondelet and Gravier Streets.
WHOLESALE GROCERY DISTRICT. Poydras and Tchoupitoulas Streets.
WHOLESALE SUGAR AND RICE DISTRICT. North Peters and Customhouse Streets.
NEWSPAPER DISTRICT. Camp Street, between Gravier and Poydras Streets.
HOTEL DISTRICT. St. Charles and Common Streets.
THEATRE DISTRICT. Canal and Baronne Streets and St. Charles Street.

In these districts are represented three major crops of the lower Mississippi at the time—cotton, sugar, and rice—and New Orleans' two long-standing major industries—shipping and "tourism," represented by the hotel district. The remaining districts manifest New Orleans' role as a local and regional hub for business, retail, journalism, and the arts. Another publication by George W. Engelhardt of the same year generally concurred with these district locations, describing Canal Street as the "retail quarter," Tchoupitoulas as the "wholesale grocery district," and Camp Street as the "financial, jobbing, and newspaper street."[213] Indicating the importance of cotton was the identification of the Cotton Exchange, corner of Carondelet and Gravier, as the hub of the "money quarter of the city," comprising banks, insurance offices, and institutions dedicated to the cotton trade. Between this fiscal precinct and the Mississippi River was what Engelhardt called "the wholesale business of the city,"[214] meaning its manufacturing, warehousing, and shipping district, occupying the batture of the upper French Quarter and the Central Business District ("Faubourg St. Mary" gradually fell out of use in this time). Wrote Engelhardt on the districts of New Orleans: "The produce and fruit trade . . . has a street or two of its own ; lumber . . . takes to the basins terminating the [Old Basin and New Basin] Canals ; and in general it is to be said that here, as in the greater cities everywhere, *concerns akin assemble together*. Thus the grocery and provision lines, the import coffee trade, the iron works, the printing and publishing houses, the horse and mule markets have each their own special locality somewhere in or about this particular quarter of trade."[215]

Politely excluded from these descriptions is Storyville, probably the most famous of historic New Orleans' "industry" districts, an eighteen-block ghetto lakeside of the French Quarter excluded from a citywide ban on prostitution by Alderman Sidney Story in 1897. By default, the first legal red-light district in the hemisphere was formed. In peak years spanning the following two decades, every structure except the St. James Methodist Church occupying the crowded blocks bounded by Basin, St. Louis, Robertson, and Iberville/Canal was dedicated to some aspect of the sex industry, from filthy cribs to lively saloons to gaudy mansions. Geographically, Storyville represented a legally forced concentration of a number of de facto red-light districts, such as the ones that had existed much earlier on Gallatin Street (now site of the French Market flea market), at "the Swamp" on Girod Street, and in houses of ill repute throughout the city. Because of the 1897 law and the high demand for these services, the "Tenderloin District" represented one of the densest concentrations of a particular enterprise in a single place that the city has ever seen—a true district. Additionally, an "Uptown District" of Storyville for black clients, operating without legal recognition but informally tolerated by the authorities, existed concurrently between Gravier and Perdido from South Franklin to Locust Street. Storyville declined in the mid-1910s and was finally closed by the Navy Department in 1917. Most of its structures were demolished around 1940 to make room for the Iberville Housing Development (1941); only about three old "District" buildings survive today.

In the 1870s-1900s, what might be called the "exchange movement" influenced a number of local wholesalers in town, often furthering the geographical concentration of certain industries into districts. Serving as central meeting places where information was shared and deals were made, exchanges represented the maturation and complication of business that came with new technology and expanding markets. Naturally, exchanges were generally sited in the heart of their respective industry's district, becoming a sort of "capitol building" for that business community. Cotton firms formed a centralized Cotton Exchange on Gravier in 1871; produce merchants followed with their Produce Exchange on Magazine in 1880, which evolved into the Board of Trade at the same location. Sugar merchants formed the Louisiana Sugar Exchange in 1883 on the French Quarter batture and expanded to include rice in 1889. A Stock Exchange formed among the brokers of Gravier Street in 1906 (replacing an earlier one at 29 Carondelet), making that area New Orleans' answer to Wall Street.[216] There was also a Mechanics, Dealers and Lumbermen's Exchange; a Mexican and South American Exchange; an Auctioneers' Exchange; a Fruit Exchange; and exchanges for the maritime, freight, and transportation industries, chambers of commerce, underwriters, and others.[217] These exchanges both reflected and reinforced the geographical concentration of competing firms, though none was stronger than the macroeconomic forces that ultimately determined the health of their industry.

Thirty-odd years later, at a time when district formation began to diminish, Works Progress Administration writers observed some old and some new concentrations:

Most of the fur dealers are still to be found along North Peters and Decatur Sts. Royal St. has become one of antique shops. . . . Coffee roasters and packers are to be found, for the most part, along Magazine and Tchoupitoulas Streets from Canal to Howard Ave. Farther uptown, Poydras St. from Camp to the river is the wholesale fruit, produce, and poultry center, while the principal meat packers are found near Magazine and Julia Sts. The section between Camp St. and the river, and Canal St. and Jackson Ave., contains most of the wholesale jobbing houses and many of the manufacturing plants. Carondelet St. has always been the street of the cotton brokers and bankers.[218]

A detailed look at three industry districts in New Orleans—the Cotton District, the Sugar District, and Newspaper Row—provides insight into the rise and fall of these economic and geographical phenomena, and the clues they've left behind in the streets of New Orleans.

The Cotton District

New Orleans exists chiefly by reason of the cotton trade it controls. Without this trade the city would actually have no industries to support its population, no reasons for such a population to live here, and, by consequence, no reason for the existence here of a town very much larger than Galveston or Mobile. Take away this cotton trade and you take away that which has created and now maintains this city.

—*New Orleans Times*, August 28, 1881

210. Cates, 4-9.
211. As quoted by Friends of the Cabildo, vol. 2, 72-73.
212. *Map of New Orleans Showing Street Railway System of the N.O. Railways Co.,* as reproduced by Chase et al.
213. Engelhardt, 11-12.
214. Ibid., 20-21.
215. Ibid., 21-21 (emphasis added).

216. *Soards' New Orleans City Directory* (1887), 1047, and Friends of the Cabildo, vol. 2, 74-75.
217. The Louisiana Sugar and Rice Exchange, 205, and Elstner, 28.
218. Federal Writers' Project, 287.

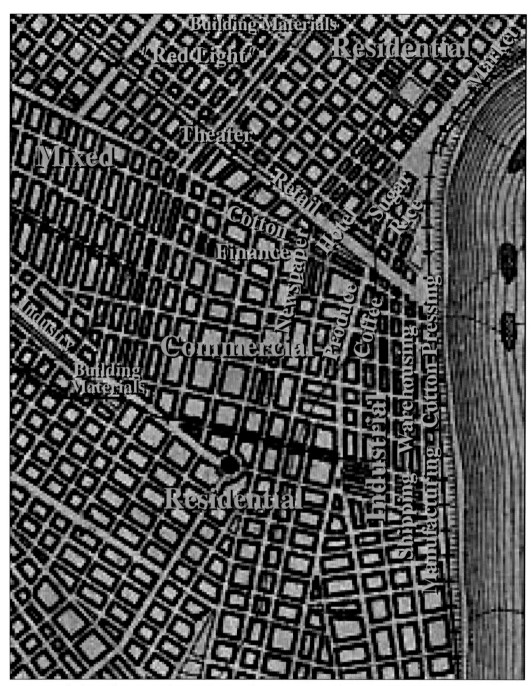

Industry districts (yellow type) and general land uses (blue type) in turn-of-the-century New Orleans. *Map by author*

Of all the commodities that passed through New Orleans from the early nineteenth to the early twentieth century, it was cotton that bestowed upon the city its greatest wealth and prestige.[219] New Orleans excelled at the cotton trade for classically geographical reasons: much of its regional hinterlands possessed ideal conditions for the cultivation of the crop; the Mississippi River provided convenient transportation for the bulky bales; and shipping access to the Gulf of Mexico made the valuable fiber deliverable to the markets of the Northeast and Europe. "New Orleans' extraordinarily favorable location on the first solid ground above the mouth of the Mississippi River conferred on its merchants a virtual monopoly of seaborne commerce for all regions that depended on the [river] and its tributaries for transportation."[220]

Southern capital was concentrated not in the manorial cotton plantations of storybook and cinema but in the urban cotton-factorage centers that financed them,[221] the biggest and best of which was New Orleans. For much of the nineteenth century, New Orleans would serve as a corner of the "Cotton Triangle," in which Northern-owned ships would ferry cotton from New Orleans to European ports like Liverpool and return to New York with cargo or immigrants, then proceed back down to New Orleans with Northern goods or ballast.[222] But it took the better part of a century for the treasured lint to rise above the traditional colonial-era crops of wheat, corn, tobacco, indigo, and rice to form the bulk of gross receipts at New Orleans.

The promise of cotton was recognized from the earliest days of New Orleans—reports to French officials in Paris in the 1720s often mentioned the beauty of Louisiana cotton—but the inability to "purge it of its seed" rendered the fiber a minor crop for decades. In 1731, only about 1.3 percent (two arpents) of the cultivated land eight leagues above and below New Orleans was devoted to cotton; indigo, by contrast, grew on 27 percent of the land.[223] The French government and colonials sought to invent an adequate "cotton engine" to separate seed from lint, and while a number of working prototypes emerged in French Louisiana, the goal of an efficient cotton gin was never reached. Speculated one modern historian, "What would have been the course of events had the French developed a successful gin and thus made cotton a profitable commodity?"[224] Perhaps, he continued, France would had resisted ceding the colony to the Spanish after its defeat in the French and Indian War, resolving instead to maintain the possession for its sudden economic fulfillment. But without the gin, cotton in Louisiana and elsewhere was, for most of the 1700s, too labor intensive, at the planting, harvesting, cleaning, transporting, and manufacturing stages, for large-scale production.

Then, at the close of the eighteenth century, a sequence of events conspired to change forever Southern agriculture, Southern society, and New Orleans. First, on the demand side, the invention and improvement of the steam engine throughout the 1700s, followed by the introduction of mechanical spinning (1760-80s), the power loom (1787), and the steam-operated loom (1790s), drastically reduced the cost of cotton garments and increased their demand in the urban centers of the North and Europe.[225] To process the cotton, the first U.S. cotton factory was built in Rhode Island in 1790, followed by others in the region, complete with power looms and other new technologies.[226] On the supply side, the introduction of Sea Island cotton and upland varieties around 1789 expanded the geographical range and quality of the commodity, unleashing the agricultural utility of the hill country. Four years later, the laborious task of separating lint from seed and trash was famously solved by Eli Whitney's cotton engine, or gin, enabling a worker to clean a thousand pounds of cotton a day, ten times more than by hand. Also on the supply side, the trickle of settlers from the Atlantic seaboard emigrating to the lower Mississippi Valley in the late 1700s grew to a steady stream after the Louisiana Purchase and expanded further after the War of 1812; many of these emigrants would settle within the Baton Rouge-Vicksburg-Jackson triangle and make it the powerhouse of Southern cotton production by the eve of the Civil War, all the while shipping their bales through New Orleans. The first Mississippi steamboat in 1812 commenced a new era in river transportation, a critical link in the chain of entities needed to make the commodity economically viable.

219. Born, 3473, and Engelhardt, 118.
220. Moore, 178.
221. Stone, 563-64.
222. Cohn, 84.
223. Daniel H. Thomas, 135-39.
224. Ibid., 148.
225. Clark, *New Orleans, 1718-1812,* 203, and Robson, 111.
226. De Bow's Review, 221-22.

New Orleans Cotton Exchange, corner of Carondelet and Gravier, once the epicenter of the cotton marketing business in New Orleans. *Photograph by author, 2000*

Slavery augmented accordingly to "solve" the cotton labor problem—in fact, the cotton boom breathed new life into the institution and would entrench it for decades[227]—while the new American government in Louisiana created a business-friendly atmosphere in comparison to the restrictive port policies of the colonial regimes. The antebellum "Golden Age" had begun.

Tens of Millions of Pounds of Cotton Funneled through a Single City
Within a few years, cotton rose from a minor crop in the regions surrounding New Orleans and Natchez to a major crop throughout the Mississippi Valley and its surrounding states and territories.[228] The 2 million pounds of cotton raised in Louisiana in 1811 quintupled in ten years, then almost quadrupled to 38 million pounds in 1826, and rose to 62 million by 1834. Mississippi production, the vast majority of which was grown in the southwestern quadrant of the state and shipped to New Orleans, rose from 10 million pounds in 1821 to 85 million pounds in 1834. The number, acreage, and productivity of plantations increased steadily in the region during the opening decades of the nineteenth century, when, before the development of competing canals and railroads, planters relied entirely on the Mississippi River to get their crop to market. Production from Louisiana and Mississippi (1835) accounted for about two-thirds of New Orleans' imported cotton, but substantial amounts also came from northern Alabama, Tennessee, Arkansas, and even from the exterior regions of Mobile, Florida, and Texas.[229] To New Orleans it went, at first on flatboats and later on steamboats, in such quantities that New Orleans in the early 1800s began to develop a cotton marketing and services industry. At first, interior planters would generally sell their crop to local merchants in cities like Nashville

or Lexington, who would then vend it to merchants in New Orleans, who in turn would transfer it North or overseas. Then:

> Local merchants were often bypassed as planters found it increasingly advantageous to sell their crop in New Orleans [where they would] deal with a merchant-agent in the Crescent City. During a visit to New Orleans in 1806, Thomas Ashe found that the most important men in commerce there were the 'commission merchants to whom the settlers of the upper and adjacent countries consign their produce.' . . . From these varied beginnings, the cotton factorage system gradually developed.[230]

Other historians view the War of 1812 as a watershed event in Southern cotton: prior to that conflict, New Orleans' cotton business was characterized by direct sales and purchases by planters and manufacturers, with a small community of independent merchants and agents. After the war, direct sales from planters faded while the professional cotton community grew and specialized, concentrating on both the selling side, by operating as factors for interior planters, and on the buying side, as agents for Northern and European buyers.[231] Purchases of agricultural produce now occurred on the wharves of New Orleans by mercantilists buying for Northern or European firms, rather than in the field by representatives of city merchants.

Cotton was quickly becoming king, but cotton marketing in New Orleans was risky, speculative, "deceptively easy"[232] to try one's hand at, and fiercely competitive. Success was by no means guaranteed: in decades to come, no firm would control more than 15 percent of the trade nationwide, and few firms made significant long-term profits.[233] Nevertheless, vast sums of money were at stake, and the lure of fortune created a "mercantile class" in New Orleans, described by one cotton buyer as comprising (in 1806) a handful of French and European establishments plus "eight or ten commission-houses, lately opened by young American merchants from New York, Philadelphia, and Baltimore."[234] Businesses like these, taking risks in this strange new American city to exploit the promise of cotton, set up shop throughout the commercial district, from the upper French Quarter to the lower streets of St. Mary and down to the river, and eventually formed a concentration around the Carondelet/Gravier Street intersection—future heart of New Orleans' Cotton District.

A District Gradually Develops
Because early city directories, from 1805 to the 1850s, did not categorize entries by profession and did not consistently distinguish among merchants of various industries, it is difficult to ascertain exactly when the Cotton District coalesced around its eventual site. A tabulation of the thousands of New Orleanians in the 1822 city directory seems to indicate that the cluster had not yet formed by that year. This source contains 357 entries described as *merchants, commission merchants, brokers, exchange brokers,* or *commercial agents* but does not identify those who dealt specifically in cotton, if in fact such a specialization occurred. In any case, 46 of the 357, or 13 percent, had addresses on Carondelet or Gravier. In addition, there were 7 entries that were specifically identified as *cotton brokers,*[235] of which all 7 operated out of offices on Magazine Street, about two blocks away from the locale that would later be the center of the Cotton District. One cotton broker, Samuel Elkins, worked at the corner of Magazine and Gravier, and another, Thomas Saul, had an alternate address at Carondelet and Common: these were the only two confirmed cotton brokers near Carondelet or Gravier in 1822.[236] Likewise, if the commission merchants advertising in an 1842 issue of the *New-Orleans Price-Current* are any indication, the cluster had still not formed by this date. Of the 50 ads that included addresses, only 4 announced Gravier Street-based merchants, while 11 were from Camp Street firms, 8 were located on Magazine, and 7 were on Poydras—though it should be noted that this is not a representative sample of the

227. Gavin Wright, 13.

228. Those plantations closest to New Orleans, along the river to Baton Rouge and westward into the Acadian parishes, were generally dedicated to sugarcane; cotton predominated north of Baton Rouge and throughout western Mississippi. But, like any port city, New Orleans profited to various degrees from its entire hinterland, not just its neighbors. Bruchey, 110-11, and Hilliard, 67-71.

229. De Bow's Review, 123; *New-Orleans Price-Current and Commercial Intelligencer;* and De Bow, 434.

230. Woodman, 12. Stone (557) traces the origins of the factorage system, in which factors served as home agents and general facilitators to colonial planters, to England's colonies in the West Indies.

231. Killick, 175-76.

232. Ibid., 171.

233. Ibid.

234. Nolte, 86.

235. The term *cotton factor* does not appear in the 1822 directory, perhaps because this occupation went by a different name at this time, such as *commission merchant* or *commercial agent.*

236. Paxton (1822), *List of Names* section (unpaged). Counting all professions that could include cotton specialists, this directory listed 265 merchants, 66 commission merchants, 24 brokers or exchange brokers, and 2 commercial agents, of whom some were undoubtedly cotton men. Additionally, there were 7 cotton brokers and 8 cotton press warehouses.

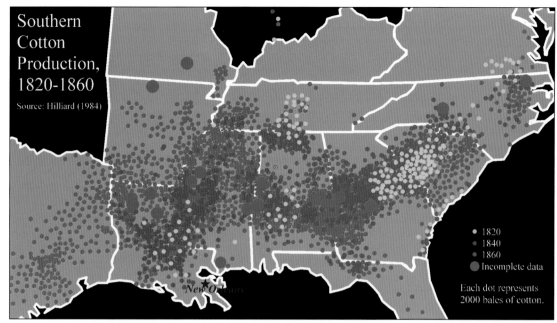

Southern
Cotton
Production,
1820-1860
Source: Hilliard (1984)

- 1820
- 1840
- 1860
- Incomplete data

Each dot represents
2000 bales of cotton.

New Orleans

Southern cotton production, 1820-60. Note the consistent and growing concentration of production in the Mississippi Valley during the forty-year period. Most of this cotton was shipped through New Orleans. *Map by author based on data in Hilliard*

city's merchants and even less so *cotton* merchants. Still, these commission merchants were clearly clustered in the streets of St. Mary, where 90 percent operated; only 2 or so worked in the old city and an equally small number worked in the uptown faubourgs.[237] These numbers were generally substantiated in other issues of the *New-Orleans Price-Current*.[238]

A Critical Mass by Midcentury

But an inspection of the *Cohen's City Directory for 1854*,[239] one of the first to categorize professions, reveals a very different picture. Of the 147 cotton receiving houses listed that year, 46 had addresses on Carondelet, and another 24 operated on Gravier Street, far more than any other street. The most common building addresses of these cotton offices were in the 40s and 50s for Carondelet Street and the 80s and 90s for Gravier Street, based on the old numbering system. The nearby streets of Common, Camp, St. Charles, and Union accounted for another 42 of the city's cotton houses. There were a few outlying locations—2 as far upriver as Poydras Street, 3 near the levee, and 9 downriver in the French Quarter—but in all about 90 percent of the operations were situated within the sixteen-block heart of St. Mary, with about half on Carondelet or Gravier. These data show that a de facto Cotton District was operating in the vicinity of the Carondelet/Gravier intersection by 1854 (and probably years earlier), a time when cotton accounted for three-quarters of New Orleans' total trade. Seven years later, 174 of the city's 465 commission merchants and cotton factors—3 out of every 8—worked in Carondelet or Gravier Street offices.[240] The draw of the district was so strong that even cotton gin offices were located in the vicinity; there were three such operations on lower St. Charles and another on nearby Union Street, though bulkier operations such as cotton pickeries, seed-oil factories, presses, and warehouses were generally located along the river from Faubourg St. Mary to the faubourgs comprising today's Lower Garden District. (A pickery is an operation that rebales loose cotton samples, spilled bolls, and damaged cotton into a low-grade but marketable product.) Gravier Street also held the offices of 7 slave dealers; another 7 were located on nearby Baronne.[241]

The reception, storage, care, sale, and exportation of over a million bales of cotton a year required, by one generous estimate, the effort of almost two-thirds the population of the city and an even greater percentage of its workforce.[242] With planters and their thousands of field hands on the supply side, and the Northern and European manufacturers and their millions of customers on the demand side, New Orleans and its competing cotton ports were vast enclaves of busy middlemen, engaged in the efficient delivery of lint from supplier to demander. At the top of this labor pyramid were the cotton commission merchants, brokers, buyers, and factors—King Cotton's "retainers," in the words of historian Harold D. Woodman.[243] Together, these professionals served as agents for principals who sought to sell or buy cotton, deciding whether a client's cotton should be sold to another merchant in the city, stored in a warehouse in anticipation of a better price, or shipped overseas to a buyer client. As these decisions were executed, the merchants were responsible for the classing of lint quality, keeping of records, and tracking of bales. Their clients on the demand side comprised manufacturers in the North or Europe; clients on the supply side included rural planters or other merchants representing other planters. Those merchants with cotton-producing clients, whose principals operated plantations or small farms, were known as cotton factors. Factors accepted cotton on consignment from planters and sold it at the highest prices obtainable, supplied planters with materials for cotton cultivation, advanced them credit when necessary and maintained an account for them (akin to a bank), and generally represented their interests in the marketplace. The enigmatic factors probably had the closest business and personal relationships with planters, and often served their clients for long terms and in capacities far beyond the business of cotton.[244] Cotton brokers, buyers, and factors specialized in various aspects of the industry and were usually listed separately in city directories, but all generally fell under the category of commission merchants.[245] These were the professionals who clustered in the streets of St. Mary around the Carondelet/Gravier intersection, undoubtedly to profit from each other and from the flow of information among them.[246] The ambience inside these cotton houses was later immortalized by Edgar Degas in his masterpiece, *A Cotton Office in New Orleans* (1873), depicting his uncle's factorage business, Musson, Prestidge, & Co.[247]

The Factorage System in the Colonial West Indies:
"The factor was the home agent of the colonial planter. He was at once his merchant and banker. He bought the goods which the planter had to purchase at home, and sold for him the products returned in exchange. He became an important link in the chain which brought Europe, Africa, and America into commercial association. If an Englishman wished to embark his son in the business of sugar planting in Jamaica or Barbadoes [*sic*], he could negotiate the entire transaction with a factor in Bristol or London. . . . He was to the individual planter what the chartered companies had been to the whole body of colonists, or to the colony itself."

And, later, in the American South:
"The importance of the Southern factorage system developed with the growth of the cotton industry. . . . The functions of the Southern factor were the same as those of his English progenitor. But the Southern system had one feature [that was] not possible with the West Indian oversea system. The relations between the cotton factor and planter were of the most intimate and confidential character, as close probably as was ever the case between business associates. The ties between them frequently were life-long, and their relations were of a social and personal as well as business nature."

—Alfred Holt Stone, 1915 (557-59)

Another specialized profession was that of the *cotton classer*, who graded the lint by color, cleanliness, and fiber length and gave it a rating that would influence its price and sellability. These men, too, worked in the Cotton District. At the opposite end of the local labor pyramid were the *roustabouts*, who worked aboard steamships loaded with cotton but whose responsibilities ended when the ship docked. *Cotton screwmen* took over at that point, unloading incoming bales to the *longshoremen* on the levee, who handled and organized the

---

237. *New-Orleans Price-Current Commercial Intelligencer*, June 22. Only those ads with addresses were counted.
238. A tabulation of the 54 commission-merchant advertisements appearing in an August 1842 issue (chosen at random) showed 11 with addresses on Camp Street, 9 on Poydras, 8 each on Magazine and Tchoupitoulas, and 5 on Gravier, with the vast majority located in Faubourg St. Mary.
239. *Cohen's City Directory*, 269-70.
240. Gardner, *Gardner's New Orleans Directory for 1861*, 472-76. Not all the commission merchants listed in this source dealt exclusively with cotton.
241. Ibid., 476, 489.

242. Zacharie, *New Orleans Guide* (1893), 81.
243. Woodman.
244. Stone, 557-65, and Sitterson, "Financing and Marketing," 190-93.
245. Terminology varied by source, time, and place. Wrote historian Harold D. Woodman (13), "Anyone buying and selling for a commission, regardless of who employed him and the article handled, was considered a commission merchant. The term 'factor,' however, was reserved for those commission merchants who were the agents of the planters growing the Southern staple crops. The distinction was not a legal one [but one] of custom and usage."
246. Zacharie, *New Orleans Guide* (1893), 81-84, and Moore, 232-35.
247. Christina Vella, "The Country for Men with Nerve," in Feigenbaum, 41.

shipments and passed them on to *draymen,* who hauled them to the cotton presses. There, *cotton rollers* got the bales to the *scalemen,* who loaded them onto scales for the *cotton weighers* to verify the weight and sometimes pull samples for the cotton classer. In other cases, a *cotton sampler* performed this task, after which the weigher would reweigh the bales.[248] While all this transpired along the river, the commission merchants on Carondelet and Gravier made their deals and decided the fate of the bales entrusted to them: sell, store, or ship; at what price, to whom, where, when, and how. When the deal was consummated, *cotton pressers* compressed the bales down to anywhere from three-quarters to one-third their original size. Then the process was reversed: the draymen hauled the compressed bales to the longshoremen, who in turn passed them to the screwmen, who then performed the more specialized task of "screwing" the bales into place on the ship (using jackscrews) so as to maximize limited space.[249] The roustabouts would then see the bales delivered to the marketplace. Each level of this labor pyramid, like any industry, had its support echelons: the professionals dealt with insurers, bankers, and lawyers specializing in cotton, who thus also set up shop in the Cotton District; the presses needed machinists and engineers; the dock workers needed tools and equipment. Ancillary parties such as cotton-seed-oil manufacturers, ginneries, pickeries, makers of screws, ties, and presses, and myriad other products and services also gathered around the district. In this manner the cotton industry fueled the New Orleans economy, enriching some professionals to a degree that is still evident today, in the palatial mansions of the Garden District and St. Charles Avenue, to which the more successful merchants retired after a long day in the Cotton District.

Why did the Cotton District form around the Carondelet/Gravier intersection? A paucity of hard data from the formative years makes this question difficult to answer. It is likely that the centrality of the location, the desire to associate with other professionals, the prevalence of Americans in the cotton industry, and a desire to be neither too close to the river, nor the crowded old city, nor the swamp, nor the rural uptown faubourgs destined the Cotton District to be situated in the heart of St. Mary. Perhaps the high number of cotton houses on Gravier originated from the fact that this street, from Tchoupitoulas to Magazine, was one of the first to be paved (with pebble stone) in the area, probably around 1807.[250] Since Common and Canal streets hardly existed at this time, Gravier then would have been the first Faubourg St. Mary street to provide paved access between the interior blocks of the neighborhood and the riverside cotton presses and warehouses of Rillieux, Debuys and Longer, Palfrey, Beckmann, Millaudon, Freret, and others, an area that would soon become the "Cotton Press quarter of the city."[251] The Cotton District's perpendicular spread into Carondelet Street may have occurred on account of an early cotton press located on Carondelet between Union and Perdido, when this was practically the outskirts of the urbanized area.[252] Additionally, chance real-estate opportunities, around which a critical mass of competing firms would eventually develop, may partially explain why and where the Cotton District formed.

Heart of the Cotton District: The New Orleans Cotton Exchange

As America industrialized and its factories competed with European textile manufacturers, more opportunities and thus more complexity entered the world of the cotton merchant. Add to this the development of Northern canals and railroads[253]—the manmade enemies of New Orleans' natural geographical advantage—and the upheaval of the Civil War to form a very different industry outlook by 1870. With no central place to conduct this increasingly intricate business, "most of the cotton business was conducted in the open air, up and down Carondelet Street" or "in saloons, which called themselves 'exchanges.'"[254] Need arose in New Orleans' cotton community for a central exchange for marketing, price determination, and the gathering and analysis of agricultural economic data. A Merchant's Exchange attempted to satisfy this need in 1867, but, in trying to accommodate all commercial interests instead of mastering one, it petered out quickly. Then, in February 1871, a group of about one hundred cotton men and a few bankers organized the New Orleans Cotton Exchange, chartered for the following purposes:

1. Provide and maintain suitable rooms.
2. Adjudge controversies between members.
3. Establish just and equitable principles, uniform usages, rules and regulations, and standards for classifications to govern all transactions connected with the cotton trade.
4. Acquire, preserve, and disseminate information.
5. Decrease risks incident to the cotton trade.
6. Generally to promote the interests of the trade and to increase the facilities and amount of the cotton and other businesses in New Orleans.

Under the astute leadership of Col. Henry G. Hester, the "Father of Cotton Statistics," the New Orleans Cotton Exchange modernized and streamlined the role of the city in the cotton marketplace. One of Hester's early contributions in his incredible sixty-three-year career with the Exchange was the creation of a telegraphic news service and other information services, reducing the wide fluctuations in price and the guesswork in marketing. He also introduced futures trading, which dramatically increased business volume, and campaigned to improve cotton quality and promote modern production techniques.[255] The Exchange accommodated a new era in the cotton industry, one of speedier transactions, better information, and fiercer competition, sometimes to the lament of older merchants from the antebellum era.[256] "During its formative years from 1871 to 1880 the Exchange . . . enabled New Orleans to regain its position as the principal spot market of the world and to become a leading futures market, outranked only by Liverpool and New York."[257]

While the Exchange brought together the world of Mississippi Valley cotton, it also consummated the identity of Carondelet/Gravier as *the* heart of New Orleans' Cotton District. At first operating out of rented rooms, the Exchange contracted for a three-story building erected "on the corner of Gravier Street and Theater Alley"—a narrow passage also known as Varieties Alley or Varieties Place, about one hundred feet off Carondelet.[258] Across Gravier Street from the Exchange was a row of three-story structures, "one of the finest in our city," housing "the offices of some of our most worthy and influential Cotton Factors," including the firms of John Phelps & Co. and Welshans & Woods.[259]

The organization quickly outgrew the Theater Alley building and finally came into its own in 1883, when the magnificent four-story Cotton Exchange Building was completed and opened on the lakeside/downtown corner of Carondelet and Gravier. Behind the highly florid façade of the $380,000 structure, variously described as Second Empire, Renaissance, and Italian, was a spacious Exchange Room with Corinthian columns, gold ceiling medallions, fresco murals, sculptures, and a fountain around which cotton futures were sold, topped with numerous well-appointed offices and meeting rooms on four floors serviced by an elevator.[260] For almost four decades, this building functioned as the "capitol" of New Orleans' Cotton District, just as New Orleans served as the "capital" of Mississippi Valley cotton production. "Carondelet and Gravier streets are considered the centre of the cotton business, and in this neighborhood are clustered all the large houses dealing in cotton," one guide writer stated succinctly (1893) in the opening line of his chapter on the local cotton trade.[261] Attesting to this clustering are the 283 Cotton Exchange members listed with their business addresses in the organization's 1894 charter.[262] Ninety-five percent of these members worked in St. Mary, 1 percent

248. Zacharie, *New Orleans Guide* (1893), 81-84; Arnesen, 38-40; and New Orleans Press, 271-74.
249. Arnesen, 39.
250. Paxton (1823), 118-19.
251. Zacharie, *New Orleans Guide* (1893), 84.
252. Waldo, *Illustrated Visitors' Guide,* 149.
253. Arnesen, 37-38. See also Clark's article on competing transportation systems in nineteenth-century America, "New Orleans and the River."
254. Boyle, 69.

255. Born, 3478-79.
256. Woodman 267.
257. Ellis, 322.
258. Boyle, 78, and *Sanborn Fire Insurance Map* (1885), block 227.
259. Waldo, *Illustrated Visitors' Guide,* 149.
260. Zacharie, *New Orleans Guide* (1893), 83, and New Orleans Press, 280.
261. Zacharie, *New Orleans Guide* (1893), 81.
262. New Orleans Cotton Exchange, 81-87.

worked in the French Quarter or uptown, and the remainder had out-of-town addresses. Of the 270 based in St. Mary, fully 99 percent of them worked within two streets of the Cotton Exchange. Categorized by street,

- 40 percent were on Gravier;
- 19 percent were on Union;
- 17 percent were on Carondelet, including the Cotton Exchange Building itself;
- 9 percent were on Common;
- 7 percent were on Baronne;
- 6 percent were on Perdido;
- and 3 percent were on other St. Mary streets and alleys. (Percentages are rounded.)

So prevalent was the cotton trade in this district that even the lint itself abounded: in 1885, about 37 percent of the buildings in the blocks bounded by Carondelet, Common, Baronne, and Perdido contained enough lint samples—a fire hazard—to have been labeled "COTTON SAMPLES" on the *Sanborn Fire Insurance Map*.[263] Some blocks, like Factors' Row on Perdido (site of Degas's *A Cotton Office in New Orleans*), consisted exclusively of such buildings, which housed offices of merchants, brokers, and factors. Edward King captured the ambience of a typical day in the Cotton District in his 1875 book, *The Great South:*

This detail of Currier & Ives' *The City of New Orleans* (1885) shows the New Orleans Cotton Exchange (center) two years after it was built. The adjacent streets were home to scores of cotton offices. Nearby are the columned St. Charles Hotel and the domed Church of the Immaculate Conception. *American Memory Panoramic Maps Collection, Library of Congress*

The New Orleans Cotton Exchange, established in 1871 and briefly housed in rented offices, had its first home constructed on Gravier and Theater (Varieties) Alley, a half-block down Gravier Street at extreme left. The elaborate second home of the New Orleans Cotton Exchange, seen here, was built on the corner of Carondelet and Gravier in 1883, when the organization outgrew the small structure on Theater Alley. This building was torn down in 1920-21 and replaced by a third, simpler edifice, which still stands today. A cluster of cotton factors, merchants, brokers, and other professionals dedicated to the crop operated out of offices in this vicinity—Carondelet and Gravier, the Cotton District—at least since the early 1850s, probably earlier. *Craig, "Cotton Exchange"*

Occupants of buildings on this block, bounded by Carondelet, Gravier, Baronne, and Common, show the predominance of the cotton industry here in the mid-1890s. *Map by author based on data in Sanborn Fire Insurance Map (1896)*

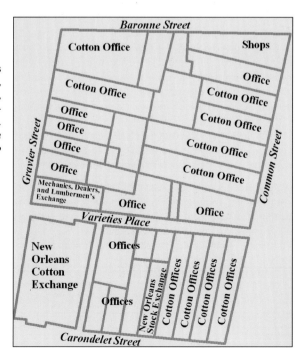

263. Sanborn Fire Insurance Map (1885), blocks 227-229.

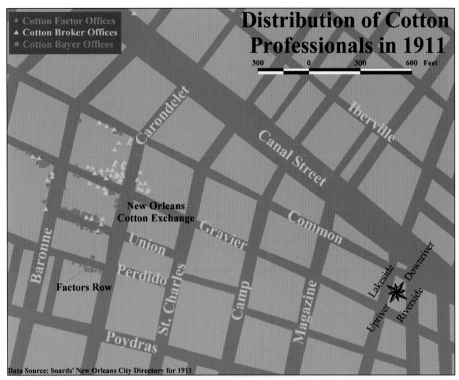

Distribution of Cotton Professionals in 1911

- ● Cotton Factor Offices
- ▲ Cotton Broker Offices
- ■ Cotton Buyer Offices

300　0　300　600 Feet

Carondelet

Iberville

Canal Street

New Orleans
Cotton Exchange

Gravier

Common

Union

Baronne

Perdido

Factors Row

St. Charles

Camp

Magazine

Lakeside

Downriver

Upriver

Riverside

Poydras

Data Source: Soards' New Orleans City Directory for 1911

Distribution of cotton factor, broker, and buyer offices in New Orleans in 1910-11, based on the city directory of 1911. Note the clustering of brokers around the Carondelet/Gravier intersection, the preference of buyers for Union Street, and the concentration of factors in the aptly named Factors' Row on Perdido Street. Also note the degree to which cotton professionals preferred the Central Business District for their offices; the French Quarter was largely a slum by this time. The laborers' end of the business was located on the wharves, in presses, and in warehouses lining the downtown riverfront. *Map and analysis by author. Points may be within one to two doors of actual locations; multiple offices on upper floors of same building are represented by adjacent points.*

In the American quarter, during certain hours of the day, cotton is the only subject spoken of; the pavements of all the principal avenues in the vicinity of the Exchange are crowded with smartly-dressed gentlemen, who eagerly discuss crops and values, and who have a perfect mania for . . . the favorite staple; with young Englishmen, whose mouths are filled with the slang of the Liverpool market; and the skippers of steamers from all parts of the West and South-west, each worshipping at the shrine of the same god.

From high noon until dark the planter, the factor, the speculator, flit feverishly to and from the portals of the Exchange, and nothing can be heard above the excited hum of their conversation except the sharp voice of the clerk reading the latest telegrams.[264]

From this commercial hearth, the business of cotton dominated city life, monopolized newspaper space, permeated conversations, and forged relationships. Degas, as visitor and observer to the city in the early 1870s, "had come to realize that people in New Orleans talked of nothing else, [repeatedly expressing] his exasperation with 'this climate of cotton' where everyone lived 'for cotton and by cotton.'"[265] Then he too succumbed, finding a fascination in the topic that led to the painting of his masterpiece.

The Dethroning of Cotton and Dispersion of Its "Retainers"

While the number of businesses engaged in the cotton trade in New Orleans gradually declined by a rate of about three or four per year from the 1880s to the 1920s,[266] gross receipts continued to rank the crop near the top of the city's moneymakers, and the city at or near the top of the nation's cotton markets. World War I

264. Edward King, 50-51.
265. Christina Vella, "The Country for Men with Nerve," in Feigenbaum, 41.

brought with it rocky times for American cotton: suddenly, major European markets were closed off and for a while in 1914, market quotations ceased and some exchanges temporarily closed. But the war also pumped up domestic demand for cotton and rejuvenated America's use of the Mississippi River for transportation. The South produced its first $1 billion crop during these years, then doubled it in 1919.[267]

The New Orleans Cotton Exchange, counting on a rosy future, tore down its 1883 building due to structural concerns and replaced it in 1921 with a modern seven-story structure with a corner entrance at Carondelet and Gravier. Unfortunately, the life of the new building would instead coincide with a bleak era in American cotton, one that would eventually lead to the demise of the Exchange, the Cotton District, and New Orleans' historic role in the cotton trade. That the new building included offices specifically for government representatives, along with space for brokers and bankers, testified to changes already taking place in American cotton in this era: the federal government became increasingly involved in the control and stabilization of the nation's cotton trade, using methods developed by the New Orleans Cotton Exchange that nonetheless had the effect of rendering the Exchange redundant.[268]

The Cotton Futures Act, which went into effect in 1915, leveled a penal tax against the cotton exchanges in New York and New Orleans if they traded on the cotton futures market without conforming to new government regulations.[269] What was once a wide-open market of myriad players and wild price fluctuations, countered by the regulations and "hedging" (protection from fluctuations) offered by the Exchange, was now becoming a mature business overseen by laws and government regulators. Additionally, starting in 1913, the Federal Reserve was established in Dallas, a city with better rail connections to Southern and new Western cotton lands and stronger ties to Northern banking institutions, making it more central and New Orleans more peripheral to the cotton industry.[270]

Then, in 1920-21, the cotton market crashed. Demand dropped, and competition from Brazil and Egypt increased. The Great Depression further sapped demand, and the movement of cotton cultivation to dry Western lands denied those yields to the Mississippi Valley. New Deal agricultural programs further negated the roles of the Exchange as enforcer of regulations and overseer of transactions. Market information, once a scarce resource obtained by specialists, became widespread and obviated the dependence of producers upon port-city agents for sales. Transportation options, formerly limited to the Mississippi, now included rails, roads, canals, and other rivers. More radical change lay ahead: mechanization and diversification on the farm drastically decreased the rural South's dependence on agriculture in general and cotton in particular, sending many field hands to the North or to urban centers in the South in search of a new life.[271] Cotton acreage in Louisiana declined steadily from almost 2 million acres in 1930 to a few hundred thousand in later decades.[272]

In New Orleans, the total number of cotton-related businesses, from marketers to pressers to manufacturers, declined by 70 percent in twenty-five years, from 152 in 1921 to only 47 in 1945-46. Cotton factors, the quintessential profession of the high-rollers of antebellum times, declined in numbers after the Civil War and gradually faded from the scene as railroads detoured cotton away from New Orleans, land-mortgage companies allowed planters to finance their obligations on the basis of their land, and market information became more widespread and reliable.[273] There were 93 factors in New Orleans in 1880, 15 in 1921, and only 1—the last self-described cotton factor in New Orleans—in 1949. The firm was an old name in the local cotton scene, Weis, Julius & Co., located at 819 Gravier Street, on the site of the first New Orleans Cotton Exchange building and about one hundred feet away from the famous second and extant third building on the corner Carondelet and Gravier.[274] (By the 1950s, the term *factor* was almost never used; most cotton businessmen described themselves as *merchants* or *shippers,* as they do today. Additionally, the Carondelet/Gravier intersection was no longer referred to as the Cotton District by this era.)[275]

266. The decline of New Orleans' cotton-market domination was a constant matter of concern in the late 1880s. Stated the *New Orleans Times* on August 28, 1881, "It is a startling fact that other cities with their railway facilities and great aggregations of capital are trying to take [our cotton market] away, and they have succeeded to an alarming extent. St. Louis has carried off 400,000 bales of it, and Norfolk twice as much. . . . New Orleans does not receive as much of [cotton] by several hundred thousand bales as was handled and marketed in this city twenty years ago."
267. Soltow, 14.
268. Born, 3480-81.
269. Hoffmann, 465-67.
270. Murphy.
271. Soltow, 14-15.
272. Kniffen and Hilliard, 179.
273. Stone, 564.
274. All data are extracted from cotton sections of Gardner (1861), *Soards' New Orleans City Directory* (1880, 1885, 1911, 1921, 1925, 1930, 1935), and Polk's New Orleans city directories (1940, 1945-46, 1952-53, 1960, 1965, 1971, 1980, 1990, 2000).
275. Herman S. Kohlmeyer, Jr., interview by author, June 6, 2001.

The number of other cotton-related businesses on Carondelet or Gravier hovered around twenty-five in the early 1950s, while about the same number operated in surrounding streets, enough to keep the Exchange's trading ring one of the city's financial hot spots. But cotton surpluses and competition from synthetic fibers brought about a third of these businesses down by the late 1950s. "We went from trading thousands of contracts in the early fifties to maybe five contracts in all of 1962," recalled Eli Tullis, a retired cotton broker and a member of one of New Orleans' last active cotton families.[276] Another merchant of that era recalled that the New Orleans cotton trade was brisk in the years after World War II but took a blow when the government imposed price ceilings on cotton during the Korean War.

The Exchange itself declined in relevance as government price supports in this era smoothed out once-volatile prices and communication technology decreased the importance of the trading floor as a place to do business. The building was sold off in 1962—to the Universal Drilling Company, symbolizing the upcoming oil boom that would rock New Orleans roughly to the same degree that cotton did eighty years earlier—and the Exchange finally closed in 1964, though by one first-person account, the nearly century-old institution "just petered out" after the 1962 sale, when the rent was no longer worth paying and "the lights were just turned out."[277] In the 1970s, some merchants started the New Orleans Cotton and Commodity Exchange, nominally similar but otherwise unrelated to the old exchange. This new organization appeared under *Brokers-Cotton* in city directories as the New Orleans Cotton Exchange (in Room 404 of the Exchange Building at 231 Carondelet) up to 1978. In 1979, the organization was listed as the New Orleans Commodity Exchange; a year later, according to city directories, it had left the former Exchange Building and departed the historic intersection of Carondelet and Gravier.[278] The lack of "locals"—that is, merchants showing up and trading on the floor—brought down this last attempt at an exchange.

The former Cotton District area remained a hot business location into the 1960s—in 1959, the Exchange block had the highest employment density in the CBD, with 4.63 employees per 100 square feet of land area[279]—but cotton was no longer the topic of conversation or the fuel in the economic engine. The closure of Gould & Company in the mid-1970s signified the end of sizable merchant organizations. During the 1980s and 1990s, the former Exchange building served as an office building and home to the main branch of the Dryades Savings Bank; then, in 2000, its owners proposed refurbishing the building for New Orleans' current boom crop: tourists. Like many old landmarks in the Central Business District, the old Cotton Exchange and the adjacent Security Homestead Association structure were slated for renovation into a 200-room hotel and restaurant. "You could say cotton is becoming king again in New Orleans, but more for the sheets covering tens of thousands of hotel beds than for the heavy bales that dominated trade on the Mississippi River 150 years ago," commented one journalist on the ironic and symbolic transformation.[280]

Since 1980, there have been fewer than five or so cotton-related businesses in New Orleans listed in the city directory (which have been known to undercount actual numbers, especially in these latter decades) for a given year, most of which were small value-added firms that may be found in any city. The last cotton warehouse was the Port Compress at 1421 South Peters Street, last listed in 1983, the same year that the last listing appeared for a Carondelet Street-based cotton dealer (in the former Exchange Building). The last pickery (waste cotton dealer) had operated at 4811 Annunciation into the late 1960s. The city directory of 1990 was devoid of a single entry for the 200-year-old trade that once made New Orleans one of the most important places in North America.[281] In the twenty-first century, the powerhouse of American cotton is Memphis, a once-small river city that formerly bowed to the Queen of the South. Centrally located, convenient to the cotton-growing regions, and generally more progressive and business friendly than the Crescent City, Memphis is home to three of the five premier "cotton shipping" firms, Allenberg Cotton Company, Hohenberg Bros. Company, and Dunavant Enterprises, Inc., while two other major players operate out of Dallas and Montgomery. None calls New Orleans home, and not one of the twenty-seven officers and directors of the Memphis-based American Cotton Shippers Association (whose member firms control 80 percent of the

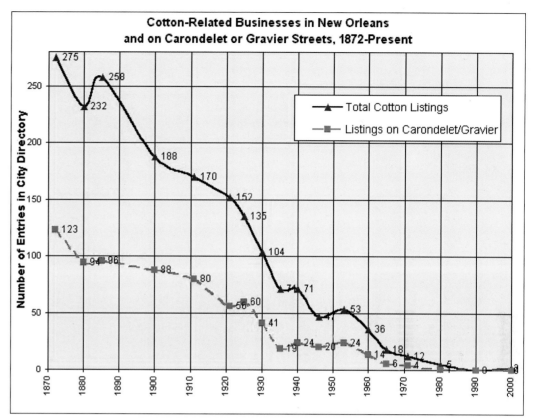

Cotton-Related Businesses in New Orleans and on Carondelet or Gravier Streets, 1872-Present

The gradual decline of the New Orleans cotton industry and the Cotton District is graphed through tabulations of city-directory listings. Numbers reflect all cotton-related businesses, professional and industrial. The rise of the city's cotton market, from about 1790 to the Civil War, is difficult to quantify, because early city directories did not clearly and consistently identify businesses by their field. For example, New Orleans was home to 147 "cotton receiving houses" in 1854 and 465 "commission merchants and cotton factors" in 1861, but it is difficult to verify the degree to which these numbers reflect the entire local cotton scene. *Analysis by author. Note: Directory listings are not always a reliable source of such data. Figures for the 1950s-70s probably underestimate the true number of cotton businessmen in the city, though the general trend remains true.*

nation's cotton) has a New Orleans address. Cotton is now traded on the commodities market under the auspices of the New York Cotton Exchange, and "producers" (they are no longer called "planters" or "farmers") across the "Cotton Belt" (now spanning the entire southern tier of the United States, Georgia to California) no longer have a need to market their harvest at the nearest seaport. While cotton remains one of Louisiana's largest agricultural commodities, earning $328 million in 1997, New Orleans' end of the business lies more with the T-shirts sold in the French Quarter than in the buying and selling of the commodity. Herman S. Kohlmeyer, Jr., a descendent of the founders of H & C Newman Cotton Factors in the 1880s, is perhaps the last active cotton-futures trader in the New Orleans area, lured back to the family business by a return of some fluctuation in the price of cotton in the 1970s. Though his office today occupies not a nineteenth-century row building in the Cotton District but a high-rise in suburban Metairie, his ties to the district are still evident: in his lobby hangs a framed print of *A Cotton Office in New Orleans,* many of the figures of which he can identify by name. And above his desk hangs an 1889 calendar of his ancestors' firm, featuring an etching of its office building at 218 Gravier Street, in the heart of the Cotton District.[282]

276. Ronette King.
277. Kohlmeyer, interview.
278. *Polk's New Orleans (Orleans Parish, La.) City Directory* (1971-80).
279. Transportation Advertisers, Map of Employment Density—By Block.
280. Greg Thomas, "Old Cotton Exchange Building."
281. *Polk's New Orleans (Orleans Parish, La.) City Directory,* (1965-90).

282. Kohlmeyer, interview. See also Ronette King.

For over a century, New Orleans was the great Southern node of the cotton marketing business. The men behind the business operated out of offices clustered near this intersection of Carondelet and Gravier Street in Faubourg St. Mary, today's Central Business District. This was the center of New Orleans' Cotton District. The factors and brokers are gone, but their opulent homes still stand in the Garden District and their imposing offices still line the streets of downtown New Orleans. *Photograph by author, 2000*

On Perdido Street between Carondelet and Baronne stands Factors' Row (1858), one of the greatest extant monuments to the city's historic cotton trade. Factors were essentially the city-based agents of wealthy rural planters, though their roles often extended far beyond cotton vending to one of financial consultant and family advisor. It was in this building that the great French Impressionist Edgar Degas captured his uncle's cotton office in his 1873 masterpiece, *A Cotton Office in New Orleans*. The statuary are recent additions. *Photograph by author, 2000*

Few office workers in downtown New Orleans can identify Varieties Alley today, but in the late 1800s and early 1900s, it was filled with cotton men spilling out from adjacent offices and the Exchange, carrying their business into the streets. The narrow alley, also known as Varieties Place or Theater Alley, was lined with a number of offices; to its immediate left was the first Cotton Exchange (1871-83); to its immediate right were the second (1883-1921) and third (1921-present) Exchange buildings. According to the 1949 city directory, New Orleans' last self-described cotton factor—the firm of Weis, Julius & Co.—operated at 819 Gravier Street, next door to the left. Today, Varieties Alley is unmarked, dark, and lonely, home only to the homeless. *Photograph by author, 2000*

The Cotton District Today

Entrance to the former New Orleans Cotton Exchange (1921). The building was sold in 1962 and the organization "just petered out" over the next two years, according to one merchant. Beginning in the 1980s, the former Exchange building served as an office building and home to the Dryades Savings Bank. Then, in 2000, its owners proposed refurbishing the building as a 200-room hotel and restaurant. "You could say cotton is becoming king again in New Orleans, but more for the sheets covering tens of thousands of hotel beds than for the heavy bales that dominated trade on the Mississippi River 150 years ago," commented one journalist. *Photograph by author, 2000*

The third and last New Orleans Cotton Exchange building was constructed in 1921, preceding an era of radical change in the regional cotton industry and the eventual demise of the city's Cotton District. The organization is gone today, as are the cotton merchants and factors who dominated these streets a hundred years ago. Gone too is the first Exchange office, demolished in the 1960s and replaced by the modern building (left side of image on right), although many other nineteenth-century cotton offices still stand in the Central Business District, especially on Gravier Street. Memphis, Tennessee, a once-small river city formerly dwarfed in every way by the Queen of the South, is now home to the most powerful cotton merchants and shippers. *Photographs by author, 2000*

Lower Carondelet Street exhibits a great 1920s ambience; a movie set designer could do no better. Most of these buildings arose in the latter decades of the Cotton District era. The Hibernia Bank Building (1921), with its prominent cupola, was the tallest building in the city (355 feet) for over forty years. The Hennen (Maritime) Building, with the bay windows, was an early steel-frame high-rise in the city and home to many cotton professionals after its 1895 completion. *Photograph by author, 1996*

  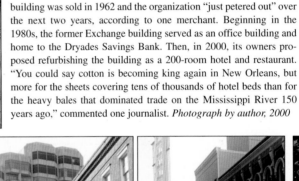  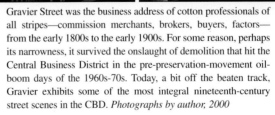 

Gravier Street was the business address of cotton professionals of all stripes—commission merchants, brokers, buyers, factors—from the early 1800s to the early 1900s. For some reason, perhaps its narrowness, it survived the onslaught of demolition that hit the Central Business District in the pre-preservation-movement oil-boom days of the 1960s-70s. Today, a bit off the beaten track, Gravier exhibits some of the most integral nineteenth-century street scenes in the CBD. *Photographs by author, 2000*

Offices of cotton professionals clustered in the Central Business District, but the homes of these men were located uptown, predominantly in Lafayette (now the Garden District) in the early days and on St. Charles Avenue and elsewhere uptown in later years. Few lived in the old city or below it; few, for that matter, worked there. One of the most opulent "cotton mansions" is William Perry Brown's home on St. Charles Avenue, built in 1905 in the Richardson Romanesque style. *Photograph by author, 2000*

New Orleans' Cotton District is completely extinct in function but may still be seen in form in the great 1920s-ambience of lower Carondelet Street, the surprisingly intact nineteenth-century streetscape of lower Gravier, and in neighboring streets throughout the core of the Central Business District. Even Varieties Alley—that narrow passage that abutted all three Cotton Exchange buildings and was home to a number of cotton firms—still exists, though it is now lonely, foreshortened, and eerily quiet. The Maritime (Hennen) Building, the Hibernia Bank Building, Factors' Row on Perdido, and dozens of other structures from the late nineteenth and early twentieth centuries recall the era of the Cotton District, though none so clearly and so prominently as the former New Orleans Cotton Exchange Building on the corner of Carondelet and Gravier, whose frieze and plaque remind current CBD denizens who owned the streets of downtown New Orleans a hundred years ago.

The Sugar District

While states throughout the lower Mississippi Valley contributed cotton to New Orleans, it was mostly the subtropical lowland parishes of Louisiana itself that sent sugar through the Crescent City. So intimate was the relationship between this crop and this city that sugarcane plantations proliferated within the confines of present-day downtown into the late eighteenth century, within uptown to the mid-nineteenth century, and within the present-day metropolitan area until the late twentieth century and to some extent even today. Sugar earnings were truly indigenous to the region, from planting to processing to marketing. For almost a century, two of these three activities occurred practically upon the very site where, in 1718, Bienville's men first scratched a foothold into the marshes. River-deposited sediments had since extended this land into the water, forming a batture at a time when—and a place where—extra space along the levee was highly valued for the shipping industry. It was upon this upper French Quarter batture, from present-day Iberville to Toulouse and from Decatur to the Mississippi, that a "sugar landing" formed from the early 1800s and eventually evolved into New Orleans' Sugar District, operating from 1870 to the early 1930s.

The regional sugar industry was smaller but geographically more concentrated and industrially more complex than the area's cotton industry. It is also older and more deeply rooted in Louisiana's colonial origins. Native to New Guinea, sugarcane had been wildly lucrative in the Caribbean colonies since the early 1500s but, as a tropical crop, did not fare well at first in subtropical Louisiana, restricted by labor shortages and technology gaps but primarily by an eight-month growing season. A smattering of attempts to grow sugarcane in French Louisiana appeared in various accounts of the colony's first fifty years: Iberville himself, for example, planted some cuttings unsuccessfully in Quinipissas territory in 1700; his brother Bienville reported that some fellow colonists in New Orleans tried the crop in 1733. The Jesuits reportedly experimented with the crop as early as 1742,[283] but probably the first serious, large-scale effort at sugarcane cultivation in the area was not made until 1751, when the Jesuits imported Malabar-variety seeds (which became known as "Creole cane") and forty skilled slaves from Saint-Domingue to grow the crop on their landholding in what is now the Central Business District (see page 88). Though the Jesuits' endeavor did not do especially well, it did serve to introduce sugarcane to the colonists as something more than an experimental crop. This first large sugarcane field was located in the block bounded by present-day Canal, Baronne, Common, and Carondelet and is indirectly recalled today by the Church of the Immaculate Conception ("The Jesuits' Church"), built on land reacquired by the Jesuits well after their expulsion from Louisiana in 1763.[284]

Locals picked up small-scale cultivation of the grass for the purposes of producing *taffia* (rum), sweet pastes, and syrups and for chewing. But for the crop to be truly profitable, producers had to match the West Indians' skills in crystallizing cane juice into granulated sugar, because the Caribbean techniques and other methods, some centuries old, did not work for Louisiana cane. The underlying problem was that the eight-month growing season—far below the fourteen- to twenty-four-month cycle used in the tropics—cut short the maturing of the grass and yielded a juice high in acids and impurities, making the clarification and granulation process more difficult. Leaving the crop in the ground as long as possible put the crop at high risk for a frost, which would destroy the sucrose content of the grass and render it waste.[285] A number of men strove to overcome these challenges: Claude-Joseph Dubreuil de Villars[286] built a sugar mill on his plantation near present-day Esplanade Avenue in the mid-1750s and probably produced some sugar; the Chevalier de Mazan took over

283. Joseph George Tregle, Jr., 24, and Henry P. Dart, "The Career of Dubreuil," 276.

284. Gayarré, vol. 2, 62-63, and The Sugar Journal, 1-2.

285. Le Gardeur, 4.

286. The handiwork of this prominent early citizen of New Orleans is still with us today: Claude-Joseph Dubreuil de Villars was the contractor who, in 1749-53, built the Ursulines Convent on Chartres Street, oldest building in the city and region. Ibid., 5; see also Henry P. Dart, "The Career of Dubreuil," 267-331.

Church of the Immaculate Conception ("The Jesuits' Church"), originally constructed in 1851-57 and rebuilt in the same style in 1929, marks part of an old Jesuit plantation on which sugar was successfully cultivated for the first time on a large scale in Louisiana, in 1751. *Photograph by author, 2000*

this mill in 1757 and, by one record, produced a suspiciously amazing 26,000 pounds of sugar probably after the 1763 growing season.[287] Juice from the cane of one Sieur La Chaise finally "yielded sugar of the most beautiful grain" after trials conducted in November of 1764.[288] But the threat of an excessively cold winter made the investment in sugarcane too risky for Louisiana planters; this, coupled with the traditional reliability of the indigo crop (the plant for blue dye traditionally cultivated on plantations surrounding New Orleans), the domination of the Sugar Islands in the world sugar market, and instability of the early Spanish colonial years, made planters abandon sugarcane cultivation in Louisiana for a quarter-century starting in the late 1760s.

Then, in the 1790s, economic and political conditions began to make Louisiana sugarcane look more attractive. The indigo crop was afflicted with moisture and pest problems, lowering its price and nearly ruining many planters. Slave insurrection in Saint-Domingue destabilized the Sugar Islands' control of world sugar, depleting their labor supply while sending sugar-savvy refugees to Louisiana's shore.[289] The time was right for Louisiana to exploit this opening economic niche; the only thing missing was a renewed demonstration of the complex and risky granulation process for Louisiana's particular cane crop.

Those demonstrations, breakthroughs that would do for Louisiana sugar what Eli Whitney's cotton gin did for Southern cotton, transpired on plantations near New Orleans in the 1790s. Many credit Antonio Méndez, Joseph Solís, and Antoine Morin with this success, when they produced and refined some sugar on a Terre aux Boeufs plantation in 1791—not enough, or not prominently enough, for historical recognition.[290] That came four years later, on a plantation just below present-day Audubon Park, where the distinguished Creole planter Jean Etienne de Boré (see page 95) sowed 100 arpents of Creole cane and invested in a sugar maker (probably Antoine Morin),[291] a grinding shed, a sugar mill and drying house, and the labor of thirty slaves in a risky attempt to recoup losses from last year's blighted indigo crop.[292] In 1795, Boré successfully granulated his cane—in front of a deliriously happy and adoring local audience, according to historian Charles Gayarré, who happened to be Boré's grandson—and was able to replicate the success and conduct it on a commercial scale in ensuing years.

The $12,000 Boré earned from the 1795 crop (augmented in following years) convinced many local planters that the time of indigo had passed and the time of sugar had arrived, a trend recognized by French diplomat Pierre Clement de Laussat, who visited the plantation in 1803. "It was in this place," wrote Laussat, "that the first attempt to raise sugarcane in Louisiana was made and sustained. This cultivation is still carried out successfully there and has had, since, many prosperous imitators in the neighboring area."[293]

Clearly, Boré was not the first to granulate sugar in Louisiana; his credit for this achievement derives in large part from the sensational and oft-quoted account ("It granulates! . . . It granulates!")[294] of the event later scribed by his historian grandson, Charles Gayarré. But Boré does deserve ample credit for demonstrating the process in the right way at the right time, and sustaining it economically over a number of years. This achievement led directly to the growth of a true Louisiana sugar industry, a feat more historically significant than the superlative of being "first." The business end of Boré's plantation was located in the area now bounded by Annunciation, Henry Clay, Constance, and Calhoun streets; the actual site of the famous granulation probably occurred here or toward Audubon Zoo, where a historical sign marks the event. This site may be considered the birthplace of the Louisiana sugar industry and the New Orleans sugar market. Sugarcane cultivation spread rapidly throughout the lower Mississippi River "Coast" as the eighteenth century closed and the new century dawned, rising to prominence as indigo faded from the local agricultural scene and the Sugar Islands diminished in importance on the world sugar market. Sugar experts, escaping the slave revolt in the Caribbean, sought refuge in the New Orleans area.[295]

"On the day when the grinding of the cane was to begin, a large number of the most respectable inhabitants had gathered in and about the sugar-house, to be present at the failure or success of the experiment. Would the syrup granulate? Would it be converted into sugar? The crowd waited with eager impatience for the moment when the man who watches the coction of the juice of the cane, determines whether it is ready to granulate. When that moment arrived, the stillness of death came among them, each one holding his breath, and feeling that it was a matter of ruin or prosperity for them all. Suddenly the sugar-maker cried out with exultation : 'It granulates!' and the crowd repeated : 'It granulates!' . . . All flocked around Etienne Boré, overwhelming him with congratulations, and almost hugging the man whom they called their saviour—the saviour of Louisiana."

—Charles Gayarré, 1903 (vol. 3, 349-50. Dramatized account of the 1795 sugar-granulation experiment of his grandfather, Jean Etienne de Boré, that is generally recognized as the birth of the Louisiana sugar industry. In fact, Louisiana sugar had been granulated years earlier, but in small quantities.)

Most first-generation sugarcane cultivators were Creole planters who switched to the crop in the years after Boré, joined by sugar-savvy refugees from the Saint-Domingue revolt as well as an increasing number of agriculturists lured down from the North and upper South to cultivate the region (as was occurring concurrently with cotton). Southeastern Louisiana produced 2,500 tons of sugar in 1802, just seven seasons after Boré's success; a year or so later, sixty to seventy sugar plantations lined both banks of the river from present-day Kenner to English Turn, many of which were constructing their own mills and most of which were producing around 70,000 pounds each and selling at roughly ten cents a pound.[296] American domination further fueled the growth of Louisiana sugarcane, through the imposition of tariffs against West Indian sugar, the introduction of new technologies, the insatiable demand for sweets among Americans, and the construction of flood-protection levees along the lower Mississippi.

By 1816, with over $40 million invested regionally in the sugar industry, "the great impetus thus given to the trade was felt in every direction and the city of New Orleans rapidly increased in wealth and population, tripling the same within twenty years after the opening of the sugar industry."[297] Plantations were established, augmented, and/or converted to sugar along the Mississippi from below New Orleans up to Pointe Coupée and westward to Bayou Lafourche and Bayou Teche.[298] Accompanying many plantations were the steaming, smoking, chimneyed red-brick

In the area behind this imposing building on Henry Clay and Laurel, near Audubon Zoo, Jean Etienne de Boré successfully demonstrated that locally cultivated sugarcane could be granulated (1795) and made into an economically viable crop. The accomplishment, which was old hat in the Caribbean islands but a tricky process for subtropical Louisiana-grown cane, kicked off sugar agriculture in southern Louisiana as Eli Whitney's 1793 invention of the cotton gin spread cotton cultivation throughout the interior South at about the same time. Both crops injected vast fortunes into New Orleans. *Photograph by author, 2000*

287. D'Abbadie (1764), as quoted in Le Gardeur, 7.
288. Ibid., 8. Nineteenth-century historians Charles Gayarré and Henry Rightor dismissed some of these apparent successes as failures, either because they considered this sugar "so inferior that it all leaked out before reaching port" or because they rigidly viewed Jean Etienne de Boré—Gayarré's grandfather—as the first to granulate Louisiana sugar. Rightor, 649.
289. Le Gardeur, 9-10.
290. Stubbs and Purse, 5-7.
291. Le Gardeur, 21.
292. James Pitot, 73.
293. Wilson, "The Uptown Faubourgs," 25-26.
294. Gayarré, vol. 3, 349.
295. Clark, *New Orleans, 1718-1812,* 183, 217-18, and Le Gardeur, 4-10. The banks of the lower Mississippi River were known as "the Coast" in the 1800s. (This term still survives in the "Lower Coast" section of Algiers.)

296. Clark, *New Orleans, 1718-1812,* 219. By another count, Louisiana's sugar-related production in 1802 comprised 5,000 hogsheads of sugar, 5,000 barrels of molasses, and 5,000 casks of rum. Address by J. Dymond, "The Sugar Exchange: Formal Opening of the Beautiful Building," *New Orleans Times-Democrat,* 3, columns 3-5.
297. Address by Dymond, 3, columns 3-5. This passage is repeated in The Louisiana Sugar and Rice Exchange, 37.
298. Prichard, 315.

distilleries where juice was ground out of the harvested cane, purified, boiled, and cooled to the point of granulation; later, the molasses was drained off as a separate product and the remaining brown sugar grain was sent to market.

New Orleans itself got its first sugar mill prior to 1802, when it produced 100 tons, but in general, from Boré's breakthrough in 1795 to the Civil War, sugar mills were not centralized in the city but located on the manor proper, making the plantation the "constitutive cell of the sugar civilization. . . . It was a farm where cane was grown, a factory where sugar was produced, and a home to the proprietor and his family and retinue of slaves. The nature of the sugar-making process prevented use of centrally located custom mills, with the result that every plantation, regardless of size, had its own sugarhouse."[299] There were, however, some large mills or refineries that served surrounding plantations; one was the Louisiana Sugar Refinery (1832), which produced sugar and rum on a riverside site near the present-day Industrial Canal. A wide range of technologies developed during this era expanded Louisiana sugar: steam-operated engines and cane mills (1820) would supplant cattle and horse power; coal would replace firewood; and specialized equipment such as the vacuum pan, the "Rillieux train," the centrifugal machine (1844), and the filter press (1855) would facilitate processing.[300] One historian cited the early Louisiana cane sugar industry as an example of the successful "application of science and technology to agriculture."[301]

With the help of tariffs restricting foreign competition, the industry grew steadily into the 1820s then surged between 1824 and 1830, when the number of sugar plantations grew from 193 to 691.[302] While a reduction in foreign tariffs in 1835 and the Panic of 1837 derailed growth for a few years, production rebounded to 43,000 tons in 1840 and surged again in 1845-49, when there were 1,536 sugar plantations. At this point, Louisiana's "sugar bowl" expanded from the New Orleans region to the highlands north of Baton Rouge, westward to the Attakapas and Opelousas prairies, and up the Red River to Natchitoches.[303]

In 1850, 105,000 tons were produced, and in 1861, 230,000 tons went to market,[304] making output just before the Civil War ninety-two times greater than that just before the American domination, a time span in which New Orleans' population grew by a factor of twenty-one (8,000 in 1803 to 168,000 in 1860). These nearly quarter-million tons, worth around $25 million, were produced on 1,291 plantations spread across twenty-three Louisiana parishes. Louisiana sugar accounted for 95 percent of Southern sugar in these years, and more than half of it passed through a single point: New Orleans.[305]

The "Coffee House Era," 1800-1830

The buying and selling of Louisiana sugar was, in the early days, based largely on the geography of its supply and demand. Roughly half of Louisiana sugar production in the early 1800s was shipped through New Orleans; the other half was sold "on plantation" to merchants representing firms in distant cities. Production from the upper part of Louisiana's sugarcane region—the Red River and Baton Rouge vicinity—was often sold to merchants from western cities such as St. Louis, Cincinnati, and Louisville. The lower regions of sugar country would often ship directly to cities of the Northeast based upon sales to merchants visiting those plantations. As the industry matured, New Orleans would become more central to sugar negotiations, largely because merchants dealing with individual planters were denied the benefits of comparison shopping, rendering difficult the assessment of quality, supply, demand, and other price-affecting factors. Likewise, planters "could hardly expect to make a particularly advantageous sale on plantation,"[306] where competitive bidding was limited to a handful of merchants. On-plantation sales generally declined as the antebellum era progressed, while in New Orleans a professional class of sugar businessmen grew. Increasingly, planters would sell or consign their production to commission merchants in New Orleans, who would in turn advertise it to wholesalers or buyers through newspapers and fliers. Buyers and sellers would also associate at the Exchange Coffee House (known through the years as Maspero and Elkins, Maspero's Exchange, or the New Exchange) and like establishments in the city, to negotiate, auction, and observe the trends of the market.[307] A 2 percent duty on auction sales discouraged the disposal of large quantities of sugar (as well as cotton and other staples) through auctioning, possibly retarding the development of a centralized location for large-scale sugar business. This and other factors

led to a dispersed geography of sugar business in New Orleans during the first three decades of the industry's life, when sugar professionals "networked" not in a specific district but in coffeehouses, public venues, and on the street and levee.

"We went to the French coffee house or as the sign over the door proclaims it to be the New Exchange. It is a very large room with two columns in the centre [from which] are suspended four splendid chandeliers that make a blaze of light in the apartment. Around the walls are the usual notices of an exchange, sales, arrivals departures, &c, &c. A large portrait of Napoleon of full size in oil is on one side of the apartment with General Washington for his vis a vis on the other. Here as elsewhere there is a bar, or counter, where the usual refreshments are to be obtained. The Coffee house has always a crowd of frequenters who lounge and get and relate the news, and comprising people from every quarter of the globe who are here gathered together in the commercial bustle of a great mart."
—John H. B. Latrobe, 1834 (as quoted in Wilson, *Southern Travels*, 49-50)

Sugar merchants and other businessmen in the early 1800s gathered in the Exchange Coffee House (known through the years as Maspero and Elkins, Maspero's Exchange, or the New Exchange). The shop was a prominent rendezvous: on September 16, 1814, citizens met here to plan defenses against a rumored British assault, which transpired four months later. The structure was built in 1810 and demolished in 1838 for the famous St. Louis and City Exchange Hotel, which was in turn razed in 1916 and replaced in 1960 by the Royal Orleans Hotel, seen at top with the shadow of the Girod (Napoleon) House upon it. The name Maspero's lives on in the restaurant at 440 Chartres (bottom) diagonally across from the original coffee shop, which occupies a late-1790s Spanish Colonial structure that probably resembled the old exchange. In antebellum times, slaves were sold at both locations. *Photographs by author, 2000*

299. Roland, 3.

300. The Louisiana Sugar and Rice Exchange, 35-41, and Huber, *New Orleans*, 307.

301. Clark, *New Orleans, 1718-1812*, 219.

302. Galloway, 190.

303. Prichard, 315.

304. Address by J. Dymond, "The Sugar Exchange: Formal Opening of the Beautiful Building," *New Orleans Times-Democrat*, 3, columns 3-5. These data are repeated in The Louisiana Sugar and Rice Exchange, 37.

305. Roland, 1-5; Galloway, 190; and Sitterson, "Financing and Marketing," 194.

306. Sitterson, *Sugar Country*, 188.

307. Ibid., 185-86. The Exchange Coffee House was located not in the late-1790s structure known today as Maspero's Exchange (corner of Chartres and St. Louis) but diagonally across from it, at the Chartres Street end of the present-day Royal Orleans Hotel. The structure housing this original Exchange Coffee House was built in 1810 and demolished in 1838 to make room for the famous St. Louis Exchange Hotel, which stood until 1916. Both the Exchange Coffee House and the later hotel served as principal centers for business and finance, especially for Creole businessmen. Wilson, *Southern Travels*, 50.

The Sugar Landing Era, 1830-70

In 1827, the 2 percent tax on auction sales was repealed by the state legislature, eliminating this impediment to large auctions. Three years later, the levee in front of the city, part of which had been naturally expanded by the development of the batture, was repaired and renovated with new wharves and warehouses. "From this time on," wrote J. Carlyle Sitterson, "a regular sugar market with daily transactions operated on the levee."[308] The viability of this area as a major freight deposit was further enhanced in 1836 when the First Municipality reserved the riverside from Canal to Toulouse for the exclusive use of steamboats.[309] Proximity to the financial institutions of Royal and Chartes streets, which provided some of the credit that factorage firms passed on to planters, helped attract sugar merchants to these blocks. With spacious acreage now conveniently available within the limits of the old city and directly accessible to steamboat traffic, the refurbished riverfront promised to be a valuable port asset, one that would be monopolized by the sugar industry, informally at first as the "sugar landing" or "sugar levee" and later as the "Sugar District," for the next 100 years. Over the decades of the mid-nineteenth century, when 45 to 60 percent of the entire Louisiana sugar crop was sold in New Orleans,[310] the sugar landing generally covered from where Customhouse Street (present-day Iberville Street) met the river and later expanded inland to Decatur Street and downriver to about Toulouse Street. Recalling the origins of sugar brokerage in New Orleans, John Dymond reminisced about life on the sugar landing in a speech delivered a half-century later:

> In the early days sugars, when landed, were examined by the consignees, who left word with some one on the levee concerning what price he would accept for them. Even "Old Joe," the colored weigher of forty years ago, acted under some of the instructions, but we can hardly call him the first broker. Adolph Fontenette seems to have been the first to make first hand sugar brokerage his regular business, and this was about 1840. Soon after William Robinson also became a regular broker, and then with the increasing business, Richard Milliken and John Flathers engaged in it. . . . In the early days there were [also] many prominent factor and dealers [as well as] many prominent Western buyers, whose long visits here made them feel as much at home as in their Western cities.[311]

Gibson's Guide and Directory (1838) listed the A. J. Fontenette mentioned above as a sugar broker working at 42-43 New Levee, a street that was only about a few decades old at the time, having been laid out upon the fresh batture deposited by the river in the upper corner of the city in the early 1800s (see page 62). If Fontenette was indeed among the first sugar brokers, it is fitting that he worked on New Levee Street (renamed North and South Peters Street by 1856), as this street would eventually form a principal corridor through the Sugar District. Other sugar men operated offices on nearby streets: Edmund J. Forstall's New Orleans Sugar Refinery, for example, had its office on Royal between Toulouse and St. Louis, though the refinery itself was outside the city.[312]

> "It is one of the striking facts in southern history," wrote J. Carlyle Sitterson in 1944, "that one who played so important a role in the ante-bellum economy appears so little in recorded history." Sitterson was referring to "that noted, yet enigmatic southern financier, the factor." A sugar factor served not only as a planter's agent in the city but also as his adviser, insurer, lender, marketer, purchaser of supplies, and informant of market trends. "On occasions, the factor even visited and advised the planter's children who were at school in the city" ("Financing and Marketing," 190).

These professionals conducted their business outdoors on the sugar landing, directly in front of present-day North Peters, in the manner that cotton brokers conducted business in the open air of Gravier Street and along the wharves in the days before the Cotton Exchange. This era of outdoor negotiations on the sugar landing, in the antebellum "Golden Age," formed a scene remembered nostalgically by merchants of later decades. In those days, planters would consign their sugar and molasses to factors in the city and ship their hogsheads on steamboats bound for New Orleans. Upon docking at the sugar landing, the steamboats were immediately boarded by clerks verifying to whom the lots had been consigned. Brokers with lots to sell met with interested buyers on the levee to sample and examine the hogsheads and confer on a price, while second buyers interjected in the hope of scoring a bargain. Western merchants and their hired commission merchants purchased supplies and conducted their business in sending sugar to their distant cities, while local dealers and their aides negotiated for their clients and sugar factors looked after their receipts. Weighers hauled their bulky scales to the scene of deals that would call for their services, as draymen towed hogsheads to waiting vessels or to storage. The pace was bustling not just because of the nature of negotiation but because a local law stipulated that produce on the levee had to be sold within thirty-six hours or removed to storage,[313] to keep the levee clear.

Fees incurred by the planter for the privilege of selling in the New Orleans market were numerous and the source of bitter complaint: the factor received a 2.5 percent commission; insurance for shipping added another 1 percent; then there were charges for transportation, cooperage, weighing, tarpaulin, and drayage, plus a charge of thirty to fifty cents per hogshead per month if the product had to be stored. In all, about "10 per cent of the gross return on a hogshead of sugar" stayed with Crescent City sugar men, from the lowly dock worker to the urbane factor. "In other words, a 1,100 pound hogshead bringing 5 cents a pound for a gross of $55 would bear total freight and marketing charges of about $5.50, leaving a net of $49.50 due to the planter."[314]

While the various players maneuvered on the sugar levee to earn their portion of that 10 percent, "our sugar levee presented a gay scene":[315] street urchins circulated among the merchants with samples of sugar still under consideration, perhaps hired by brokers to stimulate interest among potential buyers. Steamboat captains anxiously sought freight to carry back upriver. Grocers purchased sugar for retail sale in local shops, vendors peddled oranges, pies, tarts, and water among the workers, and coffee shops and eateries catered to negotiating businessmen along the periphery of the sugar landing. On the buying side, about 50 percent of the sugar passing through the sugar landing in this era was purchased for consumption in the West (that is, up the Mississippi); another 30 to 35 percent went to the Northeast; and the remainder was mostly consumed locally, with a small portion purchased by speculators in the hope of exploiting a day-to-day price fluctuation.[316]

Who were these businessmen and where were their offices? Unfortunately, reliable comprehensive data are hard to come by: early city directories did not categorize citizens by profession and did not clearly and consistently identify professions in the general residential listings. The 1861 *Gardner's New Orleans Directory* does not distinguish among commission merchants specializing in particular crops—they are all merged with cotton factors—although one source cited 63 sugar and molasses factors in New Orleans a few years before, 1858.[317] The 1861 directory does, however, identify 19 sugar brokers among the city's 122 brokerage firms. About half of these 19 sugar firms were loosely clustered in the upper French Quarter, on or a few blocks from the sugar landing:

- 9 worked in the city, on Conti, Bienville, St. Louis, and St. Philip streets;
- 2 worked behind the city;
- 2 worked downriver from the city;
- 2 worked upriver from the city, in Faubourg St. Mary;
- 4 worked upriver from Faubourg St. Mary.[318]

308. Sitterson, 190.
309. Winston, 204.
310. Sitterson, "Financing and Marketing," 194.
311. Address by J. Dymond, "The Sugar Exchange: Formal Opening of the Beautiful Building," *New Orleans Times-Democrat*, 3, columns 3-5. This passage is repeated in The Louisiana Sugar and Rice Exchange, 43.
312. *Michel's New Orleans Annual and Commercial Register,* 245. Edmund J. Forstall was a prominent planter and industry expert from the antebellum era. Prichard, 317.

313. "In the 1840's the limit was twenty-four hours, but was increased to thirty-six during the 1850's." Sitterson, "Financing and Marketing," 196.
314. Sitterson, *Sugar Country,* 191. Subtracted from this net were a planter's voluminous costs to operate his plantation.
315. Address by J. Dymond, "The Sugar Exchange: Formal Opening of the Beautiful Building," *New Orleans Times-Democrat*, 3, columns 3-5.
316. Sitterson, "Financing and Marketing," 196-97.
317. Sitterson, *Sugar Country,* 196.
318. *Gardner's New Orleans Directory for 1861,* 469-70. See 472-76 for commission merchants and cotton factors.

The rather loose concentration of sugar professionals indicates that the sugar landing at this time was not an established "district" with its own dedicated brick-and-mortar infrastructure but rather a generalized site where sugar was deposited and merchants congregated to conduct business. It is for this reason that it is probably apropos to refer to this era (1830-70) as the time of the *sugar landing* and not quite yet the *Sugar District*. Like the scattered distribution of sugar refineries before the war, the loose concentration of sugar merchants around the landing would change in the postwar years, when both the industrial and professional components of New Orleans' sugar scene would cluster to form a genuine district.

Missing also from the sugar landing was the industrial end of the business, sugar processing. In fact, there was none conducted on the sugar landing in the antebellum era. Refining before the Civil War generally occurred in sugarhouses located on or among plantations, not in centrally located urban plants. Early photographic images and bird's-eye lithographs of the city made during the 1850s reveal no massive distilleries or belching chimneys on the sugar landing (though a very different picture would appear a half-century later). Rather, the landing in the prewar era served as a break-of-bulk site and point of sales for processed sugar and molasses.

Another shortcoming of the sugar landing was the inadequacy of its wharf and storage facilities, years after the 1830 renovation. The landing was just that: a broad expanse of riverside land, lacking colonnades to protect produce from the elements during unloading and sans nearby warehouses to store it if not quickly sold. One Rapides Parish planter wrote in 1856 that "parts of the wharf were breaking in from the weight [of cotton, sugar, and molasses on the levee] and produce [was] sacrificed to get it out of the way." He came home "thoroughly impressed with the conviction that New Orleans is the meanest commercial port in the world."[319] Another planter from West Baton Rouge Parish described the levee in 1858 as "more of a hog-litter-slush and filthy mud, than anything else—a place so miserably kept up that a person wishing to pass from the pavement on Front Levee street, is often compelled to walk a considerable distance out of his way to get on a narrow plank or gunwale, in order to reach the wharves."[320] Lack of cohesion among merchants also hindered business at the sugar landing. "There was no special association of the sugar factors or businessmen in New Orleans which purported to protect and advance the sugar industry," wrote historian J. Carlyle Sitterson. "Such important matters as adequate levee facilities, investigation of complaints, consideration of marketing improvements, and regulation of credit practices were all left to agencies having no special interest in the industry as a whole."[321] One observer in 1855 commented that Louisiana sugar probably stood alone among American business interests in its lack of association and coordination. In response to these concerns, a Sugar Planters Convention was held in the city in January 1856; a few months later, the convention's marketing committee recommended (1) extending the thirty-six-hour rule to seventy hours hours before unsold sugar had to be removed to storage, (2) expanding the levee itself, (3) constructing sheds and other permanent structures, and (4) forming a corporation of planters to be called the Louisiana Sugar Mart. Construction activities would be funded by a ten-cent tax on a hogshead of sugar and a five-cent tax on a barrel of molasses. If these recommendations were not heeded, the group proposed relocating the sugar landing across the river to Algiers or Gretna—a move that would have significantly changed the urban and economic geography of the city in general and the French Quarter in particular. Committees began soliciting contributions from the sugar parishes, but momentum for the radical reform was derailed by a poor sugar crop in 1856. No changes were made on the sugar landing for the remainder of the antebellum era, and when that era closed, so did a chapter of the local sugar industry.

> "I don't care if one half of [my sugar] melts away, so these rascally loafers on the Lévée, makes nothing out of me. I heard so much of their schemes, that I am like an enrager against them all, some making $70,000 in one year out of the poor hard working planters."
> —complaint of planter Andrew Durnford in a letter to John McDonogh, 1844 (As quoted in Sitterson, *Sugar Country*, 192. "The Lévée" refers to New Orleans' sugar levee, along the river in the upper French Quarter, where much of Louisiana's sugar was marketed. Ill feelings sometimes prevailed between rural planters and New Orleans merchants.)

Louisiana sugar took a severe but not fatal blow during the Civil War. Sugar mills and the manorial plantations they served were targeted for destruction by Union troops, dropping sugar production by a staggering 98 percent (230,000 down to 5,000 tons) between 1861 and 1864. Total value of the Louisiana sugar industry, approximated at $200 million before the war, dropped to about one-eighth that figure in 1865, with one contemporary estimating financial losses to be over 99 percent.[322] "By 1865, the Southern sugar industry lay in ruins with its traditional labor force gone, its mills and equipment destroyed, and with much of the cane land under water, thanks to the neglect of the levees."[323] With a new tariff against foreign sugar, production slowly climbed to 9,000 tons in 1865, 20,000 the next year, and 75,000 in 1870. But it was not until 1893 that output matched prewar levels, produced under very different circumstances than in the days of the lost "sugar civilization." Although the plantation survived as a production unit, greatly depreciated land values forced many old planters to sell out to speculating merchants, bankers, and corporations, the majority of which had Northern roots. Because sugar processing became increasingly costly and complicated in the postwar era, "a gradual divorcement of sugar agriculture and manufacture occurred,"[324] slowly pushing the old plantation sugarhouse off the landscape in favor of centralized refineries—a trend furthered by the postbellum growth of railroads, which naturally favor centralized locations, and a shift in taste from raw to refined sugar.[325] A watershed event for the sugar landing was the laying of tracks for the Pontchartrain Railroad (1867) and New Orleans, Mobile, and Texas Railroad (1871, expanded 1873) through the batture of the upper French Quarter, a step toward modernization of the port in general and sugar industry in particular. At about this time—particularly in 1866—many of the new blocks surveyed upon the batture, of which some had been conveyed to the city by a U.S. Supreme Court judgment in 1836, were subdivided into lots and sold off by the City of New Orleans, putting many acres of the old sugar landing into private hands. New French Quarter streets with such un-French names as Clay, North Front, and Wells were designated here from the 1860s to the 1880s, while the older streets of Customhouse (now Iberville), Bienville, Conti, and St. Louis were extended perpendicularly toward the river. All the ingredients for the development of a modernized Sugar District—industry centralization, technological development, transportation access, location—fell into place.

The Sugar District Era, 1870-1930s

The old sugar landing transformed into a bona fide Sugar District a few years after the Civil War, when the slowly recuperating sugar industry renewed its demands for better facilities in the Crescent City. In response, the Reconstruction-era city government approved a plan by Francis B. Fleitas to build permanent fireproof sheds on the sugar landing for the storage of sugar and molasses. The location was especially valuable because it paralleled the railroad tracks along Wells Street. Fleitas was awarded a twenty-five-year exclusive right to the area and permitted to collect up to twenty-five cents for sugar hogsheads and fifteen cents for molasses barrels, plus other charges, in return for a 10 percent payment on gross revenues to the city.[326] Fleitas organized the New Orleans Sugar Shed Company in January 1870, capitalized at $1,200,000, and promptly began work on the sheds. In 1870-71, the company constructed 308-foot-long molasses and sugar sheds with a distinctive saw-tooth roofline, a feature that would visually characterize this industrial landscape for years. More followed. Actually open-air pavilions, the sheds' floors were "arranged to slope along to gutters which will convey the drippings of the molasses or sugar into [thirty-eight eighty-gallon] tanks places under the floor."[327] A newspaper recorded that "operators in sugar now meet in the sheds on 'change, instead of on the landing."[328] These "Sugar & Molasses Shed Warehouses," as they were labeled in the Sanborn Fire Insurance Maps, lined the railroad tracks through the Sugar District from Customhouse (Iberville) to St. Louis Street from 1870 to the 1910s. The construction of the sheds marked the first major structural improvement on the old sugar landing, the first major corporate involvement in the area's real estate, and the beginnings of a true concentration of sugar's shipping, industrial, and professional elements at this locale. One may view Fleitas's sheds as the turning point from the old sugar landing era to the new Sugar District era, though both terms would be used for

319. As quoted in Sitterson, *Sugar Country,* 193.
320. Ibid., 195-96.
321. Ibid., 193.

322. Roland, 137.
323. Galloway, 191.
324. Roland, 139.
325. The centralization of sugar processing after the war was gradual: there were 1,291 sugarhouses in operation in 1861; 1,130 in 1879; 998 in 1884; 347 in 1898; 214 in 1910; and only 60 by 1957. Roland, 139; Elstner, 45; Begnaud, 38, 45; and Galloway, 191.
326. *Charter of the New Orleans Sugar Shed Company* (Tulane University Special Collections, January 25, 1870).
327. *New Orleans Republican,* 1, column 5.
328. Ibid., 8, column 3.

years to come. Meanwhile, smaller sugar-related businesses were built on adjacent blocks, notably the units in the Italianate-style edifice designed by Henry Howard in 1867, built by 1873, and known as the Importers Bonded Warehouse, along North Peters between Conti and St. Louis.[329] Many adjacent batture lots were originally purchased by private individuals from the city, but in time, most were obtained by sugar-refinery and warehouse interests, lumbering mills, railroads, and ancillary businesses such as cooperage shops, which made barrels for sugar when hogsheads became a thing of the past. Upon these lots additional sugar-related buildings went up during the 1870s. By 1876, sugar and sugar-related businesses occupied about 40 percent of the blocks bounded by Crossman, North Peters, Toulouse, and the river, not including railroads and wharves.[330]

While the shed-construction effort was applauded, the New Orleans Sugar Shed Company was criticized in 1880 as a corrupt Carpetbagger-regime monopoly known for mishandling produce and overcharging for its storage. Frustration with the company—in fact, efforts "to bring suit against the Sugar Shed Company and destroy it"[331]—led members of the Louisiana Sugar Planters' Association to consider forming a Sugar Exchange, where sugar could be sold by sample and merchants could share information and agree upon standards.[332] The idea came to fruition at the association's meeting in February 1883, perhaps in recognition of the success of the New Orleans Cotton Exchange and the realization that many other industries in town were forming similar organizations.

Working zealously, the group obtained a charter on March 6 and decided upon a constitution, bylaws, elected officials, and committees. Four lots at the corner of Bienville and Conti—dead center of the Sugar District—were purchased from a Madame Blanche for $16,262 plus fees, and noted local architect James Freret won the competition to design the structure. The Louisiana Sugar Exchange Building was built by Joseph R. Tureck during the next year for a total of $52,000 and dedicated on June 3, 1884.[333]

Comprising planters and producers on the supply side and dealers and buyers on the demand side, the Exchange had as its purpose "to govern and direct how commodities offered on our floor may be sold, purchased, and delivered; to fix penalties for failure to comply with contracts . . . ; to establish standards of articles bought and sold . . . ; to establish rules for the government of inspectors, weighers and gaugers, and to determine the order of meetings of the Exchange, and for the conduct of member and of visitors."[334] The pressing need to coordinate efforts in the sugar industry was voiced more passionately by John Dymond on the occasion of the Exchange's inauguration. After recounting the quaintly efficient days of the old sugar landing, he asked,

Then why do we change? All the world has changed and our turn has come. The Western merchant tells us to-day that he does not want our sugar unless it is white . . . the local dealers, sending away samples and soliciting orders, receive in return orders less than cost. What does all this mean? It means that in sugar we are now competing with all the world, and that the sugar business contains little or no margin, and that to succeed in it every device suggested by modern economy must be availed of. Sugars must be bought and sold quickly and correctly, and at a minimum of expense; disputes must be quickly settled by arbitration; abuses must be settled by authority; new, good methods must be brought out, and old, bad ones rejected; and modern experience shows that this can be best done by an Exchange.[335]

Freret's graceful Beaux Arts design featured triptych walls in front and rear, large windows, a landmark clock in the pediment, and a skylight atop a sixty-five-foot-high dome supported by four fluted Ionic columns within the main hall. The Louisiana Sugar Exchange marked the heart of the Sugar District, in function and location, just as the New Orleans Cotton Exchange connoted the center of the Cotton District—the main difference being that the former operated among its crop's professional, industrial, warehousing, and transportation sectors, while the latter's neighbors were exclusively professionals. Members circulating around the Sugar Exchange in its early days lived in a world of sugar: there were sugar and molasses warehouses in almost every direction, steamships and freight trains unloading and loading the commodities in various forms, cooperages and mixing shops, "The Brokers' Charm" Saloon at 35 (now 335) North Front, and even a small triangular "Sugar Park" sandwiched among Bienville, North Front, Conti, and Wells, a site once used to dump old sugar machinery until the city and the Exchange had it landscaped. Acres of sugar barrels covered the ground, punctuated by itinerant clusters of weighers, samplers, and merchants going about their tasks. Laborers loaded barrels of the commodity in various stages of production on and off steamships and schooners docked along the river.

That the Sugar District coalesced around 1870 is supported by statistics on sugar businesses located within or near its riverside confines. These data are recorded in the business sections of the annual city directories and were tabulated by the author starting with data in 1861. Although the sugar landing/Sugar District comprised only about 1 percent of the land area of New Orleans' built environment, about 35 percent of the city's sugar businesses had addresses there in 1861 and 1869, representing a fairly intense concentration of firms. By 1882, that relative concentration increased to 45 percent, and by 1892, fully 62 percent of those sugar businesses listed in the New Orleans city directory had addresses in the Sugar District. The percentage of all New Orleans' sugar entities—brokers, dealers, factors, firms, wholesalers, importers, growers, suppliers, machinists, and operators of refineries, mills, and evaporators—located in the Sugar District would vary from about 45 percent to 60 percent from the 1880s to 1920s before finally tailing off during the depression. In absolute numbers, the Sugar District counted an average of thirty-nine entities dedicated to sugar (many of which also worked with molasses) in its peak turn-of-the-century years of 1890-1920, a time when the entire city had a mean of seventy such firms. Data representing sugar professionals only (brokers, factors, dealers, and others, excluding industrial entities) are fairly similar to the above patterns.

Within those professions, it is interesting to note that some were far more likely than others to settle in the Sugar District to do business. Sugar brokers, for example, were big fans of the district: an average of 77 percent of their ranks had district addresses between 1881 and 1921. Sixty percent of those professional firms listed under the heading of "Sugar and Molasses" in the city directories also called the Sugar District home in those years. But one profession eschewed the locale: only 13 percent of those identifying themselves as sugar factors operated in the Sugar District; the majority worked across Canal Street in the Central Business District, particularly in the vicinity of the Cotton District. This may indicate that these professionals identified themselves by function first and by crop second, and because the majority of their factor colleagues worked in the CBD, perhaps they had no inclination to relocate to the wharves of the old city. Sugar factors, of whom there were rarely more than three in the Sugar District and a dozen in the entire city, disappeared entirely as a profession in the early 1930s, about a decade before the last of their cotton-dedicated colleagues found new callings.

The Sugar District's most salient constituents, the Planters Sugar Refining Company (1881) and the Louisiana Sugar Refining Company (1884), built their refineries almost concurrently with the Sugar Exchange during the second quarter of the 1880s. The two new refineries reflected the consolidation of sugar processing from numerous rural sugarhouses to a few major urban refineries, the beginning of a scientific and technological revolution

329. Drastically modernized into a truck-loading dock in the 1950s, this block was refurbished with a more fitting exterior motif in 1987 and is now home to theme restaurants and retail shops. To the extent that this building retains its original parts, it is the only major structure ever to stand on this block, which was subdivided, sold, and developed all within 1866-67. *Vieux Carré Survey,* Binder for Square 5B.
330. Estimate based on *Sanborn Fire Insurance Map* (1876).
331. Louis Bush, *Louisiana Sugar Bowl,* February 19 and April 22, 1880, as quoted by Heitmann, *The Modernization of Louisiana Sugar Industry,* 95.
332. Sitterson, *Sugar Country,* 299-300.
333. "The Sugar Exchange: Formal Opening of the Beautiful Building," *New Orleans Times-Democrat.*
334. Ibid.
335. Address by J. Dymond, "The Sugar Exchange: Formal Opening of the Beautiful Building," *New Orleans Times-Democrat,* 3, columns 3-5.

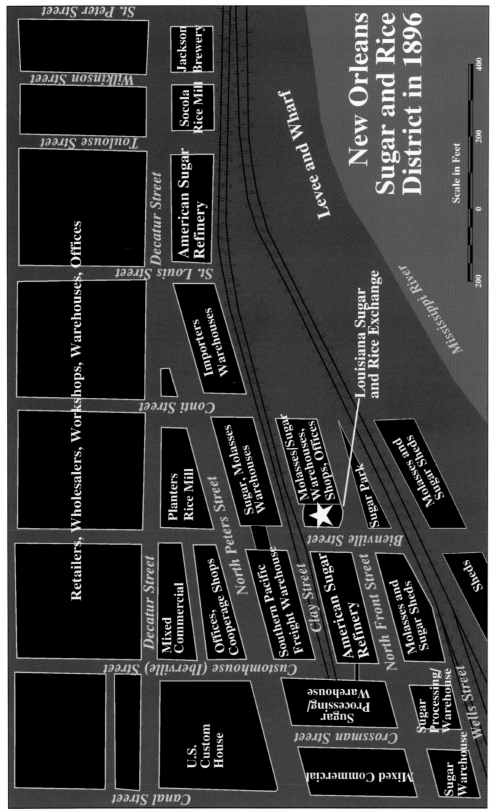

New Orleans Sugar and Rice District in 1896

St. Peter Street

Wilkinson Street

Toulouse Street

Decatur Street

St. Louis Street

Conti Street

Decatur Street

Customhouse (Iberville) Street

Crossman Street

Canal Street

Jackson Brewery

Socola Rice Mill

American Sugar Refinery

Importers Warehouses

Planters Rice Mill

Sugar, Molasses Warehouses

Molasses/Sugar Warehouses, Shops, Offices

Molasses and Sugar Sheds

Mixed Commercial

Offices, Shops Cooperage

Southern Pacific Freight Warehouse

American Sugar Refinery

Molasses and Sugar Sheds

Sheds

Sugar Processing/Warehouse

Sugar Processing/Warehouse

U.S. Custom House

Mixed Commercial

Sugar Warehouse

Retailers, Wholesalers, Workshops, Warehouses, Offices

North Peters Street

Clay Street

North Front Street

Wells Street

Bienville Street

Sugar Park

Louisiana Sugar and Rice Exchange

Levee and Wharf

Mississippi River

Scale in Feet

400 200 0 200

Former Sugar and Rice District in 1989

4.

3.

2.

1.

From the epicenter of the Louisiana sugar industry to a staging ground for the tourism industry: the Sugar District in 1896, based on Sanborn Fire Insurance Maps of that year, compared to a 1989 aerial photograph of the same area. There are only four remnants of the industrial side of the Sugar District: (1) the 111 Rue Iberville Building, built in 1884; (2) a ca.-1900 addition to the Old Filter House, now in ruin; (3) four well-preserved row structures on North Front Street; and (4) the former Importers Bonded Warehouse (1873), restored in 1987 and now a popular retail strip. While the industrial Sugar District is almost all gone, the professional offices of sugar men are mostly preserved on the blocks of North Peters and adjacent streets. *Map and analysis by author; aerial image courtesy U.S. Geological Survey*

This detail of Currier & Ives' *The City of New Orleans* (1885) shows the Sugar District in its heyday, on the batture of the French Quarter. Some liberties were taken in this perspective, but all the major components of this busy industry cluster are depicted: the spacious landing lined with steamships; the saw-tooth rooflines of the sugar and molasses sheds; the chimneyed refineries of the Louisiana Sugar Refinery; the Louisiana & Texas Railroad tracks; the sugar merchants' office buildings on North Peters; even the Louisiana Sugar Exchange, near the base of the lower smokestack. Unlike the Cotton District, which comprised a cluster of marketing professionals, the Sugar District was the home of professional offices as well as storage, refinery, transportation, and marketing facilities. Both blue and white collars worked here. *American Memory Panoramic Maps Collection, Library of Congress*

Ground view of the Sugar District in 1890, looking up Wells Street and North Front Street from Sugar Park (right foreground) toward the facilities of the Louisiana Sugar Refinery (later American Sugar Refinery). The sugar and molasses sheds at left, built by Francis Fleitas throughout the area in the early 1870s, formed a distinctive signature of the Sugar District for decades. The Louisiana Sugar and Rice Exchange is just out of view on the extreme right. Every building in this scene is gone with the exception of the high-rise sandwiched between the two taller structures at center, now called the 111 Rue Iberville Building. *Craig*

Bird's-eye view of the Sugar District in 1890, looking down Clay Street and North Front Street toward Jackson Square. At bottom left is the Louisiana Sugar and Rice Exchange; most other structures in the mid- and foreground of this scene served as sugar sheds, refineries, warehouses, or offices. Note Sugar Park at lower right and St. Louis Cathedral at upper left. The photographer captioned this scene as "Birds-Eye View From Top Of Custom House," but in fact it was taken from the upper stories of the Louisiana Sugar Refinery (later American Sugar Refinery) Filter House, possibly from its chimneys. *Craig*

Bird's-eye view of the Sugar District around 1906, viewed from the American Sugar Refinery Filter House at the intersection of North Front and Bienville Street, looking toward Jackson Square. *Detroit Publishing Company, Library of Congress*

The American Sugar Refining Company's processing facilities in the Sugar District dominated the skyline of the upper French Quarter in turn-of-the-century New Orleans. These scenes were taken from the Maritime (Hennen) Building on Carondelet Street, looking toward the Mississippi River, around 1905. *Detroit Publishing Company, Library of Congress*

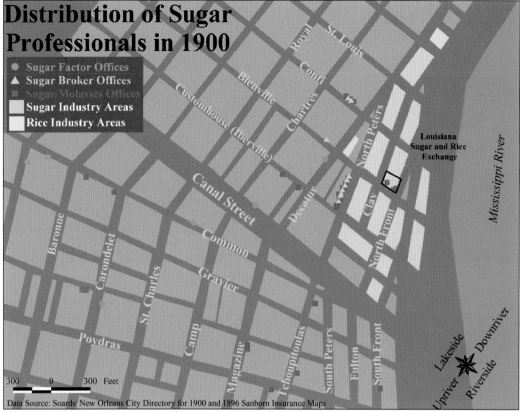

Distribution of Sugar Professionals in 1900

- ● Sugar Factor Offices
- ▲ Sugar Broker Offices
- ■ Sugar/Molasses Offices
- Sugar Industry Areas
- Rice Industry Areas

300   0   300 Feet

Data Source: Soards' New Orleans City Directory for 1900 and 1896 Sanborn Insurance Maps

Distribution of sugar factor, broker, and sugar/molasses offices in 1899-1900, based on the city directory of 1900, and sugar and rice industry areas, based on the Sanborn Fire Insurance Maps of 1896 and 1908. Note the cluster of offices on the second block of North Peters and in the Louisiana Sugar and Rice Exchange. Sugar offices were more dispersed throughout the French Quarter and the Central Business District than were cotton offices, which were entirely in the CBD. *Map and analysis by author. Points may be within one to two doors of actual locations; multiple offices on upper floors of same building are represented by adjacent points.*

(1880-1910) in sugar production,[336] and the increasing demand for refined white sugar rather than the more easily produced brown sugar. The Planters Refinery, occupying the block between St. Louis and Toulouse on the riverside of Decatur, changed the skyline of the aging city (barely 400 feet from Jackson Square) with its four smokestacks and various tanks and kilns. Three blocks upriver, across Bienville Street from the Exchange, was the Louisiana Sugar Refinery (1883-84), "the largest and most substantial structure in the city" and "the largest sugar refinery in the South,"[337] built by Alexander Muir for $300,000. Its Filter House was the only ten-story building in the city, rising to 120 feet and exceeded at the time only by its 130-foot smokestack—all just a few blocks from Jackson Square. The two companies competed fiercely for two years, then colluded in 1886.[338] In 1891, the refineries came into the possession of the newly incorporated American Sugar Refining Company (ASRC), a firm of the Sugar Trust dominated by America's first family of sugar, the Havemeyers, and a player that would have a significant impact on the local sugar economy and the Sugar District for years to come.[339] The

company erected a second Filter House in 1899-1900 across from the Sugar Exchange at the corner of North Front and Bienville. It was the second-highest structure (162 feet) ever to exist within the official confines of the French Quarter.[340] These two refineries linked with their neighboring warehouses by means of elevated barrel conveyors at the second-story level, adding another distinguishing physical characteristic to the landscape of the Sugar District. Given that the era of 1881-84 saw all lots acquired and major construction activity for both refineries and the Exchange, these years may be seen as the "Golden Age" of New Orleans' Sugar District. By the mid-1880s, about 65 percent of the total land area in the core blocks of the Sugar District, bounded by Crossman, North Peters, Toulouse, and the river, were dedicated to sugar and sugar-related business, up from 40 percent a decade earlier.[341] Another building boom occurred in 1906, when the American Sugar Refining Company replaced its six-year-old Filter House with a new fourteen-story structure (though not as lofty, at 150 feet) and constructed a three-story power house and twin 50-foot boiler stacks.[342]

Sugar Grinding

"The cane is cut and hauled in mule carts to the sugar mills, where it is thrown on a cane carrier and conveyed to a set of huge rollers, turned by steam, through which the cane passes, and the juice is extracted by pressure. The juice, a milkish white liquid, with a peculiar sweet odor, is purified with lime and the fumes of sulphur, is then boiled in a series of mammoth open iron kettles, until it reaches the granulating point. It is then conveyed to large vats, called coolers, and left there to cool and granulate into sugar. After a few days this mass of cooked juice, which has become sugar is carried to the purgery and packed into hogsheads of a thousand pounds each. After draining off in the purgery all the molasses mixed in with the sugar the article is ready for the market as brown sugar. White sugars are produced by several different processes in refineries, and all the large plantations have machinery for producing such grades of sugar."

—James S. Zacharie, 1885 (*The New Orleans Guide and Exposition Handbook*, 124)

The square blocks between now-erased Crossman Street and present-day Iberville predated the main blocks of the batture by two decades and were home to general port businesses in those years, such as ice storage, cooperage, and lumbering. But they were eventually absorbed into the Sugar District in 1888-91, when two substantial multistory brick-and-timber warehouses were erected on the small blocks. Owned by the Louisiana Sugar Refinery until 1891 and the American Sugar Refining Company as late as 1943, these impressive brick structures were known in their latter years as the Maloney "Block X" Warehouse[343] and the Douglas Public Service "Block Y" Warehouse. The Maloney Warehouse adjoined a much different edifice, in both form and function, at the corner of North Peters and Iberville: the main office of the American Sugar Refining Company (132 North Peters), a two-story building of Egyptian and Greek Revival style from which the domineering corporate presence at the Sugar District was managed. The Southern Pacific Company, another major corporate player in the area, constructed in 1888-90s two block-long three-story warehouses built of ship timbers and ornate brickwork with Romanesque arches and Greek Revival details. Paralleling the railroad tracks and North Peters Street from Iberville all the way to Conti, the warehouses were used for storing sugar and molasses and were connected by an elevated conveyor. By 1896, at least 80 percent of the Sugar District (bounded by Crossman, North Peters, Toulouse, and the river) was occupied by sugar and sugar-related industries, almost a quarter more acreage than 1885 and double the size of 1876. It would remain at this level into the 1910s.[344]

The marketing activities of another Louisiana crop, rice from the southwestern prairies, settled in this vicinity almost concurrently with the sugar industry. A. Maureau operated the New Orleans Rice Depot at 43 North Peters between Customhouse and Bienville as early as 1870, while Isaac Levy's Rice Mill functioned one

336. Begnaud, 44-45, and Heitmann, *Scientific and Technological Change*, ii. The initial milling and subsequent processing steps, in which the raw cane was crushed to separate the cane juice from the *bagasse* (woody matter), were still carried out in rural sugar mills, since it would have been impractical to haul cane to the city. The refining process, however, was concentrated in the city.

337. *New Orleans Daily Picayune*, and Elstner, stored in *Vieux Carré Survey*, Binder for Square 3A.

338. Eichner, 81-82.

339. The New York-based American Sugar Refinery Company became the New Jersey-based American Sugar *Refining* Company in 1891 as a result of litigation by the State of New York against the company's monopolistic status.

340. Works Progress Administration, and Russell Wright. The latter source records the height as 196 feet. The highest present-day structure in the "official" French Quarter (that is, excluding the Canal Street blocks) is the annex to the Monteleone Hotel.

341. This estimate is based on *Sanborn Fire Insurance Map* (1885).

342. Works Progress Administration.

343. "In digging the foundations [for the structure later known as the Maloney Warehouse,] the workmen came in contact with the timbers of an old wharf built 60 years ago when the river was a half mile West of where it is at present. The timbers are 5 feet beneath the surface and are yet comparatively sound." *Daily States*, December 19, 1888, as quoted in *Vieux Carré Survey*, Binder for Square 2. Note: the "half mile" estimate is an exaggeration; the river was originally no more than a few hundred feet west of this spot.

344. This estimate is based on *Sanborn Fire Insurance Map* (1896 and 1908). The percentage reflects those structures specifically identified as sugar related; actual percentage may be higher.

block down in the 1880s. Angelo Socola, one of the founders of the state's rice industry, owned the Louisiana Rice Depot on the corner of Decatur and Toulouse in the 1870s. Socola was also president of the Louisiana Rice Exchange (46 Decatur), founded a full decade before the sugar men organized their exchange.[345] In 1889, the Sugar Exchange expanded to include this increasingly important crop, and was thence known as the Louisiana Sugar and Rice Exchange. With rice not as extensively grown and not nearly as industrially intensive, its marketing was secondary to sugar in the Sugar District, though many merchants and workers tended to both commodities.

While both industries benefited from the Sugar District's prime downtown-riverside location, the major drawback of the locale was its limited space. Even in the district's boom days, not all sugar refineries were located there; in 1881, for example, four refineries were scattered along the wharves of Faubourg St. Mary. The American Sugar Refining Company grew to dominate the local sugar scene in general and the Sugar District in particular in the 1890s, crowding out space for expansion and competition. This would be part of a series of intertwined events that would eventually eliminate the sugar industry from the Sugar District.

Decline of the Sugar District
In the 1910s, a series of events undercut the geographical and economic advantages of the Sugar District and the health of the Louisiana sugar industry on which it depended. First, the American Sugar Refining Company built its state-of-the-industry Chalmette Sugar Refinery (1909-12 and expanded periodically) in the spacious semirural locale of Arabi in St. Bernard Parish. The fourteen-story complex, with its own docking and railroad facilities, a 6-million-gallon-a-day filtering plant, and a total annual capacity of 600,000 tons of sugar, nudged the fulcrum of the sugar processing industry from the crowded Sugar District on the French Quarter batture to the semirural riverside of St. Bernard Parish. At about the same time, competing refineries, such as the Colonial Sugars holding in Gramercy acquired by the Cuban-American Sugar Company, challenged the supremacy of the ASRC in the region. Second, the year 1912 saw the beginning of a decline in Louisiana sugar that would last for over two decades. Mosaic disease and root rot struck; late spring frosts and heavy or insufficient rainfall took their toll; and prices dropped after World War I. Crops of 300,000 tons per year, achieved regularly in Louisiana in the early 1900s, were reached only twice between 1912 and the 1930s. In 1926, the worst year, planters harvested a crop one-eighth the size of the record-breaking 1904 yield: less than 50,000 tons compared to almost 400,000.[346] Increasing costs and decreasing yields reduced the number of raw sugar factories in rural parishes from 300 in 1900 to only 54 in 1926. These sugar-producing parishes suffered economically and passed it on to the Sugar District, which was already feeling the impact of the Chalmette refinery.

Third, in 1913, Congress passed the Underwood-Simmons Bill to reduce and eventually eliminate duties on sugar imports by 1916. Bitterly opposed by the sugar lobby, the threat of "free sugar" was rescinded a few years later to avert a sugar shortage caused by the war. Nevertheless, the bill arrested investment in the local industry and led to more shutdowns and reinvestments in other enterprises. The issue of sugar duties also characterized the increasingly bitter feud between the growers and the Sugar Trust, the former supporting all import tariffs but the latter favoring a reduction in tariffs on raw sugar and an increase in those on refined sugar, for obvious reasons of self-interest. Growers accused the Trust of price exploitation in their handling of competing Cuban sugarcane and processing facilities in New York City, and of striving to destroy the Louisiana and Texas sugar industries for access to cheaper imports. The hostility came to a head in 1914, when the State of Louisiana filed suit to cancel the license of the American Sugar Refining Company—*the* major player in the Sugar District—to do business in the state, on the grounds of monopolization. One of the complaints against the ASRC was its attempt "to keep other refiners from buying in the New Orleans market"[347]—a reference to its domination of the Sugar District. Impatient with the court system, irate planters took their case to the legislature, which, in June 1915, declared sugar refining to be a public utility subject to the control of the state. Fueled in part by a national antitrust sentiment, the issue pitted not only Southern growers against a Northern trust but rural Louisiana against urban New Orleans, which stood to lose if this major corporate player (and the merchants and laborers who depended on it) was held to what it claimed to be uncompetitive pricing policy. The grievances were eventually resolved through compromises between the growers and the ASRC, and the ouster suit was withdrawn, but the controversy further jolted the status quo in the Sugar District.[348]

World War I provided temporary relief from the rocky times in Louisiana sugar, as increased demand and rolled-back free-sugar bills coincided with bumper crops and led to a brief resurgence in the industry. But in the streets of New Orleans, the damage was done. In the latter 1910s, the number of sugar businesses in the city as a whole and in the Sugar District started to decline, having peaked at over eighty in the city and over forty in the District around the war years. The two American Sugar Refining plants—the former Planters and Louisiana Sugar refineries—were sold off in 1917 and 1920, respectively,[349] and partially demolished in the 1920s, as sugar was processed instead at the Chalmette refinery. The saw-tooth sheds first built by Francis B. Fleitas in 1870 were quickly antiquated and removed, as new wharves and tracks severed the old landing's direct access to the river. Price collapses in 1920-21 further exacerbated the postwar decline, and the consistently disastrous crops of 1923-28 led to large-scale abandonment of numerous old sugar plantations (many of which were damaged by the Great Flood of 1927) and an exodus of black laborers to better lives elsewhere. As quickly as it had risen in the 1870s and 1880s, the Sugar District had come apart at the seams by the late 1920s and early 1930s. Government involvement in agriculture and in crop prices in this era eliminated the role of many local players in the sugar industry, while the congressional decision in 1933 to end the import tariffs that had protected Louisiana sugar since 1803 further altered the traditional structure of the industry.[350] Competition from Western sugar-beet production also shook Louisiana sugar, making it about as productive in the early 1930s as it was fully eighty years earlier, when it produced 200,000 tons of cane sugar for a much smaller nation. Louisiana's share of the national market fell from 11 percent around 1900 to only 4.5 percent in 1937.[351] These trends were felt strongly in the Sugar District. Brokers, factors, and sugar and molasses firms almost all completely disappeared from its buildings in the early 1930s, remaining at no more than two or three firms into the 1960s. In 1937, the American Sugar Refining Company Office still operated at North Peters and Iberville, but its refineries were completely gone from the district and its sugar and molasses warehouses were now general storage warehouses. The Louisiana Sugar and Rice Exchange sold its property and ornate building to the Construction and General Laborers for $13,520 on August 12, 1941, after which it was operated—somewhat ironically—as a meeting hall for the Laborers Local Union 689.[352]

Disappearance of the Sugar District
In the decades following the depression, a walk through the former Sugar District would have revealed an industrial landscape of aging brick storage structures interspersed with parking lots and brewing and bottling facilities, namely those of Coca-Cola at the Canal Street end of the batture and Jax Beer at the Jackson Square end. Long metal sheds and a series of railroad tracks divorced the river from the batture. In 1946, a city ordinance excluded all blocks bounded by Iberville, Decatur, St. Peter, and the river from Vieux Carré Commission jurisdiction—essentially defining them out of the French Quarter—leading to the alteration or demolition of many old Sugar District structures. In this era, the Sugar Park created in the early days of the Louisiana Sugar Exchange was eliminated when an electrical transmission tower was located there, and the remnant ten-story shell of the Old Filter House came down.[353] Perhaps the biggest blow to the historical memory of the Sugar District came in 1963, when the former Louisiana Sugar and Rice Exchange Building, in ruinous condition, was sold and promptly demolished. By the time the State Supreme Court nullified the 1946 ordinance and returned the riverside area to Vieux Carré Commission control (1964), the former Sugar District had lost much of its form.

These were also the years when the highly controversial Riverfront Expressway (Interstate Route 310) was in its planning phase; the former Sugar District was slated for radical change as a key portion of the route designed to connect the Mississippi River Bridge with the main Interstate 10 trunk at Elysian Fields. The elevated expressway would have emerged from a tunnel near the "Block Y" Warehouse and skimmed over the former district, past Jackson Square and the French Market, and up Elysian Fields Avenue. The plan, which threatened the historic heart and soul of the city and helped launch the preservationist movement, was finally rejected in 1969.

Abandonment of the expressway plan opened up a wide range of land-development proposals for the former Sugar District and the rest of the French Quarter riverfront, few of which came to fruition.[354] The 1970s saw the

345. *Vieux Carré Survey*, Binder for Square 5-D, and Waldo, *Visitor's Guide*, 169.
346. Sitterson, *Sugar Country*, 343.
347. Ibid., 351.
348. Ibid., 348-52.

349. *Vieux Carré Survey*, Binder for Squares 5C and 3A.
350. Shea, abstract.
351. Dalton, 167-68.
352. *Vieux Carré Survey*, Binder for Square 4A.
353. Russell Wright.
354. See Tulane University School of Architecture, *New Orleans and the River* and *Study of the Vieux Carré Waterfront*.

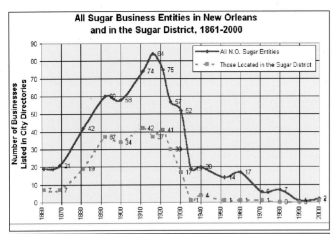

All Sugar Business Entities in New Orleans and in the Sugar District, 1861-2000

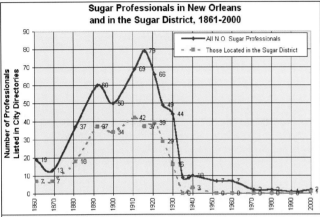

Sugar Professionals in New Orleans and in the Sugar District, 1861-2000

New Orleans Sugar Brokers, Factors, and Firms Located in the Sugar District, ~1861-1960

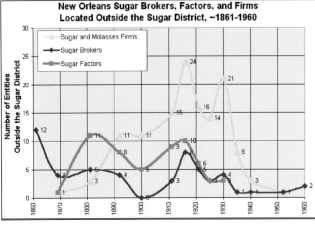

New Orleans Sugar Brokers, Factors, and Firms Located Outside the Sugar District, ~1861-1960

One way to retrace the rise and fall of an industry district is by tracking business listings in annual city directories.

Top: Total number of all sugar-related businesses in New Orleans from 1861 to 2000, and those with addresses within or very near to the Sugar District (bounded by present-day Iberville, Decatur, St. Peter, and the river).

Second: *Professional* sugar entities in the city and in the Sugar District. These data include mostly brokers, sugar and molasses firms, and factors, and also some wholesalers, dealers, importers, and grower representatives, but not operators of refineries, mills, evaporators, or suppliers. Both graphs clearly show the boom days of the Sugar District lasting from about 1870 to 1930.

Bottom Two: These graphs show the numbers of the three major professional sugar occupations—sugar and molasses firms, brokers, and factors—by the location of their businesses inside or outside the Sugar District. Broker and sugar and molasses firms generally operated within the District, though the latter group branched out in the latter years. Sugar factors stayed away from the Sugar District.

Sources: These data were categorized and counted by the author from the Gardner's, Soards', and Polk's New Orleans City Directories of 1861, 1869, 1881, 1892, 1900, 1911, 1916, 1921, 1925, 1930, 1935, 1940, 1952, 1960, 1971, 1980, 1990, and 2000. Entities had to describe themselves as sugar related to be considered as sugar businesses and had to be listed under "Sugar," "Brokers-Sugar," or "Brokers-Food Products" in the business sections of the city directories. (Hence, modern-day commodities brokers would not have been counted unless they described themselves as sugar brokers in the city directory.) Because of changing terminology, some firms were combined with similar entities to allow for tabulations across many decades. The vast majority of cases was easily categorizable in terms of occupation and location; less than 5 percent involved some difficulty in grouping. *Analysis by author*

Last moments: The demolition of the former Louisiana Sugar and Rice Exchange in 1963, shortly after these Historic American Buildings Survey (HABS) photographs were taken, removed an architecturally and historically significant structure from what was once a major industrial district and is now a concrete no-man's land. The elegant columns and skylight of the interior would have made a spectacular public space today. *Historic American Buildings Survey (HABS), American Memory Collection, Library of Congress*

first breath of appreciation for and preservation of the uncharming old sugar structures, but also more destruction. The seven-story edifice built by the ASRC in 1884 was restored as an office building in 1971 by Curtis & Davis and named 111 Rue Iberville; this handsome white brick high-rise is now the premier landmark of the sugar era, though no sign describes its significance and no walking tours ponder its working days. Also in 1971, the Jax Brewing Company Warehouse—originally the Southern Pacific Railroad Sugar and Molasses Warehouse, the huge brick-and-timber structure on North Peters—burned in a ferocious blaze apparently ignited by a nearby railroad car that had exploded. The twin of this warehouse had succumbed to the same fate in 1939.[355] The nearby Douglas Public Service "Block Y" Warehouse and Maloney "Block X" Warehouse, both built in the boom days of the district and later distinctive for their supersized advertisement messages painted on the brickwork, met their fate by a Mardi Gras fire and a wrecking ball, respectively, in 1975 and 1979. The adjacent American Sugar Refining Company Office, local headquarters for the Sugar District's heaviest hitter, fell for the Canal Place complex mall in 1979; a Pottery Barn and Starbucks now occupy the site. The Importers Bonded Warehouse designed by Henry Howard in 1867 and built by 1873 had been drastically modernized into a truck-loading dock in the 1950s, and was renovated in 1987 to resemble its original appearance. It now houses a series of retail outlets and restaurants, with offices on the second floor.[356] If a "district" still exists in the acreage of the old sugar landing, it is now one dedicated to three aspects of the tourism economy: the ambitious riverfront projects of Woldenberg Park, Aquarium of the Americas (1989-90), and adjacent attractions; expansive acres of bleak parking lots punctuated by transmission towers and the occasional relict building from the sugar era; and the numerous theme restaurants and retail shops lining the North Peters/Decatur corridor.

Today, while sugar marketing has long since moved from the port-city scene to the worldwide commodity market tracked by organizations such as the New York Coffee, Sugar, & Cocoa Exchange, most former offices of New Orleans sugar merchants still stand in good condition lakeside of North Peters and on Decatur and intersecting blocks. The merchants are gone, the upper stories are generally vacant, and ground floors house souvenir shops blaring incongruous Cajun music over trinkets hyperbolizing stereotypes of the city: vulgar T-shirts, glassy-eyed lockjawed alligator heads, mass-produced voodoo trinkets, ceramic mammies. Starting in the early 1990s, ubiquitous theme restaurants, with their penchant for "designer folk" ambience, have flocked to this area, making it something of a franchised Bourbon Street. There is no reference to the true historic dedication of this area, with the possible exception of a hand-painted sign for "Public Weighers" on a granite column at 235 North Peters[357] and the word *RICE* (possibly a name) spelled out in bas-relief letters on the pediment of 233 North Peters. Despite the economic shift to this entertainment district—some may argue because of it—this portion of the former Sugar District is structurally alive and well. But across North Peters, in the heart of the Sugar District and the "sugar landing" of antebellum days, only a few landmarks remain. The well-restored 111 Rue Iberville (1884) is the best example, followed by four contiguous late-1860s row buildings that amazingly survived at the corner of North Front and Conti, an island of historical structures surrounded by a sea of parking lots. One of these buildings (335 North Front) housed "The Brokers' Charm" Saloon, a wateringhole frequented by 1880s sugar men. There is also a ruinous brick remnant of a ca.-1900 addition to the Filter House standing across from the now-vacant corner of North Front and Bienville, where the graceful Sugar Exchange once stood. To the extent that the Henry Howard warehouse contains original structural components—original interior walls and ceilings may be seen inside Bookstar—this too may be considered a survivor of the Sugar District. But one element from the heyday of New Orleans' sugar economy is structurally and economically intact. The Chalmette refinery in Arabi, built by the American Sugar Refining Company in 1909-12, which later became Amstar and, until 2001, Tate & Lyle North American Sugars, Inc. (makers of Domino's Sugar), dramatically breaks the skyline of St. Bernard Parish with its fourteen stories of intricate brickwork, smokestacks, and industrial atmosphere. To a degree, the architecture and atmosphere of New Orleans' turn-of-the-century Sugar District survives here on the Mississippi, still on North Peters Street but now in the 7400 block, four miles downriver from one of the Crescent City's most historic industrial districts.

355. Jenkins.

356. *Vieux Carré Survey,* Binder for Squares 5A-5B.

357. The 2000 New Orleans Polk city directory actually lists a sugar brokerage at this address—the last and only one in the former Sugar District. *BellSouth Yellow Pages* has only two sugar entries for the entire metropolitan area: a brokerage/wholesaler in Jefferson Parish and the refinery in Arabi.

Vestiges of the Sugar District *Photographs by author, 1999-2000*

1. The former Sugar District today: brokers' offices in the foreground, now professional offices; the Filter House ruins behind them; and the white brick 111 Rue Iberville Building. Looming behind is the early-1980s high-rise hotel that is currently the Wyndham.

2. Broker offices on North Front Street, built in the late 1860s and now standing alone in a desert of parking lots. "The Brokers' Charm" Saloon operated here (335 North Front) in the 1880s, at a time when the Louisiana Sugar and Rice Exchange stood a few doors down. These well-preserved structures, which remarkably survived the gradual demolition of the Sugar District, are now professional offices.

3. The parking lot in the foreground was once occupied by the Planters Refinery, which, with its four smokestacks and various tanks and kilns, changed the skyline of the aging city barely 400 feet from Jackson Square. In 1891, the refinery was taken over by the American Sugar Refining Company, a corporation which would have significant impact on the local sugar economy and the Sugar District in later years. The building in the midground is the former Importers Bonded Warehouse, designed by Henry Howard and built in 1873, and later heavily modernized into a truck-loading dock by the 1950s. It was returned to a more traditional appearance in 1987, when it was renovated into a tourist retail-and-restaurant strip.

4. Remains of the ca.-1900 addition to the Old Filter House.

5. 111 Rue Iberville Building, built in 1884 by the American Sugar Refining Company as a sugar processing warehouse and restored in 1971 as office space, viewed from the garage of Canal Place. During renovation, some timber beams were found to be "pickled" from spilled molasses.

6. DANGER OPEN SHAFT, reads a sign on a window of the 1884 American Sugar Refining Company structure that is now the 111 Rue Iberville Building. The sign may be a leftover from the latter years of building's sugar-processing days; if so, it is one of the very few textual reminders of the Sugar District remaining in the streetscape.

7. Moonrise over the Mississippi, December 23, 1999. In 1900, the land below was bustling with the processing and marketing of Louisiana sugar. Now, at the end of the 1900s, it is largely devoted to parking for tourists. It is probably inevitable that the French Quarter batture, the only major open land within the confines of the Vieux Carré, will be utilized for something more relevant than auto storage. But it is safe to say that its industrial days are past.

8. This corner at Bienville and North Front was once home to the beautiful Louisiana Sugar and Rice Exchange Building, epicenter of the Sugar District. The Beaux Arts-style structure was built in 1884 and demolished in 1963.

9. The Sugar District was also the Rice District. This turn-of-the-century structure on North Peters Street in the French Quarter once faced the Planters Rice Mill.

10. This sign for public weighers on a building on North Peters Street may reflect a resident from the Sugar District era. The occupant at the time of this 2000 photograph was associated with Tipitina's night club, part of the entertainment scene that took over Decatur and North Peters during the 1990s. The employee inside had no idea what the sign referred to, never having noticed it.

Vestiges
of the
Sugar District

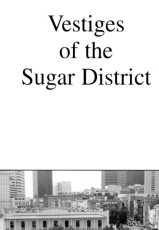

The former Sugar District, viewed from above the river near Jackson Square (far left) in the early 1980s and from the World Trade Center in the mid-1990s (near left). This riverside area, devoted primarily to the buying, selling, shipping, storage, and/or processing of sugar from the 1830s to the 1930s, had been transformed into a warehouse district in the midcentury years and then to a parking and infrastructure zone by end of century. One major change was the removal of riverside sheds for the construction of the Woldenberg Park green space along the river. The former Sugar District occupies the French Quarter's batture, an area that was in the river when the city was founded, formed when sediments were deposited by the shifting Mississippi starting in the late eighteenth century. *1980s photo courtesy Army Corps of Engineers; 1996 photograph by author*

In the turn-of-the-century era, most of New Orleans' sugar brokers worked out of this particular block on North Peters, between Iberville (formerly Customhouse) and Bienville. *Photograph by author, 2000*

The sugar landing, and later the sugar-processing plants of the American Sugar Refining Company, occupied these parking lots a hundred years ago. Last remnants of the industrial era are represented by the 111 Rue Iberville Building (1884, extreme lower right) and the red-brick ruins of a circa-1900 addition to the Old Filter House behind it. *Photograph by author, 2000*

(Center) The American Sugar Refining Company built this refinery in Arabi in 1909-12, helping shift the nucleus of the local sugar-processing industry from North Peters Street in the French Quarter to semirural St. Bernard Parish, which still exhibited its plantation roots at the time (note the Three Oaks plantation house, built in 1831 and demolished in 1965, at right). The plant was later owned by Amstar and Tate & Lyle North American Sugars, Inc., makers of Domino's Sugar. In 2001, a Florida investment group planned to acquire the brand and the operation. Ironically, the plant is still on North Peters Street, but now on the 7400 block, rather than the 200 block. The impressive brickwork of the massive structure, viewed from the levee in Arabi and from Algiers (bottom), evokes the ca.-1880s processing plants that once dominated the French Quarter riverfront. *Historic image courtesy American Memory Collection, Library of Congress; other photographs by author, 2000*

Newspaper Row

No newspapers circulated in New Orleans until the 1790s, and by the 1990s, the Crescent City, like so many other American cities, was a decidedly one-newspaper town. But in the intervening centuries, especially from the 1830s to the 1950s, New Orleanians enjoyed a wealth of local periodicals—morning and evening newspapers; weeklies and semiweeklies; papers in French, German, Spanish, English, or a combination thereof; papers catering to just about every major segment of the population and many minor ones. In the early years, when French culture (both Creole and foreign) still prevailed throughout the city, most newspaper and periodical offices operated in the *Vieux Carré de la Ville*, principally on Chartres Street. Later, when Americans came to predominate and English became the first language, publishers gradually established their offices in Faubourg St. Mary. By the mid-nineteenth century and lasting into the twentieth century, those offices would form a small but distinct district on Camp Street from Gravier to Poydras, a stretch that would be known as Newspaper Row, described variously as New Orleans' answer to Rue St. Jacques in Paris or Park Row in Manhattan (also known as Newspaper Row).[358] By the 1920s, the fulcrum of the local press drifted up Camp Street toward Lafayette Square and, forty to fifty years later, finally dispersed to a dozen different locations, to address the new suburban communities developing around the Crescent City. In his book, *Early Printing in New Orleans 1764-1810,* Douglas C. McMurtrie observed that the city's typographic history reflected its political history, especially during those years of shifting sovereignty.[359] By examining "typographic geography"—that is, the spatial patterns of newspaper and publishing offices—we see a reflection of the city's physical and demographic development. The historical geography of New Orleans is gleaned to some extent from the distributions of its newspaper offices, as the fulcrum of press and printing offices[360]—like the population and economy of New Orleans—moved from the old city to the up-and-coming Faubourg St. Mary, then uptown and finally off to the suburbs.

Early Newspapers in New Orleans

The French colonial era in New Orleans was in eclipse when, in what happened to be the mother country's last exclusive privilege granted in Louisiana, a merchant named Denis Braud received permission to establish the city's first printing operation.[361] Braud's shop (1764-70), followed by that of Antoine Boudousquié (1777-ca. 1780), printed official Spanish government documents and other items, leaving the isolated colonial outpost starved for the printed word except for imported materials. It was not until 1794 that a nascent printing industry was permanently established and the first newspaper appeared. After lying mostly dormant for three-quarters of a century, journalism and publishing awoke slowly in New Orleans in the late colonial era and then flourished in the early American years. Some papers came and went within a few years; many would hardly be considered newspapers by modern standards, devoting most space not to news articles but to advertisements, announcements, eccentric philosophical essays, and the "occasional flurry of vindictiveness."[362] The newspapers' choice of language, in this polyglot city, revealed the cultural stance of the editor, readership, and all that was printed. Early newspapers were all French, all English, French-English, English-French, or Spanish-English, but in the first quarter of the nineteenth century, French was the key to a larger readership and most publishers responded accordingly. When, from the late 1820s to the Civil War, French and English claimed roughly equal numbers of speakers in the city, the newspapers reflected this fact; after the war, English came to prevail in the spoken and printed word, and French gradually disappeared from both.[363] The bilinguals, which predominated in the antebellum era, generally kept the two languages in separate sections of the paper, each under its own masthead and each often containing unique text. One interesting phenomenon was the predominance of foreign French refugees (from France as well as its Caribbean colonies) in the publishing business, who along with Americans contributed more to early Crescent City journalism than the thousands of natives (Creoles) of the city.

The first newspaper in New Orleans, *Moniteur de la Louisiane,* which was also the first in Louisiana and the entire Mississippi Valley, appeared in February or March 1794 and lasted until 1814. Known more for notices, documentations, and quirky proclamations than for news reporting and editorials, the *Moniteur* came into being during the Spanish colonial era but was published in French and staffed in part by foreign French refugees. The *Moniteur* was the only paper of the Spanish colonial era, and was joined on parlor tables and saloons by New Orleans' only French-colonial-era newspaper, *Le Télégraphe,* which started during the very brief period between France's repossession of Louisiana from Spain in November 1803 and official turnover of the colony to the United States in December of that year. *Le Télégraphe,* which was also partially staffed by French refugees, recorded these historic events and published its items in both French and English, symbolic of the changing times. In the first year of American New Orleans (1804), the city's first significant English-language paper, a weekly called the *Louisiana Gazette,* went to press. With English speakers the exception and French speakers the rule, the *Gazette* decided to go bilingual in 1817, nearly tripling its circulation. The *Gazette* is also noteworthy in that it introduced the first columnist to the city, Alexis Daudet, who went by the pen name "Feuilleton." Setting the precedent for future generations of columnists, Feuilleton used his column for commentary and philosophy but also to harangue the city for the shortcomings of its municipal services. The *Gazette* ended its run in 1826. *Courier de la Louisiane,* another bilingual publication, started in 1807 and thrived throughout the antebellum period, folding in 1860. A year later, a Spanish-English semiweekly called *El Misisipi* appeared but folded in 1810, the year that another Spanish paper started, *El Mensajero.* In 1809, Jean Le Clerc started *L'Ami des Lois,* which gradually evolved into the famous *L'Abeille de la Nouvelle Orléans* (the *Bee*). Some early papers, like the *Trumpeter* (1811-12) and the *Chronicle* (1818-19), had very brief life spans, and few if any copies survive. In addition to these examples, another ten or so minor periodicals hit the streets of New Orleans in the early 1800s.[364] Another important milestone in this early era of publishing was the appearance, in late 1806, of the *Calendrier de Commerce de la Nouvelle-Orléans* for the year 1807, the first almanac in Louisiana and the first in the lineage of city directories that are still published today and have served as a fundamental source of historical data about New Orleans.[365]

In and Around Chartres Street: The First Newspaper "District," 1790s-1840s

Early newspaper offices and printing shops operated in the upriver/riverside quadrant of the Vieux Carré, with many but not most on Chartres Street. Offices (sometimes located on upper floors) were too few to form a true district, and it is probable that the beat of the newspaper business did not dominant the streetscape as it would elsewhere in later decades. The newspapers set up shop in this area simply because the upper blocks of Chartres Street were the "central business district" of the day. Professionals of various stripes worked here; naturally, publishers in this small and remote city sought to be in the heart of things. Areas downriver or toward the lake were either too residential or completely undeveloped, areas toward the river were too industrial, and Faubourg Ste. Marie was too young a suburb with not yet enough clout. By default, New Orleans' first newspaper "district," if it may be called that, spanned the same few blocks centered around upper Chartres that bankers, lawyers, businessmen, and retailers preferred. (A map of exact newspaper-office locations is difficult to make due to the lack of reliable sources on the very erratic street-address system in early-nineteenth-century New Orleans.) The 1807 *Calendrier de Commerce* listed these five *imprimeurs* in the city:[366]

Newspaper/Periodical (1807)	Editor	Location of Editorial Office
Gazette d'Orléans	Bradford & Anderson	13 Chartres Street
Gazette le Télégraphe	Claude Beleurgey	13 Bourbon Street south
Gazette le Moniteur	J. B. L. S. Fontaine	19 Royal Street north
Gazette la Louisiane	John Mowry	36 Bienville Street
In addition, the printing office of Jean Renard, *Imprimeur de la Ville,* which printed the *Calendrier de Commerce,* was located at 8 Chartres Street.		

Two years later, two more printing companies, owned by Dacqueny and Thierry et Co., opened in the same building at 37 Chartres.[367] In that year, *L'Ami des Lois,* a French and English journal originally issued on a triweekly basis, was started by publisher Jean Le Clerc and, after many convolutions and changes of ownership,

358. McMurtrie, 74-76, and Friends of the Cabildo, vol. 2, 117.

359. McMurtrie, 13.

360. This section examines the geographical distribution primarily of newspaper offices, but also includes the offices of magazine, book, directory, and other publishers, some of which were oriented toward niche markets.

361. One of the earliest extant documents from Braud's press is an extract of King Louis XV's edict, dated April 21, 1764, announcing that he had ceded New Orleans to his Spanish cousin a year and a half earlier (November 3, 1762). McMurtrie, 21-22.

362. Marino, 320.

363. Ibid., 313, 320, and John S. Kendall, 364-65.

364. Marino, 309-21, and Kendall, 363-80.

365. McMurtrie, 78. Directories of residents and listings of census data had been published earlier, such as in 1805.

366. Lafon, *Calendrier,* 75.

367. Lafon, *Annuaire,* 213.

eventually became—in 1827 according to the paper; in 1835 according to historian John S. Kendall—the famous *L'Abeille de la Nouvelle Orléans* (the *New Orleans Bee*). The *Bee* anchored the journalistic presence in the Vieux Carré from the era when this was the most important place in town to the era when progress had faded its glory. Originally located at 94 St. Peter, between Royal and Bourbon, the *Bee* moved its editorial and printing offices in 1830 to the busy corner of Chartres and St. Louis, across the street from Maspero's Exchange, frequented by sugar traders (see page 135). A few years later, it moved again to the block of Chartres between Conti and Bienville, enumerated variously as 63 Chartres, 81 Chartres, and 110 Chartres.[368] It would remain on this block for almost ninety years, for a number of decades at the extant buildings of 323-25 Chartres. The *Bee* played an active role in the politics of the day and the happenings of the city for the rest of the nineteenth century, reporting to all citizens of the community but reflecting the French Creole and foreign French element like no other paper.[369] To the extent that a newspaper district existed in the upper Vieux Carré in this era, the offices of the *Bee* may be considered the node of the district. Its neighbors in the newspaper and periodical business in the late 1830s included the *Louisiana Courier* (80 Chartres), the *Louisiana Advertiser* (around the corner at 41 Bienville), and Benjamin Levy's operation at Chartres and Bienville.[370]

New Orleans' first newspaper "district," home to only handful of publishers and printers from the 1790s to the 1840s, was located in and around upper Chartres Street in the old city. *L'Abeille de la Nouvelle Orléans* (the *New Orleans Bee*), the famous French-language paper that lasted into the early twentieth century, had its office at 323-25 Chartres (four-story green building at center) and other locations on this block for many years. *Photograph by author, 2000*

Benjamin Levy, a Jewish emigrant from New York City, was one of the most important early publishers in New Orleans and a notable industry representative on Chartres Street. Starting with a book and stationery store on Chartres in 1811, Levy became "one of the most active publishers in New Orleans during the period of 1822-41, and was undoubtedly the first important Jewish printer-publisher not only in the South, but probably in the entire country." After utilizing four different offices within a block or so of upper Chartres, Levy "apparently reached a high point of business success in 1825, when he moved his store and printing office . . . to [the] corner of Chartres and Bienville Streets, with the store at the ground floor and the presses on the third floor."[371] Levy published and sold law books, medical books, the influential business journal *The New-Orleans Price-Current and Commercial Intelligencer,* almanacs, and a plethora of pamphlets and the like. (He also made the important contribution of reviving, in 1822, the annual city directory, which had not been published in eleven years. Today, city directories are a vital source of data to historians.) Levy also was an enthusiastic advertiser of literature, calling the attention of New Orleanians to a wide range of reading material and to his shop on Chartres Street. His fortunes and those of the smattering of publishers on Chartres Street diminished during the 1830s and, in 1840, Levy made a significant move from the Chartres/Bienville corner four blocks upriver to the very different scene at Camp and Gravier. He went bankrupt in 1843.

> "For many years the 'Rue de Chartres,' in the old French days the most important street of the city, was to be a popular address with the printers, much as was the Rue St. Jacques in old Paris."
>
> —Douglas C. McMurtrie, 1929 (74-76)

By this time, the rise of the Northern-born American element in the upriver faubourgs had gradually pulled the nucleus of the newspaper and publishing business, as well as other enterprises and the city in general, beyond the confines of the old city. While 100 percent of New Orleans' seven editorial and printing offices were located in the old city in 1809, only 40 percent (of ten) remained there in 1838; the other 60 percent were all in Faubourg St. Mary. The *Herald,* the *Commercial Bulletin,* and the *Merchant* operated at various sites on Magazine Street, while the *True American* was on St. Charles and the religious weekly the *Observer* was on Poydras. Statistical data extracted from annual city directories indicate that, in both relative and absolute numbers, the geographical center of gravity of the New Orleans newspaper and publishing scene marched upriver, from the old city to Faubourg St. Mary, in the mid-1840s (see graphs on page 151). Levy's 1840 move from old Chartres to new Camp was thus symbolic of changing times in the growing and Americanizing city. But it was the Camp Street home of the new morning English-language daily, the *Picayune,* that would form the nucleus of New Orleans' new newspaper district, "Newspaper Row," in the booming American sector of the city.

Newspaper Row, 1850s-1920

Volume 1, number 1 of the *Picayune,* published by F. A. Lumsden and G. W. Kendall, hit the cold, rainy streets of New Orleans on January 25, 1837, selling for a *picayune,* the Spanish silver coin worth one-sixteenth of a dollar. The proprietors first set up shop in a twelve-by-fourteen-foot room at 38 Gravier Street, then relocated a few months later to slightly more spacious quarters on 74 Magazine. Before completing its first year, the operation moved once again, this time to a solid granite structure at 72 Camp Street, where it was the only newspaper operation on that street (although five other papers and journals functioned within a few blocks).[372]

On this spot on Camp Street, New Orleans' most famous newspaper would not only prosper for more than eighty years but would attract colleagues and competitors to its flanks, forming a true district of the press in the Crescent City. The *Picayune* made a name for itself during the Mexican War, which G. W. Kendall covered as a war correspondent, sending back stories to the presses on Camp Street via chartered steamboat and pony express—an innovation the paper had used successfully since 1837 to get scoops from Northeastern papers to the readership prior to the competition. The *Picayune* became the most-quoted paper in America for its stories on the war, assuring its place as a premier journal in this major American city (and frustrating its rival, *L'Abeille,* on Chartres Street in the old city).

On February 16, 1850, a fire destroyed the Picayune office and twenty-two adjacent buildings on both sides of the third block of Camp Street. It was a blessing in disguise: the cleared area allowed the publishers to purchase the lot and construct a custom-made building at 66 Camp to suit the editorial and publishing needs of the growing operation. Builders Jamison and McIntosh finished the handsome four-story Greek Revival structure by late 1850, the first plant erected by a newspaper in the city.

There was no mistaking the office of the *Picayune:* a copper spread-winged eagle was dramatically perched upon the prominent parapet, an ornate iron-lace verandah clung to the second story, and between the third and forth floors were etched the words *THE PICAYUNE* into the granite. The excessive depth of the building from its Camp Street entrance to its rear on Bank Place (now Picayune Place) detracted from the amount of natural light reaching the offices and necessitated the installation of a glass sunlight on the roof. White interior paint reflected the light for the benefit of the editors and typesetters inside. The building was also fitted with a steam elevator, a dumbwaiter, a network of gas jets, and three Hoe cylinder presses powered by a coal-burning steam engine, all of which were made in New Orleans. At this time, the *Picayune* employed its proprietors plus six men in the business office, eight editors, twelve in the press room, up to fifteen in the job shop, and forty in the composing department.[373]

The reputation of the *Picayune* and its state-of-the-art headquarters served to associate this block with the newspaper and publishing business: Within four years, four of the city's fifteen newspapers and periodicals were located on Camp Street, while another seven functioned on nearby streets in Faubourg St. Mary. Transplanted Northerners, especially New Yorkers, controlled many of them.[374] Only three remained in the old city, with one more in the Faubourg Marigny. While a true district had yet to develop on Camp Street, the fulcrum of newspaper publishing in New Orleans had clearly moved from the old city to the suburb of St. Mary, reflective of the fact that New Orleans was growing, Americanizing, and modernizing.

368. John S. Kendall, 368. See also city directories of 1838 (Gibson), 1842 (Pitts & Clarke), and 1854 (Cohen). In the 1860s and 1870s, the *Bee* had its *bureaux* at 83 Chartes and 73 Chartres, respectively.

369. As discussed on pages 115-20, this part of the old city was a mixed American/Creole commercial neighborhood, not nearly as Creole-dominant as people may think but more so than Faubourg St. Mary, and physically closer to the truly Creole-dominant neighborhoods below present-day Jackson Square.

370. *Gibson's Guide and Directory,* 356.

371. Korn, 27, 32.

372. Dabney, *One Hundred Great Years,* 1, 14, 22, 30, and *Gibson's Guide and Directory,* 356.

373. Dabney, 90-91, and Friends of the Cabildo, vol. 2, 116.

374. Chenault and Reinders, 239-40.

Newspaper/ Periodical (1854)	Characteristics	Office Address	Office Location
Balloon	Weekly	24 Commercial Place	Faubourg St. Mary
New Orleans Bee	Morning daily, in French and English	63 Chartres Street	Vieux Carré
New Orleans Commercial Bulletin	Morning daily, in English	37 Gravier Street	Faubourg St. Mary
Crescent	Morning daily	93 St. Charles Street	Faubourg St. Mary
Delta	Morning daily, in English	112 Poydras Street	Faubourg St. Mary
Louisiana Courier	Evening daily, in French and English	24 Customhouse	Vieux Carré
Daily Orleanian	Daily, in French and English	Marigny Buildings, Third District	Faubourg Marigny
Picayune	Morning daily, in English	66 Camp Street	Faubourg St. Mary
New Orleans Price Current	Weekly business paper	51 Camp Street	Faubourg St. Mary
True Delta	In English	103 St. Charles Street	Faubourg St. Mary
German Gazette	Morning daily, in German	31 Poydras Street	Faubourg St. Mary
De Bow's Commercial Review	Monthly	22 Exchange Place	Vieux Carré
New Orleans Medical and Surgical Journal	Bimonthly	6 Carondelet Place	Faubourg St. Mary
Semi-Weekly Creole	Semiweekly	94 Camp Street	Faubourg St. Mary
Southern Organ	Weekly	94 Camp Street	Faubourg St. Mary
Source: *Cohen's New Orleans Directory for 1854,* 296.			

First signs of a cluster of publishing offices on Camp Street appeared during the 1850s, a few years after the industry had migrated across Canal Street to Faubourg St. Mary. Why Camp Street? First, this street, like Chartres in the old city, was as busy as any in mid-nineteenth-century Faubourg St. Mary. The blocks between Gravier and Poydras, where most publishers settled, were centrally located between the uptown faubourgs and the city, while not too close to either the river or the back-of-town. Major banks, hotels, and offices occupied adjacent blocks, followed by City Hall, which, in 1853, relocated to Lafayette Square, only a couple of blocks from this part of Camp Street. In other words, there were no compelling reasons *not* to locate on Camp Street. Probably the main reason *to* locate on Camp Street was the presence of major players in the local newspaper scene, first the *Picayune* and later the *Times-Democrat, Daily States, City Item, Daily News,* and others. The success of the early-comers to Camp Street, who may have selected the site for purely incidental reasons such as building availability or reasonable rent, lured rivals for the simple survivalist instinct to be *in the heart of it all,* especially in a competitive information-dependent business like journalism. Once a critical mass of major newspapers was established on Camp Street, support services such as printers and binders also settled in the area, which reinforced and perpetuated the trend. The convenience of nearby printing facilities and suppliers of all that goes into the publishing process surely made an address on or near Newspaper Row a competitive advantage. It should be noted, however, that a Camp Street address was by no means critical to the success of a newspaper. While it had more newspapers and publishers than any other street for most of the years between the Civil War and World War I, Camp Street never had more than 57 percent of all such offices in the city, averaging about 35 percent between 1870 and 1918.[375] Still, most of the highest-circulating papers called Camp Street and nearby Bank Place and Natchez Alley home.

"In 1891 . . . the *Daily Picayune* had a circulation of 19,000 on weekdays, 30,000 on Sundays[; second] was the *Times-Democrat,* formed by the merger of the *Times* and the *Democrat* in 1881—17,738 on weekdays, 28,480 on Sundays. The *Daily States* was third—12,750 daily, 12,200 Sundays."
—Thomas Ewing Dabney, 1944 (*One Hundred Great Years,* 313-14. At the time, these papers were the "big three" of Newspaper Row, all headquartered on the riverside of Camp Street between Gravier and Poydras.)

375. Based on data from the Edwards and Soards city directories of 1870, 1871, 1872, 1873, 1874, 1875, 1876, 1877, 1878, 1879, 1885, 1890, 1895, 1900, 1906, 1910, 1915, and 1918.

Lower Camp Street in 1890, misidentified by the photographer as "New Orleans Feb 1890 St. Charles St.," viewed from the upper floors of the new Morris Building looking uptown toward St. Patrick's Church (distant center). Most of New Orleans' newspapers, typesetters, printers, and binderies had their offices on these blocks. Newspaper Row was located in the blocks in front of the utility tower straddling Camp Street. *Photographer unknown, New Orleans Views Collection, UNO Special Collections*

View of Camp Street from Newspaper Row (300 block) looking downtown in 1892. The Morris Building, from which the 1890 photograph of Camp Street was captured, is the high-rise in the distance, at the corner of Camp and Canal. *Craig, "Camp Street—Looking North"*

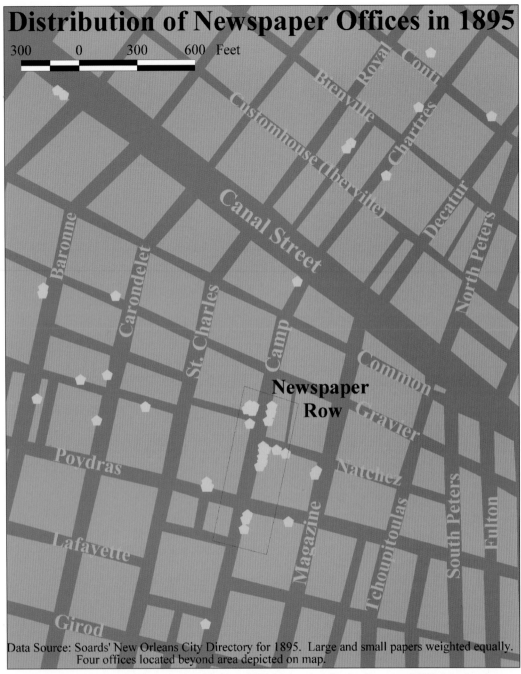

Distribution of Newspaper Offices in 1895

300   0   300   600 Feet

Newspaper Row

Data Source: Soards' New Orleans City Directory for 1895. Large and small papers weighted equally.
Four offices located beyond area depicted on map.

Distribution of newspaper offices in New Orleans in 1894-95, based on the city directory of 1895. It is clear from this distribution that "Newspaper Row," the third, fourth, and fifth blocks of Camp Street, was aptly named. These blocks were also the home base of the city's print shops and binderies. *Map and analysis by author. Points may be within one to two doors of actual locations; multiple offices on upper floors of same building are represented by adjacent points.*

A Stroll Up Newspaper Row

A visitor walking up Camp Street from Canal in the mid-1880s may have sensed the presence of a nearby newspaper district by the scurry of newsboys and the sounds of their singsong sales pitch. To his left, immediately on the riverside corner of Canal, he would have noticed the first print shop on Camp Street, above which was published the *Louisiana Sugar Bowl and Farm Journal.* After passing the City Hotel at the corner of Camp and Common, he would come across a composing and printing shop at 28-30 Camp, indicative of Newspaper Row's related businesses of "job" (contract) printing. The corner shop at Gravier and Camp was also occupied by a hand-printing business (type set by hand), while a job-printer shop with a press room occupied a building a few doors down on Gravier. The third and fourth floors of 56 Camp were utilized by a hand printer and bindery, respectively, while all floors of 58 Camp were occupied by one of the largest-circulating papers in the city, the *Times-Democrat,* an operation running straight back to Bank Place.

The *New Orleans Picayune,* headquartered prominently at 66 Camp (now 326 Camp), had its offices, composing rooms, and press rooms spread out across all floors and a number of adjacent buildings. This was the heart of Newspaper Row: the riverside of Camp Street between Gravier and Poydras, including the rear of those Camp Street structures lining narrow Bank Place (now Picayune Place). Here, newsboys from the competing papers might offer the visitor the latest edition, while the curbside conversations of reporters on the beat or workers on an errand may be overheard. He might hear a reverent reference to Pearl Rivers (born Eliza Jane Poitevent and married into the Nicholson family), owner of the *Picayune* and a beloved citizen, poet, and progressive activist of New Orleans. If the windows were open, the clicking of hand-set type may have been audible, a pleasing sound to be replaced a few years later (1891-92) by the noisy but more efficient Linotype machines.

Directly across the street from the *Picayune* office, at the intersection of Commercial Place with Camp Street, were the offices of the *Louisiana Sugar and Rice Report* (61 Camp) and the *Soards' Business Directory of New Orleans,* an annual publication that is the source of much of these data. Back on the riverside of the street, the building at 68 Camp was home to the *Mascot* (as well as to the *Picayune* at other times), while the rear of the building at 72 Camp, which fronted Bank Place, was the cramped office of the *Evening Chronicle.* Insurance offices and banks, also customers of the local print shops, filled the storefronts and upper floors between and among the publishing establishments.

After passing another composing/binding shop, our visitor would cross Natchez Alley (home to its own cluster of lithographers, paper warehouses, printers, the main office of the *City Item,* and the smaller operation of the *Southwestern Christian Advocate*). There may have been a cluster of paper boys gathered across this narrow alley, at the door of the Newsboys' Home, biding time until the latest edition came off the press by rolling dice, racing each other, or playing ball in the alley. Our visitor would then pass another print shop and the 90 Camp office of the *Daily States,* another major paper. Three more publishing-related shops, plus the *Southwestern Presbyterian,* the *Baptist Advocate,* and the *Orion,* occupied portions of buildings in this block before Poydras Street. Above Poydras, the visitor might notice a number of smaller shops—the influential *German Gazette,* the *New Orleans Christian Advocate,* and *Der Familien Freund* between 108-12 Camp, as well as some other print shops.[376] By the time our friend made it to a park bench at Lafayette Square, he would have had plenty of opportunities to pick up some reading material.

Peak and Decline

Camp Street's glory days as New Orleans' newspaper district peaked in 1890-1910, when as many as twenty of the city's fifty or so publishing-related offices (and almost all of the major ones) were located there, mostly concentrated on the riverside stretch between Gravier and Poydras (Newspaper Row) plus Bank Place and Natchez Alley a few steps away. The tight cluster of aggressive newsmen in this fiercely competitive marketplace made for a bustling and colorful atmosphere, one that sometimes boiled over with political passions and personal vendettas. Brawls, shootouts, and even Wild West-style gunfights, one right outside the office of the *Picayune,* were not unheard of on Newspaper Row.[377] Mostly, though, the antebellum Greek Revival row buildings lining the district were filled with diligent journalists, editors, typesetters, and workers intent on meeting deadlines and surviving in the crowded newspaper market. The streets around Newspaper Row were the domain of newsboys,

---

376. Based on *Sanborn Fire Insurance Map* (1885); *Soards' New Orleans City Directory* (1885); Wilds, 177-82; and sketches of street scenes from various newspaper and directory advertisements depicting this area.
377. Wilds, 107-59.

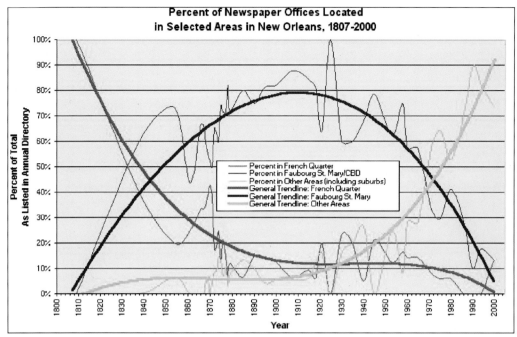

Percent of Newspaper Offices Located in Selected Areas in New Orleans, 1807-2000

Legend:
- Percent in French Quarter
- Percent in Faubourg St. Mary/CBD
- Percent in Other Areas (including suburbs)
- General Trendline: French Quarter
- General Trendline: Faubourg St. Mary
- General Trendline: Other Areas

Percent of all New Orleans newspaper and publishing offices located in the French Quarter, Faubourg St. Mary, and elsewhere, 1807-2000. Because different categorization standards were employed by various directories over the years, year-by-year variation is sometimes wide. However, the general trend is clear: the New Orleans publishing industry moved in the 1840s from the French Quarter to Faubourg St. Mary and then "elsewhere"—primarily the suburbs—by the 1970s. This geographical shift serves as a metaphor for the historical development of the New Orleans metropolitan area. These data include all offices of newspapers and periodicals as listed in the city directories, regardless of circulation. For 1980s-2000, "elsewhere" may include suburban parishes, even though only the Orleans Parish directory was consulted. Analysis by author based on data from Lafon, Gibson, Gardner, Edwards, Soards, and Polk city directories of 1807, 1809, 1838, 1854, 1861, 1866-79, 1885, 1890, 1895, 1900, 1906, 1910, 1915, 1918, 1921, 1925, 1930, 1935, 1940, 1945, 1953, 1958, 1960, 1965, 1971, 1975, 1980, 1986, 1990, 1994, and 2000

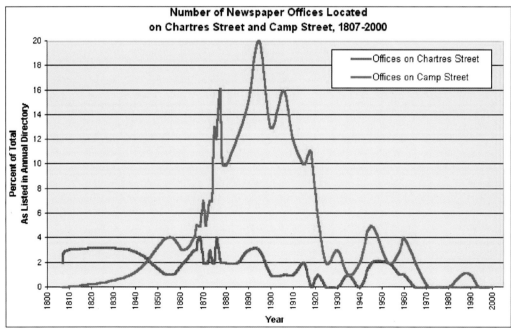

Number of Newspaper Offices Located on Chartres Street and Camp Street, 1807-2000

Legend:
- Offices on Chartres Street
- Offices on Camp Street

Number of newspaper and publishing offices located on New Orleans' two most famous historical publishing streets, Chartres Street and Camp Street, 1807-2000. Wide annual variation is explained mostly by directories' different categorization standards, but the general trend reveals Chartres Street's domination of the tiny publishing industry up to the 1840s, and Camp Street's ("Newspaper Row") domination from the 1840s to around 1920. The *Times-Picayune*'s move to the 300 block of Camp Street in 1837 initiated the era of "Newspaper Row" on that street; its relocation to Lafayette Square in 1919 (which also happened to be on Camp Street) signified the end of the famous publishing district on lower Camp Street. *Analysis by author based on data from the city directories of same years as previous graphic*

most of them orphans, on whom the papers (especially those issued in the evening) depended for distribution before trucks and vending machines did the job. On cold winter nights in the 1860s-80s, some waifs would sleep in the corners of press rooms on Newspaper Row, "huddled together as thick as kittens in a rag basket."[378] The number of street urchins was such that, in 1879, the Society of St. Vincent de Paul and the Sisters of Mercy of St. Alphonsus moved their newsboys' home from the back-of-town to 20 Bank Place (now 324 Picayune Place), directly behind the *Picayune* office, where homeless newsboys were offered the amenities of a school, dormitory, kitchen and chapel tucked among three floors that were also used for warehousing. The home testifies to the round-the-clock intensity of work on Newspaper Row, operating with such bustle that charities relocated there to serve effectively the beneficiaries of their kindness. These years were also the era of domination of Faubourg St. Mary (a term that by this time was antiquated) in the city's publishing industry: about 80 percent of such businesses were located within the historical confines of this former suburb, with another 12 percent hanging on in the French Quarter and the remainder uptown (notably Carrollton) or across the river. The French Quarter and its large Creole populace had long since lost its grip on the city and on the press; by the latter decades of the 1800s, the few news offices still located there were mostly specialized papers with small circulations. In addition to the old-line *L'Abeille*, the French-language *Trait-D'Union*, *L'Opinion*, and *L'Orleanais*, all based in the Quarter in the late 1880s, appealed to the diminishing Creole element, while the *Italo-Americano* published on Decatur Street for the local (mostly Sicilian) immigrant population and the *Daily Crusader*, the "only Republican paper south of the Mason-Dixon Line," came out of Exchange Alley and went to the black community.[379] Except for *L'Abeille*, all shut down after a few years in production.

> Abeille de la Nouvelle Orleans,
> PUBLISHED IN FRENCH,
> IS
> THE OLDEST PAPER IN THE SOUTHWEST.
> CIRCULATES EXTENSIVELY IN THE
> FRENCH AND CREOLE PARISHES OF LOUISIANA.
> IS RECEIVED IN
> FRANCE, MEXICO AND THE WEST INDIES.
> A Very Valuable Medium for Advertising.
> OFFICE, NO. 73 CHARTRES STREET,
> NEW ORLEANS.
> —part of an advertisement for the *New Orleans Bee*, in Waldo, 1879
> (*Illustrated Visitors' Guide*, advertisement section following 224)

While the industry remained geographically stable in the Central Business District, its members opened, closed, changed hands, merged, and bought out each other at a rate almost like Internet startups in the late 1990s. "From the simple operation it had once been, newspaper publication was [becoming] a highly specialized and tremendously costly manufacturing process. Machinery grew larger and more expensive; telegraph tolls increased; the cost of news service rose; paper; ink; and other materials climbed; so did labor."[380] A major merger occurred in 1914, when the *Picayune* consolidated with the *Times-Democrat* (the product of an 1881 merger of the *Times* and *Democrat*) and became the *Times-Picayune*. Now owned by the Nicholson Publishing Company rather than the Nicholson family, "the old lady of Camp Street" became a corporate entity, less influenced by the strong and charming personalities of its owners.

With many papers swallowed up by rivals or hobbled by wartime costs, the number of offices on Camp Street declined from about sixteen in previous years to about ten. The Newsboys' Home on Bank Place closed in 1917. Then, in the post-World War I boom, the rapidly expanding *Times-Picayune* made a major decision to relocate its main office from the third block of Camp Street—the core of Newspaper Row and its home since 1837—to a larger building next to Lafayette Square near City Hall. The announcement came on June 21, 1919; the cornerstone was laid on September 24; and a public housewarming was held only six weeks later, on November 8. The new building, which was technically at 601-15 North but still maintained a front on Camp, "occupied a site 150 by 85 feet, and contained, in its four stories and basement, 75,000 square feet of floor space—a handsome structure of tapestry brick and concrete, with an iron-grille balcony suggestive of the Vieux Carré. With equipment, it cost $1,000,000."[381] The move was necessitated by the need for more space, especially for the new Hoe press, which could print 80,000 sixteen-page papers in an hour.

---

378. *States*, November 8, 1885, as quoted in Wilds, 178.
379. Wilds, 71-75.
380. Dabney, *One Hundred Great Years*, 377.
381. Ibid., 443.

At the same time that the *Times-Picayune* was packing up and moving out of Newspaper Row, it bought out the *Bee* (L'Abeille), the French-language periodical that traced its origins back to the early days of publishing in New Orleans and was a fixture on Chartres Street for close to ninety years. The *Bee*'s death knell came in 1914, when the state legislature rescinded the law that required certain legal documents to be published in French, a requirement that kept *L'Abeille* in business even after the melodious sounds of Creole French dissipated from the streets of this former French colony. The *Bee* lived out its last three years at the new building of the *Times-Picayune* and was finally discontinued in December 1923.

These events were correlated to—probably causative of and certainly symbolic of—the dramatic decline of the cluster of newspaper and publishing offices specifically on Camp Street and eventually in the former Faubourg St. Mary, called at this point the Central Business District. During the 1920s, the number of these offices with Camp Street addresses plunged from over ten down to one to three. The Central Business District would enjoy a monopoly on publishing offices into the 1930s but began to lose it to places uptown or in Mid-City, as trucks and new highways allowed access to cheaper real estate and more elbow room. The spread of the population to the new lakeside communities starting in the 1910s and continuing to the suburbs and neighboring parishes today further pushed the fulcrum of the local newspaper industry away from a single, concentrated downtown district toward a dispersion of points throughout the metropolitan area. Since 1930, there have been no more than five publishers on Camp Street (none today), while the number throughout the Central Business District during the same period declined from eighteen to two (60 percent to 13 percent of all in the city). By the 1940s, newsboys also vanished from the streets of New Orleans, replaced by men stationed on street corners and honor-system coin boxes.[382]

Dispersion of the Newspaper and Publishing Industry

The *Times-Picayune* acquired the *New Orleans States* in 1933 and the *New Orleans Item* in 1958. Operations occurred within a few blocks of each other, on Camp Street and Union Street, where local journalists recorded the historic events of those midcentury years—the depression, Huey Long's administration, World War II, postwar prosperity, the civil rights movement—and congregated in their favorite restaurant hangouts, Marble Hall near City Hall and Abadie's on Camp.[383] In 1968, when downtown New Orleans was in decline and white residents fled to the suburbs, the morning and Sunday paper *Times-Picayune* and its afternoon daily *New Orleans States-Item* (at this time editorially separate papers but both under the ownership of S. I. Newhouse) moved from Lafayette Square to a modern structure at 3800 Howard Avenue in Mid-City, convenient to the new interstates providing access to suburban subdivisions.[384] According to Carl McArn Corbin, former editor of the *States*, another reason for the move was to save on the costs of rail and truck delivery of paper to the office at Lafayette Square. The new Mid-City office was right by the railroad, eliminating the need for trucking of paper before printing, and also convenient to the Pontchartrain Expressway, allowing for truck delivery after printing.[385]

In the 1970s, the percentage of New Orleans' downtown-based newspaper and publishing companies fell below those located elsewhere, a trend that continues strongly today, when almost 90 percent of those firms listed in the Orleans Parish city directory under the category *Newspapers* have addresses in places other than the Central Business District and the French Quarter. One of the last Newspaper Row-based publications was the Archdiocese of New Orleans' biweekly *Clarion Herald,* housed at 523 Natchez Alley into the 1970s and now published from the archdiocese's headquarters at 1000 Howard Avenue. In the 1980s, the afternoon daily *New Orleans States-Item* was folded into its parent paper to become the rather unwieldy *Times-Picayune/States-Item,* and finally the *Times-Picayune* in 1986. After almost two hundred years of rich journalistic heritage, New Orleans was at last a one-newspaper town. One *major daily* newspaper, that is: there were still fifteen to thirty papers of various sizes and stripes operating in the city by the close of the twentieth century, including the widely read free alternative *Gambit Weekly.*

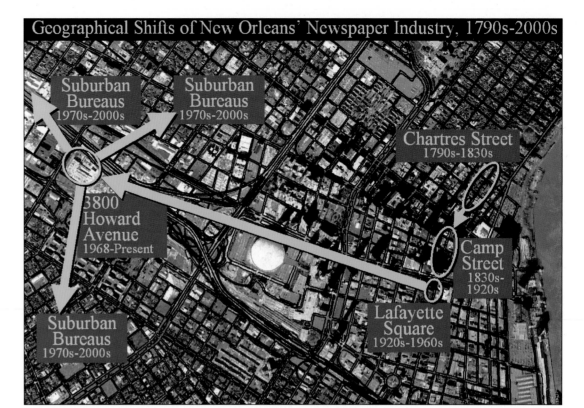

Geographical Shifts of New Orleans' Newspaper Industry, 1790s-2000s

Suburban Bureaus 1970s-2000s

Suburban Bureaus 1970s-2000s

Chartres Street 1790s-1830s

3800 Howard Avenue 1968-Present

Camp Street 1830s-1920s

Suburban Bureaus 1970s-2000s

Lafayette Square 1920s-1960s

The geographical shift of New Orleans' newspaper-industry centers over 200 years reflects the general movement of the New Orleans population and economy, originally housed in the old city, then migrating up to Faubourg St. Mary, then farther uptown, then toward the lake, then off in all directions to the suburbs. *Map and analysis by author; street data from New Orleans City Planning Commission; aerial image courtesy U.S. Geological Survey*

Perhaps most symbolic of the trend of institutional consolidation of newspapers and geographical dispersion of newspaper offices is the development of suburban *Times-Picayune* bureaus throughout the metropolitan area, in east Jefferson Parish, Kenner, St. Bernard Parish, St. Charles/St. John Parish, and St. Tammany Parish and on the west bank. To address the news interests of the increasingly dispersed population, the newspaper started geographically specialized supplements: *Downtown Picayune, Uptown Picayune, Lakefront Picayune, East New Orleans Picayune, Algiers Picayune, Gretna Picayune, Marrero Picayune, Westwego Picayune, Kenner Picayune, Metairie Picayune, Harahan Picayune, St. Bernard Picayune, River Parishes Picayune, Slidell Picayune,* and the *St. Tammany Picayune.* This startling dispersion of suburban subnewspapers is controlled from the six bureaus located throughout the region, all answering to the *Times-Picayune*'s headquarters under the distinctive tower with the circular sign that marks 3800 Howard Avenue, close to the geographical centroid of the entire metropolitan area. In 1999, the *Times-Picayune* was ranked as "the best-read newspaper in the nation's top 50 metropolitan markets," reaching 60.3 percent of the metropolitan area's adult population on an average weekday—a statement on both the paper's success as well as its lack of competition.[386]

From a smattering of tiny print shops on Chartres Street in the *Vieux Carré de la Ville* at the turn of the nineteenth century, to the distinct Newspaper Row on Camp Street at the turn of the twentieth century, to the consolidation and scattering of the written press at the turn of the twenty-first century, the geography of New Orleans' publishing industry echoes the historical development of the city itself. Newsmen rushing to meet deadlines and newsboys hawking their daily papers are no longer part of the ambience of downtown New Orleans, nor are the chatter of telegraph machines, the rumble of Linotype devices, and the smell of wet ink on pulpy paper. A stroll up former Newspaper Row today reveals some reminders of the bustle that was 100 years ago: about half of the structures from district days still stand, many of them protected by the Historic District Landmarks Commission as the aptly named Picayune Place Historic District. A number of units on Camp

---

382. The charming image of the corner newsboy in knickers and an oversized hat contrasts with the stark reality of his existence. Many were delinquents, undernourished, and out of school and engaged in smoking, drinking, gambling, and even prostitution. As late as 1928, most New Orleans newsboys were between the ages of ten and fifteen. Stricter enforcement of child labor laws and mandatory school attendance, as well as newspaper innovations such as the honor-system newspaper stands, ended the time of the newsboy. He did not go quietly: by one account, the stands were unsuccessful at first, because the newsboys would confiscate the papers. Kaplan, and Wilds, 182.

383. Carl McArn Corbin, interview by author, July 9, 2000.

384. In its *Guide to New Orleans Architecture* (111), the otherwise staid New Orleans Chapter of the American Institute of Architects commented about the *Times-Picayune*'s new building, "It is one of the city's great unsolved mysteries how such a strikingly progressive modern building could have been built by such an ultra-conservative newspaper publisher."

385. Corbin, interview.

386. *New Orleans Times-Picayune,* November 13, 2000, Metro section, p. 3, announcement of results of Scarborough Report, a syndicated media study that monitors newspaper readership. Data reflect latter half of 1999.

Newspaper

Row

Today

Newspaper Row Today *Photographs by author, 2000*

1. Newspaper Row, New Orleans' newspaper and publishing district from the 1850s to the 1920s, comprised these row structures on the 300 block of Camp Street plus a number of adjacent streets. This particular block is well preserved, but the newspaper industry has long since departed.

2. Heart of Newspaper Row: The *Picayune*, New Orleans' oldest and most famous newspaper, occupied the site on the left starting in 1837 and this particular structure (originally enumerated as 66 Camp Street, now 326 Camp) after its construction in 1850. At times, the *Picayune*'s facilities spilled over into the neighboring buildings. For seventy years, most of New Orleans' vibrant publishing industry clustered around this site.

3. Occupying the former Picayune Building today is Ed. Smith's Stencil Works, a local landmark that has occupied the building for many years and maintains at least a distant connection to the publishing and printing activity that once prevailed here. The old-fashioned signs and window display of Mr. Smith's business add a great touch to Camp Street, one of the most historic and best-preserved streets in the Central Business District.

4. A faint palimpsest of THE PICAYUNE, etched into the façade of the newspaper office when it was constructed in 1850, is still visible between the third and fourth floors of 326 Camp Street.

5. Around the corner from the 300 block of Camp Street was Natchez Alley, home to the main office of the high-circulation *City Item* (building with protruding sign at center), the smaller operation of the *Southwestern Christian Advocate*, lithographers, binderies, printers, and paper warehouses. Idle newsboys would play ball in this narrow alley until the afternoon edition hit the streets, sending them scurrying in fierce competition to hot vending spots throughout downtown. A few decades ago, this block was ragged and decaying, but recent prosperity and an appreciation for these classic antebellum row structures have made well-kept professional offices out of them.

6. A half-block riverside of Newspaper Row on the 300 block of Camp is a narrow street once known as Bank Place and now called Picayune Place. Most structures along this quiet alley had some connection to the publishing industry in the late nineteenth and early twentieth centuries. The units above the orange taxi, which faced the rear of the *Picayune* office, housed the Newsboys' Home of the Society of St. Vincent de Paul and the Sisters of Mercy of St. Alphonsus, founded in 1879 to provide with the homeless and neglected boys with room and board, schooling, and spiritual guidance in a building that doubled as a warehouse. The home closed in 1917, when Newspaper Row was in decline. Time has swept away the bustle, the smell of fresh ink, and the fighting newsboys from this back alley; eerily motionless and always in some degree of shadow, Picayune Place is a vestige of the past in the middle of the Central Business District.

7. Like the Cotton District, Newspaper Row is fairly well preserved structurally. One exception is this parking lot on the 300 block of Camp Street, which put an unfortunate hole in the otherwise integral row. The surviving corner edifice, once a printing business, exhibits ghostly palimpsests of staircases and doorframes of the attached building. One can almost imagine stock boys and clerks scurrying about in the airspace, attending to the demands of a long-ago workday.

8. In late 1919, the *Times-Picayune* moved to a spacious state-of-the-art structure on the corner of North and Camp on Lafayette Square, demolished a few decades ago and now occupied by this skyscraper. The move marked the end of Newspaper Row. In 1968, the *Times-Picayune* moved out of downtown to its present location at 3800 Howard Avenue, and has since started a number of suburban bureaus, following the dispersion of the New Orleans population.

between Gravier and Poydras have been demolished and replaced by early-1900s-era high-rises; others have succumbed to parking lots or recent skyscrapers. Best preserved is the narrow alley called Picayune Place, formerly Bank Place, which maintains almost all its historic facades. Back on Camp, the best surviving landmark of Newspaper Row is the Picayune Building (1850) at 326 Camp. Operating inside is the long-lived Ed. Smith's Stencil Works, a fixture on Camp Street for decades, distinctive for its old-fashioned signage and window displays. The shop, which recalls the printing heritage of Newspaper Row through its manufacture of rubber stamps and signs, allows one to imagine the activity within its four walls as local journalists prepared stories on the triumphant, mundane, and tragic pageantry of events occurring between 1850 and 1920. Stepping outside and glancing up to the wall space between the third and fourth floors, with the sun at just the right angle, you can make out the faint palimpsest of the words *THE PICAYUNE* etched in the masonry, part of its original design from 150 years ago. The sense of loss diminishes somewhat when a newspaper vending machine captures your attention on a nearby corner, showing through its glass window the dignified masthead and the curious name of the *Times-Picayune*, revealing just enough of the main headline to compel you to stuff fifty cents—eight *picayunes*, that is—into the coin slot.

Other Industry Districts in Modern New Orleans

- Mention the word "district" to New Orleanians today and many will think of the Warehouse District, officially eighteen blocks bounded by Magazine Street and Convention Center Boulevard, from Poydras up to Howard. Warehouses predominated here from the mid-1800s to the mid-1900s—many still stand and some are still warehouses—but did not cluster here to the exclusion of other riverside areas. Rather, warehouses dominated the riverside from the present-day Industrial Canal practically up to Audubon Park, with the most intense concentrations between the former Sugar District and the present-day Lower Garden District. Identification of the aforementioned area as *the* Warehouse District came ex post facto, in the 1970s and especially after the 1984 Louisiana World Exposition, which shined a light of appreciation on these fascinating old industrial structures and the intriguing paving-block streets among them. (New Orleans was not alone in "finding" its Warehouse District: Cleveland, Minneapolis, Austin, Oakland, Toledo, and a number of other cities have discovered and refurbished theirs.) In the years since, New Orleans' Warehouse District has become the principal expansion zone for the convention trade as well as one of the hottest real-estate markets in town, a mecca for condominiums and apartment development, art galleries, night clubs, trendy restaurants, and—in 1998-2000—an astounding boom in hotels. Combined with the CBD, the Warehouse District saw a 31 percent increase in its residential population during the 1990s, to 1,794, the largest percent change of any census tract in the city.

The Warehouse District in 1996, viewed from the World Trade Center. *Photograph by author*

- The year 2000 also saw the coming together of a "museum district" around the intersection of Camp and Howard, renamed Andrew Higgins Place. The home since 1891 of the Confederate Museum, oldest museum in the state, this area is now also the proud site of the D-Day Museum, the affiliated Eisenhower Center for American Studies, and the Ogden Museum of Southern Art (in the old Howard Memorial Library). Around the corner is the Contemporary Arts Center (former office of the *States*), followed by the Louisiana Children's Museum and art galleries. Banners hanging from lampposts in 2000 declared this area the "Arts District," anchored by Julia Row, home to a number of art galleries and the summertime White Linen Night art festival. Following another successful outdoor art event, Art for Art's Sake, a headline in the *Times-Picayune* observed, "Lee Circle emerging as center of new arts district."[387] A brochure issued in 2001 went a step further and dubbed four institutions in this area the "Warehouse Museum District," excluding, for some reason, the Confederate Museum. This neighborhood received worldwide attention on June 6, 2000, for the parade and dedication of the D-Day Museum, noted at the time to be

387. MacCash, "The Picture of Success."

the last major ceremony for America's dwindling population of World War II veterans. Evidence that these museums are mutually benefiting from their adjacency—a necessary trait for a district to survive—came a month after the grand opening, when the area's museums reported dramatic increases in attendance since of the opening of the D-Day Museum.[388]

- Like warehouses, the city's "shipping district" was also distributed broadly along the river, originally clinging to the banks of the old city and spreading up, down, and across the river as the city grew. The major shift in the geography of the port started in the 1920s and accelerated in the 1960s, when the excavation of the Industrial Canal and the Mississippi River-Gulf Outlet Canal opened up deepwater docking opportunities in the former swamps of eastern New Orleans (see page 73). Additionally, the old Harvey Canal in Jefferson Parish was expanded in the 1920s-30s for industrial use. Shipping facilities migrated off the river to these manmade canals. In 1970, planning work commenced on the CENTROPORT, envisioned as a "spacious industrial complex for port, manufacturing, and distribution facilities" at the Industrial Canal/MR-GO turning basin, an effort that would "free the banks of the Mississippi of the unsightly steel sheds . . . for development of choice high-rise riverfront apartments, hotels, tourist terminals, [and] riverfront parks."[389] Geographer Peirce Lewis predicted in 1976 that this shift in the shipping district from the old riverside wharves to the eastern canals "would be the most drastic change in New Orleans economic geography since the city's founding."[390] Numerous major container terminals and other port facilities now cram the docks lining the Industrial Canal, their cranes punctuating the skyline as masts once did along the riverbank, but the bottleneck of the canal's lock, the environmental damage caused by the MR-GO, the relatively few industries that moved to eastern New Orleans, and other factors have ensured that a significant presence of the maritime industry remain on the Mississippi, with more to return there in the future. Recently, for example, the Dock Board decided to expand and consolidate the Napoleon and Nashville terminals to create a "mega-wharf" along the river in uptown New Orleans.[391] Nevertheless, the eastward move of the port opened up parts of the riverfront, from the French Quarter to beyond the bridge, for tourism, convention, and recreational use. New Orleans today has two separate major shipping districts: (1) the Mississippi River Terminal Complex and a nearly contiguous line of wharves stretching from Henry Clay Avenue down to the Faubourg Marigny, and (2) the five berths of the France Road Container Terminal and the Jourdan Road Terminal fronting the turning basin of the Industrial Canal and MR-GO.[392] Many other private dockside facilities also line the Industrial Canal, such as grain elevators and storage sheds.

- One of New Orleans' few industry districts to have survived most of the twentieth century is its small but vibrant theater and performing arts district, centered around the intersection of two of downtown New Orleans' widest streets, Canal and Basin. In 1910, this general vicinity—the twelve blocks straddling Canal and bounded by Bourbon, Rampart, Common, and Conti, to be exact—was home to eight theaters: the Plaza, Trianon, Crescent, Tulane, Alamo, Lyric, Greenwall, and Dauphine. Another six venues were located within five blocks.[393] As the century progressed, most were closed and demolished, replaced

388. Mullener, "Crowds Keep Coming"; and *New Orleans Times-Picayune,* July 28, 2000, Lagniappe section.
389. Huber, *New Orleans,* 352.
390. Lewis, 71.
391. Darcé, "Dock Board Chooses Design."
392. Port of New Orleans, *Port of New Orleans Annual Directory, 1997-1998,*12-13, 39-46.
393. *All Theaters and R.R. Depots Lead to the New Hotel Ranson* (1910), map of downtown New Orleans, courtesy Jack Stewart, reproduced by Hennick and Charlton, 73. Canal Street was also an early home of cinema in New Orleans, at Vitascope Hall near Exchange Place in the late 1890s. By 1915, eleven of New Orleans' eighty picture theaters had an address on Canal Street.

Shipping districts: wharves, terminals, and other facilities of the Port of New Orleans along the Industrial Canal (left) and the Mississippi River (top). Photographs at middle and bottom show the canalside France Road complex and the riverside Nashville Avenue Complex. *Maps by author based on 1999 annual directory for the Port of New Orleans; aerial photographs by Donn Young, courtesy the Port of New Orleans*

For a century, a number of New Orleans' most famous theaters have been located within a few blocks of the spacious Canal/Basin intersection (center). Those currently in operation in this area include the Orpheum (1918) on University Place, the Saenger (1927, marquis at center) on Canal between Rampart and Basin, the State Palace (formerly Loew's, 1926), and the Joy Theater. *Photograph by author, 2000*

Magazine Street, one of the most picturesque and interesting thoroughfares in uptown New Orleans, is home to one out of every three antiques dealers in the entire metropolitan area, forming perhaps the most elongated district in the city. It is also a mecca for art galleries, boutiques, coffee shops, and restaurants. On Friday and Saturday nights, locals flock to Magazine Street the way tourists head for Bourbon Street. *Photographs by author, 2000*

Bourbon Street from Iberville to Dumaine is New Orleans' most famous industry district, home to a door-to-door cluster of bars, night clubs, restaurants, and trinket shops. It may be the only district in the city famous enough to serve as a metaphor for its vocation, as "Wall Street" implies finance and "Madison Avenue" advertising. One often hears of places like Beale Street in Memphis or Sixth Street in Austin described as "the Bourbon Street" of those cities. *Photograph by author, 1995*

Royal Street (below), a block away from Bourbon but a world away in its atmosphere, is home to some of the most famous antiques shops in the nation. The cluster of antiques dealers on upper Royal has existed at least since the late 1800s. *Photograph by author, 2000*

The immense Art Deco-style Charity Hospital marks the core of downtown New Orleans' "medical district," along Tulane Avenue from Loyola to South Galvez plus adjacent blocks. The area is home to a number of major private and public hospitals and internationally known medical-research facilities, including the downtown campus of Tulane University. There has been a significant medical presence at this location since 1833, when Charity Hospital first moved here. *Photographs by author, 2000*

This and adjacent commercial strips in the Faubourg Marigny are often referred to as the Decatur Street-Frenchmen Street (seen here) music corridor, for their cluster of acclaimed jazz venues and night clubs. *Photograph by author, 2000*

Storyville, the legal prostitution district, viewed from the Hotel Grunewald (later the Roosevelt, now the Fairmont) in 1909. The "Tenderloin District" operated from 1897 to 1917 and, in its heyday, rivaled other industry districts in New Orleans in terms of spatial extent and concentration of businesses—though the comparisons end there. Most of Storyville's structures were demolished by 1940 for the Iberville Housing Development. *Detail of panoramic photograph courtesy American Memory Collection, Library of Congress*

by new theaters constructed a few blocks toward the lake and closer to Canal Street. Those theaters and cinemas currently in operation in this area include the Orpheum (1918) on University Place, the Saenger (1927) on Canal between Rampart and Basin, the State Palace (formerly Loew's, 1926) across the street, and the Joy Theater one block toward the lake. In the nineteenth century, New Orleans was world famous for some of its theaters and opera houses, most notably the spectacular St. Charles Theater in Faubourg St. Mary and the cherished French Opera House in the French Quarter, both victims of fire.

- Small districts thrive in the French Quarter, nurtured by the predominance of pedestrian traffic and the nature of tourist-oriented retail. Bourbon Street is, of course, the world-famous night club and bar district and has been so since World War II; it is the only district in the city famous enough to serve as a metaphor for its vocation, as "Wall Street" implies finance and "Madison Avenue" advertising. One often hears of places like Beale Street in Memphis or Sixth Street in Austin described as "the Bourbon Street" of those cities. (Storyville once achieved a similar role in the American vernacular, as a synonym for red-light districts, but is now a name recognized only by history buffs and jazz lovers.) Decatur Street and parts of North Peters have given Bourbon a run for its money as an entertainment district in recent years, attracting the theme-restaurant scene at the upriver end and the dog-collar-and-combat-boot crowd at the downriver end. Far across the social spectrum, upper Royal and Chartres Street form the backbone of the upscale antiques marketplace: in 2000, Royal Street was the address to about 28 of the metropolitan area's 208 antiques dealers listed in the Yellow Pages; though Magazine Street had over 70, Royal Street had a greater concentration, and certainly more famous old dealerships.[394] (The cluster on Royal has been around at least since the late 1800s; one 1902 city guide stated that "antique and bric-a-brac shops abound on all sides"[395] of the lower blocks of the street, as they do today.)

- Magazine Street has long been a haven for bric-a-brac shops and colorful dives, and has recently attracted a plethora of art galleries, coffee shops, and upscale restaurants (paralleled by a doubling of property values between 1993 and 1998). But it is best known for its assemblage of antiques dealers, forming what must be the city's most elongated retail district. In 2000, over one out of every three antiques dealers (75 out of 208) in the entire metropolitan area was listed in the Yellow Pages with Magazine Street addresses, more than any other street. An Internet search under the heading of antiques and collectibles in New Orleans alone showed 44 of 100 listings to be on Magazine Street.[396] One suspects that the browse-and-search nature of antiques shopping encourages dealers to gather together. The 2000, 3000, 4200, and 5400 blocks of this fascinating street are especially clustered with such enterprises.

"It's been called the Street of Dreams and 'a vast linear flea market,' and it once marked a kind of DMZ between Uptown proper and what was loosely known as the Irish Channel. . . . In many ways, Magazine between Race Street and Jackson Avenue epitomizes much of what is colorful and unique about this city. For a long time, as other areas became progressively gentrified, the Lower Garden District simply became more bohemian, as the more colorful denizens of the subculture fled high rents elsewhere. . . . Cool shops and galleries sprouted amidst the blight as the area became rife with innovation, and the Utne Reader even called it the 'coolest neighborhood in America,' a flattering, if ominous, declaration."
—D. Eric Bookhardt, 2000 ("The Scene on Lower Magazine," 53)

- New Orleans' "medical district," one of its largest industry districts, spreads out around the intersection of Tulane and Claiborne avenues. Here, the medical, educational, and research facilities of Tulane University, Charity Hospital, University Hospital, Veteran's Administration, Louisiana State University, Delgado Community College, and other organizations function out of a variety of structures with architectural styles ranging from Art Deco to International. The cluster of these internationally important institutions in this particular area may be traced back to the topography of New Orleans and the related patterns of urban development in the nineteenth century. While the original Charity Hospital (1736) operated out of a provisional convent within city limits (Chartres and Bienville), the second (1743) and third (1785) hospitals of that name were located near the backswamp edge of the original city, in part to keep the infirmed segregated from the rest of the population (living on higher lands) according to the public-health standards of the day. Charity Hospital was moved in 1815 to Canal Street between Baronne and present-day University Place, near the fringes of the city, and, in 1833, to a point on Common Street on the outskirts of the American Sector, again near the edge of the backswamp. The site was convenient to the rapidly developing faubourgs of St. Mary and uptown yet was far enough from the masses to minimize fears of contagion, especially in these years of yellow fever epidemics. The presence of the impressive new Charity Hospital attracted other medical institutions to the general area, such as the Maison de Santé (1840, at Canal and Claiborne, two blocks away) and the Hotel Dieu (1859, Common and South Johnson, five blocks away). After over a century of service, while New Orleans expanded far beyond what was once the edge of the city, old Charity Hospital was demolished and replaced in 1939 by the huge Art-Deco structure that still operates in the same location (by this time called Tulane Avenue and considered downtown).[397] The medical-services industry that continued to develop around the legendary hospital attracted still other institutions of medicine to the area, and within a few decades, a bone fide district had developed. The "Tulane Avenue medical corridor" now includes Tulane University's downtown campus and may be home to a future biomedical technology district, a research arena in which New Orleans hopes to establish leadership in the future.[398] That this technological progress in medicine occurs in this particular corner of the city may be traced back to New Orleans' underlying historical-geographical characteristics.

- Poydras Street, once an unremarkable four-lane route through the CBD, was widened in 1966 and built up during the oil-boom years of the 1970s and early 1980s as the city's "skyscraper district," dominated by the petroleum industry. With the Rivergate Exhibition Hall (1968) at one end and the Superdome (1975) at the other, the effort was described by Peirce F. Lewis as an attempt to reverse the blight that had frayed the upper CBD as well as to keep up with Houston by building things on a "Texan" scale.[399] One Shell Square (1972), the city's tallest structure at 697 feet, became the premier landmark on the gleaming private-sector showcase of Poydras Street, and a monument to the local oil and gas industry. The bottoming-out of this market in the mid-1980s left Poydras overbuilt and underoccupied. It partially recuperated in the prosperous 1990s, but with less than half the petroleum industry. There were 28,000 oil and gas jobs in New Orleans in 1982, with Poydras Street hosting the best-paying positions; by 1997, there were only 14,440, and by 2000, only 11,600 jobs remained, and these of dubious future.[400] Some of these jobs were lost to normal industry cycles, but more were eliminated as the industry, on a nationwide scale, centralized itself in cities such as Houston, for the same reasons that form industry districts in the first place: to "offer greater access to information from other insiders, provide a specialized labor force and attract a core number of suppliers and financiers."[401] This provides a good example of how industry-district formation at the microlevel (within a city) may be supplanted by the same clustering instinct carried out at the macrolevel (throughout the nation). Poydras Street today is the daytime address of thousands of white-collar office workers in the private and public sectors, the largest concentration in the city, but because they cut across dozens of professional lines, they do not form an industry district. The same may be said of the cluster of city, state, and federal government offices along Loyola Avenue.

394. *BellSouth Yellow Pages,* 41-43. An Internet survey conducted through *Yahoo!* on August 3, 2000, for antiques and collectibles listed ten antiques stores on Royal and another eight on Chartres. The discrepancy in the counts for Royal Street may be due to multiple listing of the same enterprise or different standards of categorization.
395. Zacharie, *New Orleans Guide* (1902), 93.
396. *BellSouth Yellow Pages,* 41-43; Internet survey conducted through *Yahoo!* on August 3, 2000. The discrepancy in the counts for Magazine Street may be due to multiple listing of the same enterprise or different standards of categorization.

397. Salvaggio, 11-12.
398. Yerton, "Bio-Medical Firm."
399. Lewis, 93-95.
400. Biers, "City Is Still Leaking" and "N.O. Bears Brunt."
401. Bill Gilmer, economist for Federal Reserve Bank of Dallas, as quoted by Biers, "N.O. Bears Brunt."

- The city's "University District," now past the century mark, comprises Tulane University, Newcomb College, and Loyola University in and near the old Foucher tract (see page 97) in the heart of uptown New Orleans. These schools first located here in the 1890s-1900s, after downtown proved too crowded for a decent university campus and semirural uptown invited such developments during the boom following the 1884 World's Industrial and Cotton Centennial Exposition. The span of St. Charles Avenue between Audubon Park and the campuses of Tulane and Loyola is one of the most beautiful spots in the nation, especially on cool late-winter mornings when the azaleas are in full bloom. Following the former limits of the Foucher tract to its Mid-City terminus, one finds Xavier University, one of the nation's premier (and largest Catholic) historically black institutions of higher learning.
- A cluster of seafood restaurants exploits the balmy lakefront ambience at West End. At the opposite end of the city, among the "camps" of the Rigolets, is a linear district of shrimpers, oystermen, and fishermen plying the waters where Lake Pontchartrain is subsumed into the Gulf of Mexico. They are there, of course, for purely physical-geographical reasons. Roughly between is a community of Catholic Vietnamese immigrants living in subdivisions along Chef Menteur Highway in eastern New Orleans, an ethnic enclave complete with its own retail district, Saturday-morning markets, and extensive vegetable gardens like those of the residents' homeland.

Industry districts are a fading phenomenon in most American cities, and New Orleans is no exception. Automobiles, suburban sprawl, chain retailers, telecommunications, and corporate consolidation diminish and sometimes even reverse the mutual advantages once gained by *concerns akin assembling together*.[402] As evidenced by the oil and gas industry and the marketers of sugar and cotton, the centralization instinct that forms districts in the streets of a particular city sometimes ends up wiping out these local districts in favor of a new clustering at the national level, in Houston or Manhattan. It is not by coincidence that New Orleans' few surviving industry districts tend to sell locally relevant products and services (antiques, art, food and drink, entertainment) in pedestrian-scale parts of the city (the French Quarter, the CBD, Magazine Street), and more often than not comprise locally owned enterprises. The dispersion of industry districts subtracts an elusive sense of purpose and place from a city, leaving behind fading palimpsests and curious toponyms—or sometimes not a single apparent clue—to remind information-age laborers of the profundity of change that sweeps through the streets and structures of old cities.

Nodes: Essential Places

"Nodes are points, the strategic spots in a city into which an observer can enter, and which are the intensive foci to and from which he is traveling. They may be primarily junctions, places of a break in transportation, a crossing of convergence of paths, moments of shift from one structure to another."[403] So Kevin Lynch described the concept of nodes as urban elements in *The Image of the City* (1960). New Orleans' strategic geographical situation invites a recasting of Lynch's nodes to signify key spots in the city that are rooted in its physiography and indicative of its role linking river and sea. Following is a set of criteria proposed to identify "geographical nodes" throughout Orleans Parish.
- A geographical node should be, as the name implies, fairly compact in size—a specific site rather than an extended linear feature like a levee or an expansive areal element such as a neighborhood.
- Geographical nodes should be rooted to some degree in the physical geography of the city, natural or man-made.
- Most importantly, a geographical node should reflect the fundamental premise for the existence of New Orleans: the nexus of the exterior world beyond the Gulf of Mexico with the interior world of the Mississippi River and the basin it drains.
- Relatedly, a geographical node should serve to place New Orleans in the larger scheme of things, regarding the city's role in the world as a major river/sea port.

Locations fulfilling these requirements are, literally and symbolically, *essential places* to New Orleans, just as New Orleans is an essential place among the nations and seas of the Western Hemisphere.

The Rigolets and Chef Menteur Pass

The far eastern fingers of Orleans Parish form a complex barrier of wetlands separating the eastern tip of Lake Pontchartrain from a bay of the northern Gulf of Mexico, called Lake Borgne. The barrier comprises three features: a small body of water known as Lake Catherine bordered on the east by marshes and on the west by a narrow, twisting island bridging the rest of Orleans Parish with the "mainland" of St. Tammany Parish and the piney woods of Mississippi. Geologically, this land bridge is a product of ancient sandbars that once transected the coast, were overlaid by Mississippi River sediments deposited 8,500 years ago and again 3,200 year ago, then subsided and were built up again by Bayou Sauvage (eastern terminus of the Bayou Metairie/Bayou Gentilly distributary system), and now are being eroded away by persistent wave action and the occasional hurricane.[404] The fragile swath of land, known as the Rigolets, has an edge-of-the-world atmosphere today, windswept and vulnerable, populated by spindly fishing camps and salty characters, shored up from erosion by concrete riprap left anxiously along the encroaching coastline. Many family-owned fishing camps and weekend bungalows here are marked with whimsical roadside signs, some laced with irony and dark humor regarding impending storms. A rebellious and independent streak seems to run through this linear community: Confederate flags and David Duke placards, a rarity in the rest of the city, are occasionally visible here, just a few miles from the mostly black and Vietnamese communities of Chef Menteur Highway. Some New Orleanians do not realize that this rural peninsula is as much a part of their city as Carrollton or Gentilly or anywhere else in the 181 square miles of Orleans Parish, so different is the environment here. Its modern physical link to the city is Highway 90, the lifeline to the Rigolets as the Mississippi River is to southeastern Louisiana, providing both access and topographic relief where isolation and inundation would otherwise prevail. Three hundred years ago, the Rigolets provided two major lifelines to the city that was eventually founded to its south and west, partially explaining the site selected for the city and providing it with accessibility into the twentieth century. The lifelines were two sluggish brackish-water tidal streams meandering across the land bridge connecting Lake Borgne and Lake Pontchartrain, one called Chef Menteur Pass and the other the Rigolets, both under 10 miles in length.[405] These were the waterways that provided the Indians, the first European explorers and settlers, and early New Orleanians with the least-cost/minimum-distance access from the coastal settlements of Biloxi, Mobile, Pensacola and points in the Caribbean and beyond to the interior region of Lake Pontchartrain, Bayou St. John, Bayou Road, and the Mississippi River.

Aboriginal use of the region may date as far back as 9,000 years, according to evidence unearthed at the Garcia site at the northern tip of the island, and continued as the landscape changed well into historic times.[406] European utilization of these two prized shortcuts commenced with the earliest voyages of Iberville and Bienville in 1699, during their exploration of routes between the present-day Mississippi Gulf Coast and the Mississippi River. (Iberville named one point along the Rigolets waterway *Les Petites Coquilles* for the mounds of shells there.) Early maps of the region attest to the importance of these routes by portraying them in a prominent and sometimes exaggerated cartographic manner compared to adjacent geographical features. Guillaume de L'Isles's *Carte de la Riviere de Mississipi* (1702), for example, shows the Rigolets route as a veritable superwaterway, a straight and unobstructed coastal connection wider than the Mississippi. Thus, according to our criteria, the Rigolets and Chef Menteur Pass may be considered the first geographical nodes in the region, links in the chain of geographical features that had to be crossed to gain access between sea and river. The Rigolets, being wider and more conveniently oriented than Chef Menteur Pass, saw more traffic than Chef Menteur Pass, and far more than lesser sea/river routes such as Bayou Bienvenue and Bayou Dupré in present-day St. Bernard Parish.

It is difficult to assess how much traffic en route to colonial New Orleans came through these waterways ("the lake route") as opposed to the mouth of the Mississippi ("the river route")—usage probably depended on the seasonal conditions at the silty and turbulent delta—but it is likely that most smaller watercraft would have taken this lake route, especially in the early years. The English, too, utilized these waterways to access the interior during the era of Spanish control of New Orleans, when Spain refused them passage on the lower Mississippi. Spanish governor Carondelet, recognizing the vulnerability of what he called "the entry of the lakes," recommended in 1794 that a fort be built at *Los Rigolets*,[407] though it is unclear if the Spanish eventually built one.

---

402. Paraphrased from Engelhardt, 21-22.
403. Lynch, 47.

404. Castille, 1-1-3.
405. Rigolets is French for channel, canal, or little river. It is from the early explorers' identification of this waterway that the entire land bridge gained the name of "the Rigolets." It is interesting that ensuing generations of English speakers did not rename the waterway with a redundancy such as "Rigolets Channel" or "Bayou Rigolets." Nevertheless, for clarity in this passage, "the Rigolets" will denote the land bridge while "the Rigolets waterway" will mean the channel.
406. Castille, 2-1.
407. Letter of Baron de Carondelet to the Duke of Alcudia (November 24, 1794), as reproduced in Turner, 497.

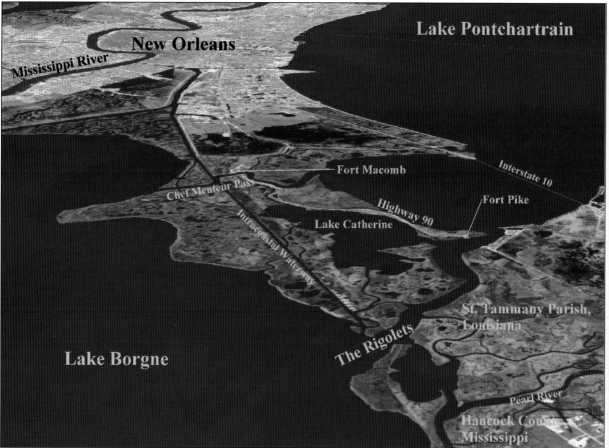

Oblique view of the Rigolets land bridge from Lake Borgne through the twin passes—Chef Menteur Pass and the Rigolets—toward Lake Pontchartrain and New Orleans. Early explorers and settlers used this backdoor route to the interior so as to avoid the long and arduous journey up the mouth of the Mississippi River. *Image processing and cartography by author; Landsat/SPOT satellite image courtesy Louisiana State University*

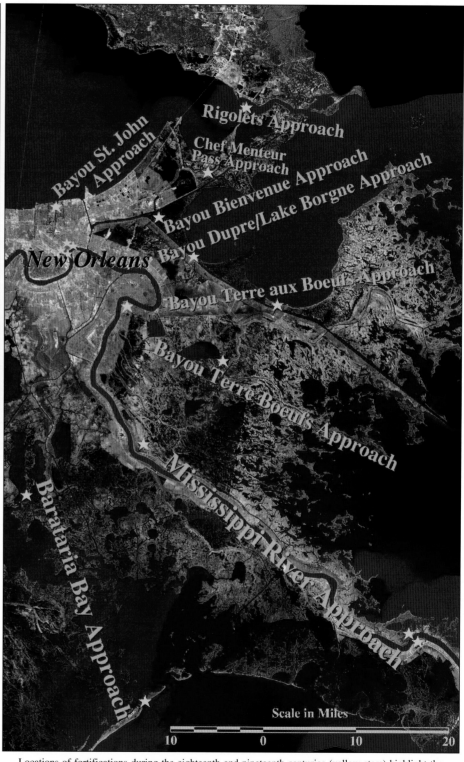

"Fort Petite Coquilles, at the junction of the Rigolets with Pontchartrain, is one of the most important posts in Louisiana. It is the key to West Florida, and effectually covers one flank of New Orleans. While this excellent position is maintained, it would be extremely difficult for an enemy to get into the rear of the city, and if well constructed, strongly garrisoned, and skillfully commanded, few places could present a more formidable aspect to a besieging army."

—William Darby, 1816 (188)

Fort Pike, one of a number of forts built along the Gulf Coast after the British attempt on New Orleans in 1815, guarded the Rigolets from enemy invasion. It is now a state commemorative area. *Photograph by author, 1999*

Locations of fortifications during the eighteenth and nineteenth centuries (yellow stars) highlight the various approaches to New Orleans in historic times. *Map and analysis by author; Landsat/SPOT satellite image courtesy Louisiana State University*

From 1763 to 1783, the Rigolets formed part of the international border between Spanish Louisiana and British West Florida; twenty years later, it separated French Louisiana from Spanish West Florida (1803) and American Louisiana from Spanish West Florida (1803-10). The Americans did build a small fort at the Garcia site (Fort Petite Coquilles) in 1813, followed by a much more substantial fortress started in 1818 and expanded in the 1820s and 1830s, in response to foreign threats such as that of the British invasion famously defeated at Chalmette in 1815.[408] This was Fort Pike, now a state commemorative area and a reminder that the Rigolets was a major backdoor, for friend but also potentially foe, to New Orleans and the American interior. At the other end of the island, Fort Wood (later Macomb, also started in 1818) was constructed to guard Chef Menteur Pass; it too still stands, though in poignant ruin amid flooded moats and eroding waves.

As the threat of foreign invasion of America's underbelly subsided, Fort Pike and Fort Macomb served variously as garrisons, prisons, and outposts before being abandoned in the 1890s and ending up in state hands in the 1920s. Throughout the 1800s, the waterways they guarded were still quite active with traffic transporting cargo and passengers between coastal cities and communities within the Lake Pontchartrain basin. Oceangoing vessels, however, had long since resorted to the river route, their hulls too broad for narrow Bayou St. John and their cargo too bulky to deposit behind the city.

All coastal shipments arriving to New Orleans via the Old Basin Canal (Carondelet Canal, 1790s) and the busy New Basin Canal (1830s) necessarily passed through the Rigolets or Chef Menteur Pass, as did passengers from the coast bound for the Pontchartrain Railroad depot at Milneburg. But with improved shipping technology, increased trade volume, and better engineering control of the Mississippi, the importance of these two geographical nodes waned at the turn of the century. The closing of the Old Basin Canal in 1927-38 and New Basin Canal in 1937-50 deprived the Rigolets waterways of their inner-city port destinations, while railroads and highways replaced waterborne transportation to and from towns around the lake. The construction of the Intracoastal Waterway, which cuts perpendicularly across both Chef Menteur Pass and the Rigolets waterway, gave barge traffic a much more efficient route between river and sea.

While the fairly shallow waters of Chef Menteur Pass limit its usage, the Rigolets waterway is still well utilized by small commercial and recreational watercraft entering Lake Pontchartrain from the gulf, many destined for New Orleans' lakefront harbors. The Rigolets land bridge remained an important terrestrial access route—Highway 90 was the only way to get to points east along the Gulf Coast—until Interstate 10 was opened in 1968 well to its west, relegating the community to a rural future that, in many ways, may have saved the place. Today, motorists heading out of New Orleans on Highway 90 pass the city's most isolated neighborhood, Venetian Isles, and get a fleeting glimpse of the ruins of Fort Macomb before crossing the excruciatingly narrow ca.-1921 drawbridge at Chef Menteur Pass (frequently raised for fishing vessels) and arriving onto "the Island." After nine winding miles of landscape that ranges from the spectacular to the ragged, and a built environment that varies from the sublime to the ridiculous, one arrives at the well-kept state park of Fort Pike, providing the best views and most fitting monument not just to the military history of the bastion but to the geographical significance of the placid waterway it overlooks.[409] Then it's over another hair-raising 1920s-era drawbridge and off to the piney woods of Mississippi.

Bayou St. John at the Bayou Road Portage
After traversing the Rigolets into Lake Pontchartrain, early voyagers destined for nascent New Orleans would sail the southern shore of the lake toward the twisted, log-strewn channel of Bayou St. John. About 3.5 miles up this bayou, they disembarked at a certain spot from which a slight upland would allow foot passage to the Mississippi River—and the frontier city established on its banks. This was the Bayou St. John portage (see pages 20-25). The point at which the arrivals disembarked from their saltwater voyage and walked 2 miles to the fresh waters of the Mississippi is another major geographical node in the history of New Orleans.

Where, precisely, was this node, the point at which passengers debarked from their voyage across ocean, gulf, and lake and walked to the river? The original jumping-off point was probably near the intersection of present-day Bell Street and Moss Street. A small waterway connecting Bayou Metairie and Bayou Gentilly, called Bayou Fanchon (later Clark), had deposited sediments along this swath, which allowed for passage to the Gentilly Ridge topographic feature. The Bayou Road portage followed these slight uplands to their fusion with the far edges of the Mississippi River's natural levee, at which point it veered to the right and followed a curving path toward the river—the only walkable portage between Bayou St. John and the river and, of course,

a major reason why New Orleans exists here today. One can retrace this historical topographic corridor (now known as the Esplanade Ridge but much broader than the avenue of that name) by strolling down Bell Street to Bayou Road to Governor Nicholls Street—different names for the same historic portage—into the French Quarter and finally to the banks of the Mississippi.

The location of Bayou Road's origin is the subject of some debate in the present-day neighborhood of Faubourg St. John. Many identify the Grand Route St. John/Moss Street intersection as the start of the portage, where stands today a stately structure known as the Old Spanish Custom House (1784), one of the oldest extant buildings in this beautiful faubourg. With its raised construction, airy gallery, and double-pitched roof, it seems to mark a place of former great importance; the imposing name for the quaint street to its side, *Grand Route St. John*, adds to the aura. But this appears to be the case about a century after the formative years of New Orleans. In 1777, the road was moved a small distance toward present-day Grand Route so that it would be shared by two plantation owners; in 1809, a bridge was built over Bayou St. John at Grand Route, either reflecting or causing the rerouting of Bayou Road traffic from the present-day Bell/Desoto Street area to Grand Route St. John. Evidence for this comes from Barthélémy Lafon's *Plan du Faubourg St. Jean* (1809), the original plat for the neighborhood of today.[409] Some confusion may arise from the fact that present-day Bell Street was once called St. John Street, while Grand Route St. John was named St. John Route. There is also the possibility that the intervening Desoto Street, which used to be called Washington, hosted the portage at some point. Whether at Bell, Desoto, or Grand Route, the sites are only two blocks apart and one may assume that, at least prior to the first surveying of properties in 1708, people milled about at this miniature port and took various footpaths along the upland to the river.

Bayou Road's monopoly on lake-route traffic to New Orleans was superceded by the excavation of Carondelet Canal in the 1790s (see page 66), especially after it was widened in the 1810s and later challenged by the Pontchartrain Railroad and New Basin Canal as alternate lake routes into the city. But by this time, ancient Bayou Road was embedded into the street network and cadastral patterns of the city, a permanent artifact of New Orleans' urban geography. The significance of the Bayou Road portage is detectable today by the angular orientation of many adjacent properties, originally surveyed when Bayou Road was the only street around, compared to the orthogonal orientation of neighboring blocks that were developed afterwards.

At the intersection of Bell Street and Bayou St. John, a historical marker explains the significance of the spot. While I was photographing this area in 1999, a gentleman came out of his house and warned me that the sign was mislocated by two blocks; the real portage, he said, started along Grand Route St. John. Both he and the sign are probably right if the larger history of Bayou Road is considered. In this sense, the two-block stretch of Bell Street, Desoto Street, and Grand Route St. John along the southern meanders of Bayou St. John all comprise a significant geographical node in historic New Orleans, and perhaps the most tranquil and beautiful.

---

408. The British, incidentally, entered Louisiana around Christmas 1814 via Lake Borgne to Bayou Bienvenue and Mazant, then followed the Villere Canal to reach the natural levee of the Mississippi near present-day Meraux. A month earlier, Andrew Jackson had led his American troops into New Orleans via the Rigolets land bridge. The two armies clashed at Chalmette on January 8, 1815, resulting in an astounding victory for the Americans in one of the most significant battles in American history. After the war, Pres. James Monroe fortified all vulnerable frontdoor and backdoor entrances to the Atlantic and Gulf Coast, fearing more foreign infiltration. Many of these forts still stand.

409. See Freiberg, footnote on 15.

Greater Jackson Square

The sense of historical and architectural centrality in New Orleans reaches an apex at Jackson Square. With its harmonious ensemble of historical structures, the graceful and dignified square was for about 140 years the most significant site in the city, home of colonial and city government, the church, military and civic bodies, and the site of important public functions and everyday private gatherings. Its relevance waned by the mid-nineteenth century, when the old city lost its clout to the uptown neighborhoods, but revived when appreciation for the Vieux Carré blossomed in the 1920s-30s. Today, most people—locals and tourists alike—would readily identify Jackson Square as the "heart of the city." It is one of the busiest pedestrian spots in the nation. Jackson Square's geographical nodality, in accordance with our criteria, comes when we loosely expand the limits of the square to include not just the park and adjacent buildings but the one or two blocks surrounding it: greater Jackson Square. This locale is rooted in the physical geography of the region because it represents (1) the high natural levee of the Mississippi at (2) a point close to the intersection of the Bayou Road/Esplanade Ridge with the levee, on (3) a commanding bend of the river. According to a 1723 map by Le Blond de la Tour, Bienville's original clearing of the forest from 1718 to 1721 fell mostly within this riverside acreage, specifically along present-day Decatur Street from Conti to St. Ann, and up to the intersection of Royal and St. Ann. This initial incursion of man's order upon this wilderness, in and of itself, elevates the significance of this area. More order came in the spring of 1721, when La Tour's diligent assistant, Adrien de Pauger, began adapting La Tour's design for Biloxi to the riverside clearing, siting a *Place d'Armes* front and center in the eleven-by-six-block city in the deltaic wilds. Around the square he located key structures to be built, the *Eglise, Presbitaire, Corps de Garde, Prison,* and *Gouvernement,* with the main *quay* only a few feet in front. Pauger's decision and execution of the plan guaranteed the three-and-a-half-acre square a central place for all the life of the city, which at the time was not foreseeable too far beyond the next heavy rain or high water. Selection of New Orleans as the capital of Louisiana in late 1722 injected further relevance to the city in general and the *Place d'Armes* in particular, and was followed during the mid-1720s by the construction of the first generation of church and state buildings around the *place.* The quay in front was naturally the first port of New Orleans (excepting the 1708 arrivals at Bayou St. John), making greater Jackson Square part of the sea/river connection that is New Orleans' raison d'être. The second generation of church and state structures—the St. Louis Cathedral (1794), followed by the Cabildo (1796-99) and the Presbytère (1791-1813)—arose around the square during the late Spanish colonial administration, when it was called the *Plaza de Armas,* and early American years, when it was the Public Square. It was in the Cabildo on November 30, 1803, that France regained formal possession of Louisiana from Spain and, on December 20, that France formally transferred the great drainage of the Mississippi to the Americans in the Louisiana Purchase. Few acts of greater historical and geographical significance than the signing of the Louisiana Purchase could have taken place here.

The architectural rebirth of greater Jackson Square came in 1846-56, when the present-day St. Louis Cathedral and the twin Pontalba Buildings were constructed, the Cabildo and Presbytère were renovated with distinctive Mansard roofs and cupolas, the Andrew Jackson statue was installed, and the newly landscaped and fenced plaza was renamed Jackson Square. It was one of the most inspired urban-renewal projects in the city's history, transforming a dusty commons into a place of splendor. But the relocation of city government to Lafayette Square in 1853, the ebbing of Creole influence and the ascension of the Americans, the Civil War, Reconstruction, and civic strife detracted from the prestige of Jackson Square. In 1879, the city leased the area across Decatur Street in front of the square to Morgan's Louisiana and Texas Railroad, which built a warehouse along the tracks and severed the square's visual connection with the river. It was an eyesore that would last for decades, but it symbolized the fact that Jackson Square continued to occupy part of an important transportation corridor for rail and sail, serving everything from the Sugar District a few blocks upriver, the French Market a few blocks downriver, and the vast cotton presses and other facilities all along the riverfront. This particular warehouse was demolished after its fifty-year lease expired, but other railroad and riverside structures were added to the general area in exploitation of its geographical nodality.[410]

Greater Jackson Square's days as a cog in New Orleans' river/sea connection gradually faded in the 1920s-30s, when the Sugar District folded and the Industrial Canal began to draw port activity off the river. At about this time, the preservation movement gained momentum in the Vieux Carré, and tourism became increasingly important to the economy. But the pressure to route transportation infrastructure through this node resurfaced in a new way during the 1960s, when planners proposed to route Interstate 310—the infamous Riverfront Expressway—directly in front of the entire French Quarter riverfront to connect the Mississippi River Bridge with Interstate 10 at Elysian Fields. The proposal, which polarized the city and fueled the preservationist movement, was finally scrapped in 1969.

Today, Jackson Square's historical, cultural, and architectural relevance is assured for as long as New Orleans clings to the Mississippi. Reminders of its geographical nodality arise whenever a freight train rumbles past the mimes and street performers at the Washington Artillery Park, or when a Coast Guard cutter or navy destroyer docks nearby for a special occasion, or when an oceangoing freighter glides down the river just high enough for its superstructure to be visible from the balcony of the Cabildo.

Turning Basins of Carondelet Canal and New Basin Canal

Carondelet (Old Basin) Canal and the New Basin Canal, two monuments to New Orleans' sea/river shipping mission, play metaphorical roles in the city's history (see the detailed discussion on pages 66-73). In these long-gone murky waterways, we see references to the earliest schemes of the city fathers, the later rivalry between the Creoles and the Americans, the suffering of slaves and Irish immigrants, the draining of the back-swamps and the growth of the city, and the economic development of local and regional industries. Their turning basins, where schooners docked to transfer cargo, qualify as geographical nodes in historic New Orleans, starting in the late colonial era and ending prior to World War II.

The turning basin of Carondelet Canal was located in Faubourg Tremé, one block behind the city, at the intersection of eponymous Basin Street and Toulouse Street, covering an area of roughly one rectangular city block. The canal extended from the basin's upper right corner, forming the shape of a golf club, and extended 1.6 miles to Bayou St. John, which continued 3.5 miles to the lake. The surrounding neighborhood, dating from the late eighteenth and early nineteenth centuries, was an intimate streetscape of cottages and tenements with a mostly Creole populace, though the presence of the canal would also attract functional land uses such as lumberyards, coal depots, and workshops. A mile uptown was the New Basin Canal's turning basin, shaped like a crooked laboratory beaker and nestled among Julia Street, Triton Walk (now Howard Avenue), and present-day South Rampart, four blocks lakeside of Lee Circle. It too was surrounded by the utilitarian and the commercial, not the aesthetic or the residential. Both canals were, at various times and in various places, paralleled by shell roads, streets, and railroads, making each basin that much more a geographical node.

These turning basins were miniature local ports, not expansive depots teeming with activity. Their channels were too narrow for large riverboats or oceangoing vessels; with some exceptions, their locations were too far from the levee to receive cotton bales, hogsheads of sugar, and other bulky cargo. Besides, the regional hinterlands served by these canals—mostly the North Shore and the Gulf Coast—were not agricultural districts. Rather, one might find construction materials such as lumber, bricks, sand, shells, shingles, and staves; charcoal and firewood for cooking and heating; tar, turpentine, and rosin; and oysters, fish, fruits, vegetables, meats, and wild game around the docks of the turning basins. Local consumption and production played a much bigger role in the cargo at the turning basins than at the levee, which of course had a national and international clientele. In some regards, the turning basins of Carondelet Canal and New Basin Canal were the antithesis of the great levee along the Mississippi, which nearly every visitor to nineteenth-century New Orleans marveled at for its excitement and commotion. Few visitors ventured to the grungy, back-of-town basins with their rough characters and nearby red-light districts.

A pedestrian in the 1880s-90s strolling down Carondelet Walk, the quaint cobblestoned, cottage-lined street paralleling the canal, would have smelled the turning basin before seeing it. Seafood, rotting vegetable scraps, filthy water, the aromas of a nearby brewery, coal and wood smoke, and sewage permeated the steamy air. The sounds of a tin shop and a steam-operated wood-planing mill emanated from across the canal between Marais and Tremé streets, near the drawbridge. Two blocks in the opposite direction was the Tremé Market, a picturesque emporium with a landmark cupola where canal-borne produce was sold. Lumberyards and junkyards dominated the scene around the canal, with the exception of a two-story Masonic Hall at the intersection of St. Claude and Carondelet Walk. Opposite the hall, the 200-by-400-foot turning basin was now in full view, cramped with dozens of luggers, schooners, and other watercraft, no two alike, most with masts silhouetted against the dusk sky. Each was its own enterprise, specialized to haul coal in some cases, oysters in others, lumber in others still. The landings surrounding the basin were dirty and unprotected by levees, piled in places with lumber, cords of firewood, and sundry items in transit, tended to by dockworkers and their beasts of burden. Turning past a number of charcoal distributors and an incongruous bakery, the visitor would arrive at Basin

---

410. Huber, *Jackson Square,* 91-93.

Summer twilight in the heart of the French Quarter, looking down Chartres Street toward Jackson Square, with the Cabildo and St. Louis Cathedral facing the Mississippi River. *Photograph by author, 2000*

Hundred-and-fifty-year-old roofscape: the St. Louis Cathedral's steeples, the cupola of the Cabildo, and the multifaceted roofs and courtyards of the Upper Pontalba Building. This view is gained from the fourth floor of the Jax Brewery annex. *Photograph by author, 2000*

The greater Jackson Square area in 1989:
1. Dashed line indicates approximate riverbank at the time of the city's founding, 1718;
2. Approximate location of first clearing of forest by Bienville's men, starting in March-April 1718;
3. St. Louis Cathedral (1849-51);
4. The Cabildo (1796-99);
5. The Presbytère (1791-1813);
6. Jackson Square, originally the French *Place d'Armes* and later the Spanish Plaza de Armas;
7. Upper Pontalba Building (1849-50), owned by the city;
8. Lower Pontalba Building (1849-51), owned by the state;
9. French Market (1810s-20s, renovated 1930s and 1970s);
10. Former wharves and Sugar District into the 1930s;
11. Jax Brewery, a remnant of the area's industrial history, converted to a festival marketplace in 1984;
12. Moonwalk, the popular riverside promenade, which reopened the Mississippi River to French Quarter residents and visitors after well over a century of industrial and transportation usage.
Map by author, aerial image courtesy U.S. Geological Survey

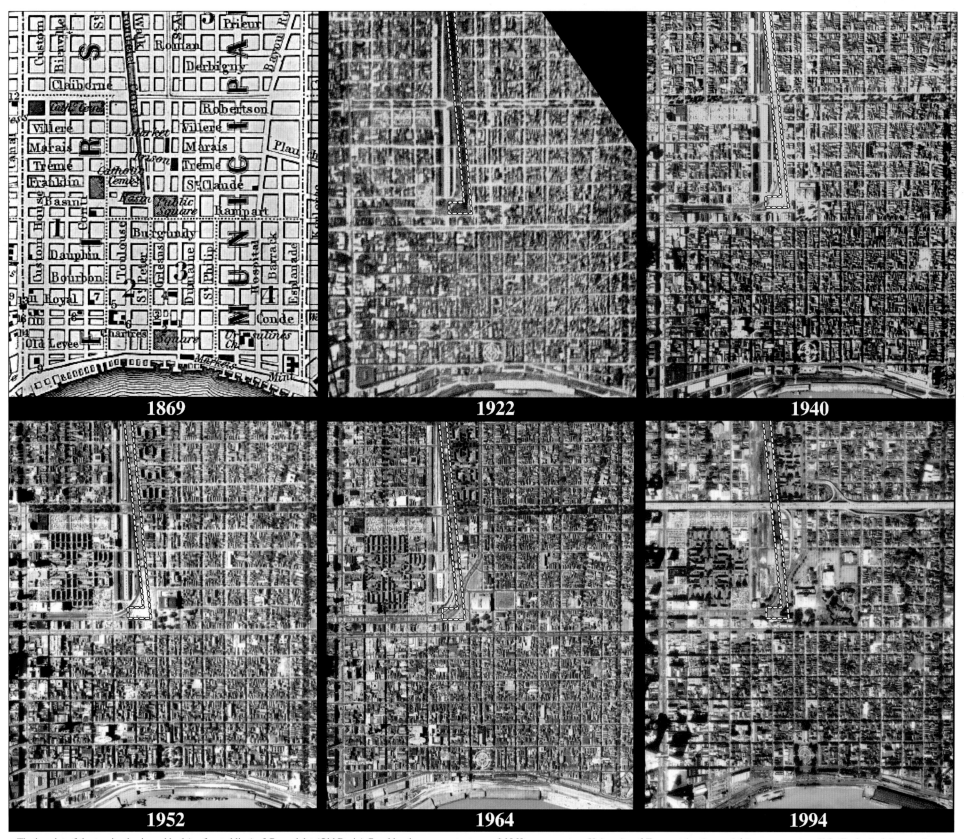

The imprint of the turning basin and bed (perforated line) of Carondelet (Old Basin) Canal has been a constant part of New Orleans' evolving urban geography for over two hundred years. These perspectives cover the French Quarter (bottom) and Faubourg Tremé from Canal Street to Esplanade Avenue. *Map by author; detail of 1869 map courtesy University of Texas at Austin; aerial images courtesy U.S. Geological Survey, Army Corps of Engineers, and the Port of New Orleans*

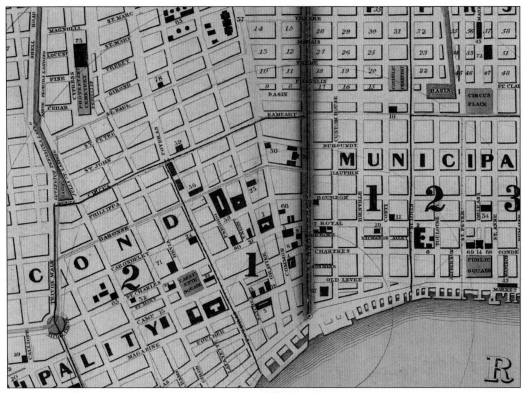

Turning basins of the New Basin Canal (triangular feature at left) and the Old Basin Canal (rectangular basin at right) in 1845. *Norman (detail)*

Passenger Depot was constructed directly across present-day Howard Avenue from the basin, giving the area a level of street and foot traffic that did not exist at the downtown basin.

But neither canal could survive the obsolescence rendered by the railroads that paralleled them, the highways that replaced them, or the Industrial Canal that superceded them. Carondelet Canal was declared unnavigable and filled in, starting with its turning basin in 1927 and completed in 1938. Today, the canal's corridor is apparent to anyone driving over Interstate 10, where a large open swath (Lafitte Street) connects the rear of the French Quarter to Bayou St. John. But all signs of the turning basin, a geographical node in New Orleans for over 130 years, have been wiped away, with the exception of an old Southern Railway office, built there on account of the canal, and the name of the street that was its home, made famous worldwide through the jazz tune "Basin Street Blues." The Louisiana state legislature passed a constitutional amendment in 1936 to close the New Basin Canal; its turning basin was filled in 1937, and by 1938, the portion from South Rampart to Claiborne was covered over. The remaining portion operated until 1946 but was entirely filled in by the early 1950s, except for the extreme lakeside tip at West End, which still exists. Lost amid parking lots, rerouted streets, and the expanded lanes of Loyola Avenue near the Plaza Tower, the turning basin of the New Basin Canal is erased from the modern streetscape, but the canal's corridor is well utilized as the path of the Pontchartrain Expressway. The turning basin, a geographical node for 100 years, lives on vicariously through the transportation node it helped create: the Union Passenger Terminal and bus station serving today as one of the gateways into New Orleans.

Foot of Canal Street

New Orleans aficionados arrive early for screenings of the 1951 film adaptation of *A Streetcar Named Desire,* occasionally presented at the annual Tennessee Williams Festival and other cultural events. While the world remembers the movie for its sultry balcony scenes and masterful performances, this local crowd also anticipates the fleeting opening scenes filmed on location in downtown New Orleans. The camera pans the broad expanse of lower Canal Street past the Liberty Place Monument to the swirling junction of taxicabs, trains, streetcars, and pedestrians at the L & N Station near the river, where, amid blaring whistles and clanging bells, Blanche DuBois emerges from lingering locomotive steam into the Crescent City evening and boards Desire streetcar #922 to the metaphorical Elysian Fields. The scene works as well for the story as it does in capturing the bustling excitement that once prevailed at the foot of Canal Street.

From the antebellum age to the mid-twentieth century, the foot of Canal Street[412] was one of the liveliest places in town, for it was here that river traffic, port activity, railroad and streetcar lines, and the downtown street network all came together at a single node. It was also the point at which the city's oldest neighborhood, its central business district, its most prominent thoroughfare, and its most important geographical feature were all staked together. The foot of Canal Street is high on the crest of the natural levee and lined with a batture, and its historical relevance as a port, landing, and transportation hub makes it one of the city's geographical nodes. It is also a transient node, starting near the present-day corner of Canal and North Peters when the city was platted in 1723 (neither street would exist for almost another century) and slowing expanding riverward as nature and man annexed about 1,500 feet of the Mississippi into the urban realm.

Fittingly, Bienville himself lived near this site in the early 1720s, followed by a Jesuit compound in the 1730s, when this area formed the rural outskirts of the city. Settlers in the frontier village would have known the spot as the site of a windmill and the point at which the smattering of houses dissipated into field and forest.[413] A lock and navigation canal was planned for what would be the foot of Canal Street as early as 1721, a proposal that would surface and die periodically for well over a century, eventually bestowing upon the street its simple, common, yet unforgettable name. The intersection of the *Chemin Real* (now Tchoupitoulas Street) through the future Canal Street foot made this point the upriver gate of the city for both land and river traffic. Fortifications built during the French era guarded this and all sides of the city but were reconstructed more substantially by the Spanish in the 1790s, when the foot of future Canal Street was the site of Fort San Luis. This bastion was located at the present-day intersection of Magazine with Canal. (Its powder magazine, which exploded disastrously during the 1794 city fire, probably accounts for the name of this intersecting street.) The Spanish also built the first of four historical custom houses near here; its Spanish word, *aduana,* was used for an adjacent street, later Customhouse Street, now Iberville Street.

Street and pass the lugger landing along the broad side of the basin, at which point a penetrating new aroma wafts through the air: the output of the Southern Vinegar Company. At the far corner of the turning basin was the McDonogh School No. 18 and a line of tenements, an indigent residential community living in and among industries and wharves. Perhaps an occasional dialogue in Creole French would be heard from old-timers.[411]

Had he visited again around 1910, the visitor would have observed some significant changes in and around the turning basin. There was now the three-story Globe Hall (Globe Exchange) where the Masonic Hall used to be, from which he might have heard the newfangled sounds of jazz and dancing, for it was to become an important site in the development of New Orleans' most famous cultural export. Storyville, the legalized red-light district of 1897-17, may have also been audible a few blocks up Basin Street. The North Franklin/Toulouse Street corner of the basin itself was, by 1908, filled in and paved over with railroad tracks, which exploited the canal's right-of-way and curved onto Basin Street to deposit passengers at the beautiful new train station designed by Daniel Burnham on Canal Street. The Parish Prison was gone from its site a few blocks down, and new drainage devices had been installed. But all in all, the Old Basin Canal still maintained its timeless, Dickinson atmosphere, and would for another two decades.

The New Basin Canal's turning basin formed a similar landscape at the rear edge of the Faubourg St. Mary, but it and its surroundings were almost a half-century younger than those of Carondelet Canal. This uptown port, sometimes called Mobile Landing, had a steadier stream of traffic and a higher tonnage that the Old Basin; the streets around it were paved with asphalt, gravel, and sand; and its shell road and towpath to the lake at West End were well-used transportation routes. Lumber sheds, cement and lime distributors, planing mills, and wagon shops were intermixed with tenements of poor blacks, a situation similar to downtown. A historic Protestant graveyard, the Girod Street Cemetery, lay nearby, just as the St. Louis No. 1 Cemetery neighbored the downtown canal, and many sites in the adjacent neighborhood were noted for their role in the birth of jazz. Railroad tracks also followed the canal to its basin, as they did downtown, and in 1892, the Illinois Central

---

411. Street scenes based on *Sanborn Fire Insurance Map* (1885, 1896, and 1908) plus various photographs and descriptive accounts.

412. Some people use the metaphor "foot of Canal Street" to mean the cemeteries end of Canal Street in Mid-City. In fact, such usage makes sense, since this end of Canal Street is physically lower and farther from downtown activity than the river end. But this is not the majority usage. Most people immediately understand "the foot of Canal Street" to mean the busy river end of the boulevard.
413. Bienville's plantation house was near the present-day corner of Common and Magazine, a short block from Canal. The windmill was near the corner of Canal and North Peters and is depicted in the panoramic sketch of the city made by Jean Pierre Lassus in 1726. Wilson, *The Vieux Carre*, 20.

By the early American years, the original city was mostly developed, the batture was expanding into the river, and Faubourg Ste. Marie was growing. The only unformed element was the open commons nestled among these three zones. This commons finally came into its own on March 3, 1807, when an Act of Congress created what would become Canal Street (see pages 66 and 110). Within the year, the foot of Canal Street began to take shape when Benjamin Latrobe, the architect responsible for the U.S. Capitol, designed a second custom house for the block of Canal Street riverside of Decatur Street; it was built in 1808-9 in the new Greek Revival style, one of the first in the former French colony. Lower Canal developed with American-style row structures mixed with some colonial-era styles, one of which, a five-bay storehouse built in 1821 by Felix Pinson and Maurice Piseta, still exists, though heavily remodeled.[414] An expansive landing/wharf was laid out and well utilized as the heart of New Orleans' amazing riverside port, at a time when the city was routinely predicted to become one of the largest and most important in the nation. At this time, an alley of sycamore trees shaded the neutral ground of Canal Street down to its riverside foot. The scale of the area would change substantially in 1848, when construction commenced on the immense Custom House that currently anchors the street, a monument to its strategic location and maritime mission.

For the next few decades, the foot of Canal Street melded into the spacious riverside landing where ships docked and cargo was deposited, while inland it was surrounded by mostly two- to four-story row structures occupied by warehouses, port services, wholesalers, retailers, and professionals. The site was made salient in 1859 when a landmark cast-iron City Water Works Building was built directly in the middle of the Canal Street foot; though never used for this purpose and removed a few decades later, it figured prominently in Reconstruction-era sketches of the area for its centralized location. It was joined by the distinctive Harbor Station/Canal Street Ferry House, notable for its cupola and graceful roof. Streetcar lines laid in 1861 and railroads installed after the Civil War would help carry the foot of Canal Street to a significance beyond its mere status as a terminus of a major downtown thoroughfare.

Reconstruction-era political enmities boiled over at the foot of Canal Street, in front of the Custom House, on September 14, 1874, when the White League, a Democratic militia vehemently opposed to the Republican presence, engaged carpetbagger governor W. P. Kellogg's predominantly black Metropolitan Police in a violent fifteen-minute clash precipitated by the White League's attempt to oust the governor after his seizure of an arms shipment. The defeat of the Metropolitans in the Battle of Liberty Place, which cost thirty-two lives, provided the White League with a momentum that would eventually lead to the withdrawal of all federal troops in 1877. Memories of the battle, both deferential and bitter, would draw citizens to the Liberty Place Monument every September 14 for over a century to come, contributing to the mystique of the foot of Canal Street.

But what cinched the fame of this spot was its happier role as the landing site of Rex on the day before Mardi Gras. From the mid-1870s to 1917, the King of Carnival arrived at the foot of Canal Street on a steamboat or yacht, where throngs would welcome him and chariots would carry him to various social engagements in preparation for his one-day reign on Mardi Gras. The tradition was revived decades later and, starting in 1987, was formalized into a series of events taking place on a "new" holiday called Lundi Gras (Fat Monday). In any other city, such a notion would seem like a bewildering collective indulgence in fantasy and escapism, but in New Orleans it is part of a civic act as important to the city's identity as a defining historical event is to other communities. And it happened—and happens—at the foot of Canal Street.

Intermodal transportation dominated the scene at the foot of Canal Street in the early 1900s: a landmark pedestrian viaduct allowed commuters to board the ferry to Algiers while locomotives hauled passenger cars into the thousand-foot-long Louisville & Nashville (L & N) Station and shed. Nearby was a comparatively more peaceful setting, Eads Plaza, named after Capt. James Eads, who contributed substantially to New Orleans' prosperity through his river engineering in the late 1800s. From 1899 to 1930, lower Canal hosted a major eight-track layover terminal for the streetcars that serviced the surrounding areas. "The terminus at Liberty Place, the loop at the foot of Canal Street, saw in 1902 more lines terminating and grouping there than did the famous streetcar terminus at the Ferry Building in San Francisco. . . . The cars of twenty lines could be seen at the layover terminus, and as none of these lines had a greater headway than five minutes, the mass of cars there congregated inticed [sic] the imagination."[415] In 1929, this same site was also the scene of violent riots during one of the most divisive street railway strikes in the nation. Streetcar transportation took a severe blow that year but recovered in 1930, the same year when a beautification program spruced up Canal Street's lighting fixtures and sidewalks. Ten years later, the foot of Canal Street saw the first major troop departure from New Orleans for the impending hostilities of World War II.[416]

The foot of Canal Street diminished as a geographical node in the 1950s and 1960s, when passenger trains and streetcar lines were removed from the spot and only ferries and tour boats docked at the river. While the rest of the street remained economically vibrant far longer than most of America's major downtown thoroughfares—into the 1970s—the foot of Canal Street took on a shabby appearance. Then a new relevance arrived, godsend to some, anathema to others: the tourist and convention trade and its need for immense structures. Starting in the mid-1960s and continuing to the present, Canal Street in general and the foot in particular transformed to modern, postindustrial times. In 1966, one of New Orleans' first true skyscrapers (on the heels of the forty-five-story Plaza Tower), the cruciform thirty-three-story International Trade Mart, was constructed on the prized real estate immediately adjacent to the foot of Canal Street. The International Trade Mart and Plaza Tower were the first skyscrapers built upon "Brunspiles," steel-reinforced octagonal concrete pilings fitted end to end and driven through 50 to 200 feet of millennia-old river sediments to rest upon the local version of bedrock: the firm point-bar sand or hard Pleistocene-Epoch clay strata stable enough to bear a skyscraper. Based on research and designs by engineers Thomas Bruns, William Mouton, and others, the Brunspile revolutionized construction in New Orleans and forever altered its 1920s-era skyline.[417] It started at the foot of Canal Street. The landmark skyscraper, now called the World Trade Center, provided office space for the city's maritime industry as well as the Louisiana Maritime Museum, a perfect location for such entities. Joining the Trade Mart were a series of higher skyscraper hotels along lower Canal built in the late 1960s and 1970s, the visually astonishing freeform Rivergate Exhibition Hall (1968), and the Canal Place complex (started in 1979), practically a city unto itself. The demolition of a full block of antebellum Greek Revival row buildings—occupied mostly by grungy bars and lounges in the early 1970s—to make room for the huge mall/hotel/office/parking complex eliminated the last major historical streetscape from the foot of Canal Street. One of the more unusual developments on (rather, under) lower Canal was the excavation of a 300-foot-long, 1.5 million-cubic-foot tunnel in the 1960s from Poydras to Canal in preparation for the ill-fated Riverfront Expressway, abandoned in 1969. For the 1984 Louisiana World Exposition, the riverfront from the French Quarter to the Warehouse District, including the portion in front of Canal, was landscaped and developed into an attractive and popular promenade loaded with New Orleans-themed shops, eateries, and features. The beautiful fountains at Spanish Plaza (1976) form a very different scene in what was once a gritty cargo landing.

The last decade of the twentieth century saw further alteration, both physical and social, to the foot of Canal Street. Infrastructural changes to the area led to the temporary removal in November 1989 of the controversial Liberty Place Monument, erected in 1876 at the intersection of North Front and Canal to commemorate the White League's casualties in the 1874 street battle. For 113 years, the obelisk anchored Canal Street—streetcars did 360-degree turns around its landscaped base—but its message was long considered an affront to the black community, and it is a comment on the city that it lasted almost to the 1990s in such a prominent locale.[418] The monument's pending reinstallation in the early 1990s sparked a citywide debate at a time of heightened racial tension in the city and state. The rededication ceremony for the monument, reinstalled in early 1993 in an obscure corner a few hundred feet away from its original site, ended up in nearly violent confrontation, creating a street spectacle broadcast on national news. Its contentious inscription paneled over with a diplomatically worded homily, the Liberty Place Monument now stands exiled from its once-prominent location.[419] Controversy aside, the elimination of the obelisk deprived the foot of Canal Street of a single, prominent anchor, detracting from its sense of place and significance in the streetscape. City officials would do well to replace it with a statue or sculpture, though current traffic patterns may not allow this.

The Aquarium of the Americas (1990) and Riverwalk Marketplace (1986) formed links in a riverside chain of tourism and convention-related facilities that now stretches from the French Market flea market to beyond the bridges, with the foot of Canal Street and the foot of Poydras Street intersecting the heart of the strip. In the early to mid-1990s, a heated competition among national gambling interests unfolded over control of that intersection, which, convenient to the French Quarter, downtown hotels, and the convention center, was considered prime real estate for a major casino with all the accouterments. The Rivergate Exhibition Hall was demolished (amid controversy, for its architectural significance) in 1995 for the construction of Harrah's Casino, but news later that year that gambling in New Orleans was proving to be far less lucrative than had been anticipated led to a long stall in the construction. Harrah's finally opened in October 1999. As a major new component to the foot of Canal Street,

414. This is the oldest surviving structure on Canal Street, at 507 Canal, now home to a Wendy's, a package store, and a pension. It was heavily remodeled from its Spanish colonial style in 1899.

415. Hennick and Charlton, 56, 194.

416. John Burke, "Pictures from the Past: 1940 First Troop Train Leaves N.O. as U.S. Nears WWII Entry," *New Orleans Times-Picayune*, May 28, 2000.

417. Swoboda, "Piled High," 30-31, and Russell, "William J. Mouton."

418. The city had placed a bronze plaque next to the monument in 1974, disavowing association with the White League. Mayor Dutch Morial later had bushes planted around it, in an attempt to obscure the monument he could not legally remove.

419. Gill, *Lords of Misrule*, 259-78. Even in exile, the Liberty Place Monument still invokes rancor: lone protesters have batted away all four of its ornamental columns, one by one, over the past few years.

These panoramic photographs capture the excitement of the waterborne arrival of Rex to the foot of Canal Street on the day before his annual Mardi Gras reign. The year was 1910. The upper photograph pans across the riverfront from the wharves of the Sugar District to the foot of Canal Street; the building with the cupola is the Canal Street Ferry House. The lower photograph spans from the ferry house up Canal Street proper. The Liberty Place Monument is barely discernible in the middle of Canal Street, left of the turret of the L & N train station (far right). The tradition of Rex's arrival at this spot was revived many years later and is now part of Lundi Gras activities. *Photographs by A. L. Barnett, Library of Congress*

(Right) The Liberty Place Monument stood for many years at the intersection of Canal Street and North Front, commemorating the racially charged street battle of September 14, 1874, which led to the end of Reconstruction. The white-supremacist tone of the monument's inscription made it a controversial landmark right up to its removal from the foot of Canal Street in 1989. Four years later, it was reinstalled at an obscure corner a few hundred feet away from its original site (far right), its columns batted away by protestors and its contentious inscription paneled over with a reflective message. Controversy aside, the foot of Canal Street has lacked the sense of geographical terminus that the obelisk formerly provided. City fathers would do well to replace it with a statue or monument all can agree on—perhaps to Judah Touro, the great philanthropist who lived on Canal Street and invested in its beautification. *Photographer of 1890 scene unknown, New Orleans Views Collection, UNO Special Collections; 2000 photograph by author*

The foot of Canal Street, once a prominent and well-defined transportation terminus marking New Orleans' greatest boulevard at its intersection with the Mississippi, is unfortunately rather indistinct today, curving into side streets and lined with infrastructure. Despite its conspicuous buildings—the World Trade Center (1966), Canal Place (early 1980s), the Aquarium of the Americas (1990), and Harrah's Casino (1995-99)—the foot of Canal Street lacks the sense of place it once had. *Photograph by author, 2000*

The foot of Canal Street in its mid-twentieth-century heyday, when streetcars, autos, railroads, ferries, and pedestrian traffic all came to a node. Note the streetcars rounding the Liberty Place Monument at center. Streetcar lines "looped" at the foot of Canal Street from 1869 to 1964. *Photograph from pamphlet, "Way Down Yonder in New Orleans" (1946)*

the casino added alien elements to the street scene, in the form of the flamboyant, sprawling structure[420] itself as well as the illuminated palm trees and signage, features more at home in Las Vegas or Miami than in this historic port city. The vast majority of traffic (pedestrian and vehicular) around the Canal Street foot now comprises non-locals engaged in tourism-related activities.[421] Even the World Trade Center, whose name implies the importance of international commerce to the city, planned to take advantage of the area's tourism dependency by partially converting to a 700-room Crowne Plaza hotel. Then, in 1997, streetcar tracks were reinstalled on the Great Wide Way, thirty-three years after the termination of the famous Canal Street lines. The streetcar comeback, providing satisfying I-told-you-so's for the preservationist community, marks one of the few returns to historical circumstances for the foot of Canal Street. The new tracks curve from the Riverfront Streetcar line onto Canal, giving the foot of Canal Street a new angle for the twenty-first century; if funding comes through, streetcars will once again travel down the great corridor all the way to Mid-City.

No longer is the intersection of New Orleans' greatest thoroughfare with the Father of Waters the geographical node it once was, when the foot of Canal Street was a distinct place that served as the jumping-off point between the city and the world. As one looks down on it from Canal Place or ventures across its treacherous traffic patterns, it is apparent that the once-conspicuous site has been engineered to a lesser distinctiveness, feeling a bit like an infrastructural staging ground for the daily goings-on of the tourist and convention industry. City buses now make awkward traffic-stopping U-turns where streetcars once made graceful 360-degree turns around the Liberty Place Monument. But you can still catch the ferry here, see great ships sail the river, wait out slow-moving freight trains, or jump on a streetcar or bus. That the node still occupies a special place in New Orleans popular culture was made apparent by local musician John Boutte's 1999 song, "At the Foot of Canal Street."

Algiers Ferry approaching the foot of Canal Street. *Photograph by author, 2000*

Lock and Turning Basin of the Inner Harbor Navigational Canal

On January 29, 1923, on the site of the old Ursuline Nuns property in the Ninth Ward, two hydraulic dredges tore away the final earthen barrier separating the silty fresh waters of the Mississippi River from the clear brackish waters of Lake Pontchartrain. When the waters mixed in the forebay of the completed Inner Harbor Navigational Canal—the Industrial Canal—New Orleans had created a physical connection of river and lake, a single point epitomizing its ancient mission to serve both the North American hinterland and the world beyond the Gulf of Mexico. The lock of the Industrial Canal best symbolizes the nexus, followed by the turning basin excavated when the Gulf Intracoastal Waterway and Mississippi River-Gulf Outlet Canal were added to the seaway scheme. Together, these assets represent the greatest of New Orleans' geographical nodes, as well as the last: other nodes discussed here have largely played out their days as foci for New Orleans' connection with the world, most before the close of the nineteenth century.

The concept behind this waterway forms a thread connecting the earliest days of the city—when Company agents recognized the need in 1718 and a river-to-lake canal was sketched on the first plan of New Orleans in March 1721—with its ambiguous future, when environmental concerns may lead to the closing down of the tangential Mississippi River-Gulf Outlet Canal. The lock itself, an engineering marvel in the 1920s but now a notorious shipping bottleneck, is also the subject of controversy at the turn of the twenty-first century, as the Army Corps of Engineering commences the long-awaited, long-dreaded, and very expensive expansion. But few question that the canal has been and is vastly important to New Orleans and its hinterland. Lining the turning basin of the Industrial Canal, where the Gulf Intracoastal Waterway and Mississippi River-Gulf Outlet Canal branch off for the open seas, four immense container-terminal berths along France Road and another one across the basin on Jourdan Road serve vessels bearing cargo to and from millions of people around the globe. In these rugged and uncharming environs far from the balconies of the French Quarter and the streetcars of St. Charles, New Orleans continues to execute its historic mission, its raison d'être, its central organizing principle: link between river and sea.

Lock of the Industrial Canal. *Photograph by Donn Young, courtesy the Port of New Orleans*

420. For alternative views of Harrah's Casino, see Douglas MacCash's architectural review, "Bricks and Mortality," and the editorial comments of Barbara L. Allen, professor of architecture at the University of Louisiana at Lafayette.
421. Palm trees are not new to Canal Street, its neutral ground having been lined with them into the 1970s, nor will they be confined to the foot of Canal Street. In the near future, the Downtown Development District will plant 220 Medjool date palms along the street from the foot to Claiborne Avenue. Gordon Russell, Gordon, "Urban Jungle."

Turning basin of the Industrial Canal and Mississippi River-Gulf Outlet Canal. *Photographs by Donn Young, courtesy the Port of New Orleans*

Landmarks: Clues of Identity

Landmarks, according to Kevin Lynch's *Image of the City,* are not only famous historic sites like St. Louis Cathedral or cherished places like Preservation Hall, but any object in the cityscape clear in form, contrasting with its background, and prominent in its spatial location. Landmarks provide "clues to identity" and "trigger cues" to one's route down paths, through districts, to nodes, and across edges.[422] A landmark may be a single sign or cupola, a row of distinctive houses, or a massive skyscraper, as long as it sends conscious or subconscious messages that inform observers of where they are: *You know you're in (neighborhood, district, place) when you see (landmark).*

Landmark recognition develops gradually and naturally as one travels routinely about a place, but at the macroscopic level, they may be known vicariously through countless pictographic references. Show anyone a scene of iron-lace galleries and they will immediately identify it as New Orleans, though it may take a visit to understand that such landmarks characterize the French Quarter more so than other parts of the city. Airlines know the power of landmarks, using them in airport waiting-room posters to promote "destinations" such as London, Paris, and Sydney with cliché images of Big Ben, the Eiffel Tower, and the Sydney Opera House. Our discussion is at the microlevel, and at that scale New Orleans is rich in quirky, odd, and majestic landmarks[423] that trigger a sense of spatial understanding.

Two qualifications. First, unlike paths, edges, districts, and nodes, landmarks are personal and unquantifiable. What one individual identifies as a symbol of an entire neighborhood may not even be noticed by another. Second, while Dr. Lynch described landmarks to be single, isolated objects serving as clues of identity, I have expanded the concept to mean particular types or styles of objects that are ubiquitous in a certain area, thus informing observers of their spatial context via dozens of clues, not just one. This accommodates the fact that architectural styles play a major role in visually indicating location in the city, through hundreds of point sources, rarely just one.

422. Lynch, 48, 78-83.
423. See Bookhardt and Newlin for the final word in bizarre landmarks.

Landmarks of the French Quarter

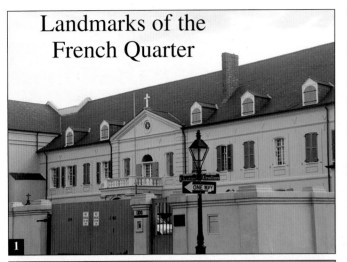

1. Oldest building in the Mississippi Valley, the Ursuline Convent on Chartres Street is the only major physical remnant of New Orleans' first French colonial era. It was designed in 1745 and built in 1749-53, serving variously as a convent, school, orphanage, bishop's residence, rectory, and archive. The Ursuline Nuns, major figures in New Orleans history since 1727, moved to a new complex at the present-day mouth of the Industrial Canal in 1824 and to their present-day campus on State Street in 1912.

2. Steeples of St. Louis Cathedral (1851) above the rear quarters of the Upper Pontalba Building.

3. Distinctive cupola of the Girod (Napoleon) House on Chartres Street at the St. Louis intersection in the French Quarter, built in 1814 with some components dating from the 1790s.

4. Dramatically illuminated statue of Christ in St. Anthony's Garden behind St. Louis Cathedral, one of the most beautiful and serene spots in the city.

5. Silhouette of the Cabildo viewed from Jackson Square during an August sunset.

6. Everyone, from weekend tourists to lifelong residents, knows where Café Du Monde is located.

7. Cupola of the Cabildo (1799) above the Upper Pontalba Building. The Cabildo's Mansard roof and cupola were rebuilt following the disastrous fire of May 1988; the building reopened in 1994.

8. Antoine's, oldest restaurant in the nation and most famous in a city known for restaurants, has occupied this St. Louis Street townhouse since 1868. Founded a block away by Antoine Alciatore in 1840, Antoine's has been managed by the same family for five generations and remains an institution of local history, Creole cuisine, and fine dining. Antoine's is New Orleans at its best. Note, in this 1995 scene, the Confederate battle flag: once a common sight on galleries in the Quarter, the few remaining ones quietly came down during the 1990s.

9. Archway into the French Market flea market in front of slant-roofed servant quarters of Decatur Street townhouses, at the lower corner of the French Quarter. The row structures of Gallatin Street once occupied this site prior to their demolition in the 1930s to create the present-day flea market.

Photographs by author, 1995-2001

Landmarks of Faubourg Tremé, New Marigny/St. Roch, Faubourg Marigny, Bywater, and Holy Cross

1. The swirling brick patterns of Congo Square, former site of Fort Ferdinand, made famous as a Sunday gathering spot for slaves from the 1810s to the 1850s.

2. The New Orleans Italian Mutual Benevolent Society Tomb (1857) is visible from most perspectives as one passes St. Louis Cemetery No. 1, the city's oldest surviving cemetery (1789), on Basin Street in Faubourg Tremé.

3. Our Lady of Guadeloupe (Mortuary Chapel of St. Anthony, 1826), a landmark of Rampart Street across from the French Quarter, has served New Orleans for funerals of yellow-fever victims, as a parish church for Irish, Italian, Filipino, Hispanic, and African-American populations, and as a chapel for the local fire and police departments. Its current steeple replaced the original dome that complemented the Spanish Colonial style of the structure.

4. This imposing Greek Revival mansion on North Rampart and Ursulines, now a hotel, recollects the prosperous residential living that once intermixed with cottages and slums on and near Rampart Street at the edge of the French Quarter. Passing in front is a parade marking the closing of the twentieth century, December 31, 1999.

5. A nineteenth-century townhouse painted bright pink looks just fine in New Orleans. Gene's Po-Boy is a kind of gateway into the funky historic district of Faubourg Marigny and the lower French Quarter for motorists and pedestrians heading down Elysian Fields Avenue toward the river.

6. Ten blocks of 150-year-old Creole cottages, their residents relocated elsewhere, were cleared out of Faubourg Tremé in 1956-73 and developed into Louis Armstrong Park (1980) and the Theater for the Performing Arts. The project, seen in retrospect as a regrettable example of misguided "urban renewal," caused ill feelings and cost the city dozens of historical and architectural treasures. But the mistake is past and irreversible, and today Louis Armstrong Park takes its place in the fabric of the city as a peaceful green spot with lagoons and berms, a site for music festivals and home to the local radio institution, WWOZ. The park is slated to be the home of the New Orleans Jazz National Historic Park.

7. St. Augustine Roman Catholic Church, designed by J. N. B. de Pouilly and built in 1842 on St. Claude and Governor Nicholls (formerly Bayou Road), has been a distinguished landmark for most of the life of what has been called America's oldest black neighborhood, Faubourg Tremé (1810). Its graceful patinous bell tower, the signature symbol of Tremé, is visible from strategic points throughout the French Quarter and the Creole faubourgs. The event in this photograph was a whimsical jazz funeral for the twentieth century on December 31, 1999.

8. St. Bernard Circle Market (ca. 1920s), like the nearby St. Roch Market, is an old municipal marketplace now utilized as a grocery store. A landmark of the Seventh Ward, it is especially distinctive from elevated I-10, from which motorists get a good view of its Spanish Revival-style tower and charging-bull weathervane. The market gets its name from the traffic circle at the intersection of St. Bernard Avenue and North Claiborne, similar to Lee Circle but sans a monument. The circle was eliminated when the interstate came in 1966 (a forested neutral ground once passed in front of the market); some of the old buildings in this vicinity reflect the former street pattern with their curving fronts.

9. St. Roch Market on St. Claude Avenue, in the neighborhood of St. Roch, is one of the handful of old municipal markets that survived the passing of that era, operating today as a local food store serving some of the dishes that make New Orleans famous.

10. Another landmark of St. Roch is Saint Roch's Campo Santo, one of the most poignantly beautiful burial grounds in the city. Its Gothic chapel (1876), famous for its display of votives, was built by Fr. Peter Leonard Thevis in thanksgiving for the survival of his parishioners during the 1868 yellow fever epidemic.

11. Three historic Catholic churches in the Faubourg Marigny and Bywater closed on a very sad Friday—June 29, 2001—for lack of congregation. St. Vincent de Paul on Dauphine Street in Bywater, with which the other parishes will be combined, was the happy exception: its congregation was already large and vibrant, mostly comprising a Latino community. The bonds to this church are so strong that many attendees live in distant suburbs but still make the long trip to its doors every Sunday for afternoon mass. The bell tower, visible from afar and across the river, is mysteriously spectacular, with its clock illuminated a dim yellow against a moonrise in the east, a sunset in the west, or a starry night above. It has been overlooking these downriver neighborhoods since 1908, added forty years after the church was built and seventy years after the parish was founded. St. Vincent de Paul was renamed Blessed Francis Xavier Seelos in 2001 following the consolidation.

12. Faubourg Marigny is home to a number of graceful old Catholic churches erected by and for various ethnic groups that resided in this historic neighborhood in the late nineteenth century. These are the twin bell towers of Holy Trinity on St. Ferdinand Street, founded for German Catholics in 1853; it closed a few years ago when its parishioners dwindled to a number too few. The weathered old church gives a distinctly Caribbean or Latin American ambience to the neighborhood.

13. Something for everyone at King Roger's, where McShane Place cuts off North Rampart Street on the edge of the Faubourg Marigny. McShane Place, laid out in 1927, efficiently transfers heavy traffic flow from North Rampart Street to St. Claude Avenue as one heads downriver toward the Industrial Canal.

14. Twin landmarks of the Holy Cross riverfront: the Doullut "Steamboat" Houses (1905-13), arguably the most unusual and imaginative buildings in a city famous for interesting architecture. Located in an area geographically isolated from the heart of the city, the "steamboat houses" probably are viewed more by tourists on passing riverboats than by visitors to the Holy Cross neighborhood.

Photographs by author, 1995-2001

Landmarks of the Central Business District

1. The Pickwick Club, on Canal Street at St. Charles Avenue, was built in a much simpler design in 1826, remodeled into a hotel in 1858, converted to a billiard hall in 1865, and renovated in 1874 with ornate Italian Renaissance and Greek Revival features.

2. Streamline-modern styling of Walgreen's (1938) on Canal Street at the corner of Baronne. The drugstore originally served the patients of the physician offices in the upper floors of the Maison Blanche Building, across the street. The doctors are gone, as is Maison Blanche, but Walgreen's prospers. Two years after this 1995 photograph was taken, the units to the right of the corner store were demolished and Walgreen's was expanded into the space.

3. Spectacular pearl-white Maison Blanche Building (1909) on Dauphine and Canal, in 1995, when it still was occupied by the famous retailer. Maison Blanche closed in 1998, marking the end of the era of great downtown department stores. Two years later, a Ritz-Carlton Hotel opened within its walls, indicative of Canal Street's economic shift from local retail toward tourism.

4. One of the most conspicuous landmarks of the Central Business District is the lantern cupola of the Hibernia Bank Building (1921), the city's high point—355 feet—for over forty years. It is illuminated a glowing white on most evenings, switching to holiday colors during Carnival, July 4, Halloween, and Christmas. So salient is the cupola, it is used as a navigation landmark by pilots on the Mississippi.

5. Poydras Street Branch of Whitney Bank, corner of Poydras and Camp Street.

6. Poydras Street landmarks from two very different eras, Le Pavillon Hotel (1906) and One Shell Square (1972). Actually, the part of Le Pavillon visible here is a recent addition. Poydras Street was widened in 1966, allowing the 1906 hotel, which originally was oriented toward Baronne, to expand toward Poydras. That the hotel now addresses Poydras Street with this gigantic façade reflects the street's newfound importance during the oil-boom years. One Shell Square (697 feet) is the tallest building in the city and the lower Mississippi Valley. It is 196 feet higher than the highest natural point in Louisiana.

7. Former Masonic Lodge, built in a modernized Gothic style in 1926 on the site of an earlier cathedral-like temple. An office building since 1982, it was recently converted to a hotel.

8.-9. Ultimate landmark: The Louisiana Superdome (1975) drastically changed the skyline of downtown New Orleans with a look that, even in the twenty-first century, appears futuristic. Controversial from the beginning, the Superdome made the important contribution of keeping business and attention focused on the Central Business District during times when money was fleeing to the suburbs. Most would agree that it has been a tremendous success, and many New Orleanians harbor a sense of pride and affection for the stunning marvel. In 2001, however, the New Orleans Saints aired their complaints about the structure's limitations for professional football, raising questions about the future of both the Superdome and the Saints. In aerial photographs and satellite images of the city, the bright white 9.7-acre roof of the 273-foot-high stadium provides instant orientation to viewers.

10. Four of the tallest structures in New Orleans scrape the twilight sky of New Year's Eve 1999, two on Canal and two in the interior of the Central Business District: the Marriott Hotel, the Sheraton Hotel, One Shell Square (tallest in the city, 697 feet), and the post-modern First NBC Center (Place St. Charles, 645 feet). All four were built between 1972 and 1985.

Photographs by author, 1995-2000

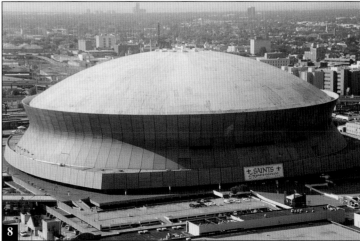

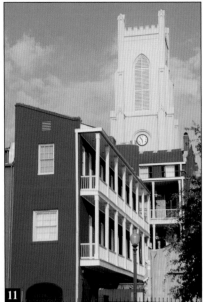

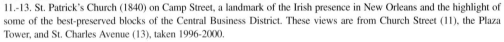

11.-13. St. Patrick's Church (1840) on Camp Street, a landmark of the Irish presence in New Orleans and the highlight of some of the best-preserved blocks of the Central Business District. These views are from Church Street (11), the Plaza Tower, and St. Charles Avenue (13), taken 1996-2000.

14. Tower of the Maginnis Cotton Mill, one of the impressive landmarks of the Warehouse District dramatically visible to commuters arriving over the bridge from the west bank. The building was converted into luxury apartments in the mid-1990s.

15.-16. The Thirteen Sisters of Julia Street (1833)—Julia Row, between St. Charles and Camp—tell many stories: American architectural styles in the Creole city; childhood home of famed architect Henry Hobson Richardson; spectacular example of an integral row block; epitome of urban decay in the 1970s; interesting contrast between restoration (Camp Street end) and rough handling (St. Charles end, visible here, 15). The Preservation Resource Center of New Orleans initiated the resurrection of Julia Row in 1976 when it moved into the Camp Street unit; today, nine of the thirteen units are restored. Twelve of the thirteen service wings also survive, making for an impressive sight from Camp Street (16).

17. Classic Warehouse District ensemble along Tchoupitoulas Street.

18. Old advertisements painted on walls are typical of the Warehouse District. This is on St. Joseph Street.

19. This port-city montage is briefly visible from St. Charles Avenue near the I-10 overpass: Mississippi River bridge, Cotton Mills water tower, and an isolated Victorian building on Camp Street, loaded with dependencies, that somehow survived the twentieth century.

20. The former Howard Memorial Library (1888) at Lee Circle, the only design of Louisiana-born architect Henry Hobson Richardson built (posthumously) in the Crescent City, is a massive landmark for motorists curving around Lee Circle. The "Richardson Romanesque"-style building houses the Ogden Southern Art Museum. Another museum, commemorating D-Day and other amphibious landings of World War II, opened to worldwide acclaim on June 6, 2000. Around the corner is the Confederate Museum, oldest in the state. This area has made tremendous gains recently as an art, museum, dining, and upscale living district, after years as practically a slum. Note the shadow of the Lee Monument cast upon the foreground.

21. The Lee Monument (1884), one of the landmarks that people consciously and subconsciously use to separate downtown from uptown.

Photographs by author, 1996-2000

1

10

2

11

3

4

5

GROCERY

6

7

8

9

Landmarks of the Lower Garden District, Irish Channel, Garden District, and Magazine Street Corridor

1. Coliseum Theater and St. Theresa of Avila Roman Catholic Church (1849), two very different landmarks of the Lower Garden District built about a century apart.

2. You know you're in the Lower Garden District, and approaching Coliseum Square, when you see the Half Moon Bar and Restaurant.

3.-4. The amazing architecture and brickwork of St. Alphonsus (1857) and St. Mary's Assumption (1860) say "Irish Channel" to New Orleanians. In fact, the Irish Channel is one of New Orleans' most nebulously delineated neighborhoods; over the years, people have described a wide range of areas between Magazine and the river as "the" Irish Channel. Recent historic districts have formalized the boundaries, but there is still disagreement as to the location of the original Irish Channel, home to dense populations of Irish immigrants in the mid-1800s.

5. This great corner building on Magazine and Felicity marks the gateway from residential to commercial Magazine, one of the most interesting streets in the city. Harkins the Florist occupies the Caribbean-style structure, notable for its unique enclosed gallery.

6. Mom-and-pop corner store on Amelia and Magazine. Such locally owned neighborhood stores and restaurants, landmarks to the residents of that neighborhood, make their last stand in New Orleans; they are especially common in mixed and poorer communities, where national chains have no interest in investing.

7. The striped steeple of immense St. Stephen Church (1868-87) is a landmark of the present-day neighborhoods of Touro/Bouligny. It is viewed here from the corner of Magazine and Napoleon.

8. The former Arabella Streetcar Barn on Magazine Street was a bus depot in recent years and is slated for conversion to a health-food supermarket. The century-old "barn" marks the gradual petering out of commercial Magazine Street, after which a residential tone emerges.

9. Splendid corner structure on Magazine and Jefferson, now home to a coffee shop on the ground floor.

10. Commander's Palace, one of the best restaurants in the city and a turquoise-colored landmark of the Garden District, opened in 1880 and has been in the Brennan family since 1974. Zoning laws in most cities may prohibit a restaurant next to a cemetery (Lafayette Cemetery in this case, across the street) in the middle of an old residential neighborhood, but New Orleans is made only more interesting by such juxtapositions.

11. A block away from Commander's Palace is The Rink, originally built as the Crescent City Skating Rink in 1885 and successfully transformed into a gallery of shops in the late 1970s after years as a rundown service station. The coffee shop and bookstore inside have become integral parts of the fabric of this historic neighborhood.

Photographs by author, 2000

Landmarks of Uptown St. Charles Avenue

1. The historic Pontchartrain Hotel (1927), once the tallest structure in the Garden District area at twelve stories, now marks the point at which mixed commercial St. Charles Avenue gives way to a leafy residential thoroughfare.

2. The Columns, built in 1883 as a mansion for the tobacco merchant Simon Hernsheim, is now a prominent hotel.

3. The Academy of the Sacred Heart, an acclaimed Catholic girls' school, is the local representative of the Society of the Sacred Heart, a teaching order founded in France in 1800. Nuns of the order established a convent and school in the French Quarter in the late 1800s but moved uptown, following the bulk of the population and their student body, in the late 1880s. Their present-day Colonial Revival structure, designed by Diboll and Owen, built in 1900, and expanded in 1906 and 1913, highlights one of the most beautiful blocks on St. Charles Avenue.

4. Bultman Funeral Home occupies three old houses joined together and is distinguished by its great clock.

5. Tulane University was founded in 1834 as the Medical College of Louisiana and operated downtown until the early 1890s, when it moved to the former Foucher tract and established its present-day uptown campus. Named for benefactor Paul Tulane in 1884, it still operates its medical school and related departments on a downtown campus in the "medical district" along Tulane Avenue. Gibson Hall (1894), the symbolic heart of the institution, appears on the left.

6. Landmark LOYOLA sign standing on the great lawn of Loyola University—backed up by "Touchdown Jesus" and the distinctive Tudor Gothic style of Marquette Hall (1910).

7. Holy Name of Jesus Church (1913-18) keeps the peace between Tulane and Loyola universities on St. Charles Avenue.

8. St. Charles Avenue entrance to Audubon Park. This urban Eden combines with the magnificent campuses of Loyola and Tulane, Holy Name of Jesus Church, streetcars, azaleas, oak trees, and nearby mansions to make this locale one of the most stunningly beautiful places in the nation. The sight of all these elements says "uptown" to passersby.

9. Graceful statue in Audubon Park, with Gibson Hall in the distance.

Photographs by author, 2000

Landmarks of Carrollton, Mid-City, and Bayou St. John

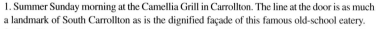

1. Summer Sunday morning at the Camellia Grill in Carrollton. The line at the door is as much a landmark of South Carrollton as is the dignified façade of this famous old-school eatery.

2. Carrollton Courthouse bypassed by the St. Charles Avenue streetcar on South Carrollton Avenue. The predecessor of the streetcar, the New Orleans & Carrollton Rail Road (1835), fueled the development of this remote area and led to its status as a separate town (hence the courthouse) until 1874, when it was annexed into New Orleans. The building currently houses a public school, one of the oldest structures in the nation serving that role.

3. The Carrollton Streetcar Barn (1893) on Dublin Street in Carrollton. This is the origin and destination for the city's world-famous fleet of 1920s-era streetcars, traveling a route established in 1835. All tracks lead to this barn, where highly specialized mechanics and their equipment are based.

4. Movable landmark: Saturday morning on St. Charles or South Carrollton usually features a fruit and vegetable vendor, a picturesque throwback to the days of outdoor vending, which survived in New Orleans long after it disappeared from most other big cities.

5. Steep roofs and cupola of Notre Dame Seminary (1923) on South Carrollton Avenue, an institution of strikingly impressive structures that appear to be extracted from the French countryside.

6. "Cemetery" can mean any one of dozens of burial places in New Orleans, but "Cemeteries" means only one—the remarkable termination of Canal Street at a maze of historic cemeteries built upon the Metairie Ridge, followed by Metairie Road to the west and City Park Avenue to the east. The area, in the heart of Mid-City, once lent its name to the streetcar line that served here and is now the destination of the Canal Street bus that travels all the way to the foot of Canal at the Mississippi River. The word CEMETERIES scrolling across the busses' digital sign causes the same double take in people today that the streetcar signs might have in Tennessee Williams, who saw in it a metaphor for life.

7. The streamlined Art Moderne-style Blue Plate Fine Foods building on Jefferson Davis is a landmark of Mid-City.

8. Despite its location in a rather bland strip mall in Mid-City, everyone knows where Mid-City Lanes is. The local institution has built up widespread fame on the clever idea of combining bowling with live music—a classic example of this city's uncanny ability to make the ordinary extraordinary. This same creative genius is seen in New Orleans' architecture, cuisine, and music.

9.-11. The vicinity of the Canal Street/North Carrollton Avenue intersection is home to many great locally owned restaurants and nightspots. The prominent intersection marks the literal and figurative center of Mid-City, one of New Orleans' most interesting neighborhoods—and one not yet discovered by tourists.

12. The Crescent City Steak House, a favorite local restaurant operated by the Vojkovich family since the 1930s, is a landmark on North Broad Avenue, a classically quirky New Orleans commercial thoroughfare through interesting Mid-City neighborhoods.

13. Classical architecture on the campus of Dillard University, as prominent a landmark on Gentilly Boulevard as Tulane University's Gibson Hall is on St. Charles Avenue.

14. Entrance to the New Orleans Fair Grounds (1872) on Gentilly Boulevard, one of the premier horseracing arenas in the South. To many people, this landmark signifies an event as well as a place: Jazz Fest, the annual springtime celebration of local music that has grown into one of the nation's premier festivals and has served to enshrine New Orleans' tremendous contributions to the world's musical heritage.

15. The lions of the Peristyle (1907) overlook the remnant of Bayou Metairie in City Park. The Peristyle is a favorite destination for family reunions and weddings, and every child involved can't resist climbing up on these sculptures to be king of their world for a moment. The swans in the lagoon, the cypress and oak trees, and the festive ambience make for memorable weekend afternoons in City Park.

16. P. G. T. Beauregard statue at the head of Esplanade Avenue, in the Bayou St. John neighborhood.

17. Dome of Our Lady of the Most Holy Rosary Roman Catholic Church viewed from a Bayou St. John bridge. In front is the 1830s-era mansion that now serves as the church's rectory.

18. The American Can Company factory, near the "headwaters" of Bayou St. John, was converted to apartments in 2001, extending into Mid-City the decades-old downtown trend of renovation of old industrial buildings into residential units. *Photographs by author, 1996-2001*

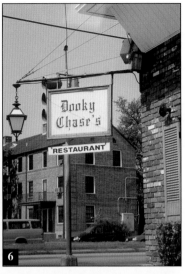

Landmarks of Central City, Freret, Sixth Ward, and Tulane Avenue

1. The distinctive bell tower of the Holy Ghost Catholic Church, on Louisiana at Daneel, overlooks the neighborhoods of Central City and Milan.

2. Serene Spanish Revival domes of Our Lady of Lourdes Roman Catholic Church on Napoleon Avenue rise dramatically above the cluttered streetscape as one travels downriver along the ever-interesting Freret Street. A business district since the 1880s, this section of Freret is a bit ragged today, and will soon participate in the National Trust for Historic Preservation's Main Street revitalization initiative.

3.-4. The gilded onion dome of St. John the Baptist Church (1872) is the landmark of Central City, visible throughout the neighborhood and most prominently to Pontchartrain Expressway motorists, who pass a few hundred feet from it. Located on what used to be the busy retail district of Dryades Street, now Oretha Castle Haley Boulevard, the church stands like a sentinel at the gateway of Central City from the Central Business District. The Plaza Tower (1966), one of New Orleans' first modern skyscrapers, is a landmark of the upper/lakeside corner of the CBD.

5. Uglesich's is one those famous and wildly popular local eateries one encounters throughout New Orleans, thriving despite the economically depressed condition of its neighborhood—in this case, Central City.

6. Dooky Chase's Restaurant, a monument to Creole cooking and an institution on the local culinary scene, has operated on Orleans Avenue in the Sixth Ward since 1939.

7. Cluttered streetscape on Tulane Avenue, emerging from the CBD and heading toward Mid-City, with the Dixie Brewery in the background.

8. The Central Business District ends and the Tulane/Gravier neighborhood begins at the St. Joseph Roman Catholic Church (built in stages from 1871 to 1892) on Tulane Avenue, largest church in the city and one of the grandest in the South.

9. Mid-City landmark: the Falstaff Brewery, which once broke the skyline of mid-twentieth-century New Orleans, now stands empty after its 1978 closing. The tower with the ball and the name FALSTAFF was, starting in 1952, illuminated in a manner that indicated the weather forecast. Note the statue of Falstaff toasting the city (upper left). Plans to renovate the old brewery have circulated in recent years.

10. This place of worship on North Roman Street is St. James African Methodist Episcopal Church, small in scale and modest in style but as old as the present-day St. Louis Cathedral, in service since 1851. Many New Orleanians know St. James from this distant perspective, visible from the portion of Interstate 10 that passes over Faubourg Tremé.

Photographs by author, 2000-2001

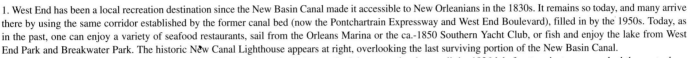

Landmarks of the Lakefront and Algiers

1. West End has been a local recreation destination since the New Basin Canal made it accessible to New Orleanians in the 1830s. It remains so today, and many arrive there by using the same corridor established by the former canal bed (now the Pontchartrain Expressway and West End Boulevard), filled in by the 1950s. Today, as in the past, one can enjoy a variety of seafood restaurants, sail from the Orleans Marina or the ca.-1850 Southern Yacht Club, or fish and enjoy the lake from West End Park and Breakwater Park. The historic New Canal Lighthouse appears at right, overlooking the last surviving portion of the New Basin Canal.

2. The Hellenic Cultural Center in the Filmore neighborhood overlooks Bayou St. John at a point that, until the 1926 lakefront project, once marked the spot where the bayou flowed into the lake. The domed church and tower are landmarks of lakeside New Orleans and headquarters for the city's Greek community.

3. University Center of the University of New Orleans, built on reclaimed land formerly occupied by the Naval Air Station (now in Belle Chasse) starting in the late 1950s, and now part of the neighborhoods of Lake Terrace/Lake Oaks.

4. What the New Basin Canal did for West End, the Pontchartrain Railroad (also a product of the 1830s) did for Milneburg, creating a resort community where the railroad terminated at the shores of Lake Pontchartrain (now Elysian Fields at Leon C. Simon). This lighthouse was once out in the water but is now landlocked near the University of New Orleans and a recently established technology center. This area was oriented toward local recreation until the early 1980s, when the Pontchartrain Beach amusement park closed.

5. The UNO Lakefront Arena, a bold landmark of sprawling, Florida-like lakefront New Orleans, looks even more otherworldly than the Superdome.

6. New Orleans Lakefront Airport, built as Shushan Airport in 1931-33 as an extension of the lakefront project, is one of the most prominent features of New Orleans when viewed from air or space, because it juts into Lake Pontchartrain like a peninsula. At the time, it was one of the best airports in the nation, later serving as a training station and staging ground for World War II-era pilots. Today, the airport is used for private planes and corporate jets, averaging about 200,000 takeoffs and landings a year. The modernistic exterior of the main terminal, seen here, masks a classic 1930s-era Art Deco design with friezes by famed local sculptor Enrique Alférez. Inside survives one of the best examples of Art Deco styling in the city, and in the adjoining Walnut Room restaurant, one can almost hear the Andrews Sisters playing in the background. It is one of the lesser-known treasures of New Orleans.

7.-8. Opelousas Street is to Algiers Point what St. Charles Avenue is to uptown or Esplanade Avenue is to downtown: the residential thoroughfare lined with beautiful homes, shaded by graceful oak trees, and anchored by picturesque mom-and-pop corner stores such as this one (8).

9. The most notable landmark in the historic neighborhood of Algiers Point on the west bank is the Algiers Courthouse (1896), built upon the ashes of the Duverjé House and other buildings destroyed in the Great Fire of 1895. The courthouse's crenellated asymmetrical towers are as distinctive from Morgan Street (seen here) as they are from across the river, on the French Quarter riverfront.

10. As the Algiers Courthouse indicates Algiers Point to people on the east bank, the St. Louis Cathedral marks the French Quarter for people on the west bank. In the foreground is the Algiers Ferry, about to head across the river to the foot of Canal Street.

11.-12. Entrance to Lakeshore, West End Boulevard at Robert E. Lee. This neighborhood, built on land created along the southern edge of Lake Pontchartrain in 1926-34, exhibits an architecture and ambience for which New Orleans is not famous: ranch-style residences in a suburban setting. But many of them are generations old now, and some nearby areas, most notably Lakeview, are finally gaining recognition for their historical status and contribution to New Orleans architecture.

Photographs by author, 2000

Conclusion: Isle of Orleans

Geography influences the appearance and character of all cities, port cities especially, New Orleans in particular. Because its physical situation is quantifiably unique, its topographic variation measurably minute (and therefore more influential), and its cultural experience unusually multifaceted, New Orleans may be viewed as a veritable laboratory for historical geography, an ideal place to study the relationships between people and place through time and space.[424] It is also a test bed for studying the struggles of an old city in an inhospitable environment whose original mission is no longer as critical to the world economy as it once was.

That mission—gatekeeper of the North American interior—made New Orleans the marvel of the nation and the city of the future just as long as the Mississippi River remained the primary ingress and egress to the heart of the continent. That monopoly began to end as early as 1825, when the 363-mile Erie Canal was excavated across upstate New York, connecting the Great Lakes region with the Hudson River and putting New York City in commercial contact with the Western frontier. There was a bit of a lag time before New Orleans felt the impact—the city was, in fulfillment of expectations, the richest in the nation in the 1830s—but with the Panic of 1837, New Orleans slipped behind New York in commercial supremacy[425] and, after the tumult of the Civil War and Reconstruction, gradually declined with the ensuing development of railroads, waterways, highways, and other lateral penetrations into the Mississippi Valley.

Myriad other factors have since sent New Orleans through a series of boom and bust cycles, seemingly more severe than those of other major American cities, making it today a city that is as troubled as it is charming, as superlative in social dysfunction as it is in physical splendor. Only the deluded would predict a future for New Orleans as magnificent as that foreseen by great men in the early 1800s. More so than in any other major American city, a common topic of conversation in coffee shops and parlors throughout New Orleans today is the question of *how* and *when,* not *if,* the Crescent City will finally sign off. Frank assessment of the city's situation—geographic, economic, social, and otherwise—leads some observers to conclude that, a century or two hence, historic New Orleans may end up a deltaic Harpers Ferry, occupied only by park rangers and concessionaires who tend to daily waves of tourists, then lock up the visitors' center after the last shuttle boat leaves.

A prevailing sentiment among present-day residents is that the city—and they themselves—are under the siege of a litany of problems akin in scope and magnitude to the biblical plagues. Crime rates, though lower than a few years ago, are still tragically high. Poverty in some areas is almost Haitian in intensity and appearance. The population and tax base continue to dwindle, making New Orleans the only major Southern city on the Census Bureau's list of ten most rapidly shrinking cities. Income distributions resemble those of third-world societies: many very poor, a few very rich, and a depleted (compared to America in general) and beleaguered middle class. Public schools are among the worst in the nation, depriving local children of a decent education and discouraging businesses and families from relocating here. Cherished neighborhood churches and landmark businesses fold with almost monthly regularity. Governmental services are underfunded, stretched thin, and sometimes stymied by subtropical lethargy. Much of the petroleum industry and many locally based corporations have quietly slipped out of town or gone out of business, while high-technology firms visit only for conventions.[426] Cotton merchants, once synonymous with the Crescent City, now call Memphis home. Magnificent old office buildings that once housed local enterprises paying white-collar salaries now employ chambermaids earning minimum wage. The Mississippi River, while still an internationally important transportation route, is now one of many ways to transport goods in and out of the American heartland. No major airline uses New Orleans as a hub, and, in 2001, the city's only Fortune-500 company (Entergy) nearly departed for Florida while the city's sole remaining big-league sports franchise (the Saints) threatened to leave and a market-seeking NBA basketball team (the Vancouver Grizzlies) opted for Memphis. There is a pervasive sense that New Orleans' greatest years are past, and that its modern-day role is one of selling history, not making it. "Like a risqué old madam, we live off our history, not our present charms," lamented one writer in a recent editorial.[427]

424. Tulane University professor H. W. Gilmore made a similar observation in 1944 (385-94), stating that "New Orleans is sufficiently different from the general run of American cities to make it an interesting laboratory for studying ecological principles evolved on the basis of data from other cities." Dr. Gilmore is using "ecology" to mean patterns in man's relationship to the land—in a word, geography.

425. Crété, 32.

426. In response to Mayor Marc Morial's confidence that New Orleans can become a high-technology center in the twenty-first century, a corporate relocation specialist from Austin stated, "The economy hasn't brought people here. Frankly, we've never brought anybody to New Orleans. It's not on the short list. [My clients] think this is a place to play. . . . You guys have a perception problem. People come down here to get sick on the sidewalk." Associated Press, *Mayor, Technology Expert Differ on New Orleans' High-Tech Future* (June 21, 2001). Available from World Wide Web: http://www.nola.com.

427. Nolan.

Then there are the physical challenges: rapacious Formosan termites swarm and devour two of the most endearing aspects of the city, the historical architecture and ancient live oaks. Decay, conflagration, and demolition continually deplete the city's stock of historical houses. Subsidence cracks walls, brickwork, and asphalt—the streets are the worst in the nation—and occasionally blows up a gas line. Heavy rains flood low-lying areas and strain the century-old drainage system. Polluted street runoff and poorly treated sewage throughout the metropolitan area end up in Lake Pontchartrain, forcing the closure of the famous beaches that once lined its shores. High river waters still pose a threat to the city, as does the possibility that the river may lunge past the Old River Control Structure into the Atchafalaya Basin and leave New Orleans on an elongated lake, making the Atchafalaya the new Mississippi and Morgan City the new New Orleans. Summertime brings with it the ultimate sudden threat: the chance that a Category-5 hurricane scores a direct hit on Lake Pontchartrain, surging its waters into the New Orleans basin and inundating the pumps designed to remove them.[428] Finally, there is the ultimate gradual threat: the erosion of coastal soils, caused mostly by the very levees designed to protect the city from a watery death and destined, if present trends continue, to make New Orleans a peninsula city, then a coastal city, and finally an island city—at which point the park rangers take over. Pundits often comment that it is the city's alleged laissez-faire attitude and penchant for merriment that temporarily alleviates but ultimately exacerbates the severity of these ills. Indeed, many of these coffee-shop conversations conclude when the group decides to seek out a nightspot for music and spirits!

Before defeatism is granted victory, however, some historical perspective is in order. People have doubted New Orleans since the day it was created—and before, when Company agents first debated potential sites, as discussed in chapter 1. Too low, said some. Isolated. Vulnerable to flood and hurricane. Soils too soft. Too hot, humid, and fetid. Infested by mosquitoes and prone to disease. Exposed to invasion. Too far from the coast, too far inland. They were right in every case, but they were wrong in assessing man's ability to solve problems, especially when the promise of a superior geographical situation outweighs the burden of a lousy site. The doubters certainly had evidence to support their reservations: since the beginning, the young city has been buffeted by hurricanes, flooded, burned, rotted, plagued by pestilence, targeted by invaders, blockaded, mismanaged, swindled, held hostage to world shipping trends, and used as a pawn among competing powers. Yet it survived and prospered. The hazard of river floods was alleviated by the construction of levees. Military threats were repelled by the heroics of a local militia in 1815 and by an extensive series of forts built afterwards. The silting of the mouth of the Mississippi was cleared by Capt. James Eads' jetties. The rechanneling of the Mississippi into the Atchafalaya was prevented by the control structures at Old River. Overreliance on levees for flood protection was rectified through the construction of spillways at Morganza and Bonnet Carré. The challenge of draining the bowl-shaped city was solved through the concerted effort of thousands and the ingenuity of Albert Baldwin Wood. The threat of storm surge was lessened by the lakefront project, hurricane-protection levees, and ongoing disaster planning. Coastal erosion and saltwater intrusion are confronted by massive freshwater diversion projects at Caernarvon and Davis Pond and interagency initiatives such as the Coast 2050 program. Yellow fever, which routinely decimated large percentages of the population for over a century, was conquered once its vector was understood. Competition from other ports and railroads was answered through the construction of the Industrial Canal and modernization of port infrastructure. The Mississippi River, while no longer holding a monopoly on hinterland trade, is still the most economical option for shipping many types of cargo. The diminished relative importance of maritime commerce was mitigated by new revenue generated by the petroleum industry and now the tourism and convention trade. An abundance of fresh water courtesy the Mississippi River makes New Orleans one of the few major American cities without a water-supply problem, and may prove to be an exportable commodity someday. Skyscrapers, once thought impossible on this alluvial silt, arose when specialized pilings and homegrown engineering techniques afforded them a stable foundation. Reckless, unanswered demolition of the city's architectural heritage was arrested by citizens who banded together and, through activism and legislation, achieved protection of many historic

428. Experts differ in their predictions of the damage that a direct hit of a Category-5 hurricane would inflict upon New Orleans. In November 2000, a draft report released by the Army Corps of Engineers forecasted that such a storm would push twenty-five feet of water into the New Orleans basin, inundating the entire city except for levee crests and rooftops and rendering the floodgates and pumps inoperable. Floodwaters would be heavily polluted with waste, gas, and corpses. Levees would have to be breached to let the water out, then rapidly reconstructed. It would probably be at least six months before the city would be pumped dry—and then the devastation of its ruined infrastructure would be confronted. So extreme would be the devastation that the Corps' New Orleans District would not be involved in the rescue effort—the Memphis District would move in—under the assumption that the local staff and assets would be evacuated or lost. But engineers at the New Orleans Sewerage and Water Board, who for some reason were not consulted in the Army Corps report, say that these scenarios are excessive. The surge would likely be significantly less than twenty-five feet, and the high lake water would flow back to the sea in a matter of days, after which a section of the lakefront levee would be dynamited to drain the city. While devastation would be widespread, the city would not be flooded for six months. Based on Schleifstein, "Corps' Storm Plan Grim," and New Orleans Sewerage and Water Board engineers, interviews by author.

neighborhoods and, more importantly, inspired a broad appreciation and sense of value for them. Federal and local entomologists have turned the corner in the battle against the invasive swarms of Formosan termites, which posed a seemingly insuperable threat to structures and trees as recently as 1998. The waters of Lake Pontchartrain have been cleaned up to the point that the reopening of the beaches for bathing is imminent. Old streetcar lines are staging a comeback after decades of domination by the automobile on congested arteries; even the famous Desire line may return. Gentrification, a phenomenon not applauded by everyone, nevertheless injects new money and community spirit into old neighborhoods and is the premier force behind the renovation of decaying historical structures. Even the population decline is abating—the -10.9 percent population change of the 1980s slowed to -2.5 percent in the 1990s—a trend encouraged by a new organization called New Orleans 24-7, dedicated to attracting new residents to the city. It is true that some of these solutions are only partial or short term, and others may incur long-term environmental problems that dwarf the original challenge. But this heritage of hometown problem solving in the face of biblical-scale predicaments should give New

Orleanians hope that their city's current dilemmas, while daunting, are no more insurmountable than those of earlier eras, which have long since been resolved.

Geography underscores the history of New Orleans, helping decipher the city's provenance, purpose, appearance, and character. But ultimately it is, of course, New Orleanians who made the city what it is today, a vivacious and magnificent sentinel on the southern brink of the North American continent, a cog between the sea and the Father of Waters of the richest valley on earth, an architectural and cultural treasure recognized worldwide for its unique charms. What draws the world to New Orleans is not geography per se but its cultural fruits—the iron-lace balconies of the French Quarter, the streetcars of St. Charles, the sounds of jazz and the taste of Creole cooking—all influenced by place and seasoned by time, but created by New Orleanians. It will be New Orleanians who save them. The historical geography of New Orleans tells a fascinating story of this place through times past, but the challenges of the future warrant that greatness will always find a home in this splendid and distinguished American city.

A sense of place through the dimension of time. *Photographs of New Orleans Board of Trade on Magazine Street in 2000 and cottage on St. Bernard Avenue in 1999 by author. The cottage did not survive into the twenty-first century.*

Appendix

On Geography, History, and Historical Geography

"Geography is the science of place. Its vision is grand, its view panoramic[;] it sweeps the surface of the Earth, charting the physical, organic, and cultural terrains, their areal differentiation, and their ecological dynamics with man."

—Leonard Krishtalka, 1990, Carnegie Museum of Natural History (as quoted by Jordan and Rowntree, 1)

"Of the three great parameters of concern to scientists, space, time, and composition of matter, geography is concerned with [the first] two. . . . It seeks to explain how the subsystems of the physical environment are organized on the earth's surface, and how man distributes himself over the earth in his space relation to physical features and to other men."

—Ad Hoc Committee of Geography, Earth Sciences Division, *The Science of Geography* (1965) (as quoted by Haring, Lounsbury, and Frazier, 5-6)

"The changing patterns and associations of geographical phenomena through time inevitably give rise to those of the present. A change in one feature may produce changes in others, which in turn may become causes for further change . . . and are prerequisite to the complete geographic interpretation of the region."

—Douglas Crary, 1959 (25)

"Historical geography has come to mean simply the geography of the past,—human ecology in past times."

—Harlan H. Barrows, "Historical Geography," *Annals of the Association of American Geographers* 3 (1923): 11-12 (as reproduced in Green, 3)

"Every event occurs both in space and time. Hence it may be deduced that every event concerns both the Geographer and the Historian."

—Sir Halford Mackinder, 1932 (as paraphrased by Fawcett, 6)

"Historical Geography is essentially that part of Geography in which we are studying the influence of Historical events on Geographical facts. . . . A large proportion of the so-called Historical Geography [conducted in England up to the 1930s] is essentially Geographical History; since its aim is the better and truer explanation of historical events by reference to those facts of Geography which have influenced them."

—C. B. Fawcett, 1932 (6-7)

"At least five different meanings could be given to the term 'Historical Geography'[:] The history of the changes of political frontiers of states, the history of geographical discovery and exploration, the history of geography as a science, the influence of environment on the course of history . . . [and] the reconstruction of the regional geography of the past."

—E. W. Gilbert, 1932 (as reproduced in Green, 8)

"Most scholars of history and geography stand united in their skepticism of universal laws of social behavior[;] on these grounds both have been denied time and again the status of a real 'science.' It is hardly necessary to add that in spite of this both will live on because the deep-seated urge to understand the human scene, in terms of time as well as space, cannot be suppressed by dogmatic reasoning."

—Jan O. M. Broek, "The Relationship Between History and Geography," *Pacific Historical Review* 10, no. 3 (1941): 321-25 (as reproduced in Green, 29)

"Those North American geographers who have assumed the misleading title of 'historical geographers' are, at heart, persons incurably in love with particular places . . . as these places were in the past or as they are now (whatever 'now' may mean)."

—Wilbur Zelinsky, "In Pursuit of Historical Geography and Other Wild Geese," *Historical Geography Newsletter* 3 (fall 1973): 1-5 (as reproduced in Green, 193)

"If every year were identical—and the same events occurred over and over again—no academic study of history would be needed. In the same way, if every place on earth were identical, we would not need geography."

—Terry G. Jordan and Lester Rowntree, 1990 (3, citing the philosophy of Immanuel Kant)

Development of New Orleans with Respect to Topographic Characteristics

Development Name	Initial Subdivision	Current Section/Neighborhood	Topographic Nature (elevations represent modern ranges, excluding manmade levees)	Location with respect to original city limits ("streetcar distance")
Original city of *La Nouvelle Orléans*	1722	French Quarter, Vieux Carré	Natural levee of Mississippi, at intersection of Bayou Road/Esplanade Ridge upland; 3-12 feet above mean sea level (m.s.l.), later expanded into the batture	Original city
Faubourg Ste. Marie (St. Mary)	1788	Central Business District	Broad natural levee of Mississippi, 3-14 feet above m.s.l., later expanded into the batture	Upriver and adjacent, separated by 2-block-wide commons until 1810
Faubourg Delord/Duplantier	1806	Howard Avenue corridor through Central City and Lee Circle and into Lower Garden District	Very broad natural levee of Mississippi, 3-14 feet above m.s.l., later expanded into the batture; upriver and adjacent to Faubourg Ste. Marie	Upriver by about 1 mile
Faubourg Saulet (Solet)	1810	Central City and Lower Garden District	Very broad natural levee of Mississippi, 3-14 feet above m.s.l., later expanded into the batture; upriver and adjacent to Faubourg Delord	Upriver by about 1 mile
Faubourg de La Course	1807	Central City and Lower Garden District	Very broad natural levee of Mississippi, 3-14 feet above m.s.l., later expanded into the batture; upriver and adjacent to Faubourg Saulet	Upriver by about 1.5 miles
Faubourg de L'Annunciation	1807	Central City and Lower Garden District, to Felicity Street	Very broad natural levee of Mississippi, 3-14 feet above m.s.l.; upriver and adjacent to Faubourg de La Course	Upriver by about 1.5 miles
Faubourg Marigny	1805-6	Faubourg Marigny	Narrow natural levee of Mississippi, 2-12 feet above m.s.l.; slightly wider in historic times before riverbank erosion	Downriver and adjacent
Faubourg Washington (comprising Faubourgs Daunois, Montegut, Clouet, Montreuil, Cariby, and deLesseps)	1809-40s	Lower portion of Marigny and Bywater, from present-day Franklin Avenue to the Industrial Canal	Narrow natural levee of Mississippi, 2-10 feet above m.s.l.; below and adjacent to Faubourg Marigny; slightly wider in historic times before riverbank erosion	Downriver by about 1 mile
Faubourg Nouvelle Marigny/ Faubourg Franklin	1830s	New Marigny, St. Roch, Seventh Ward	Edge of former backswamp behind the narrow natural levee of Mississippi at Faubourg Marigny, -5 to 3 feet above m.s.l. This area was developed because the Pontchartrain Railroad, running on Elysian Fields between the river and the lake, opened access to the lowlands.	Lakeside and downriver by about 1 mile
Faubourg St. John	1809	Bayou St. John	Metairie/Gentilly Ridge at the intersection of the Esplanade Ridge, about 3 feet above m.s.l.	Lakeside by about 2 miles
Faubourg Tremé	1810	Tremé	Trunk of the Bayou Road/Esplanade Ridge, as it fuses with the natural levee of Mississippi, 1-4 feet above m.s.l.	Lakeside and adjacent, in the downriver direction
City Commons near Faubourg Tremé	1810s	Iberville Housing Development, Cultural Center	Edge of former backswamp within the curve formed by the Bayou Road/Esplanade Ridge and the natural levee of Mississippi, 0-2 feet above m.s.l.	Lakeside and adjacent, in the upriver direction
Faubourg Hagan	1840-41	Tulane, Sixth Ward	Edge of former backswamp, downriver from Tulane Avenue between South Galvez, North Claiborne, and Bayou Road, 0-1 foot above m.s.l.	Lakeside by about 0.5 mile
Faubourg Nuns (des Religieuses, the Ursuline Nuns)	1810, developed 1830s	Upriver portion of Lower Garden District, above Felicity Street; formerly part of City of Lafayette (1833-52)	Very broad natural levee of Mississippi, 2-14 feet above m.s.l., upriver and adjacent to Faubourg de L'Annunciation	Upriver by about 1.5 miles
Panis Plantation (Faubourg Lafayette)	1813-18, developed 1830s	Jackson Avenue corridor between Lower Garden District and Garden District; formerly part of City of Lafayette	Natural levee of Mississippi, 2-14 feet above m.s.l., upriver and adjacent to Faubourg Nuns	Upriver by about 1.5 miles
Faubourg Livaudais	1832	Garden District, Irish Channel, and Central City; formerly part of City of Lafayette	Broad natural levee of Mississippi, 2-14 feet above m.s.l., upriver and adjacent to the former Panis Plantation	Upriver by about 2 miles
Faubourg Delassize	1836	Between Harmony Street and Toledano Street in Garden District and Irish Channel	Broad natural levee of Mississippi, 2-14 feet above m.s.l., Upriver and adjacent to Faubourg Livaudais	Upriver by about 2 miles
Faubourg Plaisance	Surveyed 1807, developed 1830s	Louisiana Avenue corridor in former Jefferson City (1850-70), now parts of the uptown neighborhoods of Touro, Garden District, Irish Channel, and Riverside	Natural levee of Mississippi in the main portion of the crescent, 2-14 feet above m.s.l., upriver from Faubourg Delassize and Livaudais	Upriver by 2.5 miles
Faubourg Delachaise	1855	Uptown neighborhoods of Touro and Riverside, in former Jefferson City	Natural levee of Mississippi in the main portion of the crescent, 4-12 feet above m.s.l., upriver and adjacent to Faubourg Plaisance	Upriver by 2.5 miles
Faubourg St. Joseph	1849	Uptown neighborhoods of Touro and Riverside, in former Jefferson City	Natural levee of Mississippi in the main portion of the crescent, 4-12 feet above m.s.l., upriver and adjacent to Faubourg Delachaise	Upriver by 3 miles

Development Name	Initial Subdivision	Current Section/Neighborhood	Topographic Nature (elevations represent modern ranges, excluding manmade levees)	Location with respect to original city limits ("streetcar distance")
Faubourg Bouligny	1834	Uptown neighborhoods of Touro and Riverside, in former Jefferson City	Natural levee of Mississippi in the "belly" of the crescent, 4-12 feet above m.s.l., upriver and adjacent to Faubourg St. Joseph	Upriver by 3 miles
Faubourg Avart	1841	Uptown neighborhood of Riverside, in former Jefferson City	Natural levee of Mississippi in the "belly" of the crescent, 4-12 feet above m.s.l., upriver and adjacent to Faubourg Bouligny	Upriver by 4 miles
Rickerville	1849	Jefferson Avenue corridor and upper limit of former Jefferson City, now parts of University, Uptown, and Riverside	Natural levee of Mississippi in the main portion of the crescent, 2-12 feet above m.s.l., upriver and adjacent to Faubourg Avart	Upriver by 4.5 miles
Hurstville	1834-37	Nashville Avenue corridor through University and Riverside neighborhoods between present-day Audubon Park and former Jefferson City	Natural levee of Mississippi in the main portion of the crescent, 2-12 feet above m.s.l., upriver and adjacent to Rickerville	Upriver by 4.5 miles
Bloomingdale	Surveyed in 1836, developed in 1880s	University and Riverside neighborhoods between Audubon Park and former Jefferson City	Natural levee of Mississippi in the main portion of the crescent, 2-12 feet above m.s.l., upriver and adjacent to Hurstville	Upriver by 4.5 miles
Burtheville	Surveyed in 1854, developed in 1880s	University and Riverside neighborhoods immediately downriver from Audubon Park	Natural levee of Mississippi in the main portion of the crescent, 2-12 feet above m.s.l., upriver and adjacent to Bloomingdale	Upriver by 5 miles
Foucher tract	Never subdivided; first landscaped in 1880s and improved in early 1900s	Audubon Park and the campuses of Tulane and Loyola universities	Natural levee of Mississippi at the upriver bend of the crescent, 0-12 feet above m.s.l., between Burtheville and Greenville	Upriver by 5 miles
Greenville, Friburg	Surveyed in 1836, developed in 1880s	Portions of present-day Carrollton and Black Pearl/Uptown Triangle neighborhoods adjacent to Audubon Park; formerly just downriver from City of Carrollton	Fairly narrow and lower natural levee of Mississippi on the western edge of the crescent, 0-8 feet above m.s.l., upriver from Burtheville and adjacent to Foucher tract (Audubon Park)	Upriver by 5.5 miles
Carrollton (Macarty Plantation)	1833	Carrollton, West Carrollton, and Black Pearl/Uptown Triangle formerly City of Carrollton (1845-74)	Low but wide natural levee of Mississippi on western portion of crescent, 1-8 feet above m.s.l. Carrollton occupies the spur of relief that underlies Carrollton Avenue and comes within 1 mile of the Metairie/Gentilly Ridge; if the "Carrollton Spur" actually touched this ridge (as does the Esplanade Ridge), a settlement in the Riverbend-Carrollton area might have developed a century earlier than Carrollton eventually did.	Upriver by 6 miles
Allard Plantation	Never permanently subdivided; first landscaped in 1890s and expanded in 1920s	City Park	Metairie/Gentilly Ridge (3 feet above m.s.l); park was expanded in the 1920s into the low country (5 feet below m.s.l.) toward the lake	Lakeside by 2 miles
Faubourg de Montluzin (Michoud Tract)	1960s	Eastern New Orleans neighborhoods of Pines Village, Plum Orchard, Read Boulevard West, Read Boulevard East, Edgelake/Little Woods, West Lake Forest, Village De L'Est, Michoud, Venetian Isles, and numerous subdivisions	Anchored upon Gentilly Ridge, 0-3 feet above m.s.l.; expanded in recent decades into some of the lowest areas of the city, to beneath 10 feet below m.s.l. Land reclamation and the construction of I-10 enabled the development of these areas.	Lakeside and downriver by about 7 miles
Lakeview Area	1910s, developed after 1920s	Neighborhoods west of City Park: Lakeview, Lakewood/West End, Navarre, Lakewood, Lakeshore/Lake Vista	Anchored upon Metairie Ridge, 0-4 feet above m.s.l.; subdivided upon former backswamps (0-6 feet below m.s.l.) after early-twentieth-century land reclamation.	Lakeside and downriver by about 4 miles
Lakefront Area	1939-60	Lake Vista, Lakeshore West and East, Lake Terrace, and Lake Oaks	Occupies the artificial lakefront land constructed in 1926-34 by the Orleans LeveeBoard, which pumped sediment from the bottom of Lake Pontchartrain into the area between the original shoreline and a bulkhead 3,000 feet offshore. The constructed land is 2-8 feet above m.s.l.	Lakeside by about 5 miles

Sources: Freiberg; Friends of the Cabildo, vol. 1, 4, and 7; New Orleans City Planning Commission, "Planning District Seven," *1999 Land Use Plan* (1999); Meloncy C. Soniat, "The Faubourgs"; Starr. *GIS processing by author based on data from New Orleans City Planning Commission*

Selected Geographical and Socioeconomic Facts about New Orleans (Orleans Parish)

Land Surface	Total surface area of New Orleans/Orleans Parish (including southeastern quadrant of Lake Pontchartrain)	~ 350 square miles
	Total land area of New Orleans (excluding Lake Pontchartrain)	~ 181 square miles
	Total urbanized area of New Orleans, 1990s	~ 84 square miles
	Percent of land area of New Orleans that was urbanized by the 1990s	46 percent
Elevation	Mean elevation (includes all terrestrial areas of Orleans Parish on both banks except the undeveloped wetlands east of Paris Road/Michoud)	0.1 feet above mean sea level (m.s.l)
	Standard deviation of elevation, same area	5.1 feet
	Extent of New Orleans that is above sea level (includes all terrestrial areas of Orleans Parish on both banks except the largely undeveloped area east of Paris Road/Michoud)	38 square miles
	Percent of New Orleans' urbanized area above sea level	45 percent
	Extent of New Orleans that is at or below sea level (includes all terrestrial areas of Orleans Parish on both banks except the largely undeveloped area east of Paris Road/Michoud)	46 square miles
	Percent of New Orleans' urbanized area at or below sea level	55 percent
	Highest substantial area in urbanized New Orleans (excludes landscaped hills, overpasses, and minor isolated features)	Mississippi River levee/batture in (1) uptown, roughly from Soniat Street to Broadway (especially Riverview Park) and from the riverside terminus of Perrier Street to Benjamin; and (2) the French Quarter from St. Louis to Canal. These areas are over 20 feet above m.s.l.
	Lowest substantial area in urbanized New Orleans (excludes drainage canal beds and minor features)	Area bounded by Paris, Morrison, Jourdan, and Dwyer roads in Little Woods, Lake Forest East, and Lake Forest West, parts of which are lower than 10 feet below m.s.l.
Port Activity	Total freight tonnage handled at the Port of New Orleans, 1998	88,768,246 tons (fourth after Houston, New York/New Jersey, and South Louisiana)
	Total freight tonnage handled at Port of South Louisiana (ports throughout region exclusive of New Orleans), 1998	196,645,563 tons (first in nation)
	Total freight tonnage handled at Port of South Louisiana plus Port of New Orleans, 1998	285,413,809 tons (69 percent more than Houston, 88 percent more than New York/New Jersey)
Demographics and Socioeconomics	Population, 2000	484,674
	Population ranking among large U.S. cities, 2000	31st
	Population of eight-parish metropolitan area, 2000	1,337,726
	Population ranking among metropolitan areas, 2000	35th
	Population per square mile of urbanized land area of New Orleans, 2000	5,770 persons
	Percent change, population, 1980-90	-10.9 percent
	Percent change, population, 1990-2000	-2.5 percent
	Percent change, population, 1960-2000 (1960 population = 627,525)	-22.8 percent
	Percent white, 2000	28.1 percent
	Percent black, 2000	67.3 percent
	Percent Hispanic, 2000	3.1 percent
	Percent Asian, 2000	2.3 percent
	Percent of population under 19 years old, 2000	30.1 percent
	Percent of population 65 and over, 2000	11.7 percent
	Family households with children under 18, 2000	55,053
	Percent of family households with children under 18 that have female heads-of-household, 2000	47.9 percent
	High-school graduates, persons 25 and over, 1990	68.1 percent
	College graduates, persons 25 and over, 1990	22.4 percent
	Median household income, 1995 model-based estimate	$22,285
	Average annual earnings of full-time workers in eight-parish metropolitan area, 1999-2000	$29,901
	Percent of population below poverty line, 1995 model-based estimate	33.6 percent
	Percent of children below poverty line, 1995 model-based estimate	51.6 percent
	Total housing units, 2000	215,091
	Percent renter occupied, 2000	46.8 percent
	Percent owner occupied, 2000	40.7 percent
	Percent unoccupied, 2000	12.5 percent

Neighborhood Population Trends, 1990-2000, Sorted by Percent Change

Neighborhoods (grouped according to Census Blocks)	2000 Population	Percent Change Since 1990	1990			2000		
			Percent White	Percent Black	Percent Other	Percent White	Percent Black	Percent Other
CBD/Warehouse District	1,794	+31%	66	28	6	57	33	10
Lower Coast Algiers/English Turn	33,656	+10%	63	32	5	46	46	8
Eastern New Orleans lakefront neighborhoods	44,311	+8%	33	65	2	10	87	3
St. John/Fair Grounds/Mid-City/City Park	34,158	+7%	41	53	6	32	62	6
Venetian Isles	1,760	+6%	99	0	1	95	2	3
French Quarter	4,176	+5%	93	5	2	92	4	4
Eastern New Orleans neighborhoods	50,292	+4%	24	64	12	8	79	13
Gentilly West/Dillard	18,772	+1%	40	57	3	26	69	5
Gentilly East/Pontchartrain Park	23,199	+1%	43	56	1	22	74	4
Lakeview	19,469	+1%	98	1	1	96	1	3
Marigny/Bywater	8,241	-2%	46	51	3	51	45	4
Tremé/Downtown/7th Ward	36,921	-2%	4	92	4	5	93	2
Carrollton/Gert Town/Broadmoor	36,364	-3%	27	72	1	24	73	3
Garden District / Uptown / University	35,447	-3%	69	25	6	73	22	5
Lakefront neighborhoods	5,777	-5%	93	5	2	88	8	4
Algiers Point	7,760	-5%	29	69	2	29	68	3
St. Claude/St. Bernard	30,123	-7%	9	89	2	5	93	2
Riverfront uptown/Irish Channel	12,722	-7%	44	54	2	42	54	4
Lower Garden District/St. Thomas	9,073	-11%	35	63	2	42	54	4
Lower 9th Ward	19,515	-13%	7	93	0	3	96	1
Middle Algiers/Fischer	15,366	-15%	29	67	4	16	78	6
Central City	26,552	-15%	12	87	1	14	84	2
Desire/Florida	9,226	-39%	2	97	1	2	97	1

Notes:

Declining populations in gentrifying neighborhoods often reflect replacement of households with children with childless households.

Certain important trends are masked by aggregation of distinct neighborhoods, such as the gentrifying Lower Garden District and impoverished St. Thomas.

Source: U.S. Census Bureau (as interpreted by Coleman Warner, "Neighborhoods Win, Lose")

References

Abbey, Kathryn T. "The Land Ventures of General Lafayette in the Territory of Orleans and State of Louisiana." *The Louisiana Historical Quarterly* 16, no. 3 (July 1933).

Abbot, Henry L. *Approaches to New Orleans.* Department of the Gulf Map No. 5 Prepared by Order of Maj. Gen. N. P. Banks (1863). Reproduction. Louisiana Collection. University of New Orleans Earl K. Long Library.

Allen, Barbara L. "Casino Building an Improvement." *New Orleans Times-Picayune,* January 7, 2000, editorial page.

Allison, James E., & Co. *Report on the Street Railway Service of the City of New Orleans.* New Orleans: Committee on Transportation Facilities of New Orleans, 1917.

Alpert, Bruce. "La. May Feel Heat in Grilling of Army Corps of Engineers." *New Orleans Times-Picayune,* March 3, 2000.

Arnesen, Eric. *Waterfront Workers of New Orleans: Race, Class, and Politics, 1863-1923.* New York and Oxford: Oxford University Press, 1991.

Arnold, Morris S. "The Iberville Prospectus." *The Historic New Orleans Collection Quarterly* 18, no. 2 (spring 2000).

Associated Press. "Corps Suggests Island for Millennium Port." *New Orleans Times-Picayune,* October 5, 2000.

Association of Levee Boards of Louisiana. *The System That Works to Serve Our State.* 1990.

Barbier, Sandra. "Less Louisiana." *New Orleans Times-Picayune,* February 8, 1999.

———. "Winds of Change." *New Orleans Times-Picayune,* June 1, 2000.

Barry, John M. *Rising Tide: The Great Mississippi River Flood of 1927 and How It Changed America.* New York: Simon & Schuster, A Touchstone Book, 1997.

Barton, Edward H. "Report Upon the Sanitary Condition of New Orleans." In *Cause and Prevention of Yellow Fever in New Orleans.* 1854.

Basso, Etolia S., ed. *The World From Jackson Square: A New Orleans Reader.* New York: Farrar, Straus and Company, 1948.

Baughman, James P. "A Southern Spa: Ante-Bellum Lake Pontchartrain." *Louisiana History* 3, no. 1 (winter 1962).

Beech, Jack, and Amman-International. *Vieux Carre Aerial Survey* (1966). Large-scale aerial photographs. The Historic New Orleans Collection, New Orleans, La.

Begnaud, Allen. "The Louisiana Sugar Cane Industry: An Overview." In *Green Fields: Two Hundred Years of Louisiana Sugar.* Lafayette, La.: University of Southwestern Louisiana, Center for Louisiana Studies, 1980.

Behrman, Martin. "New Orleans—A History of Three Great Public Utilities: Sewerage, Water and Drainage, And their influence upon the Health and Progress of a Big City." Paper presented at the Convention of League of American Municipalities, Milwaukee, Wis., 1914.

Bell, Rhonda. "N.O. Area Can Put Aside Fear of Flooding, Corps Official Says." *New Orleans Times-Picayune,* March 18, 1997.

BellSouth Yellow Pages. New Orleans: May 2000-2001.

Biers, John. "N.O. Bears Brunt of Oil Job Reductions." *New Orleans Times-Picayune,* September 3, 2000.

Biers, John M. "City Is Still Leaking Oil-Industry Jobs." *New Orleans Times-Picayune,* August 8, 2000.

Bolding, Gary A. "The New Orleans Seaway Movement." *Louisiana History* 10 (1969).

Bookhardt, D. Eric. "The Scene on Lower Magazine." *Gambit Weekly* (September 5, 2000).

Bookhardt, D. Eric, and Jon Newlin. *Geopsychic Wonders of New Orleans.* New Orleans: Temperance Hall, 1992.

Born, W. "The Cotton Trade of New Orleans." *Ciba Review* (April 1953).

Boyle, James E. *Cotton and the New Orleans Cotton Exchange: A Century of Commercial Evolution.* Garden City, N.Y.: Country Life Press, 1934.

Bragg, Marion. *Historic Names and Places on the Lower Mississippi River.* Vicksburg, Miss.: Mississippi River Commission, 1977.

Brasseaux, Carl A. "The Image of Louisiana and the Failure of Voluntary French Emigration, 1683-1731." 1979. In *The Louisiana Purchase Bicentennial Series in Louisiana History,* vol. 1, *The French Experience in Louisiana,* edited by Glenn R. Conrad. Lafayette, La.: University of Southwestern Louisiana, Center for Louisiana Studies, 1995.

———, ed. *A Comparative View of French Louisiana, 1699 and 1762: The Journals of Pierre Le Moyne d'Iberville and Jean-Jacques-Blaise d'Abbadie.* Lafayette, La.: University of Southwestern Louisiana, Center for Louisiana Studies, 1979.

Briede, Kathryn C. "A History of the City of Lafayette." *The Louisiana Historical Quarterly* 20, no. 4 (October 1937).

Brown, Douglas Stewart. "The Iberville Canal Project: Its Relation to Anglo-French Commercial Rivalry in the Mississippi Valley, 1763-1775." *The Mississippi Valley Historical Review: A Journal of American History* 32, no. 4 (March 1946).

Brown, Ralph H. *Historical Geography of the United States.* New York: Harcourt, Brace & Co., 1948.

Bruchey, Stuart, ed. *Cotton and the Growth of the American Economy, 1790-1860.* New York: Harcourt, Brace & World, 1967.

Bureau of Government Research, City of New Orleans. *Plan and Program for the Preservation of the Vieux Carré.* New Orleans: City of New Orleans, 1968.

Burns, Francis P. "The Spanish Land Laws of Louisiana." *The Louisiana Historical Quarterly* 11, no. 4 (October 1928).

Cable, George Washington. "New Orleans Revisited." *The Book News Monthly* (April 1909).

Campanella, Richard, and Marina Campanella. *New Orleans Then and Now.* Gretna, La.: Pelican, 1999.

Canal Bank and Trust Company. *Through Ninety-Five Years.* New Orleans: Canal Bank and Trust, 1926.

Cant, R. G. "The Dilemma of Historical Geography." 1969. In *Historical Geography: A Methodological Portrayal,* edited by D. Brooks Green. Savage, Md.: Rowman & Littlefield Publishers, 1991.

Carte Particuliere du fleuve St. Louis dix lieites au dessus et au dessous de la Nouvelle Orleans où sont marqué les habitations et les terrains concédés a Plusieurs Particuliers au Mississipy (ca. 1723). Reproduction. Louisiana Collection. University of New Orleans Earl K. Long Library.

Castellanos, Henry C. *New Orleans As It Was: Episodes of Louisiana Life.* 1895. Reprint, Gretna, La.: Pelican, 1990.

Castille, George. *Archaeological Investigations at Fort Pike: The 1978 Excavation.* Baton Rouge: Coastal Environments, 1982.

Cates, Michael. *New Orleans Banking in the Nineteenth Century* (1997). Self-published research document.

Chambers, Henry E. *A History of Louisiana: Wilderness-Colony-Province-Territory-State-People.* Vol. 1. Chicago and New York: American Historical Society, 1925.

Charlevoix, Pierre François Xavier de. *Historical Journal of Father Pierre François Xavier de Charlevoix in Letters Addressed to the Dutchess of Lesdiguieres.* In *Historical Collections of Louisiana, Embracing Translations of Many Rare and Valuable Documents Relating to the Natural, Civil and Political History of That State,* translated by B. F. French. New York: D. Appleton, 1851.

Chase, John Churchill. *Frenchmen, Desire, Good Children . . . and Other Streets of New Orleans!* Reprint, Gretna, La.: Pelican, 2001.

Chase, John Churchill, Hermann B. Deutsch, Charles L. Dufour, and Leonard V. Huber. *Citoyens, Progrès et Politique de la Nouvelle Orléans 1889-1964.* New Orleans: E. S. Upton, 1964.

Chenault, William W., and Robert C. Reinders. "The Northern-born Community of New Orleans in the 1850s." *The Journal of American History* 51, no. 2 (September 1964).

City Planning and Zoning Commission. *Major Street Report.* New Orleans: City Planning and Zoning Commission, 1927.

Claiborne, J. F. H. *Mississippi as a Province, Territory and State.* 1880. Reprint, Baton Rouge: Louisiana State University Press, 1964.

Claiborne Avenue Design Team. *I-10 Multi-Use Study.* New Orleans: Claiborne Avenue Design Team, 1976.

Clark, John G. "New Orleans and the River: A Study in Attitudes and Responses." *Louisiana History* 8 (1967).

———. *New Orleans, 1718-1812: An Economic History.* Baton Rouge: Louisiana State University Press, 1970.

Cohen's City Directory for 1854.

Cohn, David L. *The Life and Times of King Cotton.* New York: Oxford University Press, 1956.

Conrad, Glenn R., ed. *The Historical Journal of the Establishment of the French in Louisiana.* Lafayette, La.: University of Southwestern Louisiana, Center for Louisiana Studies, 1971.

Copeland, Fayette. "The New Orleans Press and the Reconstruction." *The Louisiana Historical Quarterly* 30, no. 1 (January 1947).

Cowdon, John. *New York and New Orleans Contrasted in Their Commercial Relations.* New York, H. J. Hewitt, 1885.

Cowdrey, Albert E. *Land's End: A History of the New Orleans District, U.S. Army Corps of Engineers.* New Orleans: U.S. Army Corps of Engineers, 1977.

Craig, James P. *New Orleans Illustrated in Photo Etching.* Chicago: James P. Craig, 1892.

Crary, Douglas. "A Geographer Looks at the Landscape." *Landscape—Magazine of Human Geography* 9, no. 1 (autumn 1959).

Crété, Liliane. *Daily Life in Louisiana 1815-1830.* 1978. Translation, Baton Rouge and London: Louisiana State University Press, 1981.

Cross, Marion E., trans. *Father Louis Hennepin's Description of Louisiana: Newly Discovered to the Southwest of New France by Order of the King.* Minneapolis: University of Minnesota Press, 1938.

Cruzat, Heloise H., and Henry P. Dart. "Documents Concerning Bienville's Lands in Louisiana, 1719-1737." Installments 1-4. *The Louisiana Historical Quarterly* 10, no. 1 (January 1927); no. 2 (April 1927); no. 3 (July 1927); no. 4 (October 1927).

Dabney, Thomas Ewing. *The Industrial Canal and Inner Harbor of New Orleans: History, Description and Economic Aspects of Giant Facility Created to Encourage Industrial Expansion and Develop Commerce.* New Orleans: Board of Commissioners of the Port of New Orleans, 1921.

———. *One Hundred Great Years: The Story of the Times-Picayune From Its Founding to 1940.* Baton Rouge: Louisiana State University Press, 1944.

Daily States, November 8, 1885.

Dalrymple, Margaret Fisher. *The Merchant of Manchac: The Letterbooks of John Fitzpatrick, 1768-1790.* Baton Rouge and London: Louisiana State University Press, 1978.

Dalton, John E. *Sugar: A Case Study of Government Control.* New York: Macmillan, 1937.

Darby, William. *Geographical Description of the State of Louisiana.* Philadelphia: John Melish, 1816.

Darcé, Keith. "Board to Launch First Phase of Massive Wharf Renovation." *New Orleans Times-Picayune,* December 17, 1999.

———. "Cargo Ship a Huge Hit." *New Orleans Times-Picayune,* March 25, 2000.

———. "Dock Board Chooses Design for Its Uptown Mega-Wharf." *New Orleans Times-Picayune,* June 29, 2000.

———. "N.O. Port Plans Huge Uptown Expansion." *New Orleans Times-Picayune,* February 26, 1999.

———. "Officials Take to Air in Search for Port Site." *New Orleans Times-Picayune,* June 27, 2000.

———. "Prompt Steps Urged To Build Interim Port." *New Orleans Times-Picayune,* July 20, 1999.

Dart, Henry P. Introduction to "Allotment of Building Sites in New Orleans (1722)." *The Louisiana Historical Quarterly* 7, no. 4 (October 1924).

———. "The Career of Dubreuil in French Louisiana." *The Louisiana Historical Quarterly* 18, no. 2 (April 1935).

———, trans. "The First Law Regulating Land Grants in French Colonial Louisiana." *The Louisiana Historical Quarterly* 14, no. 3 (July 1931).

Dart, Henry P., III. "The Arpent." Parts 1 and 2. *Loyola Law Review* (New Orleans) 13, no. 1 (1966); no. 2 (1967).

Davis, Edwin Adams. *The Story of Louisiana.* Vol. 1. New Orleans: J. F. Hyer, 1960.

Day, John W., Jr., Louis D. Britsch, Suzanne R. Hawes, Gary P. Shaffer, Denise J. Reed, and Donald Cahoon. "Pattern and Process of Land Loss in the Mississippi Delta: A Spatial and Temporal Analysis of Wetland Habitat Change." *Estuaries* 23, no. 4 (August 2000).

De Bow, J. D. B. *The Commercial Review of the South and West.* Vol. 6. New Orleans: B. F. De Bow, 1848.

De Bow's Review. *The Southern States, Embracing a Series of Papers Condensed from the Earlier Volumes of De Bow's Review.* 1856.

Detro, Randall Augustus. "Generic Terms in the Place Names of Louisiana, An Index to the Cultural Landscape." Ph.D. diss., Louisiana State University, 1970.

De Vorsey, Louis, Jr. "La Salle's Cartography of the Lower Mississippi: Product of Error or Deception?" *Geoscience and Man.* Vol. 25. Baton Rouge: Geoscience Publications, 1988.

Din, Gilbert C. "Spain's Immigration Policy in Louisiana and the American Penetration, 1792-1803." In *The Louisiana Purchase Bicentennial Series in Louisiana History,* vol. 2, *The Spanish Presence in Louisiana 1763-1803.* Lafayette, La.: University of Southwestern Louisiana, Center for Louisiana Studies, 1996.

Donze, Elizabeth. "Home Tour Highlight." *New Orleans Times-Picayune,* March 25, 2000.

Dufour, Charles L. "The People of New Orleans." In *The Past as Prelude: New Orleans 1718-1968,* by Hodding Carter. Gretna, La.: Pelican, 1968.

———. *Ten Flags in the Wind: The Story of Louisiana.* New York: Harper & Row, 1967.

Dumont, M. "Arrival of the Royal Commissaries at New-Orleans—Establishment of a Council in That Capital." In *Historical Memoirs of Louisiana, From the First Settlement of the Colony to the Departure of Governor O'Reilly in 1770,* translated by B. F. French. New York: Lamport, Blakeman & Law, 1853.

Duncan, Jeff. "Game Plan." *New Orleans Times-Picayune,* May 13, 2001.

East, W. Gordon. *The Geography behind History.* Scranton, Pa.: W. W. Norton, 1967.

Edwards' Annual Directory to the City of New Orleans. 1870-73.

Eggler, Bruce. "DDD Turns 25." *New Orleans Times-Picayune,* August 11, 2000.

Eichner, Alfred S. *The Emergence of Oligopoly: Sugar Refining as a Case Study.* Baltimore and London: Johns Hopkins Press, 1969.

Ekberg, Carl J. "The English Bend: Forgotten Gateway to New Orleans." In *La Salle and His Legacy: Frenchmen and Indians in the Lower Mississippi Valley* edited by Patricia K. Galloway. Jackson: University Press of Mississippi, 1982.

———. *French Roots in the Illinois Country.* Urbana and Chicago: University of Illinois Press, 1998.

———. "The Illinois Country: The Veritable New France." Paper presented at the France and Louisiana: Journée D'Étude Symposium, The Historic New Orleans Collection, New Orleans, La., January 2000.

Elie, Lolis Eric. "Indians Get Alternative to Overpass." *New Orleans Times-Picayune,* February 26, 2001.

Ellis, L. Tuffly. "The New Orleans Cotton Exchange: The Formative Years, 1871-1880." In *The Louisiana Purchase Bicentennial Series in Louisiana History,* vol. 16, *Agriculture and Economic Development in Louisiana,* edited by Thomas A. Becnel. Lafayette, La.: University of Southwestern Louisiana, Center for Louisiana Studies, 1997.

Elstner, J. M. *The Industries of New Orleans.* New Orleans: J. M. Elstner, 1885.

Engelhardt, George W. *New Orleans, Louisiana, The Crescent City: The Book of the Picayune.* New Orleans: Picayune, 1903-4.

Evans, Oliver. *New Orleans.* New York: Macmillan, 1959.

Fahrenthold, David A. "Neighbors Split on Pharmacy Plan." *New Orleans Times-Picayune,* August 5, 1999.

Falconer, Thomas. *On the Discovery of the Mississippi, and on The South-Western, Oregon, and North-Western Boundary of the United States.* 1844. Reprint, Fredericksburg, Tex.: Shoal Creek Publishers.

Farber, Joseph C., and Wendell D. Garrett. *Thomas Jefferson Redivivus.* Mass.: Barre, 1971.

Fawcett, C. B. 1932. Quoted in *Historical Geography: A Methodological Portrayal,* edited by D. Brooks Green. Savage, Md.: Rowman & Littlefield Publishers, 1991.

Federal Writers' Project of the Works Progress Administration. *New Orleans City Guide.* 1938. Reprint, New York: Pantheon Books, 1983.

Feigenbaum, Gail. *Degas and New Orleans: A French Impressionist in America.* New Orleans: New Orleans Museum of Art in association with Ordrupgaard, 1999.

Filipich, Judy A., and Lee Taylor. *Lakefront New Orleans: Planning and Development 1926-1971.* New Orleans: Urban Studies Institute, 1971.

Freiberg, Edna B. *Bayou St. John in Colonial Louisiana, 1699-1803.* New Orleans: Harvey Press, 1980.

French, B. F., trans. *Historical Collections of Louisiana, Embracing Translations of Many Rare and Valuable Documents Relating to the Natural, Civil and Political History of That State.* New York: D. Appleton, 1851.

Fricker, Donna. "Gentilly Terrace Added to National Register of Historic Places." *Preservation in Print* 27, no. 1 (February 2000).

Friends of the Cabildo. *New Orleans Architecture.* Vol. 1, *The Lower Garden District.* Gretna, La.: Pelican, 1971.

———. *New Orleans Architecture.* Vol. 2, *The American Sector.* Gretna, La.: Pelican, 1972.

———. *New Orleans Architecture.* Vol. 4, *The Creole Faubourgs.* Gretna, La.: Pelican, 1974.

———. *New Orleans Architecture.* Vol. 6, *Faubourg Tremé and the Bayou Road.* Gretna, La.: Pelican, 1980.

———. *New Orleans Architecture.* Vol. 7, *Jefferson City.* Gretna, La.: Pelican, 1989.

———. *New Orleans Architecture.* Vol. 8, *The University Section.* Gretna, La.: Pelican, 1997.

Frost, Meiga O. "Zulu King to Change His Scene of Arrival; Canal is Being Filled." *New Orleans States,* July 18, 1937.

Galloway, J. H. *The Sugar Cane Industry: An Historical Geography from its Origins to 1914.* Cambridge: Cambridge University Press, 1989.

Gardner's New Orleans Directory for 1861, 1866-69.

Gayarré, Charles. *History of Louisiana.* Vol. 2, *The French Domination.* 1882. Reprint, Gretna, La.: Pelican, 1999.

———. *History of Louisiana.* Vol. 3, *The Spanish Domination.* 1903. Reprint, Gretna, La.: Pelican, 1999.

———. *History of Louisiana.* Vol. 4, *The American Domination.* 1866. Reprint, Gretna, La.: Pelican, 1999.

Gibson's Guide and Directory of the State of Louisiana and the Cities of New Orleans and Lafayette. 1838.

Gill, James. "Goodbye, Gulf Outlet, Goodbye." *New Orleans Times-Picayune,* July 11, 1999.

———. *Lords of Misrule: Mardi Gras and the Politics of Race in New Orleans.* Jackson: University Press of Mississippi, 1997.

Gilmore, H. W. "The Old New Orleans and the New: The Case for Ecology." *American Sociological Review* 9, no. 4 (August 1944).

Giraud, Marcel. *A History of French Louisiana.* Vol. 1, *The Reign of Louis XIV, 1698-1715.* 1953. Translation, Baton Rouge and London: Louisiana State University Press, 1990.

———. *A History of French Louisiana.* Vol. 2, *Years of Transition, 1715-1717.* 1958. Translation, Baton Rouge and London: Louisiana State University Press, 1993.

———. *A History of French Louisiana.* Vol. 5, *The Company of the Indies, 1723-1731.* 1987. Translation, Baton Rouge and London: Louisiana State University Press, 1991.

Grace, Stephanie. "Funky Meters." *New Orleans Times-Picayune,* June 22, 2000.

Green, D. Brooks, ed. *Historical Geography: A Methodological Portrayal.* Savage, Md.: Rowman & Littlefield, 1991.

Guelke, Leonard. *Historical Understanding in Geography: An Idealist Approach.* Cambridge: Cambridge University Press, 1982.

Guilbeau, James. *The Saint Charles Streetcar or the History of The New Orleans and Carrollton Railroad.* New Orleans: Louisiana Landmarks Society, 1992.

Hahn, S. M. "Goodbye, New Orleans." *New Orleans Times-Picayune,* January 18, 2000.

Hall, A. Oakey. *The Manhattaner in New Orleans Or, Phases of "Crescent City" Life.* 1851. Reprint, Baton Rouge: Louisiana State University Press, 1976.

Hall, John Whitling. "Louisiana Survey Systems: Their Antecedents, Distribution, and Characteristics." Ph.D. diss., Louisiana State University, 1970.

Hallenbeck, Cleve, *Álvar Núñez Cabéza de Vaca: The Journey and Route of the First European to Cross the Continent of North America 1534-1536.* Spokane, Wash.: Arthur H. Clark, 1939.

Hardee, T. S. *Topographical and Drainage Map of New Orleans and Surroundings.* 1878.

Hardy, Jeannette. "A Slice of Woods." *New Orleans Times-Picayune,* January 19, 2001.

Haring, L. Lloyd, John F. Lounsbury, and John W. Frazier. *Introduction to Scientific Geographical Research.* Dubuque, Iowa: Wm. C. Brown, 1992.

Harmon, Nolan B., Jr. *The Famous Case of Myra Clark Gaines.* Baton Rouge: Louisiana State University Press, 1946.

Hartshorn, Truman Asa. *Interpreting the City: An Urban Geography.* New York: John Wiley & Sons, 1980.

Hartshorne, Richard. "Time and Genesis in the Study of Present Cultural Features." 1959. In *Historical Geography: A Methodological Portrayal,* edited by D. Brooks Green. Savage, Md.: Rowman & Littlefield Publishers, 1991.

Hauck, Philomena. *Bienville: Father of Louisiana.* Lafayette, La.: University of Southwestern Louisiana, Center for Louisiana Studies, 1998.

Heard, Malcolm. *French Quarter Manual: An Architectural Guide to New Orleans' Vieux Carré.* New Orleans: Tulane School of Architecture, 1997.

Heitmann, John Alfred. *The Modernization of the Louisiana Sugar Industry, 1830-1910.* Baton Rouge and London: Louisiana State University Press, 1987.

———. "Scientific and Technological Change in the Louisiana Sugar Industry, 1830-1910." Ph.D. diss., Johns Hopkins University, 1983.

Hennick, Louis C., and E. Harper Charlton. *The Streetcars of New Orleans.* 1965. Reprint, Gretna, La.: Pelican, 2001.

Hero, Alfred Olivier, Jr. *Louisiana and Quebec: Bilateral Relations and Comparative Sociopolitical Evolution, 1673-1993.* Lanham, Md.: University Press of America, 1995.

Higginbotham, Jay. *Fort Maurepas: The Birth of Louisiana.* Mobile, Ala.: Colonial Books, 1968.

———, trans. and ed. *The Journal of Sauvole: Historical Journal of the Establishment of the French in Louisiana by M. de Sauvole.* Mobile, Ala.: Colonial Books, 1969.

Hilliard, Sam Bowers. *Atlas of Antebellum Southern Agriculture.* Baton Rouge and London: Louisiana State University Press, 1984.

Hirsch, Arnold R., and Joseph Logsdon, ed. *Creole New Orleans: Race and Americanization.* Baton Rouge: Louisiana State University Press, 1992.

Hoffmann, I. Newton. "The Cotton Futures Act." *The Journal of Political Economy* (University of Chicago) 23, no. 5 (May 1915).

Holmes, Jack D. L. "Dauphin Island in the Franco-Spanish War, 1719-22." In *Frenchmen and French Ways in the Mississippi Valley,* edited by John Francis McDermott. Urbana: University of Illinois Press, 1969.

———. *A Guide to Spanish Louisiana, 1762-1806.* New Orleans: Louisiana Collection Series, 1970.

———. "The Value of the Arpent in Spanish Louisiana and West Florida." *Louisiana History* 24, no. 3 (summer 1983).

House Executive Documents. *Report on the Internal Commerce of the United States.* 50th Cong., 1st sess., 1887, 6, pt. 2.

Howell, Walter G. "The French Period, 1699-1763." In *A History of Mississippi.* Vol. 1, edited by Richard Aubrey McLemore. Jackson: University & College Press of Mississippi, 1973.

Huber, Leonard V. *Jackson Square Through the Years.* New Orleans: Friends of the Cabildo, 1982.

———. *New Orleans: A Pictorial History.* 1971. Reprint, Gretna, La.: Pelican, 1991.

Hudson, Charles. *Knights of Spain, Warriors of the Sun: Hernando de Soto and the South's Ancient Chiefdoms.* Athens and London: University of Georgia Press, 1997.

Hunt, Charles B. *Natural Regions of the United States and Canada.* San Francisco: W. H. Freeman, 1967.

Ingraham, Joseph Holt. *The South-West by a Yankee.* Vol. 1. New York: Harper and Brothers, 1835.

Inner-Harbor Navigation Canal Dedication Pamphlet (1923). Tulane University Special Collections, New Orleans, La.

Irish Cultural Society of New Orleans. "Dedication of New Basin Canal Park and Monument" (November 4, 1990). Flier. Louisiana Collection. University of New Orleans Earl K. Long Library.

Irvin, Hilary S. *The Nineteenth Century Development of the Riverfront Between Erato and Poydras Streets and the Nineteenth Century Usage of Property Now Vacant or Occupied by Inappropriate Structures Within the Boundaries of the 1984 Louisiana World Exposition.* New Orleans: Preservation Resource Center of New Orleans, 1982.

Jackson, Joy J. *New Orleans in the Gilded Age: Politics and Urban Progress 1880-1896.* Lafayette, La.: University of Southwestern Louisiana, Louisiana Historical Association and Center for Louisiana Studies, 1997.

Janssen, James S. *Building New Orleans: The Engineer's Role.* New Orleans: Waldemar S. Nelson, 1987.

Jenkins, Kay. "Preservation/Fireway Robbery." *Vieux Carre Courier* (March 26-April 1, 1971). In *Vieux Carré Survey: A Pictorial Record and Study of the Land and Buildings in the Vieux Carré.* 1966. Rev. ed. New Orleans: Historic New Orleans Collection, Binders for Squares 4-5E, 1979.

Jensen, Lynne. "City Park Readies Arboretum, Trails." *New Orleans Times-Picayune,* May 17, 2000.

Johnson, Brent M. "Development of the Mississippi River-Gulf Outlet." *Journal of the Waterways Division, Proceedings of the American Society of Civil Engineers* (1969).

Johnson, Dericki. "Rebirth for Claiborne." *New Orleans States-Item,* November 4, 1976.

Johnson, Jerah. "Colonial New Orleans: A Fragment of the Eighteenth-Century French Ethos." In *Creole New Orleans: Race and Americanization,* edited by Arnold R. Hirsch and Joseph Logsdon. Baton Rouge: Louisiana State University Press, 1992.

Johnson, Walter. *Soul by Soul: Life Inside the Antebellum Slave Market.* Cambridge, Mass., and London: Harvard University Press, 1999.

Jordan, Terry G., and Lester Rowntree. *The Human Mosaic: A Thematic Introduction to Cultural Geography.* New York: Harper & Row, 1990.

Kaplan, Benjamin. "A Study of Newsboys in New Orleans." Master's thesis, Tulane University, 1929.

Kellogg, John. "Negro Urban Clusters in the Postbellum South." *The Geographical Review* 67, no. 3 (July 1977).

Kelman, Ari. "A River and its City: Critical Episodes in the Environmental History of New Orleans." Ph.D. diss., Brown University, 1998.

Kendall, John S. "The Foreign Language Press of New Orleans." *The Louisiana Historical Quarterly* 12, no. 3 (July 1929).

Kendall, John Smith. *History of New Orleans.* Vol. 2. Chicago and New York: Lewis, 1922.

Kennedy, Richard S., ed. *Literary New Orleans: Essays and Meditations.* Baton Rouge: Louisiana State University Press, 1992.

Khorsandi, Mehrzad. "The Theatre District as a Component of Downtown Mixed-Use Development: The Case of Canal Street Revitalization in New Orleans, Louisiana." Master's thesis, University of New Orleans, 1989.

Kidder, Tristram R. "Making the City Inevitable: Native Americans and the Geography of New Orleans." In *Transforming New Orleans and Its Environs: Centuries of Change,* edited by Craig E. Colten. Pittsburgh: University of Pittsburgh Press, 2000.

Killick, John R. "The Cotton Operations of Alexander Brown and Sons in the Deep South, 1820-1860." *The Journal of Southern History* 43, no. 2 (May 1977).

King, Edward. *The Great South: A Record of Journeys.* Hartford, Conn.: American, 1875.

King, Grace. *New Orleans: The Place and The People.* 1895. Reprint, New York: Macmillan, 1928.

King, Ronette. "Days of High Cotton." *New Orleans Times-Picayune,* May 9, 1999.

Kirk, Susan Lauxman, Helen Michel Smith, and Thomas G. Krentel. *The Architecture of St. Charles Avenue.* Gretna, La.: Pelican, 1977.

Kniffen, Fred B. "Bayou Manchac: A Physiographic Interpretation." *The Geographical Review* (July 1935).

———. "The Lower Mississippi Valley: European Settlement, Utilization and Modification." *Geoscience and Man.* Vol. 27. Baton Rouge: Geoscience Publications, 1990.

Kniffen, Fred B., and Sam Bowers Hilliard. *Louisiana: Its Land and People.* Baton Rouge and London: Louisiana State University Press, 1988.

Knipmeyer, William B. "Settlement Succession in Eastern French Louisiana." Master's thesis, Louisiana State University, 1956

Kolb, C. R., and J. R. Van Lopik. *Geology of the Mississippi River Deltaic Plain, Southeastern Louisiana.* 1958.

Korn, Bertram Wallace. *Benjamin Levy: New Orleans Printer and Publisher.* Portland, Maine: Anthoensen Press, 1961.

Laborde, Errol. "Rediscovering Mardi Gras." *New Orleans Magazine* (February 2001).

Laborde, Peggy Scott. *Canal Street: The Great Wide Way.* New Orleans: WYES-TV. Documentary film.

Lafon, B. *Annuaire Louisianais Pour L'Année 1809.* New Orleans: B. Lafon, 1808-9.

Lafon, B. *Calendrier de Commerce de la Nouvelle-Orléans.* New Orleans: Jean Renard, 1807.

La Harpe, Jean-Baptiste Bénard de. "On the Present State of the Province of Louisiana in the Year 1720." Edited by Claude C. Sturgill and Charles L. Price. *The Louisiana Historical Quarterly* 54, no. 3 (summer-fall 1971).

Latrobe, Benjamin Henry Boneval. *Impressions Respecting New Orleans: Dairy & Sketches 1818-1820.* Edited by Samuel Wilson, Jr. New York: Columbia University Press, 1951.

Le Gardeur, René J. "The Origins of the Sugar Industry in Louisiana." In *Green Fields: Two Hundred Years of Louisiana Sugar.* Lafayette, La.: University of Southwestern Louisiana, Center for Louisiana Studies, 1980.

Ledet, Wilton P. "The History of the City of Carrollton." *The Louisiana Historical Quarterly* 21, no. 1 (January 1938).

Lemann, Susan Gibbs. "The Problems of Founding a Viable Colony: The Military in Early French Louisiana." 1982. In *The Louisiana Purchase Bicentennial Series in Louisiana History,* vol. 1, *The French Experience in Louisiana,* edited by Glenn R. Conrad. Lafayette, La.: University of Southwestern Louisiana, Center for Louisiana Studies, 1995.

Lewis, Peirce F. *New Orleans: The Making of an Urban Landscape.* Cambridge, Mass.: Ballinger, 1976.

The Literary Digest. "The Marriage of Mississippi and Pontchartrain" (April 14, 1923). Science and Invention Section. Tulane University Special Collections, New Orleans, La.

Logsdon, Joseph, and Caryn Cossé Bell. "The Americanization of Black New Orleans 1850-1900." In *Creole New Orleans: Race and Americanization,* edited by Arnold R. Hirsch and Joseph Logsdon. Baton Rouge: Louisiana State University Press, 1992.

Louisiana Advertiser, November 20, 1832.

The Louisiana Historical Quarterly (no author identified). "The Old Portage Between Bayou St. John and the Mississippi River." *The Louisiana Historical Quarterly* (April 1918).

Louisiana Statewide Flood Control Program's Project Evaluation Committee. *Flood Control in Louisiana: A Report of Flood Problem Areas and Damage Reduction Measures.* Baton Rouge: Gulf South Research Institute, 1986.

The Louisiana Sugar and Rice Exchange. *Official Merchants' and Planters' Directory.* New Orleans: Edwards & Morrison, 1896.

Louwagie, Pam. "Eye of the Storm." *New Orleans Times-Picayune,* June 1, 1999.

Lower Mississippi Region Comprehensive Study Coordinating Committee. *Lower Mississippi Region Comprehensive Study: Regional Climatology, Hydrology and Geology.* 1980.

Lynch, Kevin. *The Image of the City.* 1960. Reprint, Cambridge, Mass., and London: MIT Press, 1977.

MacCash, Douglas. "Bricks and Mortality." *New Orleans Times-Picayune,* October 30, 1999.

———. "The Picture of Success." *New Orleans Times-Picayune,* October 3, 1999.

McMurtrie, Douglas C. *Early Printing in New Orleans 1764-1810.* New Orleans: Searcy & Pfaff, 1929.

McPhee, John. *The Control of Nature.* New York: Farrar, Straus and Giroux, 1989.

McWilliams, Richebourg Gaillard. "Iberville at the Birdfoot Subdelta: Final Discovery of the Mississippi River." In *Frenchmen and French Ways in the Mississippi Valley,* edited by John Francis McDermott. Urbana: University of Illinois Press, 1969.

McWilliams, Richebourg Gaillard, trans. and ed. *Iberville's Gulf Journals.* University, Ala.: University of Alabama Press, 1991.

Maduell, Charles R., Jr. *Federal Land Grants in the Territory of Orleans: The Delta Parishes.* New Orleans: Polyanthos, 1975.

Magill, John. "A Legacy Lost—What Once Stood on the St. Thomas Site." *Preservation in Print* 27, no. 1 (February 2000).

Margavio, Anthony V., and J. Lambert Molyneaux. "Residential Segregation of Italians in New Orleans and Selected American Cities." *Louisiana Studies* 12, no. 4 (winter 1973).

Marino, Samuel J. "Early French-Language Newspapers in New Orleans." *Louisiana History* 7, no. 4 (fall 1966).

Marshall, Bob. "Grass-Roots Dilemma." *New Orleans Times-Picayune,* July 28, 2000.

Master Planning Consortium, Inc. *Tchoupitoulas Corridor Study.* Vol. 1. New Orleans: City of New Orleans and Board of Commissioners of the Port of New Orleans, 1990.

Master Planning Consortium, Inc. and Burk-Kleinpeter, Inc. *Tchoupitoulas Corridor Truck Origin-Destination Study.* New Orleans: Regional Planning Commission, 1995.

Mayoralty of New Orleans. *New Orleans Industrial and Ship Canal: An Ideal Location for Shipyards, Factories and Warehouses* (May 21, 1918). Pamphlet No. 5098—Commission Council Series. Tulane University Special Collections, New Orleans, La.

Mayoralty of New Orleans, City Hall. *Charter of the New Orleans Sugar Shed Company.* New Orleans: Stetson & Armstrong, 1870.

Meyer, William B. "Bringing Hypsography Back In: Altitude and Residence in American Cities." *Urban Geography* 15, no. 6 (1994).

Michel's New Orleans Annual and Commercial Register. 1834.

Mitchell, Harry A. "The Development of New Orleans as a Wholesale Trading Center." *The Louisiana Historical Quarterly* 27, no. 4 (October 1944).

Moe, Christine. "Yellow Fever in New Orleans." Part 2. *The Louisiana Historical Quarterly* 1, no. 1 (1973).

Montero de Pedro, José, Marqués de Casa Mena. *The Spanish in New Orleans and Louisiana.* Gretna, La.: Pelican, 2000.

Moore, John Hebron. *The Emergence of the Cotton Kingdom in the Old Southwest: Mississippi, 1770-1860.* Baton Rouge and London: Louisiana State University Press, 1988.

Mosher, Anne E., Barry D. Keim, and Susan A. Franques. "Downtown Dynamics." *The Geographical Review* 85, no. 4 (October 1995).

Mullener, Elizabeth. "Crowds Keep Coming to the D-Day Museum." *New Orleans Times-Picayune,* July 17, 2000.

———. "Ramped Up For War." *New Orleans Times-Picayune,* May 28, 2000.

Murphy, Linda Kay. "The Shifting Economic Relationships of the Cotton South: A Study of the Financial Relationships of the South During Its Industrial Development, 1864-1913." Ph.D. diss., Texas A&M University, 1999.

New Orleans Association of Commerce. *Map of Greater New Orleans, Louisiana.* New Orleans: Wm. E. Boesch, 1931.

New Orleans Bee, September 25 and 28, 1835.

New Orleans Chapter of the American Institute of Architects. *A Guide to New Orleans Architecture.* New Orleans: American Institute of Architects, 1974.

New Orleans City Planning Commission Geographic Information System (NOGIS), partially funded by a federal grant through NOAA.

New Orleans Cotton Exchange. *Charter, Constitution, By-Laws and Rules of the New Orleans Cotton Exchange.* New Orleans: L. Graham & Son, 1894.

New Orleans Daily Picayune, September 1, 1884.

New Orleans Magazine. "1999 Reader's Choice: Best and Worst of New Orleans." *New Orleans Magazine* (January 2000).

New Orleans Press, ed. *Historical Sketch Book and Guide to New Orleans and Environs.* New York: Will H. Coleman, 1885.

New-Orleans Price-Current and Commercial Intelligencer, October 10, 1835.

New-Orleans Price-Current Commercial Intelligencer and Merchants' Transcript, June 22 and August 27, 1842.

New Orleans Republican, September 10, 1870.

New Orleans Times, August 28, 1881.

New Orleans Times-Democrat, June 4, 1884.

New Orleans Times-Picayune, March 5, May 28, June 1, July 28, October 1, and November 13, 2000.

Newton, Milton B., Jr. *Louisiana: A Geographical Portrait.* Baton Rouge: Geoforensics, 1987.

Niehaus, Earl F. *The Irish in New Orleans.* Baton Rouge: Louisiana State University Press, 1965.

———. "The New Irish, 1830-1862." In *The Louisiana Purchase Bicentennial Series in Louisiana History,* vol. 10, *A Refuge for All Ages: Immigrants in Louisiana History,* edited by Carl A. Brasseaux. Lafayette, La.: University of Southwestern Louisiana, Center for Louisiana Studies, 1996.

Nolan, James. "We Watch as the Quarter Is Drained of Its Soul." *New Orleans Times-Picayune,* May 20, 2001, editorial page.

Nolte, Vincent. *Fifty Years in Both Hemispheres or, Reminiscences of the Life of a Former Merchant.* New York: Redfield, 1856.

Norman, Benjamin Moore. *Norman's New Orleans and Environs.* 1845. Reprint, Baton Rouge and London: Louisiana State University Press, 1976.

Ogden, B. F. *New Orleans and Its Environs.* 1829. Map in *New Orleans Architecture,* vol. 7, *Jefferson City,* by Friends of the Cabildo. Gretna, La.: Pelican, 1989.

Ogden, H. D. *Memorial of the Carondelet Canal & Navigation Company to the Honorable Members of the Legislature of the State of Louisiana* (ca. 1884). Tulane University Special Collections, New Orleans, La.

Ogg, Frederic Austin. *The Opening of the Mississippi: A Struggle for Supremacy in the American Interior.* New York and London: Macmillan, 1904.

Olmo, Rita. *Retail Activity in the New Orleans Central Business District: Evaluation and Prospects.* New Orleans: Mayor's Office of Industrial and Business Development, 1987.

Olmsted, Frederick Law. *A Journey in the Seaboard Slave States in the Years 1853-1854.* Vol. 2. 1856. Reprint, New York and London: G. P. Putnam's & Sons, 1904.

Orleans Levee Board. *Building a Great City.* New Orleans: Orleans Levee Board Reports, 1954.

Orleans Levee District. *The Orleans Levee District—A History* (1999). Document on World Wide Web, http://www.gnofn.org/levee/levee.htm.

Orleans Levee District, *The Orleans Levee District—The Hurricane Levee System* (1999). Document on World Wide Web, http://www.gnofn.org/levee/levee.htm.

Orleans Parish School Board. *The New Orleans Book.* New Orleans: Orleans Parish School Board, 1919.

Owens, Jeffrey Alan. "Holding Back the Waters: Land Development and the Origins of Levees on the Mississippi, 1720-1845." Ph.D. diss., Louisiana State University, 1999.

Padgett, James A., ed. "Some Documents Relating to the Batture Controversy in New Orleans." *The Louisiana Historical Quarterly* 23, no. 3 (July 1940).

Paxton, John Adems. *The New-Orleans Directory and Register.* New Orleans: Benj. Levy, 1822-23.

Pénicaut, André. *Fleur de Lys and Calumet: Being the Pénicaut Narrative of French Adventure in Louisiana.* Translated by Richebourg Gaillard McWilliams. Baton Rouge: Louisiana State University, 1953.

Peterson, Merrill D. *Thomas Jefferson and the New Nation: A Biography.* New York: Oxford University Press, 1970.

Pitot, Henry Clement. *James Pitot (1761-1831): A Documentary Study.* New Orleans: Bocage Books, 1968.

Pitot, James. *Observations on the Colony of Louisiana from 1796 to 1802.* Reprint, New Orleans: Historic New Orleans Collection; Baton Rouge and London: Louisiana State University Press, 1979.

Pitts & Clarke. *New Orleans City Directory.* New Orleans: Pitts & Clarke, 1842.

Polk's New Orleans City Directory 1940.

Polk's New Orleans (Orleans Parish, La.) City Directory 1945-46, 1952-53, 1958, 1960, 1965-90, 1994, and 2000.

Pope, John. "Refuge Running Dry." *New Orleans Times-Picayune,* July 19, 2000.

Port of New Orleans. *Port of New Orleans Annual Directory, 1997-1998.* 1997.

———. *Port of New Orleans Annual Directory, 1998-1999.* 1998.

Porteous, Laura L., trans. "Governor Carondelet's Levee Ordinance of 1792." *The Louisiana Historical Quarterly* 10, no. 4 (October 1927).

Pratz, Le Page du. *The History of Louisiana.* 1774. Facsimile edition, edited by Joseph G. Tregle, Jr. Baton Rouge: Louisiana State University Press, 1976.

Preservation Resource Center of New Orleans. *New Orleans Historic Warehouse District Study.* New Orleans: National Trust for Historic Preservation. 1983.

Prichard, Walter. "The Effects of the Civil War on the Louisiana Sugar Industry." *The Journal of Southern History* 5, no. 3 (August 1939).

Ramsey, Karen E., and Thomas F. Moslow. "A Numerical Analysis of Subsidence and Sea Level Rise in Louisiana." In *Coastal Sediments '87,* vol. 2. New York: American Society of Civil Engineers, 1987.

Reed, Merl E. *New Orleans and the Railroads: The Struggle for Commercial Empire 1830-1860.* Baton Rouge: Louisiana State University Press, 1966.

Reeves, Sally K. Evans, William D. Reeves, Ellis P. Laborde, and James S. Janssen. *Historic City Park New Orleans.* New Orleans: Friends of City Park, 1982.

Regional Planning Commission, Jefferson, Orleans, St. Bernard Parishes. *History of Regional Growth of Jefferson, Orleans, and St. Bernard Parishes, Louisiana.* 1969.

Regular Democratic Organization (Choctaw Club). *Thirty-Five Years of Progress in New Orleans.* New Orleans: Regular Democratic Organization, 1932.

Rehder, John Burkhardt. "Sugar Plantation Settlements of Southern Louisiana: A Cultural Geography." Ph.D. diss., Louisiana State University, 1971.

Reiff, Laura. "Gentilly Terrace: 'Where Homes Are Built on Hills.'" *Preservation in Print* 27, no. 1 (February 2000).

Rightor, Henry. *Standard History of New Orleans, Louisiana.* Chicago: Lewis, 1900.

Ritter, Dale. *Process Geomorphology.* Dubuque, Iowa: Wm. C. Brown, 1986.

Rivera Novo, Belén, and Luisa Martín-Merás. *Cuatro Siglos de Cartografía en América.* Madrid: Editorial MAPFRE, 1992.

Roberts, W. Adolphe. *Lake Pontchartrain.* Indianapolis and New York: Bobbs-Merrill, 1946.

Robinson, E., and R. H. Pidgeon. *Atlas of the City of New Orleans, Louisiana.* New York: E. Robinson, Publishers, 1883.

Robson, R. "Location and Development of the Cotton Industry." *Journal of Industrial Economics* 1, no. 2 (April 1953).

Roland, Charles P. *Louisiana Sugar Plantations During the American Civil War.* 1957. Reprint, Baton Rouge: Louisiana State University Press, 1997.

Rose, Al. *Storyville, New Orleans: Being an Authentic, Illustrated Account of the Notorious Red-Light District.* University, Ala.: University of Alabama Press, 1974.

Ross, Bob. "After the Flood." *New Orleans Times-Picayune,* May 8, 2000.

Rowland, Dunbar. *Official Letter Books of W. C. C. Claiborne, 1801-1816.* Vol. 2. Jackson, Miss.: State Department of Archives and History, 1917.

Rule, John C. "Jérôme Phélypeaux, Comte de Pontchartrain, and the Establishment of Louisiana, 1696-1715." In *Frenchmen and French Ways in the Mississippi Valley,* edited by John Francis McDermott. Urbana: University of Illinois Press, 1969.

Russell, Gordon. "Urban Jungle." *New Orleans Times-Picayune,* May 11, 2001.

———. "William J. Mouton, 70, Architect and Engineer." *New Orleans Times-Picayune,* July 2, 2001.

Salvaggio, John. *New Orleans' Charity Hospital: A Story of Physicians, Politicians, and Poverty.* Baton Rouge and London: Louisiana State University Press, 1992.

Samuel, Ray. *"to a point called Chef Menteur . . .": The Story of the Property Known Today as New Orleans East, Inc.* New Orleans: New Orleans East, Inc., 1959.

Sanborn Fire Insurance Maps of 1876, 1885, 1896, 1908, and 1937.

Saucier, Roger T. *Recent Geomorphic History of the Pontchartrain Basin.* Baton Rouge: Louisiana State University Press, 1963.

Sauder, Robert A. "The Origin and Spread of the Public Market System in New Orleans." *Louisiana History* 22 (1981).

Sauer, Carl O. "Foreword to Historical Geography." *Annals of the Association of American Geographers* 31, no. 1 (March 1941).

Sauer, Carl Ortwin. *Sixteenth Century North America: The Land and the People as Seen by the Europeans.* Berkeley: University of California Press, 1971.

Schleifstein, Mark. "Corps' Storm Plan Grim." *New Orleans Times-Picayune,* November 16, 2000.

———. "Lower Ground." *New Orleans Times-Picayune,* May 31, 2001.

———. "MR-GO Closing Plan Likely To Be Added to Wetlands List." *New Orleans Times-Picayune,* March 25, 1999.

———. "Virtual Destruction." *New Orleans Times-Picayune,* August 5, 1999.

———. "Wetlands Loss Threatens Lives, Property in N.O." *New Orleans Times-Picayune,* February 28, 1999.

Severin, Timothy. *Explorers of the Mississippi.* New York: Knopf, 1968.

Sewerage and Water Board of New Orleans. *Sewerage and Water Board of New Orleans: Drainage Information.* Document on World Wide Web, http://www.swbnola.org/drain_info.htm.

———. *The Sewerage and Water Board of New Orleans: How It Began, The Problems It Faces, The Way It Works, The Job It Does.* New Orleans: Sewerage and Water Board of New Orleans, 1998.

Shea, Philip. "The Spatial Impact of Governmental Decisions on the Production and Distribution of Louisiana Sugar Cane, 1751-1972." Ph.D. diss., Michigan State University, 1974.

Sibley, J. Ashley, Jr. *A Study of the Geology of Baton Rouge and Surrounding Southeast Louisiana Area.* Baton Rouge: Claitor's, 1972.

Sitterson, J. Carlyle. "Financing and Marketing the Sugar Crop of the Old South." *The Journal of Southern History* 10, no. 2 (May 1944).

———. *Sugar Country: The Cane Sugar Industry in the South, 1753-1950.* Lexington: University of Kentucky Press, 1953.

Smith, C. T. "Historical Geography: Current Trends and Prospects." 1965. In *Historical Geography: A Methodological Portrayal,* edited by D. Brooks Green. Savage, Md.: Rowman & Littlefield Publishers, 1991.

Snowden, J. O., W. C. Ward, and J. R. J. Studlick. *Geology of Greater New Orleans: Its Relationship to Land Subsidence and Flooding.* New Orleans: New Orleans Geological Society, 1980.

Soards' New Orleans City Directory for 1874-81, 1885, 1887, 1890, 1892, 1895, 1900, 1906, 1910-11, 1915-16, 1918, 1921, 1925, 1930, and 1935.

Soltow, James H. "Cotton as Religion, Politics, Law, Economics, and Art." *Agricultural History* (Washington, D.C.) 68, no. 2 (spring 1994).

Soniat, Charles T. "The Title to the Jesuits' Plantation." *Publications of the Louisiana Historical Society* (New Orleans) 5 (1911).

Soniat, Meloncy C. "The Tchoupitoulas Plantation." *The Louisiana Historical Quarterly* 7, no. 2 (April 1924).

———. "The Faubourgs Forming the Upper Section of the City of New Orleans." *The Louisiana Historical Quarterly* 20, no. 4 (January-October 1937).

Spearing, Darwin. *Roadside Geology of Louisiana.* Missoula, Mont.: Mountain Press, 1995.

Starr, S. Frederick. *Southern Comfort: The Garden District of New Orleans.* New York: Princeton Architectural Press, 1998.

Stewart, Lynn A. "The Batture: Disputed Geographies of Jurisdiction." *Urban Geography* 16, no. 8 (1995).

Stoddard, Major Amos. *Sketches, Historical and Descriptive, of Louisiana.* 1812. Reprint, Baton Rouge: Claitor's, 1974.

Stone, Alfred Holt. "The Cotton Factorage System of the Southern States." *The American Historical Review* 20, no. 3 (April 1915).

Stubbs, William C., and Daniel Gugel Purse. *Cultivation of Sugar Cane.* Savannah: 1901.

The Sugar Journal. *The Year Book of the Louisiana Sugar Cane Industry.* New Orleans: The Sugar Journal, 1939.

Sullivan, Charles L. *Hurricanes of the Mississippi Gulf Coast.* Biloxi, Miss.: Gulf, 1986.

Swanson, Betsy. *Historic Jefferson Parish from Shore to Shore.* Gretna, La.: Pelican, 1975.

Swerczek, Mary. "Water of Life." *New Orleans Times-Picayune,* March 4, 2001.

Swoboda, Ron. "Lakefront Airport Faces the Future." *New Orleans Magazine* (December 2000).

———. "Piled High: The Man Who Made High-Rise New Orleans Possible." *New Orleans Magazine* (June 2000).

Taylor, James W. "Louisiana Land Survey Systems." *The Southwestern Social Science Quarterly* 31, no. 4 (March 1951).

Taylor, Joe Gray. *Louisiana: A Bicentennial History.* New York: W. W. Norton; Nashville: American Association for State and Local History, 1976.

Thomas, Daniel H. "Pre-Whitney Cotton Gins in French Louisiana." *The Journal of Southern History* 31, no. 2 (May 1965).

Thomas, Greg. "Favored Stadium Site Off-Limits, Morial Says." *New Orleans Times-Picayune,* June 28, 2001.

———. "Grocery Store Would Serve Treme, Mid-City Residents." *New Orleans Times-Picayune,* February 24, 2001.

———. "Old Cotton Exchange Building May Become Hotel, Restaurant." *New Orleans Times-Picayune,* August 25, 2000.

Thompson, T. P. "Early Financing in New Orleans, 1831—Being the Story of the Canal Bank—1915." *Publications of the Louisiana Historical Society* 7 (1915).

Transportation Advertisers, Inc. *Population of the Core Area of New Orleans.* New Orleans: Real Estate Research, 1959.

Trautmann, Frederic, ed. and trans. *Travels on the Lower Mississippi, 1879-1880: A Memoir by Ernst von Hesse-Wartegg.* Columbia and London: University of Missouri Press, 1990.

Treat, Victor Hugo. "Migration into Louisiana, 1834-1880." Ph.D. diss., University of Texas at Austin, 1967.

Tregle, Joseph G., Jr. "Creoles and Americans." In *Creole New Orleans: Race and Americanization,* edited by Arnold R. Hirsch and Joseph Logsdon. Baton Rouge: Louisiana State University Press, 1992.

———. "Early New Orleans Society: A Reappraisal." *The Journal of Southern History* 18, no. 1 (February 1952).

———. *Louisiana in the Age of Jackson: A Clash of Cultures and Personalities.* Baton Rouge: Louisiana State University Press, 1999.

———. "On that Word 'Creole' Again: A Note." *Louisiana History* 23, no. 2 (spring 1982).

Tregle, Joseph George, Jr. "Louisiana and the Tariff, 1816-1846." *The Louisiana Historical Quarterly* 25, no. 1 (January 1942).

Trudeau, Carlos. *Plan de la Habitacion de Dn. Bertran Gravier* (1796, transcribed 1937). Reproduction. Louisiana Collection. University of New Orleans Earl K. Long Library.

Trudeau, Carlos. *Plan of the City of New Orleans and the Adjacent Plantations (Copy and Translation From the Original Spanish Plan dated 1798 Showing the City of New Orleans, Its Fortifications and Environs).* Reproduction. Louisiana Collection. University of New Orleans Earl K. Long Library.

Tulane University School of Architecture. *New Orleans and the River.* New Orleans: Tulane University School of Architecture, 1974.

———. *The New Orleans Guide.* London: International Architect, 1984.

———. *Study of the Vieux Carré Waterfront in the City of New Orleans.* New Orleans: Tulane University School of Architecture, 1969.

Turner, Frederick J. "Carondelet on the Defense of Louisiana, 1794." *The American Historical Review* 2, no. 3 (April 1897).

Turni, Karen. "Corps Battles Erosion in Gulf Outlet." *New Orleans Times-Picayune,* November 3, 1997.

———. "Task Force Urges Shutdown of Gulf Outlet." *New Orleans Times-Picayune,* November 16, 2000.

Twain, Mark. "The Metropolis of the South." 1883. In *The World From Jackson Square: A New Orleans Reader,* edited by Etolia S. Basso. New York: Farrar, Straus and Company, 1948.

Upton, Dell. "The Master Street of the World: The Levee." *Streets: Critical Perspectives on Public Space* (1994).

U.S. Army Corps of Engineers. *Final Report of Cultural Resource Investigations within the U.S. Army Corps of Engineers New Orleans to Venice Hurricane Protection Project, Annex C: Recommendations for Fort de la Boulaye, (16PL27), Plaquemines Parish, Louisiana.* Portales, N.Mex.: Eastern New Mexico University, Agency for Conservation Archaeology, 1988.

———. *Mission in the Lower Mississippi Valley* (1997). Pamphlet.

———. *The Mitigator: The Industrial Canal Lock Replacement Project Newsletter* 1, no. 2 (May 2000).

———. *National Register Evaluation of New Orleans Drainage System, Orleans Parish, Louisiana.* New Orleans: Earth Search, 1996.

———. *Research Design for the Violet Site Alternative, New Lock and Connecting Channels, St. Bernard Parish, Louisiana.* New Orleans: Louisiana State University, Museum of Geoscience, 1990.

———. *Waterborne Commerce of the United States, Part 2, Waterways and Harbors, Gulf Coast, Mississippi River System and Antilles* (1998).

———. *Waterborne Commerce of the United States, Part 5, National Summaries* (1998).

U.S. Army Corps of Engineers, New Orleans District. *Architectural and Archeological Investigations In and Adjacent to the Bywater Historic District, New Orleans, Louisiana.* New Orleans: R. Christopher Goodwin & Associates, 1994.

———. *Water Resources Development in Louisiana* (1995).

U.S. Congress. "An Act Respecting Claims to Land in the Territories of Orleans and Louisiana." March 3, 1807. In *The Debates and Proceedings in the Congress of the United States.* 1852.

U.S. Department of Agriculture Soil Conservation Service. *Soil Survey of Orleans Parish, Louisiana.* 1989.

U.S. Geological Survey 1992 1:24000-Scale Quadrangle Maps covering New Orleans area.

Veach, Damon. "First Families of Mobile Seek Kin." *New Orleans Times-Picayune,* July 1, 2001.

Vieux Carré Property Owners, Residents and Associates, Inc. *Vieux Carré Property Owners, Residents and Associates, Inc.: Its Purpose-Its Goals and Accomplishments* (2001). Brochure.

Vieux Carré Survey: A Pictorial Record and a Study of the Land and Buildings in the Vieux Carré. 1966. Rev. ed. New Orleans: Historic New Orleans Collection, Binders for Squares 1, 1A, 2, 2A, 3, 3A, 3B, 4, 4A, 5A, 5B, 5C, 5D, 5E, 6, 7, 8, 29, 30, 39, and 40, 1979.

Villiers du Terrage, Marc de. "A History of the Foundation of New Orleans, 1717-1722." *The Louisiana Historical Quarterly* 3, no. 2 (April 1920).

Waggoner, Martha. "Natural Disasters Strike Poor, Minorities Harder, Some Say." *New Orleans Times-Picayune,* February 13, 2000.

Waldo, J. Curtis. *Illustrated Visitors' Guide to New Orleans.* 1879.

———. *Visitor's Guide to New Orleans.* New Orleans: Southern Publishing & Advertising House, 1875.

Warner, Charles Dudley. "Sui Generis." 1887. In *The World From Jackson Square: A New Orleans Reader,* edited by Etolia S. Basso. New York: Farrar, Straus and Company, 1948.

Warner, Coleman. "Bottleneck." *New Orleans Times-Picayune,* April 21, 2000.

———. "Neighborhoods Win, Lose in '90s." *New Orleans Times-Picayune,* July 4, 2001.

———. "Residents Fighting Mad Over Canal Lock Project." *New Orleans Times-Picayune,* October 2, 1998.

———. "Sinking Homes Put Owners in a Panic." *New Orleans Times-Picayune,* December 2, 2000.

Webster's New World French Dictionary. Indianapolis: Macmillan General Reference, 1992.

Weddle, Robert S. *Wilderness Manhunt: The Spanish Search for La Salle.* Austin and London: University of Texas Press, 1973.

Whitaker, Arthur Preston. *The Mississippi Question 1795-1803: A Study in Trade, Politics, and Diplomacy.* New York and London: D. Appleton—Century, 1934.

Whitehill, Walter Muir, and Lawrence W. Kennedy. *Boston: A Topographic History.* Cambridge, Mass., and London: Harvard University Press, Belknap Press, 2000.

Whitney, H. *Whitney's New-Orleans Directory, and Louisiana & Mississippi Almanac for the Year 1811.* New Orleans: 1810.

Wilds, John. *Afternoon Story: A Century of the New Orleans States-Item.* Baton Rouge: Louisiana State University Press, 1976.

Williams, Tennessee. *A Streetcar Named Desire.* New York: Signet Books, 1947.

Williams, William H. "The History of Carrollton." 1876. In *The Louisiana Historical Quarterly* 22, no. 1 (January 1939).

Willie, Charles V. "Land Elevation, Age of Dwelling Structure, and Residential Stratification." *The Professional Geographer* 13, no. 3 (May 1961).

Wilson, Samuel, Jr. "Colonial Fortifications and Military Architecture in the Mississippi Valley." 1965. In *The Louisiana Purchase Bicentennial Series in Louisiana History,* vol. 1, *The French Experience in Louisiana,* edited by Glenn R. Conrad. Lafayette, La.: University of Southwestern Louisiana, Center for Louisiana Studies, 1995.

———. "Early History." In *New Orleans Architecture,* vol. 4, *The Creole Faubourgs,* by Friends of the Cabildo. Gretna, La.: Pelican, 1974.

———. "Early History of Faubourg St. Mary." In *New Orleans Architecture,* vol. 2, *The American Sector,* by Friends of the Cabildo. Gretna, La.: Pelican, 1972.

———. "Early History of the Lower Garden District." In *New Orleans Architecture,* vol. 1, *The Lower Garden District,* by Friends of the Cabildo. Gretna, La.: Pelican, 1971.

———. "The Uptown Faubourgs." In *New Orleans Architecture,* vol. 8, *The University Section,* by Friends of the Cabildo. Gretna, La.: Pelican, 1997.

———. *The Vieux Carre, New Orleans: Its Plan, Its Growth, Its Architecture. Historic District Demonstration Study.* New Orleans: Bureau of Government Research, 1968.

———, ed. *Southern Travels: Journal of John H. B. Latrobe 1834.* New Orleans: Historic New Orleans Collection, 1986.

Winston, James E. "Notes on the Economic History of New Orleans, 1803-1836." *The Mississippi Valley Historical Review* 11, no. 2 (September 1924).

Wood, Minter. "Life in New Orleans in the Spanish Period." *The Louisiana Historical Quarterly* 22, no. 3 (July 1939).

Woodman, Harold D. *King Cotton and His Retainers: Financing and Marketing the Cotton Crop of the South, 1800-1925.* Lexington: University of Kentucky Press, 1968.

Works Progress Administration. *Some Data in Regard to Foundations in New Orleans and Vicinity.* Baton Rouge: Works Progress Administration of Louisiana and Board of State Engineers of Louisiana, 1937.

Wright, Gavin. *The Political Economy of the Cotton South.* New York: W. W. Norton, 1978.

Wright, Russell. *A Report on the History and Development of the Upper Decatur Street Area of the Vieux Carre* (1978). In *Vieux Carré Survey: A Pictorial Record and Study of the Land and Buildings in the Vieux Carré.* 1966. Rev. ed. New Orleans: Historic New Orleans Collection, Binder for Square 1, 1979.

Yerton, Stewart. "Bio-Medical Firm Touted as Wave of Future in N.O." *New Orleans Times-Picayune,* March 7, 2001.

———. "Canal's Crown Jewel." *New Orleans Times-Picayune,* September 24, 2000.

Yiannopoulos, A. N. *Louisiana Civil Law System Course Outline.* Part 1. Baton Rouge: Claitor's, 1971.

Zacharie, James S. *New Orleans Guide.* New Orleans: F. F. Hansell & Brothers, 1893, 1902.

———. *The New Orleans Guide and Exposition Handbook.* New Orleans: New Orleans News, 1885.

Zimpel, Charles F. "RAILROAD From Canal street to Macarty's Point." *Louisiana Advertiser,* June 2, 1832.

———. *Topographical Map of New Orleans and Its Vicinity* (1834). Reproduction. Louisiana Collection. University of New Orleans Earl K. Long Library.

Index